FREE eGUIDE!

Enter this code at primagames.com/code to unlock your FREE eGuide:

CV59-TWQV-PKB9-CHJH

Mobile Friendly

Access your eGuide on any web-enabled device.

Searchable & Sortable

Quickly find the strategies you need.

Added Value

Strategy where, when, and how you want it.

Check Out Our Complete eGuide Library at primagames.com!

INTRODUCTION

DRAFT CHAMPIONS MODE

CONNECTED FRANCHISE MODE

MADDEN ULTIMATE TEAM

TEAMS

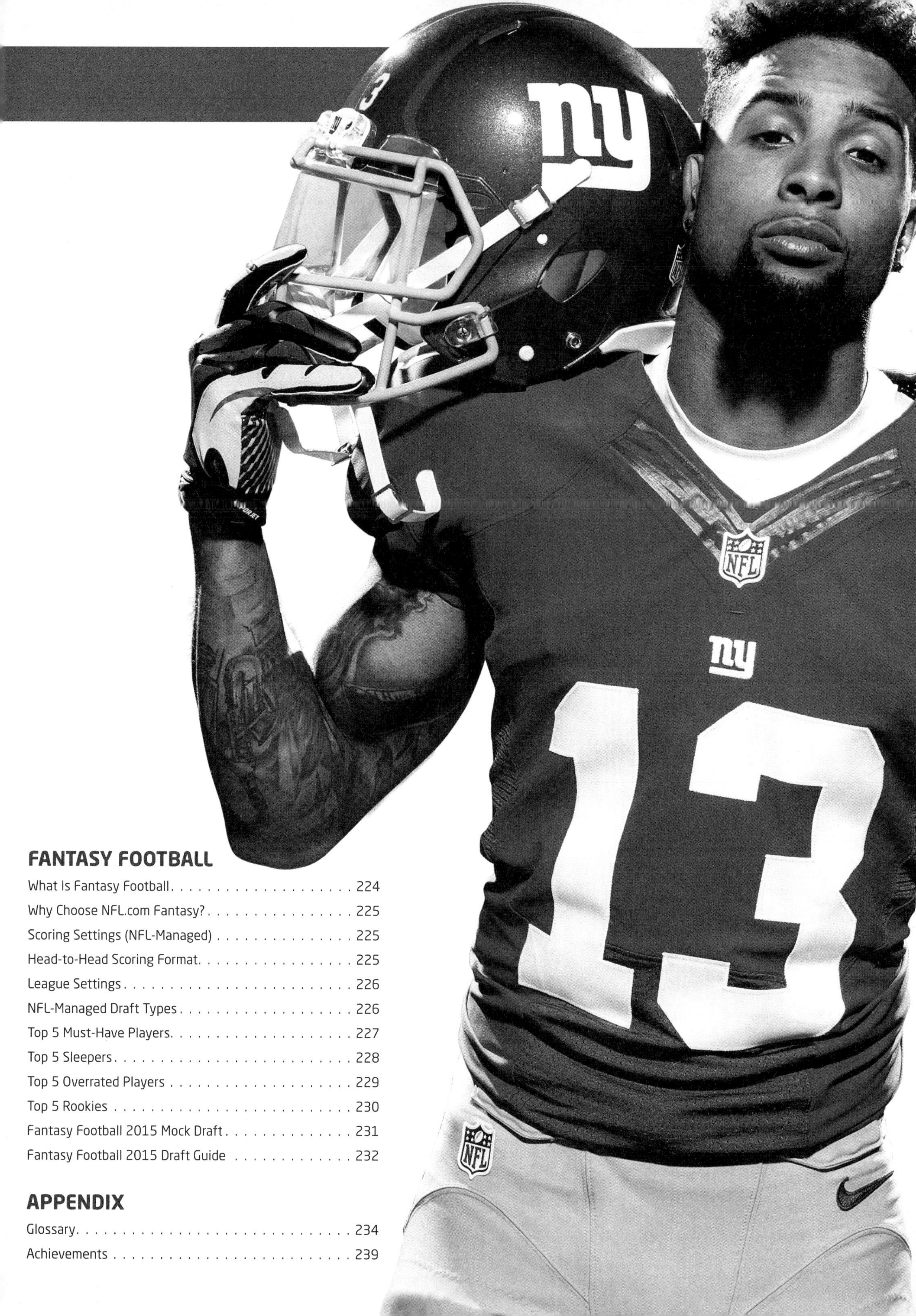

FANTASY FOOTBALL

APPENDIX

INTRODUCTION

Get a Lead

Hundreds and hundreds of hours of work and gameplay have gone into the crafting of this guide to bring you up to speed on everything you need to know to take your game to the next level in *Madden NFL 16*. By working with the community to find out their biggest needs, we have been able to put together quick tips that can change the tide of a game right in the middle of it. The goal for this guide is to spend all the time researching the best plays, so you don't have to. This means digging through every team's playbook twice, finding the best plays and making sure they work, so that in every situation you get your playmakers into position to win you games. The work is done—it is time for you to have some fun.

WHY ZFARLS

Our tournament-proven author, Zach "ZFarls" Farley, is not only a regular in the competitive scene; he also helps improve the game leading up to launch. As a respected leader of the community and official EA SPORTS Game Changer, he actually influences the game you're about to play. Each year he travels multiple times to EA SPORTS Tiburon, in Orlando, Florida, to provide feedback and advice on how to improve the new edition of Madden. There is nothing better than being able to walk down the hall to ask the developer who made the game about a certain new feature and how it should be used to get the most out of it. If you want to be the best, you need to learn from the best, and there is no one in the Madden community with more access to the developers and new features of the game than ZFarls.

- **EA SPORTS Official Game Changer**
- **Over a Decade of Madden NFL experience**
- **Creator and co-host of "This Week in Madden"**
- **Co-author of more than 35 Madden NFL Prima Games Official strategy products**
- **EA SPORTS Madden NFL Challenge Playoff Competitor**
- **Competitor in Major League Gaming EA SPORTS Madden Challenge $100,000 Final 16—Orlando**
- **Competitor in Virgin Gaming EA SPORTS Madden Challenge $140,000 NYC Final**
- **Madden NFL 25 Ultimate Team Invitational Finalist**
- **Madden NFL 25 Best Buy Tournament Finalist**
- **Commentator of the Madden NFL 15 Ultimate Team Championships Draft**

STRAIGHT FROM THE MADDEN TEAM...

"Zach is one of the most influential players in the massive Madden NFL community. He is also an official EA SPORTS Game Changer, making multiple trips to our Tiburon studio annually to help provide feedback on the game and produce quality content for the community. During my time as Community Manager for Madden, Farls has won multiple tournaments at our events and, more importantly, made *me* a better Madden player! I sincerely believe he can do the same for you. Lock up."

—Andrew Johnson, Madden NFL Community Manager

"As a former Madden professional, as seen on ESPN's Madden Nation, I know top-level talent and competition when I see it. ZFarls has proven himself to be one of the most passionate and knowledgeable Madden NFL gamers in the world. As long as he is working on the guide I know it is in good hands."

—Ryan Glick, Madden NFL Gameplay Analyst

A MESSAGE TO *MADDEN NFL 16* FANS AND COMMUNITY FROM ZFARLS

All players have different goals and dreams for their Madden NFL careers. Some want to climb the online leaderboard, while others work to build the ultimate team, try to simulate the NFL season in CFM, or simply want to beat their biggest rival and claim bragging rights. No matter what your goal is, this guide contains the strategy to help you win more games. If all else fails, remind yourself of these three things when you hop on the sticks:

1. **I have put in the work to become the best player I can be at this moment.**
2. **I am good enough to win this game and I'm going to be the playmaker with the game on the line.**
3. **I will continue to fight and keep improving no matter what the outcome.**

Make sure to find a community that lines up with your favorite game mode and goals. The best way to experience Madden NFL is with friends. We all have something to teach each other and all have areas to improve, so let's do it together. See you on the virtual gridiron.

#LockUp

—ZFarls

@Maddenbible

It is time to kick off another season with *Madden NFL 16!* Making this guide your own is the true mark of a gamer. Feel free to take notes, highlight your favorite plays, and write down every detail you uncover. Our play-calling sheets and team-building guides will help you make smart decisions no matter what mode you choose to enjoy. Each game mode has its own chapter, so make sure to dive into whatever experience you are playing at the time. We also have pages of content for each team, including our favorite plays for every situation. Keep this guide handy as you are playing; a quick glance down can find you a play to score that crucial touchdown!

Feel free to highlight your favorite tips in the guide and make notes!

What's New in *Madden NFL 16*

There are so many new things to uncover in the game this season that it would take an entire chapter just to get you up to speed. Since we know you are ready to jump in and start learning, we have covered all the new features in each individual chapter. Here is a quick overview to get you started.

PRESENTATION

Presentation has taken another leap in *Madden NFL 16,* which continues to take you beyond the broadcast and into some areas that cameramen only dream of! This season, there are new cameras to capture the action after the play that bring you right into the action. The crowd has been improved to include female fans. Fans bring their own props that are team specific, and their heads even track the action as it occurs on the field. EA Trax is the first thing you will hear when you enter the game. It is an all-new soundtrack that showcases the hottest new music in multiple genres. Also in audio, you will hear new "drive starter stories" with more than 200 unique story types.

NEW PRESENTATION FEATURES

- **EA Trax**
- **Improved Facial Likenesses via Head Scans**
- **On-the-Field Cameras**
- **Wirecam**
- **Monoliths (Augmented 3-D UI)**
- **Dynamic Feedback**
- **Living Worlds (Crowd Props and Rally Towels)**
- **Team-Specific Chants and Fight Songs**
- **Improved Post-Play Behavior**
- **Drive Starters Audio**

CONNECTED FRANCHISE MODE

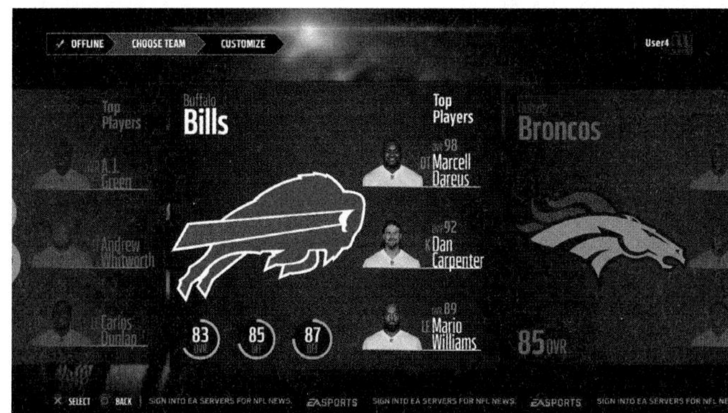

Connected Franchise Mode (CFM) was a huge area of focus for the development team this season. The first thing players will notice is their ability to start even faster. The mode looks completely different from a design standpoint, but it still has all the options that hard-core players love. If you have been too intimidated in the past to check out CFM, this is your year. Once you get in there, you will have plenty to do, from all-new scouting to dynamic drive goals. These give you something to keep an eye on all season, whether you are in or out of the game. Our CFM walkthrough follows a full season and makes sure you know how to manage all the details of your team. The game also features new commissioner tools to keep your online leagues in working order. You can add cash or reset confidence to keep franchises in the hunt.

Don't worry: You can delegate any tasks you don't want to complete to the computer to handle!

NEW CFM FEATURES

- **All-New Scouting**
- **Dynamic Drive Goals**
- **Tuning Logic for Confidence and Finances**
- **Improved Commissioner Tools**
- **New Player Cards**
- **Combine Stats**
- **Free Practice**

MADDEN ULTIMATE TEAM (MUT)

MUT is a great test of team building and on-the-field game-planning. With content that is constantly being updated throughout the season, can you build a winning team? Solo challenges have gotten an overhaul this season and can now even start in the middle of the game. These scenarios will challenge your coaching and will be based on real action you saw on Sunday. MUT is one of the easiest modes to start enjoying quickly, and all the updated content keeps it alive all season long!

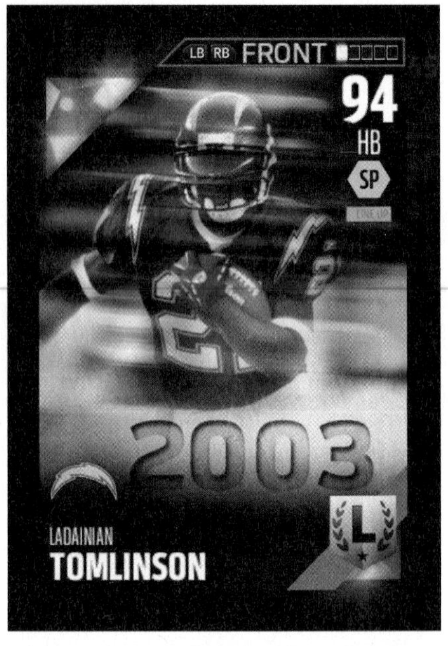

NEW MUT FEATURES

- **Brand-New Solo Challenge Experiences**
- **Improved Goals**
- **New Legends**
- **Expanded MUT Gauntlet**
- **NFL Journey Solo Challenges**
- **Batch Quicksell Increased from 20 to 100 Items**
- **Unlocks Rewards in Draft Champions**

DRAFT CHAMPIONS

Draft Champions is a brand-new mode that allows you to select your team in a 15-round draft and then bring it right onto the field to compete. Along the way, you will have some tough choices about which players to select and how they will factor into your team and scheme. Don't miss out on this fun new way to play! Check out full coverage of the mode in the Draft Champions chapter. We will get you winning games and earning rewards no matter which coach or team you draft.

GAMEPLAY

Madden NFL 16 is truly the most authentic simulation of the NFL yet. The developers put in thousands of hours of focus and sweat to make this the best game yet. In this section, developers Rex Dickson, Larry Richart, and Mike Scantlebury tell us their favorite new gameplay features and give tips on how to master them! You won't just see everything they have added—you will feel it. Everything from new tackles and catches that will leave you with wow moments! Some of our favorite small things include:

- **Penalty Improvements**
- **Improved AI QBs**
- **Organic Gang Tackles**
- **Quick Adjustments on Defense**
- **A New Handoff System**
- **Contextual Juke Behind the Line for the HB**
- **New Shot Plays**
- **Updated Team Playbooks**
- **New Extra-Point Rules**

Check out your team's play-calling sheet in the Teams chapter to see our favorites in your playbook!

New Catch Mechanics with Rex Dickson

Catching is one of the most fun aspects of *Madden NFL 16*! Now, every type of receiver has a tool to turn a basic catch into a highlight-reel play. Learn the new controls in the Skills Trainer and be ready to implement them. The difference between catch types is a quick decision that could turn a first down into a touchdown!

5 END ZONE FADE ▶ Control: Hot route, right stick up, aggressive catch

Make sure your WR gets off the jam before throwing him a fade; otherwise, it is unlikely to be a success.

If your offense slows down when you get inside the 10-yard line, try this hot route to open it back up. Target a big WR on the outside and try to throw a high-point pass for an aggressive catch! This is something you have seen on Sundays, and now, with a little practice, you can win a one-on-one matchup.

4 SIDELINE CATCH ▶ Control: Hold Ⓐ (Xbox) or ⊗ (PS) when near the sideline/back of the end zone

Use the sideline catch on passes like corner routes, especially in the fourth quarter. You can pick up big chunks of yards and keep the clock on your side!

If your WR is approaching the sideline, hold down the button and he will attempt to drag his feet. Great players use the entire field on offense, and attacking the outside of the field is crucial to making an opponent feel vulnerable.

3 CONSERVATIVE CATCH ▶ Control: Hold Ⓐ (Xbox) or ⊗ (PS) after the ball is thrown

On third and short, consider going with the conservative catch to make your WR get down after he grabs the ball. This will limit the chances of a defender coming in and ripping the ball loose, which would force a punt.

The conservative catch is perfect for balls thrown into congested areas of the field. If you like to target TEs or slot WRs on slants and drags, especially over the middle, the conservative catch is for you.

2 RUN AFTER CATCH (RAC) ▶ Control: Control: Hold Ⓧ (Xbox) ▢ (PS) after the ball is thrown

Make sure your receiver has the space to turn upfield if you go for the RAC move. If you turn into a big hit from the defender, he may drop the ball.

The RAC is perfect for turning a quick pass into a big gain. This is especially useful for tight ends and halfbacks who catch short passes in the flat. You can quickly cut upfield and get yards rather than taking "gather" steps to get your balance or running out of bounds. Now, a 2-yard gain turns into an 8-yard gain and your drive marches on!

1 AGGRESSIVE CATCH ▶ Control: Hold Ⓨ (Xbox) or △ (PS) after the ball is thrown (you do not need to be controlling the WR)

For maximum success, make sure your WR is 6'3" or taller and has the aggressive catch trait! You can use smaller WRs every now and then, but the bigger the size advantage you have over a DB, the better.

When taking a shot downfield, the high-point throw comes in handy. If you call a shot play from your playbook and see your WR with a one-on-one matchup downfield, give it a try! Hold down the Catch button as early as possible to give your WR a chance to make a play.

New Pass Mechanics with Larry Richart

The passing game received a huge overhaul this season. QBs got new tools to help them light up the scoreboards. Here are the key areas when you are looking to bring some air supremacy to your team. Keep an eye out for the all-new look of handoffs; the timing with when your holes open up along the offensive line will be better.

5 THROW ON THE RUN ▶ Control: RT (Xbox) or R2 (PS); hold to sprint, tap for rollout

Don't accidentally hold this buttonwhile in the pocket and throwing a normal pass! Your QB might shuffle his feet, which could result in a throw on the run, increasing the chances of an errant pass.

After a play-action fake, continue on the rollout and try to get outside the pocket. This is a more controlled style of rollout than an all-out sprint, and your accuracy will benefit. On plays with built-in boot action, the game will automatically start the rollout for you.

4 BACK SHOULDER ▶ Control: Low and away pass lead on left stick

Practice this pass lead in practice mode before attempting it in a game! It is very successful in the red zone, but it could lead to turnovers if you don't try it out first.

The back-shoulder throw is perfect for the "outside the numbers" area of the field. This throw type can be led with the left stick towards the sideline. If your WR has a big frame, he can shield it from the defender and pick up catches that move the chains.

3 LOW THROW ▶ Control: LT (Xbox) or L2 (PS) and the receiver's icon

Use the low throw as a way to protect the ball from the defense. This can limit your interceptions, because either your WR catches it or nobody catches it.

The low throw is very valuable when throwing into tight spaces on the field. One of the best uses is on a curl route or spot/spacing concept to keep the ball away from defenders. Although it will be very hard to get yards after the catch, you can often benefit from the extra placement on the throw. Make sure to set your feet with the QB to increase your chances of an accurate pass. One of my favorite places on the field to use this is in the red zone.

2 TOUCH PASS ▶ Control: Double-tap the receiver's icon

On horizontal routes like a deep in route, use the touch pass to give your WR more time to run under the ball and clear zones. Touch passes often go best with a conservative catch by the WR.

The touch pass puts the perfect amount of height on the ball between a lob pass and a bullet pass. By double-tapping, you will be sure to get a consistent throw. No longer will you try to hold between a bullet and a lob and accidentally throw an interception to a linebacker! Now, you have the perfect tool to consistently attack those seams over a linebacker's head but in front of the safety.

1 HIGH POINT ▶ Control: LB (Xbox) or L1 (PS) and the receiver's icon

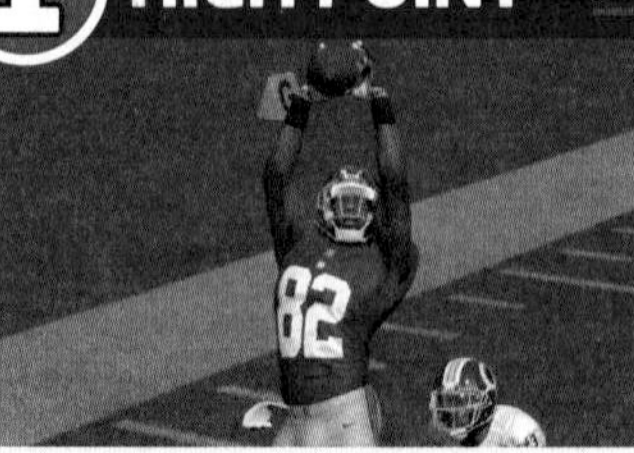

By using the high point on seam throws to the TE, you can attack a unique area of the field that is crucial to beating Cover 3 defenses!

The optimal time to throw a high point is anytime you have an advantage at the WR position against a defender one-on-one. This throw might not have the highest completion percentage, but it can reap big rewards downfield. Make sure to target a WR with an aggressive catch trait and to hold down Y (Xbox) or △ (PS) to go up and attack the ball at its peak or to rip it away from a defender.

Defensive Back Moves with Mike Scantlebury

With all new two-man interactions in *Madden NFL 16*, defenders now have a big opportunity to knock out passes against those WRs if they are in the correct position. Here are the best ways to get your defenders into position to make big plays!

5 STRAFE ▶ Control: LT (Xbox) or L2 (PS)

Learn to user-control a linebacker on defense by choosing a player in a yellow (hook) zone in Cover 3. Now you can stand near the TE, who is a favorite target for many new players, and take that option away. Even if you make a mistake, you won't hurt your team by giving up a big play in this role!

Strafing is one of the most important skills to learn on the defensive side of the ball. It squares your player up to the line, and although you can't move at full speed, it often puts you into the best position to make plays.

4 DEFENSIVE ASSIST ▶ Control: Hold LB (Xbox) or L1 (PS) after the snap

If an opposing WR is beating your CB, try calling man coverage and switching to the CB. If you hold defensive assist at the snap, you should mirror his route and can get yourself into better position to make a big play.

Defensive assist is optimal for any situation when you are unsure of where you are supposed to be as a defender. Simply hold it down and the game will direct you towards the action or your assignment. It is especially useful during tackling because it helps you with the proper pursuit angles and timing.

3 PLAY SWAT ▶ Control: Hold Ⓧ (Xbox) ▢ (PS) after the ball is thrown

Going for a swat will increase the range in which your defender can make a play verus going for a catch.

If your defender is at a size disadvantage, sometimes going for the swat can allow him to jump higher and make up ground against a big WR! While you won't get many interceptions with this method, you should see a higher number of plays getting broken up. This is a great option if you have another defender in the area, as he may be able to "tip drill" and intercept a broken-up pass that is popped into the air.

2 PLAY MAN ▶ Control: Hold Ⓐ (Xbox) or ✕ (PS) after the ball is thrown

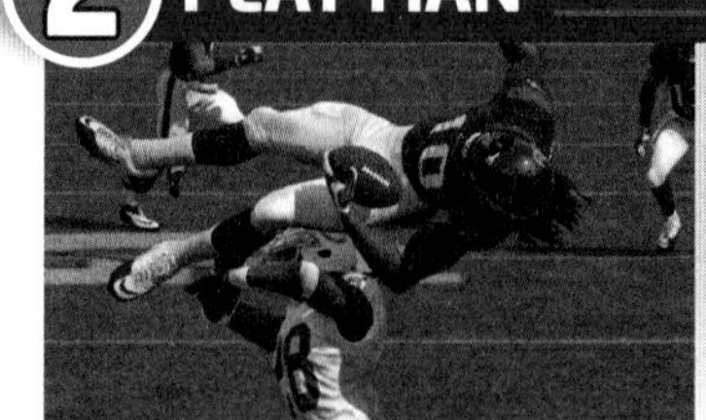

If your opponent caught the pass, you can still deliver a solid hit to knock the ball loose. Don't give up on a play until the whistle is blown.

If the WR has beaten you with a great move or arrived to the catch point earlier, try to play the body to force a drop. This is the best option when you are boxed out of a play but still in the area of the catch. If you arrive at the correct time, you can hopefully knock the ball out (unless the WR has a great Catch in Traffic rating, which would increase his ability to hang onto the ball).

1 PLAY BALL ▶ Control: Hold Ⓨ (Xbox) or △ (PS) after the ball is thrown

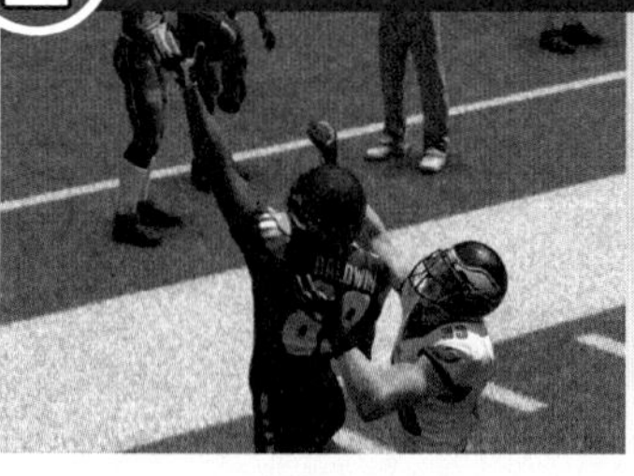

Make sure that Ball Hawk is turned on in the Settings menu. This allows you to hold the Catch button and have your defender attack the ball at the highest point.

Playing the ball can get you a big-time reward by going for the interception. Be sure to look before the snap and scout for any potential mismatches, like a tall WR against a shorter CB. If you arrive early to the ball, go for the catch! Depending on the down and distance, it can be safer to go for the swat, but nothing can turn the tide of a game like an interception. Expect to see lots of breakups that can also result in tipped balls for interceptions by a teammate.

Skills Trainer

The Skills Trainer returns in *Madden NFL 16* and is bigger and better than ever. It is still the quickest way to learn all the controls and pick up the strategy of football in a no-pressure environment. Be sure to use the Skills Trainer to get quickly up to speed on all the new gameplay mechanics. Mastering these new elements in the game will give you a day one advantage over all your friends.

Complete drills to unlock Ultimate Team packs!

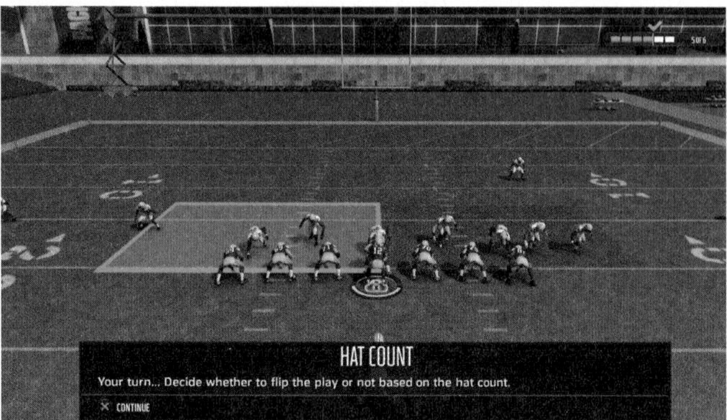

The Skills Trainer is an extremely crucial part of becoming an improved Madden NFL player. Even as an expert, I often run through the drills three times before starting the game. There is always time to go back and test yourself, and you will nearly always pick up an extra tip here or there.

SKILLS TRAINER ACTION LIST

- ❑ **Read Instructions**
- ❑ **Complete Skills Tutorial**
- ❑ **Complete Skills Drill**
- ❑ **Earn Item Reward**
- ❑ **Run the New and Improved Gauntlet**

SKILLS TRAINER LESSONS

We have put an asterisk (*) next to the most crucial drills to try out this year. Commit to getting better now!

BASIC OFFENSE

- **New: Passing Mechanics***
- **New: Catching***
- **Acceleration Burst**
- **Total Control Passing**
- **Field Goal Kicking**
- **Punting**

BASIC DEFENSE

- **New: Coverage Mechanics***
- **Tackling Mechanic***
- **Pass Rush Controls***
- **Hit Stick**

SITUATIONAL

- **New: 3 On 3 Offense (Drill Only)**
- **Oklahoma Offense**
- **Oklahoma Defense**
- **Backed Up At Goal Line**

NEW: RUN CONCEPTS

- **Hat Count***
- **Outside Zone**
- **Inside Zone**
- **Power**
- **Trap**
- **Counter**

ATTACKING COVERAGES

- **Attacking Cover 1**
- **Attacking Cover 2**
- **Attacking Cover 2 Man***
- **Attacking Cover 3***
- **Attacking Cover 4**
- **Attacking Cover 6**
- **Countering the Blitz***

READ PASS CONCEPTS

- **Curl Flat Read Concept**
- **New: Mills Read Concept**
- **Slant Flats Concept**
- **Smash Read Concept**
- **Stick Read Concept**
- **Verticals Read Concept***

PROGRESSION PASS CONCEPTS

- **Dagger Pass Concept**
- **Drive Pass Concept***
- **Flood Read Concept**
- **Levels Pass Concept**
- **New: PA Power O Concept***
- **New: PA Rollout Concept***
- **Shallow Cross Concept**
- **New: Shot Pass Concept***
- **Spacing Pass Concept**
- **Spot Pass Concept**
- **New: Switch Concept**

ADVANCED TECHNIQUES

- **New: Pocket Presence***
- **New: User Coverage***
- **Total Control Passing**
- **Precision Modifier**
- **The Option**
- **Triple Option**
- **Midline Option**
- **Inverted Veer Option**

PRE-PLAY

- **Pass Protection Adjustments**
- **Offensive Hot Routes**
- **Offensive Audibles***
- **Defensive Adjustments***
- **Adjust Coverage**
- **Defensive Audibles**

There are two main pieces to the Skills Trainer: the tutorial and the drill. The tutorial will teach you the controls and allow you to practice without any pressure. The drill will then test your knowledge and ability to implement it in a game-style situation.

 **You only need to achieve bronze to earn your pack rewards!**

PASSING CONCEPTS CHEAT SHEET

Once you get done practicing how to read defensive coverages, keep this concept cheat sheet handy. It shows which offensive concepts/plays match up well against which defensive coverages. If you go into Plays by Concept at the play-calling screen, you should find some great plays.

GOOD PLAYS VS:

COVER 0	COVER 1 (MAN)	COVER 2 ZONE	COVER 2 MAN	COVER 3	COVER 4
Verticals	Slot Cross	Four Verticals	Texas	Verticals	Stick
Screen Passes	Double Moves	Smash	Mesh	Curl Flat	Drive
Slants	Shallow Cross	Flood	Stick N Nod	Pivot	Dig/Post Combo

BAD PLAYS VS:

COVER 0	COVER 1 (MAN)	COVER 2 ZONE	COVER 2 MAN	COVER 3	COVER 4
Levels	Levels	Comebacks	Four Verticals	Slant Flat	Verticals
Smash	Spacing	Mesh	Spacing	Mesh	Curl Flats
Comebacks	HB Slip Screen	Slant Flat	Bubble Screen	Slot Cross	Mesh

Gauntlet

In *Madden NFL 16* the Gauntlet strikes back and adds a whole new level of challenges. This is a great way to test all of the skills you have learned in the Skills Trainer and to see how far you can make it! Keep an eye out for ladder and extra-life challenges that can give you more lives or allow you to skip levels.

There are some unique surprises in the Gauntlet this year, so be ready for anything...

GAUNTLET BOSS LEVEL GUIDE

The Gauntlet has some all-new bosses this year, along with all your old favorites. The game puts you up against a random defensive team this season, so you never know which opponent you are going to face. You also never know which boss challenge you are going to get at each level (we've listed all the possibilities), so be ready for anything. You have a 6 percent chance of getting a risk level at any level or a 7 percent chance of getting a bonus. Completing a risk level allows you to jump three levels forward, but if you fail, you jump two levels back.

Last season, millions of rounds were completed, but only a few hundred players completed the Gauntlet. Nobody made it higher than level 64; can you get there this season? With all of the new options and starting with six lives, it should be possible to run the Gauntlet!

LEVEL 5

HURRICANE SEASON

▶ Pro Tip: The kicking arc is your best friend on this drill. Take your time and line up the swaying arc between the uprights.

RACE TO THE BALL

▶ Pro Tip: Simply starting the meter but not trying to time the kick or stop it will result in a kick with no power and should give you a great chance at a recovery.

PUNTING INTO THE WIND

▶ Pro Tip: Don't move the kicking arrow. Click onto a different player than the punter to give yourself more speed on the recovery.

SWINGING GATE

▶ Pro Tip: Aim for full power, because it has the smallest variation, and don't forget to factor in the time to let the meter fill up!

LEVEL 10

ENTOURAGE

▶ Pro Tip: Be super patient on this level. Start towards the left side and then speed up and finish to the right.

BODYGUARDS

▶ Pro Tip: Leave the first defender unblocked and your teammates will pick him up. Look for higher priority targets downfield.

FLYING V

▶ Pro Tip: You can run through the hot spots; they will not slow you down or end the level!

LEVEL 15

RB GAUNTLET

▶ Pro Tip: If you time a move correctly, you will always fake out the defender.

RB GAUNTLET 2

▶ Pro Tip: The groups of defenders make it tough to fake out just one player. The sideline and your speed advantage are your friends here.

BEAT THE CLOCK

▶ Pro Tip: Start left or right, but never towards the middle. Keep an eye on the clock, which is small and in the right corner of the screen.

LEVEL 20

EXTEND THE PLAY

▶ Pro Tip: A completed pass that is not in the hot zone doesn't count as a fail!

HALLWAY

▶ Pro Tip: Playmaker is still great, but use conservative catches to help with the narrow sidelines.

TRICKERATION

▶ Pro Tip: Keep the HB alive with the ball and wait for the QB to finish his route before throwing it back to him.

LEVEL 25

MEDIA DAY

▶ Pro Tip: Remember that the people on the field can slow you down, *or* they can slow down your would-be tacklers.

MINEFIELD

▶ Pro Tip: This drill was only on 360 and PS3 last season. Let your center take out two tacklers.

LEVEL 30

ONE MAN D

▶ Pro Tip: Never go for an interception; use the swat option (Xbox RB or PS R1).

ONE MAN D 2

▶ Pro Tip: You have a speed advantage, so don't dive and take yourself out of the play. You can knock over blockers to trip up the back.

LEVEL 35

STAY ALIVE

▶ Pro Tip: This drill was the most difficult last season. It is still a challenge but no longer nearly impossible.

HOOK AND LADDER

▶ Pro Tip: Get the ball quickly to the last back with three pitches and then hit the corner of the end zone on the left side.

LEVEL 40

HAIL MARY

▶ Pro Tip: The final boss is still one of the toughest; remember to use your WR's speed to your advantage.

The Top 16 Plays in *Madden NFL 16*!

For the last few seasons, we have been breaking down our favorite plays in *Madden NFL* to give gamers a head start. Whether you are looking to build a custom book or choose a solid playbook for Madden Ultimate Team, these plays will win you more games. While some of our favorite plays from last year are still excellent, we always like to give you the best plays for the new game after getting our hands on it and playing it over and over. These plays take into account the new mechanics and plays in the game to really deliver a scheme that you can use all season long.

16 GUN BUNCH WK—HB CROSS SCREEN

- **TEAM PLAYBOOKS:** Bears, Broncos, Buccaneers, Chiefs, Packers, Steelers
- **CONCEPT:** HB Screen
- **PERSONNEL:** 1RB | 1TE | 3WR

- **WHAT MAKES IT GREAT:** The cross screen can really burn aggressive defenses and allows you to get your playmakers the ball in space.
- **HOW TO RUN IT:** Wait as long as possible for the HB to slip out of the backfield, then after the catch, wait for your blockers to get out in front.
- **WHEN TO USE IT:** Wait until your opponent tries to send a blitz and then crush the defense with this play.

15 GUN SPLIT VIKING—SHOVEL OPTION

- **TEAM PLAYBOOKS:** Eagles, Panthers, Vikings
- **CONCEPT:** Shovel Option
- **PERSONNEL:** 1RB | 1TE | 3WR

- **WHAT MAKES IT GREAT:** This play gives the QB plenty of players to pitch the ball to in the run game.
- **HOW TO RUN IT:** Make sure to read the pitch defenders; otherwise, this play will be tackled for a loss or could result in a turnover.
- **WHEN TO USE IT:** Use this play sparingly. However, it can really fool an opponent, especially in the red zone.

14 BIG DIME 2-3-6—COVER 4 PRESS

- **TEAM PLAYBOOKS:** Bills, Broncos, Browns, Cardinals, Chargers, Chiefs, 49ers, Jets, Packers, Ravens, Redskins, Saints, Texans
- **CONCEPT:** Cover 4
- **PERSONNEL:** Dime

- **WHAT MAKES IT GREAT:** The press look can really throw off opponents and allows you to mix in other coverages with the same look!
- **HOW TO RUN IT:** This is a great play for players who want to user-rush with a defensive lineman or LB off the edge.
- **WHEN TO USE IT:** The Cover 4 Press does a better job slowing the run than you might expect and will rarely get beaten deep against a shot play.

13 5-2 NORMAL—FIRE ZONE 2

- **TEAM PLAYBOOKS:** Giants, Lions, Panthers
- **CONCEPT:** Cover 2
- **PERSONNEL:** 5-2

- **WHAT MAKES IT GREAT:** This is an aggressive defense that forces your opponent to spread out if they want to get you out of it.
- **HOW TO RUN IT:** Make sure to shade your coverage underneath, and consider changing your deep zone defenders to man assignments.
- **WHEN TO USE IT:** This is the perfect defense to use in the red zone or against players who want to go for a two-point conversion.

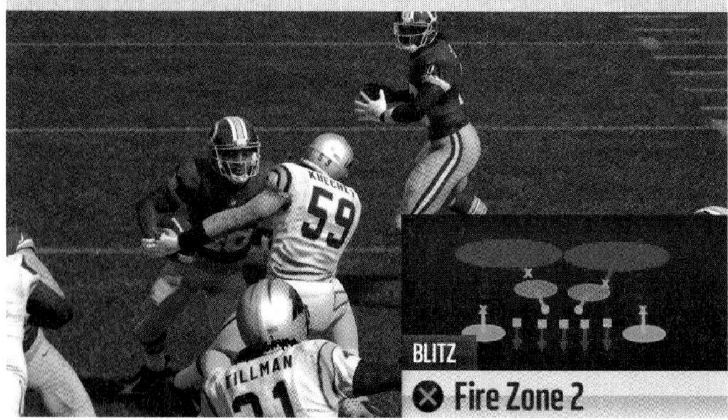

12 NICKEL 3-3-5 ODD—3 BUZZ STING PRESS

▶ **TEAM PLAYBOOKS:** Patriots

▶ **CONCEPT:** Zone Blitz 3 Deep

▶ **PERSONNEL:** Nickel

▶ **WHAT MAKES IT GREAT:** This play usually frees up a blitzer off the edge, and most QBs won't see him coming from their left side.

▶ **HOW TO RUN IT:** Crash your defensive line up and press if you aren't at a speed disadvantage at CB.

▶ **WHEN TO USE IT:** Second down is a solid time to use this play, since most players don't check down to the flats or call screen passes here.

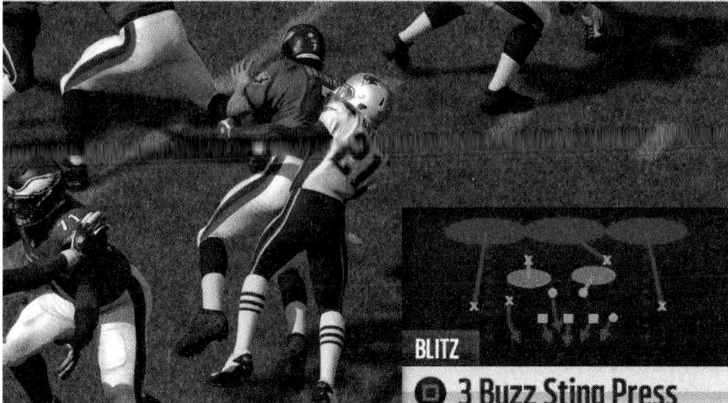

11 PISTOL ACE WING—TE CROSS

▶ **TEAM PLAYBOOKS:** Dolphins, Redskins

▶ **CONCEPT:** Y-Cross

▶ **PERSONNEL:** 1RB | 2TE | 2WR

▶ **WHAT MAKES IT GREAT:** The crossing patterns from this formation should force defenses to pinch down and potentially leave a shot open on the sideline.

▶ **HOW TO RUN IT:** Try to roll out to the open side of the field to make the throw to the crossing route easier.

▶ **WHEN TO USE IT:** This is a great second-down play after running from this excellent formation on first down.

10 PISTOL BUNCH TE—VERTICALS

▶ **TEAM PLAYBOOKS:** Saints

▶ **CONCEPT:** Verticals

▶ **PERSONNEL:** 1RB | 1TE | 3WR

▶ **WHAT MAKES IT GREAT:** This is an excellent way to attack your opponents downfield if they love to play Cover 3 all game. This formation was all new last season, and we showed off the popular PA Fork from it.

▶ **HOW TO RUN IT:** Keep an eye on the deep safety and either hit the crossing pattern or the deep ball depending on his position. You can always check down to the back for a solid gain.

▶ **WHEN TO USE IT:** This is a great call when you need a big play, but make sure you get the time you need in the pocket to unleash one.

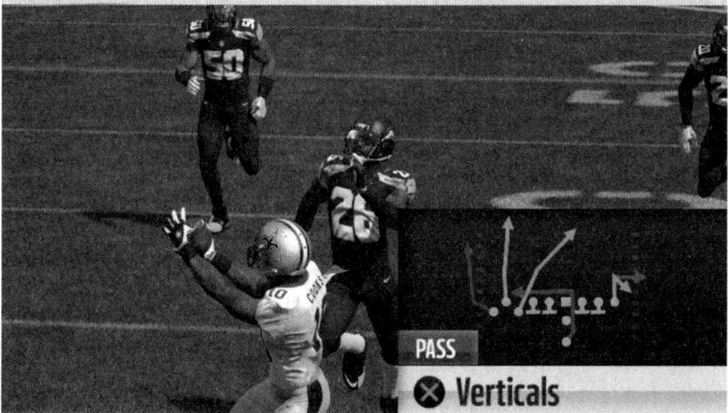

9 3-4 BEAR—COVER 2 INVERT

▶ **TEAM PLAYBOOKS:** Bears, Bills, Browns, Chiefs, Colts, 49ers, Ravens, Saints

▶ **CONCEPT:** Cover 2

▶ **PERSONNEL:** 3-4

▶ **WHAT MAKES IT GREAT:** This is a solid overall run-defense formation that is your best bet to stop the run-heavy teams out there.

▶ **HOW TO RUN IT:** Take control of the free safety and be aggressive in the box since you have no deep responsibility.

▶ **WHEN TO USE IT:** This is a stout run defense that is especially effective in the red zone. Blitz your LBs if you need a tackle for a loss.

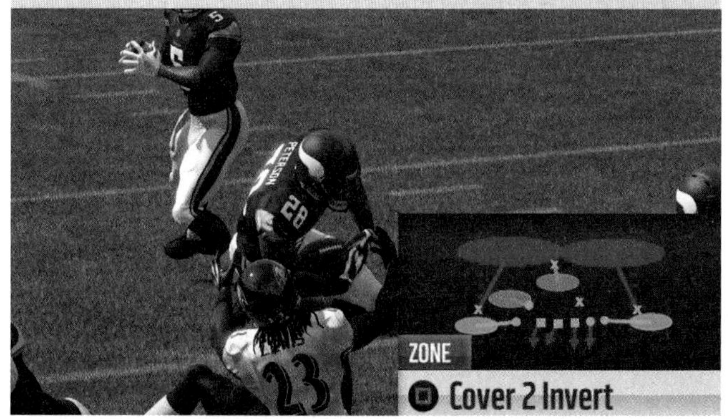

8 DOLLAR 3-2-6—COVER 2 SINK QB CONTAIN

▶ **TEAM PLAYBOOKS:** Bills, Browns, Falcons, Giants, Jaguars, Raiders, Rams, Saints, Seahawks

▶ **CONCEPT:** Cover 2

▶ **PERSONNEL:** Dime

▶ **WHAT MAKES IT GREAT:** The combo of man coverage on the outside with zones over the middle can really mess with your opponent!

▶ **HOW TO RUN IT:** User-control the blitzing LB on the left of the screen and change up your assignment depending on the situation.

▶ **WHEN TO USE IT:** Try this play if your opponent is rolling out, since the contains will prevent the QB from escaping the pocket.

7 GUN ACE TWINS OFFSET—PA VERTS SHOT

▶ **TEAM PLAYBOOKS:** Bengals, Cardinals, Seahawks, Vikings

▶ **CONCEPT:** Divide, Shot Play

▶ **PERSONNEL:** 1RB | 2TE | 2WR

▶ **WHAT MAKES IT GREAT:** The protection on this play is perfect for players looking to go downfield, and the crossing route is excellent for medium-range passers.

▶ **HOW TO RUN IT:** Change up the play action and slant the blocking TE from time to time.

▶ **WHEN TO USE IT:** Use this on second down and short when the play-action fake will be most effective; it should burn man and zone.

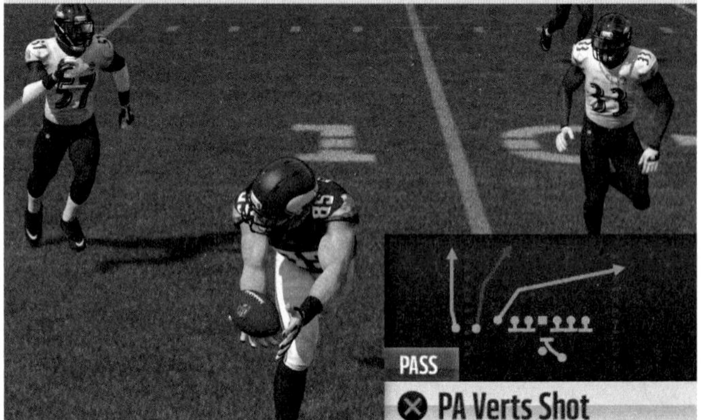

6 SINGLEBACK DEUCE WING—SKINNY POSTS

▶ **TEAM PLAYBOOKS:** Ravens, Seahawks

▶ **CONCEPT:** Slants

▶ **PERSONNEL:** 1RB | 2TE | 2WR

▶ **WHAT MAKES IT GREAT:** The depth and angle of the slants allow this play to really attack a tender area of common defenses.

▶ **HOW TO RUN IT:** There are many adjustments you can make to your TEs and HB, but the main target will always be the posts. Wait for them to clear the LBs and throw a bullet.

▶ **WHEN TO USE IT:** This play is solid at any point because it is a common run formation, and the TE in the flat can be tough to stop. You should find a similar play in many Singleback Ace formations.

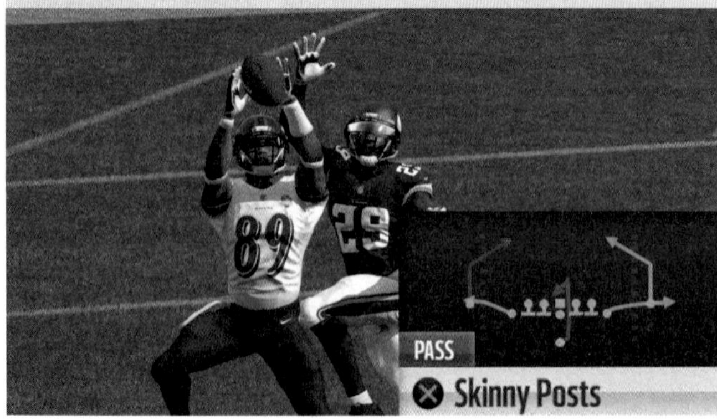

5 GUN FLIP TRIPS EAGLE—EAGLES VERTICALS

▶ **TEAM PLAYBOOKS:** Eagles, Raiders

▶ **CONCEPT:** Verticals

▶ **PERSONNEL:** 1RB | 2TE | 2WR

▶ **WHAT MAKES IT GREAT:** This formation has a concept to beat every type of defense the opponent can throw at you.

▶ **HOW TO RUN IT:** Look to attack the seam against zone coverage, but otherwise hit the drag over the middle. If you get time, look to the HB running down the sideline.

▶ **WHEN TO USE IT:** Don't wait until third down to use this play hit it early and often to get yourself in good position!

4 46 NORMAL—FIRE ZONE 3

▶ **TEAM PLAYBOOKS:** Bengals, Jaguars, Vikings

▶ **CONCEPT:** Zone Blitz

▶ **PERSONNEL:** 46

▶ **WHAT MAKES IT GREAT:** The 46 Normal is a stout run defense that provides some nice zones to stop quick passing.

▶ **HOW TO RUN IT:** Consider user-controlling the safety up in the box, and try different crashes and shifts to free up the blitzing LB.

▶ **WHEN TO USE IT:** Start with a more basic coverage early in the game, but go to this if you need to stop the run or get a key sack.

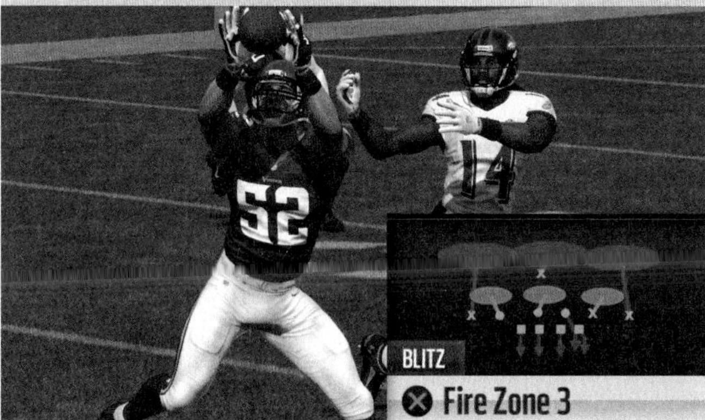

3 SINGLEBACK WING TRIPS OPEN—INSIDE ZONE SPLIT

▶ **TEAM PLAYBOOKS:** Colts, Dolphins, Eagles, Raiders, Titans

▶ **CONCEPT:** Inside Zone

▶ **PERSONNEL:** 1RB | 1TE | 3WR

▶ **WHAT MAKES IT GREAT:** This is a consistent run up the middle that won't allow your opponent to go into a full pass-defense formation.

▶ **HOW TO RUN IT:** Allow your CPU HB to make the first cut, because he does an excellent job of getting into the second level. From there look to break it outside.

▶ **WHEN TO USE IT:** This is a great way to slow down rushers off the edge who try to stop your runs in the backfield.

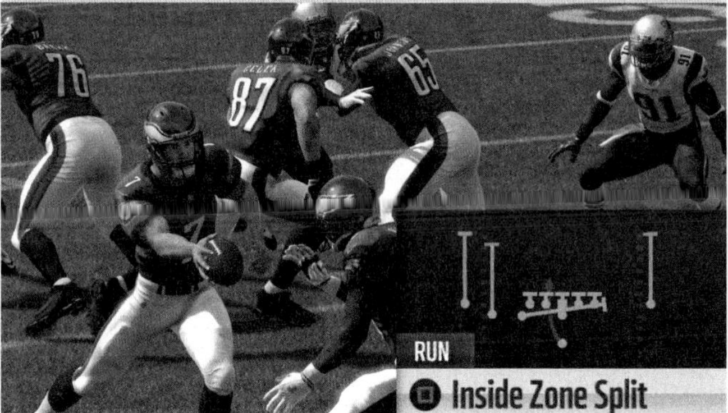

2 NICKEL 2-4-5 DBL A GAP—WILL 3 BUZZ

▶ **TEAM PLAYBOOKS:** Bears, Bills, Broncos, Browns, Cardinals, Chargers, Chiefs, Colts, Eagles, 49ers, Jets, Packers, Patriots, Ravens, Redskins, Saints, Steelers, Texans, Titans

▶ **CONCEPT:** Zone Blitz 3 Deep

▶ **PERSONNEL:** Nickel

▶ **WHAT MAKES IT GREAT:** This defense taunts the offensive line by placing defenders right up in their faces.

▶ **HOW TO RUN IT:** Utilize different crashes depending on the formation you are facing. This is a very versatile play.

▶ **WHEN TO USE IT:** Don't just save this play for third and long, although it certainly can be used there to get a sack.

1 GUN SPLIT CLOSE PATS—X DRAG TRAIL

▶ **TEAM PLAYBOOKS:** Browns, Patriots

▶ **CONCEPT:** Texas

▶ **PERSONNEL:** 2RB | 1TE | 2WR

▶ **WHAT MAKES IT GREAT:** This formation lines everyone in tight and makes it tough for man defenders to get aligned. Make sure to switch to the HB Wheel or HB Slip Screen once the defense starts to catch on.

▶ **HOW TO RUN IT:** You have options on this play to slant WRs over the middle or to block your HBs for extra time. The choice is up to you, but focus on getting the ball out quickly.

▶ **WHEN TO USE IT:** Use this play on first down to get your offense attacking the defense and forcing them into zone coverage.

DRAFT CHAMPIONS MODE

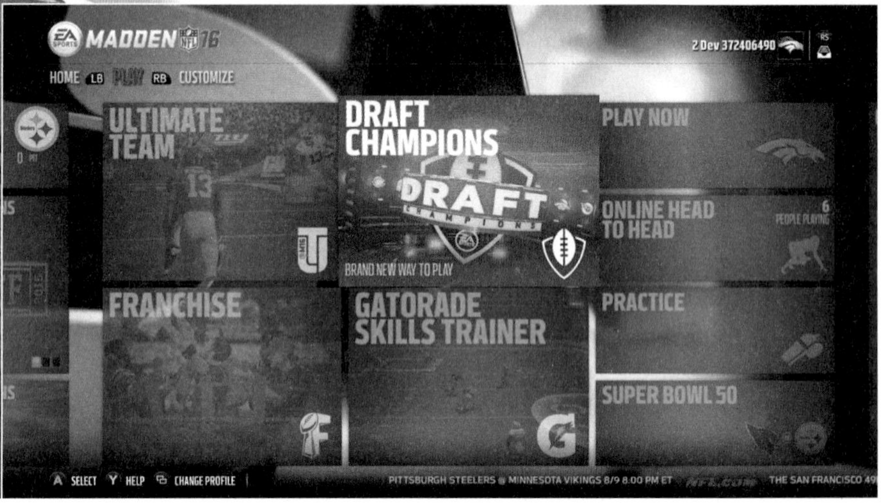

What Is Draft Champions?

Draft Champions is a brand-new way to play *Madden NFL 16*. It is a free-to-play game mode that builds in the excitement of a fantasy football draft with on-the-field Madden NFL action. Players in Draft Champions can choose to compete in a solo draft against the CPU or in a head-to-head (H2H) draft. Players start by picking a coach, which gives them their playbooks and team style. From there, the fun begins and they will draft 15 rounds of players before playing with their team. The more you win, the greater the rewards you can earn!

DRAFT CHAMPIONS CHECKLIST

- ❑ Choose Solo or H2H Draft
- ❑ Draft 15 Rounds
- ❑ Pick Your Coach
- ❑ Win to Earn Greater Rewards

Draft On

- **Check your base team for sleepers—they may change your draft plan!**
- **Keep an eye out for legends; drafting one is an excellent way to give your team an identity.**

From the main menu, select the Draft Champions panel to get started building your team. Once you select solo or head-to-head, you can enter a draft and start selecting your team. The game will give you a starting roster with base players who generally have around a 68 to 70 Overall rating. You won't have enough selections to fully create a lineup, so keep an eye on these players, as they will see the field at some point. All of these players have strengths and weaknesses, so try to get the most out of them if they make the lineup. Know which positions you need elite talent at and which ones you don't value unless something great comes up. If you grab an elite QB but keep a base left tackle, will you have enough time to consistently throw downfield? This is what makes Draft Champions so compelling. Remember that there are no wrong answers.

TEAM STYLES

Your coach will be the biggest factor in your team's style. Each coach grants +50 to style on offense and defense.

Choosing between a coach with a good playbook and one with a good style is one of the toughest decisions in Draft Champions: Lean towards playbook!

Building up your team style is a great way to get your team some boosts during gameplay. Keep an eye on what items you are starting to collect and start to build out a lineup. By flipping over an item, you can see how much style it will add to your team. Make sure to get your players in their proper positions to receive the boost. Styles and boosts work the same way as in Madden Ultimate Team, so test them there and find one you are comfortable with. This way you can experiment with the effects of style. For example, is a plus-50 boost enough or do you like to go higher?

AFTER THE DRAFT

After the draft is complete, you can adjust your lineup and play your Draft Champions game. You can also evaluate your coaching and equipment like uniforms and stadiums. Taking a few seconds to adjust your lineup can pay off in a big way once you hit the field. Make sure you get all the talent you selected into the best positions to make plays. If you selected two HBs, consider moving one to receiver if he has a high Catch rating. If you selected two OLBs who play the same side, move the backup to the other side to replace a base-level player.

All the small tweaks will help you get the most from the lineup once you get on the field. Using the Compare Items option in the Lineup screen is a great way to evaluate players' abilities and see who matches your team's play style. Finding good formations is crucial to success. For example, you want a formation to spread out the defense if you went heavy on receivers, but you'll need different options for pounding the ball if you went with a halfback and strong offensive line. Check out play-calling sheets in the Teams chapter to help find the best plays in your playbook.

Your opponent will have some great players but will also be weak at a few positions. Try to target them and get your best talent matched up against their weaker positions (but know that they will do the same). Using the matchup stick in-game is a good way to keep an eye on these potential ratings mismatches.

The game will keep you up to date on your wins and losses. Don't worry if you take a loss, because that just means you get to do another draft! If you keep racking up the wins, you will keep earning better rewards. If you chose the solo challenge route, you need to win three games before you lose one to earn rewards. If you chose head-to-head, you must win four games before you lose one. Once you lose, you get your rewards depending on how many games you won, and then you draft a new team all over again.

OFFENSIVE STYLES

- **SHORT PASS STYLE boosts Catch in Traffic and Pass Blocking to improve your ability to complete short to intermediate passes.**
- **LONG PASS STYLE boosts Route Running and Pass Blocking and improves your ability to complete intermediate to deep passes.**
- **GROUND AND POUND STYLE boosts Trucking and Run Blocking, thus increasing your effectiveness with a power running game plan.**
- **SPEED RUN STYLE boosts Elusiveness and Run Blocking, increasing the effectiveness of a running game plan built around quickness.**

DEFENSIVE STYLES

- **ZONE DEFENSE STYLE boosts Play Recognition and Zone Coverage, so there's an increased chance of success when you call zone coverage plays.**
- **MAN DEFENSE STYLE boosts Play Recognition and Man Coverage for an increased chance of success when you call man coverage plays.**
- **PASS RUSH STYLE boosts Pursuit and Block Shedding, so players blitzing the QB are more likely to escape blocks.**
- **RUN STUFF STYLE boosts Tackling and Block Shedding, so defenders have a better chance of shutting down plays.**

You will be given a heads-up if a player in the draft matches your coach's style.

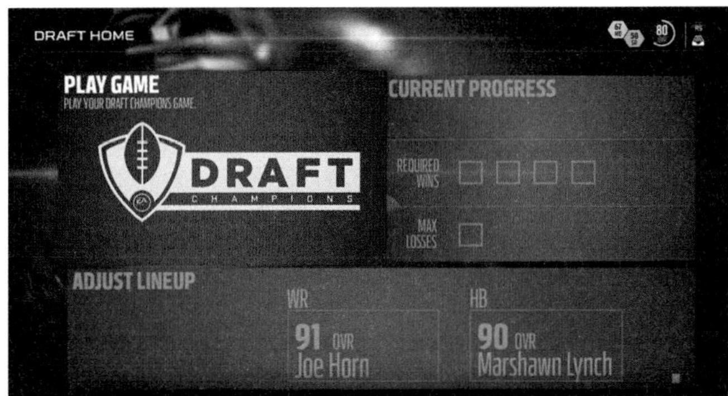

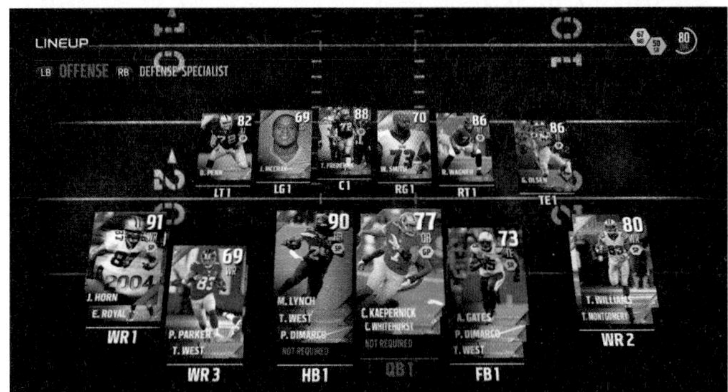

Don't forget to optimize your lineup for the 4-3 or 3-4 defense depending on which coach you selected and his playbook.

You will be able to see your opponent's best players when loading into the game, so think about how they will use them!

TIPS FOR DRAFT CHAMPIONS

Draft Champions is a brand-new mode that puts every player on equal ground when putting their team together. Since the rounds are totally random and no two drafts are the same, your results will vary. You may feel very confident about your team after one draft and the next time feel like you made a mistake. No matter what, your team will be able to win games on the field, so stay cool and be ready!

5 HAVE A PLAN

Taking on a human opponent is one of the biggest challenges. In general, they tend to draft their favorite players or skill positions and leave the offensive line weak.

Knowing what type of team you want to build is extremely important when starting a draft. Although you never know which players will appear, you can ask yourself a few questions about your play style to really have an advantage.

- **Is my defensive playbook a 3-4 or 4-3?**
- **Would I rather be a run-first or pass-first player?**
- **Which position is the most valuable to me on offense?**

QB is the most important position in Draft Champions; however, if you favor a run-heavy style and get an elite offensive line, your HB could be your most important player.

- **If a certain elite player is available, will I select him even if I already have that position covered and a need at another spot?**
- **Who would be a fun player to user-control on defense?**
- **Should I draft based on ratings or based on name recognition?**
- **How much do I value whether or not a player matches up with my team style?**

The best part is that even if you don't have quite the draft you planned for, you will still have a solid team that can win games.

4 SET YOUR LINEUP

You can always pause the game and make more changes to your depth chart if something isn't lining up like you expected.

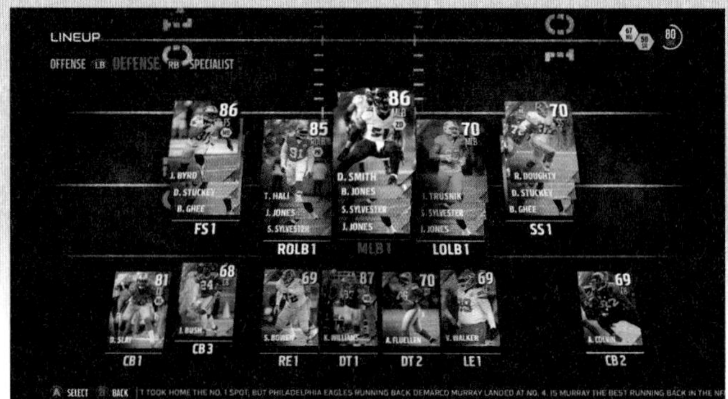

Now that you have drafted your squad, make sure to get them set up in the optimal positions before heading into a game. By taking the extra second to review your lineup and make adjustments, you can double-check your strengths and weaknesses. If you doubled up on a position, now is the time to make a move and see if you can find a spot in the lineup for both. Picking up two guards or LBs at the same position isn't a big deal since you can shift them around. You won't gain the style boost, but they will likely be better than your base player.

3 TEST EVERYTHING AND KEEP NOTES

Make sure to write down if a certain playbook fit your style, and note any specific plays from it that you liked. Chances are, most offensive concepts and defensive plays can be found in multiple playbooks, so the knowledge really helps over time!

One of the best parts of this mode is finding some talented players that seem to play even better than their ratings! On the flip side, not every elite player will catch every single pass thrown his way. Keep a notebook next to your desk and mark down any time a player makes a big play for your team. If you utilize players out of position, make a note if you feel they improved or declined. Generally, as long as the player fits into the role of the new position, it was worth it to swap positions even if it wasn't his natural listed spot.

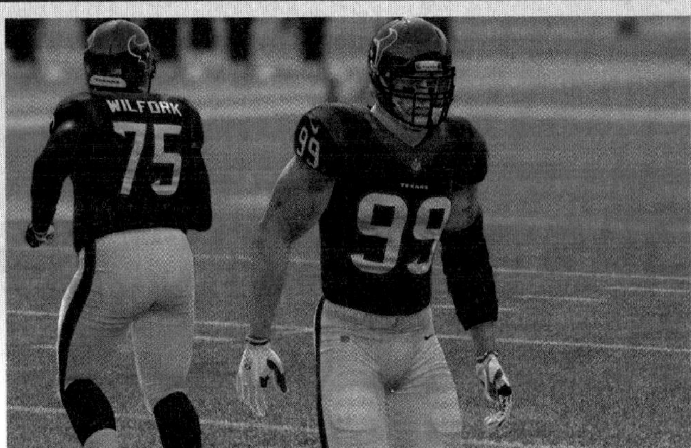

2 KNOW YOUR HOLES

Evaluate your base team before making any selections! A few solid players can be used in your lineup despite their average overall rating.

With only a 15-round draft and 22 starting spots, your team will ultimately be weak somewhere. Don't be discouraged if you didn't get to load your team up quite as you could in Madden Ultimate Team! Your backups will play a big role in the game, and they all have strengths and weaknesses. Focus on bringing out their best talents by getting them in good positions for their skill sets!

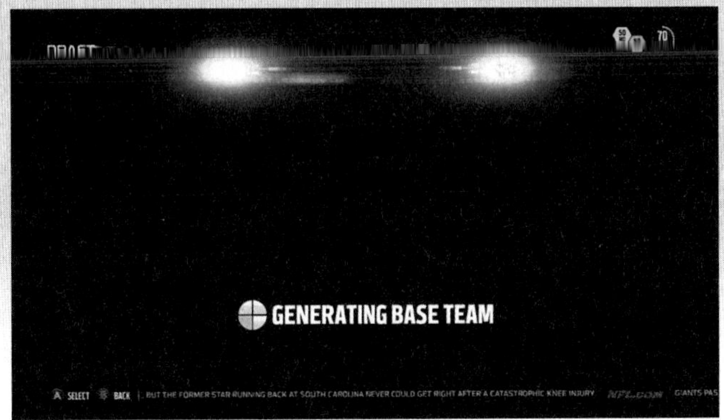

1 TAKE YOUR TIME

Once you are on the field, the stars under certain player rings indicate who the best players are, so look for them!

The draft is easily the best part of the new experience, so take your time and enjoy it. You have unlimited time to make a pick, so relax and use all the information available to you. At each new round, review the players you have already selected and make sure to look for some of those deeper hidden ratings on the back of the card. It will take a few rounds, but eventually you will get confident enough to make the pick without having to flip the cards. Until then take a deep breath and take your time!

Remember: There is no wrong pick. Even if you feel you messed up 15 times in a row, your team's Overall rating will still be high enough to win a game against someone who made 15 "perfect" selections. "Scheme over team!"

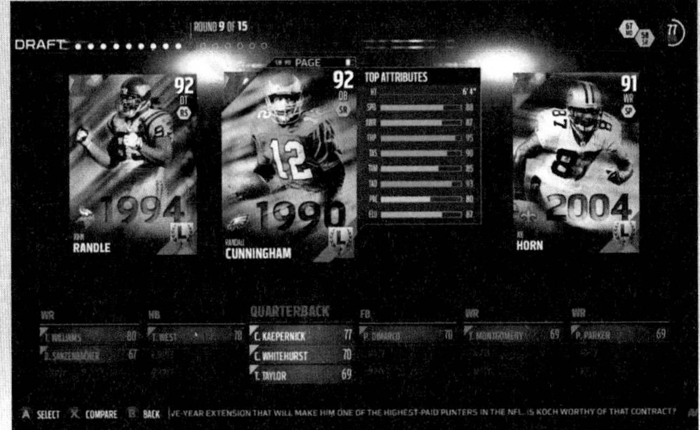

CHICAGO BEARS

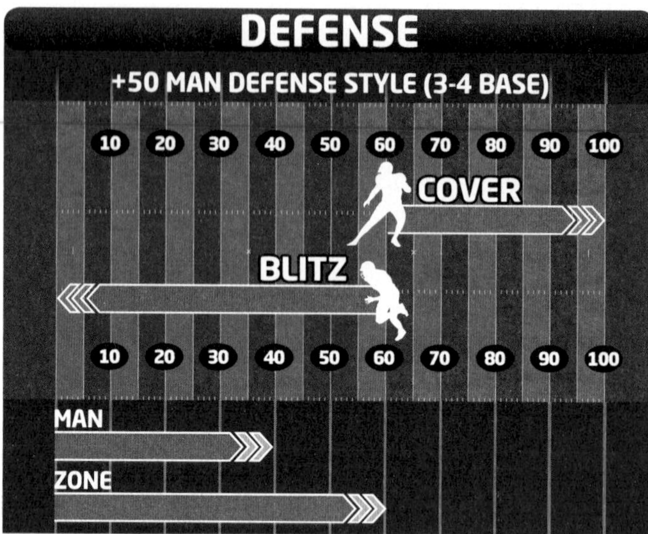

OFFENSE

The Bears' playbook has seen some big changes in *Madden NFL 16* and is now a balanced playbook with plenty of chances for big plays downfield. Run-first players will need an all-around HB, while pass-first players should aim for a big receiving target.

KEY FORMATION

Singleback Tight Flex is the optimal formation to start out in, especially if you get a balanced TE who can run-block and hit the seam. If you can't block your opponent's pass rush, drop back to shotgun.

KEY PLAYER

QB with 95+ Throw Power

FORMATIONS

- **SINGLEBACK: Ace, Ace Close, Ace Pair Twins, Doubles, Y-Trips Bear, Tight Flex**
- **I-FORM: Pro, Flex Twins, Tight**
- **STRONG: Pro, Tight Pair**
- **WEAK: Twins Flex**
- **PISTOL: Ace, Slot Wing, Y-Trips**
- **GUN: Split Offset, Doubles Wk, Y-Trips Wk, Trio, Bunch Wk, Snugs Flip, Dice Y-Flex, Trey Open, Empty Trey, 5WR Trio**

PRO TIP

▶ No matter what style you want to run, having a big arm to unleash an attempt downfield once per half will keep the defense hesitant to cram the box.

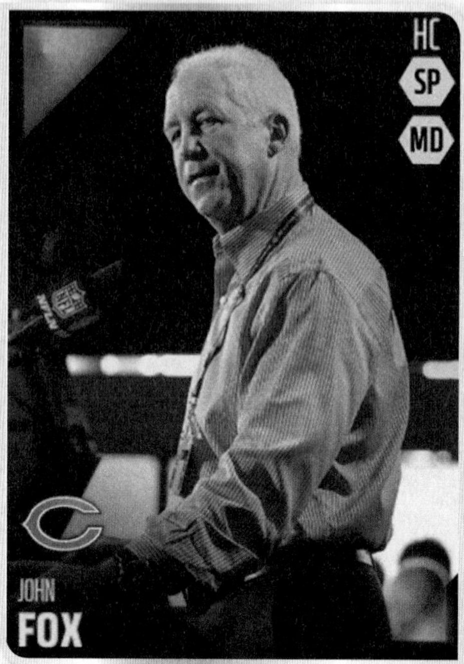

OFFENSIVE DRAFT TARGETS

- **HB (SPD, TRK, CTH)**
- **WR (6'3"+ RTE, SPC)**
- **QB (THP, DAC, PAC)**

DEFENSIVE DRAFT TARGETS

- **MLB (PRC, ZCV, SPD)**
- **DE (STR, BSH, PMV)**
- **CB (MCV, ZCV, PRS)**

DEFENSE

The Bears have changed over to a 3-4 playbook and will really benefit from pass-rushing defensive ends who won't need to drop into zone too often. No matter what, you will still want a solid MLB who is built for zone coverage.

KEY FORMATION

The Bears' Nickel 2-4-5 Prowl is a great defensive formation that can really give the offense headaches. Start with the Cover 2 Drop and see if all the commotion before the snap doesn't throw your opponent off for a while!

KEY PLAYER

MLB with 85+ Play Recognition

FORMATIONS

- **3-4: Odd, Under, Over, Even, Bear**
- **NICKEL: 2-4-5 Even, 2-4-5 Dbl A Gap, 2-4-5 Prowl, 3-3-5 Wide**
- **BIG DIME: 2-3-6 Even, 2-3-6 Will**
- **QUARTER: 1-3-7, 3 Deep**

PRO TIP

▶ Drafting a second MLB isn't a terrible move if a good one appears during your draft. This would have you using 3-3-5 Wide less often or using formation subs to get crafty.

CINCINNATI BENGALS

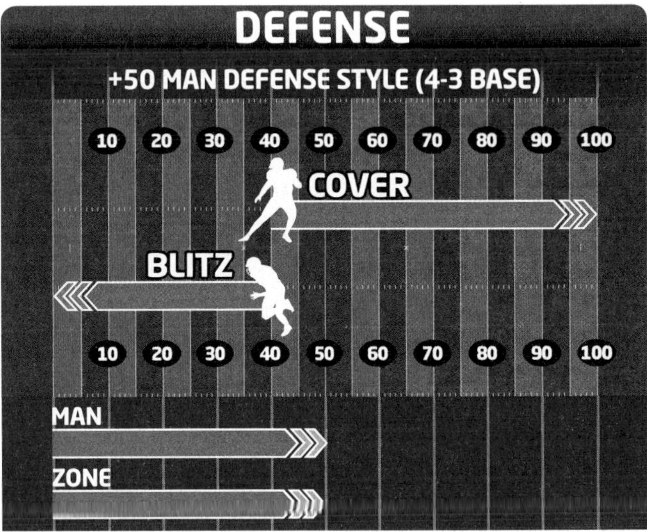

OFFENSE

The Bengals' offense is optimized for either a power or speed back, which makes it versatile. If you get a power back, stick with the under-center run formations. If you find an elusive player, get him out in space for screens and counters from shotgun.

KEY FORMATION

Gun Trips Y Iso will let your best offensive playmaker get a chance downfield!

KEY PLAYER

WR/TE with 85+ Spectacular Catch

FORMATIONS

- **SINGLEBACK: Ace, Ace Pair, Ace Pair Twins, Doubles, Y-Trips, Snugs Flip, Bunch**
- **I-FORM: Pro, Pro Twins, Tight Pair**
- **STRONG: Pro, Close, Pro Twins**
- **WEAK: Pro Twins**
- **PISTOL: Strong Twins**
- **GUN: Split Slot, Ace Offset, Ace Twins Offset, Doubles Offset, Y-Trips Bengal, Trio, Bunch Wk, Double Stack, Normal Y-Flex Tight, Trips Y Iso, Trey Open, Empty Trey, Empty Base Flex**
- **WILDCAT: Bengal**

PRO TIP

▶ The Bengals' playbook has some solid one-on-one routes if you can land a star WR, but make sure your QB has the throwing power to get the ball downfield!

OFFENSIVE DRAFT TARGETS

- WR (SPD, RTE, SPC)
- QB (THP, MAC, DAC)
- HB (SPD, CTH, ELU)

DEFENSIVE DRAFT TARGETS

- DT (FMV, ACC, STR)
- MLB (POW, ZCV, PRC)
- DE (SPD, FMV, ZCV)

DEFENSE

The Bengals' defensive book contains lots of versatility for a 4-3 playbook. By dropping defensive ends into coverage and sending LBs on blitzes, there is plenty of confusion to be created.

KEY FORMATION

The 46 Normal is perfect for slowing down the run and testing your opponent's passing game. Move your defensive linemen around to find them good rushing matchups!

KEY PLAYER

DT with 85+ Finesse Moves

FORMATIONS

- **4-3: Stack, Under, Over, Over Plus, Wide 9**
- **46: Normal**
- **NICKEL: Normal, Double A Gap, 3-3-5, 3-3-5 Wide**
- **DIME: Normal**
- **QUARTER: Normal, 3 Deep**

PRO TIP

▶ If you can draft a more athletic pass-rushing DT, it will pay off more than a stronger run-stuffing type.

BUFFALO BILLS

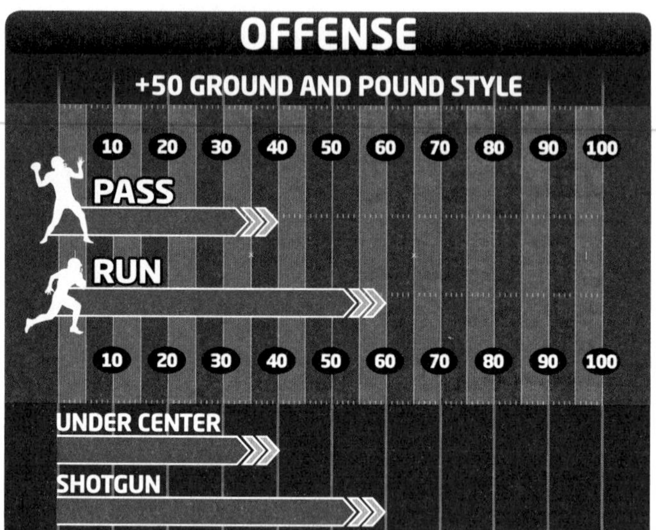

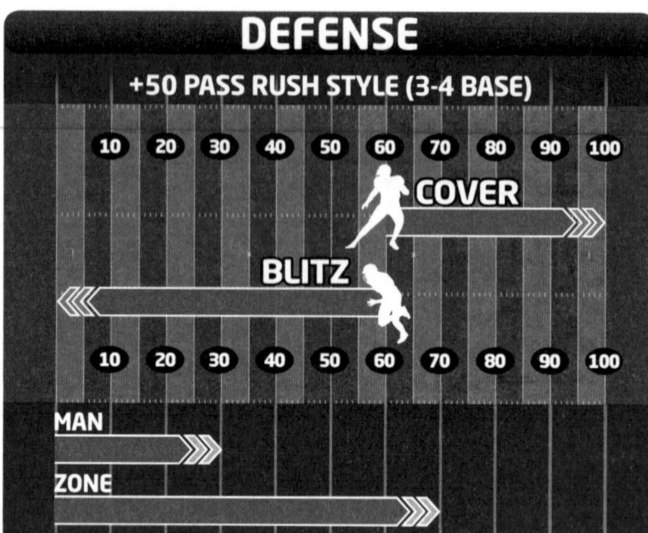

OFFENSE

The Bills' offense is perfect for players who like to mix two HBs into their game plan. If you can commit to running the ball and keeping your backs fresh, you will have great success.

KEY FORMATION

Buffalo has an excellent formation with the Dbls Wing Offset Wk. This allows you to run inside or outside to set up quick throws to the edge. Use this formation to get your fastest playmakers a mismatch on the outside.

KEY PLAYER

HB with 90+ Speed

FORMATIONS

- **SINGLEBACK: Jumbo Pair, Ace, Ace Close, Ace Pair, Ace Pair Flex, Bunch Ace, Bills Doubles**
- **I-FORM: Pro, Pro Twins, Tight, Tight Pair**
- **STRONG: Pro, Tight Pair**
- **WEAK: Pro**
- **PISTOL: Full House TE, Full House Base, Strong Twins, Weak Twins, Ace Twins**
- **GUN: Doubles, Dbls Wing Offset Wk, Y-Trips Wk, Trio Offset Wk, Bunch HB Str, Spread Flex Wk, Trey Open, Empty Trey Flex**

PRO TIP

▶ Look for a mobile QB rather than a pocket passer, especially if the difference in Overall rating is within a few points.

OFFENSIVE DRAFT TARGETS

- **HB (SPD, ACC, ELU)**
- **WR (SPD, ACC, RLS)**
- **QB (ACC, PAC, MAC)**

DEFENSIVE DRAFT TARGETS

- **OLB (ZCV, PRC, PUR)**
- **SS (PRC, SPD, ACC)**
- **DT (STR, BSH, PMV)**

DEFENSE

The Bills' playbook has always been built around solid defensive linemen and fast edge rushers. However, add more blitzes to your game plan with a new coach in town.

KEY FORMATION

Look to the Nickel 2-4-5 Even as a formation where you will be able to get the most out of your lineup. The 3-3-5 Wide is also an option if you are more comfortable and want to shut down the edge runs.

KEY PLAYER

OLB with 90+ FMV/PMV

FORMATIONS

- **3-4: Odd, Predator, Over, Over Ed, Bear**
- **NICKEL: 2-4-5 Even, 2-4-5 Dbl A Gap, 3-3-5 Wide**
- **BIG DIME: 2-3-6, 1-4-6**
- **DOLLAR: 3-2-6**
- **QUARTER: 1-3-7, 3 Deep**

PRO TIP

▶ Getting one elite player in your secondary will make you feel that much more comfortable when sending heavy pressure.

DENVER BRONCOS

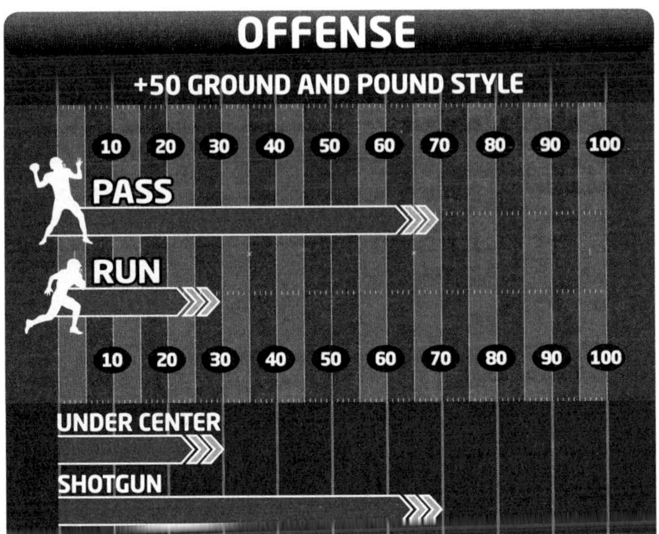

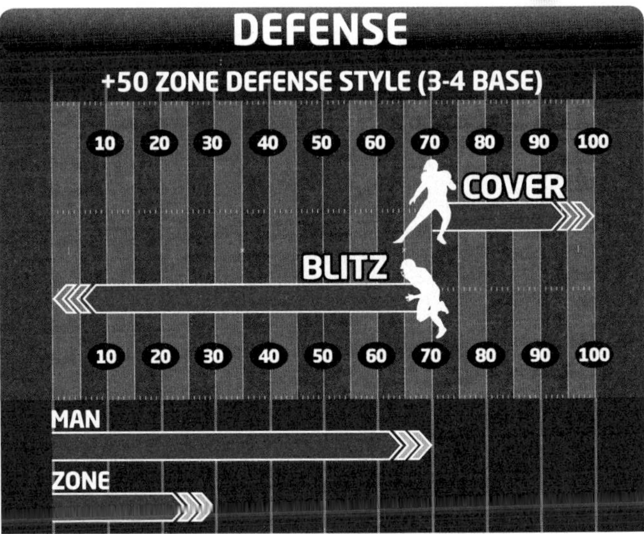

OFFENSE

The Denver offense has some unique formation names, with "dice" and "deuce" showing up, but don't be fooled, because it is one of the best playbooks for passing downfield in *Madden NFL 16*.

KEY FORMATION

Pistol Bunch TE forces the defense into a tough alignment against the offense and allows you to take any area they leave weak! Start out by targeting the flats early and often until they commit to slowing you down. Short passes not only set you up for later in the game, but one broken tackle can turn a short gain into a first down.

KEY PLAYER

WR with 90+ Route Running

FORMATIONS

- **SINGLEBACK: Jumbo Z, Deuce, Deuce Pair Twins, Dice Slot, Y-Trips**
- **I-FORM: Pro, Tight**
- **STRONG: Close**
- **PISTOL: Ace, Ace Twins, Bunch TE, Slot Wing, Y-Trips, Trips**
- **GUN: Deuce, Dice Slot, Dice Slot Wk, Y-Trips HB Wk, Bunch Wk, Snugs, Dice Y-Flex, Empty Trey, Empty Bronco**

PRO TIP

▶ This playbook has multiple receiving options from every formation; however, any time you get one-on-one coverage, take a chance downfield if you have a good matchup.

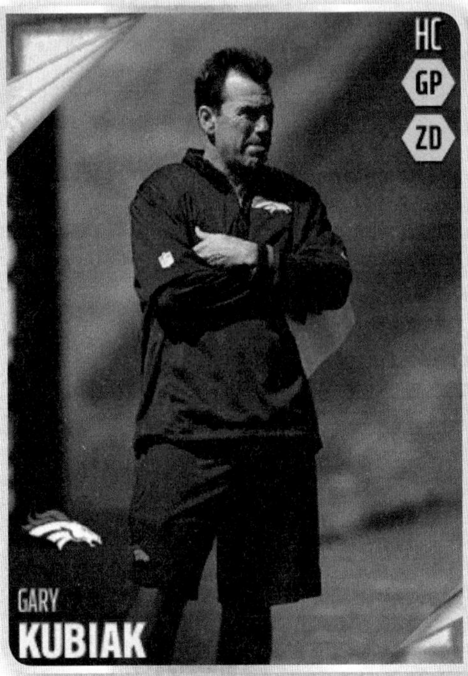

OFFENSIVE DRAFT TARGETS

- **WR (6'3", RTE, SPC, ACC)**
- **TE (RTE, ACC, SPD)**
- **QB (THP, SAC, DAC)**

DEFENSIVE DRAFT TARGETS

- **MLB (SPD, MCV, PUR)**
- **CB (MCV, PRS, TAK)**
- **OLB (STR, PMV, MCV)**

DEFENSE

The Broncos use a 3-4 defensive scheme in *Madden NFL 16* and have great coverages that allow for CBs to play physical man coverage. This is a fairly rare style, but it can be a tough matchup for players who don't face heavy man coverage.

KEY FORMATION

The Nickel 2-4-5 Dbl A Gap formation is a little aggressive, but it lets you bring serious pressure on third down. If your opponents didn't build heavily on the offensive line, they are in trouble!

KEY PLAYER

CB with 90+ Press

FORMATIONS

- **3-4: Odd, Under, Over, Even, Solid**
- **NICKEL: 2-4-5, 2-4-5 Dbl A Gap, 3-3-5 Wide**
- **BIG DIME: 2-3-6, 2-3-6 Will, 1-4-6**
- **QUARTER: 1-3-7, 3 Deep**

PRO TIP

▶ The defensive line doesn't need to be talented with pass-rush moves, but it must be strong to slow down the offensive line and keep it from getting to the second level and blocking LBs who are built for speed.

CLEVELAND BROWNS

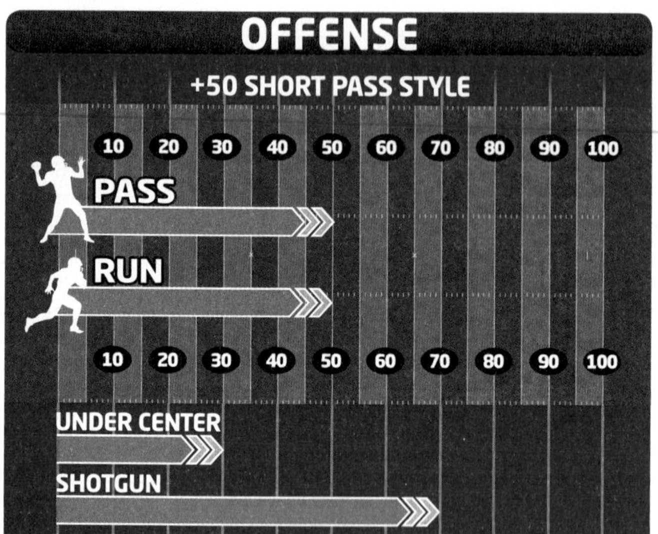

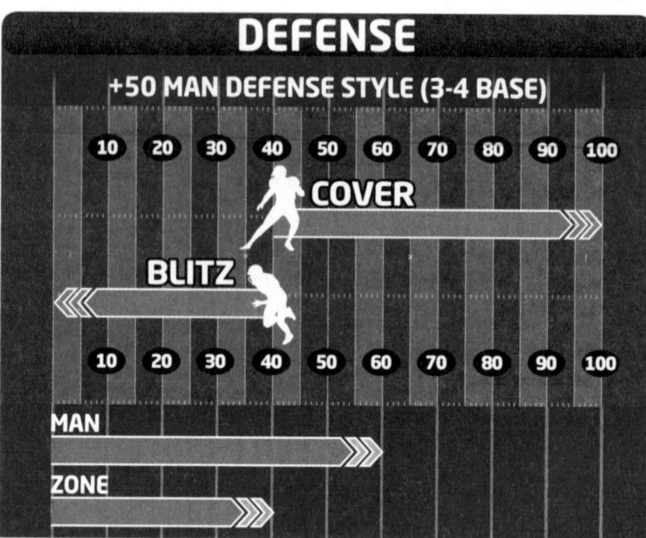

OFFENSE

The Browns have a pretty versatile offensive playbook with the ability to build schemes from under center, pistol, or shotgun. Your final scheme will vary heavily depending on what players you find in the draft.

KEY FORMATION

Gun Split Close Browns is one of the best formations in the game, especially for players who want to throw the ball. Look for a halfback who can catch out of the backfield and a big, safety-valve style tight end, who will really help make this formation tough to stop.

KEY PLAYER

QB with 88+ Short Accuracy

FORMATIONS

- **SINGLEBACK: Jumbo, Ace, Ace Pair, Ace Pair Twins, Doubles, Y-Trips**
- **I-FORM: Pro, Pro Twins, Tight Pair**
- **STRONG: Close**
- **WEAK: Pro, Pro Twins**
- **PISTOL: Strong, Ace, Slot Wing**
- **GUN: Split Close Browns, Doubles, Wing Trio Browns, Trips TE, Bunch Offset, Tight Doubles On, Snugs Flip, Spread, Trey Open Offset, Empty Browns, Empty Y-Flex**
- **WILDCAT: Trips Over**

PRO TIP

▶ Effective use of play action and new rollouts will make the Cleveland offensive playbook much more successful.

OFFENSIVE DRAFT TARGETS

- **WR (SPD, CTH, RTE)**
- **QB (PAC, SAC, ACC)**
- **LT (IPB, STR, PBK)**

DEFENSIVE DRAFT TARGETS

- **CB (MCV, SPD, PRC)**
- **MLB (SPD, MCV, PRC)**
- **OLB (PMV, STR, BSH)**

DEFENSE

The Browns' defensive scheme is best with strong players built to stop the run on the defensive line. This means the pressure will come from the OLB positions, especially if the secondary can stick with their matchups for a bit after the snap.

KEY FORMATION

Nickel 2-4-5 is a crucial formation to optimize. If you can stay in this most of the game, your opponent will be forced to make solid reads!

KEY PLAYER

CB with 85+ Man Coverage

FORMATIONS

- **3-4: Odd, Predator, Over, Over Ed, Bear**
- **NICKEL: 2-4-5, 2-4-5 Dbl A Gap, 3-3-5 Wide**
- **BIG DIME: 2-3-6, 1-4-6**
- **DOLLAR: 3-2-6**
- **QUARTER: 1-3-7, 3 Deep**

PRO TIP

▶ The longer your secondary is able to cover and even press the WRs, the better it is for your defense.

TAMPA BAY BUCCANEERS

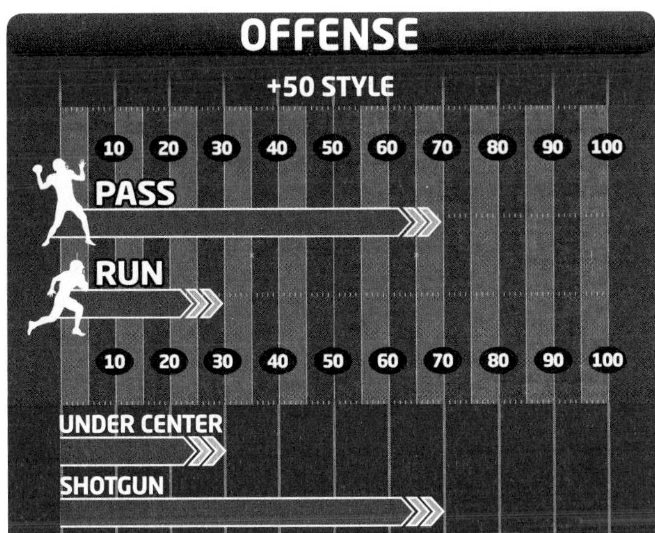

OFFENSE

If you select the Bucs' playbook, you will live and die by the big passing play downfield. If you feel comfortable with the new aggressive catch in *Madden NFL 16*, this playbook is perfect for you.

KEY FORMATION

The trio alignment in Gun Trio Buc is very tough for defenses to line up against no matter what type of talent you end up drafting. If you get your big WR, make sure to take a shot deep with PA Shot Wheel!

KEY PLAYER

Finding a big WR in the draft can pay off. If your opponent didn't land an elite CB, they will be forced to double-team your receiver nearly all game.

FORMATIONS

- **SINGLEBACK: Ace, Ace Pair, Ace Pair Twins, Doubles, Y-Trips, Bunch**
- **I-FORM: Pro, Twins Flex, Tight Pair**
- **STRONG: Close**
- **WEAK: Pro, Pro Twins**
- **PISTOL: Ace Twins, Slot, Trips**
- **GUN: Doubles, Y-Trips HB Wk, Trio Buc, Bunch Wk, Tight Flex, Spread, Buc Trips, Empty Buc, Empty Trey, 5WR Trio**

PRO TIP

▶ If you don't get a great offensive line, create more time in the pocket by blocking both of your backs in certain formations.

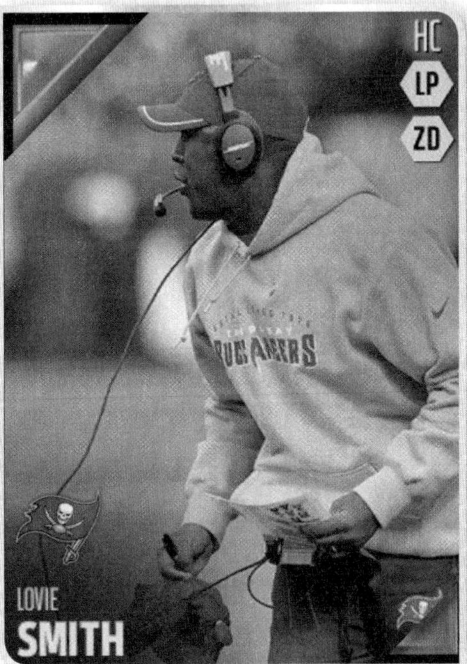

OFFENSIVE DRAFT TARGETS

- **WR (6'3"+, CIT, SPC, RTE)**
- **QB (DAC, THP, MAC)**
- **WR (6'3"+, CIT, SPC, RLS)**

DEFENSIVE DRAFT TARGETS

- **DT (PMV, STR, BSH)**
- **MLB (ZCV, PRC, SPD)**
- **SS (ZCV, PRC, PUR)**

DEFENSE

Tampa has a nice mix of 4-3 formations that can be used against a balanced offense. If they are run-heavy, get into the 46 Bear Under. If they are pass-heavy, the Big Dime can be a solid formation to get faster players on the field.

KEY FORMATION

Big Dime 4-1-6 is a unique formation that should help slow down pass-heavy teams without sacrificing too much in the run game.

KEY PLAYER

MLB with 80+ Zone Coverage

FORMATIONS

- **4-3: Stack, Under, Over, Over Plus, Wide**
- **46: Bear Under**
- **NICKEL: Normal, Double A Gap, Wide 9**
- **DIME: Normal**
- **BIG DIME: 4-1-6**
- **QUARTER: Normal, 3 Deep**

PRO TIP

▶ Having a third safety in this defense can be a benefit if the right draft situation occurs.

ARIZONA CARDINALS

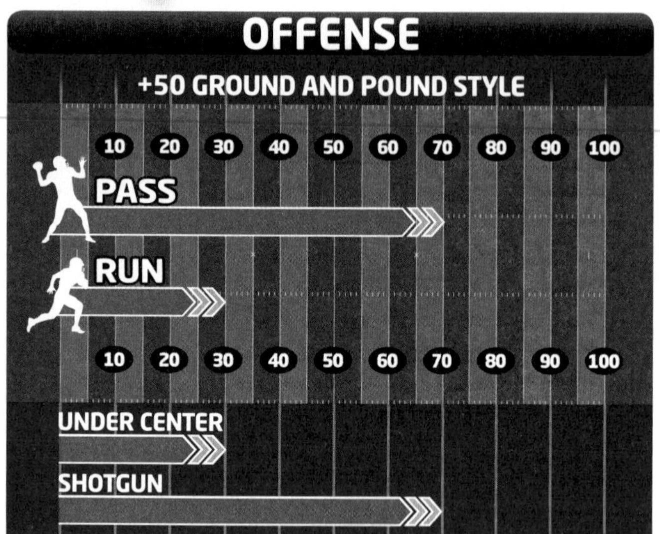

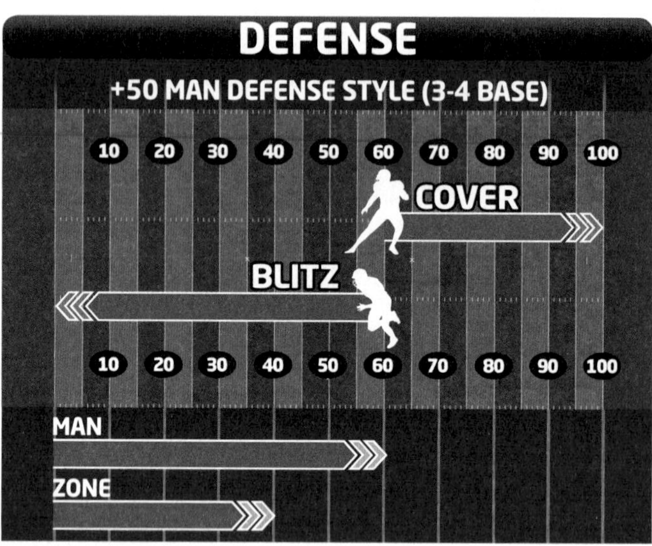

OFFENSE

The Arizona Cardinals' offense is loaded with big passing plays for players who like to attack downfield. While this isn't the style for everyone, a confident passer can really tear up defenses that don't build up their secondary. Consider drafting some linemen, too, to allow your QB the time he needs in the pocket.

KEY FORMATION

Gun Flip Trips is an excellent formation with every concept needed for a successful attack. Use the plays with built-in auto-motion to switch between attacking the corner and over the middle. Your opponent won't be able to tell what is coming next!

KEY PLAYER

90+ QB with 88+ Deep Accuracy

FORMATIONS

- **SINGLEBACK: Jumbo, Jumbo Pair, Ace, Ace Pair, Pair Tight Twins, Ace Pair Twins, Bunch Ace, Tight Doubles On, Doubles, Zona Y-Trips, Wing Trips**
- **I-FORM: Pro, Pro Twins, Tight Pair**
- **STRONG: Pro, Pro Twins**
- **WEAK: Flex Twins, Tight Pair**
- **PISTOL: Twin TE Flex**
- **GUN: Split Close, Ace Twins Offset, Doubles, Y Trips Wk, Wing Trio Wk, Trey, Bunch HB Str, Snugs, Flip Trips, Spread, Trips HB Wk, Empty Trey Flex**

PRO TIP

▶ If you don't land a big-time WR in the draft, use a tight end! They have similar size and should be able to go up for the new "high-point" throws with aggressive catch.

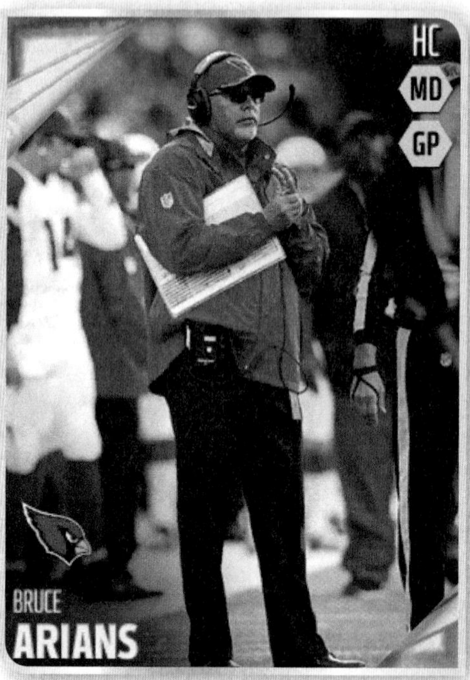

OFFENSIVE DRAFT TARGETS

- **QB (THP, DAC, MAC)**
- **LT (STR, PBK, RBK)**
- **WR (6'3"+ SPC, CIT)**

DEFENSIVE DRAFT TARGETS

- **CB (SPD, ACC, MCV)**
- **LB X 2 (SPD, MCV, ACC)**
- **DT (STR, BSH, TAK)**

DEFENSE

The strength of the Cardinals' defensive playbook is the LB corps. Since you can have up to five on the field at any time, you can never go wrong selecting just one more! Grab a big DT if available, but otherwise try to stack your LBs.

KEY FORMATION

The Nickel 2-4-5 Prowl will provide the blitzing firepower and confusion you need to get your opponent off the field on third down. It is best with man coverage, so look for good Speed and Man Coverage ratings in your back seven.

KEY PLAYER

CB with 85+ Man Coverage

FORMATIONS

- **3-4: Odd, Under, Over, Even, Solid**
- **NICKEL: 2-4-5 Even, 2-4-5 Dbl A Gap, 2-4-5 Prowl, 3-3-5 Wide**
- **BIG DIME: 2-3-6, 1-4-6**
- **QUARTER: 1-3-7, 3 Deep**

PRO TIP

▶ Adjusting an athletic defensive end to "man up" a TE or drop into a highly targeted zone area is a great way to slow down an offense.

SAN DIEGO CHARGERS

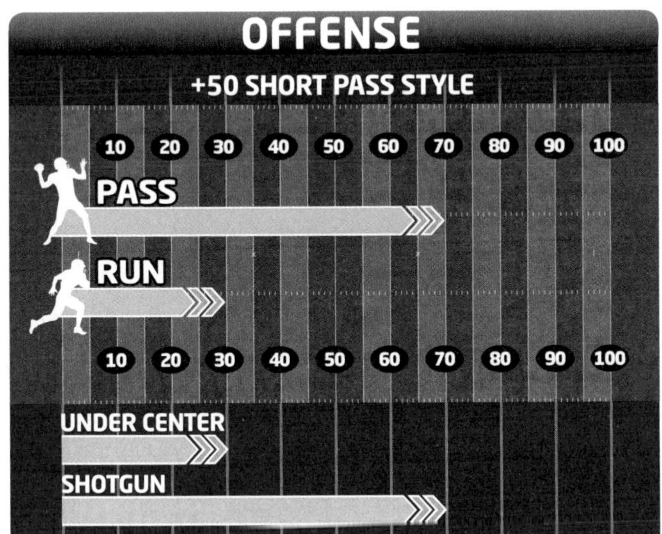

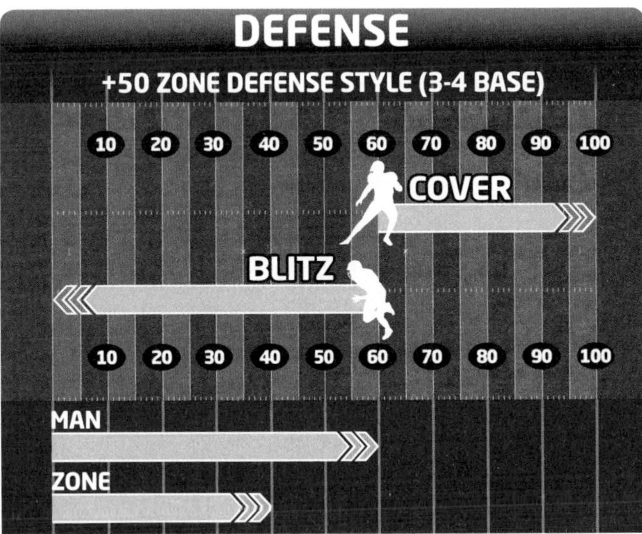

OFFENSE

The Chargers have a pretty balanced playbook that allows them to be effective running or by throwing the ball downfield. If you plan on using both options, make sure to get a QB who can get the ball into tight windows downfield to really take advantage.

KEY FORMATION

Gun Trips Y-Flex Tight formation will consistently be a tough matchup for man coverage due to the tight alignment. A TE who can run crisp routes will deliver first downs all game long.

KEY PLAYER

QB with 90+ Throw Power

FORMATIONS

- **SINGLEBACK: Jumbo, Ace, Ace Pair, Ace Pair Twins, Tight Doubles, Doubles, Y-Trips, Bunch**
- **I-FORM: Pro, Pro Twins, Tight, Tight Pair**
- **STRONG: Pro**
- **WEAK: Tight Pair**
- **PISTOL: Ace Wing, Doubles**
- **GUN: Split Y-Flex, Doubles Wk, Y-Trips Wk, Trips TE, Bunch Wk, Normal Y-Flex Tight, Spread, Y-Trips Open, Trips Y-Flex Tight, Trey Open Charger, Empty Base Flex**

PRO TIP

▶ If a second tight end catches your eye during the draft, don't hesitate to select him, because you can always find a spot in the lineup for him.

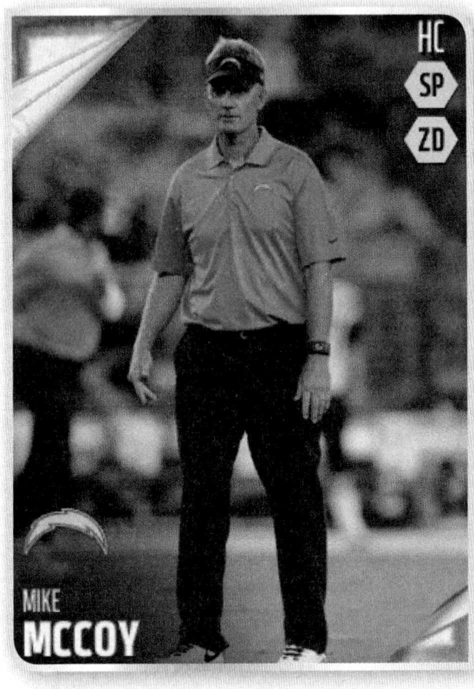

OFFENSIVE DRAFT TARGETS

- **TE (CIT, RBK, SPC)**
- **QB (THP, DAC, MAC)**
- **HB (SPD, AGI, CTH)**

DEFENSIVE DRAFT TARGETS

- **DE/DT (STR/BSH/PMV)**
- **OLB (SPD, FMV, ZCV)**
- **FS (PRC, ZCV, SPD)**

DEFENSE

The Chargers have a solid 3-4 playbook that requires good strength from the defensive line with fast finesse rushers at outside linebacker.

KEY FORMATION

Big Dime 2-3-6 Will positions your secondary players in unique spots and hopefully will confuse the offense. Don't sleep on a solid FS/SS combo!

KEY PLAYER

FS with 85+ Play Recognition

FORMATIONS

- **3-4: Odd, Under, Over, Over Ed, Solid**
- **NICKEL: 2-4-5 Even, 2-4-5 Dbl A Gap, 3-3-5, 3-3-5 Wide**
- **BIG DIME: 2-3-6, 2-3-6 Will**
- **QUARTER: 1-3-7, 3 Deep**

PRO TIP

▶ Nearly all of the Chargers' formations require a minimum of three linebackers, so don't worry about overlap in the front seven.

KANSAS CITY CHIEFS

OFFENSE

The Kansas City playbook has not only some good power running sets but also a surprising number of four-plus WR sets, so you can really pick apart the defense with short passes.

KEY FORMATION

Gun Trips TE is the best formation in the KC playbook. Try saving it for the second half to give your opponent a completely different look. It can light up the scoreboard quickly if you can't consistently pound the rock.

KEY PLAYER

HB with 88+ Overall

FORMATIONS

- **SINGLEBACK: Jumbo Pair, Ace, Ace Twins, Chief Doubles, Y-Trips**
- **I-FORM: Pro, Twins Flex, Tight**
- **STRONG: Pro, Tight Pair**
- **WEAK: Close**
- **PISTOL: Strong Twins, Weak, Ace**
- **GUN: Doubles, Y-Trips Wk, Wing Deep Offset, Trips TE, Bunch Wk, Snugs Flip, Trips Y-Flex Tight, Trey Open, Empty Chief, Empty Trey, Bunch Quads**
- **WILDCAT: Chief**

PRO TIP

▶ Aim for an all-around TE if one becomes available; you can always play him at WR if you need to air it out.

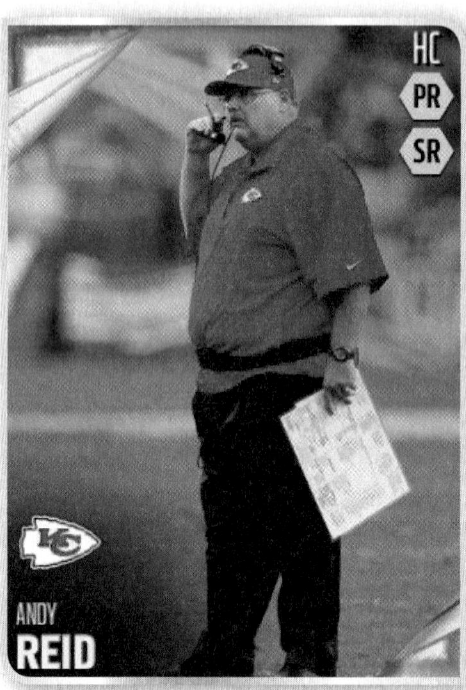

OFFENSIVE DRAFT TARGETS

- **HB (SPD, ELU, CTH)**
- **TE (RBK, CIT, RTE)**
- **QB (SAC, PAC, MAC)**

DEFENSIVE DRAFT TARGETS

- **OLB (STR, PMV, BSH)**
- **SS (POW, TAK, PUR)**
- **DT (STR, ACC, PMV)**

DEFENSE

The KC defensive playbook is another 3-4 base, so having a solid corps of LBs can't really hurt you. While picking strong defensive linemen isn't the fanciest move, they will really help stop the run!

KEY FORMATION

Nickel 2-4-5 Dbl A Gap puts tremendous pressure on the offensive line of your opponent. Send blitzes early and often!

KEY PLAYER

OLB with 85+ Block Shedding

FORMATIONS

- **3-4: Odd, Under, Over, Solid, Bear**
- **NICKEL: 2-4-5, 2-4-5 Dbl A Gap, 3-3-5, 3-3-5 Wide**
- **BIG DIME: 2-3-6, 1-4-6**
- **QUARTER: 1-3-7, 3 Deep**

PRO TIP

▶ If you get strong OLBs, the Nickel 2-4-5 can be an all-around zone defense that allows you to mix up coverage and then send solid blitzes.

INDIANAPOLIS COLTS

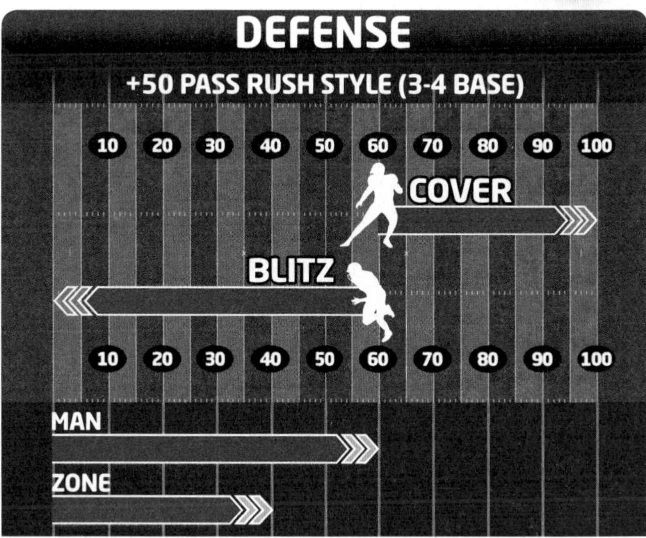

OFFENSE

The Colts' offensive playbook can be one of the most balanced in the entire game. While they have newer formations like Pistol, don't sleep on their power running sets, which have been around forever and can still be tough to stop depending on your team build.

KEY FORMATION

The Colts are the only team in the game with Gun Bunch TE, and it should be heavily used. The formation should easily beat zone coverage, and it contains nearly every concept without needing to adjust.

KEY PLAYER

QB with 85+ Deep Accuracy

FORMATIONS

- **SINGLEBACK: Jumbo, Ace, Ace Close, Ace Pair, Pair Tight Twins, Bunch Ace, Doubles, Y-Trips TE Slot, Wing Trips Open**
- **I-FORM: Pro, Twins Flex, Tight, Tackle Over**
- **STRONG: Pro, Twins Flex, Tight Pair**
- **WEAK: Pro**
- **PISTOL: Slot Wing, Y-Trips**
- **GUN: Split Close, Doubles, Y-Trips HB Wk, Bunch TE, Bunch Wk, Snugs Flip, Double Flex, Y-Trips Open, Trey Open, Empty Trey, Empty Trey Flex**
- **WILDCAT: Trips Over**

PRO TIP

▶ If you build a dominant lineup for the power run game, try the I-Form Tackle Over until your opponents prove they can stop it!

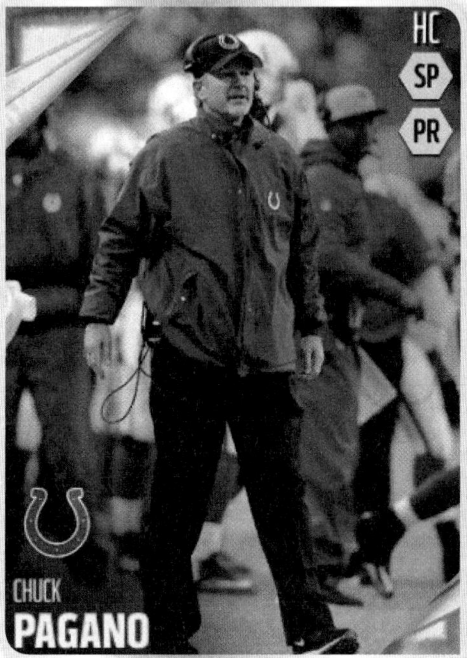

OFFENSIVE DRAFT TARGETS

- QB (DAC, SPD, THP)
- WR (SPD, RTE, CTH)
- TE (CIT, RBK, SPD)

DEFENSIVE DRAFT TARGETS

- CB (ZCV, PRS, AWR)
- MLB (ZCV, AWR, PRC)
- OLB (FMV, SPD, ACC)

DEFENSE

The Colts' defensive book is set up for quick finesse rushers to attack off the edge. This can leave them vulnerable to the run on early downs but really makes a lead valuable.

KEY FORMATION

The Nickel 2-4-5 is your most balanced formation, and it can be crucial if an opponent is looking to scramble or run off the edge. Bring a safety down by calling "show blitz" if an opponent starts to run at your weakest OLB.

KEY PLAYER

MLB with 85+ Zone Coverage

FORMATIONS

- **3-4: Odd, Predator, Over, Even, Bear**
- **NICKEL: 2-4-5, 2-4-5 Dbl A Gap, 2-4-5 Prowl, 3-3-5 Wide**
- **BIG DIME: 2-3-6 Even, 2-3-6 Flex**
- **QUARTER: 1-3-7, 3 Deep**

PRO TIP

▶ The Colts' playbook will really shine if you can secure an early lead, so this is one of the few situations where it makes sense to receive the kickoff.

DALLAS COWBOYS

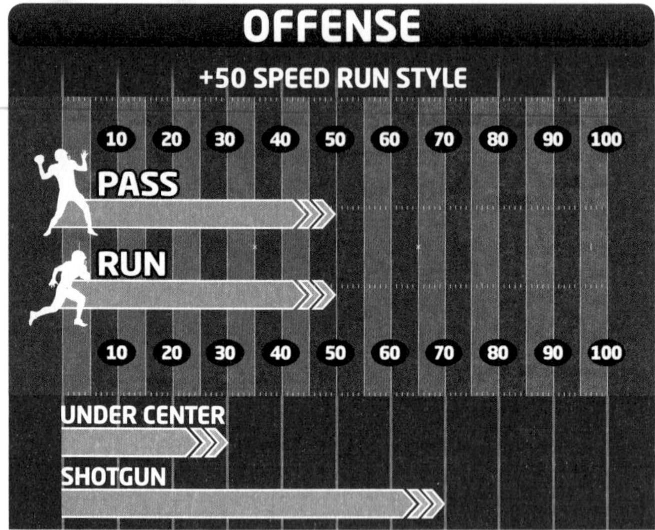

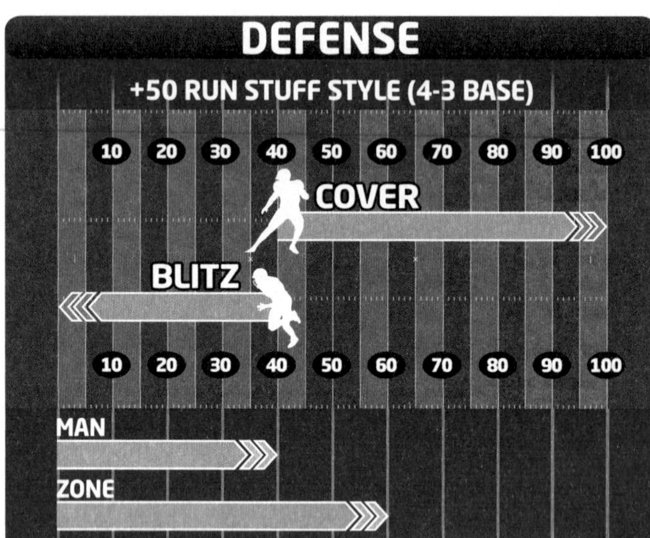

OFFENSE

The Cowboys' offensive playbook has a variety of formations that allow a balanced attack. Look for a safety valve TE who can run-block rather than a more explosive type, and use him to keep the chains moving.

KEY FORMATION

Gun Empty Trips TE is perfect if your offensive line can win the battle. The TE has some solid routes that allow him to get position on defenders for possession catches.

KEY PLAYER

TE with 70+ RBK, 85+ CIT

FORMATIONS

- **SINGLEBACK: Jumbo, Ace, Ace Close, Ace Pair, Ace Pair Flex, Doubles, Y-Trips, Bunch**
- **I-FORM: Pro, Twins Flex, Tight Pair**
- **STRONG: Close**
- **PISTOL: Ace Twins, Y-Trips, Bunch**
- **GUN: Split Cowboy, Doubles, Y-Trips Cowboy, Wing Deep Offset, Trio Cowboy, Snugs Flip, Norm Y-Flex Tight, Flip Trips, Trey Open Cowboy, Empty Trey, Empty Trips TE, Empty Cowboy**
- **WILDCAT: Cowboys**

PRO TIP

▶ You can really generate a strong ground attack with this playbook on early downs to make your third downs very manageable.

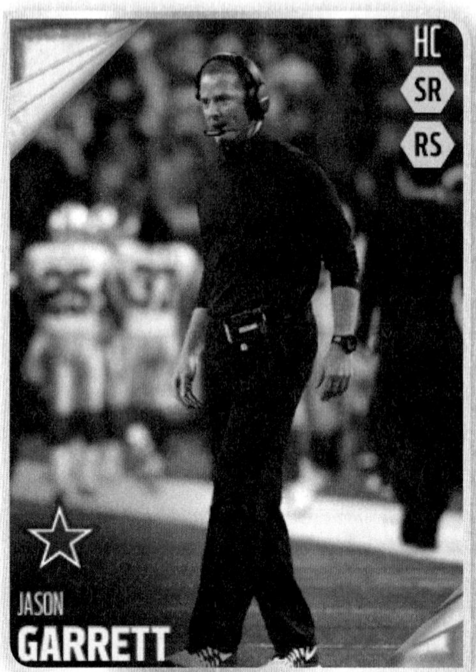

OFFENSIVE DRAFT TARGETS

- **TE (RBK, CIT, RTE)**
- **HB (TRK, SPD, CTH)**
- **LT/RT (STR, RBK, PBK)**

DEFENSIVE DRAFT TARGETS

- **SS (PRC, PUR, TAK)**
- **FS (ZCV, PRC, SPD)**
- **OLB (STR, ACC, ZCV)**

DEFENSE

The Cowboys' 4-3 defensive playbook is perfect for aggressive players who love to get eight defenders in the box and force their opponents to pass. Keep an eye out for any opposing receivers who need extra attention, and shade your safeties in that direction.

KEY FORMATION

The 46 Bear is a unique formation that isn't in available in many playbooks. Make sure to try this as your base formation to stop the run, especially up the middle.

KEY PLAYER

LB with 87+ Acceleration

FORMATIONS

- **4-3: Stack, Under, Over, Over Plus, Wide 9**
- **46: Bear**
- **NICKEL: Normal, Double A Gap, Wide 9**
- **DIME: Normal**
- **BIG DIME: 4-1-6**
- **QUARTER: Normal, 3 Deep**

PRO TIP

▶ Most players haven't seen the Bear, so you may get be able to get out to a fast start. The pressure usually generates from the right of the screen, so look out for lefty QBs.

MIAMI DOLPHINS

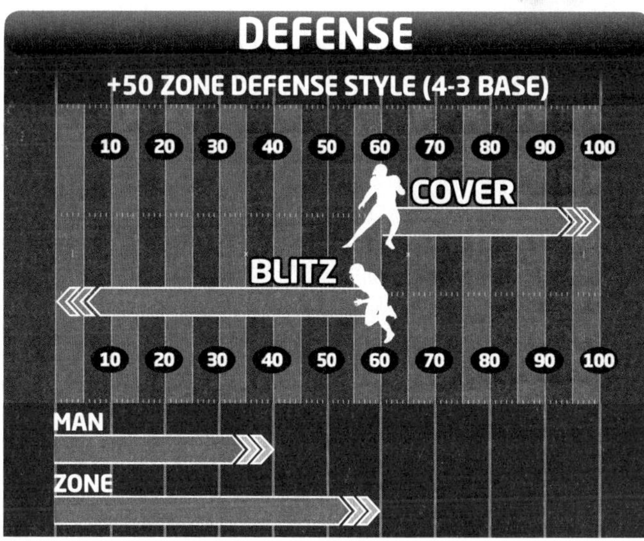

OFFENSE

The Miami playbook features multiple shotgun formations and can really be solid for a player who is balanced but has a bit more of a pass-first mentality. You don't have to run if the numbers in the box aren't in your favor.

KEY FORMATION

The Gun Wing Trips Dolphin formation is just one example of a wing formation in this playbook that allows for solid pass protection and versatility at the TE position.

KEY PLAYER

TE with 75+ RBK

FORMATIONS

- **SINGLEBACK: Ace Wing, Ace Pair, Ace Pair Flex, Doubles, Wing Trips Open, Wing Trio**
- **PISTOL: Ace Wing**
- **GUN: Split Dolphin, Ace Offset, Ace Twins Offset, Twin TE Flex Wk, Doubles Offset, Doubles Wing Offset, Doubles Offset Wk, Tackle Over Trips, Y-Trips Offset, Wing Trips Dolphin, Wing Trips Dolphin Wk, Trey Offset, Bunch, Bunch Open Offset, Tight Offset TE, Double Stack, Dbls Y-Flex Offset, Double Flex, Trey Open Offset, Empty Bunch, Empty Base Flex**

PRO TIP

▶ The Dolphins' playbook is another that only improves with the presence of a mobile QB. You don't need a speedster, but the ability to pick up a first down when scrambling on third and 5 is important.

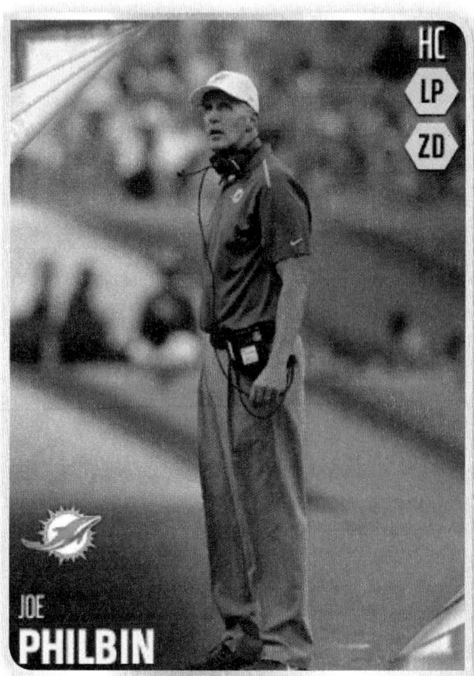

OFFENSIVE DRAFT TARGETS

- **TE (RBK, CIT, RTE)**
- **QB (SAC, PAC, ACC)**
- **HB (TRK, AGI, SPD)**

DEFENSIVE DRAFT TARGETS

- **DT (PMV, STR, TAK)**
- **SS (PRC, PUR, POW)**
- **DE (SPD, FMV, ACC)**

DEFENSE

The Dolphins have all of the traditional defensive formations of a 4-3 playbook, so generating pressure without using too many exotic blitzes will be important. If you play an opponent with a spread passing game who loaded up on receivers, use the Dollar 3-2-6.

KEY FORMATION

The 46 Bear Under provides a unique look to most defenses and can shut down the inside run if the 4-3 Wide 9 isn't getting it done!

KEY PLAYER

DT with 90+ PMV

FORMATIONS

- **4-3: Stack, Under, Over, Over Plus, Wide 9**
- **46: Bear Under**
- **NICKEL: Normal, Double A Gap, Wide 9**
- **DIME: Normal**
- **DOLLAR: 3-2-6**
- **QUARTER: Normal, 3 Deep**

PRO TIP

▶ The Dolphins have some really wide alignments on defense, so don't go for strength off the edge; look for speed instead.

PHILADELPHIA EAGLES

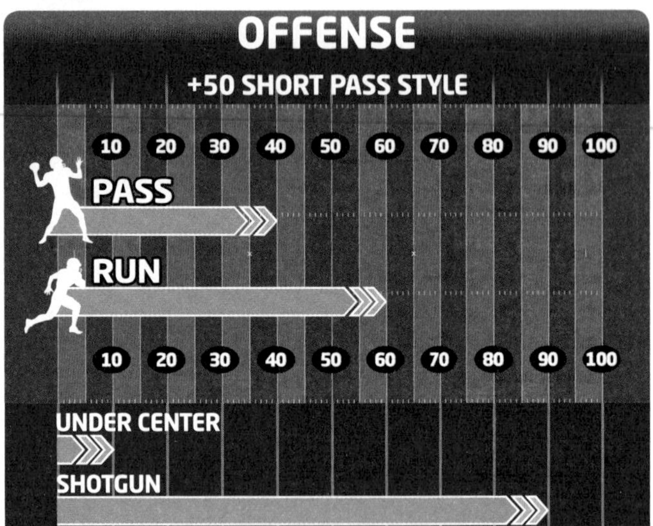

OFFENSE

The Eagles' offensive playbook is a unique one in *Madden NFL 16* and contains far and away the most shotgun formations. You must be comfortable passing and running from shotgun to have optimal success.

KEY FORMATION

In the Gun Ace Offset, learn how to run Inside Zone consistently and the rest of your offense will open up. Every formation should have an inside run, outside run, screen, and deep pass off play action.

KEY PLAYER

HB with 80+ Catch

FORMATIONS

- **SINGLEBACK: Ace, Ace Pair, Ace Pair Twins, Doubles, Wing Trips Open**
- **WEAK: Pro**
- **PISTOL: Doubles**
- **GUN: Split Slot, Slot Offset, Ace Offset, Ace Twins Offset, Twin TE Flex Wk, Doubles Offset, Doubles Wing, Doubles Offset Wk, Tackle Over Trips, Y-Trips Offset, Y-Trips Offset Wk, Wing Trips Eagle, Wing Trips Eagle Wk, Tackle Over, Trio Offset, Trio Offset Wk, Bunch Open, Bunch Open Offset, Double Stack, Spread HB Wk, Flip Trips Eagle, Trey Open Offset, Empty Trey**

PRO TIP

▶ You don't need much throw power or speed at QB, but it doesn't hurt if the right player shows up!

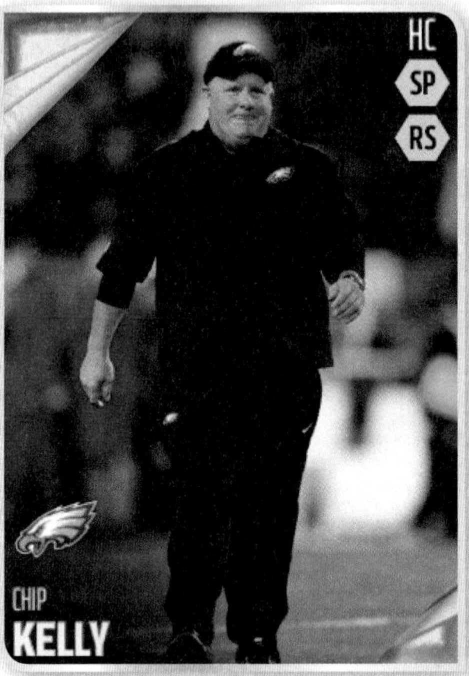

OFFENSIVE DRAFT TARGETS

- **HB (CTH, AGI, ELU)**
- **QB (PAC, SAC, DAC)**
- **WR (6'3", SPD, SPC)**

DEFENSIVE DRAFT TARGETS

- **OLB/DE (ACC, FMV, ZCV)**
- **SS (PUR, ZCV, TAK)**
- **DE (STR, BSH, TAK)**

DEFENSE

The Eagles have a solid 3-4 defensive playbook and also rely on multiple LBs moving around to create confusion.

KEY FORMATION

The 3-4 Predator allows an LB to rush from the DE position and hopefully outmaneuver a slower tackle with acceleration or finesse. Don't use this set on a running down, because this player won't be your strongest option.

KEY PLAYER

OLB with 87+ FMV

FORMATIONS

- **3-4: Odd, Predator, Over, Even, Solid**
- **NICKEL: 2-4-5, 2-4-5 Dbl A Gap, 2-4-5 Prowl, 3-3-5 Wide**
- **BIG DIME: 2-3-6 Even, 2-3-6 Will**
- **QUARTER: 1-3-7, 3 Deep**

PRO TIP

▶ Keep an eye out for a strong safety, because the Eagles' main pass-defense formations use a player up in the box.

ATLANTA FALCONS

OFFENSE

The Atlanta Falcons playbook is excellent for players who want to air the ball out! While it requires an elite WR and solid offensive line, you can certainly win some shootouts with this playbook.

KEY FORMATION

Pistol Ace is an excellent formation that will allow you to start the game very balanced as you learn the strengths of your team.

KEY PLAYER

WR with 85+ Spectacular Catch

FORMATIONS

- **SINGLEBACK: Jumbo, Ace, Ace Pair Twins, Tight Doubles, Doubles, Y-Trips, Bunch**
- **I-FORM: Pro, Twins Flex, Tight Pair**
- **STRONG: Pro, Close**
- **WEAK: Pro Twins**
- **PISTOL: Ace, Slot, Y-Trips**
- **GUN: Split Offset, Doubles On, Wing Trips, Trio Falcon, Bunch Offset, Tight Flex, Spread, Trey Open, Empty Falcon, Empty Base**

PRO TIP

▶ Try adding a pass-catching HB or TE if one becomes available, to give you the most flexibility with your lineup.

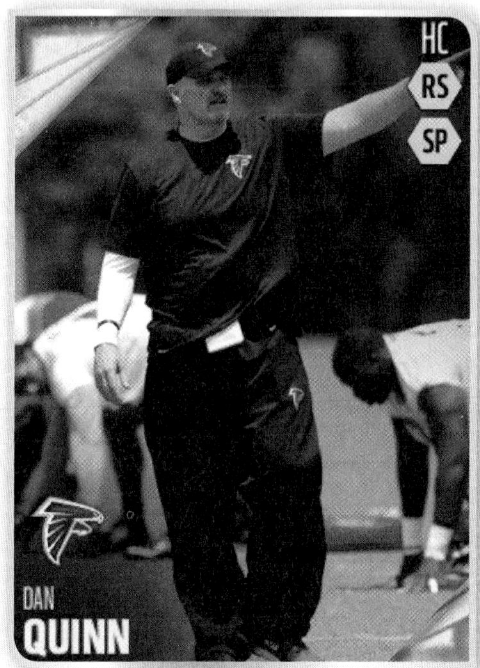

OFFENSIVE DRAFT TARGETS

- **WR (SPD, SPC, CIT)**
- **TE (6'4"+, CIT, RTE)**
- **QB (PAC, DAC, THP)**

DEFENSIVE DRAFT TARGETS

- **DE (SPD, ZCV, ACC)**
- **SS (PRC, PUR, POW)**
- **DT (STR, BSH, TAK)**

DEFENSE

The Falcons have really expanded their defensive schemes to allow for multiple DEs/LBs to rush and drop into coverage at different times.

KEY FORMATION

Nickel 2-4-5 is a perfect point to build from for this playbook. If you end up slightly off either way, you will still have plenty of options!

KEY PLAYER

DE with 75+ Zone Coverage

FORMATIONS

- **4-3: Stack, Under, Over, Over Plus, Wide 9**
- **46: Bear Under**
- **NICKEL : Normal, Double A Gap, Wide 9**
- **DIME: Normal**
- **DOLLAR: 3-2-6**
- **QUARTER: Normal, 3 Deep**

PRO TIP

▶ Adjusting an athletic defensive end to "man up" a TE or drop into a highly targeted zone area is a great way to slow down an offense.

SAN FRANCISCO 49ERS

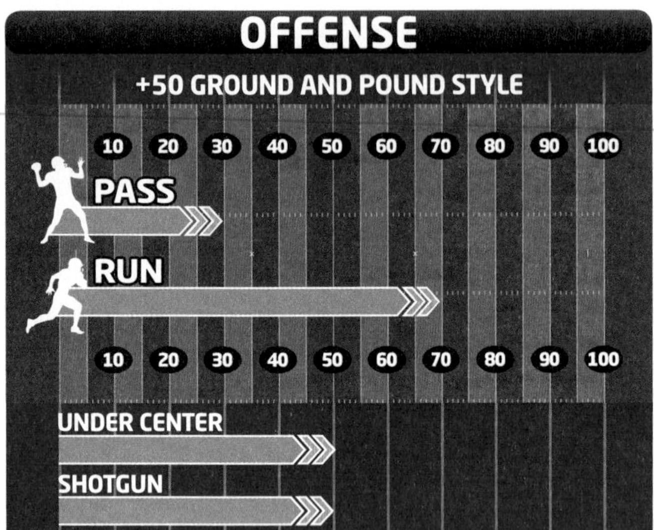

OFFENSE

The 49ers' playbook is mainly best for players who want a power rushing attack. However, players who enjoy using a mobile QB and the shotgun running game can still find success if they can strike the right balance.

KEY FORMATION

Pistol Full House TE is the best example of what this playbook has to offer. A solid power rushing attack with easy throws if the defense gets greedy.

KEY PLAYER

HB with 90+ Trucking.

FORMATIONS

- **SINGLEBACK: Jumbo Z, Ace, Ace Close, Ace Pair Flex, Doubles, Y-Trips, Bunch**
- **I-FORM: Pro, Pro Twins, Tight, Tight Pair**
- **STRONG: Pro, Tight Pair**
- **WEAK: Pro, Tight Pair**
- **PISTOL: Full House TE, Full House Base, Strong, Bunch**
- **GUN: Doubles, Dbls Wing Offset Wk, Y-Trips Wk, Wing Trips Wk, Trips TE Offset, Trio Offset Wk, Bunch HB Str, Double Flex, Trey Open, Empty Trey Flex**

PRO TIP

▶ Picking up a mobile QB for this scheme is important if you want to run the ball from pistol or shotgun.

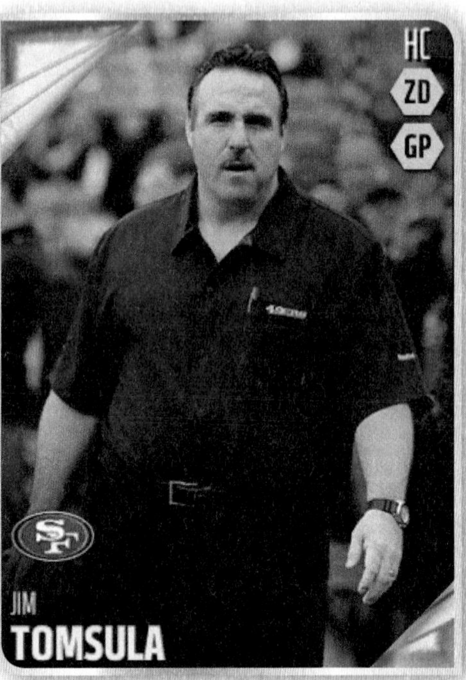

OFFENSIVE DRAFT TARGETS

- **HB (TRK, STR, BCV)**
- **QB (SPD, THP, SAC)**
- **TE (SPD, ACC, RTE)**

DEFENSIVE DRAFT TARGETS

- **MLB (SPD, PRC, ZCV)**
- **OLB (SPD, ACC, FMV)**
- **DT/DE (STR, BSH, PMV)**

DEFENSE

The 49ers' defense is best when constructed with two different linebacker types. Look for two balanced defenders at the MLB position with a strong OLB on one side and a quicker pass rusher on the other! One of your MLBs and your pass-rushing OLB will be on the field nearly every down, so go elite.

KEY FORMATION

The 3-4 Odd is a great starting formation to see if your opponent can beat your zone coverage with passing, and it doesn't give up too much in the run game.

KEY PLAYER

OLB with 85+ Acceleration

FORMATIONS

- **3-4: Odd, Under, Over, Even, Bear**
- **NICKEL: 2-4-5, 2-4-5 Dbl A Gap, 2-4-5 Prowl, 3-3-5 Wide**
- **BIG DIME: 2-3-6, 1-4-6**
- **QUARTER: 1-3-7, 3 Deep**

PRO TIP

▶ Getting a strong defensive end who can move inside to DT on passing downs is important to get the most bang for your buck.

NEW YORK GIANTS

OFFENSE

+50 GROUND AND POUND STYLE

10 20 30 40 50 60 70 80 90 100

PASS

RUN

10 20 30 40 50 60 70 80 90 100

UNDER CENTER

SHOTGUN

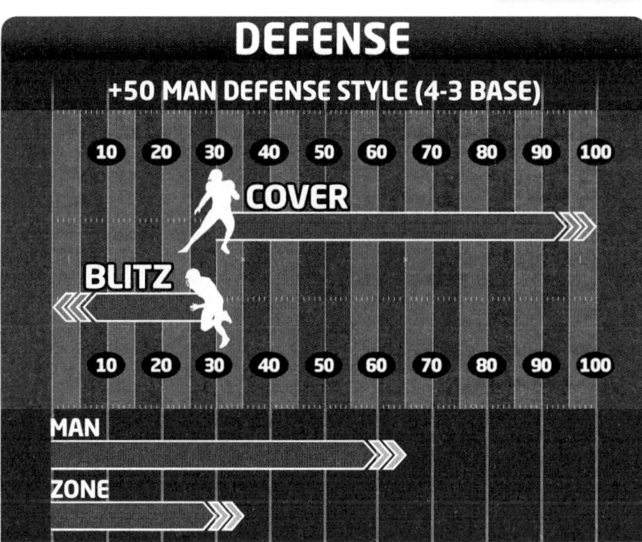

OFFENSE

The Giants' playbook has been completely overhauled in *Madden NFL 16* and is perfect for players who like to utilize quick throws and the tight end position.

KEY FORMATION

Gun Trips Y Iso is just one of many new formations in the Giants' playbook. If you pick up multiple WRs, you can use this formation to draw attention to one receiver while another gets open for a big play.

KEY PLAYER

WR with 90+ Route Running

FORMATIONS

- **SINGLEBACK: Ace, Ace Close, Ace Pair, Ace Pair Twins, Bunch Ace, Giant Doubles, Y-Trips, Wing Trio**
- **I-FORM: Pro, Pro Twins, Tight**
- **STRONG: Pro, Pro Twins**
- **FULL HOUSE: Wide**
- **GUN: Doubles Flex Wk, Doubles Flex Wing, Doubles Wing Wk, Y-Trips Wk, Wing Offset Wk, Trio Offset, Spread, Y-Trips Open, Trips Y Iso, Giant Trips, Empty Giant, Flex Trey**

PRO TIP

▶ This playbook really works well if you can master the new RAC move!

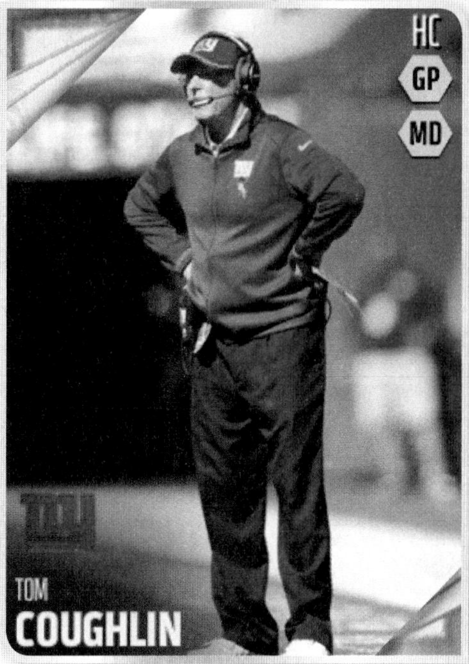

OFFENSIVE DRAFT TARGETS

- **WR (RTE, SPD, CIT)**
- **TE (CIT, RBK, RTE)**
- **QB (PAC, SAC, MAC)**

DEFENSIVE DRAFT TARGETS

- **DE (FMV, SPD, ACC)**
- **DE (PMV, SPD, ZCV)**
- **CB (ZCV, PRC, PUR)**

DEFENSE

The Giants' defensive playbook is a solid 4-3 that relies on the ability of multiple pass rushers as the bread and butter.

KEY FORMATION

Nickel NASCAR allows you to get DTs out of the game and DEs into unique spots along the line. Look for speed/size mismatches at the guard spot and get your best pass rusher in there!

KEY PLAYER

DE with 90+ FMV

FORMATIONS

- **4-3: Stack, Under, Over, Over Plus, Wide 9**
- **5-2: Normal**
- **NICKEL: Normal, Double A Gap, NASCAR**
- **DIME: Normal**
- **DOLLAR: 3-2-6**
- **QUARTER: Normal, 3 Deep**

PRO TIP

▶ Optimize your lineup before heading into game to take advantage of the Giants' unique formations.

JACKSONVILLE JAGUARS

OFFENSE

The Jaguars' offensive playbook has some very solid shotgun formations, which don't require a ton of great pass-blocking up front. Hit your quick passes to HBs and TEs before going deep, or your QB could be in trouble.

KEY FORMATION

Gun Bunch Quads is one of the most distinctive formations in the game and should crush zone defense. If you master multiple concepts, you can stay in this formation for a good chunk of the game against defenses deficient against the pass.

KEY PLAYER

HB/WR with 90+ Agility

FORMATIONS

- **SINGLEBACK: Jumbo Z, Ace, Ace Twins, Ace Pair Twins, Doubles, Bunch**
- **I-FORM: Pro, Tight, Tight Pair**
- **STRONG: Pro**
- **WEAK: Pro Twins**
- **PISTOL: Weak, Ace, Slot Wing**
- **GUN: Split Jaguar, Y-Trips HB Wk, Trips TE, Bunch Wk, Snugs Flip, Spread Y-Flex, Trips Y Iso, Trey Open, Empty Y-Flex, Empty Base, Bunch Quads**

PRO TIP

The Jaguars' playbook has plenty of ways to get the ball to an athletic player in space. Master the RAC move to become a master of this scheme.

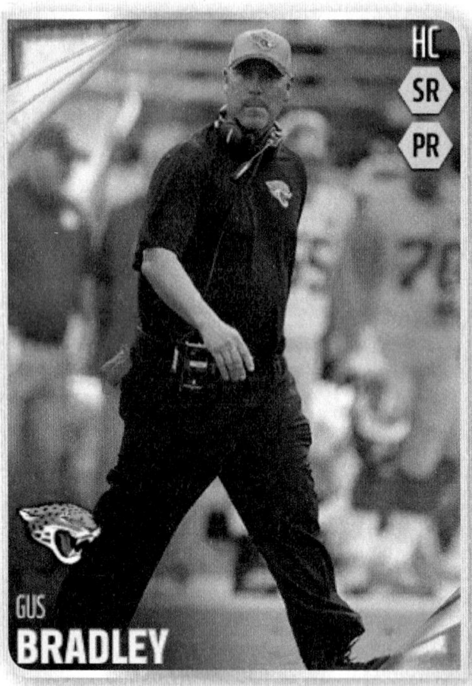

OFFENSIVE DRAFT TARGETS

- WR (ACC, AGI, CTH)
- TE (RBK, CIT, STR)
- QB (SAC, MAC, PAC)

DEFENSIVE DRAFT TARGETS

- DT (STR, PMV, BSH)
- OLB (ZCV, PRC, PUR)
- FS (ZCV, TAK, PRC)

DEFENSE

The Jaguars' playbook is built around a 4-3 defensive scheme. They don't have tons of flash in their plays, but if you can get a good pass rusher at either DE or OLB, he won't go to waste.

KEY FORMATION

The 46 Normal is a great way to shut the run game down early. It's a nice perk of the Jaguars' defensive book. If your opponent completes some passes, drop down to the Dollar 3-2-6.

KEY PLAYER

DT with 85+ Block Shedding

FORMATIONS

- **4-3: Stack, Under, Over, Over Plus, Wide 9**
- **46: Normal**
- **NICKEL: Normal, Double A Gap, Wide 9**
- **DIME: Normal**
- **DOLLAR: 3-2-6**
- **QUARTER: Normal, 3 Deep**

PRO TIP

The Jaguars' defensive book doesn't really put a premium on speed at the LB position, which is a nice difference from many of the 3-4 playbooks.

NEW YORK JETS

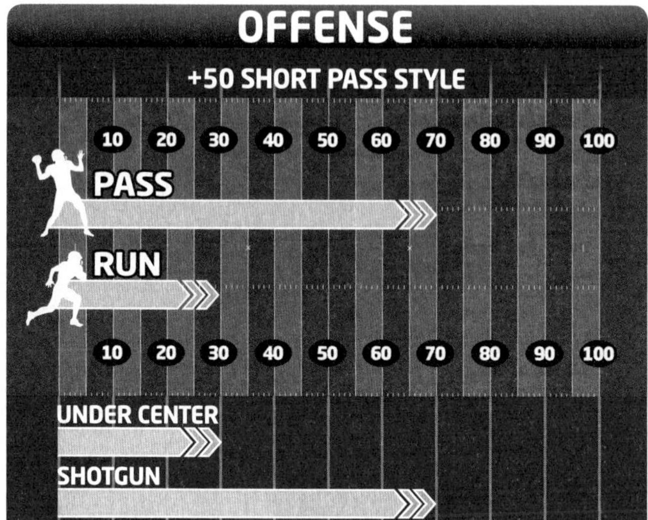

OFFENSE

The Jets' offense won't have you winning shootouts, but it works well in combination with their aggressive defense. If you can grab a lead, it will put too much pressure on your opponent. The offensive line is an underrated area in Draft Champions. Not many players love selecting the big guys up front—until they get into a game and control the line of scrimmage, resulting in a win.

KEY FORMATION

Singleback Wing Trips is just one example of the Jets' new spread-style offensive playbook. Approach it as a run-first set before looking to the quick pass.

KEY PLAYER

HB with 90+ Trucking

FORMATIONS

- **SINGLEBACK: Jumbo, Ace, Ace Pair Twins, Bunch Ace, Doubles, Y-Trips, Wing Trips**
- **I-FORM: Pro, Pro Twins, Tight**
- **STRONG: Pro, Twins Flex, Tight Pair**
- **PISTOL: Strong Slot, Slot, Wing Trips**
- **GUN: Split Jet, Doubles, Y-Trips Offset, Bunch Wk, Snugs, Spread Y-Slot, Y-Trips Open, Trips Y-Flex Tight, Trips Open Left, Trey Open, Empty Jet, Empty Spread, Bunch Quads**

PRO TIP

▶ Although you may expect to see power run sets, it is a fairly spread-heavy playbook.

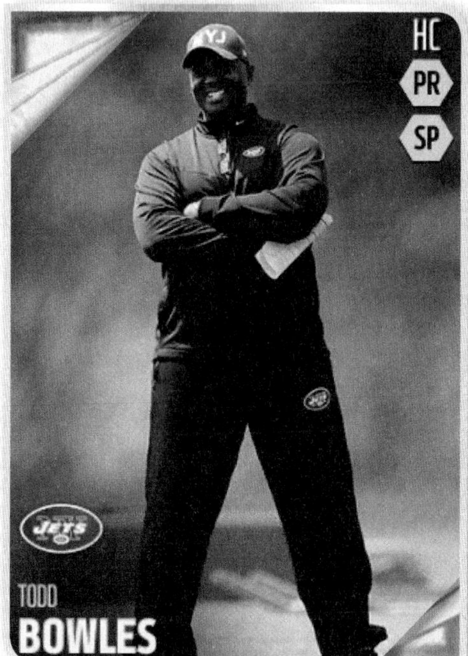

OFFENSIVE DRAFT TARGETS

- **C (STR, RBK, IPB)**
- **LG (STR, PBK, RBK)**
- **LT (STR, PBK, RBK)**

DEFENSIVE DRAFT TARGETS

- **DT (STR, BSH, PUR)**
- **CB (MCV, SPD, PRS)**
- **MLB (SPD, MCV, PRC)**

DEFENSE

The Jets have one of the most aggressive blitzing playbooks in all of *Madden NFL 16*. Take advantage of these plays on third and long to generate sacks and even some turnovers!

KEY FORMATION

Rely on the 3-4 Solid early in games to shut down the run. Be sure to pass-commit if you think your opponent is going to call play action, and try a play like Trio Sky Zone.

KEY PLAYER

CB with 90+ Man Coverage

FORMATIONS

- **3-4: Odd, Under, Over, Even, Solid**
- **NICKEL: 2-4-5 Even, 2-4-5 Dbl A Gap, 2-5-4 Prowl, 3-3-5 Wide**
- **BIG DIME: 2-3-6, 1-4-6**
- **QUARTER: 1-3-7, 3 Deep**
- **GOAL LINE: 5-3-3, 5-4-2**

PRO TIP

▶ The strength of the playbook is heavy pressure on passing downs with man coverage. This can feel risky, but if you draft the right players in the secondary and call for pressure at the right time, the rewards can be huge!

DETROIT LIONS

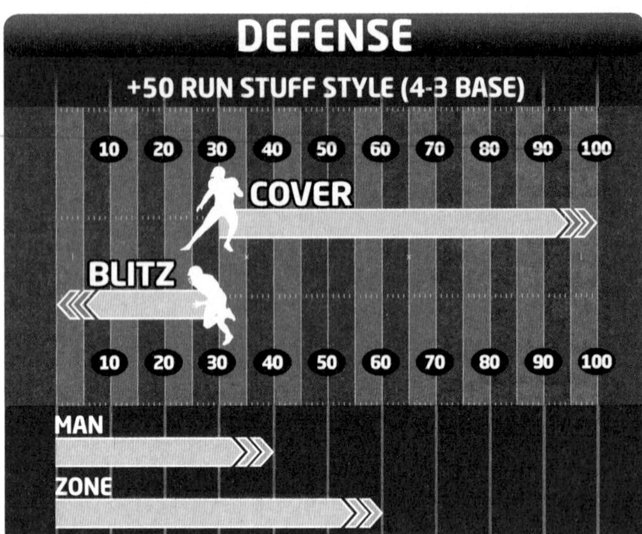

OFFENSE

The Lions' offensive playbook is built around the passing game and is one of the best to take advantage of the all-new catching in *Madden NFL 16*! Although the playbook requires a big WR and a strong-armed QB, any opponent who didn't get an elite pass-rushing or cover CB will be out-matched.

KEY FORMATION

Gun Split Lion is a great early test for your opponent. Isolate your best WR on the outside and see if you have a favorable matchup. You can always check down to your HBs or keep them in to block if you notice an elite defensive pass rusher.

KEY PLAYER

6'4"+ WR with 90+ Spectacular Catch

FORMATIONS

- **SINGLEBACK: Jumbo, Ace, Ace Pair, Ace Pair Flex, Doubles, Y-Trips Lion**
- **I-FORM: Pro, Twins Flex, Tight Pair**
- **STRONG: Close**
- **WEAK: Pro**
- **PISTOL: Strong, Ace, Slot Flex Lion, Y-Trips**
- **GUN: Split Lion, Ace Twins, Doubles, Y-Trips Wk, Snugs Flip, Spread Y-Flex, Trey Open Lion, Empty Lion, Empty Trey**

PRO TIP

▶ A smaller WR with great route running (RAC!) can shift this book to more of a short-passing one that occasionally takes big shots downfield.

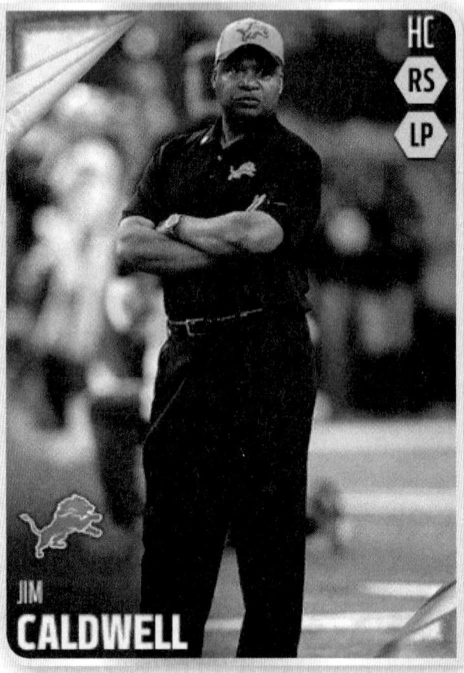

OFFENSIVE DRAFT TARGETS

- **WR (SPD, CIT, SPC)**
- **QB (THP, DAC, MAC)**
- **WR/TE (SPD, RTE, CIT)**

DEFENSIVE DRAFT TARGETS

- **DT (PMV, STR, BSH)**
- **DE (SPD, FMV, ZCV)**
- **FS (SPD, ZCV, PRC)**

DEFENSE

The Lions' defensive playbook is built around getting a solid pass rush from the defensive line. This allows gold-level LBs to stay unblocked and to make plays. Since nearly all the formations use four defensive linemen, you can't afford to come up short here, but the composition isn't a huge deal.

KEY FORMATION

The 5-2 formation can really lock down the run, even if your opponent went heavy on the offensive line in the draft.

KEY PLAYER

DT with 85+ Power Moves

FORMATIONS

- **4-3: Stack, Under, Over, Over Plus, Wide 9**
- **5-2: Normal**
- **NICKEL: Normal, Double A Gap, Wide 9**
- **DIME: Normal**
- **BIG DIME: 4-1-6**
- **QUARTER: Normal, 3 Deep**

PRO TIP

▶ Defensive ends that are capable of dropping into zone coverage to give a different look to the QB are key, especially against short-pass offenses.

GREEN BAY PACKERS

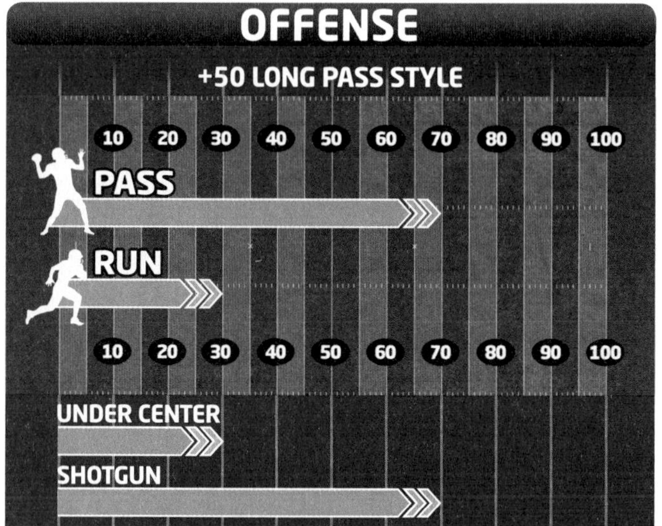

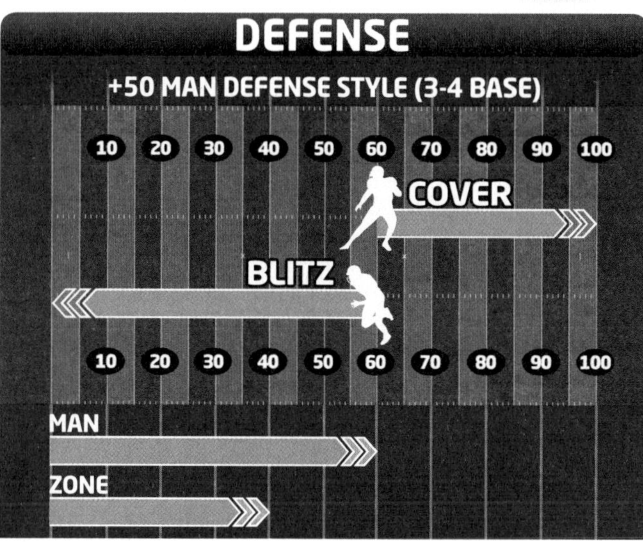

OFFENSE

The Packers' offensive playbook favors the passing game, but the right power back can really find some nice holes from the shotgun sets. Don't draft two big WRs unless an amazing opportunity appears; instead look for one that can be elusive across the middle and run after the catch (RAC).

KEY FORMATION

Gun Doubles Flex Wing is an excellent formation that provides not only a running threat but the ability to block for a deep attempt downfield.

KEY PLAYER

QB with 93+ Throw Power and 85+ Medium Accuracy

FORMATIONS

- **SINGLEBACK: Ace, Ace Twins, Ace Pair, Doubles Pack, Tight Flex, Bunch**
- **I-FORM: Pro, Slot Flex, Tight Pair**
- **STRONG: Close**
- **WEAK: Slot**
- **FULL HOUSE: Wide**
- **PISTOL: Slot Flex Packer, Y-Trips**
- **GUN: Doubles On, Doubles Flex Wing, Y-Trips Wk, Wing Offset Wk, Bunch Wk, Normal Y-Flex Tight, Double Flex, Trips Y Iso, Pack Trips, Empty Trey, Flex Trey**

PRO TIP

▶ The ability to control the pass type is huge in *Madden NFL 16,* and the Packers' book will really benefit from an accurate QB.

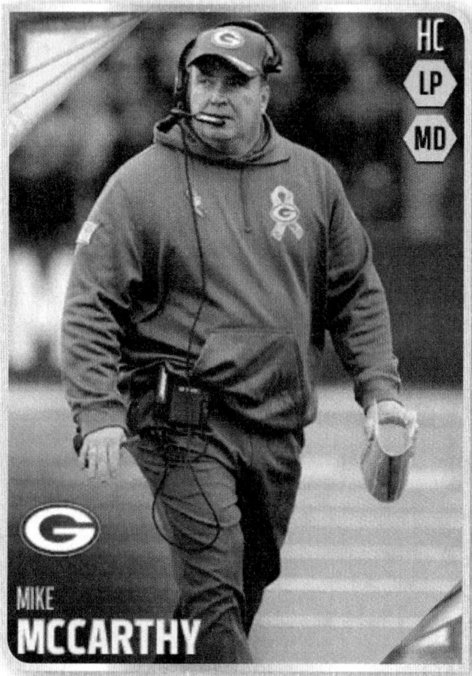

OFFENSIVE DRAFT TARGETS

- **QB (THP, SAC, DAC)**
- **WR (RLS, RTE, SPD)**
- **HB (TRK, SPD, CTH)**

DEFENSIVE DRAFT TARGETS

- **OLB (SPD, PMV, POW)**
- **CB (SPD, MCV, ZCV)**
- **DT (STR, PMV, ACC)**

DEFENSE

The Packers run a 3-4 style playbook with strong defenders up front. These players generally come off the field on rushing downs, so don't invest too much unless an elite DT is there who can be an every-down player. Selecting LBs doesn't really hurt you, as you can stack five on the field in most situations, as long as they are versatile.

KEY FORMATION

The Big Dime 2-3-6 is an excellent formation for passing downs and will really punish an opponent who didn't invest in an offensive line. Make sure to grab an extra CB or safety to maximize your effectiveness.

KEY PLAYER

OLB with 85+ PMV

FORMATIONS

- **3-4: Odd, Under, Over, Even, Solid**
- **NICKEL: 2-4-5, 2-4-5 Dbl A Gap, Psycho, 3-3-5 Wide**
- **BIG DIME: 2-3-6, 2-3-6 Will**
- **QUARTER: 1-3-7, 3 Deep**

PRO TIP

▶ Finding an OLB who can rush the passer is great, but consider moving him to DE or MLB to keep your opponents guessing.

CAROLINA PANTHERS

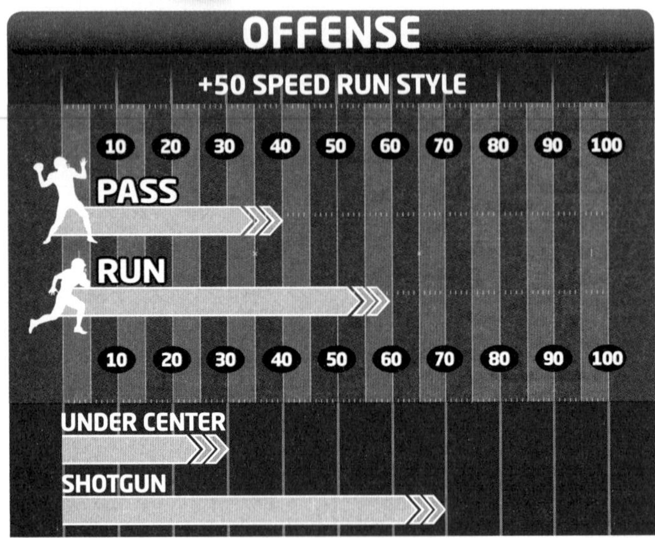

OFFENSE

The Carolina Panthers have not only one of the most fun playbooks in *Madden NFL 16*, but also one of the most effective in the hands of a skilled player who enjoys running the ball.

KEY FORMATION

Pistol Full Panther: This formation can utilize all the talent you are targeting and really foil opponents who don't bolster their front seven during the draft.

KEY PLAYER

A mobile QB is essential to getting the most out of this offensive playbook. However, you also want some depth at HB, which is tough with only 15 rounds!

FORMATIONS

- **SINGLEBACK: Ace, Ace Pair Flex, Bunch Ace, Panther Doubles, Tight Slots**
- **I-FORM: Pro, Tight Pair**
- **STRONG: H Pro, H Twins**
- **WEAK: Pro Twins**
- **PISTOL: Full Panther, Strong, Weak**
- **GUN: Split Panther, Heavy Panther, Ace, Ace Twins, Doubles Offset, Dbls Flex Wing Wk, Y-Trips TE Slot, Trips TE, Bunch Wk, Double Stack, Normal Y-Flex Tight, Trey Y-Flex, Y-Trips Open, Empty Panther**
- **WILDCAT: Slot Flex**

PRO TIP ▶ **This is one of the few playbooks where drafting a fullback might pay off big. If your opponent doesn't invest in the defensive line, you may be able to run all game.**

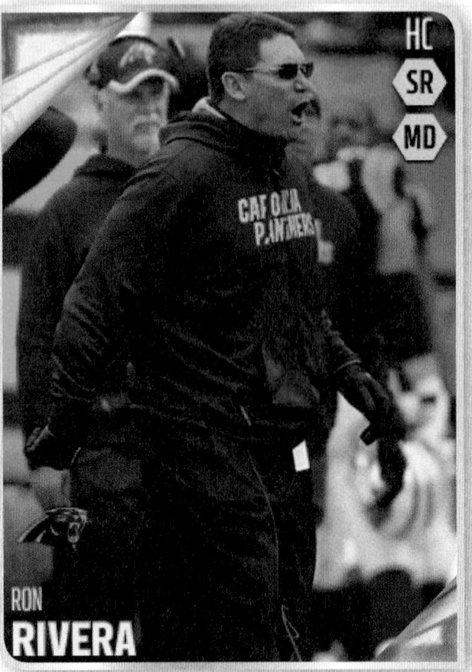

OFFENSIVE DRAFT TARGETS

- **QB (SPD, PAC, THP)**
- **HB (CTH, ACC, SPD)**
- **FB (TRK, RBK, IPB)**

DEFENSIVE DRAFT TARGETS

- **MLB (PRC, SPD, MCV)**
- **OLB (SPD, ACC, MCV)**
- **DT (PMV, STR, BSH)**

DEFENSE

This is a very solid 4-3 defensive book with some pretty standard coverages that can be tough to beat! Unless your opponent drafted multiple WRs, you should be able to play 4-3 man-to-man coverage and feel pretty confident in many situations early in the game.

KEY FORMATION

Nickel 2-4-5 Dbl A Gap is a great way to bring pressure if you aren't feeling a more passive coverage set like 4-3 Wide 9.

KEY PLAYER

Drafting a stud MLB and allowing the CPU to let him make plays is very important with this playbook. For players who don't fear user-controlling a safety or who would rather control a defensive end, this is a great move.

FORMATIONS

- **4-3: Stack, Under, Over, Over Plus, Wide 9**
- **5-2: Normal**
- **NICKEL: Normal, Double A Gap, 4 D Ends**
- **DIME: Normal**
- **BIG DIME: 4-1-6**
- **QUARTER: Normal, 3 Deep**

PRO TIP ▶ **Make your opponents prove they can beat your strength before you adjust. If you can run man coverage successfully on the first drive, stick with it until they adjust their game plan.**

NEW ENGLAND PATRIOTS

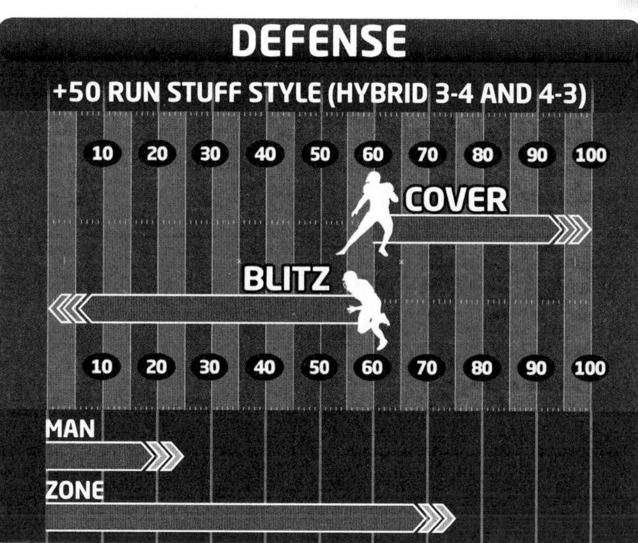

OFFENSE

The Patriots' offense is excellent for players whose focus is a quick passing attack all over the field.

KEY FORMATION

Gun Trips Y Iso allows you to use lower-rated WRs and concepts to get open on the trips side. Anytime you get a one-on-one matchup to the iso side, take a shot downfield.

KEY PLAYER

TE with 90+ Overall who has the size to be split out wide and can win one-on-one matchups downfield

FORMATIONS

- **SINGLEBACK: Jumbo Pair, Ace, Ace Overload, Ace Pair Twins, Bunch Ace, Normal Patriots, Y-Trips, Tight Slots**
- **I-FORM: Pro, Pro Twins, Tight Pair**
- **STRONG: Pro**
- **WEAK: Close**
- **GUN: Split Close Pats, Ace, Ace Pair Flex, Doubles, Normal Wing Pats, Tight Doubles On, Normal Flex Wk Pats, Pats Wing Trips, Trips TE, Bunch Wk, Normal Y-Slot, Trips Y Iso, Empty Ace Patriot, Empty Base Flex**

PRO TIP

▶ New England has great formations to get the HB the ball quickly out of the backfield, especially under center.

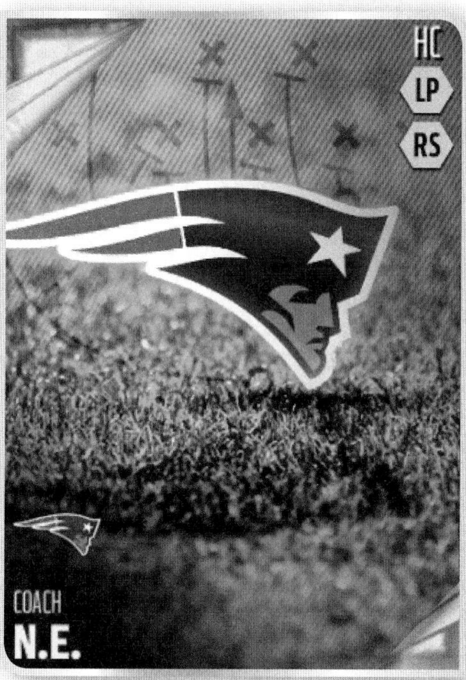

OFFENSIVE DRAFT TARGETS

- **QB (SAC, MAC, THP)**
- **WR/TE (6'4"+, CIT, SPC, JMP)**
- **WR (RTE, ACC, CIT)**

DEFENSIVE DRAFT TARGETS

- **DE/OLB (PMV/FMV, STR, ZCV)**
- **OLB (ACC, SPD, ZCV)**
- **FS (ZCV, PRC, SPD)**

DEFENSE

The Patriots' playbook is one of the most versatile in the entire game and features both 3-4 and 4-3. Drafting a strong OLB is crucial to the Patriots' success on defense! This player needs to be a hybrid rusher who can stand up in the 3-4 or drop down on early downs and hold up at end in the 4-3.

KEY FORMATION

The Nickel 3-3-5 Odd is a unique formation that should fool your opponents early in the game. Keep switching between 3-4 and 4-3 fronts to see if it throws them off.

KEY PLAYER

DE/LB with 90+ Finesse Moves

FORMATIONS

- **3-4: Odd, Under, Solid**
- **4-3: Under, Over**
- **NICKEL: 2-4-5, 2-4-5 Dbl A Gap, 3-3-5 Odd, 3-3-5 Wide**
- **BIG DIME: 2-3-6 Sam, 1-4-6**
- **QUARTER: 1-3-7, 3 Deep**

PRO TIP

▶ Taking advantage of all the Patriots' formation sub packages at the play-calling screen is the best way to get the most out of your playmakers.

OAKLAND RAIDERS

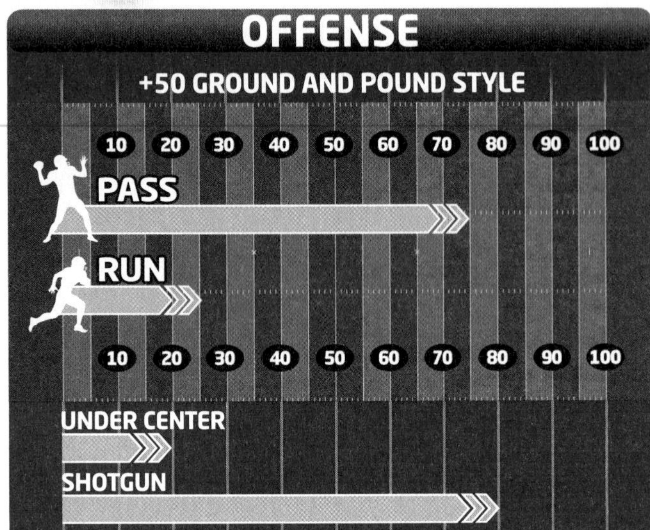

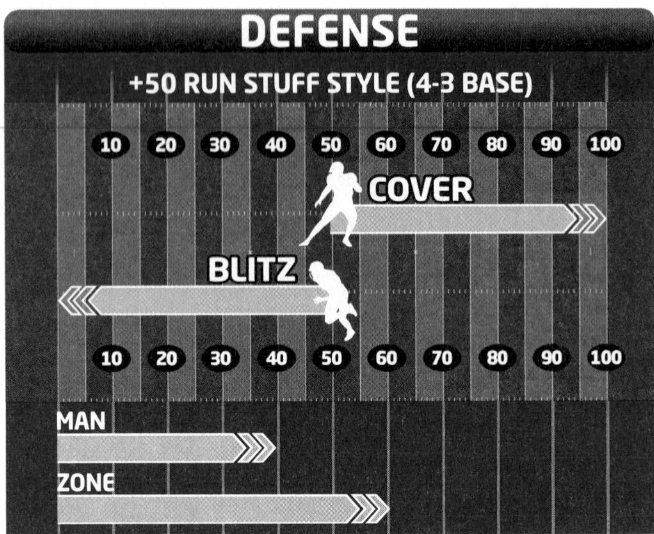

OFFENSE

The Raiders' offense was extremely popular last season and has received some brand-new formations. If you love to play out of the shotgun and utilize auto-motion, this is a playbook for you.

KEY FORMATION

Gun Flip Trips Raider is an excellent formation for offenses that pick up plenty of receivers. Learn to target short passes like Slot Trail on early downs, and take a look downfield with Oak Post Shot on third down.

KEY PLAYER

QB with 80+ Speed

FORMATIONS

- **SINGLEBACK: Ace Wing, Ace Pair, Ace Pair Twins, Doubles, Wing Trips Open**
- **I-FORM: Pro, Tight Pair**
- **PISTOL: Doubles**
- **GUN: Split Raider, Ace Offset, Ace Twins Offset, Twin TE Flex Wk, Doubles Offset, Doubles Wing Offset, Doubles Offset Wk, Tackle Over Trips, Y-Trips Offset, Wing Trips Raider, Wing Trips Raider Wk, Trio Offset, Trio Offset Wk, Bunch Open Offset, Double Stack, Dbls Y-Flex Offset, Double Flex, Flip Trips Raider, Trey Open Offset, Empty Trey**

PRO TIP

▶ This is one of a few playbooks where a FB/TE can be used in multiple formations, giving you great value if the right one appears.

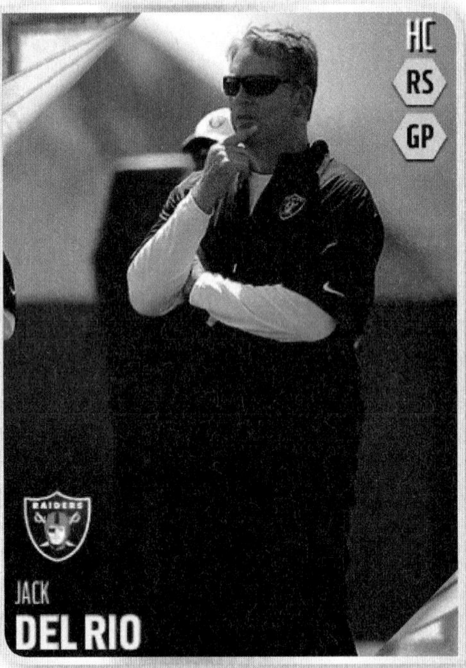

OFFENSIVE DRAFT TARGETS

- **TE (RBK, SPD, CIT)**
- **HB (TRK, AGI, CTH)**
- **QB (SPD, PAC, MAC)**

DEFENSIVE DRAFT TARGETS

- **OLB (STR, PUR, BSH)**
- **DE (STR, BSH, PMV)**
- **CB (SPD, ZCV, MCV)**

DEFENSE

The Oakland playbook contains many ways to slow down your opponent from the 4-3 formation. By using the multiple setups, you can properly align against most sets that opponents will try to use early in the game.

KEY FORMATION

The 4-3 Under Odd is a unique formation in the Raiders' playbook that can be tough for offenses to run against. Be sure to run the excellent blitzes from the LB position, which can sneak through the line and drop ball carriers in the backfield.

KEY PLAYER

OLB with 85+ Strength

FORMATIONS

- **4-3: Stack, Under, Under Odd, Over, Over Plus, Wide 9**
- **NICKEL: Normal, Double A Gap, 4 D Ends**
- **DIME: Normal**
- **DOLLAR: 3-2-6**
- **QUARTER: Normal, 3 Deep**

PRO TIP

▶ If you come up short on stud DEs in the draft, you can always look to play DTs with high Power Moves at the end position, but you shouldn't try to drop them into coverage.

ST. LOUIS RAMS

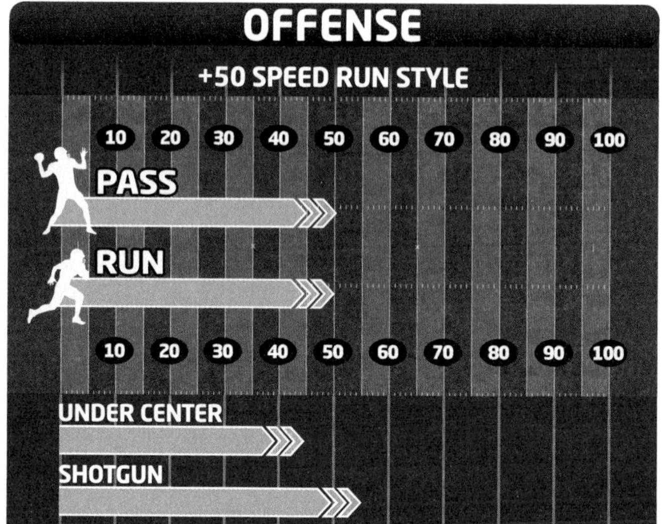

OFFENSE

The Rams have a nicely balanced offensive playbook that allows a power running back to really take over games. They also have a few formations and plays that allow a quick WR to get the ball in space and hopefully make some defenders miss.

KEY FORMATION

Gun Tight Offset TE is a great formation that allows you to take advantage of a big or fast player at tight end who will be a matchup nightmare for the defense. Use the HB Counter, HB Slip Screen, and 0 1 Trap to turn it into a great base formation.

KEY PLAYER

TE with 83+ Speed

FORMATIONS

- **SINGLEBACK: Ace, Ace Pair, Ace Pair Twins, Doubles, Bunch**
- **I-FORM: Pro, Pro Twins, Tight, Tight Pair**
- **STRONG: Pro, Twins Flex, Twins Over, Y-Flex, Tight Pair**
- **WEAK: Pro, Close, Tight Twins**
- **PISTOL: Wing Trio**
- **GUN: Split Ram, Doubles Offset Wk, Y-Trips Offset, Wings Trips Wk, Bunch Wk, Tight Offset TE, Normal Y-Flex Tight, Split Ram, Trey Open Offset, Empty Base**

PRO TIP

▶ You can get away with nearly any type of QB in this offense, but when in doubt, look for high Play Action and Deep Accuracy ratings.

HC
RS
SR
JEFF
FISHER

OFFENSIVE DRAFT TARGETS

- **HB (TRK, SPD, CTH)**
- **WR (SPD, AGI, ACC)**
- **QB (PAC, DAC, THP)**

DEFENSIVE DRAFT TARGETS

- **DE (PMV, SPD, BSH)**
- **DT (ACC, PMV, SPD)**
- **OLB (MCV, SPD, PUR)**

DEFENSE

The Rams' defensive playbook is built around their defensive ends. While you may worry about drafting four DEs and leaving weaknesses elsewhere, remember that you can also use DTs and OLBs who are solid pass rushers in your scheme.

KEY FORMATION

Nickel 4 D Ends is a great formation on passing downs if you can stop the run early and get your opponent into a third and long!

KEY PLAYER

DE with 90+ Power Moves

FORMATIONS

- **4-3: Stack, Under, Over, Over Plus, Wide 9**
- **46: Bear Under**
- **NICKEL: Normal, Double A Gap, 4 D Ends**
- **DIME: Normal**
- **DOLLAR: 3-2-6**
- **QUARTER: Normal, 3 Deep**

PRO TIP

▶ The Rams' defensive book is ideal for a players who want to lean towards more basic man coverage in their game plan. Many players will struggle to beat this type of scheme consistently.

BALTIMORE RAVENS

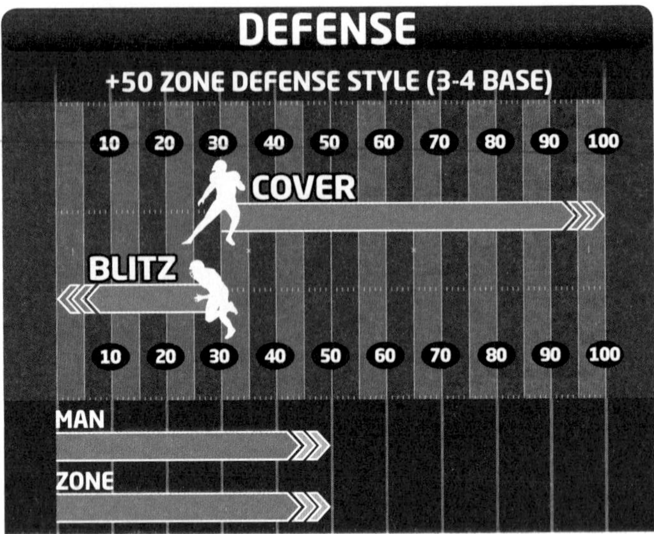

OFFENSE

What makes the Ravens' playbook unique is its variety of "tight" or "close" formations, where receivers line up close to the line of scrimmage. This makes it tough for man-to-man defenders to stick with them because of all the traffic in the area.

KEY FORMATION

I-Form Close is an example of a tight formation that can burn heavy man-to-man coverage with plays like Mesh..

KEY PLAYER

WR with 90+ Route Running

FORMATIONS

- **SINGLEBACK: Jumbo, Ace, Deuce Wing, Ace Pair, Ace Pair Twins, Bunch Ace, Tight Doubles, Doubles, Y-Trips TE Slot, Trio**
- **I-FORM: Pro, Close, Pro Twins, Tight Twins, Tight, Tight Pair**
- **STRONG: Pro, Pro Twins, Tight**
- **WEAK: Pro, Tight Twins**
- **GUN: Doubles, Y-Trips HB Wk, Bunch Wk, Spread Y-Flex, Y-Trips Open, Trips Y-Flex Tight, Flip Trips Raven, Empty Base Flex**

PRO TIP

▶ The Ravens have plenty of tight options from shotgun sets, too, if you aren't a fan of under center or didn't get to solidify your offensive line.

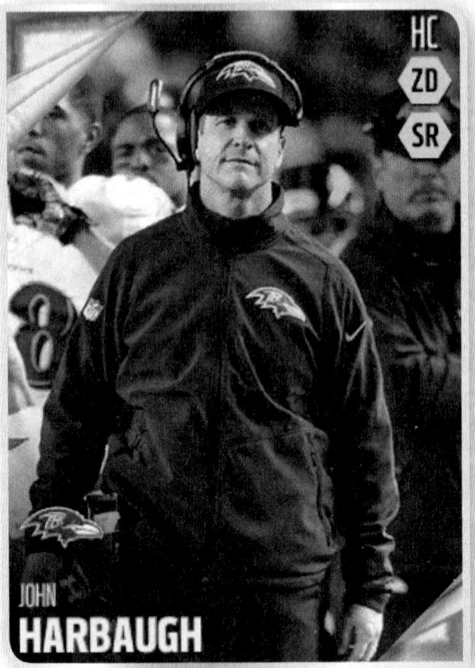

OFFENSIVE DRAFT TARGETS

- **WR (SPD, RTE, CTH)**
- **HB (ELU, CTH, SPD)**
- **QB (THP, DAC, SAC)**

DEFENSIVE DRAFT TARGETS

- **MLB (SPD, PRC, ZCV)**
- **CB (SPD, TAK, PUR)**
- **OLB (STR, BSH, PMV)**

DEFENSE

The Ravens' mixture of formations allowing their LBs to get in great matchups is second to none. Get comfortable with all of the 3-4 fronts, including the Bear, to keep your opponents off-balance.

KEY FORMATION

The Nickel 3-3-5 is an ideal formation to be balanced against any offensive attack and lineup. It requires drafting an extra CB, but if he can be physical in the run game, you will feel comfortable stopping the run from a passing set. With a solid LB holding things down in the middle, you can send pressure from the edges!

KEY PLAYER

CB with 85+ Press and 80+ Man and Zone Coverage

FORMATIONS

- **3-4: Odd, Predator, Over Ed, Even, Bear**
- **NICKEL: 2-4-5 Even, 2-4-5 Dbl A Gap, 3-3-5, 3-3-5 Wide**
- **BIG DIME: 2-3-6, 2-3-6 Will**
- **QUARTER: 1-3-7, 3 Deep**

PRO TIP

▶ While a strong OLB and DT are ideal, don't forget to move your best run defender in the secondary into the box in many situations.

WASHINGTON REDSKINS

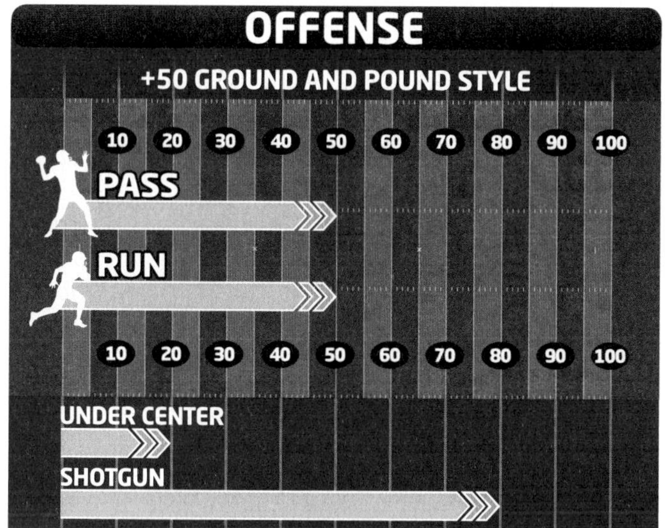

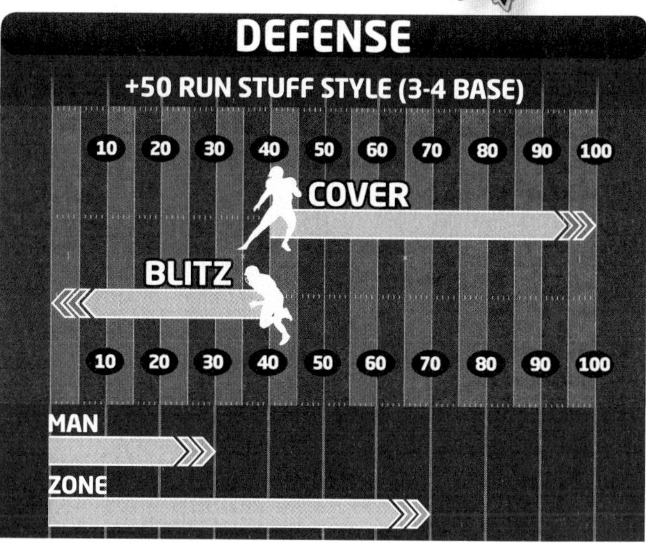

OFFENSE

The Redskins' playbook is one of the most versatile in *Madden NFL 16*. You should target a mobile QB, but if don't find any worth selecting, you can still run a scheme good enough to win.

KEY FORMATION

Pistol Ace Wing is crucial to success with the Redskins' playbook. By mixing in the Read Option and HB Stretch runs, you can add a balanced element to your offense.

KEY PLAYER

QB with 85+ Acceleration

FORMATIONS

- **SINGLEBACK: Jumbo, Ace, Ace Close, Ace Pair, Ace Pair Twins, Doubles, Wing Trio**
- **I-FORM: Pro, Pro Twins, Tight, Tight Pair**
- **STRONG: Pro, Pro Twins**
- **WEAK: Pro**
- **PISTOL: Strong, Ace Wing, Slot, Slot Wing, Y-Trips, Bunch**
- **GUN: Split Offset, Doubles Wk, Wing Trips Offset Wk, Bunch Offset, Tight Doubles On, Snugs Flip, Dbls Y-Flex Offset, Y-Trips Open, Trips Y-Flex Tight, Trips Y Iso, Trey Open, Empty Trey Flex**

PRO TIP

▶ Make sure to check the play art on option runs before the snap—knowing which defender to "read" is important for success.

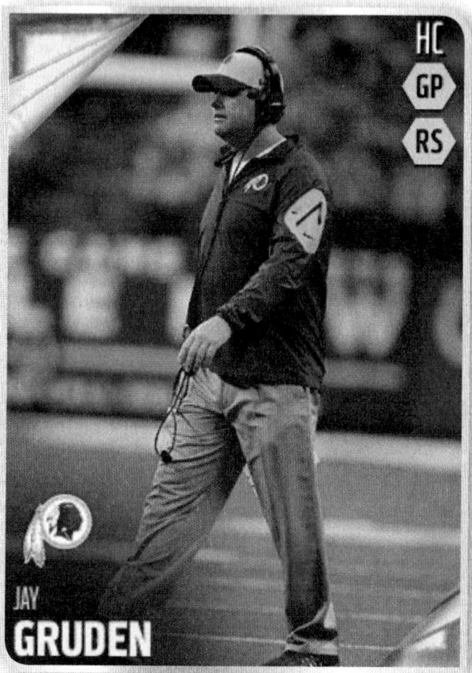

OFFENSIVE DRAFT TARGETS

- **QB (ACC, SPD, PAC)**
- **HB (TRK, STR, CAR)**
- **WR (SPD, RLS, ACC)**

DEFENSIVE DRAFT TARGETS

- **OLB (STR, PUR, BSH)**
- **DT (STR, BSH, POW)**
- **CB (SPD, MCV, PUR)**

DEFENSE

Washington has a 3-4 scheme that requires multiple LBs in most of their sets. No matter what, you can always find a spot for them: fast LBs in the middle, stronger LBs on the outside to help set the edge in the run game.

KEY FORMATION

The 3-4 Odd should be a great start against most players. Use the solid zone coverage to fan out and stop those TE routes.

KEY PLAYER

Run-stuffing OLB with 85+ Strength

FORMATIONS

- **3-4: Odd, Under, Over, Even, Solid**
- **NICKEL: 2-4-5 Even, 2-4-5 Dbl A Gap, 2-4-5 Prowl, 3-3-5 Wide**
- **BIG DIME: 2-3-6, 1-4-6**
- **QUARTER: 1-3-7, 3 Deep**

PRO TIP

▶ If you don't get the depth you need at LB, aim for big run-stopping DEs and use the Nickel 3-3-5 Wide formation.

NEW ORLEANS SAINTS

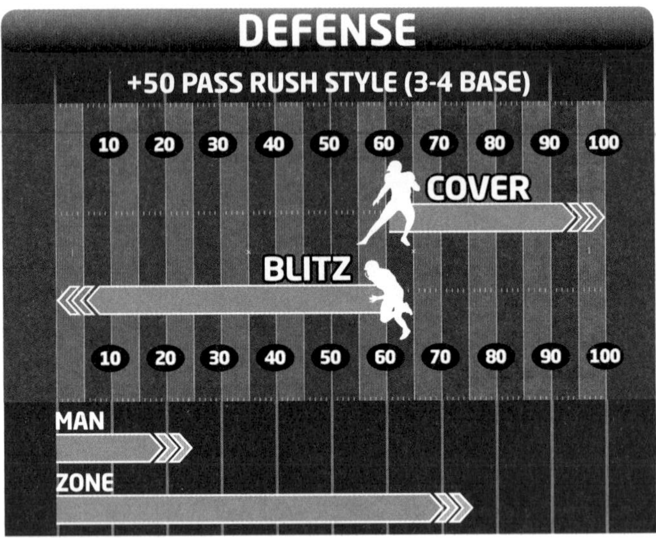

OFFENSE

The Saints' playbook has some unique plays and formations that can fool your opponent, but you can also beat your opponent by simply throwing downfield! You will need some time in the pocket, so keep linemen in mind, because a good defensive line will be a frustrating matchup.

KEY FORMATION

Gun Tight Offset TE allows you to get the most from an elite TE, who basically can be a WR in this playbook.

KEY PLAYER

6'4" TE with 85+ Catch in Traffic

FORMATIONS

- **SINGLEBACK: Jumbo, Ace, Twin TE Flex, Bunch Base, Doubles, Snugs Flip**
- **I-FORM: Pro, Close, Twins Flex, Tight**
- **STRONG: Close**
- **PISTOL: Slot Wing, Y-Trips, Bunch TE**
- **GUN: Split Offset, Doubles Wk, Wing Trio Wk, Tight Offset TE, DBL Y Flex Off Wk, Spread Y-Slot, Trips Y Iso, Trey Open Saint, Empty Saint, Empty Trey, Empty Y-Saints**

PRO TIP

▶ The Saints' playbook is still built for big WRs and deep throws downfield, which meshes perfectly with the new catching in *Madden NFL 16!*

OFFENSIVE DRAFT TARGETS

- TE (6'4"+ CIT, SPC)
- WR (6'3"+, CIT, SPC)
- QB (MAC, DAC, THP)

DEFENSIVE DRAFT TARGETS

- OLB (SPD, ACC, FMV)
- SS (PRC, POW, ZCV)
- FS (ZCV, SPD, PRC)

DEFENSE

The Saints have an excellent defensive playbook built around the 3-4. This playbook won't require much blitzing if you grab OLBs with high Speed and Finesse Moves ratings; however, it has plenty of firepower if needed on passing downs.

KEY FORMATION

Big Dime 2-3-6 is a great formation to build towards in the draft. If you come up a piece or two short, you can go to the 3-3-5 or 1-4-6.

KEY PLAYER

OLB with 87+ Finesse Moves

FORMATIONS

- **3-4: Odd, Predator, Over, Even, Bear**
- **NICKEL: 3-3-5 Will, 2-4-5 Dbl A Gap, 3-3-5 Wide**
- **BIG DIME: 2-3-6, 1-4-6**
- **DOLLAR: 3-2-6**
- **QUARTER: 1-3-7, 3 Deep**

PRO TIP

▶ The 3-3-5 Wide can be used to slow down outside runs without having to make too many adjustments.

SEATTLE SEAHAWKS

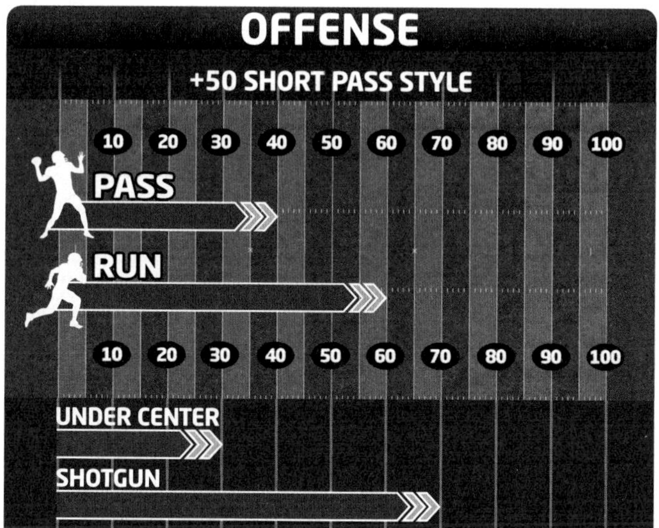

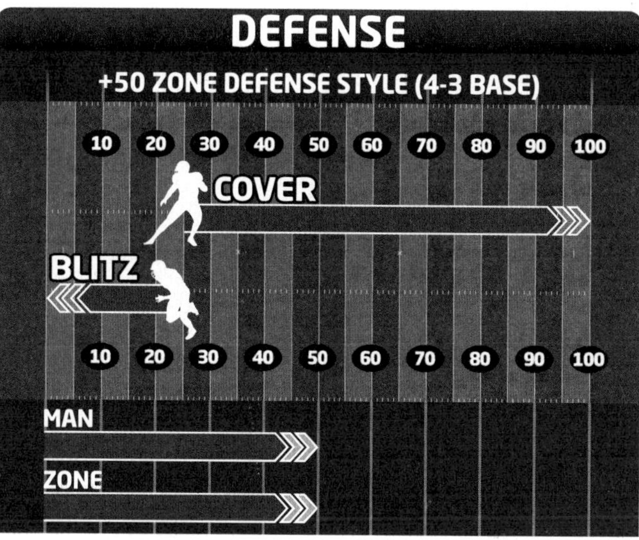

OFFENSE

For players who want a power-run-style offense without sacrificing the shotgun formations, Seattle is a great selection.

KEY FORMATION

Gun Ace Offset can be an every-down formation if you establish the run game from shotgun and learn to use play action. The Read Option in this formation really adds another dimension if you grab a mobile QB in the draft.

KEY PLAYER

While a back with 90+ Trucking is ideal, the real key is a QB who has 80+ Speed and will force the defense to commit a defender to slowing him down.

FORMATIONS

- **SINGLEBACK: Deuce Wing, Ace Pair, Ace Pair Flex, Bunch Ace, Hawk Doubles**
- **I-FORM: H Pro, H Slot, H Tight, H Twin Pair**
- **STRONG: H TE Flip, H Slot Flex, H Pair TE**
- **PISTOL: Strong Slot, Ace, Doubles Flex Wing**
- **GUN: Split Hawk, Ace Offset, Ace Twins Offset, Doubles Wing Offset, Doubles Wing Wk, Y-Trips Hawk, Wing Offset Wk, Trio Offset, Bunch Wk, Tight Slots, Double Stack, Spread Y-Slot, Trey Y-Flex, Trips Y Iso, Empty Hawk**

PRO TIP

▶ Picking up a QB who has some speed can really frustrate opponents who think they have the HB stopped only to see the QB keep the ball on a read.

OFFENSIVE DRAFT TARGETS

- HB (TRK, STR, CAR)
- QB (SPD, PAC, SAC)
- C (STR, RBK, IPB)

DEFENSIVE DRAFT TARGETS

- FS (SPD, MCV, ZCV)
- OLB (SPD, ACC, FMV)
- CB (ZCV, MCV, PRS)

DEFENSE

The mix of coverages in the Seattle playbook is outstanding if you score a rangy FS. Otherwise, find a defensive line that can overwhelm the offensive line with speed.

KEY FORMATION

The 46 Bear Under is a great way to test your opponent's commitment to the run game early.

KEY PLAYER

OLB with 90+ Acceleration

FORMATIONS

- **4-3: Stack, Under, Over, Over Plus, Wide 9**
- **46: Bear Under**
- **NICKEL: Normal, Double A Gap, Wide 9**
- **DIME: Normal**
- **DOLLAR: 3-2-6**
- **QUARTER: Normal, 3 Deep**

PRO TIP

▶ Even without drafting a dominant secondary, you should be able to mix up your coverages enough to confuse your opponent for a half.

PITTSBURGH STEELERS

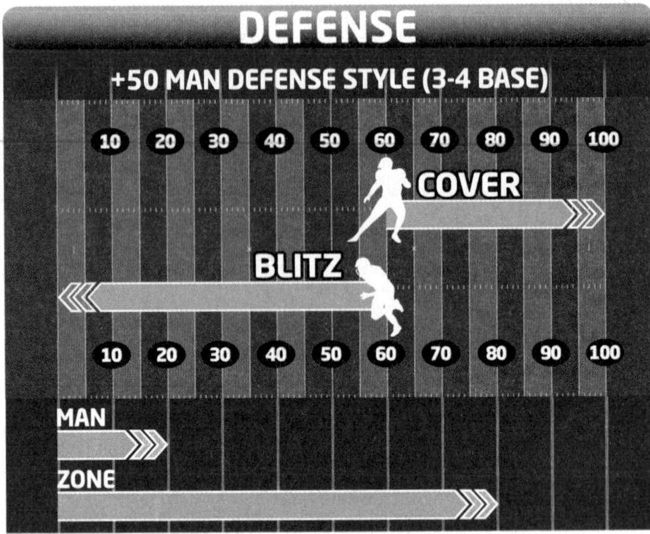

OFFENSE

The Steelers' offensive playbook is one of the best schemes for balanced players who love the short passing game. Even if you don't land a big WR, you can still have plenty of success with the concepts and RAC move.

KEY FORMATION

Singleback Pitt Doubles is a solid formation that's tough for defenses to line up against. The key is using your TE as a run blocker early and then a safety valve on third down.

KEY PLAYER

WR with 87+ Route Running and Release

FORMATIONS

- **SINGLEBACK: Jumbo, Ace, Ace Pair Flex, Bunch Base, Pitt Doubles, Y-Trips**
- **I-FORM: Pro, Pro Twins, Tight Pair**
- **STRONG: Close**
- **WEAK: Pro**
- **PISTOL: Slot Wing, Y-Trips**
- **GUN: Split Close, Doubles, Y-Trips Wk, Wing Trio Steeler, Trio, Bunch Wk, Tight Doubles On, Snugs, Spread Y-Slot, Trips HB Wk, Empty Trey, Empty Steeler**
- **WILDCAT: Normal**

PRO TIP

▶ The Steelers' playbook has added some new pistol formations this season, so don't forget to try them out!

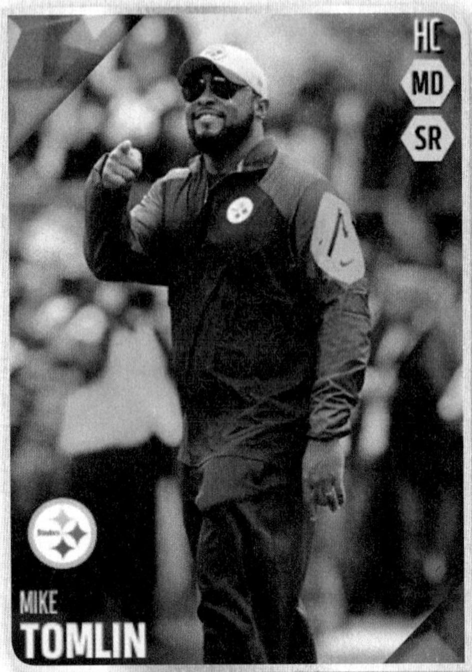

OFFENSIVE DRAFT TARGETS

- **WR (SPD, AGI, RTE)**
- **HB (TRK, SPD, CTH)**
- **TE (CIT, RBK, PBK)**

DEFENSIVE DRAFT TARGETS

- **OLB (PMV, PUR, STR)**
- **SS (PRC, ZCV, SPD)**
- **MLB (ZCV, PRC, SPD)**

DEFENSE

Pittsburgh has built their defensive scheme around the 3-4 for multiple seasons. Aim to get some strength and block-shedding on the defensive line, but don't worry about generating pressure there, as it will mainly come from your LBs.

KEY FORMATION

Nickel 2-4-5 Prowl is a solid formation that could confuse the offense and won't let any drafted LBs go to waste.

KEY PLAYER

SS with 85+ Play Recognition

FORMATIONS

- **3-4: Odd, Under, Over, Even, Solid**
- **NICKEL: 2-4-5, 2-4-5 Dbl a Gap, 2-4-5 Prowl, 3-3-5 Wide**
- **BIG DIME: 2-3-6 Will, 1-4-6**
- **QUARTER: 1-3-7, 3 Deep**

PRO TIP

▶ If you can't get enough depth at CB, try to draft an extra FS to play in the slot with mainly zone coverage.

HOUSTON TEXANS

OFFENSE

+50 SPEED RUN STYLE

10 20 30 40 50 60 70 80 90 100

PASS

RUN

10 20 30 40 50 60 70 80 90 100

UNDER CENTER

SHOTGUN

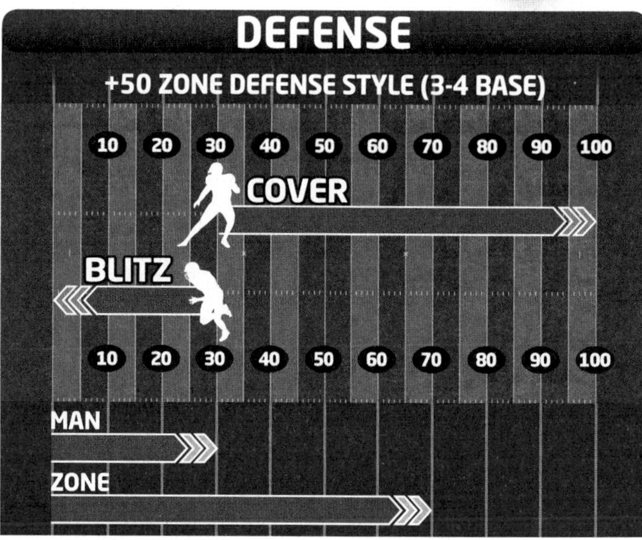

OFFENSE

The Texans' offense has some different run plays that will really benefit a patient player who can make good cuts at the line of scrimmage. Consider beefing up one side of your offensive line to run behind on most of your play calls.

KEY FORMATION

Gun Tight Doubles On is the formation you should try when you need a first down conversion. If you keep yourself in manageable situations with the run game, there are multiple ways to move the chains.

KEY PLAYER

HB with 90+ Ball Carrier Vision

FORMATIONS

- **SINGLEBACK: Jumbo Z, Ace, Ace Twins, Bunch Base, Tight Doubles, Doubles, Y-Trips Texan**
- **I-FORM: Pro, Tight Pair**
- **STRONG: Pro**
- **WEAK: Pro Twins**
- **GUN: Split Texan, Ace Pair Flex, Doubles, Y-Trips HB Wk, Wing Trips Wk, Trips TE, Bunch Wk, Tight Doubles On, Snugs Flip, Normal Y-Slot, Empty Texan, Empty Y-Flex, Empty Base**

PRO TIP

▶ This playbook has some nice rollout plays that allow you to attempt deep throws. If you an elite WR appears after you secure your HB, go for him!

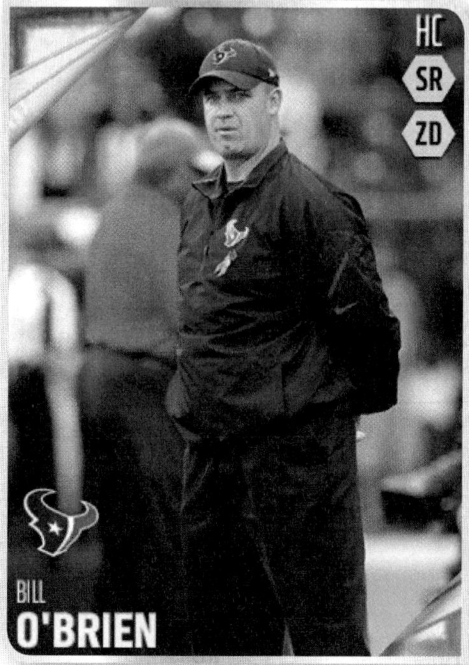

OFFENSIVE DRAFT TARGETS

- **HB (SPD, TRK, BCV)**
- **RG (RBK, IPB, STR)**
- **WR (SPD, SPC, RTE)**

DEFENSIVE DRAFT TARGETS

- **DT (PMV, STR, ACC)**
- **DE (ACC, SPD, FMV)**
- **MLB (PRC, SPD, POW)**

DEFENSE

The Texans' entire defense is built around versatility in their front seven to create an intense 3-4 scheme. The great news is that no matter who you draft, you can always use packages and substitutions to get your talent in a spot to make plays!

KEY FORMATION

The 3-4 Under is an excellent base formation that can stop the run and bring pressure off the edge if the offense tries to fool you with play action.

KEY PLAYER

DT with 75+ Speed and 80+ Acceleration

FORMATIONS

- **3-4: Odd, Under, Over Even, Solid**
- **NICKEL: 3-3-5 Will, 3-3-5 Wide, 2-4-5 Dbl A Gap**
- **BIG DIME: 2-3-6, 2-3-6 Will, 1-4-6**
- **QUARTER: 1-3-7, 3 Deep**

PRO TIP

▶ Finding a DT with enough athleticism to rush the passer from every spot is rare. If you only find a (more common) run-stuffing DT, try to use a DE to get after the QB from the inside of the line.

TENNESSEE TITANS

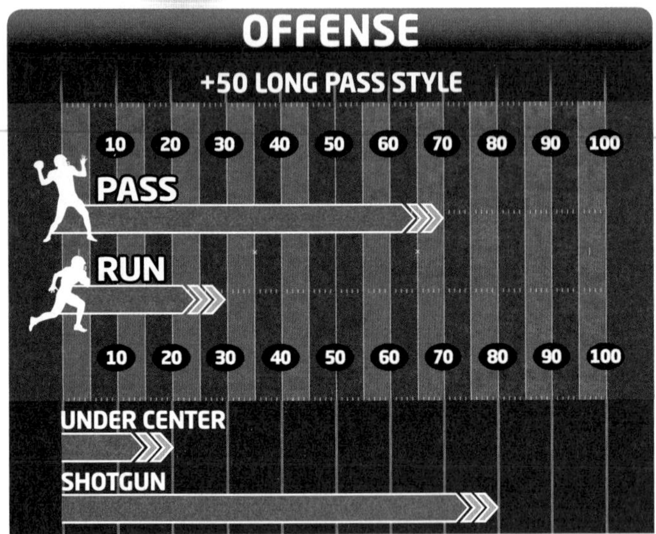

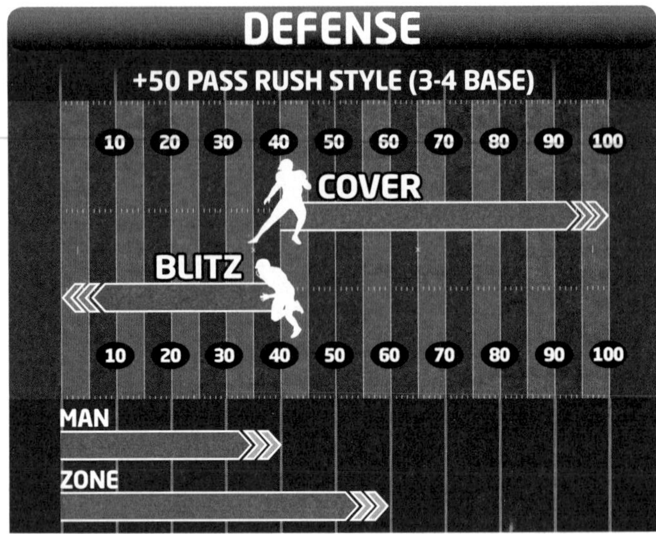

OFFENSE

The Titans' playbook is a solid way to test your opponent's pass defense. If you can come out early and spread them out, you will see your ground game open up in the second half.

KEY FORMATION

Singleback Wing Trips Open is one of the few under-center formations that have enough versatility to run all game. Pound the ball up the middle and then use quick throws to get it out in space.

KEY PLAYER

TE with 75+ Run Block

FORMATIONS

- **SINGLEBACK: Ace Wing, Ace Close, Ace Twins, Pair Tight Twins, Ace Pair Twins, Bunch Ace, Doubles, Wing Trips Open**
- **I-FORM: Pro, Pro Twins, Tight, Tight Pair**
- **STRONG: H TE Flip, Tight Pair**
- **WEAK: Close, Tight Pair**
- **PISTOL: Y-Trips**
- **GUN: Doubles, Doubles Wk, Y-Trips HB Wk, Wing Trips Titan Wk, Trips TE, Bunch Wk, Tight Flex, Double Stack, Dbls Y-Flex Offset, Y-Trips Open, Trey Y-Flex, Trey Open, Empty Base Flex**

PRO TIP

▶ The Titans' playbook is another that benefits from having two TEs available, even if the second one is mainly a run blocker.

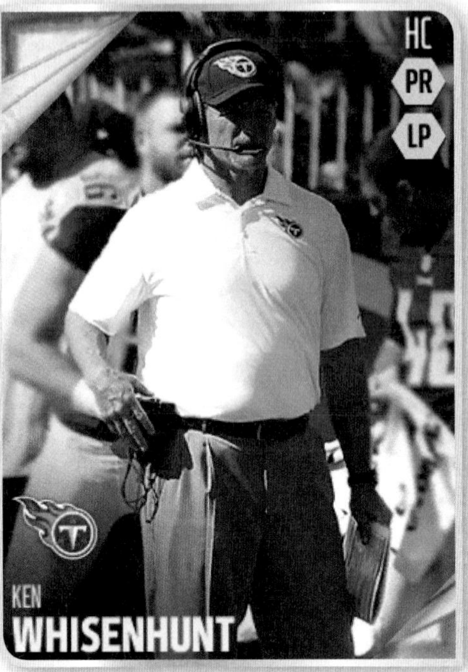

OFFENSIVE DRAFT TARGETS

- **WR (SPD, RTE, CTH)**
- **QB (SAC, MAC, ACC)**
- **TE (RBK, STR, CIT)**

DEFENSIVE DRAFT TARGETS

- **FS (ZCV, SPD, PRC)**
- **DE/DT (STR, PMV, BSH)**
- **OLB (SPD, ZCV, PUR)**

DEFENSE

Tennessee boasts a 3-4 defensive front that is built around strong defenders on the line. If you get a few options at LB, aim for whoever is the strongest of the bunch.

KEY FORMATION

The Big Dime 2-3-6 Will can give you some flexibility depending on how your draft ends up. As long as you get one strong defensive end or tackle, you will be set.

KEY PLAYER

CB with 80+ Zone Coverage

FORMATIONS

- **3-4: Odd, Under, Over, Even, Solid**
- **NICKEL: 2-4-5, 2-4-5 Dbl A Gap, 2-4-5 Prowl, 3-3-5 Wide**
- **BIG DIME: 2-3-6 Will, 1-4-6**
- **QUARTER: 1-3-7, 3 Deep**

PRO TIP

▶ Picking up the tallest defenders available is one way to make your zone coverage seem even tougher to QBs. Taller defenders can reach a higher point on their jumps and can often swat down passes that other players can't reach.

MINNESOTA VIKINGS

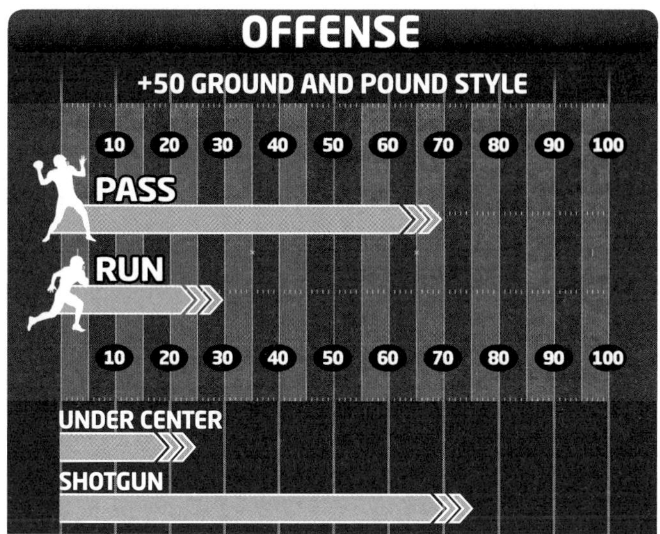

OFFENSE

The Minnesota offensive scheme is built around an elite HB who takes pressure off the QB and allows him to make short throws. If the defense over-commits, having a WR with blazing speed will pay dividends.

KEY FORMATION

Gun Split Viking is a formation that you can live in all game long. Learn to run all the different shotgun runs in this formation, and use it to set up the play action.

KEY PLAYER

HB with 90+ Speed

FORMATIONS

- **SINGLEBACK: Jumbo Pair, Ace Close, Ace Pair, Ace Pair Twins, Bunch Ace, Tight Doubles On, Doubles, Y-Trips**
- **I-FORM: Pro, Twins Flex, Tight Pair**
- **STRONG: Close, Pro Twins**
- **WEAK: Pro**
- **FULL HOUSE: Normal Wide**
- **GUN: Split Viking, Ace Twins Offset, Doubles Offset Wk, Dbls Wing Offset Wk, Y-Trips Offset, Y-Trips Wk, Wing Trips Vikes Wk, Trips TE Offset, Dbls Y-Flex Offset, Doubles Flex, Trey Y-Flex Wk, Trey Open, Empty Bunch, Empty Base Flex**

PRO TIP

▶ Being creative with screens and handoffs is a great way to get the ball in the hands of playmakers, no matter where they line up.

OFFENSIVE DRAFT TARGETS

- **HB (SPD, TRK, CTH)**
- **WR (SPD, ACC, SPC)**
- **TE (RBK, CIT, RTE)**

DEFENSIVE DRAFT TARGETS

- **DE (STR, BSH, PMV)**
- **FS (SPD, ZCV, PRC)**
- **OLB (SPD, ACC, FMV)**

DEFENSE

The Minnesota defensive scheme is a solid 4-3 book that doesn't require elite players up front to get the job done. Focus on getting solid depth and strength up front, but don't be afraid if a superstar isn't available.

KEY FORMATION

Dime 46 Normal is a unique formation that can give your opponent a different look than they are used to seeing.

KEY PLAYER

FS with 88+ Speed

FORMATIONS

- **4-3: Stack, Under, Over, Over Plus, Wide 9**
- **46: Normal**
- **NICKEL: Normal, Double A Gap, Wide 9, 3-3-5 Wide**
- **DIME: Normal**
- **QUARTER: Normal, 3 Deep**

PRO TIP

▶ Using packages (with the right stick at the play-calling screen) will allow you to get the most from the 46 Normal, depending on how your lineup shakes out after the draft.

CONNECTED FRANCHISE MODE

CFM: Tips, Tricks, and Strategies to Build a Dynasty

Connected Franchise Mode is the best way to follow the real experience of building an NFL franchise over multiple seasons while following the full calendar from preseason through the draft. This year, the experience is faster than ever before, but is also deeper for players who want to dive in and control every aspect.

If you have ever been too afraid to take the reins of your favorite team, this is the year to get involved with CFM! The CPU will help you get started quickly and will help manage all your day-to-day operations. While many players love playing with their friends in an online franchise with up to 32 total users, a good portion of players still like to play offline with CPU opponents. Why not give both a shot?

Choose Your Experience

Choosing to save in the cloud is generally the best option, even if you plan on playing solo.

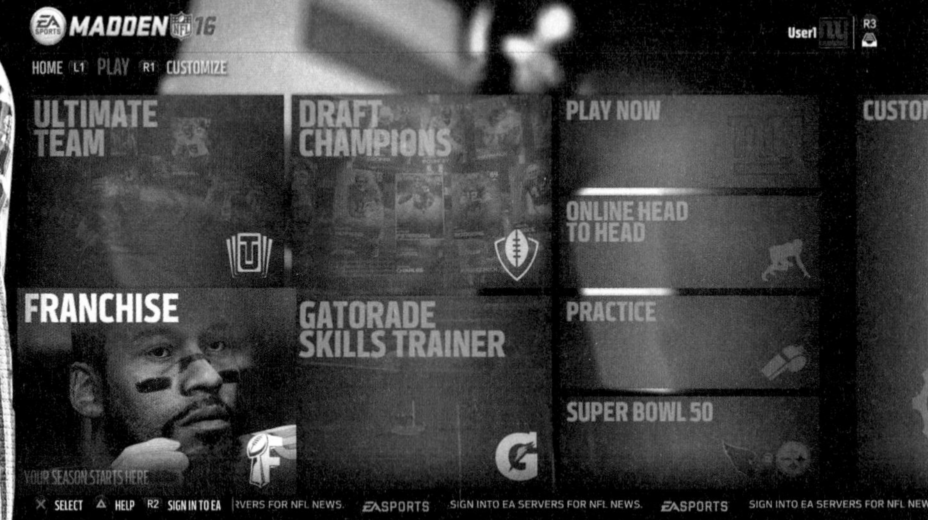

CFM QUICK START GUIDE

- ❑ Choose between Cloud and Offline
- ❑ Select a Team
- ❑ Start Regular Season as Current Coach

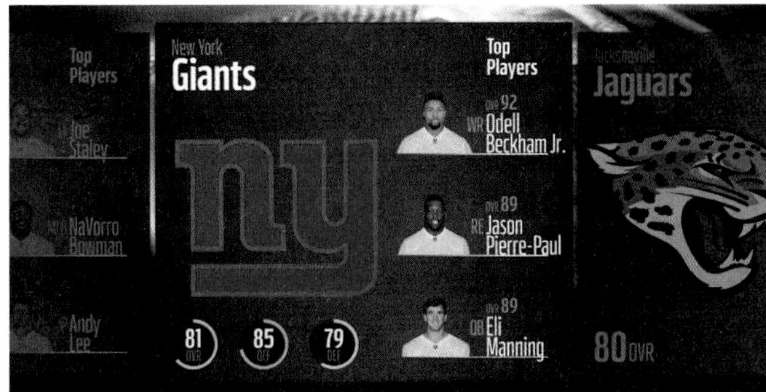

FULL START CFM CHECKLIST

- ❑ Choose Cloud or Offline
- ❑ Create or Join a League (Optional)
- ❑ Choose Preseason or Active Roster
- ❑ Select Team
- ❑ Choose Starting Point (Preseason, Regular, Fantasy Draft)
- ❑ Choose Role (Player, Coach, Owner)
- ❑ Customize League Settings (Difficulty, Quarter Length, etc.)
- ❑ Start Season

CFM SEASON RESPONSIBILITIES

- ❑ Set Depth Chart
- ❑ View Free Agents
- ❑ View Trade Block
- ❑ View Goals
- ❑ View News
- ❑ Cut Players (Preseason Start Only)
- ❑ Game Prep
- ❑ Talk to Media
- ❑ Free Practice Mode
- ❑ Start Regular Season
- ❑ Check Free-Agent Wire
- ❑ Upgrade Players
- ❑ Scout for NFL Draft
- ❑ Playoffs
- ❑ Free Agency
- ❑ NFL Draft
- ❑ Start Season 2!

Choosing a Path

No matter what role you want to play in Connected Franchise Mode this season, the first thing you need to do is to select a team. Check the lists in this chapter to find teams that fit into different categories and match your play style. You can always choose your favorite team, which is a great way to play, no matter what their ratings.

▶ You can choose to control a player, coach, or owner in CFM.

▶ PLAYER: Selecting a player allows you to focus on controlling just one player. You choose the team you want to play on and focus on earning XP to upgrade your ratings. You can choose an active player or create your own. When creating your own you start as a rookie and choose your position, player type, and backstory.

▶ Creating a coach will start you with few traits, but you can build them up over time and develop them however it will benefit your team the most.

▶ COACH: Playing as a coach gives you control over your entire team and allows you to sign, trade, and draft players. You will be responsible for offense and defense as you look to earn XP and progress and develop your players. Players can choose an active coach and take over their default traits, or they can create their own coach, which starts you as a rookie coach and allows you to choose your team.

▶ An owner can do all the same things as a coach but also has full control over the finances of a franchise. Use this option if you want to be heavily involved in all the off-the-field activities of your team, like building a new stadium or relocating.

▶ OWNER: For players who want to control every aspect of their franchise, playing as an owner is the only way to go. Owners get to set all the prices off the field and still manage and coach the team on it. You can continue the legacy of a current owner or create a new one and start as a rookie. Creating a new owner allows you to choose a backstory that will affect your finances, team happiness, and fan happiness.

▶ The "instant starter" option on league settings will let you start even if you aren't the highest-rated player on the team.

CREATE-A-PLAYER POSITION TYPES

OFFENSE

- Balanced QB
- Pocket Passer QB
- Strong Arm QB
- Mobile QB
- West Coast QB
- Balanced HB
- Speed HB
- Power Back HB
- One-Cut HB
- Receiving HB
- Balanced WR
- Speed WR
- Route Runner WR
- Red Zone Threat WR
- Possession WR
- Balanced TE
- Receiving TE
- Vertical Threat TE

DEFENSE

- Balanced LE
- Balanced RE
- Speed Rush LE
- Speed Rush RE
- Balanced DT
- Pass-Rushing DT
- Prototype DT
- Balanced MLB
- 3-4 Tackler MLB
- Prototype MLB
- Cover 2 MLB
- Balanced LOLB
- Balanced ROLB
- 3-4 Pass Rusher LOLB
- 3-4 Pass Rusher ROLB
- Prototype LOLB
- Prototype ROLB
- Cover 2 LOLB
- Cover 2 ROLB
- Balanced CB
- Man-to-Man CB
- Prototype CB
- Press Run Support CB
- Zone CB
- Balanced FS
- Balanced SS
- Playmaker FS
- Playmaker SS
- Prototype FS
- Prototype SS
- Run Support FS
- Run Support SS

POSITION TYPES

Choosing a player can be an exciting way to experience Connected Franchise Mode. While it may be hard to compete against other humans who are controlling all aspects of their team, it can certainly be fun. It doesn't take as much planning week to week, and you can build up your player quickly since you are focusing mainly on him. Keeping in mind some of the gameplay features this season, here are our top recommendations for crafting player types.

5 ROUTE RUNNER WR ▶ Player Example: Odell Beckham Jr., Giants

- ✔ Good Route Running
- ✔ Good Agility
- ✘ Decent Speed
- ✘ Decent Acceleration
- ✘ Poor Jumping
- ✘ Poor Size

Choosing between a RAC move and a conservative catch is one of the toughest decisions on a play over the middle.

Man-to-man defense is much tighter this year and will require a wide receiver with good route running to shake loose. Make sure to master the new run after catch (RAC) option, which will turn those short slants and drags into potential huge gains downfield. Until you boost your player's Catch in Traffic rating, work on the conservative catch on plays in traffic over the middle or near the sideline. Use the conservative catch to protect those crucial third-down catches and become your QB's go-to option on clutch downs.

4 STRONG ARM QB ▶ Player Example: Matthew Stafford, Lions

- ✔ Great Arm Strength
- ✔ Good Deep Accuracy
- ✘ Poor Short Accuracy
- ✘ Poor Medium Accuracy
- ✘ Decent Awareness

The new shot plays are perfect for a QB with a big arm!

Going downfield in *Madden NFL 16* is completely different with a receiver who has the ability to get up for an aggressive catch. Passing accuracy is also very important, so a QB with a strong arm can really deliver some explosive plays. Make sure to use the new shot plays and rollouts to give your QB extra time for routes to develop downfield. Focus on building up short and medium accuracy for the long term. Consider a West Coast QB if you enjoy rollout plays, but be wary of going downfield until you upgrade his throwing power.

3 RECEIVING HB ▶ Player Example: Shane Vereen, Giants

- ✔ Good Catching
- ✔ Good Agility
- ✔ OK Route Running
- ✘ Decent Awareness
- ✘ Poor Trucking
- ✘ Poor Vision

The new RAC (run after catch) move will be huge for turning short passes in the flat into big gains.

Catching the ball is more fun this year, and having a reliable option out of the backfield makes everything better. Work on your elusiveness to break more tackles in the open field. If you want a more balanced player who can be a threat in the running game, go with a speedy HB and upgrade his catching. Master the patience of a screen pass and waiting for your blockers to get out in front before accelerating.

2 PLAYMAKER FS ▶ Player Example: Eric Weddle, Chargers

- ✔ Good Speed
- ✔ Good Acceleration
- ✔ Good Play Recognition
- ✘ Decent Man Coverage
- ✘ Decent Tackling
- ✘ Decent Zone Coverage

Balls that are tipped can be intercepted, which means simply being around the ball will lead to big plays.

Defenders in *Madden NFL 16* now have tools to go up and attack the ball at the highest point too. Learn how to judge the timing of whether to play ball or to play man and you will really benefit your overall defense. Develop your zone coverage to help knock out passes when playing defenses like Cover 2 man and Cover 2 zone. Pass rushing is as fun as ever, so if you aren't comfortable controlling a safety, go for a pass rusher, depending on what scheme your team runs.

1 RED ZONE THREAT WR ▶ Player Example: Mike Evans, Buccaneers

- ✔ Good Catch in Traffic
- ✔ Good Jumping
- ✔ Good Spectacular Catch
- ✘ Decent Speed
- ✘ Decent Catching
- ✘ Decent Agility

Be sure to use the fade hot route with these players when inside the 10-yard line!

With all the new catch mechanics in *Madden NFL 16*, no player benefits more than a big tall WR who can go up and make aggressive catches. If you focus on the Catch in Traffic rating, your player will be a favorite target of QBs even when seemingly covered. The timing should be easy to learn, and by holding the new aggressive catch buttons, you should see some spectacular catches and great WR/DB interaction. Consider a possession WR if you want to be slightly more balanced and like to work the sideline and middle of the field on routes.

Selecting Your Squad

Picking a team to use in a head-to-head game is a big decision, but choosing which team to potentially start the next NFL dynasty with is an even bigger one. This isn't something you should take lightly. If you want to have success, take a minute to think about your gameplay style and what teams are going to fit it. Most players simply select their favorite team, which is a great option, but if you want to compete in a user league, maybe it is a good idea to go with the best? If you're simply playing offline for fun, maybe you want to try to get a team out of cap jail and into the playoffs? The choice is yours, and the best part is that there are no wrong answers.

If you can't figure out who you want to be, you can also control multiple teams by using the right stick, and then you can always retire your coach/owner later.

If you are having trouble picking a team, try a fantasy draft, where you can build a custom roster.

TOP 5 WIN NOW TEAMS

Bragging rights are one of the most crucial parts of playing *Madden NFL 16*, so if you want to beat your friends, this list is for you. Here are the teams that have the pieces in place to start winning now, so why wait? Match up your style with one of the teams below and a playoff berth is more than likely!

5 DALLAS COWBOYS

OFFENSIVE SCHEME	BALANCED
DEFENSIVE SCHEME	BASE 4-3
CFM OVERALL	89
OFFENSE	97
DEFENSE	85

The Cowboys have one of the best offensive lines, which makes everything so much easier.

The Cowboys went on a tear through the NFC East last season and nearly pulled off the upset win at Lambeau in January. This season, Dallas returns to the gridiron with not just an amazing QB/WR combo, but one of the youngest and most physical lines in the game. Although HB DeMarco Murray left town, you should still be able to rack up yards on the ground with a back off the free agent wire. Otherwise, allow Tony Romo to spread it out and expect to get the protection he needs to deliver a big play to star WR Dez Bryant. To extend the window, work on the defense, which won't win you any games right now but has some solid young talent in place. Expect high-scoring games and many victories in Big D this season.

4 DENVER BRONCOS

OFFENSIVE SCHEME	ZONE RUN
DEFENSIVE SCHEME	ATTACKING 3-4
CFM OVERALL	85
OFFENSE	87
DEFENSE	89

Peyton Manning has another season in him, which means the Broncos have another shot at the Super Bowl.

Most players think of the Broncos as an offensive juggernaut, which they are. However, they also have one of the best defenses in the game, led by LOLB Von Miller. QB Peyton Manning is as accurate as they come for players who like using pocket passers. Although he won't have TE Julius Thomas anymore, there are still plenty of great targets to light up the scoreboard with. Extend the window by getting backup QB Brock Osweiler plenty of XP during the season. Give Peyton plenty of rest and keep him as healthy as possible heading into January. Play plenty of man defense and focus on stopping the run, as it is your only weakness on defense.

3 NEW ENGLAND PATRIOTS

OFFENSIVE SCHEME	SPREAD
DEFENSIVE SCHEME	HYBRID
CFM OVERALL	87
OFFENSE	89
DEFENSE	91

TE Rob Gronkowski is one of the most dominant forces in *Madden NFL 16*!

The New England Patriots are the reigning Super Bowl champions and should be in consideration for players who want to win right now. QB Tom Brady is an elite pocket passer who can still make all the throws. New England is perfect for a player who wants to spread out their opponent on offense. TE Rob Gronkowski is a matchup nightmare in the seam. On defense, the Patriots did lose some veterans in the secondary, but they have more than enough young talent to make up for it at LB. This will be a season packed with high-scoring matchups, but their defense should find that crucial turnover for you in a big spot.

2 GREEN BAY PACKERS

OFFENSIVE SCHEME	WEST COAST
DEFENSIVE SCHEME	ATTACKING 3-4
CFM OVERALL	88
OFFENSE	97
DEFENSE	83

The Green Bay Packers benefit big time from the new "air supremacy" in *Madden NFL 16*!

QB Aaron Rodgers is one of the most accurate QBs in the game and will make passing the ball a breeze. Target WR Jordy Nelson on aggressive catches with WR Randall Cobb running underneath using RAC (run after catch). The Packers also benefit from having one of the top power backs in the game, which allows you to change up your scheme from week to week. On defense, Green Bay still has plenty of players left in the secondary that allow them to play some unique coverage. Send LBs Clay Matthews and Julius Peppers after the QB and you should rack up the wins.

1 SEATTLE SEAHAWKS

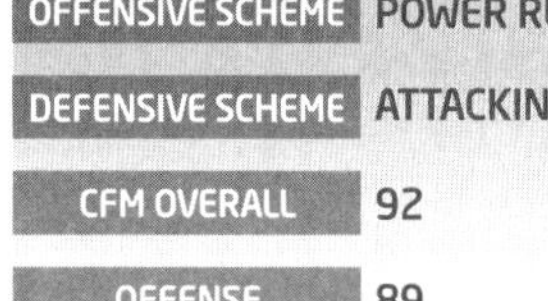

OFFENSIVE SCHEME	POWER RUN
DEFENSIVE SCHEME	ATTACKING 4-3
CFM OVERALL	92
OFFENSE	89
DEFENSE	97

Seattle was just one yard away from back-to-back Super Bowl championships.

Defense wins championships, and the Seahawks are the only team on this list with a truly lockdown D. The size and speed possessed by Seattle, especially in their secondary, make them one of a kind. On offense, they extended their own window by bringing in TE Jimmy Graham. You can extend it by making sure QB Russell Wilson sticks around for the rest of his career. Don't forget to take the pressure off by handing the ball to HB Marshawn Lynch, who is the premiere power back in the game. Seattle's formula for a third straight Super Bowl appearance is controlling the ball and playing shutdown defense.

TOP 5 TEAMS FOR THE FUTURE

One of the best parts of CFM is selecting a team that might not be ready to dominate right away but still has some solid pieces in play. With some good development and confidence building, you can turn an average team into a consistent playoff contender. Here are a few teams that your friends won't see coming in just a few seasons. Whether it is a draft pick, free agent pickup, or simply getting XP, these teams will be ready to win in the future!

▶ **Honorable Mention: Houston Texans, St. Louis Rams**

5 JACKSONVILLE JAGUARS

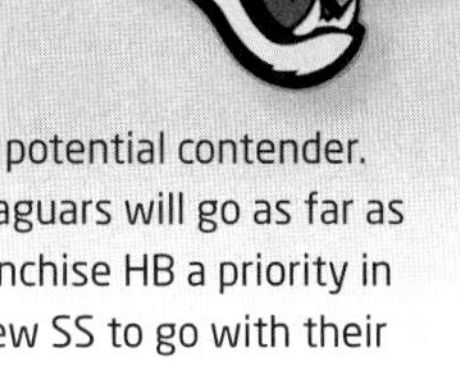

OFFENSIVE SCHEME	WEST COAST
DEFENSIVE SCHEME	ATTACKING 4-3
CFM OVERALL	80
OFFENSE	81
DEFENSE	83

The Jaguars gave promising young QB Blake Bortles a weapon in TE Julius Thomas this offseason!

The Jaguars have transformed from a team that required a serious rebuild into a potential contender. Focus on getting and keeping the confidence of QB Blake Bortles high and the Jaguars will go as far as he can take them. There is plenty of young talent at WR, so make grabbing a franchise HB a priority in the draft. On defense, the Jags are a solid group in the front seven, but grab a new SS to go with their young rushers off the edge.

4 OAKLAND RAIDERS

OFFENSIVE SCHEME	POWER RUN
DEFENSIVE SCHEME	BASE 4-3
CFM OVERALL	78
OFFENSE	81
DEFENSE	79

QB Derek Carr showed that he had a varied skill set during his rookie season.

The Raiders now have an excellent combination with rookie WR Amari Cooper and QB Derek Carr. This will be the foundation of the Raiders' return to the top tier. On defense, LB Khalil Mack proved he is the real deal and will be the centerpiece moving forward. There is also some great young talent in the secondary, but a leader will need to emerge once FS Charles Woodson closes out his career.

3 TENNESSEE TITANS

OFFENSIVE SCHEME	SPREAD
DEFENSIVE SCHEME	ZONE BLITZ 3-4
CFM OVERALL	82
OFFENSE	83
DEFENSE	85

The Titans must commit to QB Marcus Mariota's skill set to get the most out of the selection.

Tennessee made a commitment to the QB position with the #2 overall selection of Marcus Mariota. Mariota has good athleticism and a sharp command of a spread offensive system. This should be great news for the development of the offense and WRs like Kendall Wright. Defensively, the Titans should be better with the signing of veteran LB Brian Orakpo. Overall, there a solid mix of veterans on that side of the ball, but keep injecting young talent to build for the long haul.

2 TAMPA BAY BUCCANEERS

OFFENSIVE SCHEME	BALANCED
DEFENSIVE SCHEME	TAMPA 2
CFM OVERALL	79
OFFENSE	81
DEFENSE	85

Mike Evans is a dominant receiving force and should be the main focus of your offense.

Tampa Bay went with QB Jameis Winston as the #1 overall selection in the NFL Draft partly due to his excellent arm strength. Winston has two big targets on the outside and should be able to deliver a full passing offense early. Make sure to get HB Doug Martin's confidence up rather than spend another pick in the draft. Instead, focus your draft picks on defense, especially in the secondary. Tampa Bay is pretty solid up the middle, but picking up some talent for the outside will help speed up your success.

1 MIAMI DOLPHINS

OFFENSIVE SCHEME	WEST COAST
DEFENSIVE SCHEME	BASE 3-4
CFM OVERALL	81
OFFENSE	83
DEFENSE	85

The Dolphins' pass rush easily puts them atop this list.

The Dolphins solidified their place on top of this list with their offseason moves of extending QB Ryan Tannehill's contract and signing DT Ndamukong Suh. Tannehill gives the entire offense a fresh scheme going forward and allows for new signings like TE Jordan Cameron to be in position to make plays. Suh is now the leader of an already solid defense with players like DE Cameron Wake that should be a force against opposing passers. Keep building up the confidence of your young WRs and look to stack your CBs in the draft.

TOP 5 TEAMS FOR REBUILDING

CFM is excellent because it allows you to impart your knowledge of football into the game. It allows you as the fan to make the draft pick or sign the player who can turn the franchise around. Do you have what it takes to find the next Drew Brees in New Orleans? This is your chance to prove it with a team that needs some rebuilding. All of the teams on this list have a piece of the puzzle, but your vision will shape it into a winner.

▶ **Honorable Mention: Washington Redskins**

5 SAN FRANCISCO 49ERS

OFFENSIVE SCHEME	POWER RUN
DEFENSIVE SCHEME	BASE 3-4
CFM OVERALL	86
OFFENSE	91
DEFENSE	85

▶ **The 49ers had some key players retire in the offseason, including their top LB, Patrick Willis.**

The best news for 49ers faithful is that QB Colin Kaepernick and MLB Navorro Bowman are still franchise talents to build around. The 49ers must continue to develop their young HB, Carlos Hyde, who will be filling in for HB Frank Gore, who gave the team its power run identity. On defense, they must build up their depth at the LB position; fortunately, they have some good young options there. The challenge becomes whom to develop to fill in for the players who brought so much success over the last few seasons.

4 CHICAGO BEARS

OFFENSIVE SCHEME	WEST COAST
DEFENSIVE SCHEME	BASE 3-4
CFM OVERALL	82
OFFENSE	91
DEFENSE	75

▶ **Keeping QB Jay Cutler's confidence level high should be your early priority.**

The Bears have always been known for having a solid 4-3 defense but are now switching over to a 3-4. Is this a good opportunity to start a full rebuild, or do you have what it takes to get their players in a position to succeed, no matter what the scheme? QB Jay Cutler is as talented as anyone out there, but he will no longer have WR Brandon Marshall to catch passes. Thankfully, the Bears drafted an excellent rookie WR in Kevin White, who should pair nicely with red zone threat Alshon Jeffery. The Bears' line will be a piece to monitor and must be rebuilt if it can't keep Cutler upright.

3 NEW ORLEANS SAINTS

OFFENSIVE SCHEME	VERTICAL
DEFENSIVE SCHEME	ATTACKING 3-4
CFM OVERALL	80
OFFENSE	85
DEFENSE	81

▶ **Drew Brees is a veteran QB who deserves one last run for a championship.**

New Orleans traded excellent TE Jimmy Graham to the NFC Champion Seahawks in the offseason. This move earned them a first-round selection, which should help deliver some talent to QB Drew Brees, who is still capable of leading the Saints deep into the postseason. The question for the rebuild revolves around either quickly trying to reload or taking your time via the draft. The Saints could use some help at multiple positions of defense, so it is totally up to you about how to start the process. No matter what, make sure to get some big targets for Brees to take advantage of his excellent accuracy and the Saints' vertical passing attack.

2 NEW YORK GIANTS

OFFENSIVE SCHEME	BALANCED
DEFENSIVE SCHEME	ATTACKING 4-3
CFM OVERALL	81
OFFENSE	85
DEFENSE	79

▶ **The Giants found their franchise playmaker going forward in WR Odell Beckham Jr.!**

The Giants may not seem like an obvious choice for a rebuild effort, but they have some needs along both lines of scrimmage. If you can develop their young offensive linemen, this job shouldn't take long. However, the defense is in need of a playmaker at either the LB or safety spot. Push hard to make it rookie SS Landon Collins by keeping his confidence high. On offense, continue to spread the ball around to keep your playmakers happy. Consider the cost of all your talent going forward and find the best way to maximize it.

1 INDIANAPOLIS COLTS

OFFENSIVE SCHEME	BALANCED
DEFENSIVE SCHEME	BASE 3-4
CFM OVERALL	80
OFFENSE	85
DEFENSE	77

▶ **With QB Andrew Luck at the helm, it almost seems foolish to recommend a rebuild.**

The Colts geared up this offseason by signing veteran playmakers like HB Frank Gore and WR Andre Johnson. These two players will support excellent QB Andrew Luck and hopefully push Indy into the Super Bowl in the AFC. The Colts need to make sure they keep developing their young talent and can afford to keep it while making their push, which can be a delicate balance. On defense, the Colts struggle to stop the run, which can make certain matchups tough. Build your defensive line in the draft; otherwise, it won't matter how many points you can score if your opponent is always in possession of the ball.

TOP 5 SLEEPER TEAMS

Sleeper teams are a great way to surprise a player who isn't expecting much from a certain team. All the teams on this list possess special talent at a certain position or can play a challenging style that can give opponents headaches. Focus on using all the talent available to you with depth chart and formation subs to get the most out of your team on Sundays.

▶ **Honorable Mention: Houston Texans**

5 CLEVELAND BROWNS

OFFENSIVE SCHEME	POWER RUN
DEFENSIVE SCHEME	BASE 3-4
CFM OVERALL	83
OFFENSE	87
DEFENSE	89

Cleveland's defense shouldn't surprise anyone, as it is one of the best in the entire league.

Cleveland has quickly put together a solid defense that will keep them in nearly every single game. If you can generate some turnovers and win the field position battle, it will make life easy for the offense. The key to the offense is finding the right QB for the job. QB Johnny Manziel allows Cleveland to play a unique style that opponents may not be ready to defend. Make sure to run the ball and take advantage of their excellent offensive line, which is the real reason they are on this list.

4 BUFFALO BILLS

OFFENSIVE SCHEME	POWER RUN
DEFENSIVE SCHEME	HYBRID DEFENSE
CFM OVERALL	83
OFFENSE	85
DEFENSE	87

The Bills have one of the best pass rushes in all of *Madden NFL 16*!

What makes the Bills a tough team to play against is their multiple fronts, which can bring pressure from seemingly anywhere. Consistently line up the pass rushes at different angles to really throw off your opponents. On offense, QB E.J. Manuel gives the offense the best chance to run a scheme that can frustrate defenses who aren't set to stop the run. Pound the rock early to make way for WR Sammy Watkins later in the game, and then let him take over.

3 WASHINGTON REDSKINS

OFFENSIVE SCHEME	WEST COAST
DEFENSIVE SCHEME	BASE 3-4
CFM OVERALL	80
OFFENSE	85
DEFENSE	81

Washington still has one of the tougher QBs to defend in Robert Griffin III.

The Redskins can be a tricky team to defend for players who can't stop the power run game. HB Alfred Morris requires a commitment to take down, which can open up things for QB Robert Griffin III. Griffin still has the physical skills to cause nightmares for the defense but requires the right scheme to really excel. Rather than looking to take shots downfield to your speedy WRs, get them in space across the middle for running after the catch, which should really help your offense move the chains and surprise opponents.

2 NEW YORK JETS

OFFENSIVE SCHEME	SPREAD
DEFENSIVE SCHEME	ATTACKING 3-4
CFM OVERALL	82
OFFENSE	83
DEFENSE	91

The Jets' defense is tremendous, and it all starts with their defensive line.

The signing of CB Darrelle Revis in the offseason makes the Jets' defensive scheme a nightmare for opponents who rely on a number one WR. With a stacked defensive line that can stop the run without any help, the Jets will have plenty of extra defenders to move around to cause confusion for the offense. Rely on your stable of powerful HBs to shorten the game and open things up for your new playmaker at WR, Brandon Marshall. By limiting turnovers on offense, the Jets will force other teams to beat their defense, which won't be easy.

1 MINNESOTA VIKINGS

OFFENSIVE SCHEME	BALANCED
DEFENSIVE SCHEME	ATTACKING 4-3
CFM OVERALL	85
OFFENSE	85
DEFENSE	91

The Vikings still have one of the best HBs in football in Adrian Peterson.

The Vikings' offense is still built around HB Adrian Peterson. However, their QB, Teddy Bridgewater, allows them to run a unique scheme. Bridgewater proved the Vikings had talent on the outside last year and should repeat that success again this year. On defense, the Vikings have great young playmakers in the secondary who should match up well with all the good passing teams in the division. Expect to get pressure with the front four, and allow LB Anthony Barr to develop into the franchise's star.

TOP 5 REBOUND TEAMS

The teams on this list have all had runs to the playoffs in recent seasons but couldn't repeat. Their fans know they have the talent, and they want to see it manifest on the field. Take these teams that are built for success and see if you can quickly rebound them back into contention. The talent is there; try to get the most out of it.

▶ **Honorable Mention: Pittsburgh Steelers**

5 DETROIT LIONS

OFFENSIVE SCHEME	VERTICAL
DEFENSIVE SCHEME	ATTACKING 4-3
CFM OVERALL	86
OFFENSE	85
DEFENSE	89

▶ **The Lions made the playoffs last season but lost some key pieces on their defensive line.**

The Lions are looking to make back-to-back playoff appearances after a strong showing last year. While they did lose some defensive pieces in the offseason, they brought in some new players who will need to be fitted into the scheme. They are still extremely strong in the middle of their defense. On offense, they will need to find a replacement for HB Reggie Bush, who provided a great option on third down. Thankfully, they still have one of the best combos in football with QB Matt Stafford and WR Calvin Johnson.

4 KANSAS CITY CHIEFS

OFFENSIVE SCHEME	WEST COAST
DEFENSIVE SCHEME	BASE 3-4
CFM OVERALL	85
OFFENSE	85
DEFENSE	89

▶ **The Chiefs have the best defense and pass rush of any team on this list.**

The Chiefs had a winning record last season but failed to return to the playoffs, which would have been their second straight season. Kansas City has plenty of talent on offense, with HB Jamaal Charles carrying the load, and he will get support from newly signed WR Jeremy Maclin. On defense, the Chiefs can be a challenge for any team that likes to pass the ball because of the tremendous pass rush from their LBs. Can you lead the Chiefs to another winning season and their first playoff victory since 1993?

3 SAN DIEGO CHARGERS

OFFENSIVE SCHEME	BALANCED
DEFENSIVE SCHEME	BASE 3-4
CFM OVERALL	81
OFFENSE	87
DEFENSE	81

▶ **San Diego still has QB Philip Rivers, who has led them to four playoff victories.**

The Chargers finished with the same record the last two seasons, but only one led to a playoff appearance. With a tough division opponents in Denver and Kansas City, San Diego will need to rebound strongly to get a hold on the lead in the AFC West. San Diego has an excellent mix of pass catchers who should be the focal point of your offense. Use each one's unique talents. Look to turn HB Melvin Gordon into a star to keep their excellent run going even longer.

2 CAROLINA PANTHERS

OFFENSIVE SCHEME	BALANCED OFFENSE
DEFENSIVE SCHEME	BASE 4-3
CFM OVERALL	87
OFFENSE	89
DEFENSE	89

▶ **Carolina got a playoff win last season, but they'll likely need more than seven wins to return this year.**

Carolina won its first playoff game since 2005 last season, but overall the season was a struggle as they finished with a 7-8-1 record. The bulk of the talent from a 12-4 finish the year before is still there, and everyone expects the Panthers to rebound this season. Carolina committed to QB Cam Newton and his dynamic playmaking ability this offseason. With options like TE Greg Olsen and WR Kelvin Benjamin in the passing game, things should really open up. The defense is stacked, especially with MLB Luke Kuechly being the anchor in the middle of the defense. Continue to build the secondary and Carolina should be a contender for years to come.

1 PHILADELPHIA EAGLES

OFFENSIVE SCHEME	SPREAD
DEFENSIVE SCHEME	ATTACKING 3-4
CFM OVERALL	86
OFFENSE	91
DEFENSE	87

▶ **The Eagles made the biggest move during the offseason by signing HB DeMarco Murray, which should pay off big.**

No team has taken such an active approach to rebounding as the Eagles did this offseason. Out are HB LeSean McCoy and QB Nick Foles, in are QB Sam Bradford and HB DeMarco Murray, the latter from division rival Dallas. This gives the Eagles some excellent pieces to continue building their unique offensive scheme around. Keep building up the defense, especially around LB Kiko Alonso, whom they received via the McCoy trade. Their 3-4 defensive style will really improve from his presence in the lineup and could get them back to the postseason.

FANTASY Draft Guide

Choosing to start your franchise with a fantasy draft roster can make for an extremely fun experience and the chance to build the roster you have always dreamed of. All 32 teams will select from a pool of all the talent in the NFL. The draft timer moves quickly, so have some players in mind. The whole experience took about 30 minutes to complete, so set some time aside.

- **The option for a fantasy draft is located in the Starting Point panel after selecting your team.**

- **Start by drafting a few players who will define your scheme and give you an identity.**

FANTASY DRAFT SLEEPERS

OFFENSE				DEFENSE			
QB	HB	WR	TE	DL	LB	CB	SAFETY
Zach Mettenberger	Jonas Gray	Mario Alford	Blake Annen	Frank Clark	Adrian Hubbard	Jalen Collins	Gerod Holliman
Sean Mannion	Dri Archer	Breshad Perriman	Lee Smith	Danielle Hunter	Davis Tull	Tony Lippett	Adrian Amos
Joe Webb	Todd Gurley	Lestar Jean	Crockett Gillmore	Kaleb Ramsey	Daren Bates	Stanley Jean-Baptiste	Lonnie Ballentine
Tyrod Taylor	Chris Rainey	Juron Criner	Dave Paulson	Lawrence Virgil	Brandon Watts	Sanders Commings	Taylor Mays
Garrett Grayson	Cedric Peerman	Duron Carter	A.C. Leonard	Larry Webster	Max Bullough	Teddy Williams	Akeem Davis

FANTASY DRAFT RESULTS

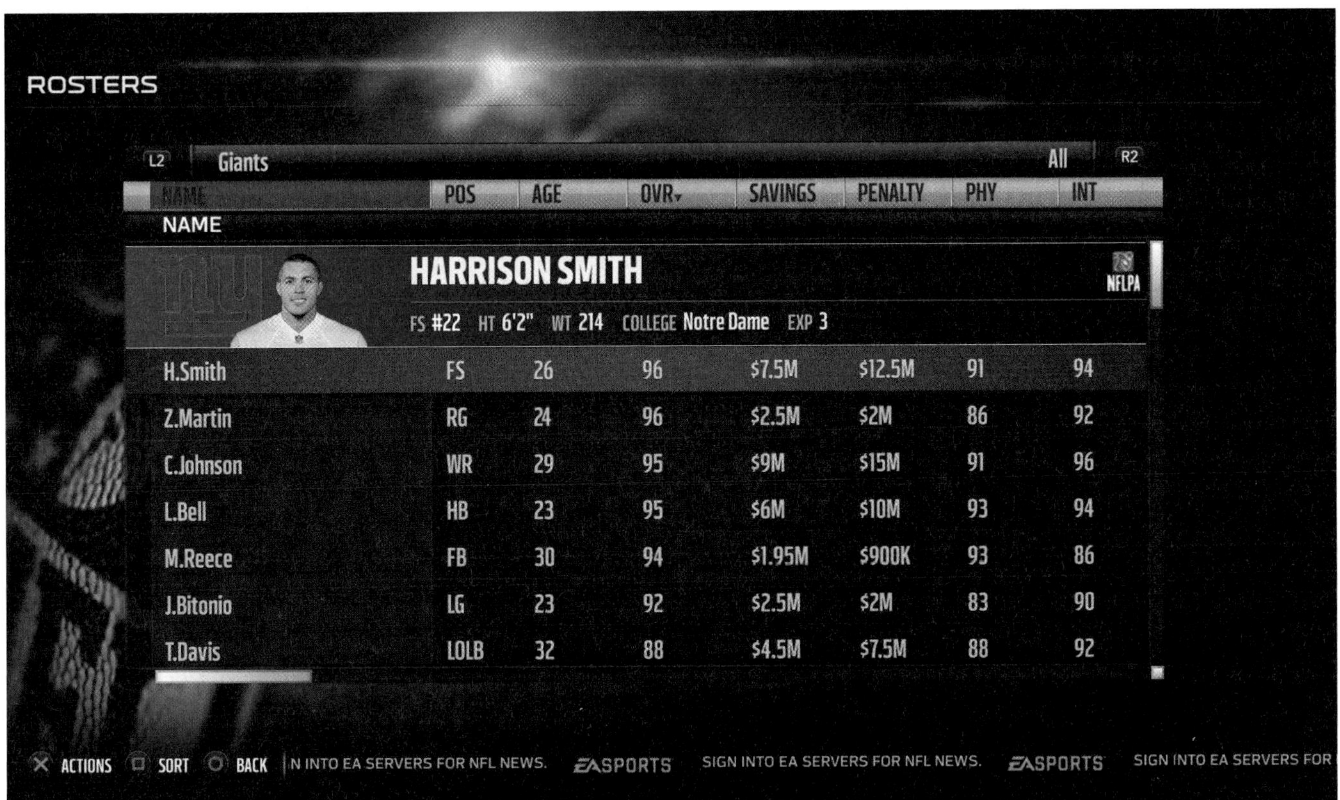

OFFENSIVE LINEUP

POS.	1	2	3	4	5
QB	Robert Griffin III	Mike Glennon	Tarvaris Jackson	–	–
HB	Le'Veon Bell	Darren Sproles	Jonas Gray	T.J. Yeldon	–
FB	Marcel Reece	–	–	–	–
WR	Calvin Johnson	Emmanuel Sanders	Andrew Hawkins	Cordarrelle Patterson	Nelson Agholor
TE	Brandon Myers	Levine Toilolo	Luke Stocker Derek Carrier	–	–
LT	David Bakhtiari	Morgan Moses	–	–	–
LG	Joel Bitonio	Edmund Kugbila	–	–	–
C	Jeremy Zuttah	Cameron Erving	–	–	–
RG	Zack Martin	Johnnie Troutman	–	–	–
RT	Zach Strief	Marcel Jones	–	–	–

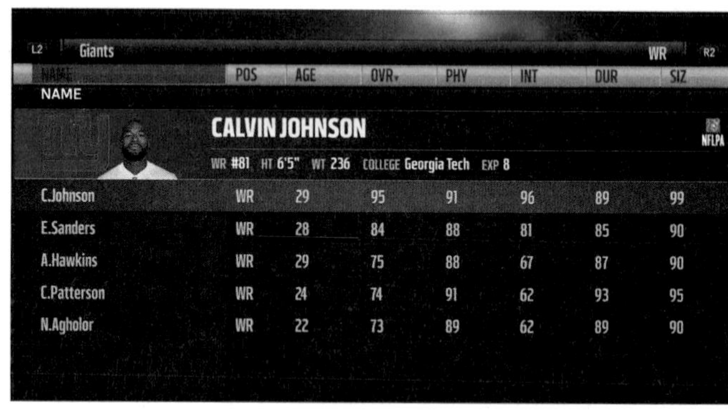

The draft started out nicely with Calvin Johnson still being available late in the first round. Although he is nearing the end of his prime, his size is exactly what our scheme calls for. He was selected over younger talent like Odell Beckham Jr., who was still available. We were surprised to see Le'Veon Bell still available but it seemed that the computer was undervaluing him; Bell is so multitalented that it was like getting two picks in one. QBs went super fast, and we didn't have the chance to get a top-tier player, so we didn't mind waiting. Instead we will try to harness the ability of RGIII and brought in a strong-armed backup just in case. Our offensive line is extremely young and strong up the middle, as that is where our main run attack will go. We picked up a great run-blocking TE along with a sure-handed pass catcher for third downs. We selected Emmanuel Sanders for his ability to run after the catch and turn shorter passes into big gains. We closed out our WR corps with a rookie to develop heading forward who can play special teams for now.

Always keep in mind how much an older player costs versus a young star with a chance to develop.

DEFENSIVE LINEUP

POS.	1	2	3	4	5
LE	Larry Webster	Michael Buchanan	–	–	–
RE	Dante Fowler Jr.	Randy Gregory	Vic Beasley Jr.	–	–
DT	Henry Melton	Isaac Sopoaga	–	–	–
LOLB	Thomas Davis	Jordan Zumwalt	–	–	–
MLB	Jon Beason	Eric Kendricks	–	–	–
ROLB	Justin Durant	Tavares Gooden	LaMarr Woodley	–	–
CB	Brandon Browner	Trae Waynes	Tharold Simon	Pierre Desir	Zack Bowman
FS	Harrison Smith	LaRon Landry	Dashon Goldson	–	–
SS	Donte Whitner	Deone Bucannon	–	–	–
K	Randy Bullock	–	–	–	–
P	Chris Jones	–	–	–	–

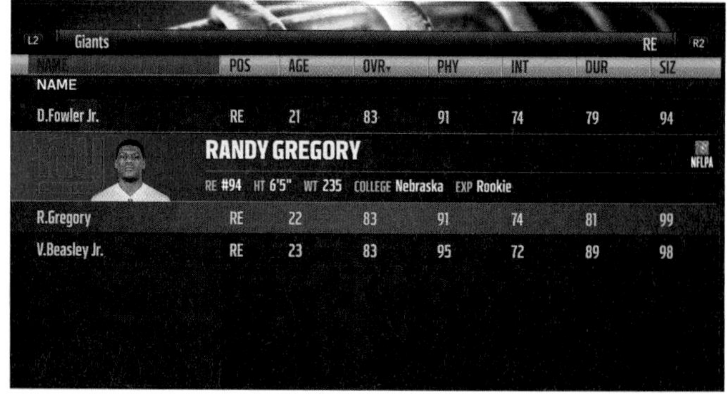

Our defense got a scheme in the second round with FS Harrison Smith, who is a big player with a zone coverage skill set. From there we wanted to fill out our defense and went with LB Thomas Davis. He is a bit on the older side but has proven to be a great player, especially in zone. We reached a bit early for CB Brandon Browner, but we loved his size and skill set. We will need to work on his penalty trait. We loaded up great young depth at CB with size and zone as the focus. Our LB corps finished out nicely with some solid veterans with high play recognition and some young stars in waiting. On the defensive line we went for one anchor with Isaac Sopoaga and one DT who can rush the passer. We loaded up with rookies at RE. All have different skills, and the smart bet is that at least one will hit! We looked for a speed rusher off the LE that we could drop into coverage, and he will be a key to our success.

Not committing to a scheme or play type gives you more options during the middle of the draft.

Start Your Franchise

LEAGUE SETTINGS

INSTANT STARTER	<> ON
If ON, all user players will start, even if they have a lower overall rating than other players at their position.	
SALARY CAP	<> ON
SKILL LEVEL	<> ALL-PRO
QUARTER LENGTH	<> 6 MINUTES
ACCELERATED CLOCK	<> ON
MINIMUM PLAY CLOCK TIME	<> 20
GAME SPEED	<> SLOW
PLAYER PROGRESSION FREQUENCY	<> WEEKLY
COACH FIRING	<> ON
GAME PLAY TUNING	<> YES
INJURY	<> ON

Players who want the most control of their franchise should set their options before heading into franchise mode. In an online league, the commissioner will control the league settings, so check them when joining. This is the last step to customizing your experience before the game starts, and you can really tailor your experience.

You can always tailor your game length and difficulty to help meet your goals.

THINGS TO DO

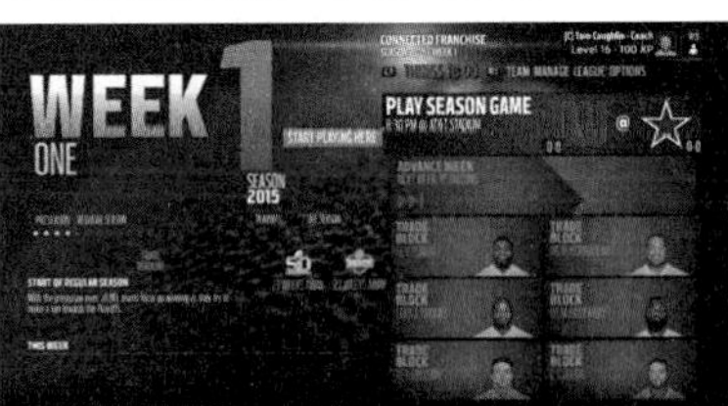

Your main screen this year will be the Things to Do tab, which will help you keep track of your weekly objectives. Early in the season, you want to check the trade block and free agents to make sure your roster is set up for the incoming season. Make sure to do the following if you want to be an active owner:

- ❑ **Trade Block**
- ❑ **Depth Chart**
- ❑ **Add Free Agents**
- ❑ **View Goals**
- ❑ **View News**
- ❑ **View Transaction Log**

The left side of the Things to Do screen helps keep your timeline in mind and alerts you of future events like the Super Bowl and NFL Draft.

PRESEASON

The preseason will be simulated on default settings during year 1 to get you into games even faster. If you wish to play it, make sure to adjust the setting before starting. You won't suffer any injuries if you choose to simulate and will still get XP and confidence.

Preseason takes four weeks, but it can be a good time to test the talent out on your roster.

OWNER MODE

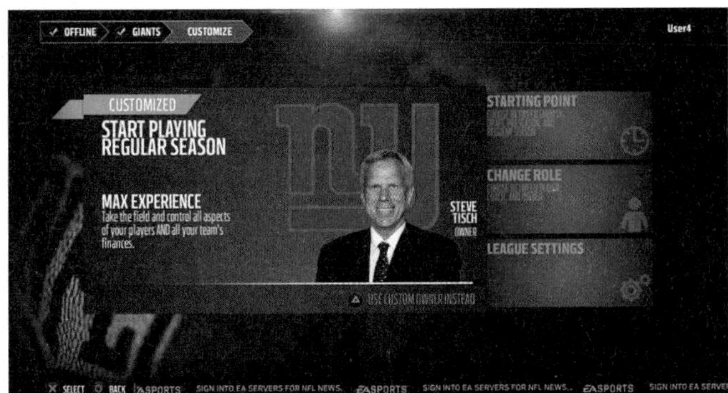

You will use your funds to pay signing bonuses in the offseason, so keep an eye on that number in the top right-hand corner.

When taking on the role of owner, you have a few additional responsibilities beyond what you would as a coach. Most of these deal with the finances of your team and keeping fans and players happy. This is once again a balancing act but is dependent on what type of owner you want to be. While most of your responsibilities are the same, there have been lots of improvements to the financial aspects of the game, which should allow you to run a successful franchise if you handle it with care. Here are the areas you will need to keep an eye on under the My Owner panel:

▶ TEAM SUCCESS: **Winning can cure almost everything, and this is where you can see how much success plays a role in your value.**

▶ MEDIA QUESTIONS: **This is your chance to let everyone know what type of owner you are and also will effect happiness in different areas, so be wise!**

▶ OWNER GOALS: **Owners have goals for adding to their legacy, just like coaches do.**

▶ TEAM VALUE: **This is a great place to get a snapshot of your value in all areas; use it to find your weaknesses and then investigate them individually.**

▶ FINANCES (TICKETS, MERCHANDISE, CONCESSIONS, TEAM REVENUE): **Finances allow you to set the price of everything from tickets to merchandise and concessions. Keep an eye on your costs, including player salaries and any potential stadium maintenance, as they will eat away at your bottom line. Respect the feedback from your fans, because they will let you know what they are comfortable paying.**

▶ MARKETING: **Player popularity and personality are very effective at increasing revenue by bringing in jersey sales! You can also see your team popularity and how your media relations affect fan happiness.**

▶ STADIUM OVERVIEW: **Stadiums are crucial to how much money you can generate and can be upgraded depending on a few different factors. For teams that don't have state-of-the-art facilities, you can always rebuild or relocate depending on your stadium rating. Keep in mind that it is costly to move a team over the first few seasons, but the move becomes more successful over time if you choose wisely. Keep an eye on your levels on amenities like parking and concessions. The higher they are, the more you can offer your fans.**

▶ FAN HAPPINESS: **This is a key area to monitor. If you can keep your fans happy, earning revenue should be a breeze. Check in on your rankings every few weeks, if your fans aren't happy, they will let you know here.**

▶ STAFF: **Staff is a crucial element to running a great franchise. While the best trainers and scouts cost more, their value is often essential to keeping fans happy and getting the best players on the field! This is also the spot to buy upgrade packages for your head coach.**

Now you know the full list of responsibilities that an owner must partake in to run a successful franchise. Test out different prices and strategies, because an active owner is usually the best one. No matter what, focus on winning on the field—it will cure almost all of your issues!

TOP 5 GAME PREP TIPS

The Game Prep section in CFM is crucial to improving your players—not just in the short term, but for developing them over the course of their careers. Game prep is limited to a certain number of hours each week based on how many days you have between games, so make sure to maximize your time. A Free Practice option is also available under Game Prep but doesn't cost hours, and while it doesn't build XP or confidence, it is still very valuable. Here are five areas to focus on each week. You can always allow the CPU to handle your game prep hours so they won't go to waste.

5 EARN PLAYER XP

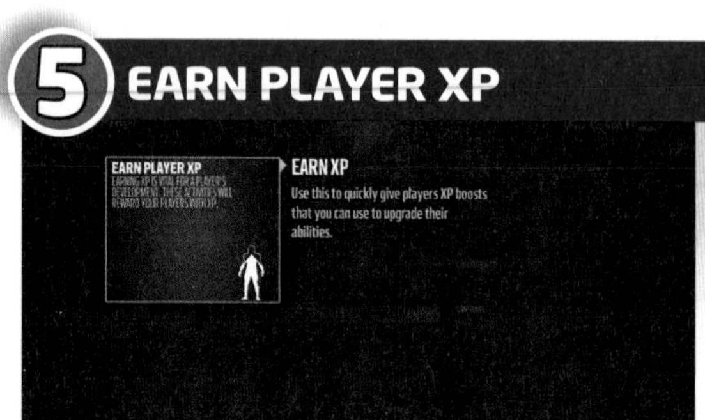

There aren't enough hours each week for every player, so try to plan ahead for which areas you would like to upgrade.

Earning XP is pretty simple and requires you to select the positions you want available to upgrade. You can usually cover most of the players at an entire position or dish it out to a few players at each. Make sure to balance the long-term gains of XP with the short-term confidence. Aim to earn XP for 3-4 players each week, generally for those on the younger side. One of the toughest things to balance is the aging of older players and how to handle their declining physical attributes. Consider changing their role or even your scheme if it becomes too costly to maintain their ratings over time.

4 EARN PLAYER CONFIDENCE

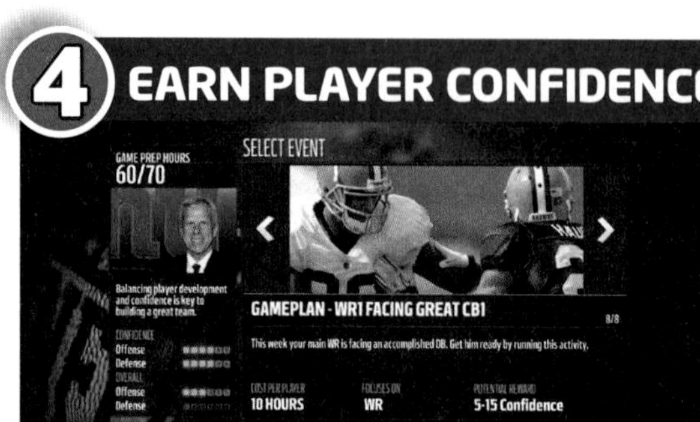

Focus on earning your drive goals to counter any potential hits to confidence!

Inside of Game Prep, you have a chance to earn player confidence each week. You can choose to work on the whole team or focus in on a specific position. These events have to do with your upcoming opponent, and different options will appear throughout the season. The more focused the drill is on a specific position, the bigger the confidence reward. Use this to keep team morale up, which can often suffer after a tough loss. Be proactive! Always remember that you can see the effects of confidence on a player's ratings by looking at his player card on the lineup screen.

3 PRACTICE IN-GAME DRILLS

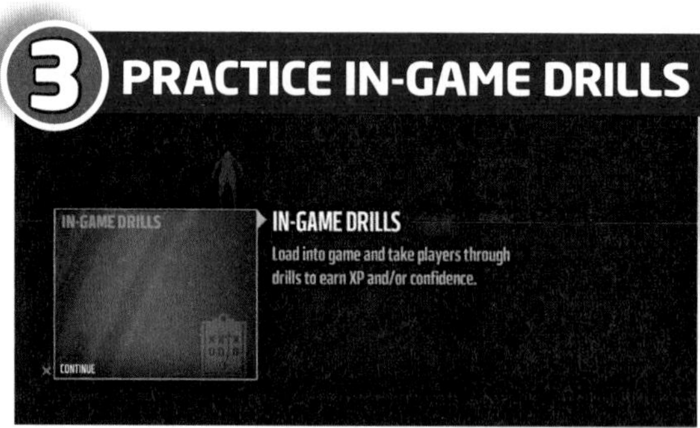

Working on the drills in the skills trainer before playing CFM can really help you maximize your earnings.

For players who want to take a more active approach to their game prep, there are in-game drills. These allow you to take players at a specific position through a series of drills to gain XP or confidence. These are especially valuable for QBs, because not only do they help gain development, but also they help you learn concepts and fundamentals to utilize in the game. On defense, make sure to use "defensive assist" with the left bumper for drills that require tackling. This will cut down the risk of missing a tackle and should help you get gold. While it takes a bit longer to go through drills with all your players, the rewards often justify the time.

2 KNOW YOUR HISTORY

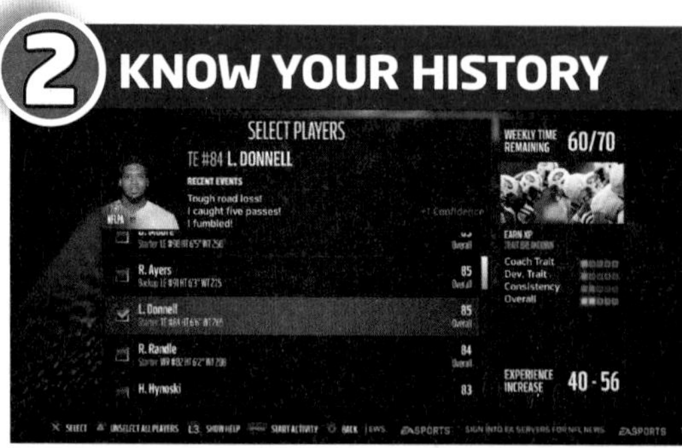

Keep an eye on modifiers like player and coach traits than can help certain players and positions progress faster. The superstar trait for players is worth it for any young players you plan on having stick around.

Each week, you should check the Progression Recap screen to see what players and positions did well and who needs improvement. The history screen will show you your game prep recap, confidence changes and progression recaps. You should monitor this to fight any downhill spiral that can happen with player confidence. Consider looking into a game prep package at a position where you have trouble developing talent. If you have a created coach, you can really start to become a force over time by investing early. The more you continue to level, the more increases you will see.

1 PROGRESS YOUR PLAYERS

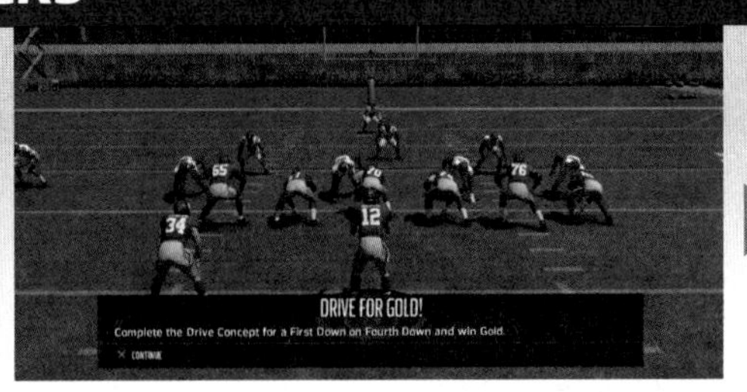

Keeping an eye on the new penalty traits is extremely important, especially for offensive linemen (to limit holding calls).

Once you have stacked some XP, head into the Upgrade Team menu and choose between automatically or manually progressing your players. If you choose to automatically do it, the game will keep in mind your team scheme and player type. We always recommend taking the time to manually progress your players, however. Abilities cost different amounts of XP and are dependent on things like current rating and position. At the start of the season, write down a target of XP to earn. You probably won't need to spend it each week, but stopping every four weeks or at the half-season mark is a good idea to see how you are doing. You can also buy traits from this screen. These are generally more expensive than abilities, but they are more of an investment, especially development traits.

XP UPGRADES BY POSITION

OFFENSE

PRIMARY	POCKET QB	MOBILE QB	SPEED HB	POWER HB	OUTSIDE WR	SLOT WR	TE	OL
1	Throw Power	Throw Power	Elusiveness	Trucking	Catch in Traffic	Speed	Catch in Traffic	Development Trait
2	Deep Accuracy	Acceleration	Speed	Ball Carrier Vision	Release	Route Running	Route Running	Run Block
3	Medium Accuracy	Speed	Agility	Agility	Spectacular Catch	Catch in Traffic	Run Block	Pass Block
SECONDARY	**POCKET QB**	**MOBILE QB**	**SPEED HB**	**POWER HB**	**OUTSIDE WR**	**SLOT WR**	**TE**	**OL**
1	Short Accuracy	Throw On Run	Catching	Speed	Speed	Release	Spectacular Catch	Strength
2	Play Action	Deep Accuracy	Juke Move	Strength	Route Running	Agility	Release	impact Block
3	Consistency	Short Accuracy	Acceleration	Carrying	Acceleration	Acceleration	Jumping	Acceleration

DEFENSE

PRIMARY	3-4 DE	4-3 DE	DT	3-4 OLB	4-3 OLB	MLB	MAN CB	ZONE CB	COVERAGE SAFETY	HARD-HITTING SAFETY
1	Strength	Power Moves	Block Shed	Finesse Moves	Zone Coverage	Play Recognition	Man Coverage	Zone Coverage	Zone Coverage	Play Recognition
2	Block Shed	Acceleration	Strength	Speed	Man Coverage	Zone Coverage	Speed	Play Recognition	Speed	Zone Coverage
3	Power Moves	Strength	Power Moves	Acceleration	Play Recognition	Block Shed	Play Recognition	Press	Play Recognition	Hit Power
SECONDARY	**3-4 DE**	**4-3 DE**	**DT**	**3-4 OLB**	**4-3 OLB**	**MLB**	**MAN CB**	**ZONE CB**	**COVERAGE SAFETY**	**HARD-HITTING SAFETY**
1	Tackle	Block Shed	Acceleration	Zone Coverage	Speed	Speed	Press	Acceleration	Acceleration	Speed
2	Pursuit	Pursuit	Play Recognition	Play Recognition	Acceleration	Strength	Agility	Man Coverage	Man Coverage	Acceleration
3	Play Recognition	Zone Coverage	Hit Power	Hit Power	Hit Power	Big Hitter Trait	Acceleration	Tackle	Awareness	Catching

GOALS

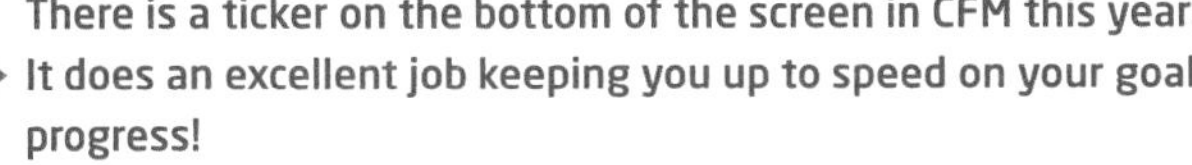

There is a ticker on the bottom of the screen in CFM this year. It does an excellent job keeping you up to speed on your goal progress!

On the My Team panel, you can head down to Team Goals to get a look at what you need to accomplish to gain even more XP from week to week. Goals are a big part of CFM and allow you to earn well beyond just your game prep upgrades. There are three main types of goals to be aware of for each player. New goals will pop up depending on how a player is performing. These vary by position, by how a player is performing, and by where they are in their career. You could see team goals that affect both the individual and the team as a whole.

Keep an eye out for new goal loading screens, which will help you keep track of what you need to do in the game that week.

GOAL TYPES:

- **Weekly Goals**
- **Season Goals**
- **Milestone Goals**

While short-term goals give XP, milestone goals take longer to achieve and provide legacy rewards for you player. Season goals are important to track to see if you are on pace. Aim for the "hard" goal to keep your player on a positive path. "Normal" goals will tend to keep them the same early in their career, while "very hard" can really change their trajectory, especially if you have a superstar trait.

Aim to hit a very hard goal with one player on each side of the ball each season. The younger they are the better.

NEW! DYNAMIC DRIVE GOALS

Dynamic drive goals are all new this year and can really tweak how you attack each drive. Now, a specific goal will appear at the start of every drive and you will be tasked to complete it to gain bonus XP or confidence! This can be a great way develop your player while in the middle of a game, and completing these will really speed up the upgrading process. But don't let a drive goal cost you a game; otherwise, you will gain confidence for one player but possibly risk it for your whole team.

You don't lose confidence or XP for failing to complete a drive goal. You simply miss out on an opportunity for bonus amounts.

KEEPING UP ON YOUR TEAM

Make sure to use the My Team panel to keep track of these of your franchise:

- **Roster**
- **Injury Report**
- **Salaries**
- **Player Progression**
- **Team Goals**
- **Depth Chart**
- **Re-signing Players**
- **Team Needs**

Try extending a young player's contract during the season, before he goes to free agency and can command big money.

TOP 5 TIPS FOR TEAM RELOCATION

MOVING YOUR TEAM CHECKLIST

- ❑ **Select Location**
- ❑ **Select Uniforms**
- ❑ **Select Nickname**
- ❑ **Select Stadium**

The owners of teams with a stadium rating under 20 have the option to relocate their franchise early in the season. This can be a strong move for an owner who wants a new stadium that can generate more revenue. Relocation settings can be set to Disabled, Normal, Users Only (stadium rating under 20; CPU cannot relocate), Everyone (regardless of stadium rating), and All Users Only (any stadium rating; CPU cannot relocate).

5 RENOVATION

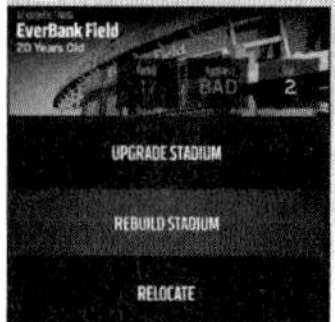

If your stadium is under level 40 but not quite at level 20, you have the option to rebuild your stadium.

Leaving town should be your last option as an owner. If you can simply upgrade your stadium or rebuild it, that may be the best option. Moving the team will upset your current fan base and will cost you money during the short term. Explore all other options before relocating.

4 LOCATION, LOCATION, LOCATION

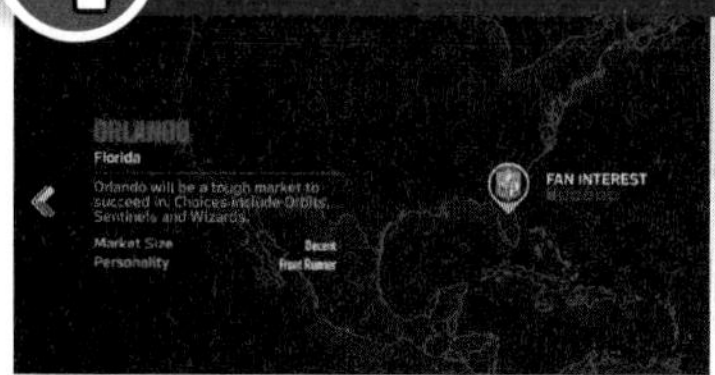

The process takes a few weeks, so don't be worried if you can't do it all at once!

After you've decided to relocate, you will have to determine who is interested. Within a few weeks, you should have some options to start exploring. Consider factors like market size, fan personality, and interest before making a move. Once you select a location, the week after you will have the option to select a nickname. You can keep your current name or go with one of three other options.

CFM RELOCATION CITIES

CITIES	NICKNAME 1	NICKNAME 2	NICKNAME 3	MARKET SIZE	PERSONALITY	FAN INTEREST
Austin, Texas	Bats	Armadillos	Desperados	Decent	Front-Runner	4
Brooklyn, New York	Beats	Bulls	Barons	Huge	Hard-Core	5
Chicago, Illinois	Tigers	Blues	Cougars	Huge	Hard-Core	4
Columbus, Ohio	Aviators	Caps	Explorers	Decent	Front-Runner	2
Dublin, Ireland	Celtic Tigers	Antlers	Shamrocks	Decent	Laid-Back	2
Houston, Texas	Oilers	Gunners	Voyagers	Huge	Loyal	4
London, England	Bulldogs	Black Knights	Monarchs	Huge	Fair Weather	6
Los Angeles, California	Crusaders	Red Dragons	Aftershocks	Huge	Fair Weather	5
Memphis, Tennessee	Hounds	Egyptians	Steamers	Small	Laid-Back	1
Mexico City, Mexico	Diablos	Conquistadors	Golden Eagles	Huge	Hard-Core	5
Oklahoma City, Oklahoma	Lancers	Nighthawks	Bisons	Small	Laid-Back	2
Orlando, Florida	Orbits	Sentinels	Wizards	Decent	Front-Runner	1
Portland, Oregon	River Hogs	Snowhawks	Lumberjacks	Decent	Fair Weather	4
Sacramento, California	Redwoods	Miners	Condors	Average	Laid-Back	2
San Antonio, Texas	Dreadnoughts	Marshalls	Express	Average	Loyal	4
Salt Lake City, Utah	Elks	Flyers	Pioneers	Small	Loyal	2
Toronto, Canada	Huskies	Mounties	Thunderbirds	Large	Laid-Back	3

3 LOOK GOOD, PLAY GOOD

Consider the impact of fan interest when choosing a new team name and uniform.

Once you've decided on a city and nickname, you will choose which uniforms you will wear for the upcoming season. These are all attached to fan opinions with a popularity poll in the bottom right-hand corner. This should be a fairly easy decision to make between three styles.

2 FRANCHISE CENTERPIECE

There are five stadium types with a basic and deluxe model for each.

Choosing a type of stadium to build is the most crucial choice in the process after location. There are many factors to take into account, including weekly cost, stadium funding, and seat capacity. Make sure to take into account the fan opinions and the number of suites, which can really help generate revenue. Here you must consider paying the big bill up front for the deluxe stadium or going with the basic style and saving some money early! Look at the advanced details before making a decision!

THE STADIUM TYPES ARE:

- **BASIC CANOPY: $0.75 billion build cost, $1.08 million weekly cost**
- **DELUXE CANOPY: $1 billion build cost, $1.58 million weekly cost**
- **BASIC FUTURISTIC: $0.85 billion build cost, $1.27 million weekly cost**
- **DELUXE FUTURISTIC: $1.35 billion build cost, $2.28 million weekly cost**
- **BASIC SPHERE: $0.70 billion build cost, $0.98 million weekly cost**
- **DELUXE SPHERE: $1.15 billion build cost, $1.88 million weekly cost**
- **BASIC HYBRID: $0.80 billion build cost, $1.17 million weekly cost**
- **DELUXE HYBRID: $1 billion build cost, $1.58 million weekly cost**
- **BASIC TRADITIONAL: $0.71 billion build cost, $1.00 million weekly cost**
- **DELUXE TRADITIONAL: $1.18 billion build cost, $1.92 million weekly cost**

Basic stadiums have level 2 facilities and will need to be upgraded.

1 LONG-TERM GAINS

Consider waiting a full season to relocate, and start saving up some cash to make it a smooth transition.

The overall goal of relocating your franchise is to generate profit. Since winning is so crucial to the whole process, make sure not to sink yourself into a insurmountable pile of debt. This could lead to a losing spiral that could be tough to climb back from. Overall, moving your team adds a great layer to CFM and really allows you to put your custom stamp on your franchise in owner mode.

OFFSEASON

Once you have played through the bulk of your season, you will get into the playoffs and the offseason. Make sure to complete these tasks:

- ❑ **Re-sign Staff**
- ❑ **Continue Scouting**
- ❑ **Hire Staff**
- ❑ **Re-sign Players**

Press Ⓨ (Xbox) or △ (PS) to franchise tag a player; it is expensive but can often keep a player you won't be able to re-sign for one more year.

- ❑ **Sign Free Agents (Four Stages)**

Signing free agents is a process that takes a few weeks and is really enjoyable when you are bidding against other users. Keep in mind how much potential interest may be in each free agent and what his value to your team could be. There are seasons when you may not have as many holes or the crop of free agents may have less quality. It is okay to save your money for the future if you already have a solid team. It is often less expensive to keep your own players than to sign new ones.

If you do have to sign some free agents, keep an eye on your available cap room. Players will be interested in your bid based on these factors:

- **Coach Ability**
- **Scheme Fit**
- **Team Need**
- **Contract Length**
- **Salary Amount**
- **Signing Bonus**
- **Location**

Remember to control everything you can when bidding on a free agent. Consider planning a year ahead with your coach abilities or scheme fit.

At the next stage, certain players will sign while other negotiations will be ongoing. Check your negotiations to see if your targets are still deciding or have signed with another team. You can also view the other signings from around the league and get an idea of similar contracts by position or rating. Before the draft, there will be a free agency recap, which will help you see who is still available and who signed where. This is crucial information that can help tip you off to some of your opponent's potential draft needs and selections.

Keep an eye on bidding teams and the highest bid. Don't let your league members come in and steal a player at the last minute!

NEW! TOP 5 SCOUTING TIPS

The scouting system in *Madden NFL 16* is all new and starts at Week 3 of the regular season. Scouting rewards players who take time each week to spend their points and helps them build a clear vision of the incoming draft class, along with finding some potential gems and busts. Here are our five best tips after multiple seasons of scouting. These got us in the best position to find playmakers during the draft.

SCOUTING GUIDE BY POSITION

OFFENSE										
GOOD UNLOCK	POCKET QB	MOBILE QB	SPEED BACK	POWER HB	BALNCED WR	SPEED/ROUTE RUNNER WR	RED ZONE WR	TE	OL	K/P
A-	Throw Power	Throw Accuracy Short	Elusiveness	Trucking	Route Running	Route Running	Catch in Traffic	Catch in Traffic	Pass Block	Kick Power
B+	Throw Accuracy Deep	Throw On Run	Catching	Ball Carrier Vision	Catch in Traffic	Catch in Traffic	Spectacular Catch	Spectacular Catch	Run Block	Kick Accuracy
B-	Throw Accuracy Short	Throw Power	Ball Carrier Vision	Carrying	Spectacular Catch	Release	Release	Run Block		
UNLOCK MORE	CONSISTENCY	CONSISTENCY	JUKE MOVE	SPIN MOVE	RELEASE	SPECTACULAR CATCH	ROUTE RUNNING	CATCHING	TOUGHNESS	AWARENESS
	Throw On Run	Throw Deep	Spin Move	Stiff Arm	Catching	Catching	Catching	Route Running	Impact Block	
			Stiff Arm	Juke Move	Kick Return	Kick Return	Kick Return			

DEFENSE											
GOOD UNLOCK	3-4 RUN STOPPER	SPEED RUSHER	DT	3-4 OLB	4-3 OLB	MLB	MAN CB	ZONE CB	COVERAGE SAFETY	HARD-HITTING SAFETY
A-	Block Shedding	Power Moves	Block Shedding	Power Moves	Hit Power	Tackle	Man Coverage	Zone Coverage	Zone Coverage	Hit Power
B+	Power Moves	Finesse Moves	Power Moves	Hit Power	Zone Coverage	Hit Power	Press	Man Coverage	Hit Power	Zone Coverage
B-		Hit Power		Zone Coverage	Man Coverage	Zone Coverage	Zone Coverage	Press	Play Recognition	Play Recognition
UNLOCK MORE	HIT POWER	PURSUIT	TACKLE	PURSUIT	PURSUIT	PURSUIT	CATCHING	CATCHING	PURSUIT	PURSUIT
	Tackle	Tackle	Pursuit	Tackle	Tackle	Catching	Kick Return	Kick Return	Catching	Catching
	Pursuit									

5 START WITH ONE SKILL

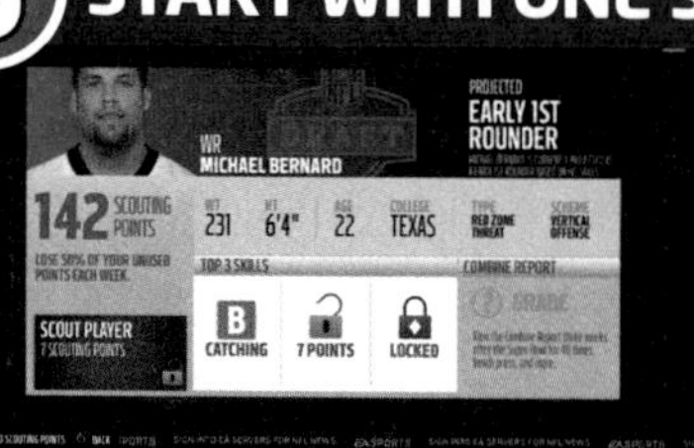

The only way to find a player's true talent is to unlock all three skills.

At the start of the draft, the entire class will be ranked by their projected draft position. From here, you will slowly uncover each player's top three skills over the course of the season. Start with just one skill for players early in the process, as the skills get more expensive for each category. The first skill will be a player's highest grade, so if you know you won't see anything better, you can often abandon a player after seeing just one skill. For example, if you choose a QB and the first grade unlocked is a D+ Throw Power, you know his Accuracy rating can't be any higher, so it isn't worth spending any more scouting points. After unlocking all three skills, you will see a player's true talent grade. Depending on if it exceeds or comes up short of your expectations, you can position him accordingly on your board. The computer won't have this inside information, so expect it to pick based on the initial ranking. If you are playing with users, they may or may not have scouted your hidden gems, so play it differently!

4 BE CONSISTENT

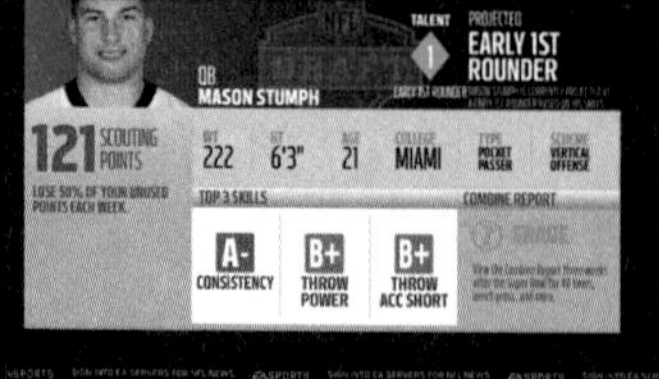

Each week you don't spend your scouting points, you lose 50 percent of them, so it really pays to follow through!

There are plenty of points to go around in scouting, as long as you do it each week. There is no worse feeling than getting to the draft and not being prepared. While you may scout plenty of players in the early rounds, most of those guys will be gone and can make your late-round picks tough. Don't forget to keep late-round picks in mind, or you will be forced to randomly select players based on their combine numbers. If you get to a point where you don't know, check their size, combine numbers, and scheme type. From there, just go with your most wanted position and cross your fingers. Which scouting package your coach has will reduce the overall cost of a position, so consider making a purchase to save in the long run.

3 COMBINE WARRIORS

You can't teach size and speed, nor do you have to pay to unlock it!

A few weeks after the Super Bowl, you will be able to review the results of the scouting combine. This will help you determine the physical skills for all the players in the draft class and help you rank them or find a specific talent. Make sure to check on the players you have already scouted to review if they performed well and are consistent with your picture of them. Scout anyone you may have missed who performed well to see if he could be a sleeper!

- **40-YARD DASH: Speed**
- **BENCH PRESS: Strength**
- **VERTICAL JUMP: Jumping**
- **3-CONE DRILL: Acceleration, Agility**
- **20-YARD SHUTTLE: Agility, Acceleration**
- **BROAD JUMP: Strength, Jumping**

40-YARD DASH	SPEED	BENCH PRESS	STRENGTH	VERTICAL	JUMP	3 CONE	ACCELERATION/ AGILITY*	SHUTTLE	AGILITY/ ACCELERATION*
4.27	98	44 Reps	98	41.1	95	6.75	93-95	4.01	94
4.33	96	41 Reps	95	38.7	91	6.85	92	4.05	90
4.41	93	39 Reps	93	35.9	86	6.95	88	4.12	89
4.57	87	38 Reps	92			7.14	82	4.18	88
4.68	83	36 Reps	90			7.2	80	4.3	87
4.74	81	34 Reps	88					4.57	72
5.34	59	31 Reps	85					4.67	68
		27 Reps	80						
		22 Reps	74						
		11 Reps	57						
		6 Reps	46						

*Acceleration and Agility varied; number is for first attribute listed.

2 SCHEME VS POSITION

Make sure to keep your "Needs" in mind; they show up on the left side of the scouting interface.

Finding a good scheme fit is important to maximize a future player's fit on your roster. Always go for talent first, but if things are equal, try to match the scheme. Every player's type can be seen without spending any points and will generally match their skills. It is rare to see a strong-arm QB without a good Throw Power rating. It is rare to see a red zone threat WR without a big frame and a solid Catch in Traffic rating. Use these to your advantage during the process. Style can help tip off what skills you may be unlocking.

1 TAG 'EM

Draft night can be very hectic, so take the extra time to tag your players or even write down who you are targeting.

When your team is on the clock, there can be a feeling of panic! You have to keep an eye on other teams' selections, and you also have the option to trade down. Keep everything organized by tagging your draft targets. This will allow you to sort the list of players you have identified as good matches for your team before the draft. Don't let time run out on you; plan ahead and be in a position to find that gem in the sixth round. The good news is that you will get instant feedback on your selection and be able to see his true talent in the class. Once the draft completes, your rookies will be signed automatically and you will be notified and able to view the deals.

FIGHT ON!

You know have officially completed your first season as an NFL player, coach, or owner—that wasn't so hard! There is always room for improvement, even for teams that bring home a Super Bowl championship. Keep developing your team, and remember that the real work is done off the field. If it didn't go according to plan, you can always try a new experience and utilize all the little tips you picked up along the way. When entering season two, continue to think about the long term and developing those young guys into future playmakers!

At the end of the season you can change a player's position, so think about how a player fits in your scheme or what skills might be valuable at another position. We moved Haloti Ngata (92 Overall) from DT to RE, and he now has an 83 Overall rating.

Next year, you will start at the preseason, so be ready to think about cutting players and chasing down the dream of a Super Bowl again.

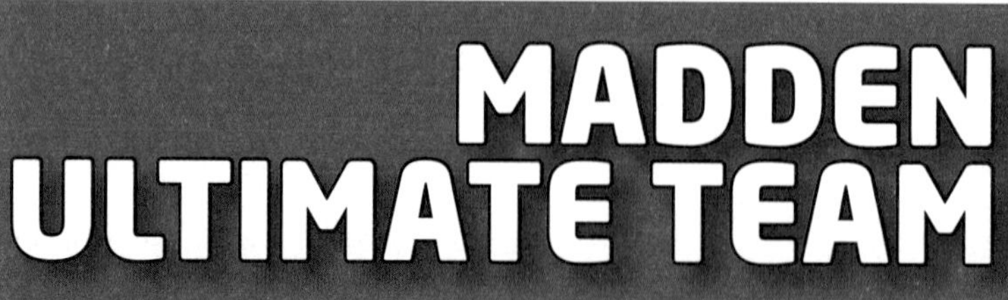

MADDEN ULTIMATE TEAM

What Is Madden Ultimate Team?

Madden Ultimate Team (MUT) is a free-to-play game mode that combines player trading items with on-the-field *Madden NFL* gameplay. MUT allows you to earn, buy, auction, and trade players to build your version of the ultimate team. The mode is loaded with player items that include not only the game's current superstars but also past NFL legends. In Madden Ultimate Team mode you put together a team that fits any style or mold you want and then compete against other players or take on the computer in solo challenges. Remember that MUT is a "live" game mode that has new content updated daily. This ranges from new items to challenges that follow the story of the NFL and the Madden season. MUT is the fastest-growing game mode in *Madden NFL*, which creates a great marketplace to auction and trade for the items you need to build your team.

GETTING STARTED

- ❑ Choose Uniform
- ❑ Choose Style
- ❑ Open Welcome Pack
- ❑ Use Best Lineup
- ❑ Play a Solo Challenge

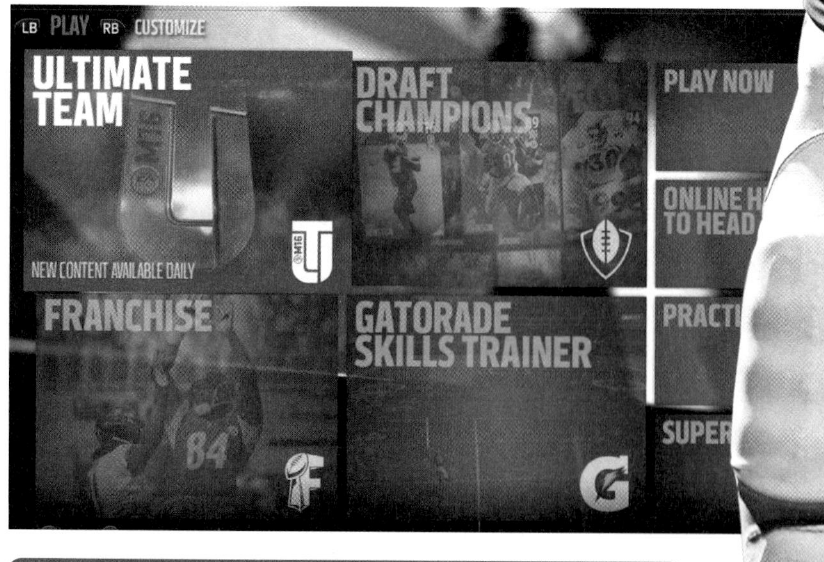

GETTING ULTIMATE

- ❑ Complete a Set
- ❑ Play a Seasons Game
- ❑ Auction Any Item
- ❑ Bid on Any Auction
- ❑ Post Any Item for Trade

Start Your Squad

> **Stay on the lookout for new content every day; it is usually most valuable right when it enters the game!**

From the main menu, select the Ultimate Team panel to get started building your team. Complete your objectives as soon as possible to continue your progress and unlock new challenges. Make sure to equip offensive and defensive playbooks, along with uniforms. The last thing to keep an eye out for is a coach who will help give your team an identity with his style.

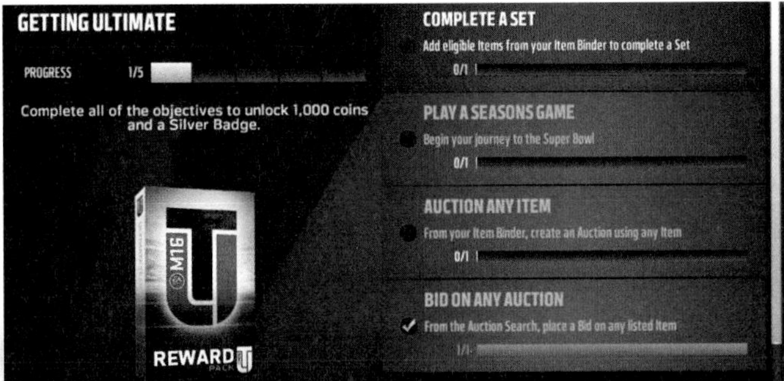

> **Keep an eye out for objective lists during the season. You will be rewarded for racking up stats.**

SOLO CHALLENGES

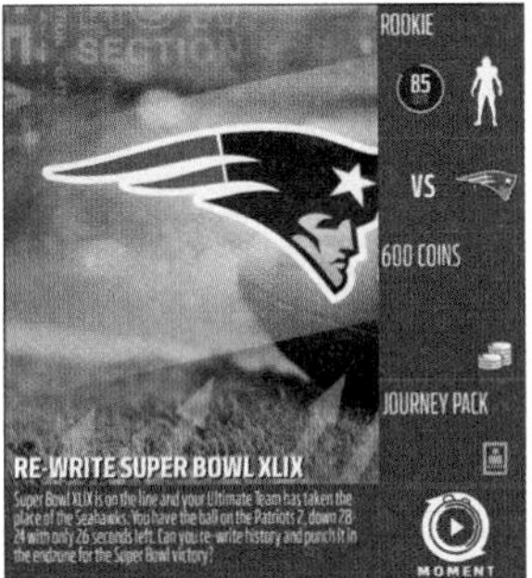

Solo challenges are an excellent place to start once you get all your positions filled out and your roster set. Don't worry if you haven't built your full ultimate team yet, since these challenges start out on an easier difficulty level before ramping up. You will have plenty of time to build your team by earning coins and items in these early challenges. Our favorite challenge is currently the Gauntlet, which requires you to defeat all 32 NFL teams on each difficulty level. Doing that unlocks a "boss" challenge. If you win those battles, you earn a Gauntlet Master collectible, which can later be used in the set. After completing those, you should have plenty of items to make lineups for different styles. Go after the Style Kickoff solo challenges next.

NFL JOURNEY

Embark on the NFL Journey, where you will play against every team in different types of games and situations while earning rewards and improving your team along the way. Take on 16 challenges at each of the 10 levels, which get more difficult as you rise.

> **The NFL Journey Solo Challenges are quick experiences that are a great place to get started and improve your team.**

LEVELS:

- **Prospect**
- **Rookie**
- **Starter**
- **Pro**
- **Veteran**
- **All-Pro**
- **Superstar**
- **All-Madden**
- **Elite**
- **Ultimate**

MADDEN ULTIMATE TEAM SEASONS

Another option to start building your ultimate team is to play Madden Ultimate Team seasons. These allow you to compete in a series of 10-game seasons against other equally skilled MUT players. If you win enough games, you will make the playoffs and advance to the next level. The higher you climb, the more coins and items you will earn as rewards. Each level has its own Super Bowl and its own rewards. Although you are taking on a human opponent instead of the CPU, there is plenty of magic in place to make sure you get a matchup of similar skill. By getting some solo challenges done early, you can get your team in a great position to compete with anyone you match up against.

WELCOME TO MADDEN ULTIMATE TEAM SEASONS

Compete in a series of 10-game seasons against other equally skilled MUT players.

Make the playoffs and advance to the next level to earn coins and items. There are 8 levels in all, and each has its own Super Bowl.

There's no time limit. Play a little or a lot, and you'll matchup with a player who has similar skills.

> **Matchmaking will find you an opponent with similar skill, so don't worry. Plus the rewards are too great to pass up!**

SUPER BOWL REWARDS

- **ROOKIE 2ND STRING:** **2,000 Coins, 1 Pack**
- **ROOKIE 1ST STRING:** **2,250 Coins, 1 Pack**
- **PRO 2ND STRING:** **2,500 Coins, 1 Pack**
- **PRO 1ST STRING:** **3,500 Coins, 1 Pack**
- **ALL-PRO 2ND STRING:** **4,550 Coins 1 Pack**
- **ALL-PRO 1ST STRING:** **5,500 Coins, 1 Pack**
- **ALL-MADDEN 2ND STRING:** **7,000 Coins, 1 Pack**
- **ALL-MADDEN 1ST STRING:** **10,000 Coins, 1 Pack**

Level	Population
ALL MADDEN - 1ST	0%
ALL MADDEN - 2ND	0%
ALL PRO - 1ST	0%
ALL PRO - 2ND	0%
PRO - 1ST	0%
PRO - 2ND	0%
ROOKIE - 1ST	4%
ROOKIE - 2ND	96%

ALL-MADDEN - 1ST STRING

POPULATION 0 PLAYERS

REG. SEASON REWARDS	
AVOID DEMOTION	250 COINS
PLAYOFF BERTH	5000 COINS, 1 PACK
1ST ROUND BYE	5500 COINS, 1 PACK
POST SEASON REWARDS	
WILDCARD	500 COINS
DIVISIONAL	4500 COINS, 1 PACK
CONFERENCE	6000 COINS, 1 PACK
SUPER BOWL	10000 COINS, 1 PACK

ADJUST LINEUP

Getting your best players into position to make plays is the key to Madden Ultimate Team. This is where the Lineup screen comes in handy. Scroll over to the Team tab and choose Adjust Lineup. This allows you to make changes to the starting lineup and depth chart. You can let the game handle it automatically, or you can do it on your own. By clicking on a player item, you can compare items in your starting lineup with those in backup roles. Then you can determine which player you want in the lineup based on his abilities and style. There are five different tabs to look at for each item, and all will help you make the best decision. You can view your entire offense, defense, or special teams on the screen at once. You can also head into your Item Binder for a different view and click on player items. From here, you can choose to promote a player to starter.

Two other important things to look at on the Team screen are the Coaching & Equipment panel and the Team Management panel. The first is where you set your coach and playbooks, and the latter is where you set your team style and name.

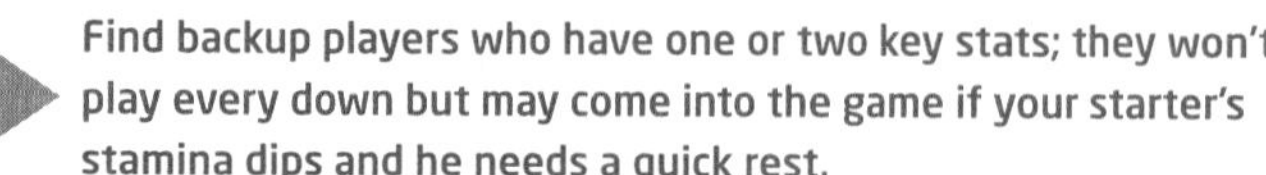

Find backup players who have one or two key stats; they won't play every down but may come into the game if your starter's stamina dips and he needs a quick rest.

ITEM BINDER

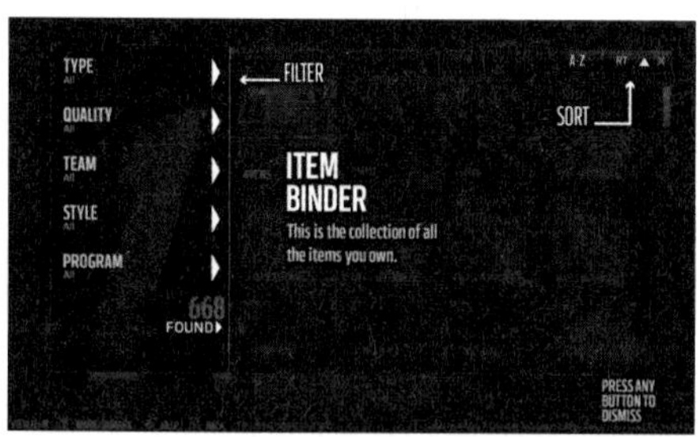

Using the Sort by Newest feature in the top right is a great way to find any new items you just picked up and want to use.

ITEM BINDER FILTERS

- **Type**
- **Quality**
- **Team**
- **Style**
- **Program**

Keeping track of all the items you collect over the season can seem overwhelming at first, but the Item Binder makes it very easy. By using different filters, you can narrow down and find the item that you want. If you are only looking for items from a certain program, the game will simply show you those, and you can quickly make a decision on how to proceed.

The Live panel on the main MUT screen will show you the freshest content in the game.

ITEM VIEWER

Once you locate the item you want, select it to bring up an extended view. From here, you can view the card in detail and perform actions. Use this screen to:

- **Compare Against Similar Items by Position**
- **Promote to Starter**
- **Extend Contracts**
- **Add to Sets**
- **Auction**
- **Trade**
- **Quick-Sell**
- **You can also navigate to other tabs on the Item Viewer screen. You can see information like player ratings, contracts remaining, style, date acquired, and full attributes!**

New sets are added during the season, so try to anticipate them to help maximize the coins you can make.

SETS

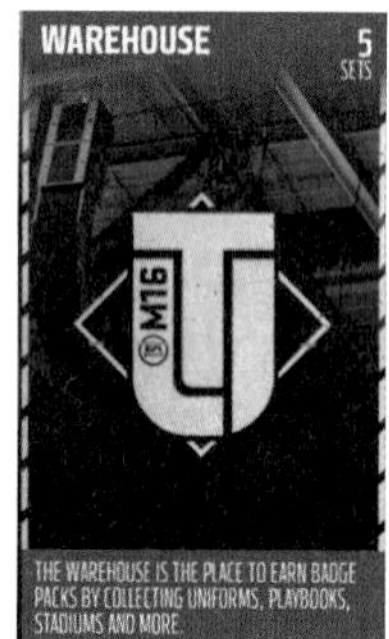

THE WAREHOUSE IS THE PLACE TO EARN BADGE PACKS BY COLLECTING UNIFORMS, PLAYBOOKS, STADIUMS AND MORE.

One of the biggest aspects of MUT is collecting items. Eligible items are placed into "sets" to earn rewards. Set rewards can be anything from coins to items that are earned when you add and complete everything in a set.

As you inspect the items required to complete a set, the ones you can use will be highlighted. Fill in all the blanks to complete the collection and claim your reward. Sets are updated throughout the year, so any items that didn't seem to have a purpose when you got them may become valuable later in the season.

If you don't have an item needed to complete a set, a Find Item icon will appear in the binder, which will take you right to the item in the Auction House to bid.

Certain sets are repeatable and keep delivering rewards during the season.

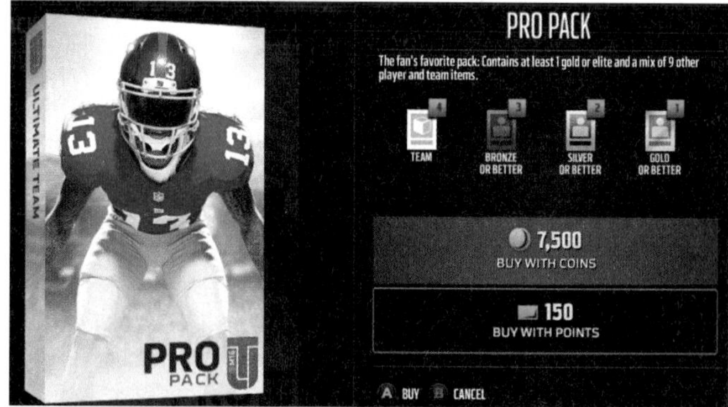

MARKETPLACE

Holding onto packs for a new promo can be a great idea. You don't have to open them all at once.

If you are looking to pick up packs without spending in-game coins, you can select the Store and buy items or packs. Opening new packs is a fun way to go hunting for new items that have been eluding you due to a lack of coins. You might even find a rare player that you don't need and put him up on the auction block. You can buy points that will allow you to purchase packs—the bigger the bundle the more points you save.

The best players rarely post a player at the Auction House without checking his price range first.

AUCTIONS

The Auction House allows players to search active auctions to find items to buy or to bid on. If you have already placed an offer or posted an item, you can view those in My Bids or My Posted Auctions. By knowing exactly which items you want to buy and how much you are willing to pay, you can find good deals. The more patient you are and the more coins you have available, the better you will do.

You can now head straight to the Auction House from your Item Binder when looking at a player item. This will save you huge amounts of time and allow you to check prices before posting a player.

You can now sell up to 100 items at a time in Quick Sell, which is an improvement from 20 last year.

Consider buying items that don't fit your style but are below current value, only to turn around and flip them for a profit!

If you replace a player in your starting lineup, make a decision to auction him or use him as a backup.

TRADE BLOCK

If you are looking for a specific item in return rather than coins, the Trade Block is where you want to be. At the Trade Block you post a specific item from your collection and specify what you would like in return. You can also search for an item if you don't have enough coins to buy it at the Auction House and offer something from your collection.

Trading players can be a great way to avoid the Auction House if you know exactly what you want.

TEAM STYLES

Getting all your styles up to 20 should be an early focus so you can unlock more solo challenges.

Selecting a style is a great way to get your team some boosts during gameplay. Keep an eye what type of items you are starting to collect and start to build out a lineup. Remember that you can find players that match your current style by using filters in your Item Binder. Focus on one, but make sure to keep some spare players around, and always test out different combinations. The higher the style, the more you can feel the boosts on the field.

To maximize your style, be sure to play players in their proper positions in the starting lineup!

STYLE PACK ROOKIES

- **SP:** Jameis Winston
- **LP:** Amari Cooper
- **GP:** Todd Gurley
- **SR:** Melvin Gordon
- **ZD:** Landon Collins
- **MD:** Trae Waynes
- **PR:** Vic Beasley
- **RS:** Leonard Williams

OFFENSIVE STYLES

- **SHORT PASS (SP) STYLE boosts Catch in Traffic and Pass Blocking to improve your ability to complete short to intermediate passes.**
- **LONG PASS (LP) STYLE boosts Route Running and Pass Blocking and improves your ability to complete intermediate to deep passes.**
- **GROUND AND POUND (GP) STYLE boosts Trucking and Run Blocking, thus increasing your effectiveness with a power running game plan.**
- **SPEED RUN (SR) STYLE boosts Elusiveness and Run Blocking, increasing the effectiveness of a running game plan built around quickness.**

DEFENSIVE STYLES

- **ZONE DEFENSE (ZD) STYLE boosts Play Recognition and Zone Coverage, so there's an increased chance of success when you call zone coverage plays.**
- **MAN DEFENSE (MD) STYLE boosts Play Recognition and Man Coverage for an increased chance of success when you call man coverage plays.**
- **PASS RUSH (PR) STYLE boosts Pursuit and Block Shedding, so players blitzing the QB are more likely to escape blocks.**
- **RUN STUFF (RS) STYLE boosts Tackling and Block Shedding, so defenders have a better chance of shutting down plays.**

By earning just a bronze in a Skills Trainer category, you will unlock rewards for MUT!

Quarterback Items in MUT

Finding an accurate passer in *Madden NFL 16* is crucial, especially with all the new upgrades to the passing game. By finding an elite passer early, you will be able to quickly gain confidence in your passing game and start moving the chains. QBs have more tools than ever before, and WRs are bigger weapons than ever before.

ANDREW LUCK ▶ Style: Long Pass

Andrew Luck is one of the rising stars in the league and continues to lead his team deeper into the playoffs each season. There isn't a throw he can't make on the field, and his accuracy allows him to fit it into questionable windows at times. Russell Wilson is the only other elite QB who can come close to matching Luck's blend of speed and throwing power.

Luck can use his speed as a threat in the red zone.

BEN ROETHLISBERGER ▶ Style: Short Pass

Big Ben is one of the best pocket-passing QBs in the league. Take advantage of his excellent strength by hanging tough in the pocket and waiting for your receivers to get open. Make sure to try a few shots downfield each game, because his arm has the range.

Big Ben can shrug off would-be tacklers and keep plays alive in the pocket.

DREW BREES ▶ Style: Ground and Pound

Brees may not have the throwing power of some of the younger QBs in the league, but his accuracy keeps him in the top 5. Aside from Peyton Manning and Tom Brady, there are no other pocket passers who can deliver throws that allow receivers to turn upfield and pick up yards after the catch. If you learn the throws Brees can and can't make he will be a star for your team.

Trust Brees to throw into tight windows in the intermediate area of the field. He is that good.

TOM BRADY ▶ Style: Speed Run

Tom Brady proved last season that, despite his age, he remains a top 5 QB. Brady still has a big arm when he needs it, but he is much better off in the intermediate passing game. Brady will rarely miss short throws, which is something very important to success in *Madden NFL 16*.

Brady is excellent at throwing accurate passes to HBs coming out of the backfield.

AARON RODGERS ▶ Style: Ground and Pound

Rodgers has slowed down a bit but remains the best all-around passer in the game. His ability to zip passes into tight windows looks simple but can't be replicated by average QBs. If you have Aaron Rodgers, there is simply no type of offense you can't run and no throw you can't make.

Rodgers can make all of the new QB passing mechanics this year look simple.

Halfback Items in MUT

Most players utilize a run-first offense early in the season while they are still looking to build confidence in their passing game. This year, both power backs and elusive backs can be effective with the right play calls. Consider grabbing a backup who is a solid receiver for third downs. However, if you get one of these elite backs, you should let him carry the load for the offense.

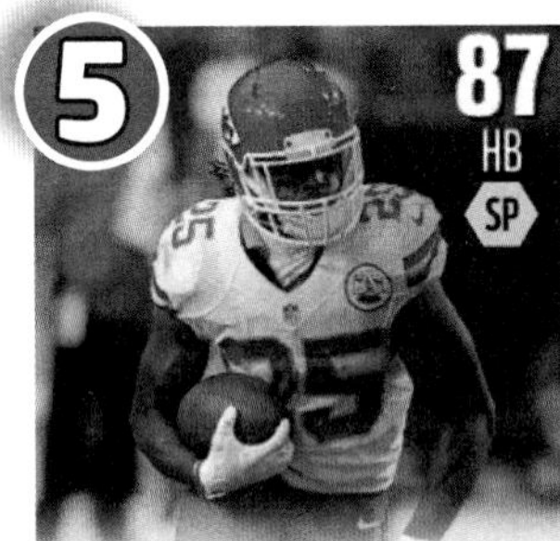

5 | 87 HB SP

JAMAAL CHARLES ▶ Style: Short Pass

Jamaal Charles is an excellent back, and not just because of his breakaway speed. Charles also has excellent hands out of the backfield and is one of the best route runners in MUT. If he gets matched up against a linebacker, he will win almost every time.

Charles is an absolute burner who can break a big play any time he touches the ball!

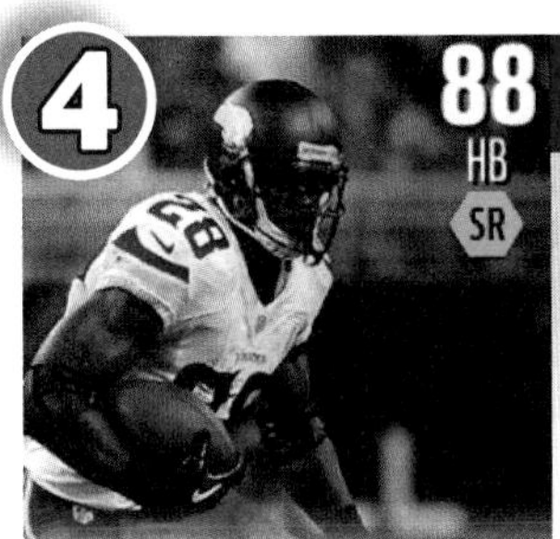

4 | 88 HB SR

ADRIAN PETERSON ▶ Style: Speed Run

Adrian Peterson can defeat tacklers with both power and elusive moves, which makes him one of the most versatile backs in Ultimate Team. To prevent fumbles, make sure to cover up the ball, and avoid taking unnecessary hits.

Peterson is very balanced between power and elusiveness, so defenders rarely bring him down on the first attempt.

3 | 89 HB GP

LE'VEON BELL ▶ Style: Ground and Pound

Bell is a powerful runner with a great arsenal of moves to defeat tacklers. While most power runners tend to be straight-ahead-style players, Bell can quickly cut and change lanes. He also is an every-down back, which provides great value to any team.

Bell proved he belonged in the top 5 last year with an excellent all-around season.

2 | 89 HB LP

DEMARCO MURRAY ▶ Style: Long Pass

Murray has such a tremendous blend of power and speed that not only can he knock over tacklers, but also he can run right past them! Murray is another rare combo player who has hands to go along with his power and is a very valuable back to an offense.

Murray is an every-down back.

1 | 90 HB SP

MARSHAWN LYNCH ▶ Style: Short Pass

Lynch is the best trucking back in the game and should be used to build a power run offense! While Alfred Morris, LeGarrette Blount, and Eddie Lacy are all solid trucking backs, Lynch is simply head and shoulders better. He will convert consistently in short yardage to keep the chains moving for your offense.

Lynch is an incredibly powerful back and should be trusted with every snap at the goal line.

Wide Receiver Items in MUT

A dominant WR is a real force in *Madden NFL 16,* especially with all the new catching mechanics. These elite-level players can bail your QB out on a bad throw and make some spectacular plays. Continue to feed these players the ball until the defense commits to double-teaming them. They may be covered, but they are always open!

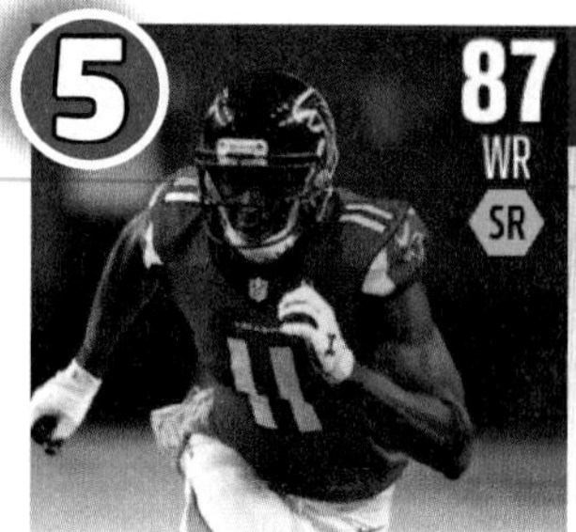

JULIO JONES ▶ Style: Speed Run

Julio Jones is capable of making every catch type look routine. With a great blend of size and speed, Julio is like a combination of A.J. Green and the more powerful Demaryius Thomas. Jones has everything in one package and can beat nearly any DB one-on-one.

Jones is the perfect option for players who want to use a speed-run style. Try pairing him with QB Tom Brady.

ODELL BECKHAM JR. ▶ Style: Short Pass

Odell Beckham Jr. exploded onto the scene last season and quickly showed off his top 5 talent. Odell Beckham Jr. is an all-around talent and has the added bonus of making highlight reel plays for your offense. If you want spectacular catches, this is your receiver.

Odell Beckham Jr. may not be the tallest WR in the game, but his Spectacular Catch rating makes him play big!

CALVIN JOHNSON ▶ Style: Ground and Pound

Johnson has one of the biggest bodies in all of Ultimate Team and can consistently make an aggressive catch downfield. There is no single defender in the game who isn't a mismatch, so adding Megatron to your lineup will pay off big.

Megatron is still the most dominant force when throwing downfield into coverage.

DEZ BRYANT ▶ Style: Long Pass

Dez Bryant has turned into a red zone machine who is able to hang onto balls in traffic. Bryant is our favorite midrange receiver because he consistently fights defenders for catches and hangs onto them.

Bryant has a knack for finding the end zone and should be trusted on fade routes.

ANTONIO BROWN ▶ Style: Short Pass

Brown is an excellent choice for the top receiver spot because he really benefits from the new RAC (run after catch) move in *Madden NFL 16*. Brown can run any type of route, so making sure to use all the different types of catches will ensure he earns his number one spot.

Brown is one of the must-have players if you struggle to beat man coverage; his route running is excellent.

TOP 5 Tight End Items in MUT

Tight ends in *Madden NFL 16* are some of the biggest and fastest players in the game. Use them to give your scheme a new level of options and deception. Will you keep your TE in to block or split him out wide in the red zone to use his size advantage? By moving these stars all over your formations, you can truly attack the defense anywhere.

JULIUS THOMAS ▶ Style: Long Pass

Thomas is an excellent option in the red zone because of his size. His ability to out-jump defenders gives him a big advantage. Thomas should get separation from most defenders unless you split him out wide against a great press corner.

Thomas can out-jump defenders, so don't worry about throwing it to him when he is one-on-one.

GREG OLSEN ▶ Style: Short Pass

Olsen is one of the best options in the game for players who can't grab Rob Gronkowski. Olsen can block and run every route that his peers can. He will also hang onto passes in traffic and has the size to steal even a bad throw from the QB away from the defense.

Olsen is a very well-rounded TE who can break big gains after the catch.

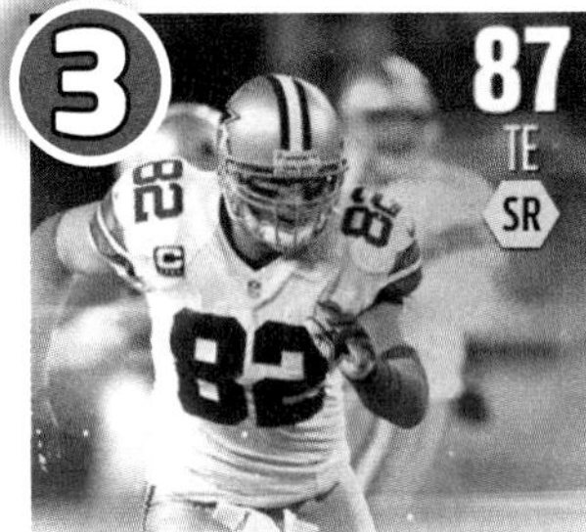

JASON WITTEN ▶ Style: Speed Run

Witten is a perfect option for players who like to use their TEs as reliable options on third down. Witten won't burn past too many defenders, but his ability to hang onto passes is extremely valuable for certain offenses. He has a big frame and can shield defenders away, especially on low throws.

Witten is an excellent safety valve who has been converting big third downs for a long time.

JIMMY GRAHAM ▶ Style: Ground and Pound

Graham is hands down the biggest and best receiving option in Ultimate Team, and he will really benefit from the offense's ability to throw high-point passes. Graham can line up anywhere in a formation and win a matchup against any type of defender. Make sure to use aggressive catches to get big over the defense!

Graham is basically a WR, and many playbooks have formations where you can split a TE out wide to get a mismatch.

ROB GRONKOWSKI ▶ Style: Long Pass

Gronk is the best TE in Ultimate Team because he can simply do it all. He is a beast when it comes to run blocking but can also run crisp routes even with his incredible size. He has the speed to attack the seam and the size to pull aggressive catches down over defenders.

Gronkowski is once again a force in the red zone—throw to him unless he is in double or triple coverage!

Defensive Linemen Items in MUT

Defensive linemen are often overlooked in MUT, but their ability to get pressure on the QB can make defending the passing game so much easier. Keep an eye out for players who have the strength and block shedding to stop the run, as they can be tough to find. While most players have one skill, the best of the best are all-around forces that the offense must pay attention to on every snap.

GERALD MCCOY (DT) ▶ Style: Man Defense

Gerald McCoy is prototypical 4-3 defensive tackle who has enough strength to stop the run but also can get after the passer. These types of players are extremely rare, so hang onto them and understand their value. McCoy is so good that he can even play in a 3-4 defense if needed.

McCoy is one of the best defenders in MUT at rushing the QB from the interior of the line.

ROBERT QUINN (RE) ▶ Style: Run Stuff

Quinn has a rare combination of size and power that allows him to attack any tackle in the game. He is capable of bringing down not only QBs with his great pursuit, but also ball carriers. Make sure to keep Quinn in a 4-3, where he will really excel at rushing off the edge.

Quinn is one of the most powerful rushing ends.

CAMERON WAKE (LE) ▶ Style: Run Stuff

Cameron Wake is perfect for 4-3 teams that want to get after the passer all game long. Wake has an array of pass moves and can even slide inside and still get pressure on passing downs. Try switching up his assignments to take advantage of his elite athletic ability.

Wake is so talented that he can drop into coverage and take away an offense's first read.

NDAMUKONG SUH (DT) ▶ Style: Zone Defense

Suh is an ideal defensive tackle in the 4-3 and will easily clog up rushing lanes. Where he becomes a nightmare for the offense is on third and long, where he can use his elite pass-rushing moves to get after the QB. Suh will consistently destroy even elite interior linemen.

Suh is so strong that he can play any position on the defensive line in a 3-4 scheme, too.

J.J. WATT (LE) ▶ Style: Pass Rush

Watt is hands down the best defensive item in Ultimate Team due to his ability to play any position on the defensive line. Watt can terrorize defenses from a 3-4 or 4-3 look and has the quickness to get pressure from the inside or the outside. He is a great run stopper and can even score off turnovers.

J.J. Watt can dominate at any position on the entire defensive line.

Linebacker Items in MUT

Finding a great LB who can control the middle of the defense or rush off the edge is imperative to building a great defense. Make sure to determine if you have a 3-4 or 4-3 defense, because it will impact the number and type of players you need. OLBs are some of the most versatile players in the game because they can rush the passer, drop into coverage, or even drop down to defensive end. You can never have enough studs at the LB position in *Madden NFL 16*.

TERRELL SUGGS (ROLB) ▶ Style: Pass Rush

Suggs is not only capable of rushing the passer and delivering big hits, he also does a great job in the run game. Allow him to play the 3-4 OLB positions, and any edge runs should get bottled up before they get outside.

Suggs is the best defender at setting the edge in the run game with his strength and block shedding.

BOBBY WAGNER (MLB) ▶ Style: Man Defense

Wagner is one of the fastest LBs in Ultimate Team, and he can unleash devastating hits that force turnovers. Wagner is the perfect player in a 4-3 defense to mix in man coverage and slow down routes to the TE.

Wagner has a rare blend of speed and hit power. He can force turnovers for your defense.

LUKE KUECHLY (MLB) ▶ Style: Zone Defense

Kuechly is one of the smartest defenders in MUT and is perfect for zone coverage. Leave him in a hook zone over the middle and allow his play recognition skill to do the work. He is a sure tackler and will lock down anything that comes through his area.

Kuechly is the ultimate set-it-and-forget-it LB. His play recognition is outstanding.

JUSTIN HOUSTON (LOLB) ▶ Style: Pass Rush

Houston is built to rush the passer from the 3-4 defense. However, he is so talented and strong that even a 4-3 defense could use him at defensive end to get pressure. No matter what defense you like to play, unleashing him at the QB is a smart idea.

Houston can be a one-man pass rush for your defense, so don't worry if it takes a ton to get him on your team.

VON MILLER (LOLB) ▶ Style: Run Stuff

Miller has excellent pass-rushing moves to go along with his speed and hit power. Miller is the best because he can drop into coverage or rush the passer and the offense can't key on him! Miller is so excellent that either a 3-4 or 4-3 defense will work for him.

Miller is an excellent pass rusher, but he can also cover most TEs pretty consistently.

Top 5 Cornerback Items in MUT

Cornerbacks have an all-new value in *Madden NFL 16* because now they can become playmakers and knock the ball away from receivers. An elite CB who can take away a number one WR on his own will make your entire defense better. Look for players who have a high Man Coverage or Zone Coverage rating depending on what style you want to play. Interceptions should be on the rise this season, and finding a CB who can get into position will be a big bonus.

5 — 86 CB MD — PATRICK PETERSON ▶ Style: Man Defense

Patrick Peterson is one of the most athletic CBs in the game, and he has the size to match up with nearly any receiver. Players who like to play man defense can look for him to be a lockdown player. If you like to mix it up a bit more, go with the more balanced but smaller Joe Haden.

In addition to being an excellent defender, Patrick Peterson is dynamic on special teams as a returner.

4 — 88 CB PR — CHRIS HARRIS ▶ Style: Pass Rush

Harris is the perfect option to match up against smaller receivers who try to use great route running to get open. If you place Harris in the slot on man coverage, he will completely lock down any quick passes over the middle and frustrate your opponent.

Harris is a lock-down man defender who won't give much separation to receivers on their cuts.

3 — 89 CB RS — VONTAE DAVIS ▶ Style: Run Stuff

Davis is one of the most physical secondary players in Ultimate Team. While he isn't enormous, his ability to press receivers at the line lets him match up with bigger players. His Man Coverage rating will have him knocking passes out of receivers' hands all game.

Take advantage of Davis's ability to jam receivers at the line of scrimmage.

2 — 89 CB MD — RICHARD SHERMAN ▶ Style: Man Defense

Sherman is always one of the most popular players in MUT because of his ability to stop bigger WRs from catching balls downfield. He often turns into a playmaker of his own and can even turn defense into offense with interceptions.

Sherman is the CB you need to shut down big WRs who want to go for aggressive catches.

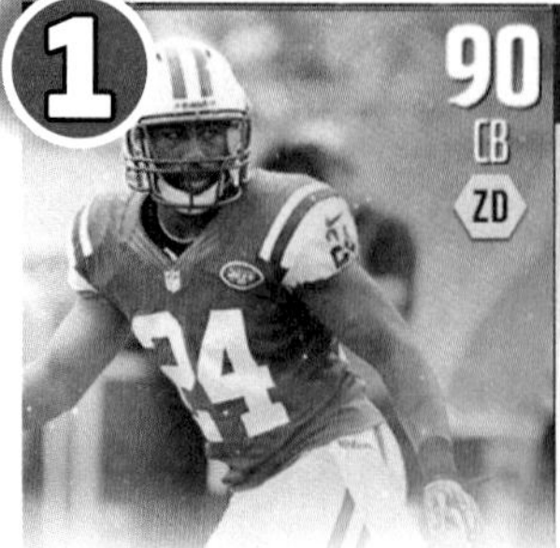

1 — 90 CB ZD — DARRELLE REVIS ▶ Style: Zone Defense

Revis is extremely balanced and can play nearly any type of coverage for your defense. Take advantage of his ability to get up at the line and slow down receivers. Mix in plenty of man coverage to get your value.

Revis can stick with nearly any WR on his own all game long!

TOP 5 Safety Items in MUT

Knowing what to look for in a safety can completely change the way you play defense in *Madden NFL 16*. A great coverage safety can quickly cover ground and make plays that will frustrate the offense. A hard-hitting safety can drop down into the box and make the offense think twice about running the ball. Use these players to disguise your defense and force turnovers, which will have you winning more games.

RESHAD JONES (SS) ▶ Style: Pass Rush

Jones's stock has been climbing consistently in Ultimate Team, and now he has cracked the top 5 with a great ability to be a stout defender in the run game. Jones has a good combination of pursuit and hit power that leads to him being a sure tackler.

▶ **Jones is a solid all-around talent who can be moved around before the snap to take advantage of his abilities.**

HARRISON SMITH (FS) ▶ Style: Pass Rush

Smith is a very young talent who is quickly getting lots of attention. Smith is the perfect safety for Cover 2 man defenses because he has great zone coverage and the size to get over and help his corners.

▶ **Smith has premiere size, which is crucial to building a great MUT secondary.**

EARL THOMAS III (FS) ▶ Style: Run Stuff

Thomas is an ideal safety for defenses that like to play a Cover 3 or commit their strong safety up in the box to stop the run. Thomas has the speed and ability to recognize plays as they are happening, which helps him play almost like two defenders in one.

▶ **Thomas is one of the quickest defenders in MUT, and his ability to break up and intercept passes is legendary!**

ERIC WEDDLE (FS) ▶ Style: Man Defense

Weddle doesn't have the best size, but he always seems to be around the ball making plays. You can rely on Weddle no matter what type of defense you want to play, and he will show up game in and game out. He may not have the hit power, but he is a sure tackler at the free safety spot, which can be rare.

▶ **Weddle is another player who has the play recognition to be in the correct spot at nearly all times.**

KAM CHANCELLOR (SS) ▶ Style: Zone Defense

With his size and hit power, Chancellor is one of the most intimidating players in Madden Ultimate Team. He is basically like an extra LB up in the box, but he can also match up with most TEs in the game and can slow down routes over the middle.

▶ **Chancellor is the perfect player to run Cover 1 Robber coverage with.**

MUT Offensive Style Builds Ground and Pound

GENERAL STRATEGY

For players who love a power running attack, the ground and pound is a great style. Focus on building a strong offensive line with great run blocking to counter the strength and block shedding of a defensive line. Pick up a halfback whose trucking is better than his elusiveness, and learn to time your ability to break tackles with the right stick. Focus on building more of a between-the-tackles run game as opposed to heading outside. Learn to control the clock and cut down on turnovers to maximize your winning.

SILVER ITEMS

TYROD TAYLOR (QB)

T.J. YELDON (HB)

GOLD ITEMS

MATT RYAN

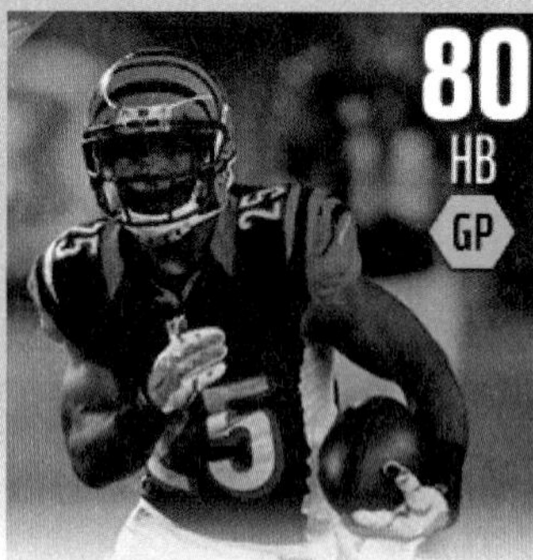

GIOVANI BERNARD

ELITE ITEMS

AARON RODGERS

LE'VEON BELL

PLAYBOOKS

1. Dallas Cowboys
2. Cincinnati Bengals
3. Houston Texans

UPGRADE ORDER

1. HB (TRK)
2. TE (RBK)
3. OL (STR)
4. QB (THP)
5. WR (CIT)

KEY RATINGS

▶ Trucking and Carry (HB), Run Blocking and Strength (OL/TE), Play Action and Throw Power (QB)

STRENGTHS

▶ The new play action "shot plays" will work well with this playbook if you get into a second and short situation.

▶ You'll have a great matchup against teams that haven't built their lineup to stop the run.

▶ The ability to convert on short yardage downs allows you to keep the chains moving.

WEAKNESSES

▶ Fumbles are the enemy. Make sure to cover up the ball to limit the damage a big hit can cause.

▶ What you save on QB and WR skill positions, you must spend on the defensive side of the ball.

▶ It can be tough to come back from a big deficit if you can't run the ball early in the game.

MUT Offensive Style Builds Speed Run

GENERAL STRATEGY

The speed-run style is perfect for a player who prefers to run outside the tackles and can make moves in the open field. While you won't have the consistency of a ground-and-pound attack, you can break off big runs that will frustrate opponents who can't contain you. Consider getting the QB involved in the run game, and look for a halfback who not only has an elusive style but can catch out of the backfield.

SILVER ITEMS

BROCK OSWEILER (QB)

RONNIE HILLMAN (HB)

GOLD ITEMS

RYAN TANNEHILL

ALFRED MORRIS

ELITE ITEMS

TOM BRADY

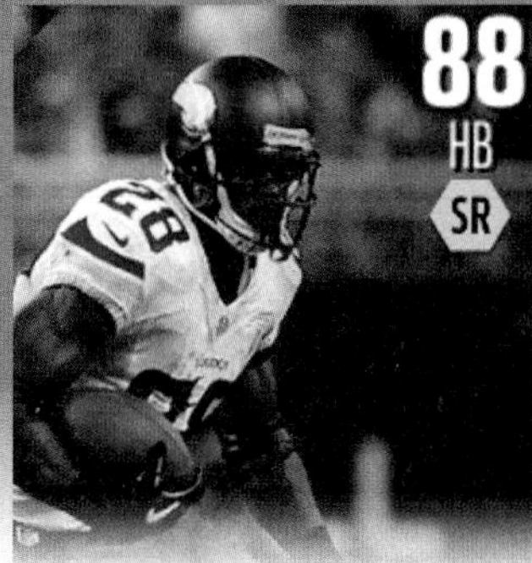

ADRIAN PETERSON

PLAYBOOKS

1. Miami Dolphins
2. Minnesota Vikings
3. Buffalo Bills

UPGRADE ORDER

1. HB (ELU)
2. OL (IMP)
3. QB (ACC)
4. TE (STR)
5. WR (RBK)

KEY RATINGS

▶ Speed and Elusiveness (HB), Run Blocking and Impact Blocking (OL/TE), Acceleration and Play Action (QB)

STRENGTHS

▶ This play style requires an extra TE or WRs with decent run blocking to hold up on the edge.

▶ Focus on finding faster offensive linemen with great impact blocking to block defenders in motion.

▶ Running formations extend to shotgun and pistol, allowing you to spread out defenses.

WEAKNESSES

▶ Learning to beat a tackler in the open field is important to maximize this offensive style.

▶ Players must learn to abandon the edge and just pick up a minimal gain rather than losing yards on certain plays.

▶ Players must commit to running the ball on second and long and can't abandon the run game early.

MUT Offensive Style Builds Short Pass

GENERAL STRATEGY

Players who want a balanced attack that is slightly in favor of passing the ball should look to build a short-pass style. If you throw quick routes to your backs and slot receiver, you can decrease how much you need to rely on the run game. Be sure to take the open read when it comes available, rather than waiting to go downfield. By making the smart consistent throw, you can limit your turnovers and keep the chains moving.

SILVER ITEMS

BRIAN HOYER (QB)

JEFF JANIS (WR)

GOLD ITEMS

CAM NEWTON

RANDALL COBB

ELITE ITEMS

BEN ROETHLISBERGER

ANTONIO BROWN

PLAYBOOKS

1. Kansas City Chiefs
2. Detroit Lions
3. Oakland Raiders

UPGRADE ORDER

1. QB (SAC)
2. WR (RTE)
3. HB (CTH)
4. TE (CIT)
5. OL (PBK)

KEY RATINGS

- Throwing on the Run and Short Accuracy (QB), Catch in Traffic and Route Running (WR), Pass Blocking (OL)

STRENGTHS

- By getting the ball out quickly on offense, you don't have to invest as much into an offensive line.
- Learning how to free up receivers from press coverage can improve your timing between the QB and WR.
- The QB's short accuracy and medium accuracy are more important than ever before, so set your feet before throwing.

WEAKNESSES

- Don't throw high-point passes with your QB into traffic over the middle.
- Learn how to use the new conservative catch when in traffic to protect the ball on third and short.
- Look out for defensive linemen dropping into coverage on zone blitzes, which can take your quick read over the middle away.

MUT Offensive Style Builds Long Pass

GENERAL STRATEGY

Teams that can throw the ball downfield can light up the scoreboard and quickly dominate opponents. While it can be a riskier way to play due to turnovers, this is often how the best offenses play. By getting big targets on the outside and a strong-armed QB, you will have everything you need to pass up and down the field.

SILVER ITEMS

RYAN MALLETT (QB)

NICK TOON (WR)

GOLD ITEMS

PHILIP RIVERS

ALSHON JEFFERY

ELITE ITEMS

ANDREW LUCK

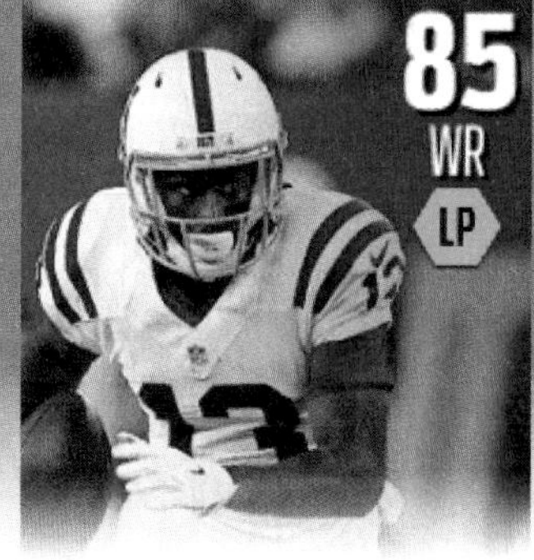

T.Y. HILTON

PLAYBOOKS

1. Denver Broncos
2. Pittsburgh Steelers
3. Atlanta Falcons

UPGRADE ORDER

1. QB (THP)
2. WR (SPC)
3. OL (PBK)
4. TE (CIT)
5. HB (PBK)

KEY RATINGS

▶ Throw Power and Deep Accuracy (QB), Spectacular Catch and Catch in Traffic (WR/TE), Pass Blocking and Strength (OL/HB)

STRENGTHS

▶ With the ability to go up for an aggressive catch in *Madden NFL 16*, this is a great offensive style to choose!

▶ If a defense doesn't have a true lockdown defender, they will be forced to double-cover your number one wideout.

▶ Players can find excellent value in pocket passers with big arms who can make all the throws downfield.

WEAKNESSES

▶ Receivers must be able to get off the press so the QB won't have to hold the ball too long in the pocket.

▶ The offensive line must be able to block the defense one-on-one, and players must learn to look for heavy blitzes.

▶ This offense can stall inside the red zone once the field dimensions get tighter.

MUT Defensive Style Builds Run Stuff

GENERAL STRATEGY

Stopping the run is one of the most crucial elements to consistently winning games in MUT. Picking the run-stuff style allows you to slow your opponents without committing extra resources into the box to stop the run. Once you get your opponent into certain passing situations, you can then ramp up the blitzing pressure. Consider the responsibilities of a 3-4 DE vs a 4-3 DE to determine what defense you want to build for the playbook you select.

SILVER ITEMS

JESSE WILLIAMS (DT)

JOHNATHAN CASILLAS (ROLB)

GOLD ITEMS

MICHAEL BROCKERS

JULIUS PEPPERS

ELITE ITEMS

CAMERON WAKE

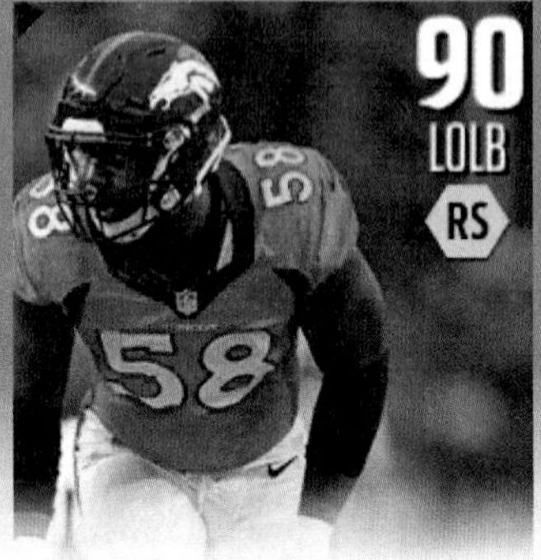

VON MILLER

PLAYBOOKS

1. New York Jets
2. Detroit Lions
3. Minnesota Vikings

UPGRADE ORDER

1. DT (BSH)
2. MLB (PUR)
3. SS (POW)
4. DE (STR)
5. OLB (TAK)

KEY RATINGS

▶ Block Shed and Strength (DT), Pursuit and Tackle (MLB), Play Recognition and Hit Power (SS)

STRENGTHS

▶ Early in the season, most players like to run the ball until they get comfortable passing, so this is a great style.

▶ Finding big, strong defensive linemen isn't too difficult, but keep an eye on their Block Shed rating, which is crucial.

▶ If you don't get a strong safety with a solid Play Recognition rating (85+), consider user-controlling him on a hook zone in the middle.

WEAKNESSES

▶ Picking up a player who can stop the run and rush the passer will cost you a solid amount of coins, so look for two players instead.

▶ If your opponent tries to spread out your defense, you may not need all the strength you picked up in the middle.

▶ Make sure to pick a second DT (4-3) or a second MLB (3-4) to maximize your base defense and match your team playbook.

MUT Defensive Style Builds Pass Rush

GENERAL STRATEGY

A QB without time to throw the ball becomes just an average player to an offense. This is the power of a great pass-rushing defense that doesn't give the offense any time to let their routes develop. If you can simply get pressure from your front four linemen without sending blitzes too often, you will force your opponents to change their entire game plan. Pass-rushing players are extremely versatile in Madden Ultimate Team and one of the best ways to get the most value for your coins.

SILVER ITEMS

MARIO EDWARDS JR (RE)

DEZMAN MOSES (ROLB)

GOLD ITEMS

CAMERON HEYWARD

ANTHONY BARR

ELITE ITEMS

J.J. WATT

JUSTIN HOUSTON

PLAYBOOKS

1. Buffalo Bills
2. Jacksonville Jaguars
3. Kansas City Chiefs

UPGRADE ORDER

1. DE (PMV)
2. OLB (FMV)
3. DT (PMV)
4. FS (ZCV)
5. CB (MCV)

KEY RATINGS

▶ Power Moves and Finesse Moves (DE/OLB), Acceleration and Speed (OLB)

STRENGTHS

▶ It will take a great offensive line (which is rare early in the season) to stop a great pass rush.

▶ If the offense has to keep an extra HB or TE in to block, you have won the battle.

▶ In *Madden NFL 16*, the QB's accuracy will suffer when under pressure, and that can lead to turnovers for the defense.

WEAKNESSES

▶ A run-heavy offense may be tough in the first half of a game, but most players will abandon it if you commit to stopping it early.

▶ Switch to man coverage if the offense is targeting HBs out of the backfield and you can't slow them down.

▶ Consider calling press coverage to slow down WRs at the line if the offense is passing the ball too quickly.

MUT Defensive Style Builds Zone Defense

GENERAL STRATEGY

Defenses that build to the strength of their players are the most successful in MUT. By looking for players in the LB corps and secondary that have solid zone coverage, you can really build an excellent defense. Learn how to use coverage shading, because it is one of the most important ways to help your players be in great position after the snap. By mixing up your coverage calls, you can send pressure and disguise your looks, which will leave the offense guessing all game long.

SILVER ITEMS

ZAVIAR GOODEN (MLB)

DAVID AMERSON (CB)

GOLD ITEMS

BRIAN CUSHING

PRINCE AMUKAMARA

ELITE ITEMS

LUKE KUECHLY

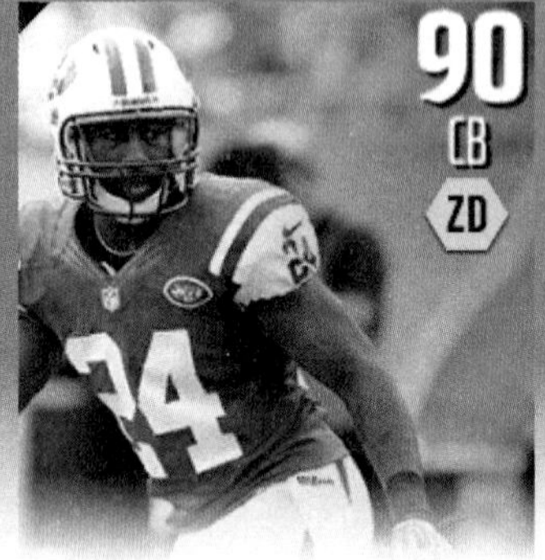

DARRELLE REVIS

PLAYBOOKS

1. Tampa Bay Buccaneers
2. Dallas Cowboys
3. Indianapolis colts

UPGRADE ORDER

1. CB (ZCV)
2. FS (SPD)
3. MLB (PRC)
4. SS (ZCV)
5. OLB (PRC)

KEY RATINGS

▶ Zone Coverage (CB/LB), Hit Power and Play Recognition (LB/S), Pursuit and Tackle (OLB)

STRENGTHS

▶ Cover 4 is a great coverage that forces offenses to connect underneath, and it can frustrate even the best teams, especially those with a long-pass style.

▶ Height is a crucial factor for zone defenders; don't let an opponent target your smaller players one-on-one downfield.

▶ Consider calling "show blitz" before the snap to slow down the run game up the middle.

WEAKNESSES

▶ Every zone coverage has a weakness, so make sure to switch up your play calls and to find a rangy free safety to help with Cover 3 calls.

▶ In short-yardage situations, your zones can drift away from the line and allow quick passes, so try man coverage.

▶ Certain formations can cause tough alignments for zone coverages. Try using base align to balance it out.

MUT Defensive Style Builds Man Defense

GENERAL STRATEGY

Man coverage is extremely improved in *Madden NFL 16* with all of the new interaction that takes place in the secondary. With many players learning how to attack zone coverage, this can be an excellent style to really cause frustration for your opponent. Stick with this style early and often and your opponents will have to work to beat it all game long and prove to you they can do it consistently. It also allows you to make adjustments to slow down their favorite targets, such as corner routes. By mixing in press and some zone from time to time, man defense can be a great way to rack up wins this season.

SILVER ITEMS

TAVON WILSON (FS)

NOLAN CARROLL (CB)

GOLD ITEMS

TASHAUN GIPSON

DOMINIQUE RODGERS-CROMARTIE

ELITE ITEMS

ERIC WEDDLE

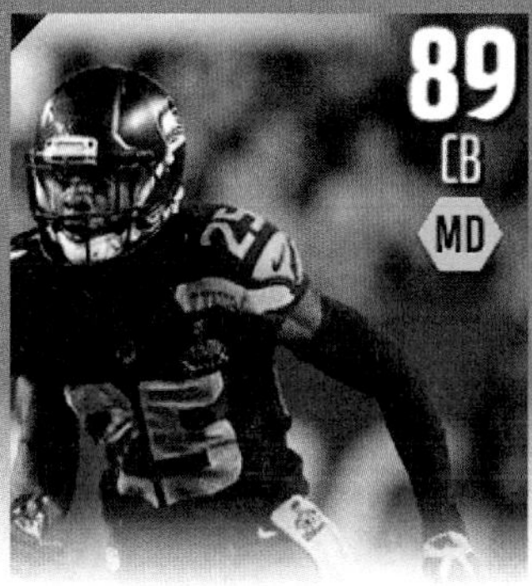

RICHARD SHERMAN

PLAYBOOKS

1. Cleveland Browns
2. Denver Broncos
3. Miami Dolphins

UPGRADE ORDER

1. CB (MCV)
2. FS (ZCV)
3. OLB (PUR)
4. SS (ZCV)
5. MLB (PRC)

KEY RATINGS

▶ Man Coverage, Speed and Agility (CB), Pursuit and Play Recognition (LB)

STRENGTHS

▶ Start with Cover 2 Man and test your opponent's ability to beat it. Keep an eye on the TE position especially.

▶ Cover 1 allows a safety to get up in the box if your CB proves he can hold his own on the outside.

▶ If his coverage assignment stays in to block, a great MLB can drop into coverage and clog up passing lanes.

WEAKNESSES

▶ Make sure to add a QB spy or contain your DEs if facing a mobile QB.

▶ If a WR has excellent route running, he can find a way to get separation on cuts, and you may need to add a zone to help.

▶ Blitzing without any safety help (Cover 0) can be perfect if timed correctly, but it shouldn't be an every-down play call.

Ways to Maximize Your Coins

Earning coins is one of the keys to building your ultimate team. Think about what your goals are when you start saving up your coins. Are you looking to be a head-to-head player or grind out solo challenges vs the CPU? Are you mainly into MUT for the collecting aspect and want to complete sets? Your focus will change your path slightly, but it doesn't change the fact that having more coins is always better than having fewer coins. By keeping a solid reserve of coins available, you will always be ready to pounce on deals and keep building your stack.

5 GRIND OUT SOLO CHALLENGES

New players are always looking for the quickest ways to earn coins, and solo challenges are a great place to start. There are plenty of great challenges that match your skill level early in the game and allow you to start building up to bigger rewards. Take a day or two and work on completing as many as you can; the sooner you get them done the more valuable the rewards will be. You should be able to get your time for each game down to a science and really maximize your coins.

Playing head-to-head seasons is a great way to earn coins, too. The rewards get bigger the higher you climb.

4 PLAY THE PROMOS

There are always great opportunities to build up your coins during promo events when new items come onto the market. Often you get rewards that go into sets, but instead you could flip yours for coins, especially if the reward doesn't interest you. Consider what the best path to making coins is and try to capitalize.

If a reward is a player who doesn't fit your team, you can always auction him on the market!

3 PULL PACKS

Opening packs is one of the best parts of building your ultimate team. The more packs you open, the more chances you have to get back valuable items that you can either use in your lineup or sell to the highest bidder at the Auction House. Manage your binder and try to get your value back from nearly all the items you pull (not just players). By spending some time checking the market, you can find some players who return more than you expect! Use all the filters available when searching to find the best deals, and then consider flipping your purchase for coins if you find a great deal.

Check the bundle topper to see if it is something you can use for your team or on the market.

2 PLAY THE WAITING GAME

For most player items in MUT, the longer you wait to pick them up on the market, the less they will cost. Over the course of a season, new content comes out each day that can lower the price of older items. Be patient and figure out the true positions, ratings, and players that are worth spending on for your scheme. If you really value QB items, consider getting the latest and greatest item, but know that you will likely spend some extra coins to get it on day 1. This also goes for players you test out and don't want to keep, so make sure to post them back as soon you know they aren't a fit for your lineup to get as much value back as possible.

It can be tough to keep up with the newest cards for a whole season, but you can look for similar items that may be a week or two older to save coins.

1 BE READY FOR SETS

The wealthiest players in MUT are the best at managing their binder and being ready for new sets to drop. They keep track of all the content in a notebook or online and are ready to strike while the values are at their peak. Consider holding onto and waiting to sell certain items in your binder when they are at their peak value, like in a set. By keeping an eye on the market each day, you will start to learn how things fluctuate each week, and you can quickly get well onto your way to becoming a MUT millionaire.

Keeping an eye on social media can be a great way to hear about the newest sets and items in MUT!

Solo Challenge Tips on Offense

Often, the team with possession last is the one that wins the game. This can be a stressful way to take on solo challenges, but it can make them go by quickly. Smart players learn to maximize their possessions: They like to kick off and score before the half, and they are always looking to win on a field goal. Here are the best ways to increase your win percentage in solo challenges, to beat them faster, and to make more coins.

5 FIND A PLAYBOOK

Madden NFL 16 has no shortage of great playbooks, so finding one to fit your style should be easy. Most playbooks cover all the basic concepts, so it really comes down to what players you have and what formations you are comfortable using. Head into practice mode with a new book just to check out all your options before starting. Find plays for each situation and develop some formations you are comfortable running and passing from. Against the CPU, quick audibles and hot routes are very valuable, so learn to use them.

You shouldn't be changing your playbooks more than once per week. When you find a good one, dig deep and stick with it.

4 GO MOBILE

One of the toughest things for the CPU to defend is a dual-threat QB who can beat the defense with both his arm and his legs. If you have a chance, get a mobile QB even just as a backup and put him in him to fool the defense. Poor decisions can lead to turnovers with a mobile QB, so be smart. Turnovers are one of the quickest ways to lose challenges, but with a smart game plan, you can eliminate opportunities to lose possession!

Using your QB's legs in the red zone can be a great way to surprise a defense!

3 TAKE THE POINTS

If your drive doesn't end with a TD, taking the points is the smart option on anything over fourth and inches. While it can feel frustrating to get stopped or to not score a TD, taking the points is consistently the smartest move when taking on the CPU. The earlier in the game you get on the scoreboard, the better the position you will be in. If you are consistently stalling in the red zone, work on some new plays in practice mode for those specific situations.

Learn whether you can rely on your defense or if you need to go for it on 4th and short to win.

2 FIND A MISMATCH

Depending on your opponent in the challenge, their lineup will have certain strengths and weaknesses. Find any advantage that you have and look to exploit it. If you have a dominant offensive line or a big tall WR, look to get them in good situations to make plays. Every team is different, so taking a second to look for your opponent's best players with the matchup stick before the snap can be a very wise move.

Take a look before the snap to see if you have an advantage at the WR position.

1 CHEW THE CLOCK

Pounding the rock is an excellent way to defeat the computer in solo challenges. Not only does it cut down on the risk of turnovers, but it keeps the clock moving and limits possessions. Use the Cover Up button to help prevent your HB from fumbling, especially at the end of games or when running up the middle. Consider keeping a good trucking HB with high carry skills on the bench to ice the game. Using the Chew Clock option at the play-calling screen can make those seconds tick off and help the coins rack up.

Winning is the only thing that matters; win quickly rather than by 100 points!

Solo Challenge Tips on Defense

Defense not only wins championships in *Madden NFL 16*, it also can help you win solo challenges with ease. Having a stout defense that can get a well-timed sack and stop the run is the key to completing solo challenges quickly. Here are our favorite ways to lock up on defense and earn more coins to build our ultimate team.

5 USE FORMATION SUBS

It will cost you coins in the long run to keep additional players on your roster, even on the bench. A big key to fielding a great team is to get value from every position. Aim to build your lineup to fit your most important defensive set and then use formation subs at the play-calling screen to fit players in. For most solo challenges, you shouldn't need to have a full roster of backups to defeat the computer consistently. You can pay up front for a highly rated player who can do it all or pick up two lower-rated players who can each do one thing well and then sub them in to maximize their ratings.

Build your defense around your favorite formation and use it on over half your play calls.

4 FIND A USER DEFENDER

Look for a big, fast defender with poor play recognition to user-control on your defense. By taking control of him, you can react to plays quickly once you read what the opponent is doing. This is a great way to take a lower-rated player and increase his level of play. This should help you save coins in one area so that you can spend them on a position like CB to match up with an opponent's number one wideout.

You always want to user-control the most vulnerable area of your defensive play call!

3 STUFF THE RUN

Stopping the run on early downs is crucial to getting the offense in a bad situation on third and long. If you don't have a solid run-defense formation that you are comfortable with, you will be vulnerable to play-action passes. Make the computer run everything inside by spreading your defensive line in early downs. Their best runs will come if you lose containment to the outside, so protect there early. If you get them to a short-yardage situation, then look for the up-the-middle run. Keeping the ball in your possession during solo challenges really speeds them up, and stopping the run is important.

Run-committing is rarely needed, but it can be a big win on third and short if it forces a punt.

2 LEARN CONCEPTS

Keep an eye on the game situation and formation that the computer is calling to give you some potential information about what play they are looking to call. On third and short, they are more likely to call a concept like stick, where you will want to be ready to jump underneath and shade your coverage down. On third and long, they are more likely to use a verticals concept, so you want to protect the deep middle, especially to the TE. You will start to recognize patterns after seeing just one route on a play, and that will let your user get into a good position. Every playbook shares similar concepts—the difference is the formation!

Using coverage shading before the snap is extremely important when playing the CPU and using zone coverage.

1 GET A BLITZ

Getting the opponent to third and long is the key to winning solo challenges. It will make them one-dimensional and force them to pass the ball, which allows you to blitz. Learn how to sneak a slot CB in on a blitz off the edge, and the QB can either dump it off for a short gain or hold the ball and take a sack. This can also lead to turnovers, which is the quickest way to get a victory.

Make sure to have a secondary blitz call that can get in when an opponent blocks the HB!

Top Offensive Budget Items in MUT

Early in the season, coins and elite players are at a premium. The key to getting ahead is to find some lower-rated players who can perform at a high level when placed into the right lineup and scheme. Here are some of our favorite offensive players if you are looking to build up your budget offense. Use these players to their strengths and they should deliver you plenty of wins early in the season to get your team on the right track.

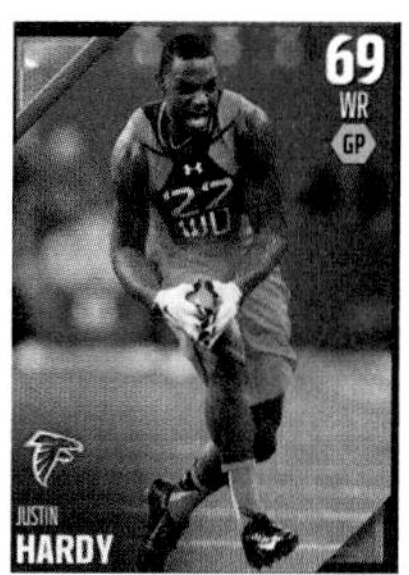

BUDGET OFFENSIVE DEPTH CHART

GOLD SILVER

QB
- 1. Marcus Mariota
- 2. Tarvaris Jackson
- 3. Ryan Mallett

HB
- 1. Todd Gurley
- 2. Matt Asiata

FB
- 1. Dorin Dickerson

WR
- 1. Dorial Green-Beckham
- 2. Nick Toon
- 3. Jeff Janis
- 4. Justin Hardy
- 5. Brian Hartline

TE
- 1. Phillip Supernaw
- 2. James Hanna

LT
- 1. Matt Kalil

LG
- 1. Laken Tomlinson

C
- 1. Daniel Kilgore

RG
- 1. Todd Herremans

RT
- 1. D.J. Fluker

BUDGET OFFENSIVE PLAYBOOKS
- 1. Chicago Bears
- 2. Houston Texans
- 3. Washington Redskins

Top Defensive Budget Items in MUT

Defense is often the side of the ball that is overlooked in Ultimate Team, as most players will try to light up the scoreboard first. The good news is that there are plenty of great value players on defense that can deliver results if fit into the right scheme and playbook. Make sure to find a good playbook and think about where you struggle. If you can't stop the run, find some strong defensive linemen to help out. Once you realize that two players can be as good as one if you're willing to make some adjustments and try new formations, you will be ready to win games with your budget lineup!

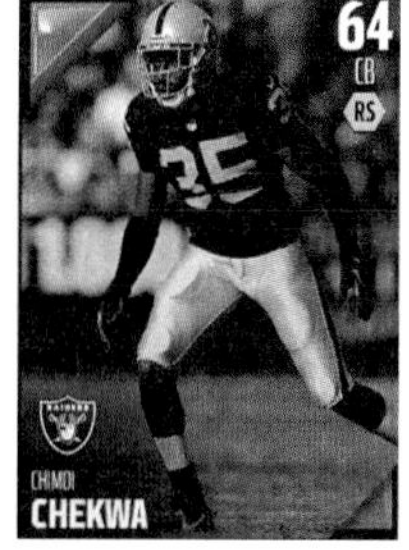

BUDGET DEFENSIVE DEPTH CHART

 GOLD  SILVER 

LE
- 1. Kendall Reyes
- 2. Margus Hunt

DT
- 1. Sammie Hill
- 2. Marvin Austin Jr.

RE
- 1. Mario Edwards Jr.
- 2. Vic Beasley Jr.

LOLB
- 1. Bruce Carter
- 2. Devon Kennard

MLB
- 1. Denzel Perryman
- 2. Stephone Anthony

ROLB
- 1. Nick Perry
- 2. Malcolm Smith

CB
- 1. Trae Waynes
- 2. Phillip Gaines
- 3. Zack Bowman
- 4. Antwon Blake
- 5. Chimdi Chekwa

FS
- 1. Rodney McLeod
- 2. Dashon Goldson

SS
- 1. Shamarko Thomas
- 2. Matt Elam

BUDGET DEFENSIVE PLAYBOOKS
- 1. San Diego Chargers
- 2. New England Patriots
- 3. Oakland Raiders

Offensive Playbooks in MUT

Working with a playbook that fits your offensive scheme is one of the biggest ways to improve your game in Madden Ultimate Team. Determine if you are a run-first or pass-first player and how your current team is made up. If you pull a big WR and a strong-armed QB, switch to a book that has some great plays for your playmakers. If you have a specific playbook you like that is run-heavy, consider selling those players and investing in your offensive line and an elite HB.

▶ **Honorable Mention: Saints, Buccaneers, Ravens**

5 NEW YORK GIANTS

The Giants' offensive playbook got an overhaul and now features some great passing formations.

- **STYLES: Long Pass, Speed Run**
- **KEY RUN SET: Singleback Ace**
- **KEY PASS SET: Gun Trio Offset**

The Giants' playbook is excellent for players who have three receiving options and love to pass the football. Check out some of the new formations that feature players in the flex. This will make it easier to pass-block and give you the time you need to look downfield. Work screen passes into the mix to maximize your scheme.

Using formation subs at the play-calling screen is one of the keys to getting your playmakers good matchup advantages.

4 PHILADELPHIA EAGLES

- **STYLES: Speed Run, Short Pass**
- **KEY RUN SET: Gun Ace Twins Offset**
- **KEY PASS SET: Gun Flip Trips Eaglet**

Philadelphia is an excellent playbook for gamers who want to pass the ball short to set up the run game inside. Drill the defense with quick throws to the outside to show them the flats must be covered. Once you get them thinking outside, mix in some inside zones to gash them up the middle. As long as you can handle shotgun formations, this playbook has it all.

The Eagles' 23 shotgun formations are the most of any team; you must be confident from these formations to win!

3 SEATTLE SEAHAWKS

- **STYLES: Ground and Pound, Short Pass**
- **KEY RUN SET: Gun Doubles Wing Offset**
- **KEY PASS SET: Gun Wing Offset Wk**

Seattle's playbook has great versatility for running the ball depending on if you prefer to run up the middle or outside. They also can succeed with running the ball from under center, pistol, and shotgun. Work on getting the opposing defense into tough alignments, and then use a mobile QB as a backbreaker to take the ball outside. You also have some good formations to take big shots downfield, but don't risk it more than once or twice per half.

Seattle can use a power-rushing attack if you are committed to the ground game.

2 MIAMI DOLPHINS

- **STYLES: Speed Run, Short Pass**
- **KEY RUN SET: Singleback Wing Trips Open**
- **KEY PASS SET: Gun Bunch Open Offset**

Miami has some excellent spread passing formations for players who love to use unique alignments. Call a diverse game plan to keep your opponent guessing which formation you will use next. You can keep using similar concepts over and over as long as they are coming from new formations. If you like this playbook, check out the Raiders and Vikings, too. You will have the most success with a mobile QB, so look for one in the Auction House.

The Dolphins' playbook benefits from a great wing style TE/FB who can lead-block and catch passes in traffic.

1 NEW ENGLAND PATRIOTS

- **STYLE(S): Short Pass, Long Pass**
- **KEY RUN SET: Singleback Tight Slots**
- **KEY PASS SET: Gun Split Close Pats**

The New England Patriots have some excellent formations for players who love to pass the football. If you have a big TE/WR, you will love the options on the outside for iso matchups. This playbook also does a nice job working with a WR using RAC over the middle. Keep your completion percentage high and work on short passes to move the chains.

TOP 5 Defensive Playbooks in MUT

The key to selecting a winning playbook is to match it to your defensive style. Think about if you would rather have a 3-4 or 4-3 base and go from there. Find a good formation that you feel comfortable using to stop the run. Consider what coverage style you like to play and how you will bring pressure on third down from your nickel and dime sets. Once you have answered these questions, picking the right defensive playbook to win you more games becomes easy! There is no problem with changing between playbooks, as many have similar concepts and can give you the edge you need.

▶ **Honorable Mention: Bengals, Seahawks, Ravens**

5 NEW ORLEANS SAINTS

- **BASE: 3-4**
- **STYLES: Zone Defense, Pass Rush**
- **RUN DEFENSE SET: 3-4 Bear**
- **PASS DEFENSE SET: Big Dime 1-4-6**

The Saints' defense has a multitude of 3-4 formations that can keep opponents guessing where the pressure is going to come from. It also has some of the best passing defenses in the game if you like to have four CBs on the field at once. Keep bringing heavy pressure off the edges to get the most out of it.

▶ Test out Cover 2 man this season and see if your opponents have what it takes to beat it consistently.

4 DALLAS COWBOYS

- **BASE: 4-3**
- **STYLES: Pass Rush, Run Stuff**
- **RUN DEFENSE SET: 46 Bear**
- **PASS DEFENSE SET: Big Dime 4-1-6**

The Cowboys' playbook requires an excellent strong safety to maximize its effectiveness. If you land a great one and prefer an aggressive 4-3 style, this is the playbook to try out. Take advantage of all the unique ways to get your secondary defenders up in the box and force opponents to try to spread you out.

▶ The 46 Bear is one of the best formations in the game for aggressive players!

3 GREEN BAY PACKERS

- **BASE: 3-4**
- **STYLES: Pass Rush, Man Defense**
- **RUN DEFENSE SET: 3-4 Solid**
- **PASS DEFENSE SET: Big Dime 2-3-6 Will**

For a 3-4 player, the Packers' defense has a great mix of formations that should have them feeling comfortable. There are plenty of great nickel formations, which will get an extra CB on the field to help slow down all the new passing features. The only thing missing is the 3-4 Bear, which can be a solid formation in the red zone and on third and short.

▶ Green Bay has the Nickel Psycho formation, which can bring heavy pressure if you have lots of LBs!

2 MINNESOTA VIKINGS

- **BASE: 4-3**
- **STYLES: Run Stuff, Zone Defense**
- **RUN DEFENSE SET: 46 Normal**
- **PASS DEFENSE SET: Nickel 2-4-5 Prowl**

The Vikings' playbook is perfect for players who prefer to play heavy zone coverage from the 4-3. The 46 Normal should figure heavily in your game plan, as early offenses may struggle to spread it out. Keep switching between the Cover 2 and Cover 4 Show 2 looks to really maximize your game plan.

▶ The Vikings have the 46 Normal formation, which can frustrate opponents.

1 PATRIOTS DEFENSE

- **BASE: Hybrid 3-4/4-3**
- **STYLE: Zone Defense, Run Stuff**
- **RUN DEFENSE SET: Nickel 2-4-5 Dbl A Gap**
- **PASS DEFENSE SET: Nickel 3-3-5 Odd**

The Patriots' defensive playbook is the only team playbook that has both 3-4 and 4-3 fronts. This allows you to mix up your looks and experiment with different lineups. Make sure to learn all of the nickel formations to really maximize the blitzes you can bring on third down.

▶ If you have extra defenders at DE and LB, consider using the Patriots' playbook.

CHICAGO BEARS

GAMEPLAY RATING 75

CONNECTED FRANCHISE MODE STRATEGY

CFM TEAM RATING: **82**
OFFENSE: **91**
DEFENSE: **75**
OFFENSIVE SCHEME: **West Coast**
DEFENSIVE SCHEME: **Base 3-4**
STRENGTHS: **WR, LOLB, TE, HB**
WEAKNESSES: **RT, FS, DT**

2014 TEAM RANKINGS

4th NFC North (5-11-0)
PASSING OFFENSE: **15th**
RUSHING OFFENSE: **27th**
PASSING DEFENSE: **30th**
RUSHING DEFENSE: **17th**

2014 TEAM LEADERS

PASSING: **Jay Cutler: 3,812**
RUSHING: **Matt Forte: 1,038**
RECEIVING: **Alshon Jeffery: 1,133**
TACKLES: **Ryan Mundy: 103**
SACKS: **Willie Young: 10**
INTS: **Kyle Fuller: 4**

KEY ADDITIONS

LB Pernell McPhee
WR Eddie Royal
S Antrel Rolle
CB Alan Ball
CB Tracy Porter

KEY ROOKIES

WR Kevin White
DT Eddie Goldman
C Hroniss Grasu

OWNER: **Ted Phillips**
LEGACY: **300**

COACH: **John Fox**
LEVEL: **18**
LEGACY: **2,500**
OFFENSIVE SCHEME: **West Coast**
DEFENSIVE SCHEME: **Base 3-4**

OFFENSIVE SCOUTING REPORT

- QB Jay Cutler will enjoy the addition of rookie WR Kevin White to replace veteran WR Brandon Marshall. Cutler won't be able to change his style at this point in his career, but if you can keep his confidence and deep accuracy up, he has the arm to make all the throws.
- HB Matt Forte has slowed down a bit but still has a versatile skill set that can take the pressure off the offense. Get him the ball in the passing game, because he is one of the best receivers coming out of the backfield.
- WR Alshon Jeffery will have to take over the lead role in WR meetings and set an example for young talent like Kevin White. WR Eddie Royal is a nice addition to the offense, not just for the slot position but for punt returner too.

DEFENSIVE SCOUTING REPORT

- The addition of LB Pernell McPhee will make a solid front of pass rushers in the right situation. You should send a combination of Jared Allen, Jeremiah Ratliff, Willie Young, and McPhee at the passer on 3rd and long.
- The Bears have quickly overhauled their CBs and now have what it takes to play a tough zone scheme. Put bigger guys like Alan Ball and Kyle Fuller on the outside with Tim Jennings sliding into the slot with his elite play recognition.
- The Bears' scheme has received an overhaul, and now it is time to see who fits where. Make sure to give veterans like Jared Allen a shot; they still have elite skill, like a 90 Power Moves rating, to get after the passer.

SCHEDULE

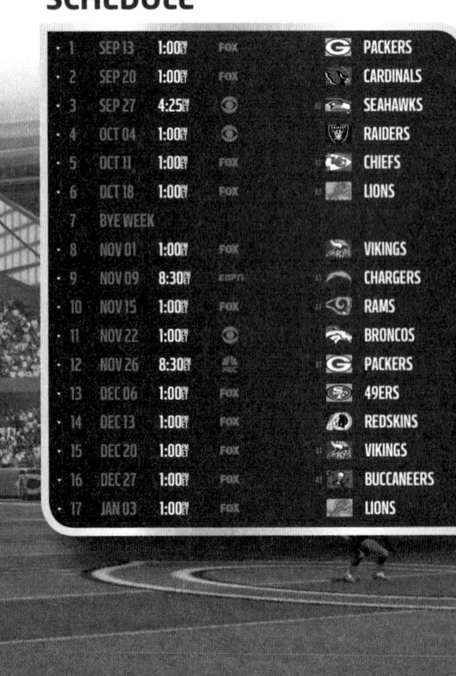

Week	Date	Time	Network		Opponent
1	SEP 13	1:00 PM ET	FOX		PACKERS
2	SEP 20	1:00 PM ET	FOX		CARDINALS
3	SEP 27	4:25 PM ET		AT	SEAHAWKS
4	OCT 04	1:00 PM ET			RAIDERS
5	OCT 11	1:00 PM ET	FOX	AT	CHIEFS
6	OCT 18	1:00 PM ET	FOX	AT	LIONS
7	BYE WEEK				
8	NOV 01	1:00 PM ET	FOX		VIKINGS
9	NOV 09	8:30 PM ET	ESPN	AT	CHARGERS
10	NOV 15	1:00 PM ET	FOX	AT	RAMS
11	NOV 22	1:00 PM ET			BRONCOS
12	NOV 26	8:30 PM ET	NBC	AT	PACKERS
13	DEC 06	1:00 PM ET	FOX		49ERS
14	DEC 13	1:00 PM ET	FOX		REDSKINS
15	DEC 20	1:00 PM ET	FOX	AT	VIKINGS
16	DEC 27	1:00 PM ET	FOX	AT	BUCCANEERS
17	JAN 03	1:00 PM ET	FOX		LIONS

KEY PLAYERS

KEY OFFENSIVE PLAYER

ALSHON JEFFERY #17

WR #17 HT 6'3" WT 216 COLLEGE South Carolina EXP 3

KEY RATINGS

- OVR 95
- SPD 88
- CIT 97
- SPC 97
- RLS 98

- There isn't a CB in the league who can consistently get his hand on Jeffery at the line.
- The red zone is a great place to use Jeffery's elite Spectacular Catch rating—throw him a high point pass

KEY DEFENSIVE PLAYER

PERNELL MCPHEE #92

LOLB #92 HT 6'3" WT 280 COLLEGE Mississippi St. EXP 4

KEY RATINGS

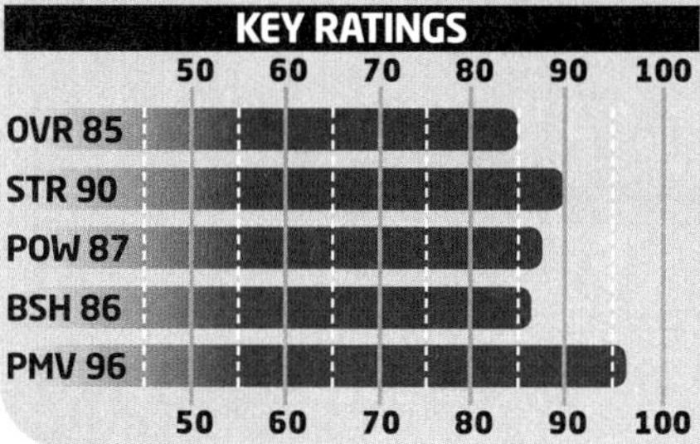

- McPhee is an excellent defender off the edge with solid strength in the run game.
- Expect McPhee to quickly become the best rusher on the Bears' defense. He can also force some turnovers with his hit power.

KEY ROOKIE

KEVIN WHITE #13

WR #13 HT 6'3" WT 215 COLLEGE West Virginia EXP Rookie

KEY RATINGS

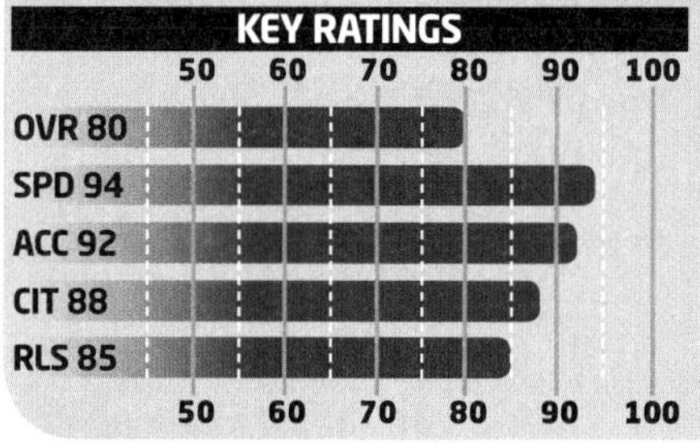

- White will have to gain his experience on the field as there is no time to waste after the departure of veteran WR Brandon Marshall.
- Start with some simple drags using White's speed to gain him confidence, then target him downfield later in the season.

KEY SLEEPER

SENORISE PERRY #32

HB #32 HT 6'0" WT 187 COLLEGE Louisville EXP 1

KEY RATINGS

- OVR 62
- SPD 92
- ELU 74
- AGI 92
- CTH 73

- Perry has the speed to get to the edge, but raise his Elusiveness rating so he can break some tackles when he gets there.
- Give Perry a shot to make the roster. He may never replace Matt Forte, but his speed brings the Bears a nice change of pace.

OFFENSIVE DEPTH CHART

POS	FIRST	LAST	OVR
QB	JAY	CUTLER	79
QB	JIMMY	CLAUSEN	72
QB	DAVID	FALES	66
QB	SHANE	CARDEN	65
QB	PAT	DEVLIN	65
HB	MATT	FORTE	90
HB	JACQUIZZ	RODGERS	76
HB	KA'DEEM	CAREY	74
HB	JEREMY	LANGFORD	71
HB	SENORISE	PERRY	64
FB	BEAR	PASCOE	82
WR	ALSHON	JEFFERY	90
WR	EDDIE	ROYAL	81
WR	KEVIN	WHITE	78
WR	MARQUESS	WILSON	73
WR	MARC	MARIANI	69
WR	JOSHUA	BELLAMY	68
WR	JOHN	CHILES	66
TE	MARTELLUS	BENNETT	90
TE	DANTE	ROSARIO	72
TE	ZACH	MILLER	71
TE	THOMAS	GAFFORD	69
TE	BLAKE	ANNEN	65
TE	CHRIS	PANTALE	64
LT	JERMON	BUSHROD	79
LT	CHARLES	LENO	65
LG	MATT	SLAUSON	84
LG	MICHAEL	OLA	74
LG	RYAN	GROY	71
C	WILL	MONTGOMERY	84
C	HRONISS	GRASU	69
RG	KYLE	LONG	88
RG	VLADIMIR	DUCASSE	72
RG	CONOR	BOFFELI	68
RT	JORDAN	MILLS	74
RT	JASON	WEAVER	68
RT	TAYO	FABULUJE	61

DEFENSIVE DEPTH CHART

POS	FIRST	LAST	OVR
LE	JEREMIAH	RATLIFF	85
LE	JARVIS	JENKINS	72
LE	BRANDON	DUNN	61
DT	WILL	SUTTON	72
DT	EDDIE	GOLDMAN	70
RE	EGO	FERGUSON	69
RE	OLSEN	PIERRE	59
LOLB	PERNELL	MCPHEE	87
LOLB	LAMARR	HOUSTON	77
LOLB	WILLIE	YOUNG	72
LOLB	DAVID	BASS	64
MLB	MASON	FOSTER	76
MLB	JON	BOSTIC	75
MLB	SAM	ACHO	73
MLB	CHRISTIAN	JONES	65
MLB	DEDE	LATTIMORE	61
ROLB	JARED	ALLEN	79
ROLB	SHEA	MCCLELLIN	78
ROLB	CORNELIUS	WASHINGTON	69
CB	TIM	JENNINGS	86
CB	ALAN	BALL	79
CB	KYLE	FULLER	78
CB	TRACY	PORTER	73
CB	DEMONTRE	HURST	68
CB	SHERRICK	MCMANIS	67
CB	BRYCE	CALLAHAN	66
CB	TERRANCE	MITCHELL	66
CB	AL	LOUIS-JEAN	61
FS	BROCK	VEREEN	75
FS	ADRIAN	AMOS	66
SS	RYAN	MUNDY	81
SS	ANTREL	ROLLE	81

SPECIAL TEAMS

POS	FIRST	LAST	OVR
K	ROBBIE	GOULD	88
KR	MARC	MARIANI	69
P	PAT	O'DONNELL	73
PR	MARC	MARIANI	69

BEST OFFENSIVE PLAYS

PRO TIPS

- These are the best two offensive plays in your playbook. They will get your playmakers in position to win you games.
- Sticking with a run that you know the timing of is usually better than calling a play you haven't practiced.
- The Bears have two big receiving options who will really stress defenses on the outside.

BEST RUN: I-FORM FLEX TWINS–HB POWER O

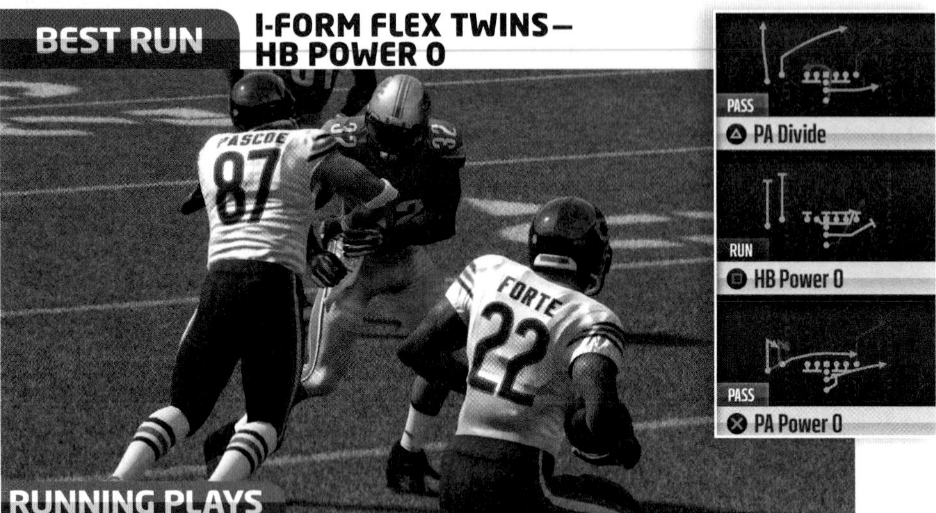

PASS △ PA Divide

RUN ▢ HB Power O

PASS ⊗ PA Power O

SETUP:

- This run is still our favorite in the playbook due to the tough alignment issues the defense must consider.
- With the new play action and ability to roll out, this play has taken on a whole new level of greatness.
- Mix in some FB Dive plays during short-yardage situations; they develop quickly.

ADVANCED SETUP:

- Playmaker the run left (optional).

RUNNING PLAYS

1ST DOWN	2ND AND SHORT	3RD AND SHORT	GOAL LINE	2ND AND LONG	3RD AND LONG
I-Form Flex Twins–HB Power O	Weak Twins Flex–HB Gut	Singleback Doubles–O 1 Trap	I-Form Pro–HB Blast	Pistol Ace–HB Counter	Gun Split Offset–Power O
Singleback Tight Flex–HB Slam	Singleback Ace–O 1 Trap	Pistol Slot Wing–Inside Zone Split	Goal Line–FB Dive	Pistol Ace–O 1 Trap	Gun 5WR Trio–Jet Sweep
Singleback Doubles–HB Cutback	Strong Tight Pair–HB Blast	Singleback Y-Trips Bear–Bears Zone Wk	Goal Line–Strong Toss	Pistol Y-Trips–Strong Power	Gun Trey Open–Inside Zone

INSIDE RUN | OUTSIDE RUN | SHOTGUN RUN | QB RUN

BEST PASS: GUN TRIO–INSIDE CROSS

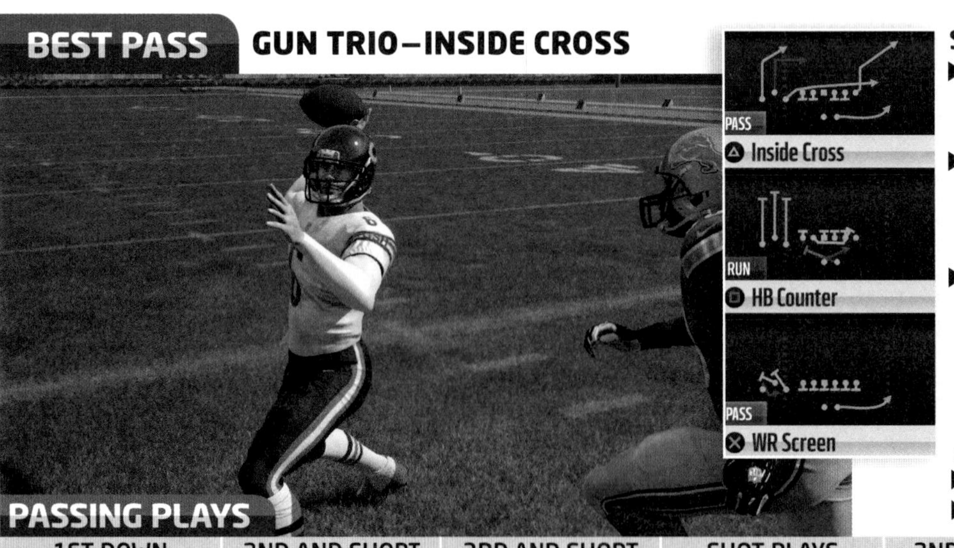

PASS △ Inside Cross

RUN ▢ HB Counter

PASS ⊗ WR Screen

SETUP/READS:

- The corner route to the TE is excellent, but it takes a few extra seconds to develop since it gets so deep downfield.
- The left side of the field can be a bit crowded, so flip this play to the open side of the field to give your receivers room to operate.
- To make this truly the best play in the playbook, learn to throw a high pass to Alshon Jeffery on the deep post, which is a back breaker route. Hitting this twice per game could mean the difference between a win and a loss.

ADVANCED SETUP:

- Curl the slot WR on the left.
- Slant the TE against man coverage.

PASSING PLAYS

1ST DOWN	2ND AND SHORT	3RD AND SHORT	SHOT PLAYS	2ND AND LONG	3RD AND LONG
Gun Bunch Wk–Divide	Singleback Ace Twins–PA Misdirection	I-Form Tight–Angle	Singleback Ace Pair Twins–PA Bears Shot	Gun Split Offset–Slot Cross	Gun Split Offset–689 Hook
Singleback Tight Flex–Slot Corner	Strong Pro–Bears Stick	Strong Pro–F Trail	Gun Trio–PA Cross Shot	Gun Bunch Wk–HB Cross Screen	Gun Bunch Wk–Verticals
Pistol Y-Trips–Smash	I-Form Flex Twins–PA Divide	Gun Trey Open–Trail Shake	Pistol Y-Trips–PA Read	Gun Snugs Flip–Mesh	Gun 5WR Trio–Four Verticals

BASE PLAY | MAN BEATER | ZONE BEATER | BLITZ BEATER

 For more plays and strategies for this team, visit your eGuide using the access code sheet provided.

BEST DEFENSIVE PLAYS

PRO TIPS

- **If you want to win more games in *Madden NFL 16*, rely on these defensive plays to lock up the run and pass.**
- **The 3-4 Odd formation should hold the edge with the talented Pernell Mcphee and Jared Allen in crucial positions.**
- **The Big Dime 2-3-6 will get your best pass defense lineup on the field.**

BEST RUN D — 3-4 ODD—WILL SAM 3

SETUP:

- The Bears' head coaching change means a change in defensive scheme. Get used to the 3-4, which can be just as stout as the 4-3 against the run.
- Don't forget to show blitz if your opponent is trying to rush up the middle. Consider calling press if you want to show an aggressive look.

PLAYER TO CONTROL:

- The SS up in the box

RUN DEFENSE

1ST DOWN	2ND AND SHORT	3RD AND SHORT	GOAL LINE	2ND AND LONG	3RD AND LONG
3-4 Bear—1 QB Contain	3-4 Bear—Sam Mike 1	3-4 Over—Sting Pinch	Goal Line 5-4-2—Jam Cover 1	Nickel 2-4-5 Prowl—Cover 1 Robber	Big Dime 2-3-6 Even—1 QB Contain
3-4 Bear—Cover 3	3-4 Bear—Cover 2 Invert	3-4 Over—Sting Pinch Zone	Goal Line 5-4-2—Flat Buzz	Nickel 2-4-5 Prowl—Cover 2 Drop	Big Dime 2-3-6 Even—Cover 4

MAN COVERAGE | ZONE COVERAGE | MAN BLITZ | ZONE BLITZ

BEST PASS D — BIG DIME 2-3-6 WILL—MIKE EDGE 3 SEAM

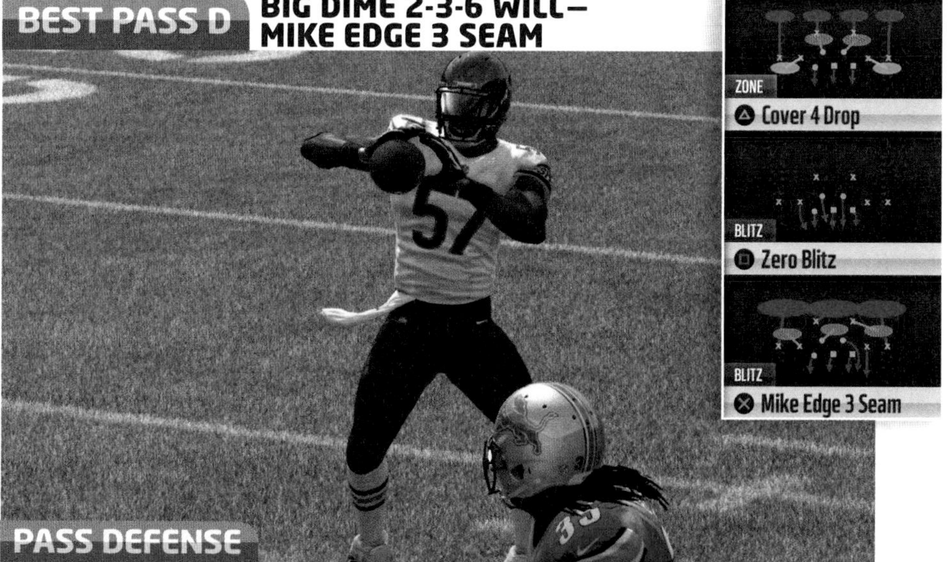

SETUP:

- This play won't get you a sack every time, but the QB will be forced to make a quicker decision than he would against regular old Cover 3.
- Consider hot routing one of the blitzing defenders to man coverage, especially against a TE.
- If your opponent starts targeting the flat, calling the Cover 4 Drop could lead to some turnovers.

PLAYER TO CONTROL:

- The hook zone defender on the side opposite the blitz

PASS DEFENSE

1ST DOWN	2ND AND SHORT	3RD AND SHORT	GOAL LINE	2ND AND LONG	3RD AND LONG
3-4 Over—Cover 2 Man	Nickel 3-3-5 Wide—Cover 1 Robber	3-4 Under—Cover 1 Hole	Goal Line 6-3-2—GL Man	Big Dime 2-3-6 Will—Mike Edge 1	Nickel 2-4-5 Dbl A Gap—Nickel Dog Meg
3-4 Over—Cover 3 Sky	Nickel 3-3-5 Wide—Sam Will 3 Blitz	3-4 Under—Will Fire 3 Seam	Goal Line 6-3-2—GL Zone	Big Dime 2-3-6 Will—Overload 3 Press	Nickel 2-4-5 Dbl A Gap—Nickel Dog 3 Buzz

MAN COVERAGE | ZONE COVERAGE | MAN BLITZ | ZONE BLITZ

CINCINNATI BENGALS

GAMEPLAY RATING 84

CONNECTED FRANCHISE MODE STRATEGY

CFM TEAM RATING: **85**
OFFENSE: **91**
DEFENSE: **85**
OFFENSIVE SCHEME: **Balanced**
DEFENSIVE SCHEME: **Base 4-3**
STRENGTHS: **WR, LT, RG**
WEAKNESSES: **C, ROLB, SS**

2014 TEAM RANKINGS

2nd AFC North (10-5-1)
PASSING OFFENSE: **21st**
RUSHING OFFENSE: **6th**
PASSING DEFENSE: **20th**
RUSHING DEFENSE: **20th**

2014 TEAM LEADERS

PASSING: **Andy Dalton: 3,398**
RUSHING: **Jeremy Hill: 1,124**
RECEIVING: **A.J. Green: 1,041**
TACKLES: **Vincent Rey: 121**
SACKS: **Carlos Dunlap: 8**
INTS: **Reggie Nelson: 4**

KEY ADDITIONS

DT Pat Sims
LB A.J. Hawk
WR Denarius Moore

KEY ROOKIES

T Cedric Ogbuehi
T Jake Fisher
TE Tyler Kroft

OWNER: **Mike Brown**
LEGACY SCORE: **250**

COACH: **Marvin Lewis**
LEVEL: **5**
LEGACY SCORE: **200**
OFFENSIVE SCHEME: **Balanced**
DEFENSIVE SCHEME: **Base 4-3**

OFFENSIVE SCOUTING REPORT

- QB Andy Dalton once again led the Bengals to the postseason, but they failed to get a win. Dalton had a solid completion percentage last season; however, the touchdown/interception ratio needs to be a little higher to consider him among the elite.
- While everyone expected HB Giovani Bernard to take over last season, rookie Jeremy Hill took the reins and scored nine TDs. Bernard is best used in bursts and deserves to be your third-down back.
- Tyler Eifert steps into the main TE role and can hopefully lead rookie Tyler Kroft to a great season. A.J. Green is the most explosive WR, but it is great for Andy Dalton to have a safety valve, and Eifert needs to be that guy.

DEFENSIVE SCOUTING REPORT

- Expect big things from DT Geno Atkins after a down season last year. With DE Michael Johnson back in town, expect the numbers for both Atkins and Carlos Dunlap to improve.
- Determine what type of defensive coverage scheme you want to lean towards, man or zone. If zone, keep Leon Hall, who has outstanding play recognition, otherwise keep Adam Jones and play more man-to-man. Dre Kirkpatrick is a zone defender with Darqueze Dennard playing more man-to-man.
- At nearly every position, the Bengals have good, but not great, players. There is not a ton of depth, so keep developing young players, especially in the LB corps. Don't pay top dollar for average performers.

SCHEDULE

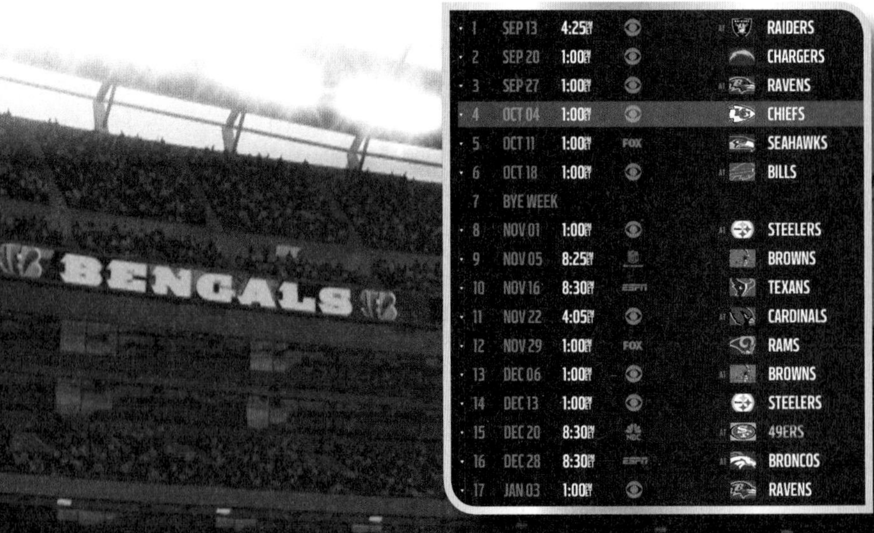

Week	Date	Time	Network	Opponent
1	SEP 13	4:25 PM ET		AT RAIDERS
2	SEP 20	1:00 PM ET		CHARGERS
3	SEP 27	1:00 PM ET		AT RAVENS
4	OCT 04	1:00 PM ET		CHIEFS
5	OCT 11	1:00 PM ET	FOX	SEAHAWKS
6	OCT 18	1:00 PM ET		AT BILLS
7	BYE WEEK			
8	NOV 01	1:00 PM ET		AT STEELERS
9	NOV 05	8:25 PM ET		BROWNS
10	NOV 16	8:30 PM ET	ESPN	TEXANS
11	NOV 22	4:05 PM ET		AT CARDINALS
12	NOV 29	1:00 PM ET	FOX	RAMS
13	DEC 06	1:00 PM ET		AT BROWNS
14	DEC 13	1:00 PM ET		STEELERS
15	DEC 20	8:30 PM ET	NBC	AT 49ERS
16	DEC 28	8:30 PM ET	ESPN	AT BRONCOS
17	JAN 03	1:00 PM ET		RAVENS

KEY PLAYERS

KEY OFFENSIVE PLAYER

A.J. GREEN #18

WR #18 HT 6'4" WT 207 COLLEGE Georgia EXP 4

KEY RATINGS

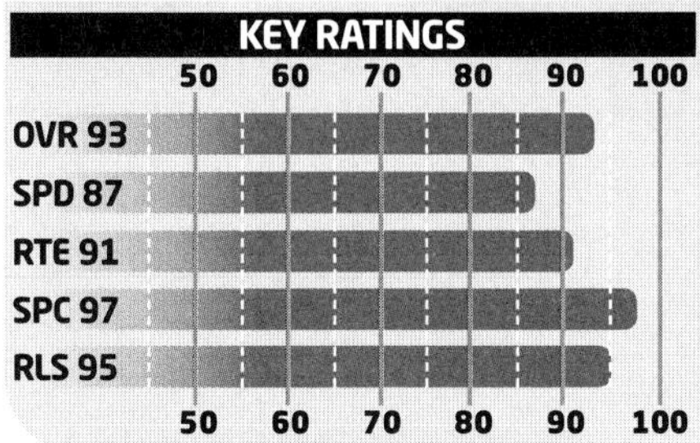

- Green isn't the faster WR out there, but his size and route running more than make up for it.
- Expect to see some amazing catches with 97 Spectacular Catch and Jump ratings for the 6'4" Green.

KEY DEFENSIVE PLAYER

CARLOS DUNLAP #96

LE #96 HT 6'6" WT 280 COLLEGE Florida EXP 5

KEY RATINGS

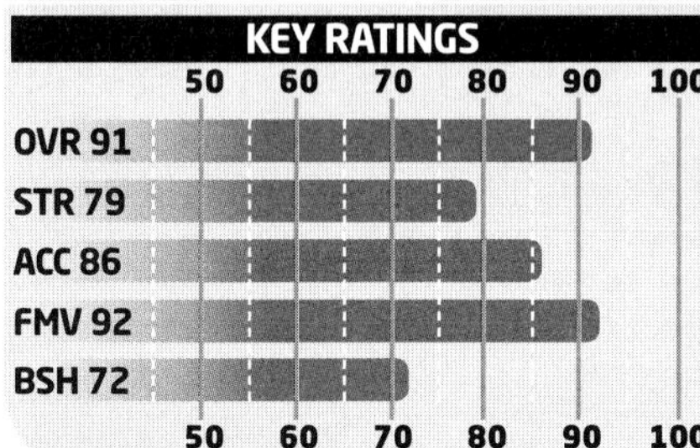

- Dunlap isn't built to stop the run; he is a pure finesse pass rusher and excels at it.
- The 6'6" frame of Dunlap goes well with 6'7" frame of line-mate Michael Johnson. Drop them into zone coverage to mess with the QB.

KEY ROOKIE

CEDRIC OGBUEHI #70

LT #70 HT 6'5" WT 306 COLLEGE Texas A&M EXP Rookie

KEY RATINGS

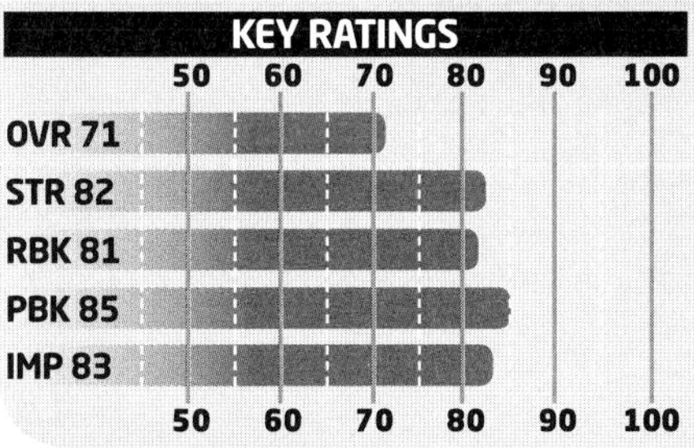

- This was a quality depth selection for the Bengals, although it may take a season or two for Ogbuehi to develop into a starter.
- The LT position is currently one of the Bengals' few truly elite positions. Focus on building Ogbuehi's strength.

KEY SLEEPER

MARGUS HUNT #99

LE #99 HT 6'8" WT 280 COLLEGE SMU EXP 2

KEY RATINGS

50 60 70 80 90 100
OVR 73
SPD 84
STR 88
ACC 87
PMV 80
50 60 70 80 90 100

- Hunt has the size to get in the rotation on defense. Try subbing him in at DT, where his acceleration could create a mismatch.
- Hunt is still a young player, and if you can increase his Power Moves rating, you never know what he could turn into for your squad.

OFFENSIVE DEPTH CHART

POS	FIRST	LAST	OVR
QB	ANDY	DALTON	80
QB	A.J.	MCCARRON	72
QB	JOSH	JOHNSON	69
QB	TERRELLE	PRYOR	65
HB	JEREMY	HILL	86
HB	GIOVANI	BERNARD	84
HB	REX	BURKHEAD	72
HB	CEDRIC	PEERMAN	72
HB	JAMES	WILDER JR.	63
FB	RYAN	HEWITT	84
WR	A.J.	GREEN	92
WR	MOHAMED	SANU	79
WR	MARVIN	JONES	78
WR	DENARIUS	MOORE	73
WR	BRANDON	TATE	72
WR	JAMES	WRIGHT	67
WR	COBI	HAMILTON	67
WR	MARIO	ALFORD	62
WR	TEVIN	REESE	61
TE	TYLER	EIFERT	81
TE	TYLER	KROFT	70
TE	JAKE	MURPHY	68
TE	CLARK	HARRIS	64
TE	C.J.	UZOMAH	63
LT	ANDREW	WHITWORTH	95
LT	CEDRIC	OGBUEHI	73
LG	CLINT	BOLING	84
C	RUSSELL	BODINE	75
C	T.J.	JOHNSON	67
RG	KEVIN	ZEITLER	89
RG	TREY	HOPKINS	65
RT	ANDRE	SMITH	85
RT	ERIC	WINSTON	75
RT	JAKE	FISHER	72
RT	TANNER	HAWKINSON	70

DEFENSIVE DEPTH CHART

POS	FIRST	LAST	OVR
LE	CARLOS	DUNLAP	88
LE	MARGUS	HUNT	73
DT	GENO	ATKINS	89
DT	PAT	SIMS	75
DT	DEVON	STILL	73
DT	DOMATA	PEKO	72
DT	KWAME	GEATHERS	69
DT	BRANDON	THOMPSON	69
DT	MARCUS	HARDISON	64
RE	MICHAEL	JOHNSON	81
RE	WALLACE	GILBERRY	74
RE	WILL	CLARKE	69
LOLB	EMMANUEL	LAMUR	74
LOLB	JAYSON	DIMANCHE	70
LOLB	MARQUIS	FLOWERS	66
LOLB	SAM	MONTGOMERY	65
MLB	REY	MAUALUGA	83
MLB	A.J.	HAWK	77
MLB	NICO	JOHNSON	73
ROLB	VONTAZE	BURFICT	86
ROLB	VINCENT	REY	78
ROLB	P.J.	DAWSON	72
ROLB	CHRIS	CARTER	70
ROLB	SEAN	PORTER	70
CB	LEON	HALL	86
CB	ADAM	JONES	81
CB	DRE	KIRKPATRICK	77
CB	DARQUEZE	DENNARD	76
CB	BRANDON	GHEE	70
CB	CHRIS	LEWIS-HARRIS	68
CB	JOSH	SHAW	68
CB	ONTERIO	MCCALEBB	60
FS	REGGIE	NELSON	86
FS	SHILOH	KEO	74
FS	DERRON	SMITH	67
SS	GEORGE	ILOKA	86
SS	SHAWN	WILLIAMS	74

SPECIAL TEAMS

POS	FIRST	LAST	OVR
K	MIKE	NUGENT	76
KR	ADAM	JONES	81
P	KEVIN	HUBER	82
PR	ADAM	JONES	81

BEST OFFENSIVE PLAYS

PRO TIPS

- These are the best two offensive plays in your playbook. They will get your playmakers in position to win you games.
- The Gun Split Slot gets both of your HBs on the field—use them according to their strengths.
- Lining up your receivers in a snugs set often means they won't get pressed by the defense.

BEST RUN: GUN SPLIT SLOT—HB OFF TACKLE

SETUP:

- If your tackle can get a push upfield, this run can be very effective.
- Try to flip the play so your speedy HB Giovani Bernard is getting the bulk of the carries. Jeremy Hill is better between the tackles.

ADVANCED SETUP:

- Motion the blocking HB out to the slot (optional).

RUNNING PLAYS

1ST DOWN	2ND AND SHORT	3RD AND SHORT	GOAL LINE	2ND AND LONG	3RD AND LONG
I-Form Pro—Power O	Singleback Ace—0 1 Trap	Weak Pro Twins—FB Dive	Goal Line Normal—QB Sneak	Gun Y-Trips Bengal—HB Base	Gun Split Slot—HB Inside
Strong Close—HB Dive	Singleback Bunch—HB Slash	Weak Pro Twins—Toss Weak	Goal Line Normal—HB Sting	Full House Normal Wide—Counter Weak	Gun Split Slot—HB Off Tackle
Singleback Snugs Flip—HB Cutback	Strong Y-Flex—Inside Zone	Strong Close—Quick Toss	I-Form Pro—FB Dive	Gun Bunch Wk—HB Mid Draw	Gun Trips Y Iso—HB Counter

INSIDE RUN | OUTSIDE RUN | SHOTGUN RUN | QB RUN

BEST PASS: SINGLEBACK SNUGS FLIP—DEEP POST

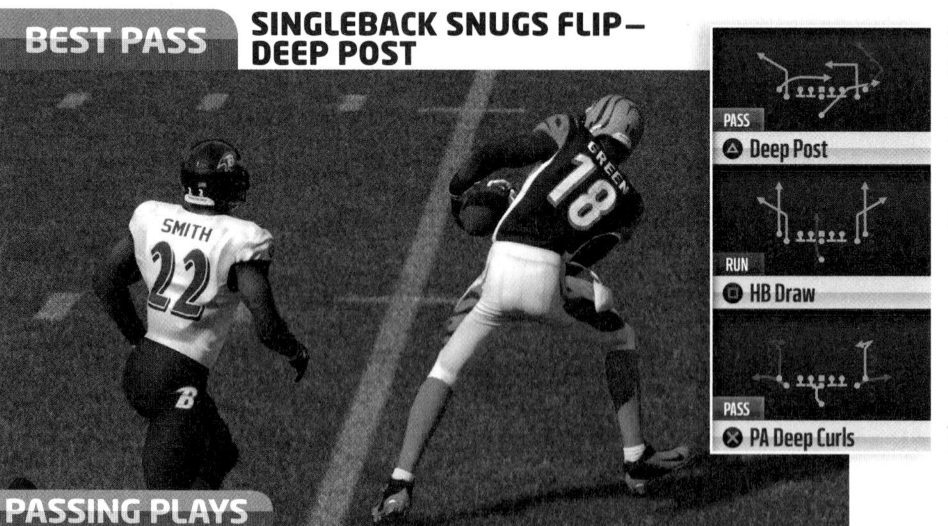

SETUP/READS:

- Against zone coverage target the corner route or wait for the post to get open.
- Against man-to-man coverage, look to the drag route and possibly playmaker it upfield if you have time.
- Against the blitz, the HB should get open quickly, or you can hot route the in to a slant if you suspect it's coming.

ADVANCED SETUP:

- Hot route the in to a slant (optional).

PASSING PLAYS

1ST DOWN	2ND AND SHORT	3RD AND SHORT	SHOT PLAYS	2ND AND LONG	3RD AND LONG
Gun Normal Y-Flex Tight—Flood Drive	Gun Split Slot—DBL Ins	Strong Pro—F Angle	Singleback Doubles—Z-Close Cross	Gun Normal Y-Flex Tight—Slot Cross	Gun Normal Y-Flex Tight—PA Deep Outs
Singleback Snugs Flip—Mesh Switch	Singleback Ace Pair—Slants	Gun Bunch Wk—PA Post	I-Form Pro—PA Draw Shot	Gun Trips Y Iso—Deep Attack	Gun Y-Trips Bengal—HB Cross Screen
Singleback Ace—Ace TE Drag	Singleback Bunch—Spacing	Strong Close—WR Out	Gun Y-Trips Bengal—PA Post Cross Shot	Singleback Bunch—Seattle	Gun Trio—Verticals

BASE PLAY | MAN BEATER | ZONE BEATER | BLITZ BEATER

BEST DEFENSIVE PLAYS

PRO TIPS

- If you want to win more games in *Madden NFL 16*, rely on these defensive plays to lock up the run and pass.
- The 46 Normal is as solid as it is unique; try to stay in it as long as possible.
- The flat zones from the 3-3-5 do a great job getting out wide and can force some big turnovers.

BEST RUN D: 46 NORMAL–COVER 2 INVERT

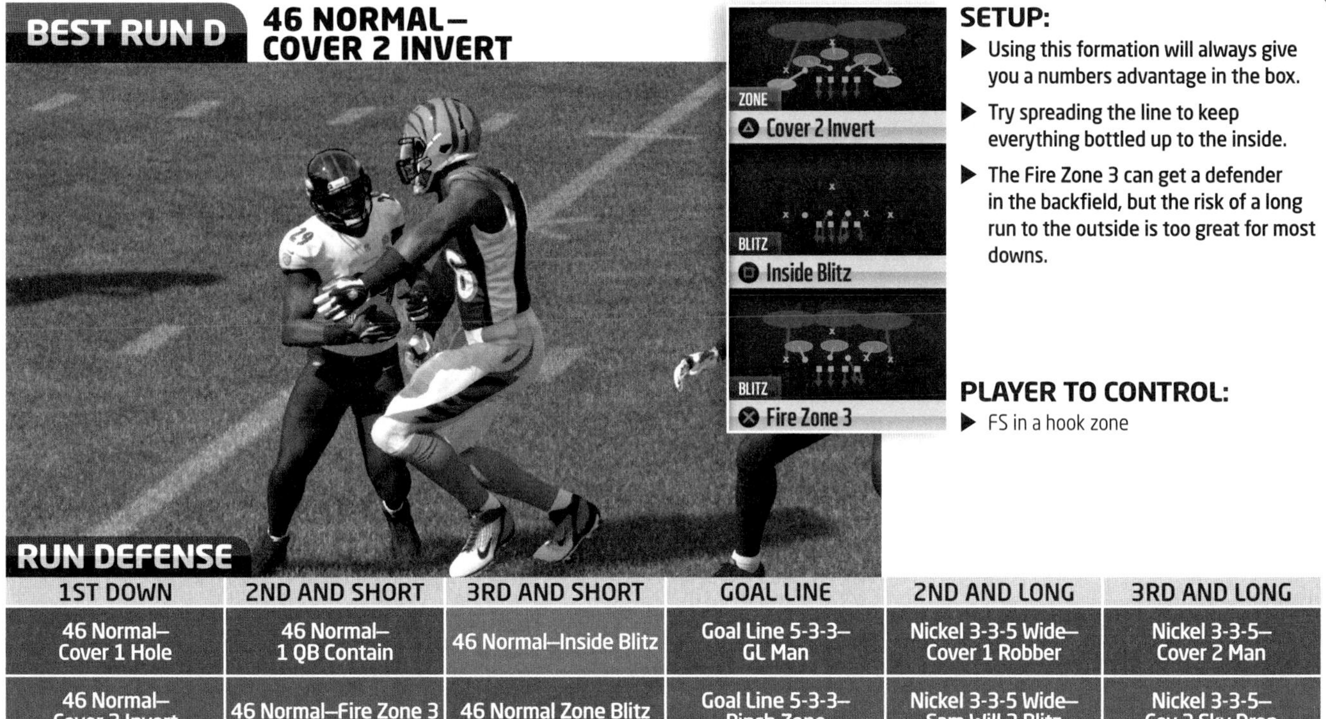

SETUP:

- Using this formation will always give you a numbers advantage in the box.
- Try spreading the line to keep everything bottled up to the inside.
- The Fire Zone 3 can get a defender in the backfield, but the risk of a long run to the outside is too great for most downs.

PLAYER TO CONTROL:

- FS in a hook zone

RUN DEFENSE

1ST DOWN	2ND AND SHORT	3RD AND SHORT	GOAL LINE	2ND AND LONG	3RD AND LONG
46 Normal–Cover 1 Hole	46 Normal–1 QB Contain	46 Normal–Inside Blitz	Goal Line 5-3-3–GL Man	Nickel 3-3-5 Wide–Cover 1 Robber	Nickel 3-3-5–Cover 2 Man
46 Normal–Cover 2 Invert	46 Normal–Fire Zone 3	46 Normal Zone Blitz	Goal Line 5-3-3–Pinch Zone	Nickel 3-3-5 Wide–Sam Will 3 Blitz	Nickel 3-3-5–Cov 3 Sky Drop

MAN COVERAGE | ZONE COVERAGE | MAN BLITZ | ZONE BLITZ

BEST PASS D: NICKEL 3-3-5–COVER 3 BUZZ DROP

SETUP:

- This is the perfect pass defense against an opponent who isn't super patient when throwing the football.
- The front three rushers for the Bengals can generate some decent pressure from this formation, but make sure to blitz on third and long.
- Swap to the Cov 3 Cloud Drop for a subtle change with the same general concept.

PLAYER TO CONTROL:

- Flat zone defender on the short side of the field

PASS DEFENSE

1ST DOWN	2ND AND SHORT	3RD AND SHORT	GOAL LINE	2ND AND LONG	3RD AND LONG
4-3 Wide 9–Cover 2 Man	4-3 Wide 9–1 QB Contain Spy	4-3 Over–Mike Will Blitz	Goal Line 5-4-2–Jam Cover 1	Nickel Double A Gap–Mid Zone Blitz	Dime Normal–Mike Dime Blitz
4-3 Wide 9–Cover 4 Press	4-3 Wide 9–Cover 2 Invert	4-3 Over–Strong Slant 3	Goal Line 5-4-2–Flat Buzz	Nickel Double A Gap–Buck Zone Blitz	Dime Normal–3 Double Sky

MAN COVERAGE | ZONE COVERAGE | MAN BLITZ | ZONE BLITZ

BUFFALO BILLS

GAMEPLAY RATING 79

CONNECTED FRANCHISE MODE STRATEGY

CFM TEAM RATING: **83**
OFFENSIVE RATING: **85**
DEFENSIVE RATING: **87**
OFFENSIVE SCHEME: **Power Run**
DEFENSIVE SCHEME: **Hybrid Defense**
STRENGTHS: **DT, LE, HB, LT**
WEAKNESSES: **QB, WR, RT, LG, S**

2014 TEAM RANKINGS

2nd AFC East (9-7-0)
PASSING OFFENSE: **18th**
RUSHING OFFENSE: **25th**
PASSING DEFENSE: **3rd**
RUSHING DEFENSE: **11th**

2014 TEAM LEADERS

PASSING: **Kyle Orton: 3,018**
RUSHING: **Fred Jackson: 525**
RECEIVING: **Sammy Watkins: 982**
TACKLES: **Preston Brown: 109**
SACKS: **Mario Williams: 14.5**
INTS: **Leodis McKelvin: 4**

KEY ADDITIONS

QB Matt Cassel
HB LeSean McCoy
WR Percy Harvin

KEY ROOKIES

CB Ronald Darby
OG John Miller
RB Karlos Williams

OWNER: **Terry Pegula**
LEGACY: **100**

COACH: **Rex Ryan**
LEVEL: **4**
LEGACY: **200**
OFFENSIVE SCHEME:
Power Run
DEFENSIVE SCHEME:
Hybrid

OFFENSIVE SCOUTING REPORT

- Kyle Orton had a solid season but took snaps away from the developing E.J. Manuel. Choose Matt Cassel or Manuel based on your scheme, but make sure to stick with one!
- LeSean McCoy is an excellent replacement for C.J. Spiller. Give him the bulk of the carries over the reliable Fred Jackson.
- Not only did rookie WR Sammy Watkins emerge as a talented player, but Robert Woods also showed he is worthy of plenty of targets!

DEFENSIVE SCOUTING REPORT

- The Bills traded away MLB Kiko Alonso and now have some holes at the LB position, so consider looking for a free agent veteran as a stop-gap.
- The Bills' three main pass rushers should generate enough heat consistently to make any secondary look great.
- Safety Aaron Williams has the speed for pass situations, but consider Bacarri Rambo for stuffing the run with his 89 Hit Power rating.

SCHEDULE

Week	Date	Time	Network		Opponent
1	SEP 13	1:00 PM ET			COLTS
2	SEP 20	1:00 PM ET			PATRIOTS
3	SEP 27	4:25 PM ET		AT	DOLPHINS
4	OCT 04	1:00 PM ET	FOX		GIANTS
5	OCT 11	1:00 PM ET		AT	TITANS
6	OCT 18	1:00 PM ET			BENGALS
7	OCT 25	9:30 AM ET		AT	JAGUARS
8	BYE WEEK				
9	NOV 08	1:00 PM ET			DOLPHINS
10	NOV 12	8:25 PM ET		AT	JETS
11	NOV 23	8:30 PM ET	ESPN	AT	PATRIOTS
12	NOV 29	1:00 PM ET		AT	CHIEFS
13	DEC 06	1:00 PM ET			TEXANS
14	DEC 13	1:00 PM ET		AT	EAGLES
15	DEC 20	1:00 PM ET		AT	REDSKINS
16	DEC 27	1:00 PM ET	FOX		COWBOYS
17	JAN 03	1:00 PM ET			JETS

KEY PLAYERS

KEY OFFENSIVE PLAYER

LESEAN MCCOY #25

HB #25 HT 5'11" WT 208 COLLEGE Pittsburgh EXP 6

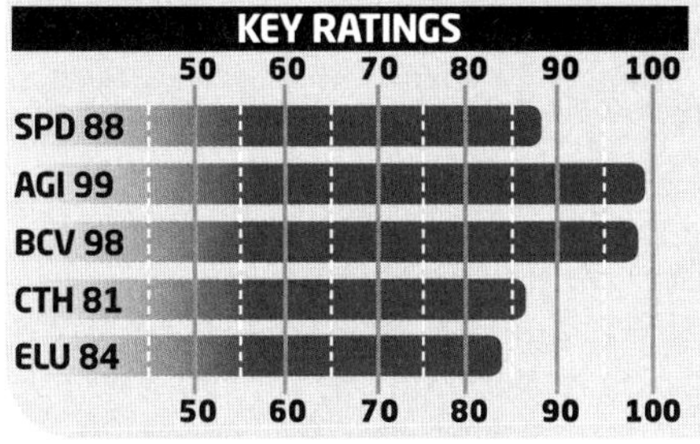

- McCoy can always cut outside against defenses that don't contain the edge.
- McCoy is a solid route runner who can't be covered by many LBs in man coverage.

KEY DEFENSIVE PLAYER

MARCELL DAREUS #99

DT #99 HT 6'3" WT 331 COLLEGE Alabama EXP 4

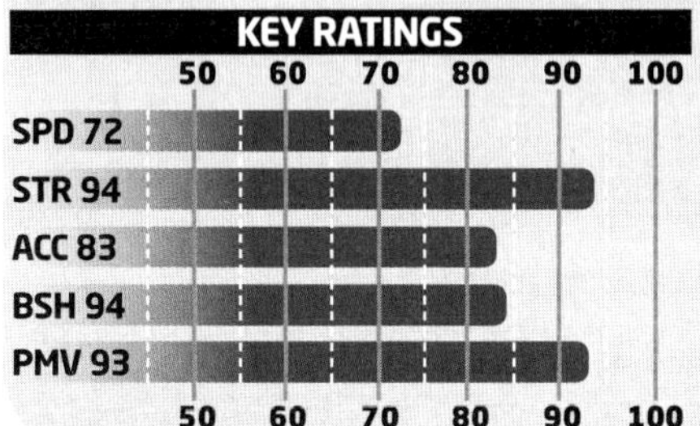

- Dareus is a tough matchup for any offensive line due to his excellent acceleration and power moves.
- Dareus benefits from having two excellent OLBs rushing the passer next to him (Jerry Hughes and Mario Williams).

KEY ROOKIE

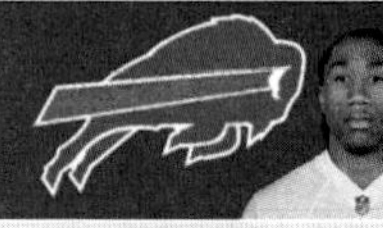

RONALD DARBY #28

CB #28 HT 5'11" WT 193 COLLEGE Florida State EXP Rookie

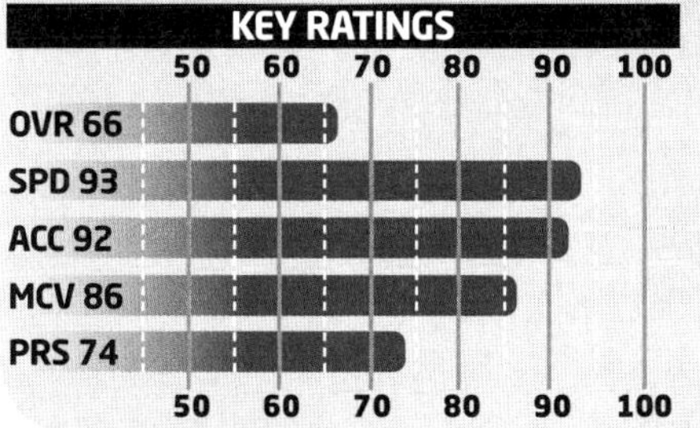

- Darby is an solid man cover corner, but he may never have the size to match up with big receivers.
- Don't invest too much in Darby's Zone Coverage ratings because the Bills already have good depth there.

KEY SLEEPER

BACARRI RAMBO #30

SS #30 HT 6'0" WT 211 COLLEGE Georgia EXP 2

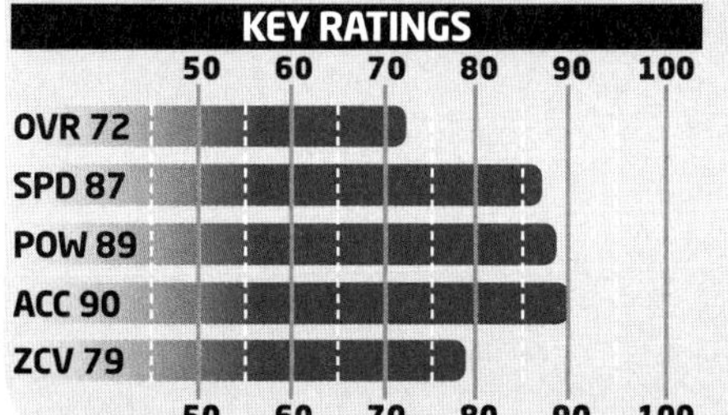

- Rambo is a solid defender whom you can attempt to use in the slot against power running teams that are attacking the edge.
- Spend some XP on upgrading the Tackle rating, because big hits are nice but consistent wrapups are better.

OFFENSIVE DEPTH CHART

POS	FIRST	LAST	OVR
QB	MATT	CASSEL	75
QB	E.J.	MANUEL	73
QB	TYROD	TAYLOR	72
HB	LESEAN	MCCOY	88
HB	FRED	JACKSON	82
HB	BOOBIE	DIXON	72
HB	BRYCE	BROWN	72
FB	JEROME	FELTON	88
FB	MARQUEIS	GRAY	65
WR	PERCY	HARVIN	86
WR	SAMMY	WATKINS	85
WR	ROBERT	WOODS	80
WR	CHRIS	HOGAN	72
WR	MARQUISE	GOODWIN	68
WR	MARCUS	EASLEY	68
TE	CHARLES	CLAY	86
TE	CHRIS	GRAGG	72
TE	NICK	O'LEARY	69
LT	CORDY	GLENN	86
LG	ALEX	KUPPER	70
LG	JOHN	MILLER	71
LG	CYRIL	RICHARDSON	64
C	ERIC	WOOD	80
C	KRAIG	URBIK	75
RG	RICHIE	INCOGNITO	79
RG	CHRIS	WILLIAMS	75
RG	WILLIAM	CAMPBELL	67
RT	SEANTREL	HENDERSON	76
RT	CYRUS	KOUANDJIO	67

DEFENSIVE DEPTH CHART

POS	FIRST	LAST	OVR
LE	MARIO	WILLIAMS	90
LE	JARIUS	WYNN	77
LE	ALEX	CARRINGTON	72
DT	MARCELL	DAREUS	94
DT	KYLE	WILLIAMS	93
DT	STEFAN	CHARLES	70
DT	CORBIN	BRYANT	69
DT	JUSTIN	HAMILTON	64
RE	JERRY	HUGHES	85
RE	MANNY	LAWSON	77
LOLB	NIGEL	BRADHAM	83
LOLB	ANDREW	HUDSON	56
MLB	PRESTON	BROWN	78
MLB	TY	POWELL	63
ROLB	RANDELL	JOHNSON	69
ROLB	TONY	STEWARD	65
ROLB	A.J.	TARPLEY	64
CB	STEPHON	GILMORE	86
CB	COREY	GRAHAM	84
CB	LEODIS	MCKELVIN	80
CB	NICKELL	ROBEY	74
CB	RON	BROOKS	69
FS	DUKE	WILLIAMS	76
FS	KENNY	LADLER	63
SS	AARON	WILLIAMS	79
SS	BACARRI	RAMBO	74
SS	JONATHAN	MEEKS	65

SPECIAL TEAMS

POS	FIRST	LAST	OVR
K	DAN	CARPENTER	89
KR	SAMMY	WATKINS	85
KR	MARQUISE	GOODWIN	68
P	COLTON	SCHMIDT	66
PR	LEODIS	MCKELVIN	80

BEST OFFENSIVE PLAYS

PRO TIPS

- **These are the best two offensive plays in your playbook. They will get your playmakers in position to win you games.**
- The far left WR can be placed on a slant for short yardage conversions.
- To take a shot downfield, use max protection blocking.

BEST RUN: SINGLEBACK NORMAL BILLS—HB COUNTER

SETUP:

- This formation allows HB LeSean McCoy to take advantage of his high Agility rating behind the line.
- Consider playmakering the run to the right if the defense looks weak.
- Don't outrun your blockers—be patient.

ADVANCED SETUP:

- Audible to the HB Dive for a more consistent gain.

RUNNING PLAYS

1ST DOWN	2ND AND SHORT	3RD AND SHORT	GOAL LINE	2ND AND LONG	3RD AND LONG
Singleback Ace Pair Flex—HB Toss Strong	Singleback Ace—0 1 Trap	I-Form Pro—FB Dive	Goal Line Normal—QB Sneak	Pistol Full House TE—Bills Read Option	Pistol Strong Twins—HB Counter
Singleback Ace—HB Zone Wk	I-Form Pro—Iso	Pistol Strong Slot Bills—Bills Inside Zone	Goal Line Normal—HB Sting	Gun Empty Trey Flex—QB Draw	Pistol Weak Twins—Lead Read Option
Strong Pro—HB Stretch	Singleback Ace Close—Tight Slots Wham	Pistol Wing Trips—Counter Y	Goal Line Normal—Strong Toss	Gun Trio Offset Wk—HB Power	Gun Doubles—HB Mid Draw

INSIDE RUN | OUTSIDE RUN | SHOTGUN RUN | QB RUN

BEST PASS: PISTOL ACE TWINS—BILLS POST WHEEL

SETUP/READS:

- This play allows you to attack the sideline behind a zone defender in a flat.
- Against man-to-man coverage, hit the crossing TE over the middle and use the new "run after catch" (RAC) option.
- Against the blitz, the HB should be open for a quick pass.

ADVANCED SETUP:

- Slant or drag the left TE (optional).

PASSING PLAYS

1ST DOWN	2ND AND SHORT	3RD AND SHORT	SHOT PLAYS	2ND AND LONG	3RD AND LONG
Gun Spread Flex Wk—Inside Cross	Singleback Normal Bills—WR Drag	I-Form Tight—Angle	Singleback Ace—PA Shot Go's	Singleback Normal Bills—Deep Attack	Pistol Ace Twins—PA Ctr Waggle
Singleback Ace Pair—TE Attack	Singleback Ace Close—Tight Slots TE Angle	Pistol Ace Twins—X Spot	Pistol Ace Twins—PA FL Stretch	Singleback Bunch Ace—Divide	Pistol Strong Twins—PA Deep In
Singleback Ace—Flanker Drive	Singleback Jumbo Pair—Y Stick	I-Form Pro—Mid Attack	Singleback Bunch Ace—All Go's	Gun Empty Trey Flex—Verticals Y Shake	Gun Trey Open—Four Verticals

BASE PLAY | MAN BEATER | ZONE BEATER | BLITZ BEATER

BEST DEFENSIVE PLAYS

PRO TIPS

- **If you want to win more games in *Madden NFL 16*, rely on these defensive plays to lock up the run and pass.**
- **Don't forget to sneak in a safety blitz each game, generally on second down.**
- **Make sure to sub your defensive tackles into the game to make the 2-4-5 an every-down set.**

BEST RUN D: NICKEL 3-3-5 WIDE–SAM WILL 3 BLITZ

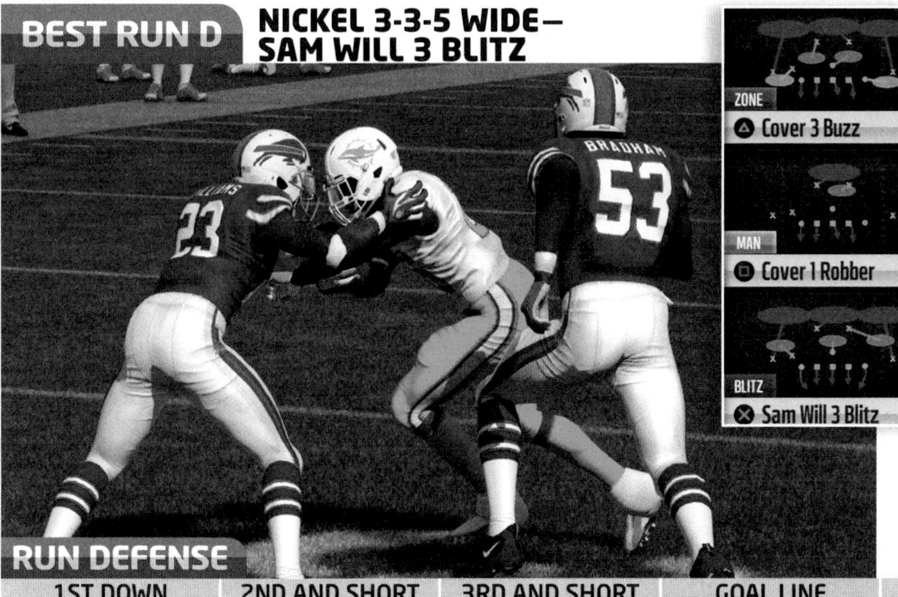

ZONE — △ Cover 3 Buzz

MAN — □ Cover 1 Robber

BLITZ — ⊗ Sam Will 3 Blitz

SETUP:

- Use formation subs to make sure Hughes and Williams are blitzing off the edge. TEs can't block them for long.
- This play is especially good vs pistol and shotgun runs.

PLAYER TO CONTROL:

- The MLB in the box (attack downhill against middle runs)

RUN DEFENSE

1ST DOWN	2ND AND SHORT	3RD AND SHORT	GOAL LINE	2ND AND LONG	3RD AND LONG
3-4 Odd–Sam Mike 1	3-4 Predator–Cov 1 Robber Press	3-4 Bear–Will Sam 1	Goal Line 5-3-3–Gaps All	Nickel 2-4-5 Even–QB Contain	Big Dime 1-4-6–Cover 1 Robber
3-4 Odd–Sam Mike 3	3-4 Predator–Will Fire 3 Seam	3-4 Bear–Cover 2 Invert	Goal Line 5-3-3–Pinch Zone	Nickel 2-4-5 Even–Cover 2	Big Dime 1-4-6–Mike SS 3 Seam

MAN COVERAGE | ZONE COVERAGE | MAN BLITZ | ZONE BLITZ

BEST PASS D: NICKEL 2-4-5 EVEN–COVER 2

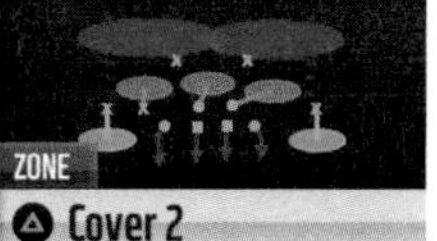

ZONE — △ Cover 2

BLITZ — □ 3 Seam Show 2

ZONE — ⊗ Cover 2 Sink

SETUP:

- Cover 2 will force checkdowns to the flat–go for the sure tackle over the big hit.
- Try this out for the first drive and mix in Cover 2 Man every third play to fool your opponent.
- Giving up a few yards in the middle early isn't a big deal; this is bend-but-don't-break defense.

PLAYER TO CONTROL:

- The LB rushing off either edge (try to contain a mobile QB)

PASS DEFENSE

1ST DOWN	2ND AND SHORT	3RD AND SHORT	GOAL LINE	2ND AND LONG	3RD AND LONG
3-4 Over Ed–Cover 2 Man	3-4 Over Ed–Cover 1 Thief	Nickel 3-3-5 Wide–Mike Blitz 0	Goal Line 5-4-2–Jam Cover 1	Dollar 3-2-6–Mike Edge 1	Big Dime 2-3-6–Over Storm Brave
3-4 Over Ed–Cover 3 Sky	3-4 Over Ed–Cover 2	Nickel 3-3-5 Wide–Sam Will 3 Blitz	Goal Line 5-4-2–3 Deep Under	Dollar 3-2-6–Overload 3 Seam	Big Dime 2-3-6–Slant 3 Press

MAN COVERAGE | ZONE COVERAGE | MAN BLITZ | ZONE BLITZ

DENVER BRONCOS

GAMEPLAY RATING 89

CONNECTED FRANCHISE MODE STRATEGY

CFM TEAM RATING: **85**
OFFENSE: **87**
DEFENSE: **89**
OFFENSIVE SCHEME: **Zone Run**
DEFENSIVE SCHEME: **Attacking 3-4**
STRENGTHS: **QB, WR, LB, CB**
WEAKNESSES: **DT, C, LG, LT**

2014 TEAM RANKINGS

1st AFC West (12-4-0)
PASSING OFFENSE: **4th**
RUSHING OFFENSE: **15th**
PASSING DEFENSE: **9th**
RUSHING DEFENSE: **2nd**

2014 TEAM LEADERS

PASSING: **Peyton Manning: 4,727**
RUSHING: **C.J. Anderson: 849**
RECEIVING: **Demaryius Thomas: 1,619**
TACKLES: **Brandon Marshall: 113**
SACKS: **Von Miller: 14**
INTS: **Aqib Talib: 4**

KEY ADDITIONS

TE Owen Daniels
DE Vance Walker
G Shelley Smith
S Darian Stewart

KEY ROOKIES

DE Shane Ray
T Ty Sambrailo
TE Jeff Heuerman

OWNER: **Pat Bowlen**
LEGACY SCORE: **8,100**

COACH: **Gary Kubiak**
LEVEL: **6**
LEGACY SCORE: **400**
OFFENSIVE SCHEME: **Zone Run**
DEFENSIVE SCHEME: **Attacking 4-3**

OFFENSIVE SCOUTING REPORT

- Another year gone by and another year with the best QB in the league in Peyton Manning. Sooner or later you will need to address the QB situation for the future.
- HB Montee Ball needs to step in and become the feature HB for this team. We aren't sold that he can carry the load long term. Make this your number one priority in the off-season.
- WR Emmanuel Sanders can catch everything, but he lacks the true size to play outside the slot. The Broncos need another big-bodied WR to complement star WR Demaryius Thomas.

DEFENSIVE SCOUTING REPORT

- The Broncos' CBs are excellent man defenders who can stick with even the best WRs. Press only on Talib's matchup, as he is the best at getting physical. Safety T.J. Ward is great in run support but shouldn't be expected to help out a ton in coverage.
- Everyone knows about Von Miller, but the Broncos have two MLBs next to him who are excellent in zone coverage. Play plenty of Cover 2 Sink because it is a great scheme fit.
- Check the free agent wire for some defensive line help in the run game. Target players with high Strength ratings to keep your LBs free to make plays.

SCHEDULE

Week	Date	Time	TV	Opponent
1	SEP 13	4:25 PM ET		RAVENS
2	SEP 17	8:25 PM ET		AT CHIEFS
3	SEP 27	8:30 PM ET		AT LIONS
4	OCT 04	4:25 PM ET	FOX	VIKINGS
5	OCT 11	4:25 PM ET		AT RAIDERS
6	OCT 18	1:00 PM ET		AT BROWNS
7	BYE WEEK			
8	NOV 01	8:30 PM ET		PACKERS
9	NOV 08	4:25 PM ET		AT COLTS
10	NOV 15	4:25 PM ET		CHIEFS
11	NOV 22	1:00 PM ET		AT BEARS
12	NOV 29	8:30 PM ET		PATRIOTS
13	DEC 06	4:05 PM ET		AT CHARGERS
14	DEC 13	4:05 PM ET		RAIDERS
15	DEC 20	4:25 PM ET		AT STEELERS
16	DEC 28	8:30 PM ET	ESPN	BENGALS
17	JAN 03	4:25 PM ET		CHARGERS

KEY PLAYERS

KEY OFFENSIVE PLAYER

DEMARYIUS THOMAS #88

WR #88 HT 6'3" WT 229 COLLEGE Georgia Tech EXP 5

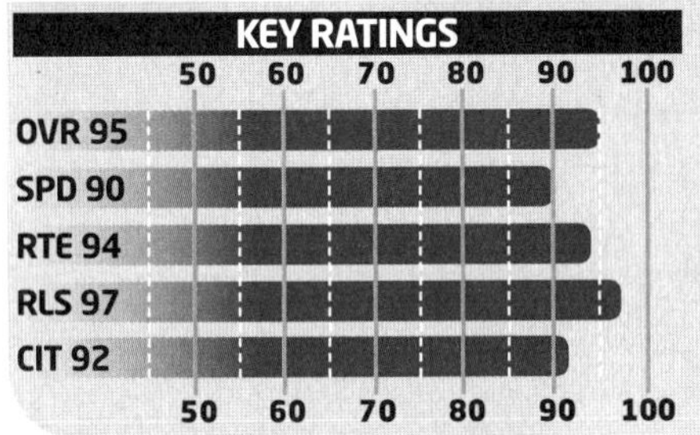

- Not only can Thomas go up for spectacular catches with his 6'3" frame, but he often hangs onto them, too.
- Thomas is the only player you can't afford to lose—he is too valuable to the offense as a whole.

KEY DEFENSIVE PLAYER

VON MILLER #58

LOLB #58 HT 6'3" WT 250 COLLEGE Texas A&M EXP 4

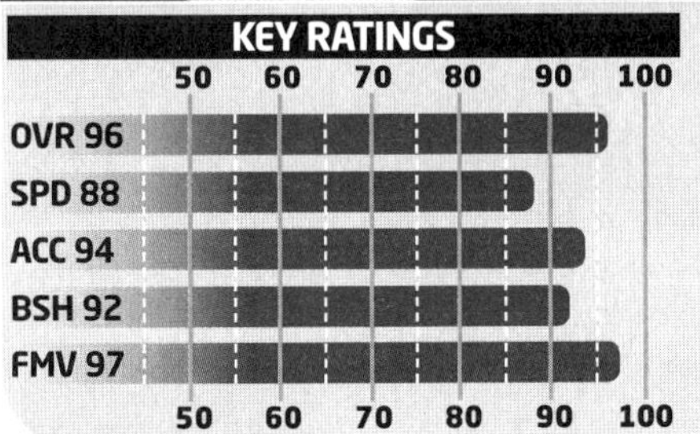

- Think of Miller as more than just a pass rusher. He really can do it all!
- Moving Miller inside on passing downs is an excellent choice because most guards won't be able to handle his finesse.

KEY ROOKIE

SHANE RAY #56

ROLB #56 HT 6'3" WT 245 COLLEGE Missouri EXP Rookie

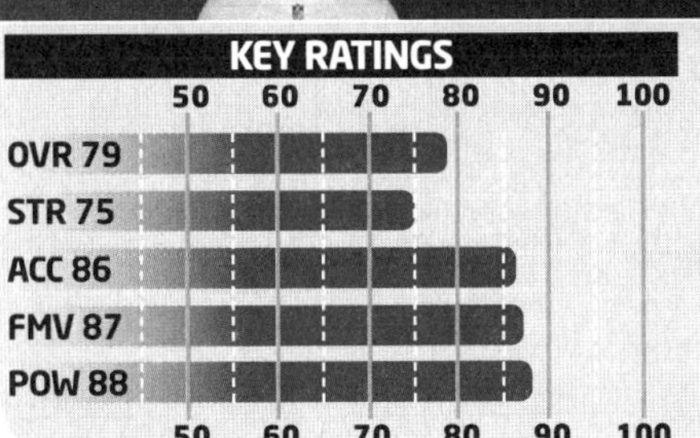

- Ray will be an excellent player to rotate in on pass-rushing downs for the first few years of his career.
- Continue to develop Ray's play recognition to help him get after the passer even quicker.

KEY SLEEPER

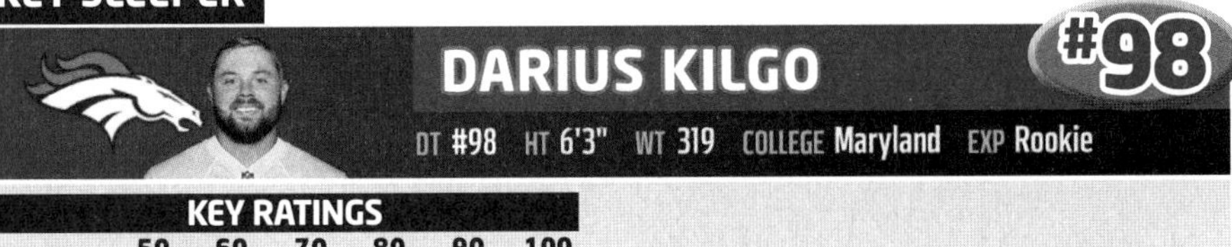

DARIUS KILGO #98

DT #98 HT 6'3" WT 319 COLLEGE Maryland EXP Rookie

KEY RATINGS

OVR 62, STR 92, ACC 77, BSH 87, PMV 69

- Kilgo is the best run stuffer on the team; give him as many snaps as you can to build his confidence.
- This is a huge position of weakness for Denver, so hopefully Kilgo will be a bright spot in a few seasons if you work on his power moves.

OFFENSIVE DEPTH CHART

POS	FIRST	LAST	OVR
QB	PEYTON	MANNING	92
QB	BROCK	OSWEILER	73
QB	ZAC	DYSERT	67
HB	C.J.	ANDERSON	85
HB	MONTEE	BALL	76
HB	RONNIE	HILLMAN	74
HB	JUWAN	THOMPSON	72
FB	JAMES	CASEY	80
WR	DEMARYIUS	THOMAS	93
WR	EMMANUEL	SANDERS	89
WR	ANDRE	CALDWELL	74
WR	CODY	LATIMER	73
WR	JORDAN	NORWOOD	64
WR	ISAIAH	BURSE	63
TE	OWEN	DANIELS	80
TE	VIRGIL	GREEN	82
TE	JEFF	HEUERMAN	71
LT	RYAN	HARRIS	76
LG	SHELLEY	SMITH	75
LG	ANDRE	DAVIS	64
C	GINO	GRADKOWSKI	70
C	MAX	GARCIA	65
C	MATT	PARADIS	63
RG	LOUIS	VASQUEZ	86
RG	BEN	GARLAND	69
RT	CHRIS	CLARK	79
RT	MICHAEL	SCHOFIELD	69

DEFENSIVE DEPTH CHART

POS	FIRST	LAST	OVR
LE	DEREK	WOLFE	82
LE	VANCE	WALKER	76
DT	MARVIN	AUSTIN JR.	72
DT	DARIUS	KILGO	62
RE	MALIK	JACKSON	84
RE	ANTONIO	SMITH	77
RE	GERALD	RIVERS	62
LOLB	VON	MILLER	97
LOLB	LERENTEE	MCCRAY	69
MLB	BRANDON	MARSHALL	84
MLB	DANNY	TREVATHAN	79
MLB	STEVEN	JOHNSON	67
MLB	REGGIE	WALKER	66
ROLB	DEMARCUS	WARE	83
ROLB	SHANE	RAY	72
CB	CHRIS	HARRIS JR.	94
CB	AQIB	TALIB	90
CB	BRADLEY	ROBY	79
CB	KAYVON	WEBSTER	73
CB	TONY	CARTER	73
FS	DARIAN	STEWART	85
FS	DAVID	BRUTON JR.	77
FS	OMAR	BOLDEN	72
SS	T.J.	WARD	87
SS	JOSH	BUSH	71

SPECIAL TEAMS

POS	FIRST	LAST	OVR
K	CONNOR	BARTH	82
KR	ANDRE	CALDWELL	74
KR	OMAR	BOLDEN	72
P	BRITTON	COLQUITT	76
PR	EMMANUEL	SANDERS	89

BEST OFFENSIVE PLAYS

PRO TIPS

- These are the best two offensive plays in your playbook. They will get your playmakers in position to win you games.
- The Broncos' playbook may have different terminology than other playbooks, but the formations are similar.
- Denver has many great pistol formations; learning to run from them is the key to making the offense work.

BEST RUN: PISTOL SLOT WING–HB COUNTER

SETUP:

- The HB Counter is no longer a sure thing, but it can still be a consistent way to pick up yards if you can seal the edge.
- Don't outrun your blockers or you will run into trouble.
- Without a mobile QB to keep contain defenders occupied, make sure to mix in plenty of play action off of these handoffs.

ADVANCED SETUP:

- Motion the TE from right to left (optional)

RUNNING PLAYS

1ST DOWN	2ND AND SHORT	3RD AND SHORT	GOAL LINE	2ND AND LONG	3RD AND LONG
Singleback Deuce Pair Twins–HB Stretch	Pistol Ace–HB Counter	Gun Deuce–0 1 Trap	I-Form Pro–FB Dive	Pistol Bunch TE–HB Counter	Gun Bunch Wk–HB Base
Singleback Deuce–HB Dive	Pistol Ace–0 1 Trap	I-Form Pro–HB Toss	Goal Line Normal–HB Sting	Pistol Slot Wing–0 1 Trap	Gun Y-Trips HB Wk–Inside Zone
Singleback Deuce–HB Off Tackle	Pistol Ace–Strong Power	I-Form Tight–Strong Stretch	Goal Line Normal–Power O	Pistol Bunch TE–Strong Power	Gun Dice Slot Wk–HB Mid Draw

INSIDE RUN | OUTSIDE RUN | SHOTGUN RUN | QB RUN

BEST PASS: PISTOL BUNCH TE–CROSS DRAG

SETUP/READS:

- Streaking the far left WR is the key to taking some safety help away on this play. Otherwise the middle can get pretty cramped.
- Against man-to-man your crossing patterns should generate some solid separation over the middle.
- Check down to a WR screen if the defense is playing off; your WRs are built to run after the catch.

ADVANCED SETUP:

- Streak the far left WR.

PASSING PLAYS

1ST DOWN	2ND AND SHORT	3RD AND SHORT	SHOT PLAYS	2ND AND LONG	3RD AND LONG
Gun Dice Slot Wk–Bronco Mesh	Gun Dice Slot Wk–Bronco Mesh	Strong Close–Y-Trail	Singleback Dice Slot–PA Draw Shot	Pistol Bunch TE–Flood	Gun Empty Bronco–Bronco Seams
Gun Snugs–Drive Corner	Gun Deuce–Inside Cross	Strong Close–WR Out	Pistol Slot Wing–PA Bronco Shot	Pistol Ace–Ace TE Drag	Gun Snugs–Bronco Seams
Pistol Ace Twins–Slot Under	Gun Bunch Wk–Bronco Cross	Gun Bunch Wk–HB Cross Screen	Pistol Ace Twins–PA FL Stretch	Pistol Trips–Verticals	Pistol Ace Twins–PA FL Stretch

BASE PLAY | MAN BEATER | ZONE BEATER | BLITZ BEATER

 For more plays and strategies for this team, visit your eGuide using the access code sheet provided.

BEST DEFENSIVE PLAYS

PRO TIPS

- **If you want to win more games in *Madden NFL 16*, rely on these defensive plays to lock up the run and pass.**
- Denver has some great depth at OLB but is slightly undersized on the defensive line for a 3-4.
- The 2-4-5 is the best way to get your talent all on the field at once.

BEST RUN D: 3-4 OVER–STING PINCH ZONE

ZONE
Cover 4

BLITZ
Sting Pinch

BLITZ
Sting Pinch Zone

SETUP:

- The Cov 3 Buzz Press is a great way to take a standard coverage and move it around after the snap.
- Call man coverage on the bulk of your snaps, because most teams will struggle to get loose from your solid CBs.
- If your edge rushers can get pressure, keep calling this play—otherwise try the 3 Buzz Blitz Show 2.

PLAYER TO CONTROL:

- Either LB rushing off the edge

RUN DEFENSE

1ST DOWN	2ND AND SHORT	3RD AND SHORT	GOAL LINE	2ND AND LONG	3RD AND LONG
3-4 Odd–2 Sink QB Contain	3-4 Solid–Cover 1 Robber	3-4 Over–Sting Pinch	Goal Line 5-4-2–Jam Cover 1	Nickel 3-3-5 Wide–Cover 1 Robber	Nickel 2-4-5–Cover 2 Sink
3-4 Odd–4 Drop QB Contain	3-4 Solid–Trio Sky Zone	3-4 Over–Sting Pinch Zone	Goal Line 5-4-2–Flat Buzz	Nickel 3-3-5 Wide–Cover 3 Buzz	Nickel 2-4-5–Cover 2 Show 4

MAN COVERAGE | ZONE COVERAGE | MAN BLITZ | ZONE BLITZ

BEST PASS D: NICKEL 2-4-5–COV 3 BUZZ PRESS

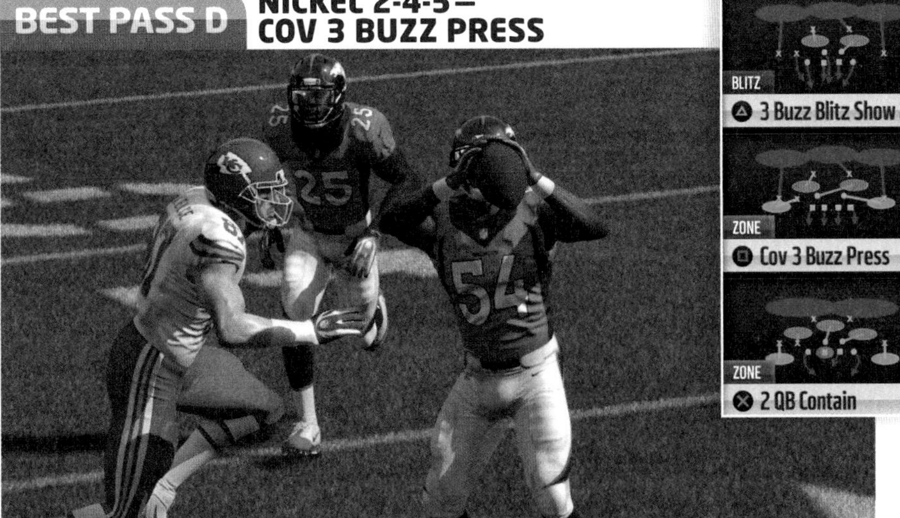

BLITZ
3 Buzz Blitz Show 2

ZONE
Cov 3 Buzz Press

ZONE
2 QB Contain

SETUP:

- The Sting Pinch Zone is an aggressive run defense, but it takes advantage of the speed of your LBs.
- You have the personnel necessary to call the man version of this blitz. Although riskier, it can shut the run down on third and short.

PLAYER TO CONTROL:

- Any blitzing LB

PASS DEFENSE

1ST DOWN	2ND AND SHORT	3RD AND SHORT	GOAL LINE	2ND AND LONG	3RD AND LONG
3-4 Odd–Cover 2 Man	3-4 Under–Cov1 Robber Press	Nickel 3-3-5 Wide–1 QB Contain	Goal Line 5-3-3–GL Man	Nickel 2-4-5 Dbl A Gap–Mid Blitz	Big Dime 1-4-6–Mike SS 1 Dog
3-4 Odd–4 Drop QB Contain	3-4 Under–Mike Scrape 3 Press	Nickel 3-3-5 Wide–Sam Will 3 Blitz	Goal Line 5-3-3–Pinch Zone	Nickel 2-4-5 Dbl A Gap–Buck Zone Blitz	Big Dime 1-4-6–Mike SS 3 Seam

MAN COVERAGE | ZONE COVERAGE | MAN BLITZ | ZONE BLITZ

CLEVELAND BROWNS

GAMEPLAY RATING 75

CONNECTED FRANCHISE MODE STRATEGY

CFM TEAM RATING: **83**
OFFENSE: **87**
DEFENSE: **89**
OFFENSIVE SCHEME: **Power Run**
DEFENSIVE SCHEME: **Base 3-4**
STRENGTHS: **LT, LG, C, S, MLB**
WEAKNESSES: **HB, RT, QB, FB**

2014 TEAM RANKINGS

4th AFC North (7-9-0)
PASSING OFFENSE: **20th**
RUSHING OFFENSE: **17th**
PASSING DEFENSE: **8th**
RUSHING DEFENSE: **32nd**

2014 TEAM LEADERS

PASSING: **Brian Hoyer: 3,326**
RUSHING: **Terrance West: 673**
RECEIVING: **Andrew Hawkins: 824**
TACKLES: **Donte Whitner: 106**
SACKS: **Paul Kruger: 11**
INTS: **Tashaun Gipson: 6**

KEY ADDITIONS

P Andy Lee
WR Dwayne Bowe
CB Tramon Williams
DT Randy Starks

KEY ROOKIES

DT Danny Shelton
C Cameron Erving
DE Nate Orchard

OWNER: **Jimmy Haslam**
LEGACY SCORE: **0**

COACH: **Mike Pettine**
LEVEL: **2**
LEGACY SCORE: **0**
OFFENSIVE SCHEME: **Power Run**
DEFENSIVE SCHEME: **Base 3-4**

OFFENSIVE SCOUTING REPORT

- Josh McCown may be the veteran in the huddle, but the Browns won't go anywhere without Johnny Manziel. It has only been one season, and there is still time to get his confidence up and develop him into an excellent player! The Browns have lots of WR options, but none really jump out. Look to see who performs best with each QB.
- The Browns have put together an outstanding offensive line, so this should make your the lives of your HBs and QBs easier. Use your starting TE at FB as a lead blocker until you find someone via free agency. Give Isaiah Crowell the nod at HB if you like power backs, but otherwise don't sleep on Duke Johnson, who is pretty elusive and shows promise.
- TE Jordan Cameron has moved on and left the door open for someone to step up. Gary Barnidge and Rob Housler are both similar in body type, but neither has an elite Catch in Traffic rating. Develop their skills and they will become reliable targets for your squad. Don't forget to target Andrew Hawkins in the slot—his agility with the new run after catch option could be a game changer.

DEFENSIVE SCOUTING REPORT

- The Browns are set nicely on the defensive line for their 3-4 scheme. It all starts with Phil Taylor in the middle, who is excellent at taking on blockers in the run game.
- Don't give up on CB Justin Gilbert in the secondary; there is still plenty of time for him to develop into a solid player. Run plenty of nickel and dime sets with heavy man-to-man coverage. Your team can certainly handle it, and not every team has what it takes to beat it.
- At LB, Barkevious Mingo and Paul Kruger are excellent to rush off the edge, and they complement each other nicely. Continue to work on developing a second MLB to play with the very intelligent Karlos Dansby.

SCHEDULE

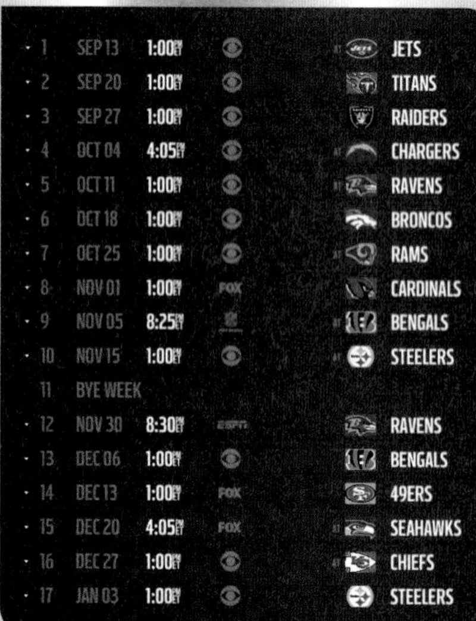

Week	Date	Time	Network		Opponent
1	SEP 13	1:00 PM ET		AT	JETS
2	SEP 20	1:00 PM ET			TITANS
3	SEP 27	1:00 PM ET			RAIDERS
4	OCT 04	4:05 PM ET		AT	CHARGERS
5	OCT 11	1:00 PM ET		AT	RAVENS
6	OCT 18	1:00 PM ET			BRONCOS
7	OCT 25	1:00 PM ET		AT	RAMS
8	NOV 01	1:00 PM ET	FOX		CARDINALS
9	NOV 05	8:25 PM ET		AT	BENGALS
10	NOV 15	1:00 PM ET		AT	STEELERS
11	BYE WEEK				
12	NOV 30	8:30 PM ET	ESPN		RAVENS
13	DEC 06	1:00 PM ET			BENGALS
14	DEC 13	1:00 PM ET	FOX		49ERS
15	DEC 20	4:05 PM ET	FOX	AT	SEAHAWKS
16	DEC 27	1:00 PM ET		AT	CHIEFS
17	JAN 03	1:00 PM ET			STEELERS

KEY PLAYERS

KEY OFFENSIVE PLAYER

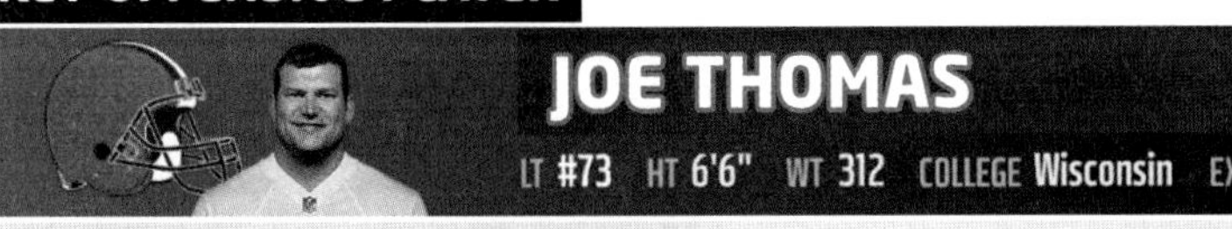

JOE THOMAS #73

LT #73 HT 6'6" WT 312 COLLEGE Wisconsin EXP 8

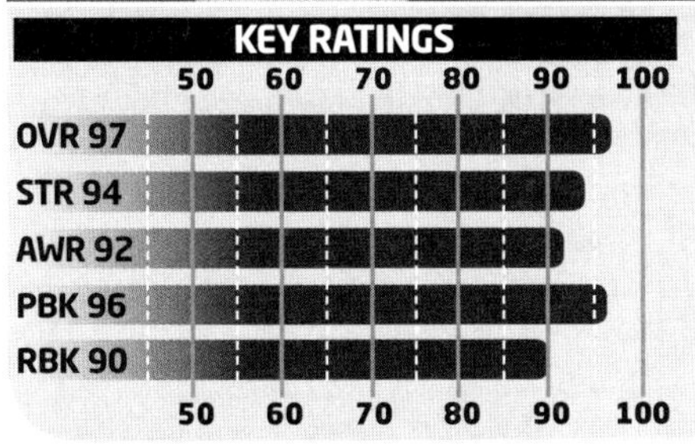

- Joe Thomas is one of the most durable linemen out there and gives the Browns' offensive line great stability.
- Try to get Thomas out in space on screen passes and pulling run plays; he has great speed and impact blocking.

KEY DEFENSIVE PLAYER

JOE HADEN #23

CB #23 HT 5'11" WT 195 COLLEGE Florida EXP 5

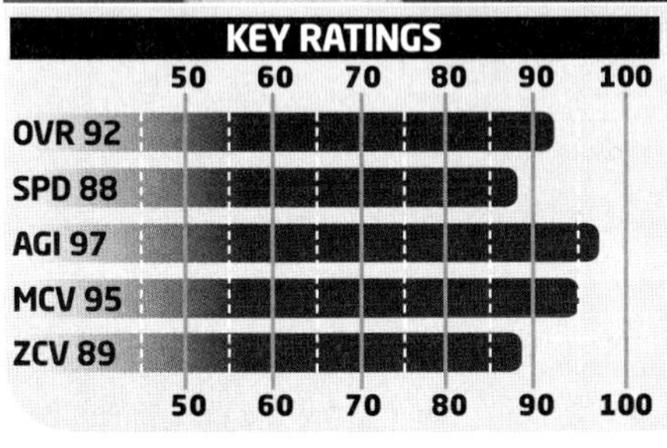

- Joe Haden should be allowed to match up with the other team's best WR and only given help if the WR proves he can get some separation.
- Haden is a solid corner who has the acceleration and agility to catch back up on a rare missed press attempt. He should be physical with any WR who has a Release rating under 90.

KEY ROOKIE

DANNY SHELTON #71

DT #71 HT 6'2" WT 339 COLLEGE Washington EXP Rookie

KEY RATINGS

OVR 79
STR 93
BSH 88
PMV 80
PUR 88

- Keep developing Shelton's Power Moves rating to turn him into an all-around defender who can get after the passer.
- Groom Shelton to take over for Phil Taylor if you can't come to an agreement on a long-term deal. You may not be able to afford both.

KEY SLEEPER

DUKE JOHNSON #30

HB #30 HT 5'9" WT 207 COLLEGE Miami EXP Rookie

KEY RATINGS

OVR 71
SPD 90
ACC 89
ELU 87
CTH 69

- Go with the juke in the open field, as it is the highest-rated move for Johnson.
- Johnson has solid strength for his play style and should break more tackles than Terrance West.

OFFENSIVE DEPTH CHART

POS	FIRST	LAST	OVR
QB	JOSH	MCCOWN	72
QB	JOHNNY	MANZIEL	71
QB	THAD	LEWIS	69
HB	ISAIAH	CROWELL	74
HB	DUKE	JOHNSON	73
HB	TERRANCE	WEST	73
HB	GLENN	WINSTON	64
FB	MALCOLM	JOHNSON	63
WR	DWAYNE	BOWE	83
WR	ANDREW	HAWKINS	80
WR	BRIAN	HARTLINE	78
WR	TAYLOR	GABRIEL	75
WR	TRAVIS	BENJAMIN	72
WR	VINCE	MAYLE	70
TE	GARY	BARNIDGE	76
TE	JIM	DRAY	74
TE	ROB	HOUSLER	71
LT	JOE	THOMAS	95
LT	RYAN	SEYMOUR	62
LG	JOEL	BITONIO	91
LG	VINSTON	PAINTER	70
C	ALEX	MACK	89
C	CAMERON	ERVING	73
RG	JOHN	GRECO	86
RG	KARIM	BARTON	60
RT	MICHAEL	BOWIE	73
RT	ANDREW	MCDONALD	70

DEFENSIVE DEPTH CHART

POS	FIRST	LAST	OVR
LE	RANDY	STARKS	79
LE	BILLY	WINN	77
LE	XAVIER	COOPER	65
DT	PHIL	TAYLOR	80
DT	DANNY	SHELTON	75
DT	ISHMAA'ILY	KITCHEN	71
RE	DESMOND	BRYANT	79
RE	JOHN	HUGHES	78
LOLB	BARKEVIOUS	MINGO	82
LOLB	ARMONTY	BRYANT	64
MLB	KARLOS	DANSBY	90
MLB	CRAIG	ROBERTSON	79
MLB	CHRIS	KIRKSEY	72
MLB	TANK	CARDER	67
ROLB	NATE	ORCHARD	68
ROLB	SCOTT	SOLOMON	69
CB	JOE	HADEN	90
CB	TRAMON	WILLIAMS	84
CB	K'WAUN	WILLIAMS	80
CB	JUSTIN	GILBERT	77
CB	PIERRE	DESIR	68
FS	TASHAUN	GIPSON	89
FS	JORDAN	POYER	69
SS	DONTE	WHITNER	90
SS	JOHNSON	BADEMOSI	71
SS	IBRAHEIM	CAMPBELL	67

SPECIAL TEAMS

POS	FIRST	LAST	OVR
K	CAREY	SPEAR	57
KR	JUSTIN	GILBERT	77
KR	TRAVIS	BENJAMIN	72
P	ANDY	LEE	89
PR	TRAVIS	BENJAMIN	72

BEST OFFENSIVE PLAYS

PRO TIPS

- These are the best two offensive plays in your playbook. They will get your playmakers in position to win you games.
- The Browns' playbook has some running options for a mobile QB depending on your play style.
- The Gun Split Close has a play for every situation, live in this formation.

BEST RUN: PISTOL STRONG–INSIDE ZONE SPLIT

SETUP:

- Make sure to use the backup QB package and run the Read Option for a change of pace.
- Your job is to pick the correct hole on this play. Don't run into the back of your lineman.

ADVANCED SETUP:

- Sub in best blocking TE at FB (optional)

RUNNING PLAYS

1ST DOWN	2ND AND SHORT	3RD AND SHORT	GOAL LINE	2ND AND LONG	3RD AND LONG
I-Form Pro–Stretch	Singleback Ace–0 1 Trap	I-Form Tight Pair–FB Dive	Goal Line Normal–QB Sneak	Pistol Ace–HB Counter	Gun Trey Open Offset–Wide Trap
I-Form Pro Twins–HB Blast	I-Form Twins Flex–HB Lead Dive	Strong Close–HB Force	Goal Line Normal–HB Sting	Pistol Slot Wing–Inside Zone Split	Gun Snugs Flip–HB Mid Draw
Singleback Jumbo–HB Ace Power	Weak Pro Twins–HB Blast	Singleback Ace Pair–HB Trap	I-Form Tight Pair–HB Lead Dive	Pistol Ace–Strong Power	Gun Bunch Offset–Read Option

INSIDE RUN | OUTSIDE RUN | SHOTGUN RUN | QB RUN

BEST PASS: GUN SPLIT CLOSE BROWNS–X DRAG TRAIL

SETUP/READS:

- Against zone coverage wait for the middle to clear out and target the post with a bullet pass.
- Against man-to-man coverage wait for the HB to cut back across the middle.
- Against the blitz throw to either player in the backfield, generally towards the open side of the field.
- While he isn't the fastest, new WR Dwayne Bowe is probably the most reliable at hanging onto passes.

ADVANCED SETUP:

- On third down, curl the far right WR.

PASSING PLAYS

1ST DOWN	2ND AND SHORT	3RD AND SHORT	SHOT PLAYS	2ND AND LONG	3RD AND LONG
Pistol Ace–Ace TE Drag	Strong Close–Read WR Out	Singleback Doubles–TE Post	Gun Trips TE–PA Shot Wheel	Gun Split Close Browns–X Drag Trail	Singleback Ace Pair–TE Attack
Gun Bunch Offset–Y Trail	Strong Close–Y-Trail	I-Form Pro–PA Scissors	Gun Wing Trio Browns–PA Cross Shot	Gun Split Close Browns–HB Slip Screen	Gun Trips TE–Verticals
Gun Tight Doubles On–Browns Cross	Pistol Ace–PA Ctr Waggle	Gun Doubles–HB Angle	Gun Tight Doubles On–Shot Fade Cross	Gun Empty Browns–Slot Stick Nod	Gun Bunch Offset–Verts HB Under

BASE PLAY | MAN BEATER | ZONE BEATER | BLITZ BEATER

 For more plays and strategies for this team, visit your eGuide using the access code sheet provided.

BEST DEFENSIVE PLAYS

PRO TIPS

- If you want to win more games in *Madden NFL 16,* rely on these defensive plays to lock up the run and pass.
- The 3-4 Bear continues to be an excellent run defense—just make sure you have enough leverage on the outside.
- The Browns have two very solid CBs, and you should consider playing heavy man coverage.

BEST RUN D 3-4 BEAR—1 QB CONTAIN

BLITZ
Will Safety Blitz 0

ZONE
Cover 2 Invert

BLITZ
1 QB Contain

SETUP:

- Spread your defensive line, because the risk of giving up a big play to the outside is too great.
- The Cover 2 Bear is a safer defense, but this stops those quick passes to the flat on third and short.
- Don't get fooled by the read option or it could be a big play!

PLAYER TO CONTROL:

- Either contain rusher

RUN DEFENSE

1ST DOWN	2ND AND SHORT	3RD AND SHORT	GOAL LINE	2ND AND LONG	3RD AND LONG
3-4 Bear–1 QB Contain	3-4 Over Ed–Cover 1 Hole	3-4 Bear–Will Sam 1	Goal Line 5-4-2–Jam Cover 1	Nickel 3-3-5 Wide–Cover 1 Robber	Dollar 3-2-6–Cover 2 Man
3-4 Bear–Cover 2 Invert	3-4 Over Ed–Sam Crash 3	3-4 Bear–Pinch Dog 3	Goal Line 5-4-2–Flat Buzz	Nickel 3-3-5 Wide–Cover 3 Buzz	Dollar 3-2-6–Cover 2 Press

MAN COVERAGE ZONE COVERAGE MAN BLITZ ZONE BLITZ

BEST PASS D BIG DIME 2-3-6–1 ROBBER SHOW 2

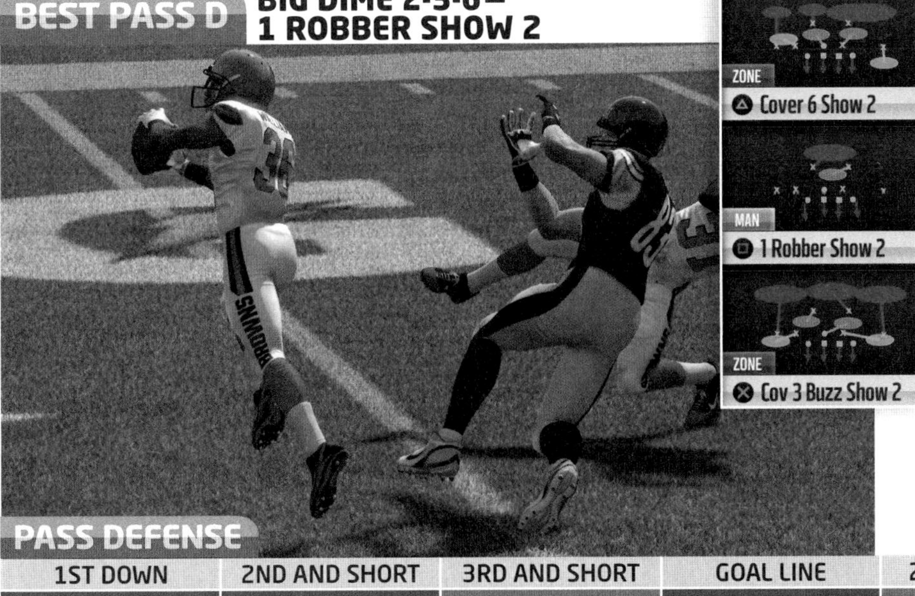

ZONE
Cover 6 Show 2

MAN
1 Robber Show 2

ZONE
Cov 3 Buzz Show 2

SETUP:

- This play is a nice change of pace from the Cover 2 Man you should be calling on most of your snaps.
- Consider subbing in an extra CB for your backup SS, who is in man coverage.
- What makes this play special is the extra defender over the middle, whom you can control to cause a headache for the offense.

PLAYER TO CONTROL:

- SS in a hook zone

PASS DEFENSE

1ST DOWN	2ND AND SHORT	3RD AND SHORT	GOAL LINE	2ND AND LONG	3RD AND LONG
3-4 Odd–2 Sink QB Contain	3-4 Over Ed–Fire Man	Nickel 2-4-5 Dbl A Gap–Mid Blitz	Goal Line 5-3-3–GL Man	Nickel 2-4-5–Cover 1 LB Blitz	Quarter 1-3-7–DB Strike
3-4 Odd–Cover 4	3-4 Over Ed–Sam Crash 3	Nickel 2-4-5 Dbl A Gap–Buck Zone Blitz	Goal Line 5-3-3–Pinch Zone	Nickel 2-4-5–Buck Slant 3	Big Dime 1-4-6–Mike SS 3 Seam

MAN COVERAGE ZONE COVERAGE MAN BLITZ ZONE BLITZ

TAMPA BAY BUCCANEERS

GAMEPLAY RATING 74

CONNECTED FRANCHISE MODE STRATEGY

CFM TEAM RATING: **79**
OFFENSE: **81**
DEFENSE: **85**
OFFENSIVE SCHEME: **Balanced**
DEFENSIVE SCHEME: **Tampa 2**
STRENGTHS: **WR, ROLB, DT**
WEAKNESSES: **HB, OL, S**

2014 TEAM RANKINGS

4th NFC South (2-14-0)
PASSING OFFENSE: **25th**
RUSHING OFFENSE: **29th**
PASSING DEFENSE: **28th**
RUSHING DEFENSE: **19th**

2014 TEAM LEADERS

PASSING: **Josh McCown: 2,206**
RUSHING: **Doug Martin: 494**
RECEIVING: **Mike Evans: 1,051**
TACKLES: **Lavonte David: 146**
SACKS: **Gerald McCoy: 8.5**
INTS: **Johnthan Banks: 4**

KEY ADDITIONS

DT Henry Melton
SS D.J. Swearinger
LB Bruce Carter

KEY ROOKIES

QB Jameis Winston
T Donovan Smith
C Ali Marpet

OWNER: **Edgar Miller**
LEGACY SCORE: **0**

COACH: **Lovie Smith**
LEVEL: **5**
LEGACY SCORE: **750**
OFFENSIVE SCHEME: **Balanced**
DEFENSIVE SCHEME: **Tampa 2**

OFFENSIVE SCOUTING REPORT

- Start rookie QB Jameis Winston over Mike Glennon at the start of the season. You must protect his confidence and allow him to develop his amazing potential.
- Give Bobby Rainey the bulk of the carries unless his 75 Carry rating becomes an issue. Practice short yardage with either Mike James or Jovorskie Lane. Neither is a great option but each has some decent trucking.
- For the Bucs to be a successful team on the field this season, they need to keep developing WR Mike Evans. With Vincent Jackson across from him, this should be an easy task, but focus on building the young player over the veteran.

DEFENSIVE SCOUTING REPORT

- The Bucs' LB corps improved during the off season by bringing in Bruce Carter. Continue building the Zone Coverage ratings for Danny Lansanah and Carter to fit your scheme.
- The Bucs have some nice players to fit into a three-safety scheme—try getting them on the field all at once and see how they fit. Don't get sucked in on play-action fakes because they don't have the speed to recover.
- McCoy will have to be the anchor on the defensive line with the departure of DE Michael Johnson. The Bucs have some rushers with decent finesse moves at DE, so see if you can shed some blocks with user control and help out the coverage by pressuring the QB.

SCHEDULE

Week	Date	Time	Network	Opponent
1	SEP 13	4:25 PM ET		TITANS
2	SEP 20	1:00 PM ET	FOX	AT SAINTS
3	SEP 27	1:00 PM ET	FOX	AT TEXANS
4	OCT 04	1:00 PM ET	FOX	PANTHERS
5	OCT 11	1:00 PM ET		JAGUARS
6	BYE WEEK			
7	OCT 25	1:00 PM ET	FOX	AT REDSKINS
8	NOV 01	1:00 PM ET	FOX	AT FALCONS
9	NOV 08	4:05 PM ET	FOX	GIANTS
10	NOV 15	1:00 PM ET	FOX	COWBOYS
11	NOV 22	1:00 PM ET	FOX	AT EAGLES
12	NOV 29	1:00 PM ET	FOX	AT COLTS
13	DEC 06	1:00 PM ET	FOX	FALCONS
14	DEC 13	1:00 PM ET	FOX	SAINTS
15	DEC 17	8:25 PM ET		AT RAMS
16	DEC 27	1:00 PM ET	FOX	BEARS
17	JAN 03	1:00 PM ET	FOX	AT PANTHERS

KEY PLAYERS

KEY OFFENSIVE PLAYER

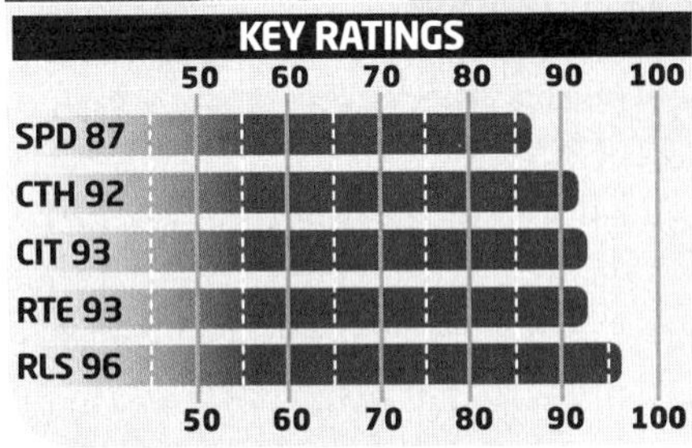

- Evans has the size to be a tremendous threat in the red zone, so have confidence in throwing high-point passes to him.
- It is extremely difficult to press Evans with his big frame and incredible Release rating.

KEY DEFENSIVE PLAYER

LAVONTE DAVID #54

ROLB #54 HT 6'1" WT 233 COLLEGE Nebraska EXP 3

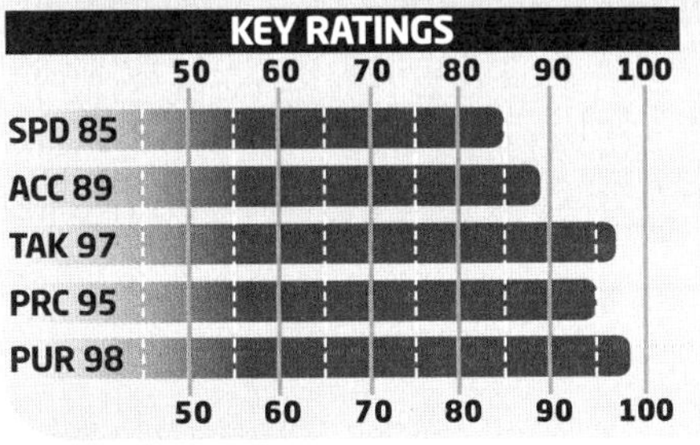

- David is the perfect LB for the Bucs' scheme; let him roam free with that 88 Zone Coverage rating.
- Make sure to lock up David for the long term, before he gets to free agency.

KEY ROOKIE

JAMEIS WINSTON #3

QB #3 HT 6'3" WT 231 COLLEGE Florida State EXP Rookie

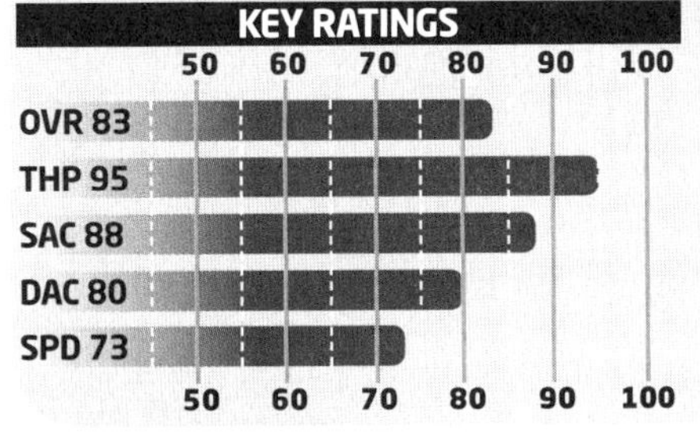

- It only takes a one draft pick to turn around a franchise. Focus on getting Winston some confidence—and watch his career take off.
- Winston will be best as a pocket passer, so build chemistry with the two outside WRs and utilize that excellent throwing power.

KEY SLEEPER

KWON ALEXANDER #58

ROLB #58 HT 6'1" WT 227 COLLEGE LSU EXP Rookie

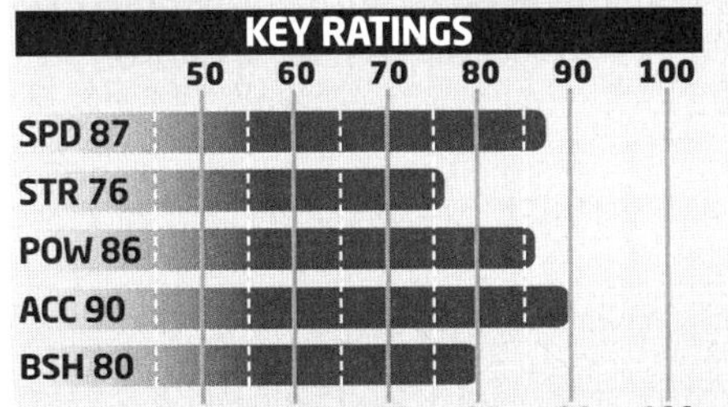

- Try to develop Alexander into the next Lavonte David. It will take time but the athleticism is there.
- Start Alexander on special teams immediately; his speed and hit power could change the tide of a game.

OFFENSIVE DEPTH CHART

POS	FIRST	LAST	OVR
QB	JAMEIS	WINSTON	81
QB	MIKE	GLENNON	73
QB	SETH	LOBATO	59
HB	DOUG	MARTIN	78
HB	BOBBY	RAINEY	75
HB	CHARLES	SIMS	72
HB	MIKE	JAMES	72
FB	JORVORSKIE	LANE	75
FB	CAMERON	BRATE	63
WR	MIKE	EVANS	87
WR	VINCENT	JACKSON	86
WR	LOUIS	MURPHY JR.	74
WR	ROBERT	HERRON	67
WR	RUSSELL	SHEPARD	67
WR	TAVARRES	KING	64
TE	AUSTIN	SEFERIAN-JENKINS	76
TE	BRANDON	MYERS	74
TE	LUKE	STOCKER	74
LT	DEMAR	DOTSON	80
LT	DONOVAN	SMITH	67
LG	LOGAN	MANKINS	86
LG	KADEEM	EDWARDS	66
C	EVAN	SMITH	79
C	GARRETT	GILKEY	64
C	JOSH	ALLEN	62
RG	PATRICK	OMAMEH	73
RG	ALI	MARPET	70
RT	KEVIN	PAMPHILE	75
RT	REID	FRAGEL	71

DEFENSIVE DEPTH CHART

POS	FIRST	LAST	OVR
LE	JACQUIES	SMITH	75
LE	WILLIAM	GHOLSTON	73
LE	T.J.	FATINIKUN	71
DT	GERALD	MCCOY	95
DT	HENRY	MELTON	83
DT	CLINTON	MCDONALD	79
DT	AKEEM	SPENCE	73
DT	MATTHEW	MASIFILO	68
RE	GEORGE	JOHNSON	75
RE	LARRY	ENGLISH	72
RE	LAWRENCE	SIDBURY JR.	72
LOLB	BRUCE	CARTER	78
LOLB	JASON	WILLIAMS	67
MLB	DANNY	LANSANAH	79
MLB	ORIE	LEMON	68
ROLB	LAVONTE	DAVID	91
ROLB	LARRY	DEAN	65
ROLB	KWON	ALEXANDER	63
CB	JOHNTHAN	BANKS	77
CB	MIKE	JENKINS	75
CB	LEONARD	JOHNSON	73
CB	STERLING	MOORE	78
CB	ALTERRAUN	VERNER	87
FS	CHRIS	CONTE	75
FS	KEITH	TANDY	73
SS	MAJOR	WRIGHT	78
SS	BRADLEY	MCDOUGALD	74

SPECIAL TEAMS

POS	FIRST	LAST	OVR
K	PATRICK	MURRAY	71
KR	BOBBY	RAINEY	75
KR	KAELIN	CLAY	60
P	MICHAEL	KOENEN	68
PR	BOBBY	RAINEY	75

BEST OFFENSIVE PLAYS

PRO TIPS

- These are the best two offensive plays in your playbook. They will get your playmakers in position to win you games.
- To get the most out of your lineup, try to work formations with three WRs, one TE, and one HB.
- The Bucs now have a QB with a huge arm to take advantage of their big WRs downfield.

BEST RUN: PISTOL TRIPS–HB COUNTER

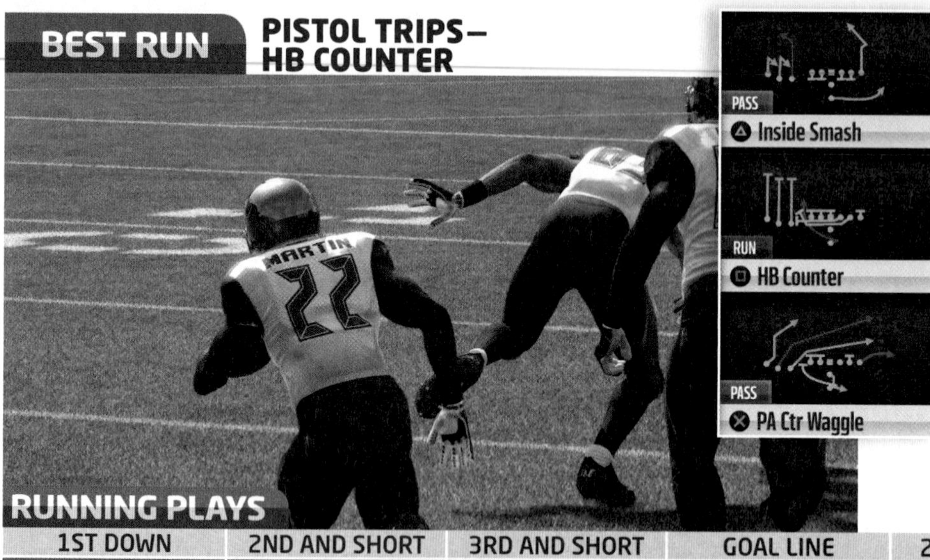

SETUP:

- You should have a good sense before the snap if the counter is going to be a success; abandon it if you don't feel confident.
- To get the most from a counter, wait as long as possible before breaking it outside.

ADVANCED SETUP:

- Motion a WR across the formation (optional).

RUNNING PLAYS

1ST DOWN	2ND AND SHORT	3RD AND SHORT	GOAL LINE	2ND AND LONG	3RD AND LONG
Singleback Ace–Outside Zone	Singleback Y-Trips–HB Zone Wk	I-Form Pro–FB Dive	Goal Line Normal–QB Sneak	Pistol Ace Twins–Read Option	Gun Buc Trips–HB Base
I-Form Pro–HB Blast	Singleback Doubles–0 1 Trap	I-Form Twins Flex–HB Search	Goal Line Normal–HB Sting	Weak Pro Twins–Toss Weak	Gun Spread–Inside Zone
Singleback Bunch–HB Counter	I-Form Pro–Counter	Singleback Doubles–HB Cutback	Strong Close–Quick Toss	Pistol Trips–Strong Power	Gun Tight Flex–HB Counter

INSIDE RUN OUTSIDE RUN SHOTGUN RUN QB RUN

BEST PASS: GUN Y-TRIPS HB WK–BUCS STREAK POST

SETUP/READS:

- Against zone coverage look across the middle or take a shot to the post.
- Against man coverage the TE/HB combo should create some separation.
- This is a big play as opposed to something that will keep the chains moving, so practice throwing downfield first.

ADVANCED SETUP:

- Slant the slot WR.

PASSING PLAYS

1ST DOWN	2ND AND SHORT	3RD AND SHORT	SHOT PLAYS	2ND AND LONG	3RD AND LONG
Pistol Trips–PA Ctr Waggle	Gun Y-Trips HB Wk–Y Trail	Gun Buc Trips–Quick Slants	I-Form Pro–PA Draw Shot	Gun Empty Trey–Bucs DBL Ins	Gun Spread–Deep Attack
Strong Close–Bucs Y-Trail	Gun Doubles–Angle Smash	Gun Empty Buc–X Slant	Singleback Ace–PA Stretch Over	Singleback Y-Trips–HB Slip Screen	Singleback Doubles–Slot Seam
Gun Tight Flex–WR Cross	I-Form Twins Flex–Flanker Curl	Gun Empty Trey–Stick	Singleback Ace Pair Twins–PA Misdirect Shot	Gun 5WR Trio–Four Verticals	Gun Bunch Wk–Bucs Verticals

BASE PLAY MAN BEATER ZONE BEATER BLITZ BEATER

 For more plays and strategies for this team, visit your eGuide using the access code sheet provided.

BEST DEFENSIVE PLAYS

PRO TIPS

- If you want to win more games in *Madden NFL 16*, rely on these defensive plays to lock up the run and pass.
- Give DT Gerald McCoy a chance to stop the run on his own before blitzing any LBs.
- The Big Dime 4-1-6 adds an extra safety into the box.

BEST RUN D: 4-3 WIDE 9—FREE FIRE 3

ZONE — Cover 2

BLITZ — Free Fire 3

ZONE — Cover 3 Cloud Show 2

SETUP:

- This play will blow up most runs without a lead blocker in the backfield.
- The Wide 9 is best against teams that like to attack the edge—you may have to switch it up against true power running teams.

PLAYER TO CONTROL:

- Either DT

RUN DEFENSE

1ST DOWN	2ND AND SHORT	3RD AND SHORT	GOAL LINE	2ND AND LONG	3RD AND LONG
46 Bear Under–Cover 1	4-3 Stack–Cover 1 Robber Press	46 Bear Under–Gap Press	Goal Line 5-4-2–Jam Cover 1	4-3 Wide 9–1 QB Contain Spy	Nickel Wide 9–Cov 1 Thief Press
46 Bear Under–Cover 3	4-3 Stack–Weak Slant 3	46 Bear Under–LB Dogs 3	Goal Line 5-4-2–Flat Buzz	4-3 Wide 9–Cover 2 Invert	Nickel Wide 9–Cov 3 Sky

MAN COVERAGE | ZONE COVERAGE | MAN BLITZ | ZONE BLITZ

BEST PASS D: BIG DIME 4-1-6 – BUCK SLANT 3

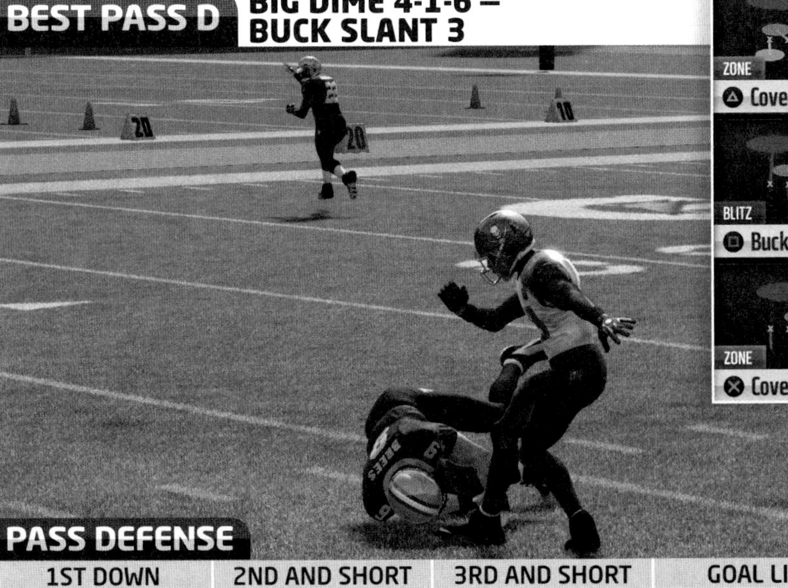

ZONE — Cover 2

BLITZ — Buck Slant 3

ZONE — Cover 2 Sink

SETUP:

- The flat will be open on this play. Let them have it early in the game before adjusting at halftime.
- When facing a left-handed QB, flip this play and bring the pressure from the other side.
- Adding a QB contain to the snap can help your defenders stay wide off the edge.

PLAYER TO CONTROL:

- Blitzing LB on the left of the screen

PASS DEFENSE

1ST DOWN	2ND AND SHORT	3RD AND SHORT	GOAL LINE	2ND AND LONG	3RD AND LONG
46 Bear Under–Cover 1	4-3 Over Plus–Cover 1	Nickel Normal–Cover 2 Sink	Goal Line 5-3-3–GL Man	Nickel Wide 9–Odd LB Dogs	Big Dime 4-1-6–Cov 1 Thief Press
46 Bear Under–Cover 3	4-3 Over Plus–Mike Blitz 3	Nickel Normal–Slant Show 2	Goal Line 5-3-3–Pinch Zone	Nickel Wide 9–Odd 4 Blitz Show 2	Big Dime 4-1-6–Buck Slant 3

MAN COVERAGE | ZONE COVERAGE | MAN BLITZ | ZONE BLITZ

ARIZONA CARDINALS

GAMEPLAY RATING 82

CONNECTED FRANCHISE MODE STRATEGY

CFM TEAM RATING: **82**
OFFENSE: **85**
DEFENSE: **81**
OFFENSIVE SCHEME: **Balanced Offense**
DEFENSIVE SCHEME: **Attacking 3-4**
STRENGTHS: **WR, LE, CB, LG, LT**
WEAKNESSES: **HB, TE, OLB, DT**

2014 TEAM RANKINGS

2nd NFC West (11-5-0)
PASSING OFFENSE: **14th**
RUSHING OFFENSE: **31st**
PASSING DEFENSE: **29th**
RUSHING DEFENSE: **13th**

2014 TEAM LEADERS

PASSING: **Drew Stanton: 1,711**
RUSHING: **Andre Ellington: 660**
RECEIVING: **Michael Floyd: 841**
TACKLES: **Rashad Johnson: 92**
SACKS: **Alex Okafor: 8**
INTS: **Rashad Johnson: 4**

KEY ADDITIONS

LG Mike Iupati
LB LaMarr Woodley
DE Cory Redding

KEY ROOKIES

T D.J. Humphries
DE Markus Golden
RB David Johnson

OWNER: **Bill Bidwill**
LEGACY SCORE: **650**

COACH: **Bruce Arians**
LEVEL: **26**
LEGACY SCORE: **500**
OFFENSIVE SCHEME: **Balanced Offense**
DEFENSIVE SCHEME: **Attacking 3-4**

OFFENSIVE SCOUTING REPORT

- Now that the left side of the line is set, give QB Carson Palmer plenty of time to look downfield. You have the size and speed at WR to make explosive plays if you can get the time in the pocket. Keeping Palmer healthy is your main goal this season; you need his consistency.
- HB Andre Ellington had a solid year catching out of the backfield, but he will average more yards per carry and stay healthy to become an every-down option for the Cardinals. Look to grab some depth early in free agency.
- Michael Floyd led the Cardinals in receiving yardage and TDs despite having only 47 catches. Develop chemistry with your QB and continue to make those big plays to your young star WR.

DEFENSIVE SCOUTING REPORT

- DE Cory Redding adds some good strength to the defensive line, but don't expect him to get into the backfield on run plays with only average block shedding. Calais Campbell is your all-around star; he will win most matchups with excellent finesse moves inside.
- The Cardinals have some young talent at the safety position. Keep developing FS Tyrann Mathieu and work on his strength to make him an every-down player. Don't forget about Rashad Johnson, who put up big numbers last year. Find a way to get him in the lineup for passing situations.
- Patrick Peterson still has the size and speed to match up with any WR in the league. However, the matchup on the other side of the field is where most teams will attack. Give extra safety help on that side of the field.

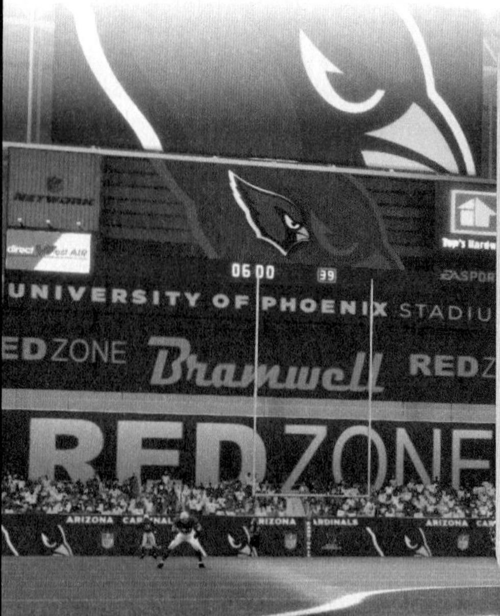

SCHEDULE

Week	Date	Time	Network	Opponent
1	SEP 13	4:05 PM ET	FOX	SAINTS
2	SEP 20	1:00 PM ET	FOX	BEARS
3	SEP 27	4:05 PM ET	FOX	49ERS
4	OCT 04	4:25 PM ET	FOX	RAMS
5	OCT 11	4:05 PM ET	FOX	LIONS
6	OCT 18	1:00 PM ET	FOX	STEELERS
7	OCT 26	8:30 PM ET	ESPN	RAVENS
8	NOV 01	1:00 PM ET	FOX	BROWNS
9	BYE WEEK			
10	NOV 15	8:30 PM ET		SEAHAWKS
11	NOV 22	4:05 PM ET		BENGALS
12	NOV 29	4:05 PM ET	FOX	49ERS
13	DEC 06	1:00 PM ET	FOX	RAMS
14	DEC 10	8:25 PM ET		VIKINGS
15	DEC 20	1:00 PM ET	FOX	EAGLES
16	DEC 27	4:25 PM ET	FOX	PACKERS
17	JAN 03	4:25 PM ET	FOX	SEAHAWKS

KEY PLAYERS

KEY OFFENSIVE PLAYER

MICHAEL FLOYD #15

WR #15 HT 6'3" WT 225 COLLEGE Notre Dame EXP 3

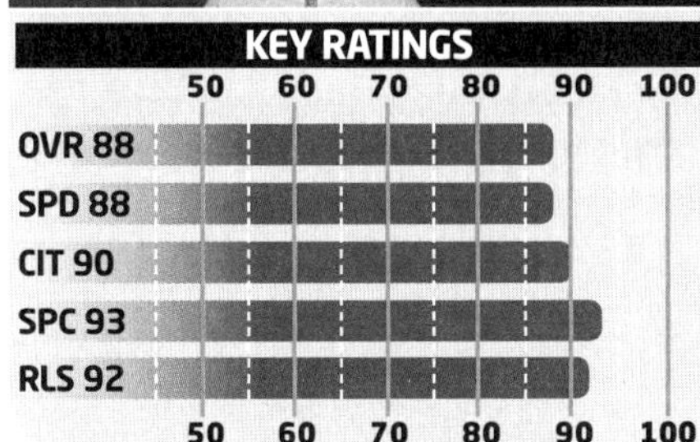

- Floyd has the aggressive catch trait, which means he will attack the ball if you give him a chance one on one downfield.
- Floyd led the team in receiving TDs last year with good reason; he is a beast in the red zone.

KEY DEFENSIVE PLAYER

CALAIS CAMPBELL #93

LE #93 HT 6'8" WT 300 COLLEGE Miami EXP 7

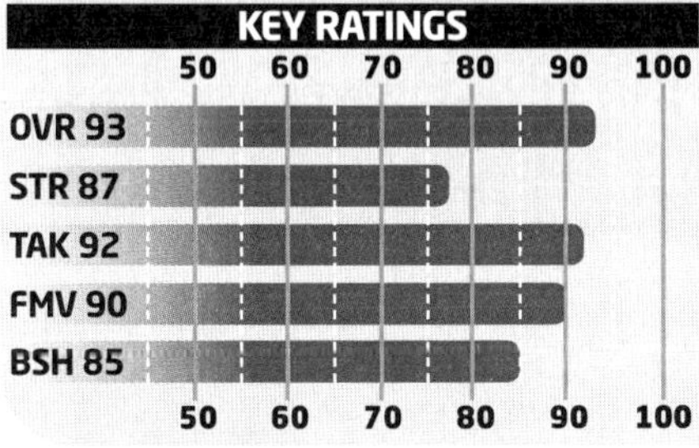

- Campbell is 6'8", which can really clog up throwing lanes for players who like to pass short over the middle.
- What really sets Campbell apart is excellent pursuit and play recognition for his size and position. Get creative with him.

KEY ROOKIE

D.J. HUMPHRIES #74

RT #74 HT 6'5" WT 307 COLLEGE Florida EXP Rookie

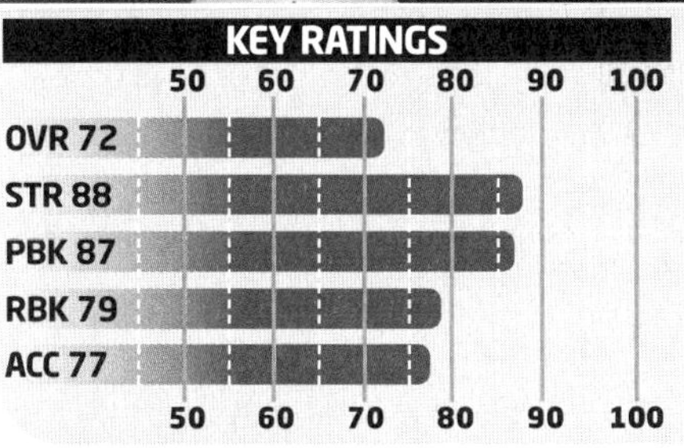

- Humphries might have a tough time playing over Jared Veldheer early, so consider giving him some snaps at RT depending on performance.
- Continue to develop Humphries as a run blocker, because pairing him with LG Mike Iupati will be an incredible combo on the left side.

KEY SLEEPER

LOGAN THOMAS #6

QB #6 HT 6'6" WT 250 COLLEGE Virginia Tech EXP 1

KEY RATINGS

50 60 70 80 90 100

OVR 71
SPD 85
THP 94
SAC 73
DAC 74

50 60 70 80 90 100

- Start grooming Thomas to take over. His consistency and accuracy need some upgrades.
- Thomas adds an extra element to your offense. Use his athleticism to surprise the defense.

OFFENSIVE DEPTH CHART

POS	FIRST	LAST	OVR
QB	PALMER	CARSON	83
QB	STANTON	DREW	73
QB	THOMAS	LOGAN	68
HB	ELLINGTON	ANDRE	77
HB	WILLIAMS	KERWYNN	72
HB	TAYLOR	STEPFAN	72
HB	JOHNSON	DAVID	70
FB	LASIKE	PAUL	65
WR	FITZGERALD	LARRY	87
WR	FLOYD	MICHAEL	86
WR	BROWN	JOHN	79
WR	BROWN	JARON	74
WR	GOLDEN	BRITTAN	64
WR	SPADOLA	RYAN	63
TE	FELLS	DARREN	73
TE	NIKLAS	TROY	72
TE	BOLSER	TED	71
LT	VELDHEER	JARED	90
LG	IUPATI	MIKE	88
LG	STEEN	ANTHONY	65
C	SHIPLEY	A.Q.	77
C	LARSEN	TED	76
RG	COOPER	JONATHAN	77
RG	WATFORD	EARL	74
RG	MCCLAIN	ANTOINE	65
RT	MASSIE	BOBBY	79
RT	SOWELL	BRADLEY	74
RT	HUMPHRIES	D.J.	74

DEFENSIVE DEPTH CHART

POS	FIRST	LAST	OVR
LE	CAMPBELL	CALAIS	95
LE	MARTIN	KAREEM	74
LE	MAURO	JOSH	60
DT	PETERS	COREY	80
DT	TA'AMU	ALAMEDA	73
RE	RUCKER	FROSTEE	82
RE	REDDING	CORY	80
RE	STINSON	CD	66
LOLB	ALEXANDER	LORENZO	76
LOLB	OKAFOR	ALEX	73
LOLB	RIDDICK	SHAQUILLE	61
MLB	MINTER	KEVIN	78
MLB	WEATHERSPOON	SEAN	76
MLB	DEMENS	KENNY	68
MLB	CARSON	GLENN	63
ROLB	SHAUGHNESSY	MATT	79
ROLB	WOODLEY	LAMARR	77
ROLB	GOLDEN	MARKUS	64
CB	PETERSON	PATRICK	89
CB	POWERS	JERRAUD	80
CB	BETHEL	JUSTIN	72
CB	LEGREE	JIMMY	66
FS	MATHIEU	TYRANN	83
FS	CLEMONS	CHRIS	78
FS	JOHNSON	RASHAD	77
SS	BUCANNON	DEONE	77
SS	JEFFERSON	TONY	77
SS	CAMPBELL	D.J.	69

SPECIAL TEAMS

POS	FIRST	LAST	OVR
K	CATANZARO	CHANDLER	83
KR	BROWN	JOHN	79
KR	NELSON	J.J.	60
P	ZASTUDIL	DAVE	78
PR	PETERSON	PATRICK	89

BEST OFFENSIVE PLAYS

PRO TIPS

- These are the best two offensive plays in your playbook. They will get your playmakers in position to win you games.
- The Cardinals' playbook has some excellent routes to get big plays downfield, especially near the sideline.
- Don't forget about your speedy slot WR—if the defense is paying too much attention outside, send him deep.

BEST RUN: PISTOL TWIN TE FLEX—STRONG POWER

SETUP:

- Do not outrun your blockers on this play; let your LG get out in front.
- This run is hit or miss—don't force it, and consider playmakering it left if it looks bad off the right edge.
- Get your best run-blocking TE or extra lineman in the game to lock down the right edge.

ADVANCED SETUP:

- Motion your far right TE out wide (optional).

RUNNING PLAYS

1ST DOWN	2ND AND SHORT	3RD AND SHORT	GOAL LINE	2ND AND LONG	3RD AND LONG
Singleback Jumbo Pair—Counter Wk	Singleback Pair Tight Twins—HB Dive	I-Form Pro—FB Dive	Goal Line Normal—QB Sneak	Pistol Twin TE Flex—Strong Power	Gun Y-Trips Wk—Outside Zone
Singleback Ace—Cards Zone Wk	I-Form Pro Twins—HB Blast	I-Form Pro—FB Dive Fake HB Flip	Strong Pro—HB Blast	Gun Ace Twins Offset—Inside Zone	Gun Trey—HB Draw
Singleback Jumbo Pair—HB Stretch	Singleback Doubles—0 1 Trap	Weak Tight Pair—HB Gut	Strong Pro—HB Stretch	Gun Doubles—HB Base	Gun Trips HB Wk—HB Base

INSIDE RUN | OUTSIDE RUN | SHOTGUN RUN | QB RUN

BEST PASS: GUN ACE TWINS OFFSET—POSTS

SETUP/READS:

- Against zone coverage your best option is a high-point throw to the corner, or you could check down to the flat and run after the catch.
- Against man-to-man get your best route-running TE in the game on the right side. Hit your HB on the cut as a backup option.
- Against the blitz max protect before the snap and go deep downfield.

ADVANCED SETUP:

- Slant the TE on the left of the screen.

PASSING PLAYS

1ST DOWN	2ND AND SHORT	3RD AND SHORT	SHOT PLAYS	2ND AND LONG	3RD AND LONG
Singleback Ace—Skinny Posts	Gun Split Close—Close X Drag	Gun Doubles—Y Cross	I-Form Tight Pair—Post Shot	Gun Snugs—Zona Seams	Gun Split Close—WR Corner
Singleback Ace Pair—TE Attack	Gun Ace Twins Offset—Stick	Gun Bunch HB Str—Y Trail	Gun Bunch HB Str—PA Bunch Shot	Gun Bunch HB Str—Verticals	Gun Ace Twins Offset—Posts
Gun Split Close—Close FB Trail	Singleback Ace Pair Slot—Slot Post	Singleback Wing Trips—Mesh	Gun Trey—PA Post Shot	Gun Trey—Verticals Y Drag	Gun Spread—Zona Post Trail

BASE PLAY | MAN BEATER | ZONE BEATER | BLITZ BEATER

BEST DEFENSIVE PLAYS

PRO TIPS

- If you want to win more games in *Madden NFL 16*, rely on these defensive plays to lock up the run and pass.
- Bringing SS Deone Bucannon into the box for passing downs should add some size and strength over the middle.
- Sending some extra LBs off the left edge should help out your run defense.

BEST RUN D: 3-4 UNDER–WILL FIRE 3 SEAM

SETUP:

- Your outside CBs won't be much help with this specific coverage—your LBs are the key.
- Blitzing the run can be good on short yardage, but if you lose the edge containment, you risk giving up a big gain.

PLAYER TO CONTROL:

- Blitzing left-of-screen LB (contain the edge)

RUN DEFENSE

1ST DOWN	2ND AND SHORT	3RD AND SHORT	GOAL LINE	2ND AND LONG	3RD AND LONG
3-4 Odd–Cover 1 Hole	3-4 Odd–Sam Buck 1	3-4 Solid–Gap Press 0	Goal Line 5-3-3–Jam Cover 1	Nickel 2-4-5 Prowl–Cover 2 Man	Nickel 3-3-5 Wide–Cover 1 Robber
3-4 Odd–Cover 3 Sky	3-4 Odd–Will Buck 3 Press	3-4 Solid–Clamp Double Go	Goal Line 5-3-3–Flat Buzz	Nickel 2-4-5 Prowl–Cover 2 Drop	Nickel 3-3-5 Wide–Sam Will 3 Blitz

MAN COVERAGE | ZONE COVERAGE | MAN BLITZ | ZONE BLITZ

BEST PASS D: BIG DIME 2-3-6–COVER 4 PRESS

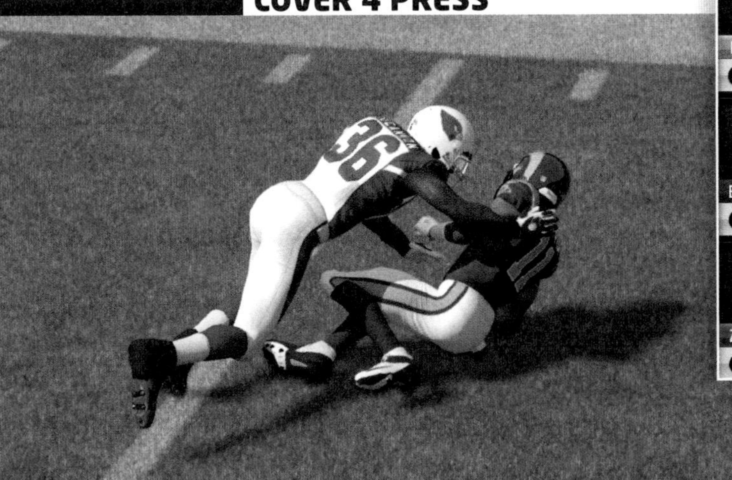

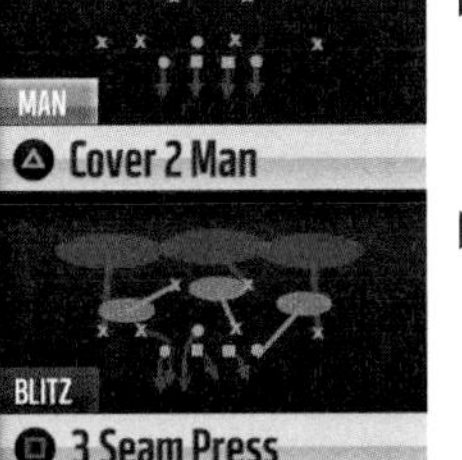

SETUP:

- Shade your coverage underneath on nearly every snap where your opponent has less than 7 yards to go for a first down.
- The press look could throw off the offense, especially with Patrick Peterson up in the WR's face.

PLAYER TO CONTROL:

- LE (finesse rush)

PASS DEFENSE

1ST DOWN	2ND AND SHORT	3RD AND SHORT	GOAL LINE	2ND AND LONG	3RD AND LONG
Nickel 2-4-5 Even–Cover 2 Sink	3-4 Even–Cov 1 Thief Show 2	3-4 Over–Sting Pinch	Goal Line 5-3-3–GL Man	Big Dime 1-4-6–DB Sting	Nickel 2-4-5 Dbl A Gap–SS Mid Combo
Nickel 2-4-5 Even–Cover 2	3-4 Even–Cover 4 Show 2	3-4 Over–Sting Pinch Zone	Goal Line 2-3-6–GL Zone	Big Dime 1-4-6–Mike SS 3 Seam	Nickel 2-4-5 Dbl A Gap–Nickel Dog 3 Buzz

MAN COVERAGE | ZONE COVERAGE | MAN BLITZ | ZONE BLITZ

SAN DIEGO CHARGERS

GAMEPLAY RATING 82

CONNECTED FRANCHISE MODE STRATEGY

CFM TEAM RATING: **81**
OFFENSE: **87**
DEFENSE: **81**
OFFENSIVE SCHEME: **Balanced**
DEFENSIVE SCHEME: **Base 3-4**
STRENGTHS: **QB, WR, TE, RE, FS**
WEAKNESSES: **LE, SS, MLB, C**

2014 TEAM RANKINGS

3rd AFC West (9-7-0)
PASSING OFFENSE: **10th**
RUSHING OFFENSE: **30th**
PASSING DEFENSE: **4th**
RUSHING DEFENSE: **26th**

2014 TEAM LEADERS

PASSING: **Philip Rivers: 4,286**
RUSHING: **Branden Oliver: 582**
RECEIVING: **Malcom Floyd: 856**
TACKLES: **Eric Weddle: 114**
SACKS: **Corey Liuget: 4.5**
INTS: **Brandon Flowers: 3**

KEY ADDITIONS

T Joe Barksdale
CB Patrick Robinson
WR Stevie Johnson
CB Jimmy Wilson
LG Orlando Franklin
WR Jacoby Jones

KEY ROOKIES

HB Melvin Gordon
LB Denzel Perryman
CB Craig Mager

OWNER: **Alex Spanos**
LEGACY SCORE: **950**

COACH: **Mike McCoy**
LEVEL: **8**
LEGACY SCORE: **60**
OFFENSIVE SCHEME: **Balanced**
DEFENSIVE SCHEME: **Base 3-4**

OFFENSIVE SCOUTING REPORT

- QB Philip Rivers is the leader in the huddle for San Diego. He has been around since 2004, and his consistency keeps the Chargers in the hunt every year. Keep him in the pocket and protected from some of the solid pass rushers in the division.
- HB Ryan Matthews is gone via free agency, and rookie Melvin Gordon is in. He will be more than ample. Use some empty sets in the passing game to take advantage of the unique skill set of Danny Woodhead. Branden Oliver could be the next Darren Sproles for the Chargers, so give him a shot on screen passes and punt returns.
- The Chargers have an excellent stable of WRs, all with different skills. Use Malcom Floyd opposite Antonio Gates in the red zone for an undefendable size advantage. Keenan Allen can run any route in the game, while TE Ladarius Green can absolutely bust seam coverage.

DEFENSIVE SCOUTING REPORT

- The Chargers have an excellent cornerstone in RE Corey Liuget. Not only is he solid against the run but he will grab some sacks and deserves to play on passing downs. At the other two spots, start Kendall Reyes and Ryan Carrethers, who aren't flashy but have the strength to hold up opposing linemen.
- LB Melvin Ingram flourished into a solid finesse rusher, but any smart coach would want to see his sack numbers increase. He will need to continue his growth because veteran Dwight Freeney is no longer in town. In the middle, you have some solid pieces that are developing into valuable starters, so keep their confidence up.
- The Chargers rebuilt their secondary in no time. Play a balanced approach between man and zone coverage because your starters can do both. The only issue could be the size against big WRs, especially in the red zone. If a mismatch happens, just add an extra defender to the area.

SCHEDULE

Week	Date	Time	Network	Opponent
1	SEP 13	4:05 PM ET	FOX	LIONS
2	SEP 20	1:00 PM ET		BENGALS
3	SEP 27	1:00 PM ET		VIKINGS
4	OCT 04	4:05 PM ET		BROWNS
5	OCT 12	8:30 PM ET	ESPN	STEELERS
6	OCT 18	4:25 PM ET		PACKERS
7	OCT 25	4:05 PM ET		RAIDERS
8	NOV 01	1:00 PM ET		RAVENS
9	NOV 09	8:30 PM ET	ESPN	BEARS
10	BYE WEEK			
11	NOV 22	8:30 PM ET	NBC	CHIEFS
12	NOV 29	1:00 PM ET		JAGUARS
13	DEC 06	4:05 PM ET		BRONCOS
14	DEC 13	1:00 PM ET		CHIEFS
15	DEC 20	4:25 PM ET		DOLPHINS
16	DEC 24	8:25 PM ET		RAIDERS
17	JAN 03	4:25 PM ET		BRONCOS

KEY PLAYERS

KEY OFFENSIVE PLAYER

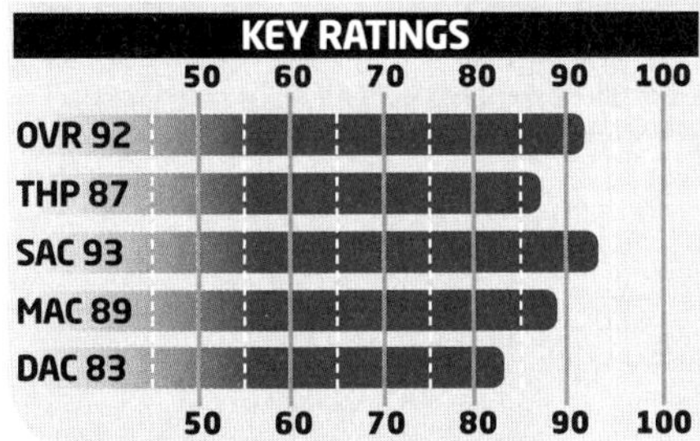

- Rivers is very effective off of play-action fakes, so make sure to establish a ground game early.
- Rivers knows when to trust his WRs to make big plays downfield. Learn the art of the "shot play" in your playbook.

KEY DEFENSIVE PLAYER

ERIC WEDDLE

#32

FS #32 HT 5'11" WT 200 COLLEGE Utah EXP 8

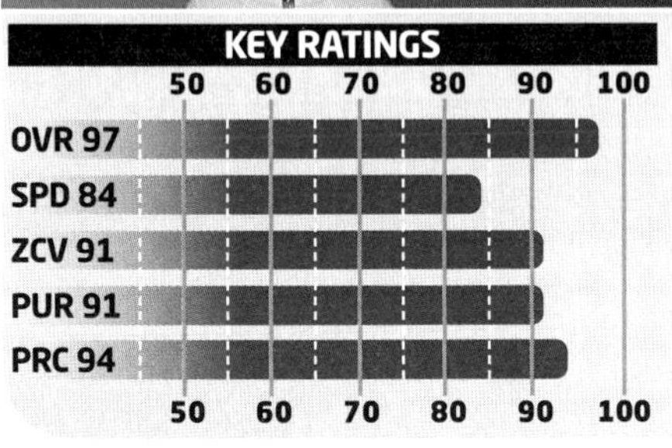

- Weddle is a player you don't have to worry about—he always seems to be around the ball no matter his assignment.
- Try to add some hit power to Weddle's game to turn him into a fumble-forcing machine; until then just go for the strip if teammates are close.

KEY ROOKIE

MELVIN GORDON

#28

HB #28 HT 6'0" WT 215 COLLEGE Wisconsin EXP Rookie

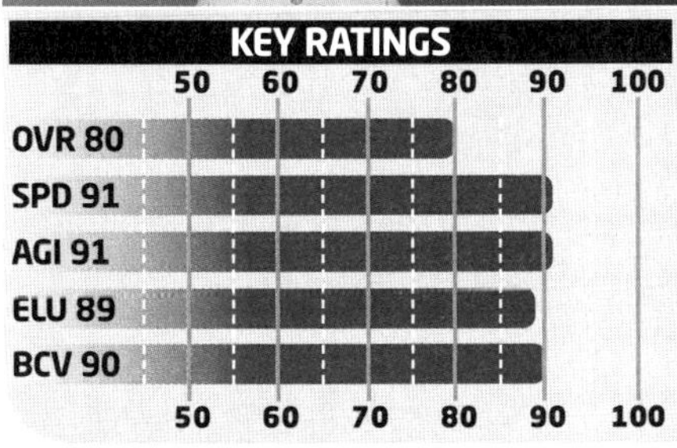

- Gordon should be your main back at the start of the season—use Danny Woodhead as a receiving option.
- Branden Oliver showed some glimpses last season, so try to find a way to use a two-back system and go with the hot hand.

KEY SLEEPER

DAVE PAULSON

#81

TE #81 HT 6'4" WT 246 COLLEGE Oregon EXP 3

KEY RATINGS

50 60 70 80 90 100

OVR 67
SPD 83
SPC 86
CIT 74
ACC 83

- Paulson could be a nice future replacement for Antonio Gates, but not until you upgrade his route running.
- Paulson has solid impact blocking and could be a nice lead blocker on runs like Inside Zone Split.

OFFENSIVE DEPTH CHART

POS	FIRST	LAST	OVR
QB	PHILIP	RIVERS	90
QB	KELLEN	CLEMENS	72
QB	BRAD	SORENSEN	63
HB	MELVIN	GORDON	78
HB	DANNY	WOODHEAD	78
HB	BRANDEN	OLIVER	77
HB	DONALD	BROWN	75
FB	DAVID	JOHNSON	78
WR	KEENAN	ALLEN	86
WR	MALCOM	FLOYD	83
WR	STEVIE	JOHNSON	83
WR	JACOBY	JONES	75
WR	AUSTIN	PETTIS	73
WR	DONTRELLE	INMAN	71
TE	ANTONIO	GATES	88
TE	LADARIUS	GREEN	78
TE	JOHN	PHILLIPS	72
LT	KING	DUNLAP	83
LT	CHRIS	HAIRSTON	74
LG	ORLANDO	FRANKLIN	90
C	CHRIS	WATT	73
C	TREVOR	ROBINSON	72
RG	JOHNNIE	TROUTMAN	70
RG	KENNY	WIGGINS	70
RT	D.J.	FLUKER	81
RT	JOE	BARKSDALE	80

DEFENSIVE DEPTH CHART

POS	FIRST	LAST	OVR
LE	KENDALL	REYES	75
LE	RICARDO	MATHEWS	75
LE	DARIUS	PHILON	63
DT	SEAN	LISSEMORE	76
DT	MITCH	UNREIN	75
DT	RYAN	CARRETHERS	72
RE	COREY	LIUGET	84
RE	TENNY	PALEPOI	68
RE	DAMION	SQUARE	66
LOLB	TOUREK	WILLIAMS	70
LOLB	CORDARRO	LAW	64
MLB	DONALD	BUTLER	78
MLB	MANTI	TE'O	78
MLB	KAVELL	CONNER	75
MLB	DENZEL	PERRYMAN	70
ROLB	MELVIN	INGRAM	79
ROLB	JEREMIAH	ATTAOCHU	73
ROLB	KYLE	EMANUEL	63
CB	BRANDON	FLOWERS	89
CB	JASON	VERRETT	82
CB	PATRICK	ROBINSON	79
CB	STEVE	WILLIAMS	75
CB	CRAIG	MAGER	67
FS	ERIC	WEDDLE	96
FS	DARRELL	STUCKEY	75
SS	JAHLEEL	ADDAE	77
SS	JIMMY	WILSON	74

SPECIAL TEAMS

POS	FIRST	LAST	OVR
K	NICK	NOVAK	81
KR	BRANDEN	OLIVER	77
KR	CHRIS	DAVIS	66
P	MIKE	SCIFRES	85
PR	KEENAN	ALLEN	86

BEST OFFENSIVE PLAYS

PRO TIPS

- **These are the best two offensive plays in your playbook. They will get your playmakers in position to win you games.**
- The Chargers are known for a downfield passing attack; make sure to set your feet to eliminate overthrown balls, which can lead to turnovers.
- The Stretch is one of the quicker handoffs in the game—flip it if the edge doesn't look open.

BEST RUN: SINGLEBACK ACE—STRETCH

SETUP:

- You should know if the stretch is going to work before the snap. Flip the run away from the strength of the defense.
- If your blockers miss their double team, cut this run back inside and fall forward for a few yards, rather than a loss.

ADVANCED SETUP:

- Playmaker to the open side of the field.

RUNNING PLAYS

1ST DOWN	2ND AND SHORT	3RD AND SHORT	GOAL LINE	2ND AND LONG	3RD AND LONG
Singleback Ace Pair Twins—HB Stretch	I-Form Pro—HB Blast	Weak Tight—FB Dive	Goal Line Normal—QB Sneak	Pistol Ace Wing—Counter Strg	Gun Split Y-Flex—Inside Zone Split
Singleback Ace—HB Zone Wk	I-Form Tight Pair—Zone Weak	Strong Pro—Stretch	I-Form Tight—FB Dive	I-Form Pro Twins—HB Lead Draw	Gun Split Y-Flex—HB Base
Singleback Ace Pair—HB Stretch	Strong Pro—HB Blast	I-Form Tight Pair—Strong Stretch	Goal Line Normal—Power O	Pistol Ace Wing—HB Stretch	Gun Y-Trips Wk—HB Counter

INSIDE RUN | OUTSIDE RUN | SHOTGUN RUN | QB RUN

BEST PASS: GUN TRIPS Y-FLEX TIGHT—VERTICALS

SETUP/READS:

- Against zone coverage wait for the deep crossing pattern to cut behind the LBs. Otherwise just hit the TE short and use the RAC (run after catch) option.
- Against man-to-man coverage, the inside WR across the middle should get open on the cut; if not, look for the curl on the left.
- This is a tough formation to blitz against. Don't forget about the HB Slip Screen in this set, which can burn aggressive opponents.

ADVANCED SETUP:

- Curl the inside slot WR.
- Block the HB (optional).

PASSING PLAYS

1ST DOWN	2ND AND SHORT	3RD AND SHORT	SHOT PLAYS	2ND AND LONG	3RD AND LONG
Pistol Ace Wing—TE Cross	Gun Spread—SD Post Trail	Gun Trey Open Charger—WR Screen	Singleback Ace Pair Twins—PA Misdirect Shot	Singleback Doubles—TE Post	Singleback Ace Pair—TE Attack
Singleback Ace—Ace Posts	Singleback Tight Doubles—PA WR Cross	I-Form Tight—Angle	Gun Trips Y-Flex Tight—PA Shot Crossers	Strong Pro—Charger Y Post	Gun Bunch Wk—Verticals
Gun Normal Y-Flex Tight—Slot Cross	Singleback Jumbo—X Post	Pistol Doubles—HB Slip Screen	I-Form Tight—Charger Fade	I-Form Pro Twins—PA Cross F Wheel	Gun Y-Trips Open—Four Verticals

BASE PLAY | MAN BEATER | ZONE BEATER | BLITZ BEATER

 For more plays and strategies for this team, visit your eGuide using the access code sheet provided.

BEST DEFENSIVE PLAYS

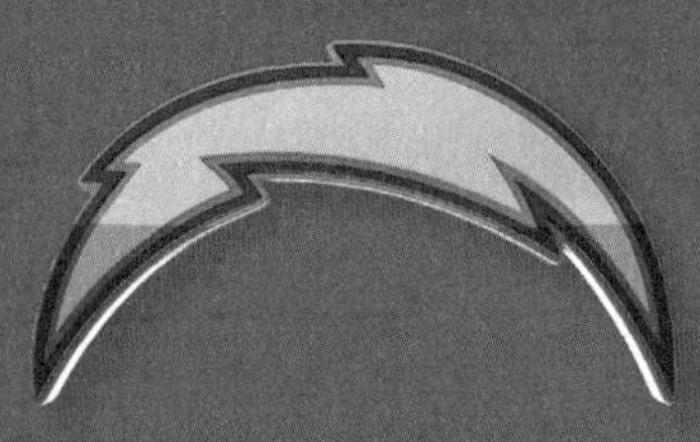

PRO TIPS

- Rely on these defensive plays to lock up the run and pass.
- Any of the Chargers' sets with three defensive linemen will be tough to run against, due to their strength.
- Melvin Ingram is your best hope to get after the QB on passing downs without sending extra pressure.

BEST RUN D: 3-4 OVER ED—SAM CRASH 3

SETUP:

- Take control of any defenders in the middle and go for a block shed.
- The Chargers should be excellent at shutting down the outside run, but you may need to blitz your LBs against runs up the gut.

PLAYER TO CONTROL:

- DT in the middle

RUN DEFENSE

1ST DOWN	2ND AND SHORT	3RD AND SHORT	GOAL LINE	2ND AND LONG	3RD AND LONG
3-4 Over—Cover 1 Hole	3-4 Odd—Cover 1 Hole	3-4 Solid—Sting Pinch	Goal Line 5-3-3—Jam Cover 1	Nickel 2-4-5 Even—Cover 2 Sink	Nickel 3-3-5—Cover 2 Invert
3-4 Over—Sam Mike 3	3-4 Odd—Sam Crash 3	3-4 Solid—Trio Sky Zone	Goal Line 5-3-3—Flat Buzz	Nickel 2-4-5 Even—Cover 2	Nickel 3-3-5—Cover 4 Drop

MAN COVERAGE | ZONE COVERAGE | MAN BLITZ | ZONE BLITZ

BEST PASS D: NICKEL 3-3-5 WIDE—COVER 4 SHOW 2

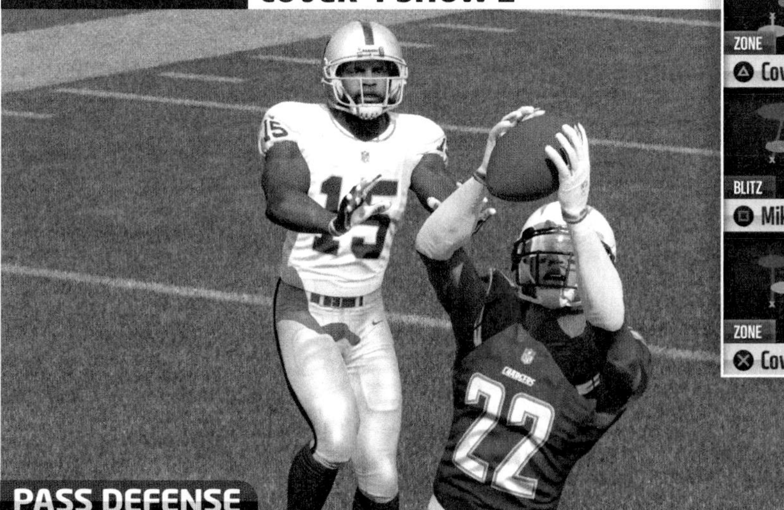

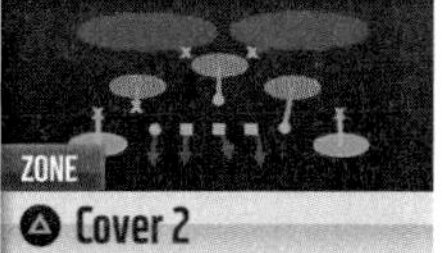

SETUP:

- The Chargers have plenty of Cover 2 looks that morph into different coverages; this is made possible by the excellent FS, Eric Weddle.
- The use of coverage shading before the snap will help your Cover 4 be more of an every-down defense. Shade underneath unless you expect a verticals concept.

PLAYER TO CONTROL:

- MLB in a hook zone

PASS DEFENSE

1ST DOWN	2ND AND SHORT	3RD AND SHORT	GOAL LINE	2ND AND LONG	3RD AND LONG
3-4 Over Ed—Cov 1 Robber Press	3-4 Under—Pinch Buck 0	Nickel 3-3-5 Wide—Cover 1 Robber	Goal Line 6-3-2—GL Man	Big Dime 2-3-6—Over Storm Brave	Nickel 2-4-5 Dbl A Gap—Mid Blitz
3-4 Over Ed—Cover 4	3-4 Under—Cross Fire 3 Buzz	Nickel 3-3-5 Wide—Sam Will 3 Blitz	Goal Line 6-3-2—GL Zone	Big Dime 2-3-6—3 Seam Press	Nickel 2-4-5 Dbl A Gap—Nickel Dog 3 Buzz

MAN COVERAGE | ZONE COVERAGE | MAN BLITZ | ZONE BLITZ

KANSAS CITY CHIEFS

GAMEPLAY RATING 82

CONNECTED FRANCHISE MODE STRATEGY

CFM TEAM RATING: **85**
OFFENSE: **85**
DEFENSE: **89**
OFFENSIVE SCHEME: **West Coast**
DEFENSIVE SCHEME: **Base 3-4**
STRENGTHS: **OLB, DT, SS, HB, TE, FB**
WEAKNESSES: **WR, C, RT**

2014 TEAM RANKINGS

2nd AFC West (9-7-0)
PASSING OFFENSE: **29th**
RUSHING OFFENSE: **10th**
PASSING DEFENSE: **2nd**
RUSHING DEFENSE: **28th**

2014 TEAM LEADERS

PASSING: **Alex Smith: 3,265**
RUSHING: **Jamaal Charles: 1,033**
RECEIVING: **Travis Kelce: 862**
TACKLES: **Josh Mauga: 103**
SACKS: **Justin Houston: 22**
INTS: **Kurt Coleman: 3**

KEY ADDITIONS

WR Jeremy Maclin
G Ben Grubbs
G Paul Fanaika
S Tyvon Branch

KEY ROOKIES

CB Marcus Peters
G Mitch Morse
WR Chris Conley

OWNER: **Clark Hunt**
LEGACY SCORE: **75**

COACH: **Andy Reid**
LEVEL: **18**
LEGACY SCORE: **2,600**
OFFENSIVE SCHEME: **West Coast**
DEFENSIVE SCHEME: **Base 3-4**

OFFENSIVE SCOUTING REPORT

- QB Alex Smith is average across the board. He won't win you many games, but with a solid rushing attack and sound defense, he won't lose you any either. Keep Smith as your starter until his Throw Power rating dips below 80.
- The Chiefs should rely on HB Jamaal Charles as much as possible; however, Knile Davis is a great short-yardage back who can keep the chains moving and give Charles a rest. FB Anthony Sherman is one of the league's best FBs, especially for a power running attack.
- The signing of WR Jeremy Maclin to go along with TE Travis Kelce should make the running game easier. Kelce is also a very solid run blocker and should almost always be on the field. Continue to develop the young talent at WR and the Chiefs' lineup will slowly get more explosive.

DEFENSIVE SCOUTING REPORT

- The defensive line for the Chiefs is strong and will do a great job against the run. DT Dontari Poe will shut down running lanes in the middle with his 97 Strength rating. LE Allen Bailey's contract is up at the end of the season, and we think you should let him test free agency.
- The Chiefs' LBs are tops in the NFL for all-around talent and rushing the passer. By user-controlling James-Michael Johnson, you add another athlete to the middle who has solid hit power and can stop the run. Continue to work on finesse moves for LB Dee Ford so he can fill in for anyone who gets injured or can't be signed long term.
- CB Sean Smith is the physical talent that teams dream of, but his deal is up at the end of the season. You will need to bring him back long term to shut down all the talented WRs in the division.

SCHEDULE

Week	Date	Time	Opponent
1	SEP 13	1:00 PM ET	TEXANS
2	SEP 17	8:25 PM ET	BRONCOS
3	SEP 28	8:30 PM ET	PACKERS
4	OCT 04	1:00 PM ET	BENGALS
5	OCT 11	1:00 PM ET	BEARS
6	OCT 18	1:00 PM ET	VIKINGS
7	OCT 25	1:00 PM ET	STEELERS
8	NOV 01	9:30 PM ET	LIONS
9	BYE WEEK		
10	NOV 15	4:25 PM ET	BRONCOS
11	NOV 22	8:30 PM ET	CHARGERS
12	NOV 29	1:00 PM ET	BILLS
13	DEC 06	4:05 PM ET	RAIDERS
14	DEC 13	1:00 PM ET	CHARGERS
15	DEC 20	1:00 PM ET	RAVENS
16	DEC 27	1:00 PM ET	BROWNS
17	JAN 03	1:00 PM ET	RAIDERS

KEY PLAYERS

KEY OFFENSIVE PLAYER

JAMAAL CHARLES #25

HB #25 HT 5'11" WT 199 COLLEGE Texas EXP 7

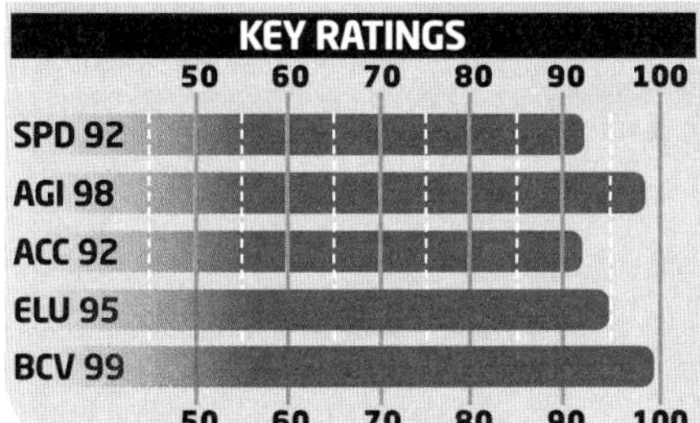

- Charles has an insane 86 Catch rating, which is higher than many WRs in the league.
- Utilize Charles on an every-down basis until he requires a rest—his juke is the best way to beat a defender in the open field if you can't simply outrun him.

KEY DEFENSIVE PLAYER

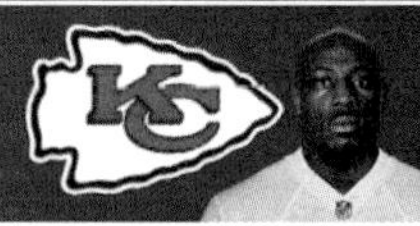

JUSTIN HOUSTON #50

LOLB #50 HT 6'3" WT 258 COLLEGE Georgia EXP 4

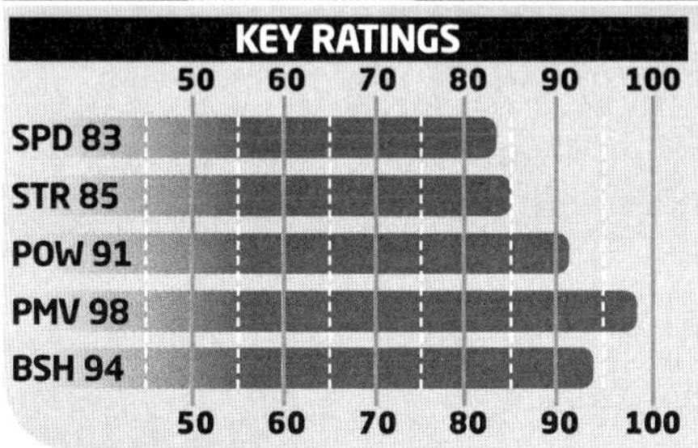

- Houston is the best pass-rushing LB in the NFL. Don't worry about his matchup or even double teams.
- Houston benefits from Tamba Hali on the other side, but he is also an excellent run defender with great ability to shed blocks.

KEY ROOKIE

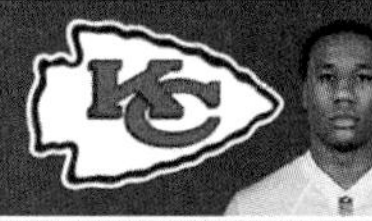

MARCUS PETERS #22

CB #22 HT 6'0" WT 197 COLLEGE Washington EXP Rookie

KEY RATINGS

OVR 75
SPD 88
ZCV 86
PRS 89
MCV 81

- Peters has solid size and an excellent Press rating at this stage of his career. He is a perfect fit to play alongside Sean Smith.
- Phillip Gaines is also a very solid corner with good size and speed. The Chiefs are a very solid zone defense team.

KEY SLEEPER

CHRIS CONLEY #17

WR #17 HT 6'2" WT 213 COLLEGE Georgia EXP Rookie

KEY RATINGS

OVR 70
SPD 94
ACC 93
CIT 84
JMP 97

- Conley is a solid physical talent, but you will need to upgrade his route running to make him an overall threat.
- While Alex Smith isn't a QB who tends to throw downfield, Conley is the type of player who could win you some one-on-one matchups.

OFFENSIVE DEPTH CHART

POS	FIRST	LAST	OVR
QB	ALEX	SMITH	84
QB	CHASE	DANIEL	72
QB	AARON	MURRAY	68
HB	JAMAAL	CHARLES	94
HB	KNILE	DAVIS	80
HB	CYRUS	GRAY	66
HB	CHARCANDRICK	WEST	64
FB	ANTHONY	SHERMAN	95
FB	SPENCER	WARE	69
WR	JEREMY	MACLIN	88
WR	JASON	AVANT	75
WR	ALBERT	WILSON	73
WR	DE'ANTHONY	THOMAS	73
WR	JUNIOR	HEMINGWAY	71
WR	FRANKIE	HAMMOND	66
TE	TRAVIS	KELCE	91
TE	RICHARD	GORDON	71
TE	DEMETRIUS	HARRIS	66
LT	ERIC	FISHER	75
LT	TAVON	ROOKS	63
LG	BEN	GRUBBS	85
LG	LAURENT	DUVERNAY-TARDIF	68
C	ERIC	KUSH	71
C	MITCH	MORSE	66
RG	JEFF	ALLEN	75
RG	PAUL	FANAIKA	74
RG	ZACH	FULTON	74
RT	DONALD	STEPHENSON	77
RT	DEREK	SHERROD	73

DEFENSIVE DEPTH CHART

POS	FIRST	LAST	OVR
LE	JAYE	HOWARD	80
LE	NICK	WILLIAMS	72
LE	VAUGHN	MARTIN	72
DT	DONTARI	POE	87
DT	CHARLES	TUAAU	59
RE	MIKE	DEVITO	85
RE	ALLEN	BAILEY	81
RE	MIKE	CATAPANO	68
LOLB	JUSTIN	HOUSTON	97
LOLB	DEE	FORD	74
LOLB	FRANK	ZOMBO	73
MLB	DERRICK	JOHNSON	88
MLB	JAMES-MICHAEL	JOHNSON	75
MLB	JOSH	MAUGA	74
MLB	RAMIK	WILSON	63
ROLB	TAMBA	HALI	90
ROLB	JOSH	MARTIN	68
ROLB	DEZMAN	MOSES	67
CB	SEAN	SMITH	91
CB	PHILLIP	GAINES	77
CB	MARCUS	PETERS	74
CB	SANDERS	COMMINGS	72
CB	JAMELL	FLEMING	71
FS	HUSAIN	ABDULLAH	81
FS	KELCIE	MCCRAY	69
FS	DANIEL	SORENSEN	64
SS	TYVON	BRANCH	84
SS	RON	PARKER	82

SPECIAL TEAMS

POS	FIRST	LAST	OVR
K	CAIRO	SANTOS	72
KR	KNILE	DAVIS	80
KR	FRANKIE	HAMMOND	66
P	DUSTIN	COLQUITT	86
PR	DE'ANTHONY	THOMAS	73

BEST OFFENSIVE PLAYS

PRO TIPS

- These are the best two offensive plays in your playbook. They will get your playmakers in position to win you games.
- The Chiefs have one of the best HBs in the entire game; call plenty of runs that take advantage of Charles's speed.
- The Kansas City offense is not known for deep passing plays, but take a shot once per half, because otherwise things get too congested.

BEST RUN: PISTOL STRONG TWINS–F LEAD READ OPTION

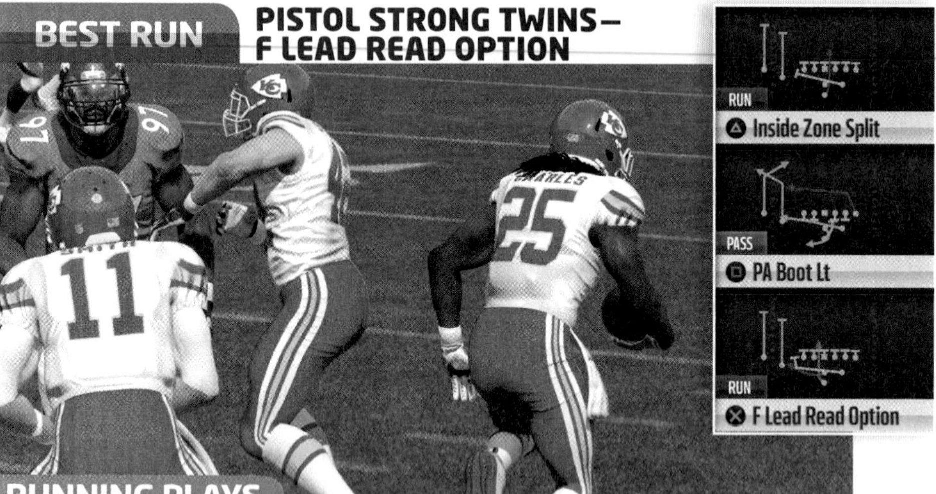

SETUP:

- This run combines the best of the HB Counter and the Inside Zone Split and into one play! You can always choose either of those runs instead.
- If you don't feel like taking a risk with the QB run, go with the HB Zone, which is still an excellent play.

ADVANCED SETUP:

- Motion the FB to the right (optional).

RUNNING PLAYS

1ST DOWN	2ND AND SHORT	3RD AND SHORT	GOAL LINE	2ND AND LONG	3RD AND LONG
Singleback Ace Twins–HB Stretch	Singleback Ace–0 1 Trap	Strong Pro–FB Dive	Goal Line Normal–QB Sneak	Pistol Strong Twins–HB Counter	Pistol Ace–Strong Power
I-Form Twins Flex–HB Zone	Weak Close–HB Gut	Singleback Jumbo Pair–KC Power 0	I-Form Pro–FB Dive Strong	Pistol Strong Twins–Inside Zone Split	Gun Trips Y-Flex Tight–Inside Zone
Strong Tight Pair–HB Toss	I-Form Tight–HB Zone Wk	Singleback Y-Trips–HB Toss Strong	I-Form Pro–FB Fake HB Flip	Pistol Strong Twins–F Lead Read Option	Gun Trips TE–HB Counter

INSIDE RUN | OUTSIDE RUN | SHOTGUN RUN | QB RUN

BEST PASS: GUN TRIPS Y-FLEX TIGHT–FLOOD HB ANGLE

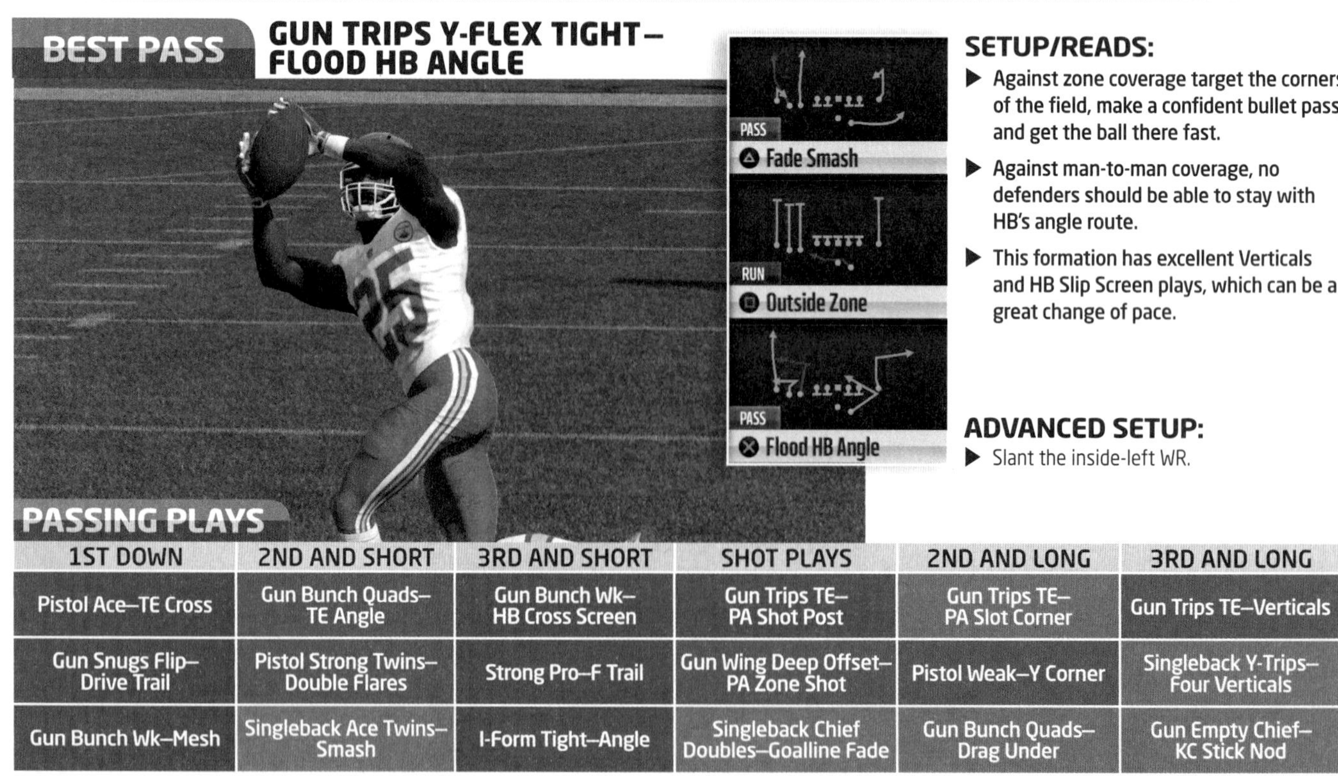

SETUP/READS:

- Against zone coverage target the corners of the field, make a confident bullet pass, and get the ball there fast.
- Against man-to-man coverage, no defenders should be able to stay with HB's angle route.
- This formation has excellent Verticals and HB Slip Screen plays, which can be a great change of pace.

ADVANCED SETUP:

- Slant the inside-left WR.

PASSING PLAYS

1ST DOWN	2ND AND SHORT	3RD AND SHORT	SHOT PLAYS	2ND AND LONG	3RD AND LONG
Pistol Ace–TE Cross	Gun Bunch Quads–TE Angle	Gun Bunch Wk–HB Cross Screen	Gun Trips TE–PA Shot Post	Gun Trips TE–PA Slot Corner	Gun Trips TE–Verticals
Gun Snugs Flip–Drive Trail	Pistol Strong Twins–Double Flares	Strong Pro–F Trail	Gun Wing Deep Offset–PA Zone Shot	Pistol Weak–Y Corner	Singleback Y-Trips–Four Verticals
Gun Bunch Wk–Mesh	Singleback Ace Twins–Smash	I-Form Tight–Angle	Singleback Chief Doubles–Goalline Fade	Gun Bunch Quads–Drag Under	Gun Empty Chief–KC Stick Nod

BASE PLAY | MAN BEATER | ZONE BEATER | BLITZ BEATER

 For more plays and strategies for this team, visit your eGuide using the access code sheet provided.

BEST DEFENSIVE PLAYS

PRO TIPS

- **Rely on these defensive plays to lock up the run and pass.**
- Any of the Chiefs' 3-4 formations should be able to stop the run off the edge, thanks to their excellent LBs.
- The Chiefs don't need to send many blitzes to get pressure on the QB, which is a huge bonus for their pass defense.

BEST RUN D: 3-4 ODD OVER–COVER 6 PRESS

SETUP:

- Start with the 3 Cloud Show 2 in this formation to see if you can get pressure only rushing four.
- Crashing your defensive line down and blitzing your LBs is the fastest way to guarantee a free rusher.
- Make sure to use QB contain before the snap when facing a mobile QB.

PLAYER TO CONTROL:

- LB on left of screen (power rush)

RUN DEFENSE

1ST DOWN	2ND AND SHORT	3RD AND SHORT	GOAL LINE	2ND AND LONG	3RD AND LONG
3-4 Bear–Cover 1 Hole	3-4 Over–Cover 2 Man	3-4 Over–Sting Pinch	Goal Line 5-4-2–Jam Cover 1	Nickel 3-3-5 Wide–Cover 1 Robber	Nickel 3-3-5 Wide–Cover 2 Man
3-4 Bear–Cover 3	3-4 Over–Will Buck 3 Press	3-4 Over–Sting Pinch Zone	Goal Line 5-4-2–Flat Buzz	Nickel 3-3-5 Wide–Cover 3 Buzz	Nickel 3-3-5 Wide–3 Sam SS Blitz

MAN COVERAGE | ZONE COVERAGE | MAN BLITZ | ZONE BLITZ

BEST PASS D: NICKEL 2-4-5 DBL A GAP–WILL 3 BUZZ

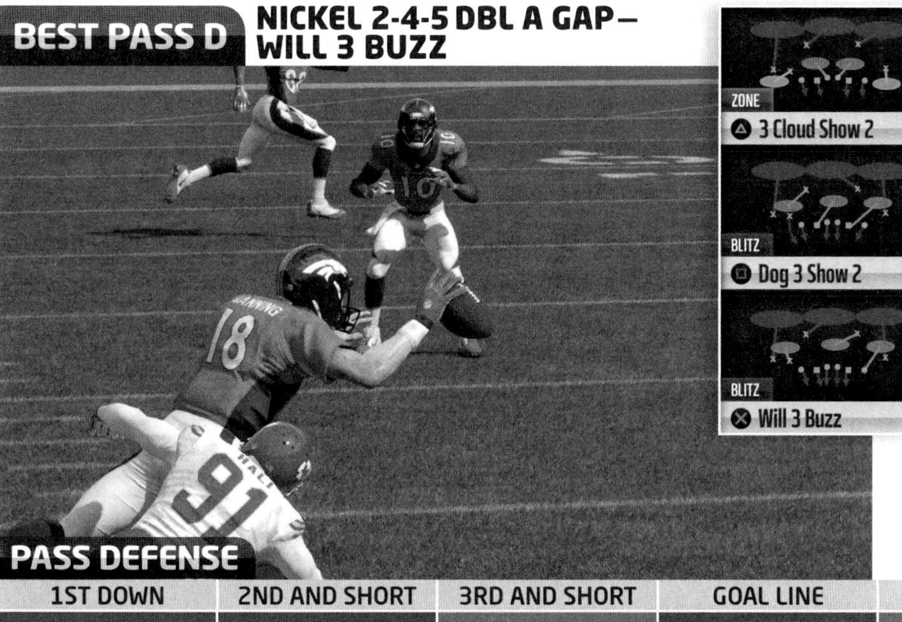

SETUP:

- The LB running out to the flat will help contain any outside runs.
- The Chiefs have an excellent front seven and shouldn't need much help from safeties in the run game. Avoid showing blitz most of the game.

PLAYER TO CONTROL:

- CB in the flat zone on the left of the screen

PASS DEFENSE

1ST DOWN	2ND AND SHORT	3RD AND SHORT	GOAL LINE	2ND AND LONG	3RD AND LONG
3-4 Solid–Cover 2 Man	3-4 Bear–1 QB Contain	3-4 Bear–Will Sam 1	Goal Line 5-3-3–GL Man	Nickel 2-4-5–Cover 1 LB Blitz	Big Dime 2-3-6–1 Robber Show 2
3-4 Solid–Trio Sky Zone	3-4 Bear–Cover 2 Invert	3-4 Bear–Pinch Dog 3	Goal Line 5-3-3–Pinch Zone	Nickel 2-4-5–Buck Slant 3	Big Dime 2-3-6–3 Bluff Press

MAN COVERAGE | ZONE COVERAGE | MAN BLITZ | ZONE BLITZ

INDIANAPOLIS COLTS

GAMEPLAY RATING 87

CONNECTED FRANCHISE MODE STRATEGY

CFM TEAM RATING: **80**
OFFENSE: **85**
DEFENSE: **77**
OFFENSIVE SCHEME: **Balanced**
DEFENSIVE SCHEME: **Base 3-4**
STRENGTHS: **QB, WR, TE, CB**
WEAKNESSES: **DT, RE, C, RT**

2014 TEAM RANKINGS

1st AFC South (11-5-0)
PASSING OFFENSE: **1st**
RUSHING OFFENSE: **22nd**
PASSING DEFENSE: **12th**
RUSHING DEFENSE: **18th**

2014 TEAM LEADERS

PASSING: **Andrew Luck: 4,761**
RUSHING: **Trent Richardson: 519**
RECEIVING: **T.Y. Hilton: 1,345**
TACKLES: **D'Qwell Jackson: 138**
SACKS: **Jonathan Newsome: 6.5**
INTS: **Mike Adams: 5**

KEY ADDITIONS

HB Frank Gore
LB Trent Cole
WR Andre Johnson

KEY ROOKIES

WR Phillip Dorsett
CB D'Joun Smith
DE Henry Anderson

OWNER: **Jim Irsay**
LEGACY SCORE: **2,400**

COACH: **Chuck Pagano**
LEVEL: **21**
LEGACY SCORE: **750**
OFFENSIVE SCHEME: **Balanced**
DEFENSIVE SCHEME: **Base 3-4**

OFFENSIVE SCOUTING REPORT

- QB Andrew Luck is worth whatever it takes to keep him as the face of your franchise. His development over the early part of his career has him on track to become one of the all-time greats.
- The Colts brought in a veteran leader in HB Frank Gore to take over the bulk of the carries. Gore is a good stop-gap, but keep developing a long-term backup or look for one in the draft. It will be tough to run behind this line for any non-elite player.
- The Colts brought in another veteran with former Texans great Andre Johnson. Keep the focus on developing T.Y. Hilton, who has been excellent and developed a great chemistry with Luck. Work on developing your two young rookies to give Luck options in the future.

DEFENSIVE SCOUTING REPORT

- Robert Mathis couldn't replicate his amazing production at LB last season, but we expect him to rebound and be a very solid option. The addition of Trent Cole gives the Colts a versatile option who can help out as a stand-up rusher or as a down lineman.
- The Colts' defensive line doesn't have the necessary strength to take on multiple blockers and free up the LBs behind them. Give Josh Chapman the start at DT, but look to improve this position through free agency or the draft.
- The Colts' secondary was above average last season but needs to be more active in the run game, or teams won't have to throw much. Allow Vontae Davis to continue to be the anchor, and help him out by finding a rangy safety to play on the other side.

SCHEDULE

Week	Date	Time	Network	Opponent
1	SEP 13	1:00 PM ET		AT BILLS
2	SEP 21	8:30 PM ET	ESPN	JETS
3	SEP 27	1:00 PM ET		AT TITANS
4	OCT 04	1:00 PM ET		JAGUARS
5	OCT 08	8:25 PM ET		AT TEXANS
6	OCT 18	8:30 PM ET	NBC	PATRIOTS
7	OCT 25	1:00 PM ET	FOX	SAINTS
8	NOV 02	8:30 PM ET	ESPN	AT PANTHERS
9	NOV 08	4:25 PM ET		BRONCOS
10	BYE WEEK			
11	NOV 22	1:00 PM ET		AT FALCONS
12	NOV 29	1:00 PM ET	FOX	BUCCANEERS
13	DEC 06	8:30 PM ET	NBC	AT STEELERS
14	DEC 13	1:00 PM ET		AT JAGUARS
15	DEC 20	1:00 PM ET		TEXANS
16	DEC 27	1:00 PM ET		AT DOLPHINS
17	JAN 03	1:00 PM ET		TITANS

KEY PLAYERS

KEY OFFENSIVE PLAYER

ANDREW LUCK

QB #12 HT 6'4" WT 240 COLLEGE Stanford EXP 3

KEY RATINGS

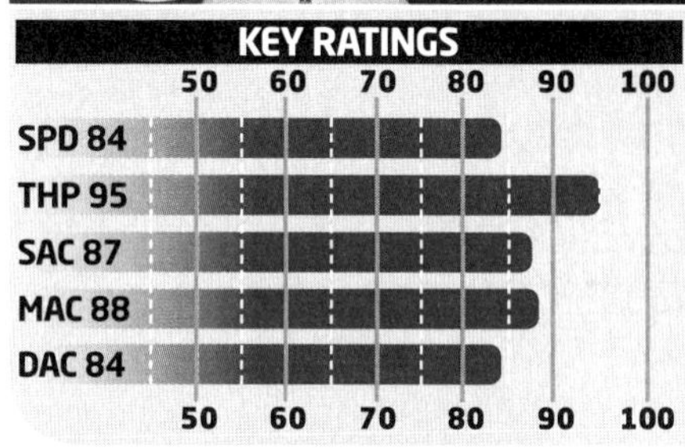

- Luck proved that he has not just a powerful arm but an accurate one by improving his deep game last season.
- Luck's speed is a small bonus, but only use it in the red zone to keep him healthy.

KEY DEFENSIVE PLAYER

VONTAE DAVIS

CB #21 HT 5'11" WT 207 COLLEGE Illinois EXP 6

KEY RATINGS

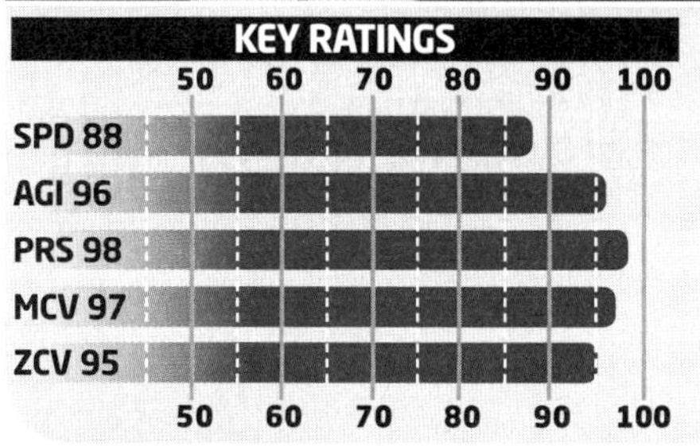

- Davis is one of the most physical corners in the league—use that Press rating to throw off the timing of the QB/WR.
- Consider giving Darius Butler the start at CB #2 to allow Davis to play more man coverage.

KEY ROOKIE

PHILLIP DORSETT

#15

WR #15 HT 5'10" WT 185 COLLEGE Miami EXP Rookie

KEY RATINGS

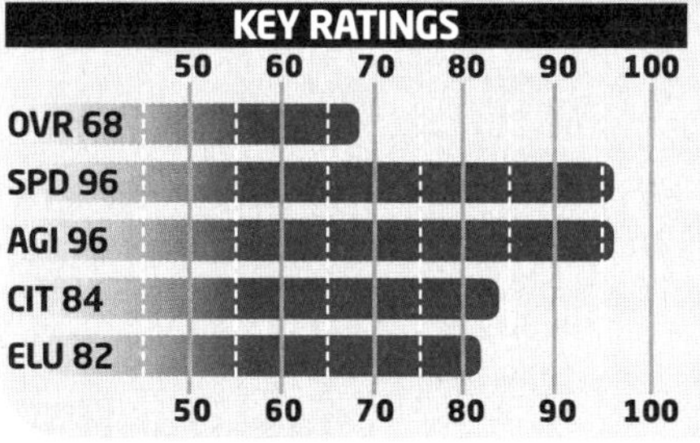

- Dorsett is a burner who can also be used on special teams. Find a few shot plays for him in practice.
- Fellow rookie WR Duron Carter has the size to make this draft class a real winner in a few seasons.

KEY SLEEPER

JONATHAN NEWSOME

LOLB #91 HT 6'3" WT 251 COLLEGE Ball State EXP 1

KEY RATINGS

50 60 70 80 90 100

OVR 79
SPD 81
ACC 87
PMV 88
POW 86

- Newsome isn't a true sleeper, because he flashed during his rookie year, but keep an eye on that hit power and find a way to harness it.
- Newsome isn't a great run defender; use him mainly as a pass rusher and upgrade those ratings first.

OFFENSIVE DEPTH CHART

POS	FIRST	LAST	OVR
QB	ANDREW	LUCK	94
QB	MATT	HASSELBECK	73
QB	BRYAN	BENNETT	60
HB	FRANK	GORE	83
HB	DANIEL	HERRON	75
HB	VICK	BALLARD	72
HB	ZURLON	TIPTON	69
FB	TYLER	VARGA	60
WR	T.Y.	HILTON	89
WR	ANDRE	JOHNSON	86
WR	DONTE	MONCRIEF	76
WR	PHILLIP	DORSETT	73
WR	GRIFF	WHALEN	72
WR	VINCENT	BROWN	71
TE	TRAVIS	KELCE	91
TE	RICHARD	GORDON	71
TE	DEMETRIUS	HARRIS	66
LT	ERIC	FISHER	75
LT	TAVON	ROOKS	63
LG	JACK	MEWHORT	80
LG	DONALD	THOMAS	78
LG	DAVID	ARKIN	67
C	JONOTTHAN	HARRISON	72
C	KHALED	HOLMES	71
RG	TODD	HERREMANS	78
RG	HUGH	THORNTON	76
RG	LANCE	LOUIS	73
RT	GOSDER	CHERILUS	80

DEFENSIVE DEPTH CHART

POS	FIRST	LAST	OVR
LE	KENDALL	LANGFORD	80
LE	KELCY	QUARLES	64
DT	JOSH	CHAPMAN	74
DT	MONTORI	HUGHES	70
DT	DAVID	PARRY	67
RE	ARTHUR	JONES	74
RE	HENRY	ANDERSON	71
RE	ZACH	KERR	69
LOLB	TRENT	COLE	82
LOLB	ERIK	WALDEN	79
LOLB	JONATHAN	NEWSOME	75
MLB	D'QWELL	JACKSON	82
MLB	NATE	IRVING	79
MLB	JERRELL	FREEMAN	76
MLB	HENOC	MUAMBA	63
ROLB	ROBERT	MATHIS	87
ROLB	BJOERN	WERNER	74
CB	VONTAE	DAVIS	95
CB	DARIUS	BUTLER	79
CB	GREG	TOLER	79
CB	JALIL	BROWN	70
CB	D'JOUN	SMITH	69
FS	DWIGHT	LOWERY	80
FS	DEWEY	MCDONALD	68
SS	MIKE	ADAMS	85
SS	COLT	ANDERSON	71
SS	CLAYTON	GEATHERS	65

SPECIAL TEAMS

POS	FIRST	LAST	OVR
K	ADAM	VINATIERI	90
KR	DANIEL	HERRON	75
KR	VINCENT	BROWN	71
P	PAT	MCAFEE	95
PR	T.Y.	HILTON	89

BEST OFFENSIVE PLAYS

PRO TIPS

- **These are the best two offensive plays in your playbook. They will get your playmakers in position to win you games.**
- **The Colts are an excellent passing team, but they still have plenty of solid under-center formations to pound the ball.**
- **The Gun Split Close has been a reliable formation for a few seasons now.**

BEST RUN: SINGLEBACK WING TRIPS OPEN—HB STRETCH

SETUP:

- The stretch is an extremely quick handoff; make sure to get in behind your TE, who is an excellent run blocker.
- Once the defense catches on, pound the ball up the middle with your veteran back, who is built for power runs.

ADVANCED SETUP:

- Playmaker the run to the left side.

RUNNING PLAYS

1ST DOWN	2ND AND SHORT	3RD AND SHORT	GOAL LINE	2ND AND LONG	3RD AND LONG
Singleback Ace—Weak Zone	I-Form Twins Flex—HB Lead Dive	I-Form Tackle Over—Inside Zone	Goal Line Normal—QB Sneak	Pistol Slot Wing—Counter Y	Gun Trey Open—Read Option
Singleback Wing Trips Open—Inside Zone Split	I-Form Pro—HB Lead	Weak Pro—Toss Weak	I-Form Tight—Iso	Pistol Y-Trips—Strong Power	Gun Trey Open—HB Counter
Strong Tight Pair—Inside Zone Split	Strong Pro—HB Dive	Pistol Slot Wing—Inside Zone Split	Goal Line Normal—Power O	Gun Split Close—Power O	Gun Double Flex—Inside Zone

INSIDE RUN | OUTSIDE RUN | SHOTGUN RUN | QB RUN

BEST PASS: GUN SPLIT CLOSE—FB TRAIL

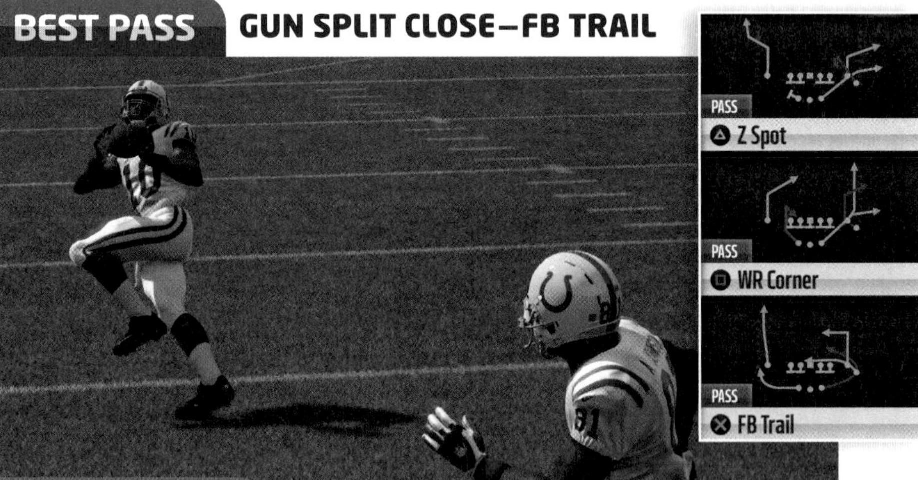

SETUP/READS:

- Against zone coverage look to swing the ball out to the flat before checking the middle of the field.
- The close alignment of the formation makes it very difficult for man defenders to line up against.
- Consider adding a second TE to the formation to give you a bigger window to throw the ball.

ADVANCED SETUP:

- Slant the slot WR.

PASSING PLAYS

1ST DOWN	2ND AND SHORT	3RD AND SHORT	SHOT PLAYS	2ND AND LONG	3RD AND LONG
Gun Split Close—HB Wheel	Gun Doubles—Drive	Singleback Ace Close—Tight Slots TE Angle	Singleback Ace—PA Misdirection Shot	Pistol Y-Trips—PA Read	Gun Bunch TE—Curl Flat Corner
Gun Doubles—Curls Slot Shakw	Gun Bunch TE—Mesh	I-Form Pro—Mid Attack	Singleback Wing Trips Open—PA Fork	Pistol Y-Trips—Smash	Gun Trey Open—Four Verticals
Gun Y-Trips HB Wk—PA Read	Singleback Bunch Ace—TE Angle	Gun Split Close—FB Trail	Gun Y-Trips Open—PA Switch Shot	Singleback Bunch Ace—Four Verticals	Gun Empty Trey Flex—Four Verticals

BASE PLAY | MAN BEATER | ZONE BEATER | BLITZ BEATER

 For more plays and strategies for this team, visit your eGuide using the access code sheet provided.

BEST DEFENSIVE PLAYS

PRO TIPS

- **If you want to win more games in *Madden NFL 16*, rely on these defensive plays to lock up the run and pass.**
- Commit to stopping the run early in the game, even if it means showing blitz before the snap.
- Nickel 2-4-5 Dbl A Gap is a new formation in the game this year, and it's extremely versatile.

BEST RUN D: 3-4 PREDATOR–MIKE SCRAPE 3 PRESS

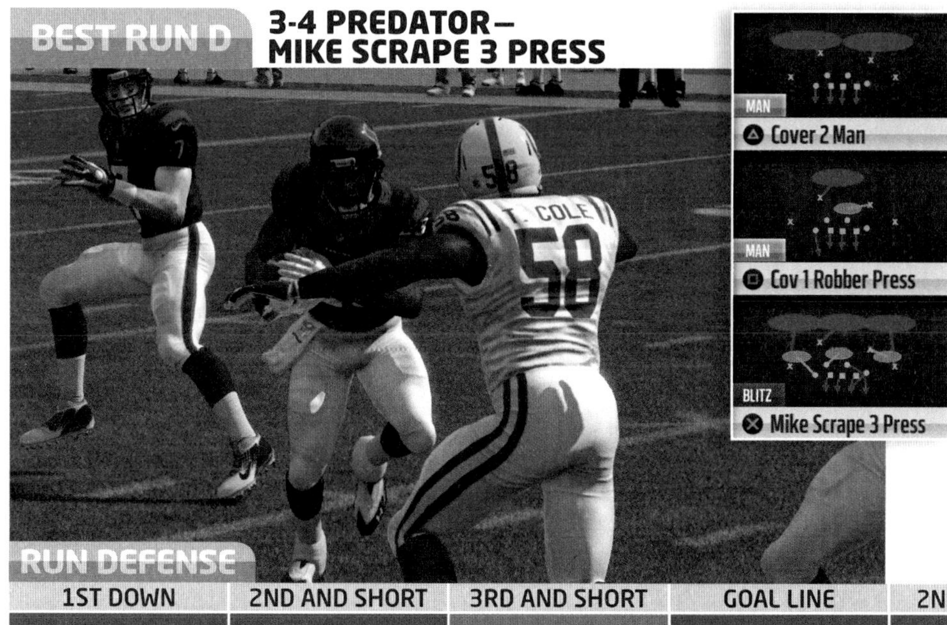

MAN — △ Cover 2 Man

MAN — ▢ Cov 1 Robber Press

BLITZ — ⊗ Mike Scrape 3 Press

SETUP:

- Notice that the blitzer takes a wide rush angle to contain the edge. If you want him to stuff a run in the middle, reblitz him straight down.
- There are more aggressive calls in the Colts' playbook, but start here to get a feel for your opponent.

PLAYER TO CONTROL:

- FS in a deep zone

RUN DEFENSE

1ST DOWN	2ND AND SHORT	3RD AND SHORT	GOAL LINE	2ND AND LONG	3RD AND LONG
3-4 Bear–Cover 1 Hole	3-4 Even–1 QB Contain	3-4 Bear–Will Sam 1	Goal Line 5-4-2–Jam Cover 1	Nickel 2-4-5 Prowl–Cover 2 Man	Big Dime 2-3-6 Flex–Cover 2 Sink
3-4 Bear–Cover 3	3-4 Even–Cross Fire 3	3-4 Bear–Cover 2 Invert	Goal Line 5-4-2–Flat Buzz	Nickel 2-4-5 Prowl–Cover 2 Drop	Big Dime 2-3-6 Flex–Max Sting 3

MAN COVERAGE | ZONE COVERAGE | MAN BLITZ | ZONE BLITZ

BEST PASS D: NICKEL 2-4-5 DBL A GAP–NICKEL OVERLOAD 3

ZONE — △ Cover 3 Show 2

BLITZ — ▢ Nickel Dog 2

BLITZ — ⊗ Nickel Overload 3

SETUP:

- This idea behind this set is to bring pressure early off the edge before retreating to a Cover 3 Show 2 to stop the flat pass.
- This formation has an excellent alignment to contain mobile QBs.
- The Colts are capable of mixing in some man-to-man coverage, so test your opponents early to see if they can beat the press.

PLAYER TO CONTROL:

- LB on the right of the screen (hook zone)

PASS DEFENSE

1ST DOWN	2ND AND SHORT	3RD AND SHORT	GOAL LINE	2ND AND LONG	3RD AND LONG
Nickel 2-4-5–Cover 2 Man	Nickel 3-3-5 Wide–Cover 1 Robber	3-4 Predator–1 Thief Show 2	Goal Line 5-3-3–GL Man	Nickel 2-4-5 Dbl A Gap–Cover 1 Hole	Big Dime 2-3-6 Even–Silver Shoot Pinch
Nickel 2-4-5–Cover 2 Press	Nickel 3-3-5 Wide–Sam Will 3 Blitz	3-4 Predator–Will Fire 3 Seam	Goal Line 5-3-3–Pinch Zone	Nickel 2-4-5 Dbl A Gap–Will 3 Buzz	Big Dime 2-3-6 Even–Cross Fire 3 Seam

MAN COVERAGE | ZONE COVERAGE | MAN BLITZ | ZONE BLITZ

DALLAS COWBOYS

GAMEPLAY RATING 86

CONNECTED FRANCHISE MODE STRATEGY

CFM TEAM RATING: **89**
OFFENSE: **97**
DEFENSE: **85**
OFFENSIVE SCHEME: **Balanced**
DEFENSIVE SCHEME: **Base 4-3**
STRENGTHS: **QB, WR, OL, TE**
WEAKNESSES: **HB, SS, FB**

2014 TEAM RANKINGS

1st NFC East (12-4-0)
PASSING OFFENSE: **16th**
RUSHING OFFENSE: **2nd**
PASSING DEFENSE: **26th**
RUSHING DEFENSE: **8th**

2014 TEAM LEADERS

PASSING: **Tony Romo: 3,705**
RUSHING: **DeMarco Murray: 1,845**
RECEIVING: **Dez Bryant: 1,320**
TACKLES: **Barry Church: 97**
SACKS: **Jeremy Mincey: 6**
INTS: **Bruce Carter: 5**

KEY ADDITIONS

DE Greg Hardy
LB Jasper Brinkley
WR A.J. Jenkins
HB Darren McFadden

KEY ROOKIES

CB Byron Jones
LB Randy Gregory
T Chaz Green

OWNER: **Jerry Jones**
LEGACY SCORE: **9,625**

COACH: **Jason Garrett**
LEVEL: **9**
LEGACY SCORE: **250**
OFFENSIVE SCHEME: **Balanced**
DEFENSIVE SCHEME: **Base 4-3**

OFFENSIVE SCOUTING REPORT

- QB Tony Romo is an incredibly consistent player and will allow your team to be in the hunt every season. While his speed may be slowing down a bit, he is smarter and more elusive against the rush, which allows him to keep plays alive until a WR breaks open downfield.
- The Cowboys lost their feature HB from last season, DeMarco Murray, when he signed with division rival Philadelphia. The good news is the Cowboys' offensive line is a dominant one and should help another player emerge to take the lead role .
- WR Dez Bryant has consistently proven that he is one of the top WRs in the game. Dallas goes to him in all their big moments, and he is worth whatever it takes to keep him a Cowboy for the long term. Keep developing the young stars at the TE position to help take the pressure off QB Tony Romo and eventually find a replacement for the reliable Jason Witten.

DEFENSIVE SCOUTING REPORT

- The Cowboys' defensive front has undergone a big transformation over the last few seasons but finally has an identity. Greg Hardy, DeMarcus Lawrence and Randy Gregory should cause some havoc for opposing passers.
- LB Sean Lee is one of the best defenders in the league when healthy, so give him plenty of zone assignments and watch him have a huge season. Consider signing MLB Rolando McClain to an extension before his contract comes up; he has proven he has more than just the size required to be a star player in the league.
- CB Orlando Scandrick has been one of our favorite CBs for a long time, and the Cowboys rewarded him with a long-term deal. Continue to build around his solid man coverage. Everyone else in the secondary is on a game-to-game basis. Stick with whatever scheme and lineup works best. CB Brandon Carr has some size and can press WRs but will need help over the top.

SCHEDULE

Week	Date	Time	Network		Opponent
1	SEP 13	8:30 PM ET	NBC		GIANTS
2	SEP 20	4:25 PM ET	FOX	AT	EAGLES
3	SEP 27	1:00 PM ET	FOX		FALCONS
4	OCT 04	8:30 PM ET	NBC	AT	SAINTS
5	OCT 11	4:25 PM ET			PATRIOTS
6	BYE WEEK				
7	OCT 25	4:25 PM ET	FOX	AT	GIANTS
8	NOV 01	4:25 PM ET	FOX		SEAHAWKS
9	NOV 08	8:30 PM ET	NBC		EAGLES
10	NOV 15	1:00 PM ET	FOX	AT	BUCCANEERS
11	NOV 22	1:00 PM ET	FOX	AT	DOLPHINS
12	NOV 26	4:30 PM ET			PANTHERS
13	DEC 07	8:30 PM ET	ESPN	AT	REDSKINS
14	DEC 13	4:25 PM ET	FOX	AT	PACKERS
15	DEC 19	8:25 PM ET			JETS
16	DEC 27	1:00 PM ET	FOX	AT	BILLS
17	JAN 03	1:00 PM ET	FOX		REDSKINS

KEY PLAYERS

KEY OFFENSIVE PLAYER

DEZ BRYANT #88

WR #88 HT 6'2" WT 222 COLLEGE Oklahoma St. EXP 5

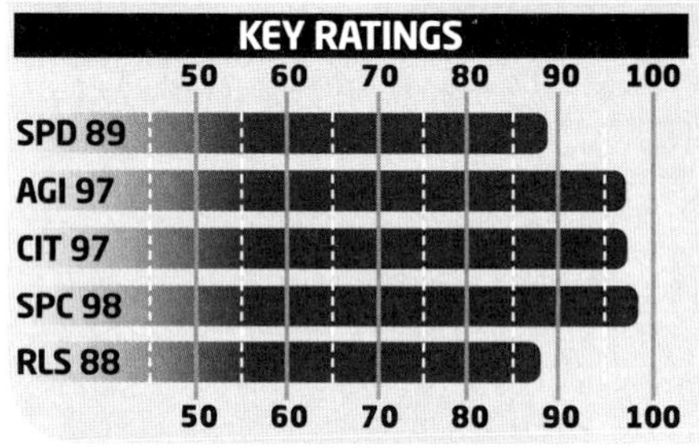

- Bryant is easily one of the best WRs at winning one-on-one matchups, even though he is only 6'2".
- Bryant has brought the Cowboys' offense to a new level and has great chemistry with QB Tony Romo.

KEY DEFENSIVE PLAYER

ORLANDO SCANDRICK #32

CB #32 HT 5'10" WT 195 COLLEGE Boise State EXP 7

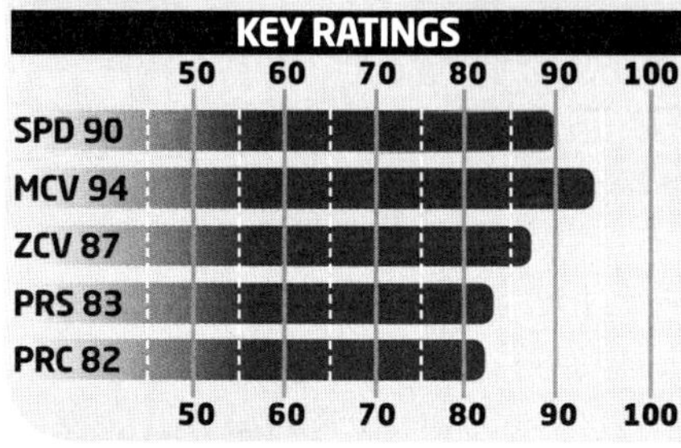

- Scandrick is a great man-to-man defender who should be able to stick with WRs on their cuts.
- Scandrick has decent press, but with his smaller size, don't expect him to cover a 6'3"-plus WR without some help from time to time.

KEY ROOKIE

BYRON JONES #31

CB #31 HT 6'1" WT 199 COLLEGE Connecticut EXP Rookie

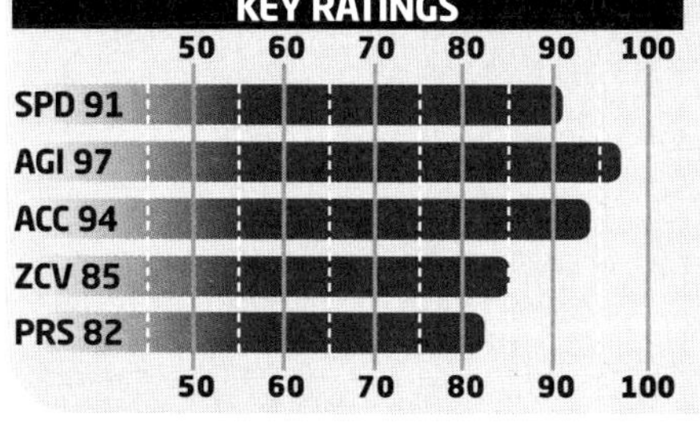

- Jones has good size and a solid combo of agility and acceleration to build around. Boost his Man Coverage rating to go with his 82 Press.
- If you want Jones to be a starter early in his career, try playing him in the flat zones on Cover 2, which will match his strength.

KEY SLEEPER

MACKENZY BERNADEAU #73

RG #73 HT 6'4" WT 333 COLLEGE Bentley College EXP 7

KEY RATINGS

50 60 70 80 90 100

OVR 85
STR 96
RBK 84
PBK 72
IMP 83

50 60 70 80 90 100

- Bernadeau may not have the best speed, but his acceleration should allow him to be an effective puller on runs like 0 1 Trap.
- If you don't want to use an extra lineman in your power run scheme, consider finding a trade partner who is weak at guard. Otherwise all his strength will go to waste.

OFFENSIVE DEPTH CHART

POS	FIRST	LAST	OVR
QB	TONY	ROMO	93
QB	BRANDON	WEEDEN	73
QB	DUSTIN	VAUGHAN	66
HB	DARREN	MCFADDEN	76
HB	JOSEPH	RANDLE	75
HB	LANCE	DUNBAR	74
HB	RYAN	WILLIAMS	73
WR	DEZ	BRYANT	96
WR	COLE	BEASLEY	77
WR	TERRANCE	WILLIAMS	82
WR	DEVIN	STREET	69
WR	GEORGE	FARMER	61
WR	REGGIE	DUNN	56
TE	JASON	WITTEN	93
TE	GAVIN	ESCOBAR	75
TE	JAMES	HANNA	74
LT	TYRON	SMITH	93
LT	DARRION	WEEMS	66
LT	RYAN	MILLER	63
LG	RONALD	LEARY	83
LG	LA'EL	COLLINS	72
C	TRAVIS	FREDERICK	91
C	SHANE	MCDERMOTT	62
RG	ZACK	MARTIN	92
RG	MACKENZY	BERNADEAU	78
RT	DOUG	FREE	87
RT	CHAZ	GREEN	68

DEFENSIVE DEPTH CHART

POS	FIRST	LAST	OVR
LE	DEMARCUS	LAWRENCE	79
LE	JACK	CRAWFORD	73
LE	RYAN	RUSSELL	64
DT	TYRONE	CRAWFORD	82
DT	TERRELL	MCCLAIN	77
DT	NICK	HAYDEN	71
DT	KEN	BISHOP	63
DT	CHRIS	WHALEY	63
RE	JEREMY	MINCEY	82
RE	RANDY	GREGORY	73
LOLB	KYLE	WILBER	77
LOLB	ANTHONY	HITCHENS	75
LOLB	CAMERON	LAWRENCE	69
MLB	ROLANDO	MCCLAIN	86
MLB	JASPER	BRINKLEY	81
MLB	ANDREW	GACHKAR	75
MLB	DAMIEN	WILSON	65
ROLB	SEAN	LEE	89
ROLB	MARK	NZEOCHA	58
CB	ORLANDO	SCANDRICK	88
CB	BRANDON	CARR	80
CB	MORRIS	CLAIBORNE	73
CB	BYRON	JONES	73
CB	COREY	WHITE	71
FS	J.J.	WILCOX	79
FS	JEFF	HEATH	71
SS	BARRY	CHURCH	81
SS	DANNY	MCCRAY	75

SPECIAL TEAMS

POS	FIRST	LAST	OVR
K	DAN	BAILEY	93
KR	COLE	BEASLEY	77
KR	LANCE	DUNBAR	74
P	CHRIS	JONES	78
PR	COLE	BEASLEY	77

BEST OFFENSIVE PLAYS

PRO TIPS

- **These are the best two offensive plays in your playbook. They will get your playmakers in position to win you games.**
- The Cowboys' offensive line is one of the best in the game, and you should feel confident running to any gap.
- When all else fails, the combination of Tony Romo and Dez Bryant should be unleashed downfield for a big play.

BEST RUN: GUN WING DEEP OFFSET—INSIDE ZONE

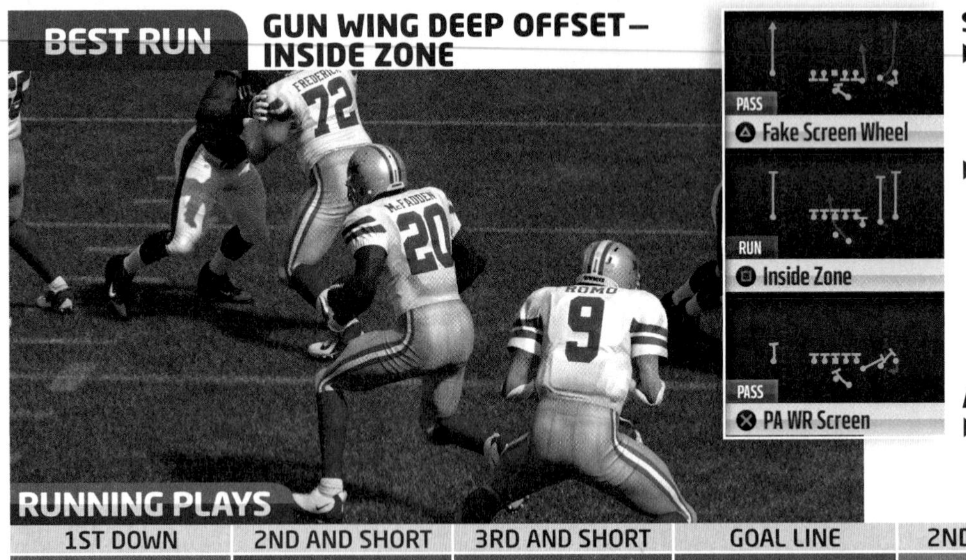

SETUP:

- The Cowboys still have some great under-center run formations, like Strong Close, if you want to use the offensive line to pound the rock.
- This run tends to go outside more than you'd think—try the 0 1 Trap if you really want to attack up the middle.

ADVANCED SETUP:

- None

RUNNING PLAYS

1ST DOWN	2ND AND SHORT	3RD AND SHORT	GOAL LINE	2ND AND LONG	3RD AND LONG
Singleback Ace—HB Stretch	Strong Close—HB Dive	I-Form Tight Pair—FB Dive	Goal Line Normal—QB Sneak	Pistol Ace Twins—HB Counter	Gun Trey Open Cowboy—HB Base
Singleback Ace Close—0 1 Trap	Singleback Ace Pair Flex—HB Dive	I-Form Twins Flex—HB Blast	Goal Line Normal—HB Sting	Pistol Bunch—HB Slam	Gun Trio Cowboys—HB Off Tackle
Singleback Ace Close—HB Stretch	Singleback Jumbo—HB Ace Power	Singleback Doubles—HB Misdirection	Goal Line Normal—Power O	Pistol Bunch—HB Counter	Gun Wing Deep Offset—0 1 Trap

INSIDE RUN | OUTSIDE RUN | SHOTGUN RUN | QB RUN

BEST PASS: GUN EMPTY TRIPS TE—FOUR VERTICALS

PASS
Four Verticals

PASS
Bubble Screen

PASS
X Dig

SETUP/READS:

- Against zone coverage wait for the deep breaking route across the middle to get behind the LBs.
- This formation has some excellent man-beating concepts, so don't feel like you need to go deep every play.
- Against the blitz, unleash the deep pass downfield if you get a one-on-one look. Otherwise, hit the flat and keep the chains moving.

ADVANCED SETUP:

- Flat or zig the left slot WR.

PASSING PLAYS

1ST DOWN	2ND AND SHORT	3RD AND SHORT	SHOT PLAYS	2ND AND LONG	3RD AND LONG
Gun Y-Trips Cowboy—Cowboys Slot Slant	Strong Close—WR Out	Strong Close—Cowboy Y Option	Gun Trio Cowboy—PA Shot Wheel	Singleback Bunch—Verticals	Gun Y-Trips Cowboy—HB Cross Screen
Pistol Y-Trips—Y Trail	Singleback Jumbo—Cowboys Verts Drag	I-Form Pro—Mid Attack	Singleback Ace—PA Stretch Shot	Pistol Bunch—Seattle	Pistol Y-Trips—Four Verticals
Singleback Ace Pair Flex—Cowboys Y-Delay	Singleback Ace Pair Flex—TE Spot	Gun Empty Cowboy—Inside Cross	Pistol Ace Twins—PA FL Stretch	Gun Y-Trips Cowboy—PA WR In	Gun Split Cowboy—Cowboy Y Circle

BASE PLAY | MAN BEATER | ZONE BEATER | BLITZ BEATER

BEST DEFENSIVE PLAYS

PRO TIPS

- **If you want to win more games in *Madden NFL 16*, rely on these defensive plays to lock up the run and pass.**
- **The 46 Bear is a rare formation, and the Cowboys should be able to stuff the run with it.**
- **Big Dime 4-1-6 is a great way to get all your talent on the field at the same time.**

BEST RUN D: 46 BEAR–BUZZ WEAK 3

BLITZ — △ Safety Fire

BLITZ — □ Buzz Weak

BLITZ — ⊗ Buzz Weak 3

SETUP:

- Try spreading your defensive line to help against edge runs. The blitzing defender should get wide, but sometimes he can get lost in the shuffle of blockers.
- If your opponent has a strong offensive line to the left, consider flipping the play to protect yourself.

PLAYER TO CONTROL:

- Any defensive lineman

RUN DEFENSE

1ST DOWN	2ND AND SHORT	3RD AND SHORT	GOAL LINE	2ND AND LONG	3RD AND LONG
46 Bear–Cover 1	4-3 Over Plus–Cover 1	46 Bear–Mid Blitz	Goal Line 5-4-2–Jam Cover 1	Big Dime 4-1-6–Cover 2 Sink	Big Dime 4-1-6–Cover 2 Man
46 Bear–Wall Stunt	4-3 Over Plus–Mike Blitz 3	46 Bear–Buzz Weak 3	Goal Line 5-4-2–Flat Buzz	Big Dime 4-1-6–Cover 2	Big Dime 4-1-6–Cov 3 Buzz Press

MAN COVERAGE | ZONE COVERAGE | MAN BLITZ | ZONE BLITZ

BEST PASS D: BIG DIME 4-1-6–COV 3 BUZZ PRESS

MAN — △ Cover 2 Man

MAN — □ Cov 1 Thief Press

ZONE — ⊗ Cov 3 Buzz Press

SETUP:

- This is a great way to start the game against pass-heavy teams. Consider containing your DEs against mobile QBs.
- Dallas will likely need to blitz to get consistent pressure; adjust at halftime and call some heat if needed.
- Switch between Cov 1 Thief Press and Cov 3 consistently to throw off your opponent's reads.

PLAYER TO CONTROL:

- Flat zone defender on the short side of the field

PASS DEFENSE

1ST DOWN	2ND AND SHORT	3RD AND SHORT	GOAL LINE	2ND AND LONG	3RD AND LONG
46 Bear–Cover 1	4-3 Wide 9–Cover 1 Hole	4-3 Wide 9–1 QB Contain Spy	Goal Line 5-3-3–GL Man	Nickel Wide 9–1 LB Blitz	Dime Normal–Mike Dime Blitz
46 Bear–Cover 3 Drop	4-3 Wide 9–Sam Blitz 3	4-3 Wide 9–Cover 2 Invert	Goal Line 5-3-3–Pinch Zone	Nickel Wide 9–Odd Overload 3	Dime Normal–Fox FZ Press

MAN COVERAGE | ZONE COVERAGE | MAN BLITZ | ZONE BLITZ

MIAMI DOLPHINS

GAMEPLAY RATING 81

CONNECTED FRANCHISE MODE STRATEGY

CFM TEAM RATING: **81**
OFFENSE: **83**
DEFENSE: **85**
OFFENSIVE SCHEME: **West Coast**
DEFENSIVE SCHEME: **Base 4-3**
STRENGTHS: **C, QB, TE, LE, DT, SS**
WEAKNESSES: **RG, ROLB, RT, WR**

2014 TEAM RANKINGS

3rd AFC East (8-8-0)
PASSING OFFENSE: **17th**
RUSHING OFFENSE: **12th**
PASSING DEFENSE: **6th**
RUSHING DEFENSE: **24th**

2014 TEAM LEADERS

PASSING: **Ryan Tannehill: 4,045**
RUSHING: **Lamar Miller: 1,099**
RECEIVING: **Mike Wallace: 862**
TACKLES: **Jelani Jenkins: 110**
SACKS: **Cameron Wake: 11.5**
INTS: **Brent Grimes: 5**

KEY ADDITIONS

DT Ndamukong Suh
TE Jordan Cameron
WR Greg Jennings

KEY ROOKIES

WR DeVante Parker
DT Jordan Phillips
G Jamil Douglas

OWNER: **Stephen Ross**
LEGACY SCORE: **0**

COACH: **Joe Philbin**
LEVEL: **5**
LEGACY SCORE: **100**
OFFENSIVE SCHEME: **West Coast**
DEFENSIVE SCHEME: **Base 4-3**

OFFENSIVE SCOUTING REPORT

- QB Ryan Tannehill has been solidified as the long-term starter in Miami; make sure to keep surrounding him with talent at WR.
- Last season, HB Lamar Miller proved he could carry the load, so be sure to utilize his strengths. Even though LaMichael James is solid on special teams, give him an opportunity to win the third-down-back role.
- Although the Dolphins prefer a short passing game, give Kenny Stills some chances downfield each game. Keep building the chemistry with Jarvis Landry, who had a solid rookie campaign. Don't forget to target TE Jordan Cameron in the red zone.

DEFENSIVE SCOUTING REPORT

- Departed DT Randy Starks will leave a big hole, but Ndamukong Suh is more than capable of filling it. Not only is he just as good in the run game, but he should also be more trouble for opposing QBs.
- Your nickel LBs should be Koa Misi and Jelani Jenkins, who are both very solid in zone coverage. Both have some nice hit power, too.
- The secondary is extremely solid, especially at the safety position. Adjust your coverage to help out CB Brice McCain, because he will be targeted by opponents.

SCHEDULE

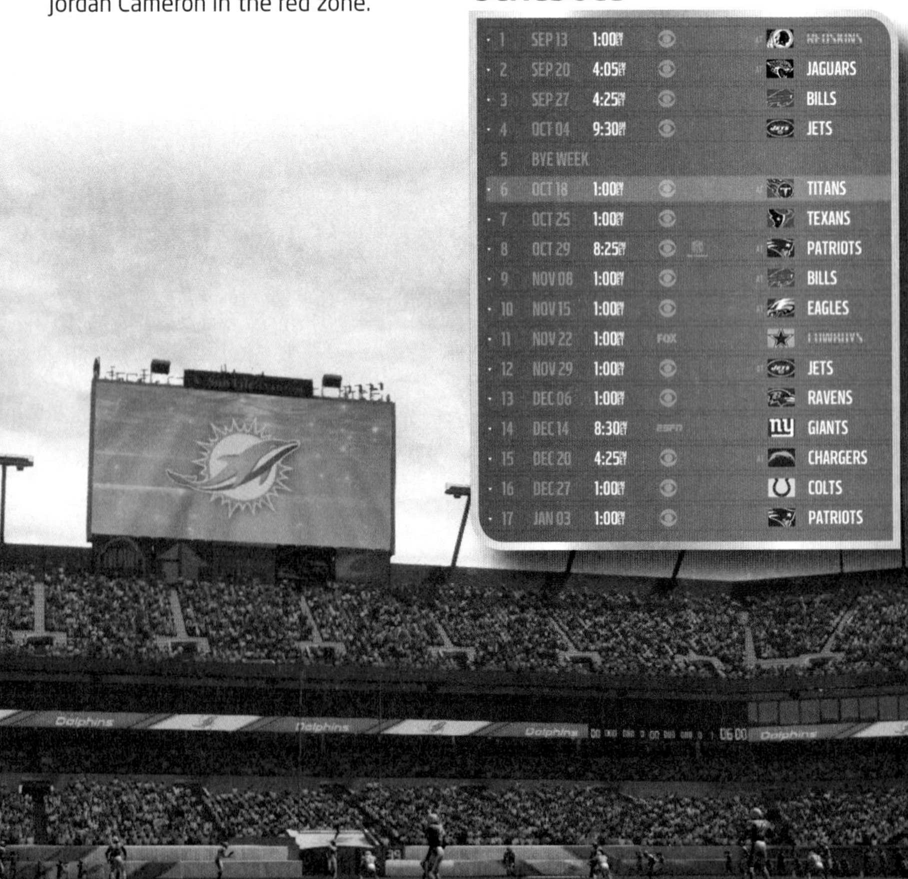

Week	Date	Time	Opponent
1	SEP 13	1:00	[illegible]
2	SEP 20	4:05	JAGUARS
3	SEP 27	4:25	BILLS
4	OCT 04	9:30	JETS
5	BYE WEEK		
6	OCT 18	1:00	TITANS
7	OCT 25	1:00	TEXANS
8	OCT 29	8:25	PATRIOTS
9	NOV 08	1:00	BILLS
10	NOV 15	1:00	EAGLES
11	NOV 22	1:00	[illegible]
12	NOV 29	1:00	JETS
13	DEC 06	1:00	RAVENS
14	DEC 14	8:30	GIANTS
15	DEC 20	4:25	CHARGERS
16	DEC 27	1:00	COLTS
17	JAN 03	1:00	PATRIOTS

KEY PLAYERS

KEY OFFENSIVE PLAYER

RYAN TANNEHILL #17

QB #17 HT 6'4" WT 222 COLLEGE Texas A&M EXP 3

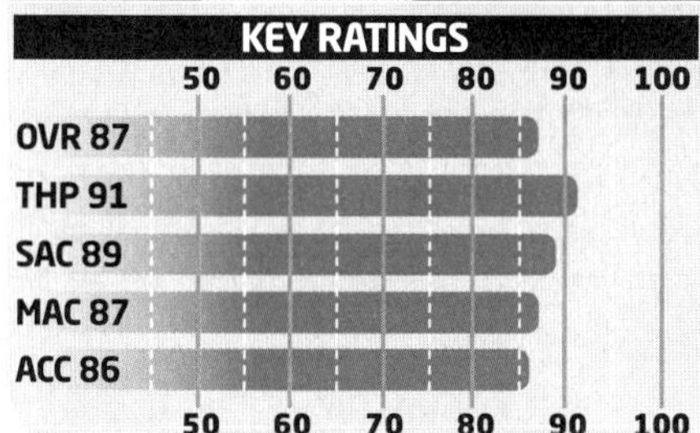

KEY RATINGS

OVR 87
THP 91
SAC 89
MAC 87
ACC 86

- Tannehill will consistently make all the open throws necessary to run a West Coast scheme.
- The Dolphins' playbook allows Tannehill to utilize his 88 Throw On Run rating.

KEY DEFENSIVE PLAYER

NDAMUKONG SUH #93

DT #93 HT 6'4" WT 307 COLLEGE Nebraska EXP 5

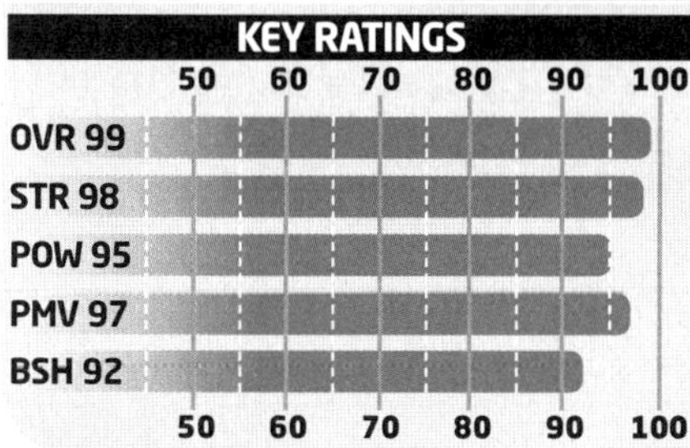

KEY RATINGS

OVR 99
STR 98
POW 95
PMV 97
BSH 92

- Suh is an every-down DT in a 4-3 scheme—he should never come off the field.
- Expect to see improved sack totals from both Olivier Vernon and Cameron Wake when they line up next to Suh.

KEY ROOKIE

DEVANTE PARKER #11

WR #11 HT 6'3" WT 209 COLLEGE Louisville EXP Rookie

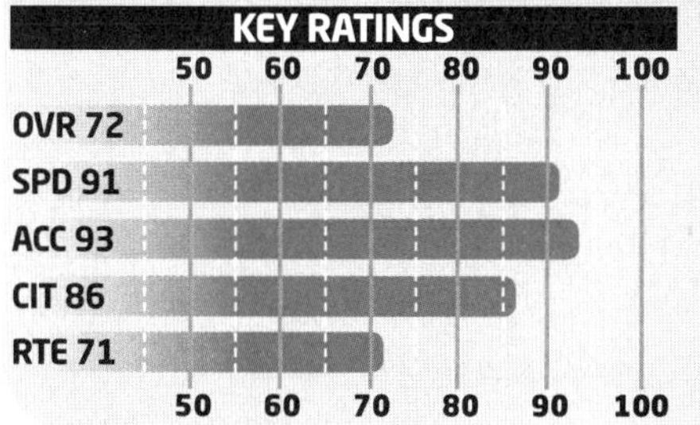

KEY RATINGS

OVR 72
SPD 91
ACC 93
CIT 86
RTE 71

- If you want to develop Parker into a superstar WR who can line up everywhere, focus on his route running.
- With his ability to get off the press and catch in traffic, Parker will be better on the outside.

KEY SLEEPER

DON JONES #38

FS #38 HT 5'11" WT 191 COLLEGE Arkansas St. EXP 2

KEY RATINGS

OVR 66
SPD 91
ACC 92
JMP 97
POW 85

- Take control of Jones yourself if you want to get the most out of him.
- With such a low Play Recognition rating, Jones can't be an every-down player until you develop him more.

OFFENSIVE DEPTH CHART

POS	FIRST	LAST	OVR
QB	RYAN	TANNEHILL	85
QB	MATT	MOORE	73
QB	JOSH	FREEMAN	67
HB	LAMAR	MILLER	84
HB	JAY	AJAYI	72
HB	DAMIEN	WILLIAMS	71
HB	LAMICHAEL	JAMES	66
FB	GERELL	ROBINSON	62
WR	GREG	JENNINGS	81
WR	KENNY	STILLS	81
WR	JARVIS	LANDRY	80
WR	DEVANTE	PARKER	76
WR	RISHARD	MATTHEWS	72
WR	MATT	HAZEL	67
TE	JORDAN	CAMERON	84
TE	DION	SIMS	77
TE	ARTHUR	LYNCH	72
LT	BRANDEN	ALBERT	90
LT	MICKEY	BAUCUS	61
LG	DALLAS	THOMAS	72
LG	SAM	BRENNER	71
LG	JAMIL	DOUGLAS	70
C	MIKE	POUNCEY	84
C	J.D.	WALTON	73
C	JACQUES	MCCLENDON	71
RG	BILLY	TURNER	75
RG	JEFF	LINKENBACH	75
RT	JA'WUAN	JAMES	76
RT	JASON	FOX	73
RT	DONALD	HAWKINS	64

DEFENSIVE DEPTH CHART

POS	FIRST	LAST	OVR
LE	CAMERON	WAKE	94
LE	DERRICK	SHELBY	76
DT	NDAMUKONG	SUH	96
DT	EARL	MITCHELL	80
DT	C.J.	MOSLEY	79
DT	ANTHONY	JOHNSON	67
DT	JORDAN	PHILLIPS	65
RE	OLIVIER	VERNON	83
RE	TERRENCE	FEDE	72
LOLB	CHRIS	MCCAIN	70
LOLB	ZACH	VIGIL	62
MLB	KOA	MISI	84
MLB	KELVIN	SHEPPARD	73
ROLB	JELANI	JENKINS	79
ROLB	SPENCER	PAYSINGER	76
ROLB	JORDAN	TRIPP	66
CB	BRENT	GRIMES	87
CB	BRICE	MCCAIN	76
CB	ZACK	BOWMAN	74
CB	WILL	DAVIS	72
CB	JAMAR	TAYLOR	68
FS	LOUIS	DELMAS	83
FS	JORDAN	KOVACS	71
FS	DON	JONES	69
SS	RESHAD	JONES	92
SS	WALT	AIKENS	66

SPECIAL TEAMS

POS	FIRST	LAST	OVR
K	CALEB	STURGIS	76
KR	JARVIS	LANDRY	80
KR	DAMIEN	WILLIAMS	71
P	BRANDON	FIELDS	82
PR	JARVIS	LANDRY	80

BEST OFFENSIVE PLAYS

PRO TIPS

- These are the best two offensive plays in your playbook. They will get your playmakers in position to win you games.
- The Lead Read Option is one of the best runs in the game—if you make the right read.
- Utilize the balance of your QB to run an unpredictable scheme.

BEST RUN: GUN TWIN TE FLEX WK–LEAD READ OPT

SETUP:

- Take a look pre-snap at the read defender; this is the key to a successful play.
- Slide! If you pick up a first down with the QB, don't get greedy and go for the TD.

ADVANCED SETUP:

- Motion the far right TE across the formation.

RUNNING PLAYS

1ST DOWN	2ND AND SHORT	3RD AND SHORT	GOAL LINE	2ND AND LONG	3RD AND LONG
Pistol Ace Wing–HB Stretch	Singleback Wing Trio–0 1 Trap	Singleback Doubles–Inside Zone	Goal Line Normal–QB Sneak	Gun Double Flex–Read Option	Gun Double Stack–Inside Zone
Singleback Ace Wing–0 1 Trap	Pistol Ace Wing–Read Option	Gun Split Dolphin–Mtn Inside Zone	Goal Line Normal–FB Dive	Gun Double Flex–HB Draw	Gun Bunch Offset–Read Option
Singleback Ace Wing–HB Stretch	Singleback Wing Trio–HB Zone	Gun Split Dolphin–HB Cross Buck	Goal Line Normal–Power O	Gun Double Flex–HB Counter	Gun Bunch–HB Base

INSIDE RUN | OUTSIDE RUN | SHOTGUN RUN | QB RUN

BEST PASS: PISTOL ACE WING–TE CROSS

SETUP/READS:

- Target the TEs against man coverage, especially if the defense is playing physical press coverage.
- Set your feet before throwing a high-point pass to the post route, because inaccuracy will lead to an interception.
- Rolling out of the pocket will help the TE routes get open against zone.

ADVANCED SETUP:

- Wheel the HB.

PASSING PLAYS

1ST DOWN	2ND AND SHORT	3RD AND SHORT	SHOT PLAYS	2ND AND LONG	3RD AND LONG
Gun Bunch–Mia Sail	Pistol Ace Wing–Slants	Gun Ace Twins Offset–Posts	Singleback Wing Trips Open–PA Mia Fork	Gun Empty Bunch–Divide Wheel	Gun Trey Open Offset–Y Cross Flood
Gun Bunch–Mia Y Trail	Gun Doubles Offset–Y Shallow Cross	Gun Doubles Offset–Angle Smash	Pistol Ace Wing–PA Deep Cross	Gun Trey Open Offset–Mtn Z Spot	Gun Double Flex–Smash HB Check
Singleback Ace Pair–TE Attack	Gun Bunch–Spacing	Gun Ace Offset–FL Spot	Gun Bunch–Mia Double Post	Gun Empty Bunch–Verticals	Gun Dbls Y-Flex Offset–Fork Wheel

BASE PLAY | MAN BEATER | ZONE BEATER | BLITZ BEATER

 For more plays and strategies for this team, visit your eGuide using the access code sheet provided.

BEST DEFENSIVE PLAYS

PRO TIPS

- If you want to win more games in *Madden NFL 16*, rely on these defensive plays to lock up the run and pass.
- Having Wake and Suh off the right edge means most teams will line up a TE over there.
- Use the LB Rush package in 46 Bear Under to get DT Suh over the center!

BEST RUN D: 46 BEAR UNDER—LB DOGS 3

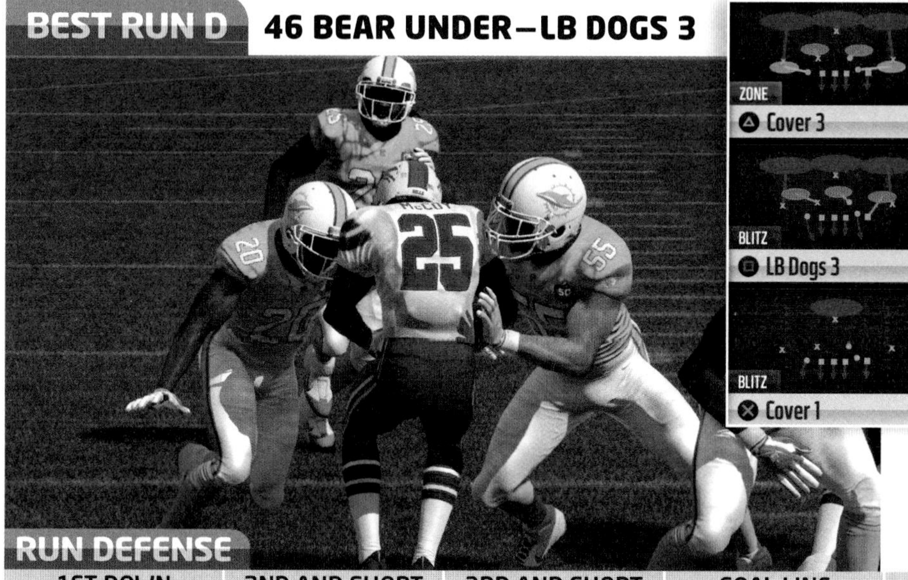

ZONE
△ Cover 3

BLITZ
□ LB Dogs 3

BLITZ
⊗ Cover 1

SETUP:

- By using contain before the snap, you can keep most runs contained to the middle.
- Spread your defensive line and crash it down.

PLAYER TO CONTROL:

- FS in a deep zone

RUN DEFENSE

1ST DOWN	2ND AND SHORT	3RD AND SHORT	GOAL LINE	2ND AND LONG	3RD AND LONG
46 Bear Under–Cover 1	46 Bear Under–LB Dogs	4-3 Stack–Free Fire	Goal Line 5-4-2–Jam Cover 1	4-3 Wide 9–Cover 1 Robber	Nickel Wide 9–Cov 1 Thief Press
46 Bear Under–Cover 3	46 Bear Under–LB Dogs 3	4-3 Stack–Free Fire 3	Goal Line 5-4-2–Flat Buzz	4-3 Wide 9–Cover 3 Cloud Show 2	Nickel Wide 9–Cover 3 Sky

MAN COVERAGE | ZONE COVERAGE | MAN BLITZ | ZONE BLITZ

BEST PASS D: DIME NORMAL—COVER 3 CLOUD

ZONE
△ Cover 6

BLITZ
□ Mike Dime Blitz

ZONE
⊗ Cover 3 Cloud

SETUP:

- Having the CB in a flat zone rather than a deep zone as in most Cover 3 setups is unique.
- For a slightly different variation, use the Cover 6 set from the same formation.

PLAYER TO CONTROL:

- Flat zone defender on the left of the screen

PASS DEFENSE

1ST DOWN	2ND AND SHORT	3RD AND SHORT	GOAL LINE	2ND AND LONG	3RD AND LONG
4-3 Under–Cover 2 Man	4-3 Wide 9–Cover 1 Hole	Nickel Double A Gap–Cover 1 Hole	Goal Line 5-3-3–GL Man	Nickel Double A Gap–SS Mid Combo	Nickel Double A Gap–SS Mid Blitz 0
4-3 Under–Cover 3 Sky wk	4-3 Wide 9–Cover 2 Invert	Nickel Wide 9–Cover 2 Press	Goal Line 5-3-3–Pinch Zone	Nickel Normal–Corner Blitz 3	Nickel Double A Gap–Nickel Dog 3 Buzz

MAN COVERAGE | ZONE COVERAGE | MAN BLITZ | ZONE BLITZ

PHILADELPHIA EAGLES

GAMEPLAY RATING 84

CONNECTED FRANCHISE MODE STRATEGY

CFM TEAM RATING: **86**
OFFENSE: **91**
DEFENSE: **87**
OFFENSIVE SCHEME: **SPREAD**
DEFENSIVE SCHEME: **ATTACKING 3-4**
STRENGTHS: **LT, HB, TE, RE, LB**
WEAKNESSES: **SS, WR, QB**

2014 TEAM RANKINGS

2nd NFC East (10-6-0)
PASSING OFFENSE: **6th**
RUSHING OFFENSE: **9th**
PASSING DEFENSE: **31st**
RUSHING DEFENSE: **15th**

2014 TEAM LEADERS

PASSING: **Mark Sanchez: 2,418**
RUSHING: **LeSean McCoy: 1,319**
RECEIVING: **Jeremy Maclin: 1,318**
TACKLES: **Mychal Kendricks: 83**
SACKS: **Connor Barwin: 14.5**
INTS: **Nate Allen: 4**

KEY ADDITIONS

HB DeMarco Murray
QB Sam Bradford
HB Ryan Mathews
CB Byron Maxwell
CB Walter Thurmond
LB Kiko Alonso
QB Tim Tebow

KEY ROOKIES

WR Nelson Agholor
CB Eric Rowe
LB Jordan Hicks

OWNER: **Jeffrey Lurie**
LEGACY SCORE: **1,150**

COACH: **Chip Kelly**
LEVEL: **13**
LEGACY SCORE: **50**
OFFENSIVE SCHEME: **Spread**
DEFENSIVE SCHEME: **Attacking 3-4**

OFFENSIVE SCOUTING REPORT

- QB Nick Foles is no longer in Philly, and taking over is former #1 pick Sam Bradford. Bradford should be a good fit for the Eagles because he has solid accuracy and should be protected from injury with quick throws and a solid offensive line.
- The Eagles' backfield is completely different from last season, and somehow it got even better! HB DeMarco Murray is an excellent runner who should pick up right where HB LeSean McCoy left off. Make sure to get Darren Sproles and Ryan Mathews involved, because they are both talented in their own ways.
- The Eagles also had an overhaul at the WR position after Jeremy Maclin left during free agency. Look to build rookie WR Nelson Agholor to take over his role. Jordan Matthews should continue to improve after a promising rookie season.

DEFENSIVE SCOUTING REPORT

- Fletcher Cox has developed into a dominant player along the defensive line and is a perfect scheme fit for the Eagles. While the rest of the line is solid, continue to develop their strength to help support the LBs in the run game.
- The LB corps had tremendous play last season from Connor Barwin, who developed into an excellent pass rusher. In the MLB spot, Mychal Kendricks showed he had the skills go with his raw ability and turned into the player many fans had been waiting to see.
- The Eagles went big at CB by bringing in excellent zone defender Byron Maxwell, who has great size. He will fit in nicely with FS Malcolm Jenkins, who will need to lead the secondary and bring up the rest of the young talent.

SCHEDULE

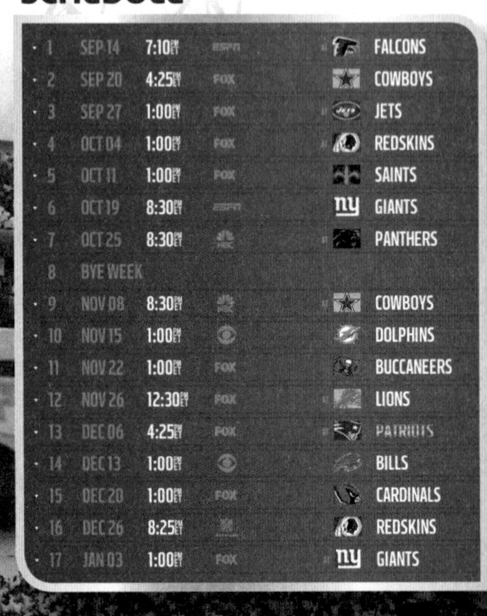

Week	Date	Time	Network	Opponent
1	SEP 14	7:10 PM ET	ESPN	FALCONS
2	SEP 20	4:25 PM ET	FOX	COWBOYS
3	SEP 27	1:00 PM ET	FOX	JETS
4	OCT 04	1:00 PM ET	FOX	REDSKINS
5	OCT 11	1:00 PM ET	FOX	SAINTS
6	OCT 19	8:30 PM ET	ESPN	GIANTS
7	OCT 25	8:30 PM ET	NBC	PANTHERS
8	BYE WEEK			
9	NOV 08	8:30 PM ET	NBC	COWBOYS
10	NOV 15	1:00 PM ET	CBS	DOLPHINS
11	NOV 22	1:00 PM ET	FOX	BUCCANEERS
12	NOV 26	12:30 PM ET	FOX	LIONS
13	DEC 06	4:25 PM ET	FOX	PATRIOTS
14	DEC 13	1:00 PM ET	CBS	BILLS
15	DEC 20	1:00 PM ET	FOX	CARDINALS
16	DEC 26	8:25 PM ET		REDSKINS
17	JAN 03	1:00 PM ET	FOX	GIANTS

KEY PLAYERS

KEY OFFENSIVE PLAYER

DEMARCO MURRAY #29

HB #29 HT 6'0" WT 219 COLLEGE Oklahoma EXP 4

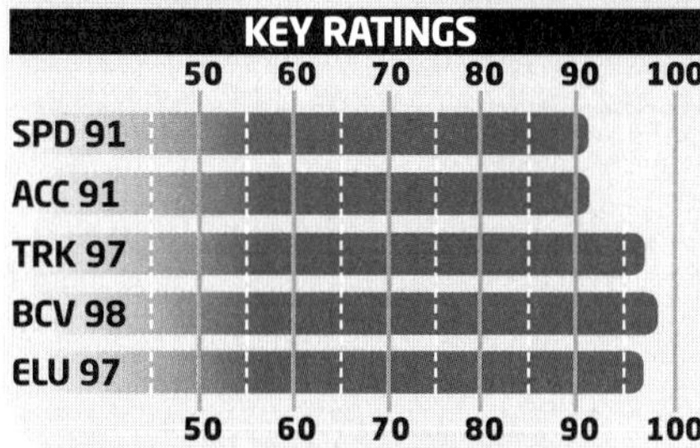

- Continue to work on Murray's Carry and Catch ratings; both are solid but can always be improved.
- Murray can do it all in the open field—expect him to break tackles with both trucking and elusiveness.

KEY DEFENSIVE PLAYER

FLETCHER COX #91

RE #91 HT 6'4" WT 300 COLLEGE Mississippi St. EXP 3

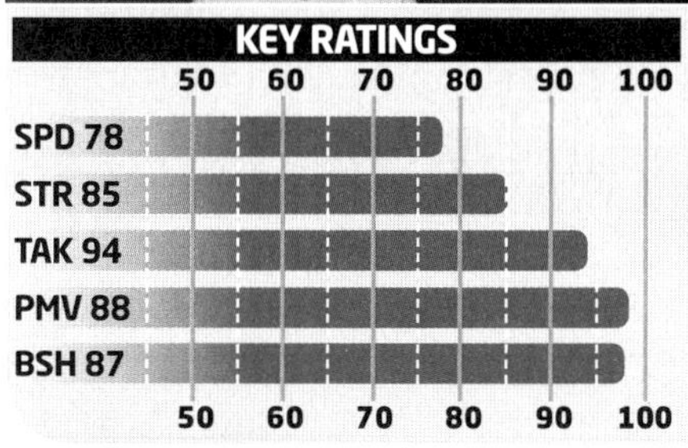

- Cox is a rare player who can rush the passer as a 3-4 end, but work on his strength in the run game.
- Cox should be in the game on all passing downs. Sub him in at DT when you go to passing defenses.

KEY ROOKIE

NELSON AGHOLOR #17

WR #17 HT 6'0" WT 198 COLLEGE USC EXP Rookie

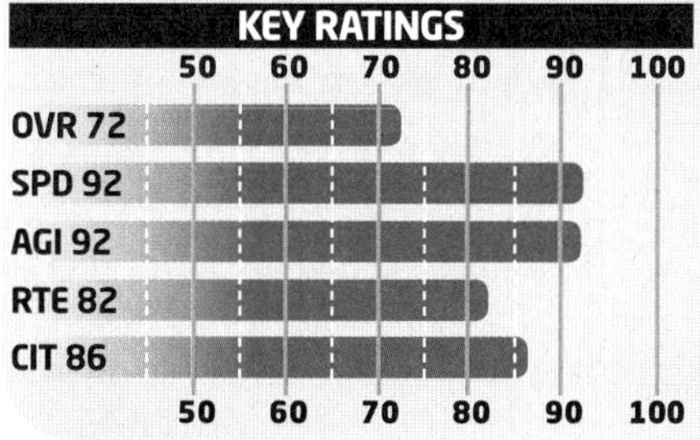

- Agholor will be a starter early in his career for the Eagles, especially with all their shotgun formations.
- Get the ball to Agholor on screen passes and quick throws and let his speed and agility do the work.

KEY SLEEPER

ERIC ROWE #32

CB #32 HT 6'1" WT 205 COLLEGE Utah EXP Rookie

KEY RATINGS

50 60 70 80 90 100

OVR 72

SPD 91

ACC 91

MCV 82

ZCV 81

50 60 70 80 90 100

- Rowe has balanced ratings in both man and zone, so consider what type of scheme you want to build and start upgrading one over the other.
- He is solid in press coverage, so consider starting him on the outside against smaller WRs.

OFFENSIVE DEPTH CHART

POS	FIRST	LAST	OVR
QB	SAM	BRADFORD	79
QB	MARK	SANCHEZ	76
QB	MATT	BARKLEY	69
HB	DEMARCO	MURRAY	94
HB	RYAN	MATHEWS	84
HB	DARREN	SPROLES	82
HB	KENJON	BARNER	67
FB	MATTHEW	TUCKER	66
WR	MATTHEWS	JORDAN	81
WR	AUSTIN	MILES	78
WR	COOPER	RILEY	76
WR	AGHOLOR	NELSON	74
WR	HUFF	JOSH	72
WR	AJIROTUTU	SEYI	69
TE	BRENT	CELEK	85
TE	ZACH	ERTZ	84
TE	TREY	BURTON	70
LT	JASON	PETERS	96
LT	ANDREW	GARDNER	67
LG	DENNIS	KELLY	72
C	JASON	KELCE	87
C	DAVID	MOLK	74
C	JULIAN	VANDERVELDE	66
RG	ALLEN	BARBRE	77
RG	MATT	TOBIN	72
RT	LANE	JOHNSON	00
RT	KEVIN	GRAF	67

DEFENSIVE DEPTH CHART

POS	FIRST	LAST	OVR
LE	VINNY	CURRY	81
LE	CEDRIC	THORNTON	81
LE	TAYLOR	HART	71
DT	BENNIE	LOGAN	80
DT	BEAU	ALLEN	69
DT	WADE	KELIIKIPI	68
RE	FLETCHER	COX	92
RE	BRANDON	BAIR	69
RE	BRIAN	MIHALIK	58
LOLB	CONNOR	BARWIN	87
LOLB	MARCUS	SMITH	70
MLB	KIKO	ALONSO	87
MLB	MYCHAL	KENDRICKS	86
MLB	DEMECO	RYANS	82
MLB	BRAD	JONES	73
ROLB	BRANDON	GRAHAM	86
ROLB	BRYAN	BRAMAN	72
ROLB	BRANDON	HEPBURN	70
CB	BYRON	MAXWELL	84
CB	BRANDON	BOYKIN	82
CB	WALTER	THURMOND	75
CB	NOLAN	CARROLL	74
CB	ERIC	ROWE	72
FS	MALCOLM	JENKINS	85
FS	CHRIS	MARAGOS	74
FS	ED	REYNOLDS	70
SS	EARL	WOLFF	77
SS	JEROME	COUPLIN	69
SS	CHRIS	PROSINSKI	69

SPECIAL TEAMS

POS	FIRST	LAST	OVR
K	CODY	PARKEY	80
KR	DARREN	SPROLES	82
KR	JOSH	HUFF	72
P	DONNIE	JONES	78
PR	DARREN	SPROLES	82

BEST OFFENSIVE PLAYS

PRO TIPS

- **These are the best two offensive plays in your playbook. They will get your playmakers in position to win you games.**
- The Eagles' playbook features over 23 shotgun formations, and you must learn to run from them to have success.
- The Eagles' playbook doesn't require a mobile QB, but it sure would make things easier for your HB.

BEST RUN: GUN WING TRIPS EAGLE WK–0 1 TRAP

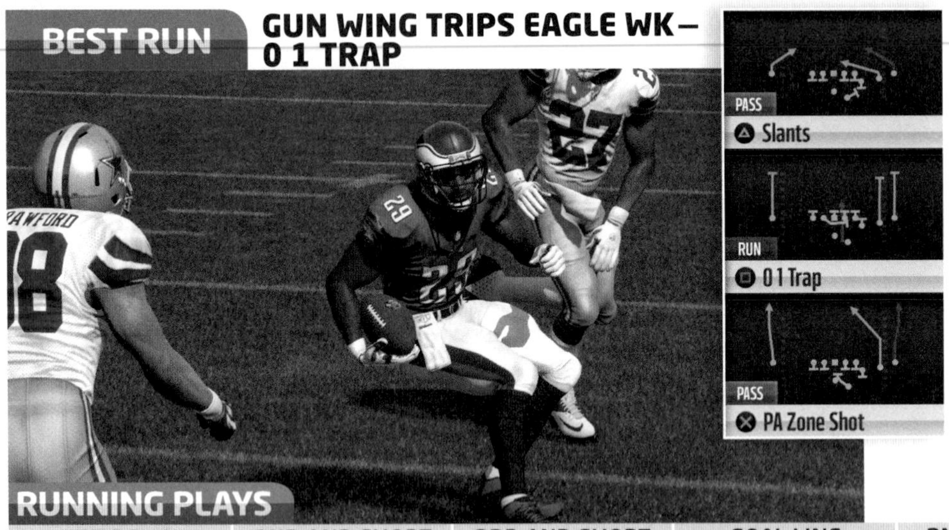

SETUP:

- The 0 1 Trap is a consistent run that you should feel confident in before the snap. If the defense shows blitz, audible out.
- The other runs in this formation contain "auto-motion," so make sure to build a scheme that fools the defense. Otherwise they can key in.

ADVANCED SETUP:

- Motion the TE left.

RUNNING PLAYS

1ST DOWN	2ND AND SHORT	3RD AND SHORT	GOAL LINE	2ND AND LONG	3RD AND LONG
Singleback Ace–HB Off Tackle	Singleback Doubles–Inside Zone	Gun Ace Offset–0 1 Trap	Goal Line–FB Dive	Gun Slot Offset–Triple Option Lt	Gun Doubles Wing–Midline Read Opt
Singleback Wing Trips Open–Inside Zone Split	Gun Slot Offset–Mtn Inside Zone	Gun Twin TE Flex Wk–Inside Zone Split	Goal Line–HB Sting	Gun Wing Trips Eagle–Inside Zone	Gun Split Slot–Shovel Option
Gun Slot Offset–HB Off Tackle	Gun Trio Offset–Inside Zone	Gun Trey Open Offset–5 6 Trap	Goal Line–Power O	Gun Trey Open Offset–HB Draw	Gun Flip Trips Eagle–Read Option

INSIDE RUN | OUTSIDE RUN | SHOTGUN RUN | QB RUN

BEST PASS: GUN FLIP TRIPS EAGLE–EAGLES HB ANGLE

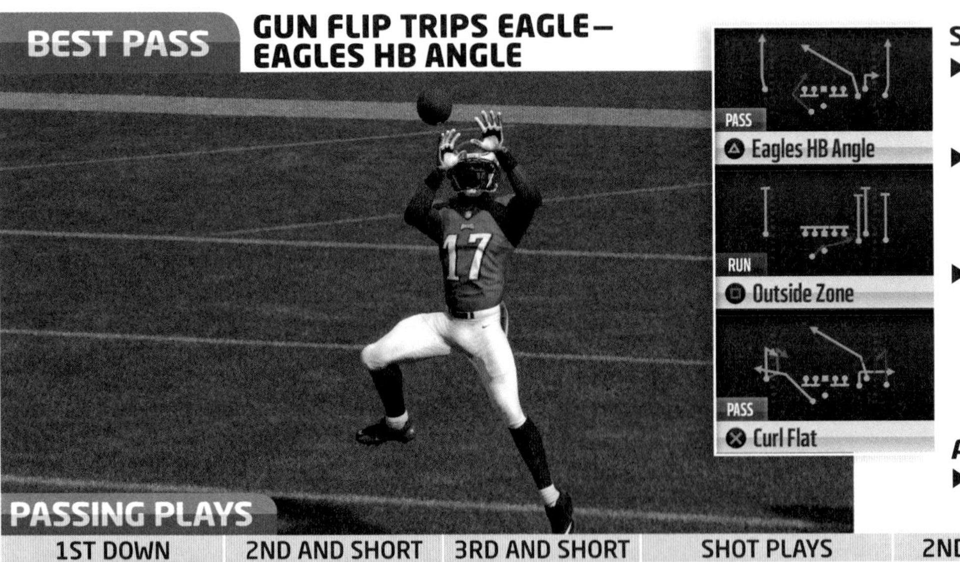

SETUP/READS:

- Against zone coverage, the combination of routes across the middle will be too tough for one defender to cover.
- Against man coverage wait for the angle to cut across the middle. Murray is an outstanding pass catcher, and no LB can hang with him in space.
- This is a play that can pick up big chunks in a hurry, but try the Slot Trail if you're looking for something more consistent.

ADVANCED SETUP:

- Slant the WR on an out.

PASSING PLAYS

1ST DOWN	2ND AND SHORT	3RD AND SHORT	SHOT PLAYS	2ND AND LONG	3RD AND LONG
Gun Doubles Offset–Drag Under	Gun Doubles Offset–Shark HB Wheel	Gun Flip Trips Eagle–Scat	Gun Spread HB Wk–PA Eagles Y Cross	Singleback Ace Pair–TE Attack	Gun Bunch Open–Eagles Flood
Gun Ace Twins Offset–Posts	Gun Wing Trips Eagle Wk–Post N Cross	Gun Split Slot–Slot Post Angle	Gun Bunch Open Offset–Fake Screen Wheel	Gun Ace Twins Offset–PA Verts	Gun Bunch Open–PA Slots Over
Singleback Ace Pair Twins–Eagles Slot Post	Gun Y-Trips Offset–All Hitch	Gun Empty Trey–Dbl Slot Cross	Gun Trio Offset–PA Post Shot	Gun Y-Trips Offset–Four Verticals	Gun Empty Trey–Go's Y Shake

BASE PLAY | MAN BEATER | ZONE BEATER | BLITZ BEATER

 For more plays and strategies for this team, visit your eGuide using the access code sheet provided.

BEST DEFENSIVE PLAYS

PRO TIPS

- If you want to win more games in *Madden NFL 16*, rely on these defensive plays to lock up the run and pass.
- The 3-4 Solid is a great formation that should stop most runs up the middle.
- The Eagles have a Prowl formation that keeps defenders moving before the snap, and the QB has to guess who is rushing at the snap.

BEST RUN D: 3-4 SOLID—TRIO SKY ZONE

SETUP:

- Work this formation to get your fastest LB blitzing on the play. This should lead to him meeting the HB in the backfield on many plays.
- Shifting your LBs will allow you to call this play against most offensive formations, even if they bring in extra TEs.

PLAYER TO CONTROL:

- Either LB on the left of the screen

RUN DEFENSE

1ST DOWN	2ND AND SHORT	3RD AND SHORT	GOAL LINE	2ND AND LONG	3RD AND LONG
3-4 Over—Cover 2 Man	3-4 Over—Cover 1 Hole	3-4 Solid—1 Will Sam Go	Goal Line 5-4-2—Jam Cover 1	Nickel 2-4-5—Cover 2 Sink	Big Dime 2-3-6 Even—1 QB Contain
3-4 Over—Will Buck 3 Press	3-4 Over—Sam Mike 3	3-4 Solid—Clamp Double Go	Goal Line 5-4-2—3 Deep Under	Nickel 2-4-5—Buck Slant 3	Big Dime 2-3-6 Even—Cover 4

MAN COVERAGE · ZONE COVERAGE · MAN BLITZ · ZONE BLITZ

BEST PASS D: NICKEL 2-4-5 DBL A GAP—NICKEL DOG MEG

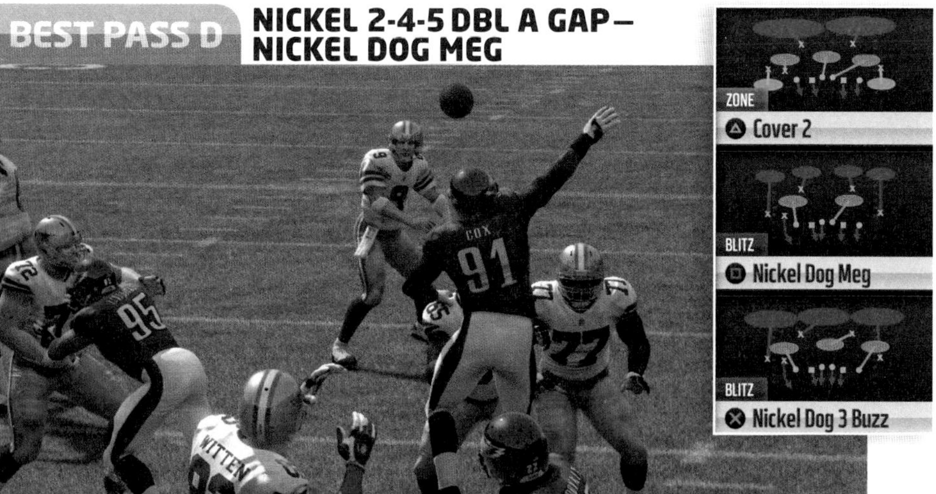

SETUP:

- Your opponent will think the short middle is open, but if they target you there the QB spy should make a play on the ball.
- If your opponent is still hitting you over the middle, switch to the Nickel Dog 3 Buzz to get some extra defenders to the area.
- If you really want to ramp up the pressure on third and long, globally blitz your LBs.

PLAYER TO CONTROL:

- Blitzing CB on a QB spy

PASS DEFENSE

1ST DOWN	2ND AND SHORT	3RD AND SHORT	GOAL LINE	2ND AND LONG	3RD AND LONG
3-4 Even—Cover 1 Hole	3-4 Predator—Cover 2 Man	Nickel 3-3-5 Wide—Mike Blitz 0	Goal Line 5-3-3—GL Man	Nickel 2-4-5 Prowl—Overload Blitz	Big Dime 2-3-6 Will—Mike Edge 1
3-4 Even—OLB Strike 2	3-4 Predator—Will Fire 3 Seam	Nickel 3-3-5 Wide—Mike 3 Show 2	Goal Line 5-3-3—GL Zone	Nickel 2-4-5 Prowl—Overload 3 Seam	Big Dime 2-3-6 Will—Mike Edge 3 Seam

MAN COVERAGE · ZONE COVERAGE · MAN BLITZ · ZONE BLITZ

ATLANTA FALCONS

GAMEPLAY RATING 77

CONNECTED FRANCHISE MODE STRATEGY

CFM TEAM RATING: **79**
OFFENSE: **85**
DEFENSE: **77**
OFFENSIVE SCHEME: **Power Run**
DEFENSIVE SCHEME: **Attacking 3-4**
STRENGTHS: **WR, QB, RG, CB**
WEAKNESSES: **MLB, FS, HB, C**

2014 TEAM RANKINGS

3rd NFC South (6-10-0)
PASSING OFFENSE: **5th**
RUSHING OFFENSE: **24th**
PASSING DEFENSE: **32nd**
RUSHING DEFENSE: **21st**

2014 TEAM LEADERS

PASSING: **Matt Ryan: 4,694**
RUSHING: **Steven Jackson: 707**
RECEIVING: **Julio Jones: 1,593**
TACKLES: **Paul Worrilow: 142**
SACKS: **Kroy Biermann: 4.5**
INTS: **Kemal Ishmael: 4**

KEY ADDITIONS

LB Justin Durant
LB Brooks Reed
WR Leonard Hankerson

KEY ROOKIES

LB Vic Beasley Jr.
CB Jalen Collins
HB Tevin Coleman

OWNER: **Arthur Blank**
LEGACY SCORE: **300**

COACH: **Dan Quinn**
LEVEL: **1**
LEGACY SCORE: **0**
OFFENSIVE SCHEME: **Power Run**
DEFENSIVE SCHEME: **Attacking 3-4**

OFFENSIVE SCOUTING REPORT

- QB Matt Ryan threw twice as many TDs as INTs last season and completed over 66 percent of his passes. That will be a tough act to follow, but if anyone can continue on that pace, it's Matty Ice.
- HB Steven Jackson vacates the role at HB, and now it is up to a few young players to carry the load. Let the battle begin between Devonta Freeman, Tevin Coleman, and Antone Smith for the starting role. Coleman is probably the best overall player but still needs time to develop.
- Star WR Julio Jones is a playmaker and should be signed for the long term immediately. With the departure of WR Harry Douglas, there is room for someone to step up. Look to Levine Toilolo at TE, who is not only young, but one of the biggest players in the league. He must become more than a run blocker if the Falcons are going to win double-digit games.

DEFENSIVE SCOUTING REPORT

- The Falcons' defensive line still has plenty of options depending on what fronts you want to use. Consider getting Vic Beasley Jr. and Ra'Shede Hageman snaps because your starters are solid but aging. Don't forget about Kroy Biermann as an option to drop into coverage if your opponent is hitting you over the middle.
- Atlanta went for upgrades in the LB corps and has a solid group with Justin Durant and Brooks Reed. Put them alongside MLB Paul Worrilow and he can develop into a solid zone defender.
- The secondary finally has a young piece to build around in CB Desmond Trufant. Consider signing a veteran for the short term while you develop someone to play opposite of him. At the safety position, don't let Overall ratings fool you; test each player and start whoever plays best. William Moore has the hit power to play up in the run game.

SCHEDULE

Week	Date	Time	TV		Opponent
1	SEP 14	7:10 PM ET	ESPN		EAGLES
2	SEP 20	1:00 PM ET	FOX	AT	GIANTS
3	SEP 27	1:00 PM ET	FOX	AT	COWBOYS
4	OCT 04	1:00 PM ET			TEXANS
5	OCT 11	1:00 PM ET	FOX		REDSKINS
6	OCT 15	8:25 PM ET		AT	SAINTS
7	OCT 25	1:00 PM ET	FOX	AT	TITANS
8	NOV 01	1:00 PM ET	FOX		BUCCANEERS
9	NOV 08	4:05 PM ET	FOX	AT	49ERS
10	BYE WEEK				
11	NOV 22	1:00 PM ET			COLTS
12	NOV 29	1:00 PM ET	FOX		VIKINGS
13	DEC 06	1:00 PM ET	FOX	AT	BUCCANEERS
14	DEC 13	1:00 PM ET	FOX	AT	PANTHERS
15	DEC 20	1:00 PM ET	FOX	AT	JAGUARS
16	DEC 27	1:00 PM ET	FOX		PANTHERS
17	JAN 03	1:00 PM ET	FOX		SAINTS

KEY PLAYERS

KEY OFFENSIVE PLAYER

MATT RYAN #2

QB #2 HT 6'4" WT 220 COLLEGE Boston College EXP 7

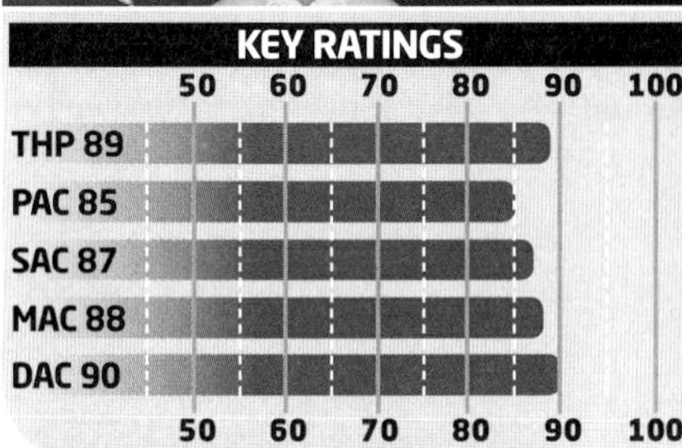

- Ryan is a master at executing shot plays—take a look for some new ones in your playbook and unleash the deep ball.
- Ryan has the outstanding playmaker Julio Jones on the outside and should target him in one-on-one situations all game long.

KEY DEFENSIVE PLAYER

DESMOND TRUFANT #21

CB #21 HT 6'0" WT 190 COLLEGE Washington EXP 2

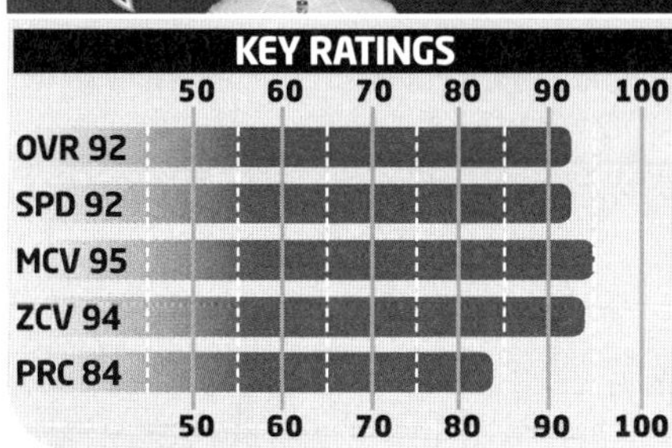

- Trufant has a crazy 97 Agility rating and is one of the best man defenders in the game.
- Having a 6'0" frame is never a bad thing when you have to face WRs in your division like Kelvin Benjamin and Mike Evans.

KEY ROOKIE

VIC BEASLEY JR.

RE #44 HT 6'3" WT 246 COLLEGE Clemson EXP Rookie

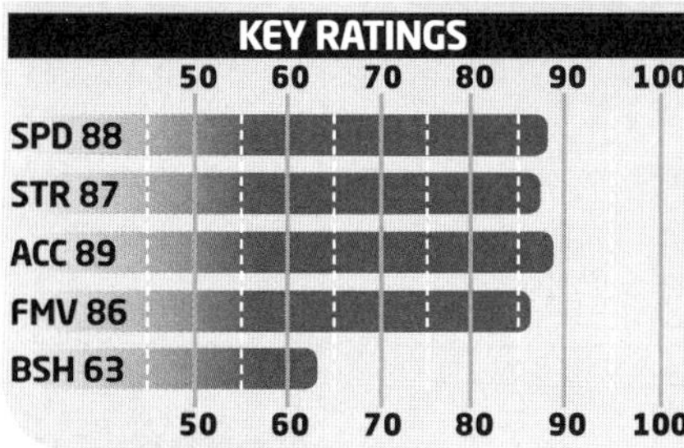

- The combination of strength and speed on Beasley is amazing. Expect big things from this rookie.
- Beasley won't get blown up in the run game, but until you improve his block shedding, he won't be in the backfield often.

KEY SLEEPER

TEVIN COLEMAN

HB #26 HT 5'11" WT 206 COLLEGE Indiana EXP Rookie

- Coleman also has the best carry rating on the team, use him to close out close games in the 4th quarter.
- Coleman's speed is undeniable, but until you get his agility up, Antone Smith may be the better play.

OFFENSIVE DEPTH CHART

POS	FIRST	LAST	OVR
QB	MATT	RYAN	90
QB	T.J.	YATES	72
QB	SEAN	RENFREE	70
HB	DEVONTA	FREEMAN	75
HB	ANTONE	SMITH	75
HB	TEVIN	COLEMAN	74
HB	JEROME	SMITH	67
FB	PATRICK	DIMARCO	79
FB	COLLIN	MOONEY	73
WR	JULIO	JONES	94
WR	RODDY	WHITE	84
WR	LEONARD	HANKERSON	76
WR	DEVIN	HESTER	74
WR	ERIC	WEEMS	72
WR	JUSTIN	HARDY	71
TE	JACOB	TAMME	77
TE	LEVINE	TOILOLO	75
TE	TONY	MOEAKI	74
LT	MATTHEWS	JAKE	75
LT	HOLMES	LAMAR	70
LG	CHRIS	CHESTER	83
LG	MIKE	PERSON	73
LG	HARLAND	GUNN	70
C	JOE	HAWLEY	74
C	PETER	KONZ	70
C	JAMES	STONE	67
RG	JON	ASAMOAH	85
RG	JARED	SMITH	72
RT	RYAN	SCHRAEDER	80
RT	TYLER	POLUMBUS	73
RT	JAKE	RODGERS	62

DEFENSIVE DEPTH CHART

POS	FIRST	LAST	OVR
LE	TYSON	JACKSON	77
LE	CLIFF	MATTHEWS	72
LE	MALLICIAH	GOODMAN	69
DT	BABINEAUX	JONATHAN	83
DT	SOLIAI	PAUL	80
DT	HAGEMAN	RA'SHEDE	73
DT	JARRETT	GRADY	67
DT	HAVILI-HEIMULI	RICKY	66
RE	ADRIAN	CLAYBORN	78
RE	VIC	BEASLEY JR.	77
RE	KROY	BIERMANN	77
LOLB	BROOKS	REED	80
LOLB	O'BRIEN	SCHOFIELD	74
MLB	PAUL	WORRILOW	77
MLB	JOPLO	BARTU	73
MLB	ALLEN	BRADFORD	66
MLB	NATHAN	STUPAR	66
ROLB	JUSTIN	DURANT	84
ROLB	MARQUIS	SPRUILL	68
CB	DESMOND	TRUFANT	90
CB	ROBERT	ALFORD	75
CB	JALEN	COLLINS	71
CB	PHILLIP	ADAMS	70
CB	RICARDO	ALLEN	68
FS	CHARLES	GODFREY	76
FS	DEZMEN	SOUTHWARD	76
FS	SEAN	BAKER	69
SS	WILLIAM	MOORE	80
SS	KEMAL	ISHMAEL	79

SPECIAL TEAMS

POS	FIRST	LAST	OVR
K	MATT	BRYANT	91
KR	DEVIN	HESTER	74
KR	ERIC	WEEMS	72
P	MATT	BOSHER	92
PR	DEVIN	HESTER	74

BEST OFFENSIVE PLAYS

PRO TIPS

- These are the best two offensive plays in your playbook. They will get your playmakers in position to win you games.
- Any formation that can isolate WR Julio Jones on the outside is a win for the Falcons.
- The 0 1 Trap is a great run that can catch your opponent off guard. If they stack the box, call an outside run.

BEST RUN: PISTOL ACE—0 1 TRAP

SETUP:

- Your opponent should be weary of bringing a safety into the box with your playmakers spread to the outside.
- Work on your acceleration and impact blocking at guard to make this solid run even more consistent.
- This run is won before the ball is snapped; if you aren't feeling it, audible to something different.

ADVANCED SETUP:

- None

RUNNING PLAYS

1ST DOWN	2ND AND SHORT	3RD AND SHORT	GOAL LINE	2ND AND LONG	3RD AND LONG
Singleback Tight Doubles—HB Stretch	Singleback Ace—0 1 Trap	I-Form Tight Pair—FB Dive	I-Form Pro—FB Dive	Pistol Ace—HB Counter	Gun Trey Open—HB Off Tackle
Singleback Jumbo—HB Off Tackle	Strong Pro—HB Blast	I-Form Tight Pair—HB Search	Goal Line—QB Sneak	Gun Split Offset—HB Off Tackle	Gun Trey Open—HB Draw
I-Form Pro—Power O	Strong Close—HB Dive	Weak Pro Twins—Toss Weak	I-Form Pro—FB Fake HB Flip	Pistol Y-Trips—HB Stretch	Gun Tight Flex—HB Counter

INSIDE RUN | OUTSIDE RUN | SHOTGUN RUN | QB RUN

BEST PASS: GUN BUNCH OFFSET—Y TRAIL

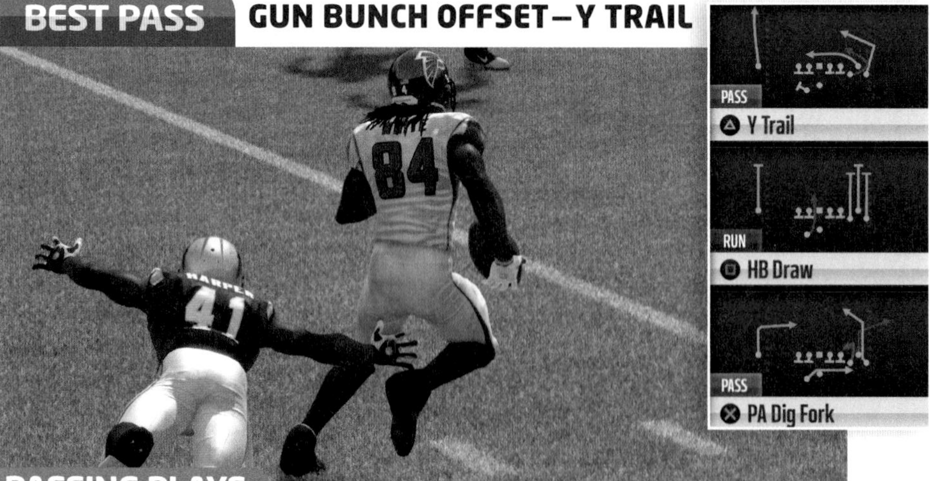

SETUP/READS:

- Against zone coverage wait for the middle to clear out and try a touch pass over the LBs.
- Against man-to-man coverage look to the drag or trail route.
- Against the blitz, keep the HB in to block and go deep on the outside left if you have a matchup advantage.

ADVANCED SETUP:

- Use the Strong Solo package.
- Flat or wheel the HB.

PASSING PLAYS

1ST DOWN	2ND AND SHORT	3RD AND SHORT	SHOT PLAYS	2ND AND LONG	3RD AND LONG
Gun Tight Flex—Falcon Cross	Strong Pro—F Angle	Gun Trio Falcon—ATL Stick	Pistol Ace—PA Shot Go's	Gun Bunch Offset—Verts HB Under	Pistol Y-Trips—PA Zone Shot
Gun Bunch Offset—Y Trail	Strong Close—ATL DBL Outs	Gun Bunch Offset—Bunch Drive	I-Form Tight Pair—Falcons Fade	Gun Trey Open—Falcons X Drag	Gun Trey Open—Four Verticals
Singleback Bunch—Falcon HB Angle	Gun Bunch Offset—Spacing	I-Form Twins Flex—WR Smoke Screen	Gun Split Offset—PA Falcons Shot	Gun Spread—Deep Attack	Gun Empty Falcon—Stick Nod

BASE PLAY | MAN BEATER | ZONE BEATER | BLITZ BEATER

 For more plays and strategies for this team, visit your eGuide using the access code sheet provided.

BEST DEFENSIVE PLAYS

PRO TIPS

- **If you want to win more games in *Madden NFL 16*, rely on these defensive plays to lock up the run and pass.**
- **The Nickel Wide 9 is especially tough if you have a fast CB to blitz off the edge on third and long.**
- **Dropping defenders into coverage from the defensive line is a great way to stop quick throws.**

BEST RUN D: 4-3 STACK—FREE FIRE 3

ZONE — △ Cover 2 Press

BLITZ — □ Free Fire 3

ZONE — ⊗ Cov 3 Cloud Press

SETUP:

- Spreading your defensive line and crashing them down is a more aggressive approach that can lead to tackles for loss.
- If you suspect a quick pass over the middle at the line, quickly use the global commands to change your blitzing LBs to zone coverage.

PLAYER TO CONTROL:

- Deep zone in the middle of the field

RUN DEFENSE

1ST DOWN	2ND AND SHORT	3RD AND SHORT	GOAL LINE	2ND AND LONG	3RD AND LONG
46 Bear Under–Cover 1	46 Bear Under–LB Dogs	4-3 Stack–OLB Fire Man	Goal Line 5-4-2–Jam Cover 1	4-3 Under–1 QB Contain	Nickel Wide 9–Cover 2 Man
46 Bear Under–Cover 3	46 Bear Under–LB Dogs 3	4-3 Stack–Wk Slant 3 Press	Goal Line 5-4-2–Flat Buzz	4-3 Under–Cov 3 Sky Press	Nickel Wide 9–CB Blitz 3 Press

MAN COVERAGE | ZONE COVERAGE | MAN BLITZ | ZONE BLITZ

BEST PASS D: NICKEL WIDE 9—ODD OVERLOAD 3

BLITZ — △ Odd Overload 4

BLITZ — □ Odd LB Dogs

BLITZ — ⊗ Odd Overload 3

SETUP:

- Flip this play depending on where the offense lines up their HB and TE as blockers.
- If you expect your opponent is going to take a shot downfield, try the Cover 4 version of this play.
- Calling press coverage will let your slot blitzer get to the QB faster.

PLAYER TO CONTROL:

- DE dropping into zone coverage

PASS DEFENSE

1ST DOWN	2ND AND SHORT	3RD AND SHORT	GOAL LINE	2ND AND LONG	3RD AND LONG
4-3 Wide 9–Cover 1 Hole	Nickel Normal–2 QB Contain	4-3 Under–Free Fire	Goal Line 5-3-3–GL Man	Nickel Double A Gap–Mid Blitz	Quarter Normal–DB Strike
4-3 Wide 9–Cover 3 Sky	Nickel Normal–Cov 3 Sky Press	4-3 Under–Will 3 Press	Goal Line 5-3-3–GL Zone	Nickel Double A Gap–Buck Zone Blitz	Dime Normal–3 Double Sky

MAN COVERAGE | ZONE COVERAGE | MAN BLITZ | ZONE BLITZ

SAN FRANCISCO 49ERS

GAMEPLAY RATING 78

CONNECTED FRANCHISE MODE STRATEGY

CFM TEAM RATING: **86**
OFFENSE: **91**
DEFENSE: **85**
OFFENSIVE SCHEME: **Power Run**
DEFENSIVE SCHEME: **Base 3-4**
STRENGTHS: **QB, LT, WR, TE, MLB**
WEAKNESSES: **LG, DT, CB**

2014 TEAM RANKINGS

3rd NFC West (8-8-0)
PASSING OFFENSE: **30th**
RUSHING OFFENSE: **4th**
PASSING DEFENSE: **5th**
RUSHING DEFENSE: **7th**

2014 TEAM LEADERS

PASSING: **Colin Kaepernick: 3,369**
RUSHING: **Frank Gore: 1,106**
RECEIVING: **Anquan Boldin: 1,062**
TACKLES: **Chris Borland: 107**
SACKS: **Aaron Lynch: 6**
INTS: **Perrish Cox: 5**

KEY ADDITIONS

HB Reggie Bush
WR Torrey Smith
DT Darnell Dockett

KEY ROOKIES

DL Arik Armstead
S Jaquiski Tartt
OLB Eli Harold

OWNER: **Jed York**
LEGACY SCORE: **750**

COACH: **Jim Tomsula**
LEVEL: **1**
LEGACY SCORE: **0**
OFFENSIVE SCHEME: **Power Run**
DEFENSIVE SCHEME: **Base 3-4**

OFFENSIVE SCOUTING REPORT

- QB is still a position of strength with Colin Kaepernick in charge. This is his season to take over the lead in the huddle now that veteran HB Frank Gore is no longer in the mix. This playbook is built to maximize his talent, which includes speed and throw power.
- The 49ers got much younger with HB Carlos Hyde taking over snaps in the backfield. Work on his agility to see if he can become an every-down back for your team. Until then, utilize Reggie Bush as your 3rd-down back and find creative ways to get him involved in the passing game.
- The 49ers picked up a missing element in their passing game by adding speedy WR Torrey Smith. Use Boldin over the middle for his catch in traffic skills, but don't expect the veteran to run past anyone downfield.

DEFENSIVE SCOUTING REPORT

- The biggest question on the defensive line: Can veteran RE Darnell Dockett step in and be the anchor that last season was Justin Smith? Thanks to his blend of strength, power, and block shedding, the smart bet is yes.
- While the 49ers may have lost talent at LB during the off-season, they still have two elite players with some young depth to build around. It's time for the young talent to step in and deliver.
- CB Tramaine Brock is solid in man coverage, while CB Chris Cook has the size to match up with WRs, so use any extra XP to build him into a lockdown man defender. The Cover 2 Sink will be an excellent way to take advantage of your lineup!

SCHEDULE

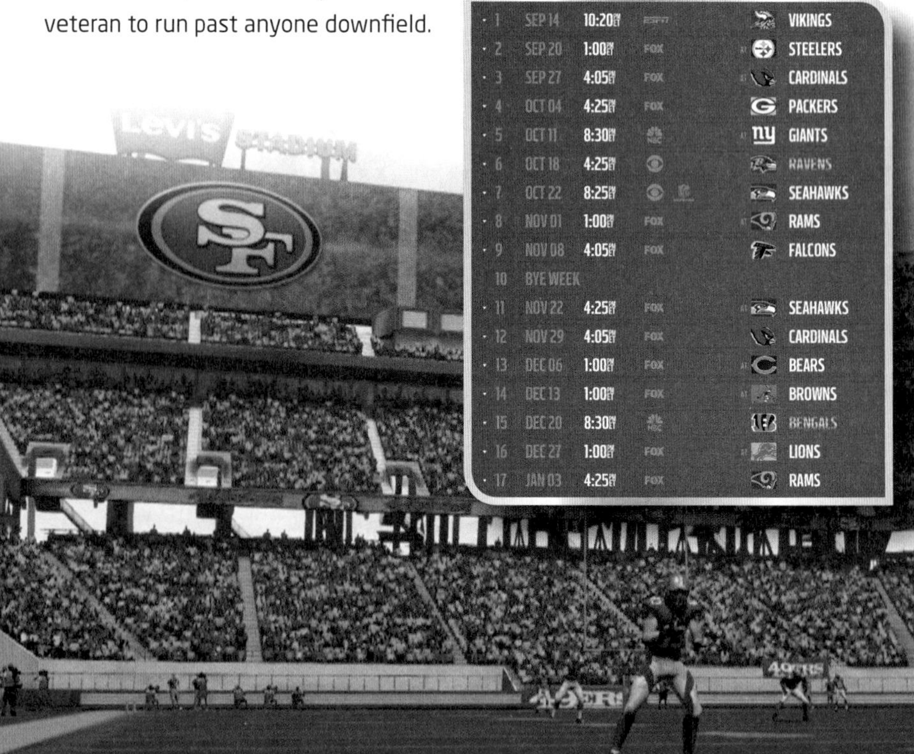

Week	Date	Time	TV		Opponent
1	SEP 14	10:20 PM ET	ESPN		VIKINGS
2	SEP 20	1:00 PM ET	FOX	AT	STEELERS
3	SEP 27	4:05 PM ET	FOX	AT	CARDINALS
4	OCT 04	4:25 PM ET	FOX		PACKERS
5	OCT 11	8:30 PM ET		AT	GIANTS
6	OCT 18	4:25 PM ET			RAVENS
7	OCT 22	8:25 PM ET			SEAHAWKS
8	NOV 01	1:00 PM ET	FOX	AT	RAMS
9	NOV 08	4:05 PM ET	FOX		FALCONS
10	BYE WEEK				
11	NOV 22	4:25 PM ET	FOX	AT	SEAHAWKS
12	NOV 29	4:05 PM ET	FOX		CARDINALS
13	DEC 06	1:00 PM ET	FOX	AT	BEARS
14	DEC 13	1:00 PM ET	FOX	AT	BROWNS
15	DEC 20	8:30 PM ET			BENGALS
16	DEC 27	1:00 PM ET	FOX	AT	LIONS
17	JAN 03	4:25 PM ET	FOX		RAMS

KEY PLAYERS

KEY OFFENSIVE PLAYER

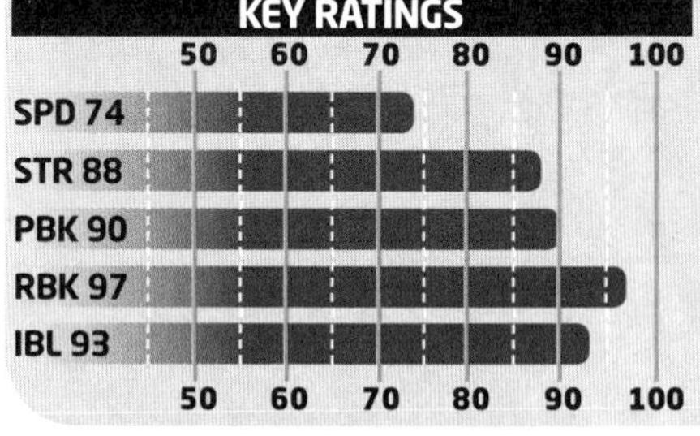

JOE STALEY #74

LT #74 HT 6'5" WT 315 COLLEGE Central Michigan EXP 8

KEY RATINGS

- SPD 74
- STR 88
- PBK 90
- RBK 97
- IBL 93

- Staley is extremely athletic for his size. If he gets out in front of the ball carrier, defenders stand no chance.
- Staley has five years left on his contract. That will allow him to be a cornerstone who builds confidence for QB Colin Kaepernick.

KEY DEFENSIVE PLAYER

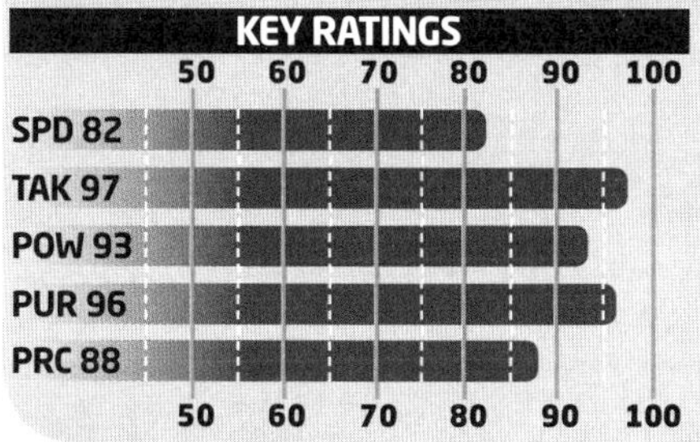

NAVORRO BOWMAN #53

MLB #53 HT 6'0" WT 242 COLLEGE Penn State EXP 5

KEY RATINGS

- SPD 82
- TAK 97
- POW 93
- PUR 96
- PRC 88

- With the retirement of MLB Patrick Willis, Bowman will have plenty of chances to prove that he is once again healthy.
- Bowman's Block Shed rating (92) makes him a star in the run game.

KEY ROOKIE

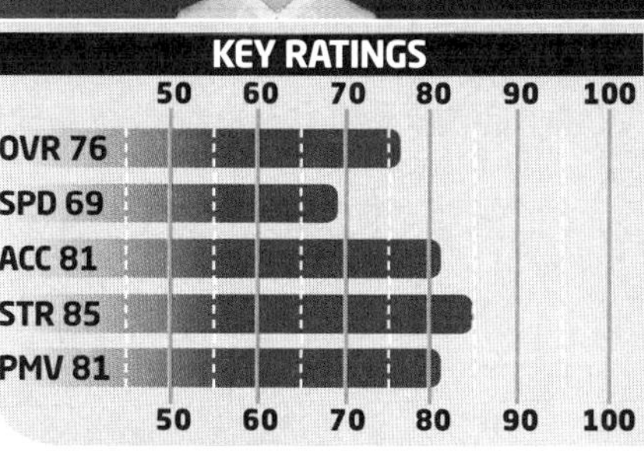

ARIK ARMSTEAD #97

LE #97 HT 6'7" WT 292 COLLEGE Oregon EXP Rookie

KEY RATINGS

- OVR 76
- SPD 69
- ACC 81
- STR 85
- PMV 81

- Armstead has a blend of acceleration and block shedding that will lead to many tackles for losses.
- Try matching him up against slower interior linemen to get a mismatch on passing downs.

KEY SLEEPER

DEREK CARRIER #46

TE #46 HT 6'4" WT 241 COLLEGE Beloit College EXP 3

KEY RATINGS

- OVR 74
- SPD 87
- AGI 91
- ACC 89
- CTH 74

- While his speed is similar to that of Vernon Davis, Carrier's route running is what you must improve to make him a starter. Use vertical routes without cuts to maximize his effectiveness until you stack XP.
- Know your scheme, and use Vance McDonald over Carrier if you plan on a power rushing attack.

OFFENSIVE DEPTH CHART

POS	FIRST NAME	LAST NAME	OVR
QB	COLIN	KAEPERNICK	81
QB	BLAINE	GABBERT	72
QB	DYLAN	THOMPSON	64
HB	REGGIE	BUSH	80
HB	CARLOS	HYDE	77
HB	KENDALL	HUNTER	74
HB	MIKE	DAVIS	71
FB	BRUCE	MILLER	88
FB	TREY	MILLARD	65
WR	ANQUAN	BOLDIN	88
WR	TORREY	SMITH	86
WR	JEROME	SIMPSON	74
WR	QUINTON	PATTON	71
WR	BRUCE	ELLINGTON	68
WR	DEANDRE	SMELTER	67
WR	DEANDREW	WHITE	66
WR	DRES	ANDERSON	65
TE	VANCE	MCDONALD	78
TE	GARRETT	CELEK	72
TE	DEREK	CARRIER	69
TE	ASANTE	CLEVELAND	68
TE	BLAKE	BELL	65
TE	BUSTA	ANDERSON	64
TE	KYLE	NELSON	50
LT	JOE	STALEY	94
LG	TRENT	BROWN	60
C	DANIEL	KILGORE	79
C	MARCUS	MARTIN	72
C	DILLON	FARRELL	65
RG	ALEX	BOONE	88
RG	CONOR	BOFFELI	68
RG	JOE	LOONEY	68
RG	ANDREW	TILLER	63
RT	ERIK	PEARS	72
RT	IAN	SILBERMAN	64

DEFENSIVE DEPTH CHART

POS	FIRST	LAST	OVR
LE	TANK	CARRADINE	77
LE	TONY	JEROD-EDDIE	76
LE	ARIK	ARMSTEAD	72
LE	KALEB	RAMSEY	64
DT	IAN	WILLIAMS	80
DT	GLENN	DORSEY	78
DT	QUINTON	DIAL	76
RE	DARNELL	DOCKETT	82
RE	LAWRENCE	OKOYE	50
LOLB	AHMAD	BROOKS	80
LOLB	AARON	LYNCH	79
MLB	NAVORRO	BOWMAN	93
MLB	DESMOND	BISHOP	76
MLB	PHILIP	WHEELER	76
MLB	MICHAEL	WILHOITE	75
MLB	NICK	MOODY	68
MLB	NICK	BELLORE	67
ROLB	ALDON	SMITH	89
ROLB	COREY	LEMONIER	71
ROLB	ELI	HAROLD	66
CB	TRAMAINE	BROCK	80
CB	CHRIS	COOK	79
CB	DONTAE	JOHNSON	74
CB	SHAREECE	WRIGHT	74
CB	LEON	MCFADDEN	71
CB	KEITH	REASER	65
CB	KENNETH	ACKER	64
CB	MARCUS	CROMARTIE	61
FS	ERIC	REID	81
FS	JIMMIE	WARD	73
FS	L.J.	MCCRAY	63
SS	ANTOINE	BETHEA	91
SS	CRAIG	DAHL	74
SS	JAQUISKI	TARTT	69

SPECIAL TEAMS

POS	FIRST	LAST	OVR
K	PHIL	DAWSON	91
KR	BRUCE	ELLINGTON	68
P	BRADLEY	PINION	51
PR	BRUCE	ELLINGTON	68

BEST OFFENSIVE PLAYS

PRO TIPS

- These are the best two offensive plays in your playbook. They will get your playmakers in position to win you games.
- The position of your TE is crucial due to his ability to outrun most LBs.
- Make sure to take advantage of your speed at the QB position.

BEST RUN: GUN DBLS WING OFFSET WK–NINERS READ OPT

SETUP:

- Look to the play PA Niner Bubble to burn aggressive defenses.
- Follow your blockers inside, and aim for consistent gains instead of home runs.

ADVANCED SETUP:

- Motion the TE behind the offensive line.

RUNNING PLAYS

1ST DOWN	2ND AND SHORT	3RD AND SHORT	GOAL LINE	2ND AND LONG	3RD AND LONG
Singleback Ace–HB Pitch	Strong Tight Pair–FB Dive	I-Form Pro–Inside Zone	Goal Line–QB Sneak	Gun Trey Open–Read Option	Pistol Full House TE–Niner Read Option
Singleback Ace Close–HB Blunt Dive	I-Form Tight–Iso	I-Form Pro–HB Toss	I-Form Tight–FB Dive	Weak Pro–HB Draw	Gun Empty Trey Flex–QB Draw
Singleback Ace Close–Tight Slots Cntr Wk	Strong Tight Pair–HB Dive	Strong Tight Pair–HB Stretch	Singleback Jumbo Z–HB Pitch	Gun Dbls Wing Offset Wk–Outside Zone	Gun Doubles–HB Counter

INSIDE RUN | OUTSIDE RUN | SHOTGUN RUN | QB RUN

BEST PASS: GUN TRIO OFFSET WK–MIDDLE SLANT

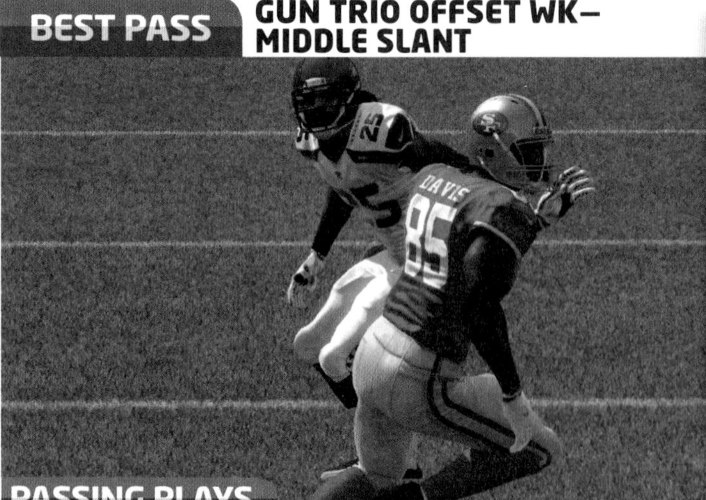

PASS
Middle Slant
RUN
QB Slot Option
PASS
Curl Flat

SETUP/READS:

- Against zone coverage, wait for the curl to settle and throw a low pass.
- Against man-to-man, either slant route should get separation on the cut.
- Against the blitz target the quick drag over the middle.

ADVANCED SETUP:

- Motion the HB to the right.

PASSING PLAYS

1ST DOWN	2ND AND SHORT	3RD AND SHORT	SHOT PLAYS	2ND AND LONG	3RD AND LONG
Gun Y-Trips Wk–Four Verticals	I-Form Pro–Bench	I-Form Pro Twins–HB Slip Screen	Gun Doubles–PA Boot	Pistol Bunch–Verticals	Gun Trey Open–Post Hitch Post
Pistol Full House TE–PA TE Corner	Strong Pro–F Angle	Gun Trips TE Offset–PA WR Screen	Weak Tight Pair–Post Shot	Pistol Bunch–Corner Strike	Gun Empty Trey Flex–Hi Lo Read
Singleback Ace–Inside Cross	Singleback Bunch–Spacing	Singleback Ace Pair Flex–PA Ctr Waggle	Singleback Y-Trips–Corner Shot	Weak Pro–TE Option	Gun Empty Trey Flex–Verticals Y Shake

BASE PLAY | MAN BEATER | ZONE BEATER | BLITZ BEATER

 For more plays and strategies for this team, visit your eGuide using the access code sheet provided.

BEST DEFENSIVE PLAYS

PRO TIPS

- If you want to win more games in *Madden NFL 16*, rely on these defensive plays to lock up the run and pass.
- The 3-4 Bear is perfect for taking on a power rushing attack.
- The Nickel 2-4-5 Prowl adds an extra element of deception to your defense.

BEST RUN D 3-4 BEAR—PINCH DOG 3

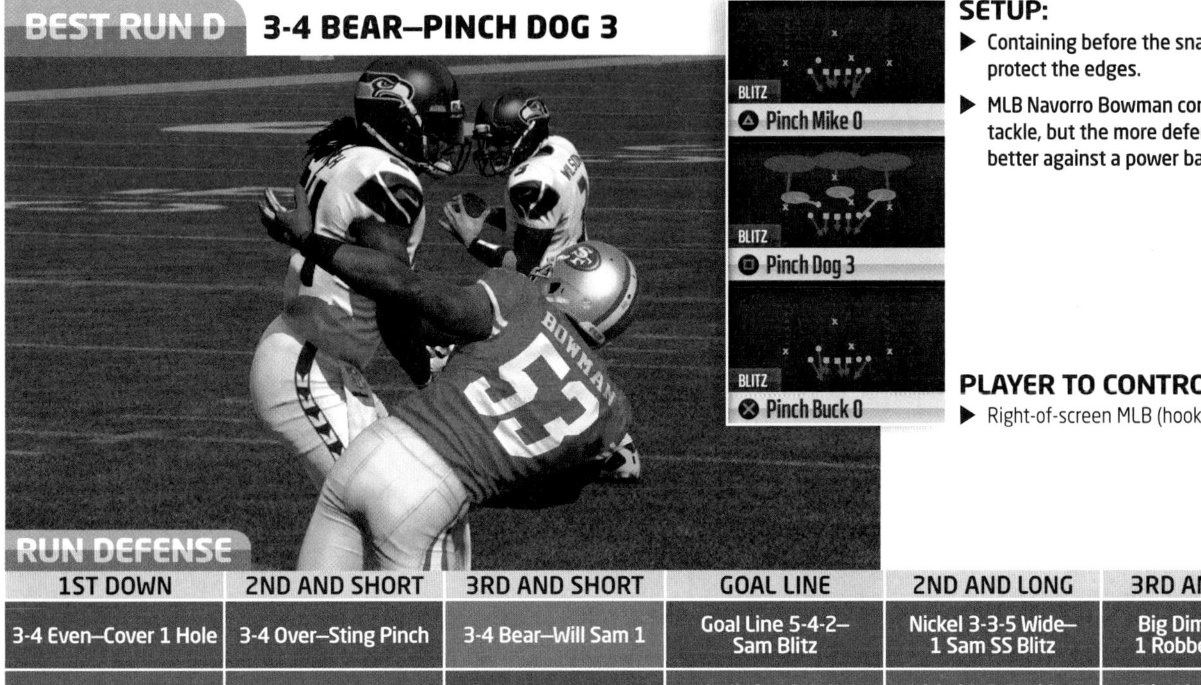

SETUP:

- Containing before the snap will help protect the edges.
- MLB Navorro Bowman comes in for the tackle, but the more defenders the better against a power back.

PLAYER TO CONTROL:

- Right-of-screen MLB (hook zone)

RUN DEFENSE

1ST DOWN	2ND AND SHORT	3RD AND SHORT	GOAL LINE	2ND AND LONG	3RD AND LONG
3-4 Even—Cover 1 Hole	3-4 Over—Sting Pinch	3-4 Bear—Will Sam 1	Goal Line 5-4-2—Sam Blitz	Nickel 3-3-5 Wide—1 Sam SS Blitz	Big Dime 2-3-6—1 Robber Show 2
3-4 Even—Will Fire 3 Seam	3-4 Over—Sting Pinch Zone	3-4 Bear—Pinch Dog 3	Goal Line 5-3-3—GL Zone	Nickel 3-3-5 Wide—Mike 3 Show 2	Big Dime 2-3-6—Cov 3 Buzz Show 2

MAN COVERAGE ZONE COVERAGE MAN BLITZ ZONE BLITZ

BEST PASS D NICKEL 2-4-5 PROWL—OVERLOAD 3 SEAM

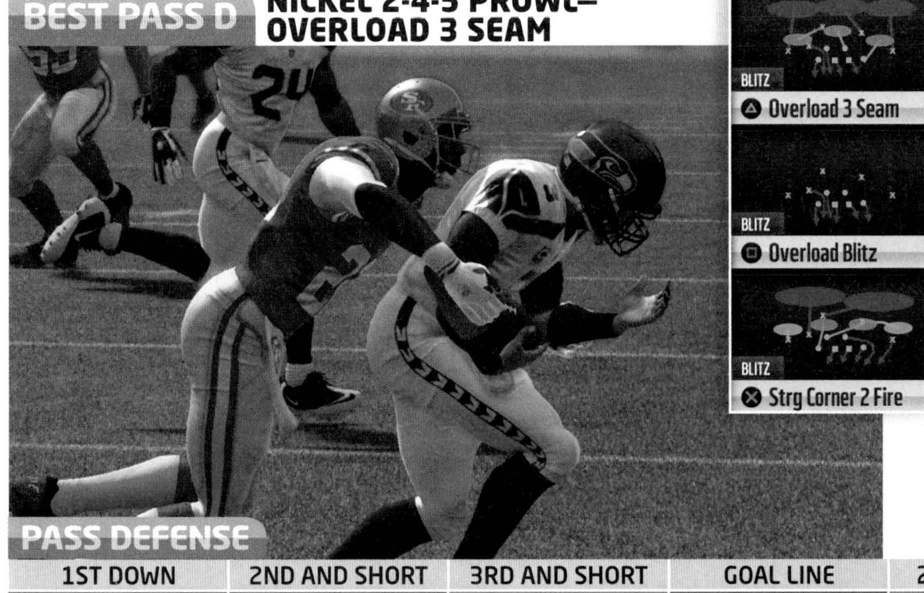

SETUP:

- Bring the blitzing CB out wide and up to the line of scrimmage before the snap.
- If you are losing a one-on-one matchup on the outside, hot route the blitzing CB to man coverage to help out.
- Try the man version of this play to really ramp up the heat on your opponent—high risk but high reward.

PLAYER TO CONTROL:

- Blitzing CB on the left of the screen

PASS DEFENSE

1ST DOWN	2ND AND SHORT	3RD AND SHORT	GOAL LINE	2ND AND LONG	3RD AND LONG
Nickel 2-4-5—Cover 2 Man	Big Dime 2-3-6—Cover 2 Man	3-4 Odd—Cover 1 Hole	Goal Line 5-4-2—Jam Cover 1	Nickel 2-4-5 Prowl—Dbl Loop	Quarter 1-3-7—DB Strike 1
Big Dime 2-3-6—Cover 3 Sky	Big Dime 2-3-6—Cover 4 Press	3-4 Odd—3 Buzz Sting Show 2	Goal Line 5-4-2—Flat Buzz	Nickel 2-4-5 Prowl—Dbl Loop 3	Quarter 1-3-7—FZ 3 Sky

MAN COVERAGE ZONE COVERAGE MAN BLITZ ZONE BLITZ

NEW YORK GIANTS

GAMEPLAY RATING 77

CONNECTED FRANCHISE MODE STRATEGY

CFM TEAM RATING: **81**
OFFENSE: **85**
DEFENSE: **79**
OFFENSIVE SCHEME: **Balanced**
DEFENSIVE SCHEME: **Attacking 4-3**
STRENGTHS: **WR, QB, CB**
WEAKNESSES: **S, OLB, C**

2014 TEAM RANKINGS

3rd NFC East (6-10-0)
PASSING OFFENSE: **7th**
RUSHING OFFENSE: **23rd**
PASSING DEFENSE: **18th**
RUSHING DEFENSE: **30th**

2014 TEAM LEADERS

PASSING: **Eli Manning: 4,410**
RUSHING: **Andre Williams: 721**
RECEIVING: **Odell Beckham Jr.: 1,305**
TACKLES: **Antrel Rolle: 87**
SACKS: **Jason Pierre-Paul: 12.5**
INTS: **Quintin Demps: 4**

KEY ADDITIONS

WR Dwayne Harris
HB Shane Vereen
TE Daniel Fells
LB J.T. Thomas
DE George Selvie

KEY ROOKIES

T Ereck Flowers
SS Landon Collins
DE Owamagbe Odighizuwa

OWNER: **Steve Tisch**
LEGACY SCORE: **4,225**

COACH: **Tom Coughlin**
LEVEL: **16**
LEGACY SCORE: **7,500**
OFFENSIVE SCHEME: **Balanced**
DEFENSIVE SCHEME: **Attacking 4-3**

OFFENSIVE SCOUTING REPORT

- QB Eli Manning really flourished last season in a new offensive system. Look for him to build on it with the young talent surrounding him, and it should lead to more wins. Focus on quick passes to help out the offensive line and keep his completion percentage up.
- The Giants got an excellent upgrade by signing HB Shane Vereen in the off-season. Use him to open up the passing game out of the backfield.
- The Giants had rookie Odell Beckham Jr. explode onto the scene last season, but defenses will be looking out for him this year. Allow his presence in the lineup to open things up for WR Rueben Randle and ease the comeback for WR Victor Cruz, who still has dancing left to do.

DEFENSIVE SCOUTING REPORT

- The Giants' defensive line will need to develop some young talent this season, or they can't afford to let Jason Pierre-Paul change uniforms. Hopefully some of their signings will help them get after the passer, or blitzing your LBs will be necessary.
- LB Jon Beason has had a nice resurgence in New York, but he is rarely at 100 percent due to injuries. The Giants will need their free agent signings of Victor Butler and J.T. Thomas to be a scheme fit for this unit to be a strength.
- The Giants' secondary lost a veteran leader with Antrel Rolle leaving; thankfully, they drafted a promising young player in Landon Collins. On the outside, their CBs are big and fast, which means they shouldn't require much help from the young safeties

SCHEDULE

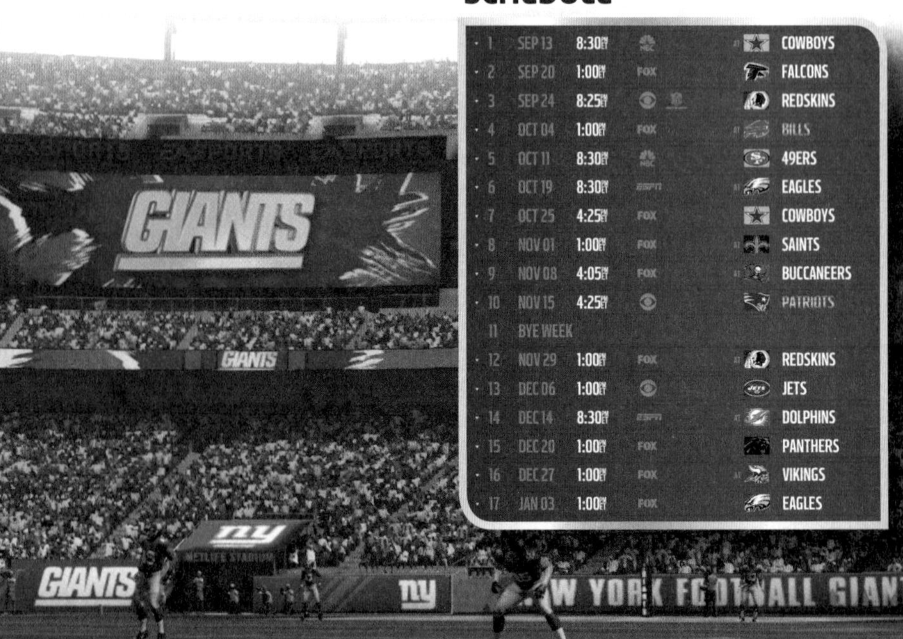

Week	Date	Time	Network		Opponent
1	SEP 13	8:30 PM ET	NBC	AT	COWBOYS
2	SEP 20	1:00 PM ET	FOX		FALCONS
3	SEP 24	8:25 PM ET			REDSKINS
4	OCT 04	1:00 PM ET	FOX	AT	BILLS
5	OCT 11	8:30 PM ET	NBC		49ERS
6	OCT 19	8:30 PM ET	ESPN	AT	EAGLES
7	OCT 25	4:25 PM ET	FOX		COWBOYS
8	NOV 01	1:00 PM ET	FOX	AT	SAINTS
9	NOV 08	4:05 PM ET	FOX	AT	BUCCANEERS
10	NOV 15	4:25 PM ET			PATRIOTS
11	BYE WEEK				
12	NOV 29	1:00 PM ET	FOX	AT	REDSKINS
13	DEC 06	1:00 PM ET			JETS
14	DEC 14	8:30 PM ET	ESPN	AT	DOLPHINS
15	DEC 20	1:00 PM ET	FOX		PANTHERS
16	DEC 27	1:00 PM ET	FOX	AT	VIKINGS
17	JAN 03	1:00 PM ET	FOX		EAGLES

KEY PLAYERS

KEY OFFENSIVE PLAYER

ODELL BECKHAM JR. #13

WR #13 HT 5'11" WT 198 COLLEGE LSU EXP 1

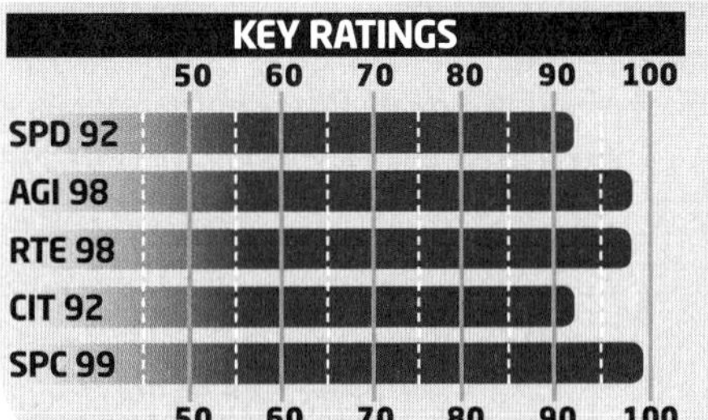

- Despite his size, Beckham is the best in the NFL at going up and making spectacular catches.
- Don't forget to get him the ball on short routes across the middle so he can pick up yards after the catch.

KEY DEFENSIVE PLAYER

DOMINIQUE RODGERS-CROMARTIE #41

CB #41 HT 6'2" WT 193 COLLEGE Tennessee St. EXP 7

KEY RATINGS

SPD 91
AGI 95
MCV 96
ZCV 80
PRC 80

- DRC is one of our favorite players in the game with his blend of size and speed.
- Get the most value out of him by not calling press, because his rating is only a 62.

KEY ROOKIE

ERECK FLOWERS #76

LT #76 HT 6'6" WT 329 COLLEGE Miami EXP Rookie

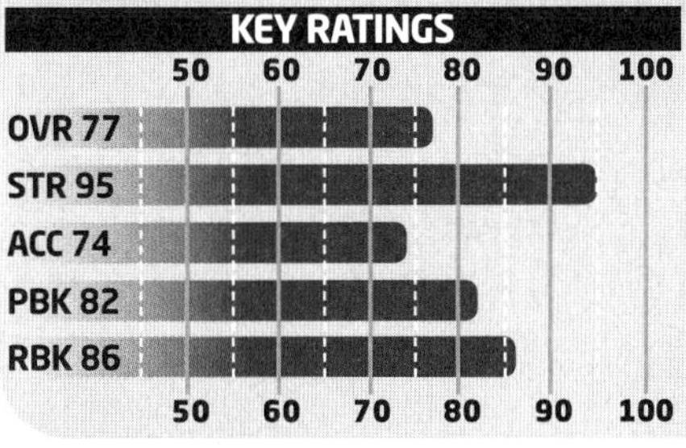

- Flowers is one of the stronger tackles in the game and should be able to get a push against almost anyone.
- While it would be nice to sit him for development, the Giants' line needs him to start right away due to injuries.

KEY SLEEPER

COREY WASHINGTON #88

WR #88 HT 6'4" WT 214 COLLEGE Newberry College EXP 1

KEY RATINGS

OVR 68
CIT 78
SPC 84
SPD 88
ACC 90

- Washington is one of the bigger targets on the Giants' roster and should be used to attack the seam.
- The Giants have tremendous depth at WR already, but try to find Washington a spot in a few formations.

OFFENSIVE DEPTH CHART

POS	FIRST	LAST	OVR
QB	ELI	MANNING	87
QB	RYAN	NASSIB	71
QB	RICKY	STANZI	64
HB	RASHAD	JENNINGS	80
HB	SHANE	VEREEN	81
HB	ANDRE	WILLIAMS	73
HB	ORLEANS	DARKWA	70
FB	HENRY	HYNOSKI	90
FB	NIKITA	WHITLOCK	61
WR	BECKHAM JR.	ODELL	94
WR	CRUZ	VICTOR	84
WR	RANDLE	RUEBEN	82
WR	HARRIS	DWAYNE	75
WR	PARKER	PRESTON	70
WR	WASHINGTON	COREY	66
TE	LARRY	DONNELL	79
TE	DANIEL	FELLS	76
TE	ADRIEN	ROBINSON	70
LT	ERECK	FLOWERS	73
LT	MARSHALL	NEWHOUSE	71
LG	JOHN	JERRY	77
LG	DALLAS	REYNOLDS	70
LG	BOBBY	HART	62
C	WESTON	RICHBURG	74
RG	GEOFF	SCHWARTZ	78
RG	ADAM	GETTIS	68
RG	ERIC	HERMAN	65
RT	JUSTIN	PUGH	79
RT	BRANDON	MOSLEY	70

DEFENSIVE DEPTH CHART

POS	FIRST	LAST	OVR
LE	ROBERT	AYERS	82
LE	CULLEN	JENKINS	78
DT	JOHNATHAN	HANKINS	86
DT	KENRICK	ELLIS	75
DT	MARKUS	KUHN	70
DT	JAY	BROMLEY	69
DT	DOMINIQUE	HAMILTON	68
RE	JASON	PIERRE-PAUL	89
RE	GEORGE	SELVIE	74
RE	OWAMAGBE	ODIGHIZUWA	69
LOLB	DEVON	KENNARD	79
LOLB	MARK	HERZLICH	75
MLB	JON	BEASON	79
MLB	JAMEEL	MCCLAIN	77
ROLB	VICTOR	BUTLER	76
ROLB	JONATHAN	CASILLAS	76
CB	DOMINIQUE	RODGERS-CROMARTIE	88
CB	PRINCE	AMUKAMARA	86
CB	TRUMAINE	MCBRIDE	75
CB	CHYKIE	BROWN	70
CB	JAYRON	HOSLEY	70
FS	COOPER	TAYLOR	71
FS	MYKKELE	THOMPSON	64
SS	LANDON	COLLINS	74
SS	NAT	BERHE	70

SPECIAL TEAMS

POS	FIRST	LAST	OVR
K	JOSH	BROWN	87
KR	ORLEANS	DARKWA	70
KR	PRESTON	PARKER	70
P	STEVE	WEATHERFORD	79
PR	ODELL	BECKHAM JR.	94

BEST OFFENSIVE PLAYS

PRO TIPS

- **These are the best two offensive plays in your playbook. They will get your playmakers in position to win you games.**
- **Rashad Jennings is a great early-down back who should be fresh this season with the added help of HB Shane Vereen on third down.**
- **The Giants have some great new shotgun formations this season. Take time to learn their strengths.**

BEST RUN: SINGLEBACK ACE PAIR SLOT–HB STRETCH

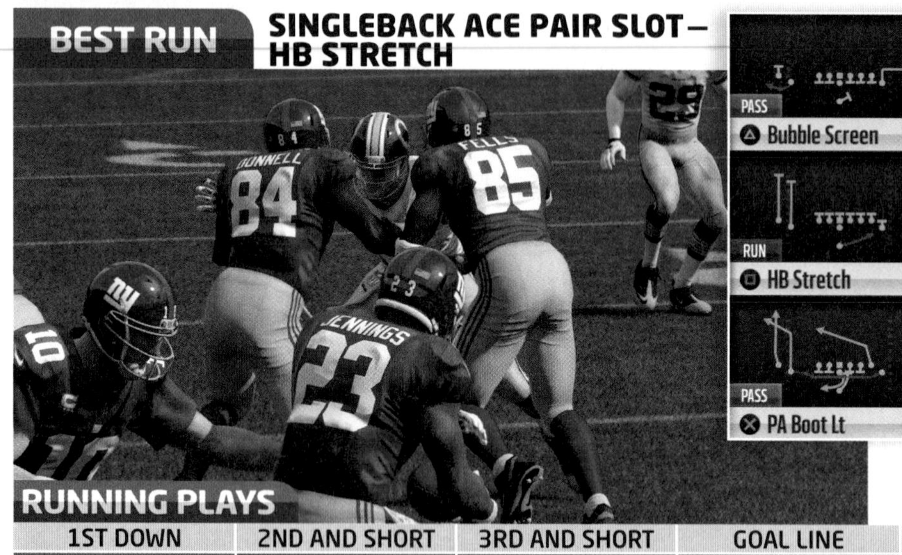

SETUP:

- Motion the slot WR or TE.
- The HB Stretch is a staple run of the Giants' playbook no matter what the formation. Look for the mismatch and playmaker the run off that edge.
- Expect opposing defenses to pay lots of attention to the two WRs in the left slot. Try adding some linemen to the right side for extra blocking.

ADVANCED SETUP:

- Playmaker the run to the left.

RUNNING PLAYS

1ST DOWN	2ND AND SHORT	3RD AND SHORT	GOAL LINE	2ND AND LONG	3RD AND LONG
Singleback Ace–HB Stretch	Singleback Ace–0 1 Trap	Full House Wide–Weak Zone	I-Form Tight–FB Dive Strong	Gun Doubles Flex Wing–HB Dive	Gun Spread–HB Draw
Singleback Ace Close–HB Blunt Dive	Strong Pro Twins–Inside Zone Split	Strong Pro–HB Stretch	Goal Line–QB Sneak	Gun Y-Trips Wk–HB Off Tackle	Gun Spread–HB Quick Base
I-Form Pro Twins–Power O	Strong Pro Twins–HB Dive	Singleback Wing Trio–HB Zone	I-Form Tight–FB Fake HB Toss	Gun Trio Offset–Inside Zone	Gun Y-Trips Open–5 6 Trap

INSIDE RUN | OUTSIDE RUN | SHOTGUN RUN | QB RUN

BEST PASS: GUN DOUBLES FLEX WK–SMASH

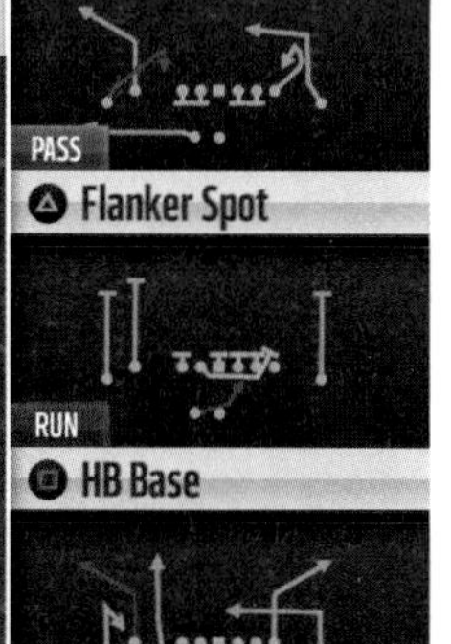

SETUP/READS:

- Against zone coverage look to throw a low pass over the middle to the HB. This is the throw that makes this play a winner.
- Against man-to-man coverage, time the throw with the TE's cut or wait for the slant over the middle.
- Against the blitz, hit the short route to the left and allow your playmakers to rack up yards after the catch.

ADVANCED SETUP:

- Slant the far right WR.

PASSING PLAYS

1ST DOWN	2ND AND SHORT	3RD AND SHORT	SHOT PLAYS	2ND AND LONG	3RD AND LONG
Gun Doubles Flex Wk–Flanker Dig	Gun Y-Trips Wk–PA Y-Out	Full House Wide–Comebacks	Gun Trio Offset–PA Post Shot	Singleback Ace Pair–TE Attack	Gun Doubles Flex Wk–HB Slips Screen
Gun Giant Trips–DBL Slants	Singleback Ace Pair–Drive	I-Form Pro–Mid Attack	Singleback Ace Pair Slot–PA Post Shot	Singleback Bunch Ace–Four Verticals	Gun Empty Giant–Giants Fork
Gun Y-Trips Open–WR Fork	Gun Trio Offset–TE In	Gun Giant Trips–Scat	Strong Pro Twins–PA Post Shot	Singleback Wing Trio–Four Verticals	Gun Doubles Wing Wk–Fork Y Seam

BASE PLAY | MAN BEATER | ZONE BEATER | BLITZ BEATER

 For more plays and strategies for this team, visit your eGuide using the access code sheet provided.

BEST DEFENSIVE PLAYS

PRO TIPS

- Rely on these defensive plays to lock up the run and pass.
- With the 5-2, you can always sub extra LBs in the game at defensive end and then drop them into coverage to make it a more versatile formation.
- The Nickel NASCAR is still a solid formation, but it needs some formation subs at the playcall screen to get everyone in the right spot to rush the passer.

BEST RUN D 5-2 NORMAL—COVER 2

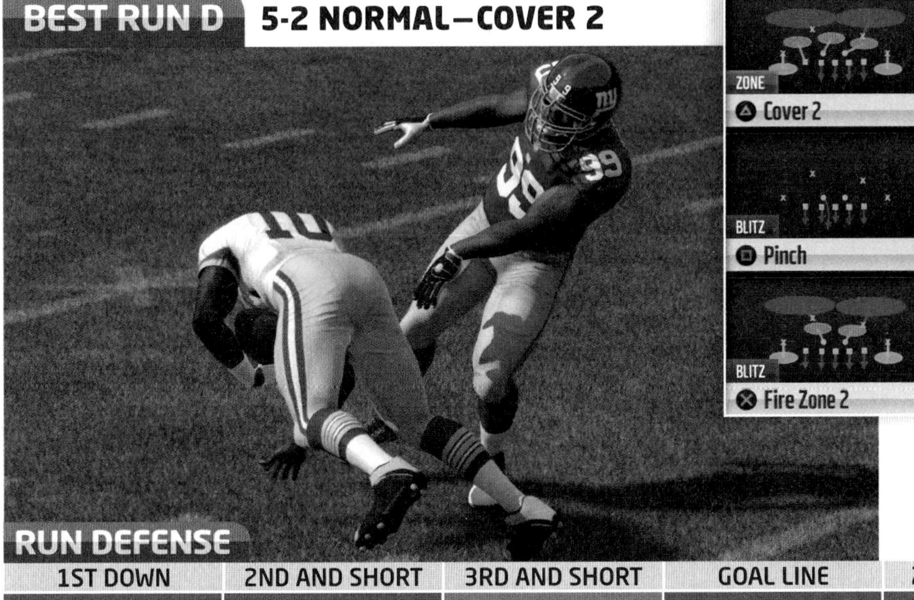

ZONE — Cover 2

BLITZ — Pinch

BLITZ — Fire Zone 2

SETUP:

- Make sure to spread the line and crash it down to make it an extremely solid front to run against.
- Use this as an every-down defense in the red zone. Make sure to shade underneath and change your deep zones to hook zones.

PLAYER TO CONTROL:

- The DE dropping into a hook zone

RUN DEFENSE

1ST DOWN	2ND AND SHORT	3RD AND SHORT	GOAL LINE	2ND AND LONG	3RD AND LONG
4-3 Stack–1 Sting Left	5-2 Normal–Cover 1	5-2 Normal–Pinch	Goal Line 5-4-2–Jam Cover 1	Dime Normal–1 QB Contain	Dollar 3-2-6–Cov 1 Robber Press
4-3 Stack–Free Fire 3	5-2 Normal–Cover 3	5-2 Normal–Trio Sky Zone	Goal Line 5-4-2–Flat Buzz	Dime Normal–3 Double Buzz	Dollar 3-2-6–SS Zone Blitz

MAN COVERAGE | ZONE COVERAGE | MAN BLITZ | ZONE BLITZ

BEST PASS D NICKEL NASCAR—COVER 4

BLITZ — FS Middle 3

BLITZ — Dbl Safety Blitz

ZONE — Cover 4

SETUP:

- The NASCAR formation should generate pressure without blitzing. Otherwise use the Double A Gap set in the Nickel formation.
- You can shade your coverage to the left or right depending on where the open side of the field is. This is one of the few times to shade.
- Your CBs in deep zones have enough speed to call press before the snap and still cover deep— use this to change the pre-snap look.

PLAYER TO CONTROL:

- The SS in a deep zone

PASS DEFENSE

1ST DOWN	2ND AND SHORT	3RD AND SHORT	GOAL LINE	2ND AND LONG	3RD AND LONG
4-3 Wide 9–Cover 1 Robber Press	4-3 Over–Cover 2 Man	Nickel NASCAR–Cover 1 Hole	Goal Line 5-3-3–MLB Gap A Zone	Nickel Double A Gap–Rush 3 Buzz	Quarter Normal–DB Strike 1
4-3 Wide 9–Cover 4 Press	4-3 Over–Strong Slant 3	Nickel NASCAR–Cover 2 QB Contain	Goal Line 5-3-3–Pinch Zone	Nickel Double A Gap–Nickel Overload 3	Quarter Normal–FZ 3 Sky

MAN COVERAGE | ZONE COVERAGE | MAN BLITZ | ZONE BLITZ

JACKSONVILLE JAGUARS

GAMEPLAY RATING 73

CONNECTED FRANCHISE MODE STRATEGY

CFM TEAM RATING: **80**
OFFENSE: **81**
DEFENSE: **83**
OFFENSIVE SCHEME: **West Coast**
DEFENSIVE SCHEME: **Attacking 4-3**
STRENGTHS: **RG, TE, DT**
WEAKNESSES: **SS, CB, HB, WR**

2014 TEAM RANKINGS

3rd AFC South (3-13-0)
PASSING OFFENSE: **31st**
RUSHING OFFENSE: **21st**
PASSING DEFENSE: **22nd**
RUSHING DEFENSE: **27th**

2014 TEAM LEADERS

PASSING: **Blake Bortles: 2,908**
RUSHING: **Denard Robinson: 582**
RECEIVING: **Allen Hurns: 677**
TACKLES: **Johnathan Cyprien: 114**
SACKS: **Sen'Derrick Marks: 8.5**
INTS: **J.T. Thomas: 2**

KEY ADDITIONS

HB Bernard Pierce
TE Julius Thomas
CB Davon House

KEY ROOKIES

LB Dante Fowler Jr.
HB T.J. Yeldon
G A.J. Cann

OWNER: **Shad Khan**
LEGACY SCORE: **0**

COACH: **Gus Bradley**
LEVEL: **4**
LEGACY SCORE: **10**
OFFENSIVE SCHEME: **West Coast**
DEFENSIVE SCHEME: **Attacking 4-3**

OFFENSIVE SCOUTING REPORT

- QB Blake Bortles had a decent start after taking over for Chad Henne last season. Continue to improve his completion percentage with easy throws and to help cut down on turnovers.
- Rookie HB T.J. Yeldon is most deserving of the carries in the backfield. While you have some nice backups with unique styles, work on turning him into a franchise back. The offensive line is coming along nicely and should help.
- The receiving corps is still very young after a big draft last season. Think young and figure out which players really fit with your scheme. Cecil Shorts has moved on, and a new leader will need to step up.

DEFENSIVE SCOUTING REPORT

- The Jags' defensive line has finesse off the edge and power in the middle. Make sure to note who can stop the run, otherwise you may never get into a long-yardage situation where you can tee off on the opposing passer.
- LB Paul Posluszny is the anchor in the middle of the defense, but Telvin Smith proved last season he has what it takes to become a starter. Continue to develop him and look for a veteran at LOLB until the draft.
- The Jaguars have a the initial pieces for a solid man coverage secondary. This will all be made easier if the pass rush can get to the QB.

SCHEDULE

Week	Date	Time	Network	Opponent
1	SEP 13	1:00	FOX	PANTHERS
2	SEP 20	4:05		DOLPHINS
3	SEP 27	1:00		PATRIOTS
4	OCT 04	1:00		COLTS
5	OCT 11	1:00		BUCCANEERS
6	OCT 18	1:00		TEXANS
7	OCT 25	9:30		BILLS
8	BYE WEEK			
9	NOV 08	1:00		JETS
10	NOV 15	1:00		RAVENS
11	NOV 19	8:25		TITANS
12	NOV 29	1:00		CHARGERS
13	DEC 06	1:00		TITANS
14	DEC 13	1:00		COLTS
15	DEC 20	1:00	FOX	FALCONS
16	DEC 27	1:00		SAINTS
17	JAN 03	1:00		TEXANS

KEY PLAYERS

KEY OFFENSIVE PLAYER

JULIUS THOMAS #80

TE #80 HT 6'5" WT 250 COLLEGE Portland St. EXP 4

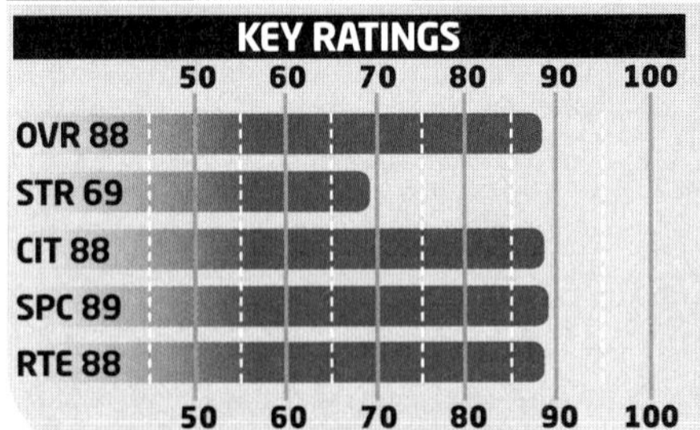

- Thomas adds great size to a TE group already featuring a big body in Marcedes Lewis.
- Find Thomas on third down and let him become Bortles's favorite target in the red zone.

KEY DEFENSIVE PLAYER

SEN'DERRICK MARKS #99

DT #99 HT 6'2" WT 294 COLLEGE Auburn EXP 6

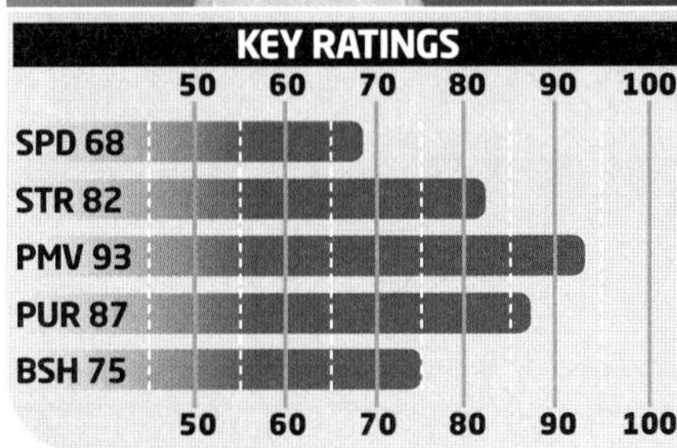

- Marks is a perfect fit for the Jags' scheme. He wouldn't be able to stop the run in a 3-4 system at DT.
- Marks is built to rush the passer from the interior of the line.

KEY ROOKIE

DANTE FOWLER JR. #56

RE #56 HT 6'3" WT 261 COLLEGE Florida EXP Rookie

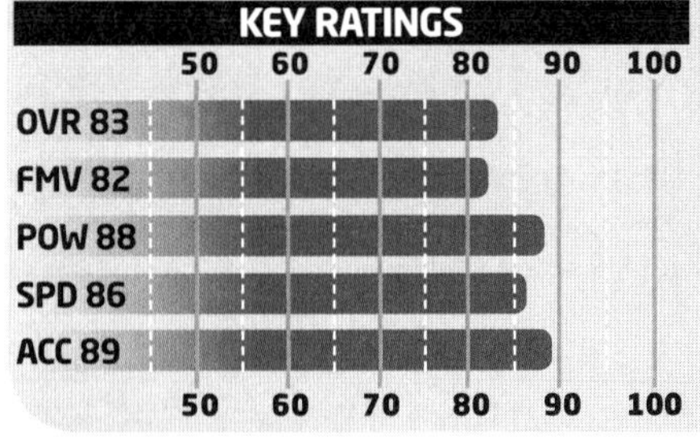

- Fowler is a promising young talent to rush off the edge. His speed means he will be perfect in Gus Bradley's defensive scheme.
- Fowler suffered an injury during training camp, so focus your development on rookie T.J. Yeldon until he returns.

KEY SLEEPER

MATT DANIELS #42

SS #42 HT 6'0" WT 212 COLLEGE Duke EXP 3

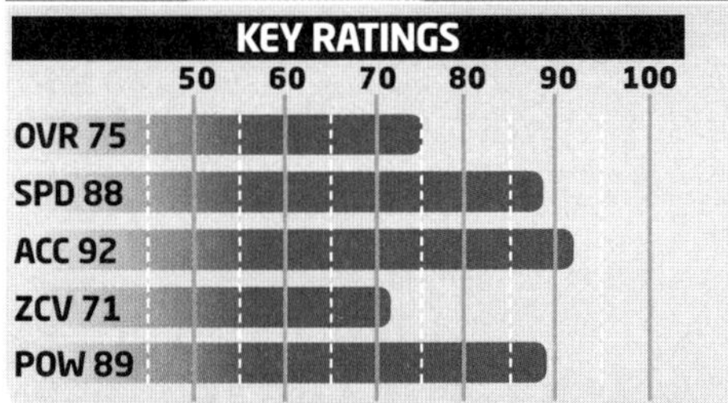

- Daniels shouldn't start over Johnathan Cyprien, but there is room for both of them on the field in some formations.
- The real key for Daniels is the 89 Hit Power; this is perfect for special teams. Keep developing him, especially his agility.

OFFENSIVE DEPTH CHART

POS	FIRST	LAST	OVR
QB	BLAKE	BORTLES	74
QB	CHAD	HENNE	73
QB	STEPHEN	MORRIS	64
HB	DENARD	ROBINSON	74
HB	TOBY	GERHART	73
HB	T.J.	YELDON	73
HB	BERNARD	PIERCE	72
FB	NIC	JACOBS	70
WR	ALLEN	ROBINSON	79
WR	MARQISE	LEE	74
WR	ALLEN	HURNS	73
WR	RASHAD	GREENE	71
WR	ACE	SANDERS	71
TE	JULIUS	THOMAS	89
TE	MARCEDES	LEWIS	81
TE	CLAY	HARBOR	74
LT	LUKE	JOECKEL	76
LT	SAM	YOUNG	65
LT	BRENNAN	WILLIAMS	60
LG	ZANE	BEADLES	83
LG	A.J.	CANN	73
C	STEFEN	WISNIEWSKI	80
C	LUKE	BOWANKO	75
RG	BRANDON	LINDER	87
RG	TYLER	SHATLEY	67
RT	JERMEY	PARNELL	84
RT	AUSTIN	PASZTOR	74
RT	JOSH	WELLS	73

DEFENSIVE DEPTH CHART

POS	FIRST	LAST	OVR
LE	TYSON	ALUALU	76
LE	ANDRE	BRANCH	75
DT	SEN'DERRICK	MARKS	87
DT	JARED	ODRICK	84
DT	ZIGGY	HOOD	78
DT	ROY	MILLER	75
DT	ABRY	JONES	68
RE	CHRIS	CLEMONS	77
RE	RYAN	DAVIS	76
RE	CHRIS	SMITH	70
LOLB	DAN	SKUTA	80
LOLB	LAROY	REYNOLDS	73
LOLB	KHAIRI	FORTT	68
MLB	PAUL	POSLUSZNY	83
MLB	JEREMIAH	GEORGE	67
ROLB	TELVIN	SMITH	79
ROLB	JOHN	LOTULELEI	68
CB	DAVON	HOUSE	80
CB	DWAYNE	GRATZ	78
CB	DEMETRIUS	MCCRAY	77
CB	AARON	COLVIN	71
CB	TOMMIE	CAMPBELL	66
FS	SERGIO	BROWN	80
FS	JOSH	EVANS	70
SS	JOHNATHAN	CYPRIEN	79
SS	CRAIG	LOSTON	71
SS	JAMES	SAMPLE	67

SPECIAL TEAMS

POS	FIRST	LAST	OVR
K	JOSH	SCOBEE	85
KR	DENARD	ROBINSON	74
KR	ACE	SANDERS	71
P	BRYAN	ANGER	86
PR	ACE	SANDERS	71

BEST OFFENSIVE PLAYS

PRO TIPS
- These are the best two offensive plays in your playbook. They will get your playmakers in position to win you games.
- Don't forget which player you have subbed in the game at HB; you need a run to fit his style.
- The Jaguars now have one of the best TEs in the game, so target him consistently.

BEST RUN: SINGLEBACK ACE TWINS–HB COUNTER

PASS — Curl Flat

RUN — HB Counter

PASS — PA Ctr Waggle

SETUP:
- Motion the inside WR across (optional).
- We prefer to use our most athletic back. As long as the blocking is sound, we won't need to break many tackles.
- Wait as long as possible before breaking the run outside.
- You can always call the stretch from this formation if you want to run to the open side of the field.

ADVANCED SETUP:
- Playmaker this run to the opposite side.

RUNNING PLAYS

1ST DOWN	2ND AND SHORT	3RD AND SHORT	GOAL LINE	2ND AND LONG	3RD AND LONG
Singleback Ace Twins–HB Counter	Singleback Doubles–0 1 Trap	I-Form Pro–FB Dive Strong	Goal Line–HB Sting	Pistol Weak–Read Option	Gun Split Jaguar–Power O
Singleback Ace Pair Slot–HB Dive	I-Form Tight Pair–Iso	Weak Pro Twins–HB Blast	I-Form Pro–FB Fake HB Flip	Pistol Slot Wing–Inside Zone Split	Pistol Ace–Strong Power
Strong Pro–HB Stretch	I-Form Tight–HB Blast	Pistol Weak–Power Option	Singleback Jumbo Z–HB Pitch	Pistol Ace–HB Counter	Gun Bunch Wk–HB Mid Draw

INSIDE RUN | OUTSIDE RUN | SHOTGUN RUN | QB RUN

BEST PASS: GUN BUNCH QUADS–DRAG UNDER

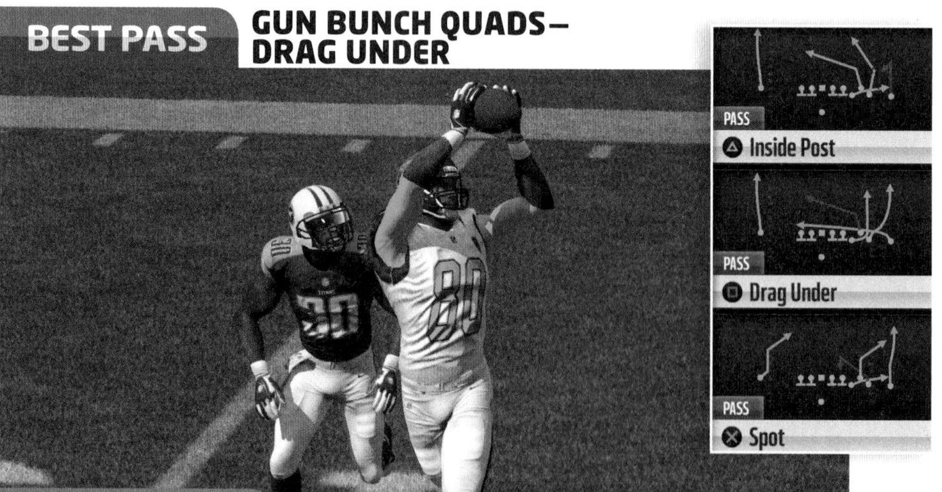

PASS — Inside Post

PASS — Drag Under

PASS — Spot

SETUP/READS:
- Against zone coverage look to throw a high pass into the seam to the TE. Find your favorite route for the solo WR on the left (slant).
- To make this more of an every-down formation, continue to hit the drag over the middle and RAC (run after the catch).
- This formation is extremely difficult to line up against and can force defenses to forget about blitzing.

ADVANCED SETUP:
- Utilize the Twin TE package.

PASSING PLAYS

1ST DOWN	2ND AND SHORT	3RD AND SHORT	SHOT PLAYS	2ND AND LONG	3RD AND LONG
Gun Bunch Wk–Y Trail	Strong Pro–F Angle	Gun Bunch Wk–PA Post	Singleback Ace Pair Slot–PA Misdirect Shot	Gun Bunch Quads–TE Angle	Gun Bunch Wk–Verticals
Pistol Slot Wing–PA Slot Cross	Gun Spread Y-Flex–Circle	I-Form Pro–Texas	Singleback Ace–PA Deep Shot	Gun Trips Y Iso–Deep Attack	Gun Bunch Quads–Drag Under
Singleback Ace Twins–Jags TE Drag	Pistol Slot Wing–PA Zone Shot	Gun Y-Trips HB Wk–PA Read	Gun Trips TE–PA Shot Wheel	Pistol Weak–PA Cross Shot	Gun Trey Open–Jags X Drag

BASE PLAY | MAN BEATER | ZONE BEATER | BLITZ BEATER

BEST DEFENSIVE PLAYS

PRO TIPS

- **If you want to win more games in *Madden NFL 16*, rely on these defensive plays to lock up the run and pass.**
- Nickel Wide 9 takes advantage of the Jaguars' best defensive options. Allow your MLBs to control the middle of the field.
- The 46 Normal–Zone Blitz will let your opponent know that you are serious about stopping the run.

BEST RUN D: 46 NORMAL–ZONE BLITZ

ZONE
Cover 3

MAN
Cover 1 Hole

BLITZ
Zone Blitz

SETUP:

- Unless it is short yardage, commit to the pass before the play; you should still stop the run and will limit any damage from play-action passes.
- Make sure that the defenders dropping into zone coverage on the play are your more athletic defenders.
- Do *not* crash the defensive line on this play. But you can base align before the snap.

PLAYER TO CONTROL:

- Safety in a deep zone

RUN DEFENSE

1ST DOWN	2ND AND SHORT	3RD AND SHORT	GOAL LINE	2ND AND LONG	3RD AND LONG
46 Normal–Cover 1 Hole	4-3 Stack–Cov 1 Robber Press	46 Normal–Inside Blitz	Goal Line 5-4-2–Jam Cover 1	Nickel Wide 9–1 LB Blitz	Dime Normal–Cover 2 Man
46 Normal–Cover 2 Invert	4-3 Stack–Aggie Cloud Star	46 Normal–Fire Zone 3	Goal Line 5-4-2–Flat Buzz	Nickel Normal–CB Blitz 3 Press	Dime Normal–Cover 2 Show 4

MAN COVERAGE | ZONE COVERAGE | MAN BLITZ | ZONE BLITZ

BEST PASS D: NICKEL 3-3-5 WIDE–3 BUZZ SHOW 2

ZONE
Cov 2 QB Contain

BLITZ
Overload 3 Seam 2

ZONE
3 Buzz Show 2

SETUP:

- By switching between the Cov 2 QB Contain and this play, we can fool our opponent and change the look of our safeties.
- The LBs running out to their zones after the snap can create some big turnovers for the defense.

PLAYER TO CONTROL:

- DE on the left side of the screen (rush)

PASS DEFENSE

1ST DOWN	2ND AND SHORT	3RD AND SHORT	GOAL LINE	2ND AND LONG	3RD AND LONG
46 Normal–1 QB Contain	4-3 Over–Sam Will Blitz	46 Normal–1 Rush Outside	Goal Line 5-3-3–GL Man	Dollar 3-2-6–Mike Edge 1	Nickel Wide 9–Odd LB Dogs
46 Normal–Cover 3	4-3 Over–Fire Zone 2	46 Normal–Zone Blitz	Goal Line 5-3-3–GL Zone	Dollar 3-2-6–Max Sting 3	Nickel Wide 9–Odd Overload 4

MAN COVERAGE | ZONE COVERAGE | MAN BLITZ | ZONE BLITZ

NEW YORK JETS

GAMEPLAY RATING 76

CONNECTED FRANCHISE MODE STRATEGY

CFM TEAM RATING: **84**
OFFENSE: **83**
DEFENSE: **91**
OFFENSIVE SCHEME: **Spread**
DEFENSIVE SCHEME: **Attacking 3-4**
STRENGTHS: **WR, C, LT, DE, DT, CB**
WEAKNESSES: **QB, HB, TE, SS, LOLB**

2014 TEAM RANKINGS

4th AFC East (4-12-0)
PASSING OFFENSE: **32nd**
RUSHING OFFENSE: **3rd**
PASSING DEFENSE: **14th**
RUSHING DEFENSE: **5th**

2014 TEAM LEADERS

PASSING: **Geno Smith: 2,525**
RUSHING: **Chris Ivory: 821**
RECEIVING: **Eric Decker: 962**
TACKLES: **David Harris: 123**
SACKS: **Sheldon Richardson: 8**
INTS: **Darrin Walls: 2**

KEY ADDITIONS

CB Darrelle Revis
QB Ryan Fitzpatrick
HB Zac Stacy
HB Stevan Ridley
WR Brandon Marshall

KEY ROOKIES

DE Leonard Williams
WR Devin Smith
LB Lorenzo Mauldin

OWNER: **Woody Johnson**
LEGACY SCORE: **200**

COACH: **Todd Bowles**
LEVEL: **12**
LEGACY SCORE: **150**
OFFENSIVE SCHEME: **Spread**
DEFENSIVE SCHEME: **Attacking 3-4**

OFFENSIVE SCOUTING REPORT

- Bringing QB Ryan Fitzpatrick into town doesn't mean the Jets have given up on Geno Smith. If you can get him some confidence early in the season, he should be your starting QB.
- The Jets have built up a stable of powerful HBs. Keep an eye out to see who has the hot hand and stick with him. In the passing game, the best option is Bilal Powell unless you can trade or find someone in free agency.
- The WR position has really filled out nicely and should give the QB some confidence when throwing to the outside. Keep developing your young TE, Jace Amaro, as he has the size and speed to become a dominant TE in this league.

DEFENSIVE SCOUTING REPORT

- The Jets' defensive line doesn't have to bring up extra defenders in the box to stop the run. This will allow you to focus on your LBs and getting them into good position to make plays.
- The Jets' LBs could be pretty solid in a 4-3 style defense. This would be something to keep in mind after year one with all the depth available; consider going with a hybrid scheme. If you don't have the guts to blitz heavily, this would let you send your front four after the passer.
- The Jets are back to having a dominant secondary. Utilize their speed and man coverage ability to send aggressive blitzes that will get your defense off the field on third down.

SCHEDULE

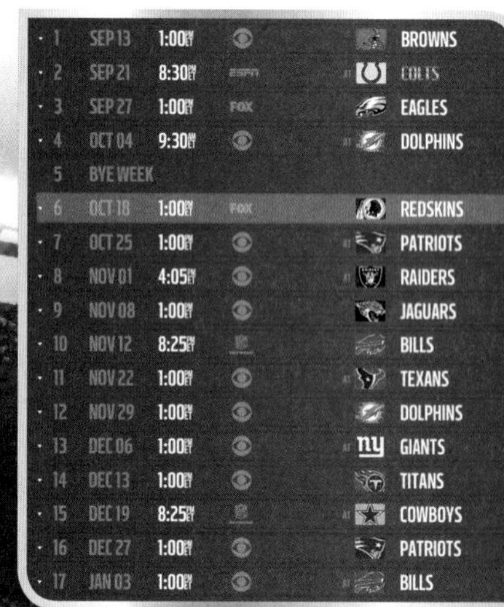

Week	Date	Time	TV		Opponent
1	SEP 13	1:00 PM ET			BROWNS
2	SEP 21	8:30 PM ET	ESPN	AT	COLTS
3	SEP 27	1:00 PM ET	FOX		EAGLES
4	OCT 04	9:30 AM ET		AT	DOLPHINS
5	BYE WEEK				
6	OCT 18	1:00 PM ET	FOX		REDSKINS
7	OCT 25	1:00 PM ET		AT	PATRIOTS
8	NOV 01	4:05 PM ET		AT	RAIDERS
9	NOV 08	1:00 PM ET			JAGUARS
10	NOV 12	8:25 PM ET			BILLS
11	NOV 22	1:00 PM ET		AT	TEXANS
12	NOV 29	1:00 PM ET			DOLPHINS
13	DEC 06	1:00 PM ET		AT	GIANTS
14	DEC 13	1:00 PM ET			TITANS
15	DEC 19	8:25 PM ET		AT	COWBOYS
16	DEC 27	1:00 PM ET			PATRIOTS
17	JAN 03	1:00 PM ET		AT	BILLS

KEY PLAYERS

KEY OFFENSIVE PLAYER

BRANDON MARSHALL #15

WR #15 HT 6'4" WT 230 COLLEGE UCF EXP 9

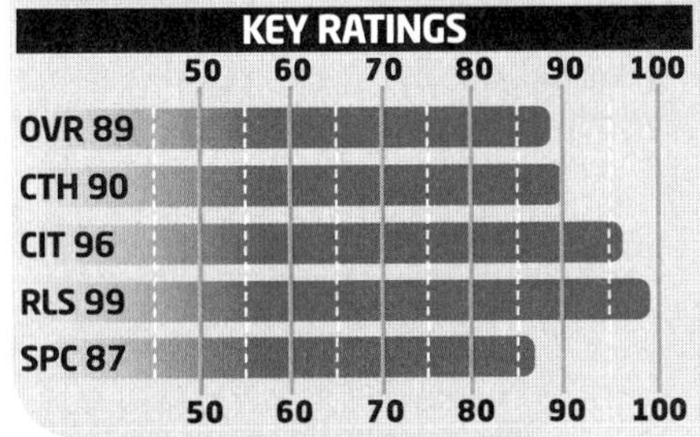

- Marshall no longer has the speed to burn anyone downfield, but he can be counted on in the red zone.
- There won't be a CB in the league who can consistently win a battle at the line of scrimmage with Marshall, so use that to your advantage.

KEY DEFENSIVE PLAYER

MUHAMMAD WILKERSON #96

LE #96 HT 6'4" WT 315 COLLEGE Temple EXP 4

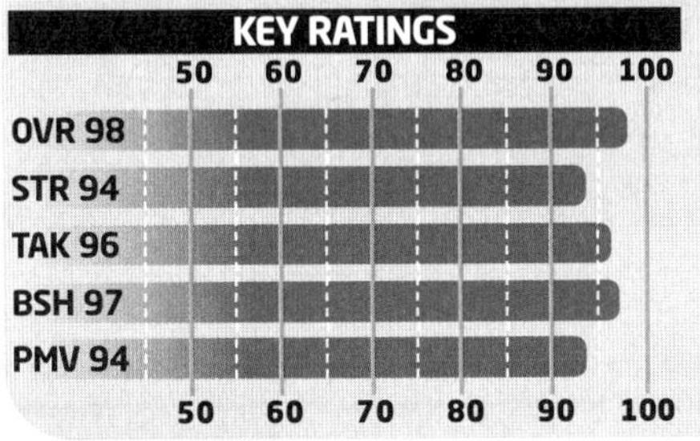

- Wilkerson is an amazing talent who should be the face of your franchise for the long term.
- Having Wilkerson in the lineup allows you to worry less about the run and focus on setting up to stop the pass.

KEY ROOKIE

LEONARD WILLIAMS

LE #62 HT 6'5" WT 302 COLLEGE USC EXP Rookie

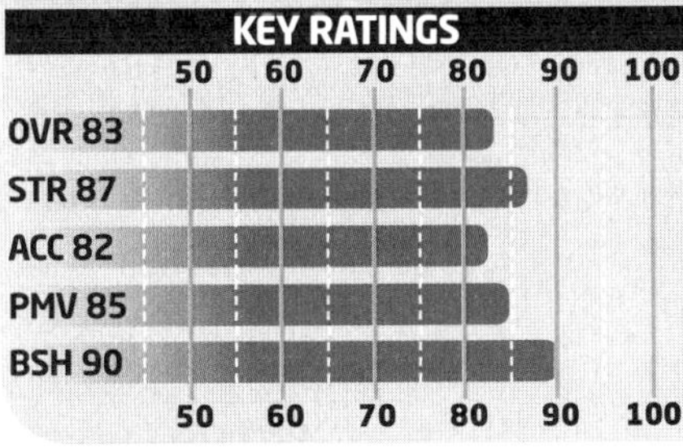

- Williams wasn't a necessity for the Jets, but his presence adds depth and makes an already great unit even greater.
- With so many other pieces around Williams, be sure to put him into the best situation to grow as a player before using him on an every-down basis.

KEY SLEEPER

SAALIM HAKIM

WR #19 HT 5'11" WT 188 COLLEGE Palomar College EXP 3

KEY RATINGS

Rating	Value
OVR	52
SPD	96
CTH	70
ACC	95
RLS	39

- It can be hard to justify a roster spot for a player with only one true ability, but that speed is a potential game changer.
- Hakim may even be solid as just a decoy—he could get the defense to back off just a few steps.

OFFENSIVE DEPTH CHART

POS	FIRST	LAST	OVR
QB	RYAN	FITZPATRICK	78
QB	GENO	SMITH	76
QB	BRYCE	PETTY	70
HB	CHRIS	IVORY	80
HB	STEVAN	RIDLEY	76
HB	ZAC	STACY	76
HB	BILAL	POWELL	74
FB	TOMMY	BOHANON	76
WR	BRANDON	MARSHALL	89
WR	ERIC	DECKER	86
WR	JEREMY	KERLEY	76
WR	DEVIN	SMITH	72
WR	T.J.	GRAHAM	71
WR	DEVIER	POSEY	68
TE	JACE	AMARO	76
TE	JEFF	CUMBERLAND	74
TE	KELLEN	DAVIS	74
LT	D'BRICKASHAW	FERGUSON	84
LT	BEN	IJALANA	66
LG	WILLIE	COLON	77
LG	JAMES	BREWER	74
LG	BRIAN	WINTERS	69
C	NICK	MANGOLD	95
C	DALTON	FREEMAN	69
C	WESLEY	JOHNSON	67
RG	JAMES	CARPENTER	80
RG	DAKOTA	DOZIER	69
RG	JARVIS	HARRISON	68
RT	BRENO	GIACOMINI	78
RT	ODAY	ABOUSHI	75

DEFENSIVE DEPTH CHART

POS	FIRST	LAST	OVR
LE	MUHAMMAD	WILKERSON	96
LE	LEONARD	WILLIAMS	80
LE	KEVIN	VICKERSON	74
DT	DAMON	HARRISON	88
DT	DEON	SIMON	64
RE	SHELDON	RICHARDSON	92
RE	STEPHEN	BOWEN	73
RE	T.J.	BARNES	62
LOLB	CALVIN	PACE	77
LOLB	TREVOR	REILLY	69
LOLB	LORENZO	MAULDIN	67
MLB	DEMARIO	DAVIS	81
MLB	DAVID	HARRIS	81
MLB	JOE	MAYS	77
MLB	JAMARI	LATTIMORE	72
ROLB	JASON	BABIN	79
ROLB	QUINTON	COPLES	79
ROLB	IKEMEFUNA	ENEMKPALI	68
CB	DARRELLE	REVIS	97
CB	ANTONIO	CROMARTIE	86
CB	BUSTER	SKRINE	78
CB	DEE	MILLINER	77
CB	MARCUS	WILLIAMS	71
FS	CALVIN	PRYOR	82
FS	ANTONIO	ALLEN	79
FS	RONTEZ	MILES	71
SS	MARCUS	GILCHRIST	79
SS	JAIQUAWN	JARRETT	79

SPECIAL TEAMS

POS	FIRST	LAST	OVR
K	NICK	FOLK	80
KR	T.J.	GRAHAM	71
KR	WALTER	POWELL	62
P	RYAN	QUIGLEY	84
PR	JEREMY	KERLEY	76

BEST OFFENSIVE PLAYS

PRO TIPS

- These are the best two offensive plays in your playbook. They will get your playmakers in position to win you games.
- Don't get fancy with the run game. If the run is built to go straight ahead, keep it there.
- Any pressure you can take off the QB with play action and simple reads will improve your offense.

BEST RUN: GUN TRIPS OPEN LEFT—INSIDE ZONE

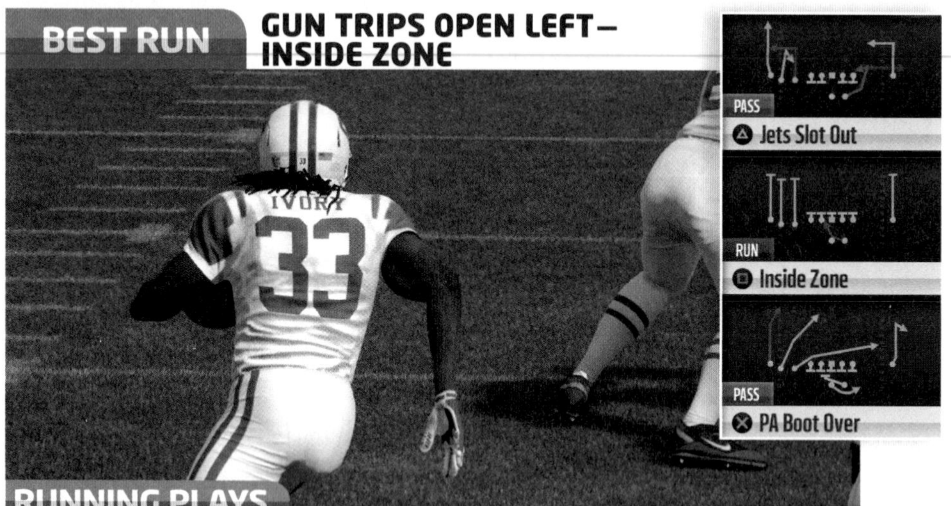

SETUP:

- The left guard is the key to knowing which hole to hit. If he doesn't get any push, try to make an adjustment.
- This formation has strong play-action options, so work this run early to set up for later in the game.

ADVANCED SETUP:

- Motion a WR across the formation (optional).

RUNNING PLAYS

1ST DOWN	2ND AND SHORT	3RD AND SHORT	GOAL LINE	2ND AND LONG	3RD AND LONG
Singleback Ace Pair Twins—Outside Zone	Singleback Ace—0 1 Trap	I-Form Pro—Inside Zone	Goal Line—QB Sneak	Pistol Wing Trips—Counter Y	Gun Trips Open Left—Inside Zone
Singleback Bunch Ace—Inside Zone	Singleback Jumbo—HB Dive	Strong Tight Pair—HB Toss	Goal Line—FB Dive	Pistol Strong Slot—HB Draw	Gun Trips Open Left—HB Counter
Singleback Bunch Ace—Quick Pitch	I-Form Pro Twins—HB Blast	Pistol Strong Slot—FB Belly	Strong Twins Flex—HB Toss	Gun Split Jet—Power O	Gun Spread Y-Slot—HB Draw

INSIDE RUN | OUTSIDE RUN | SHOTGUN RUN | QB RUN

BEST PASS: GUN TRIPS Y-FLEX TIGHT—HB ANGLE

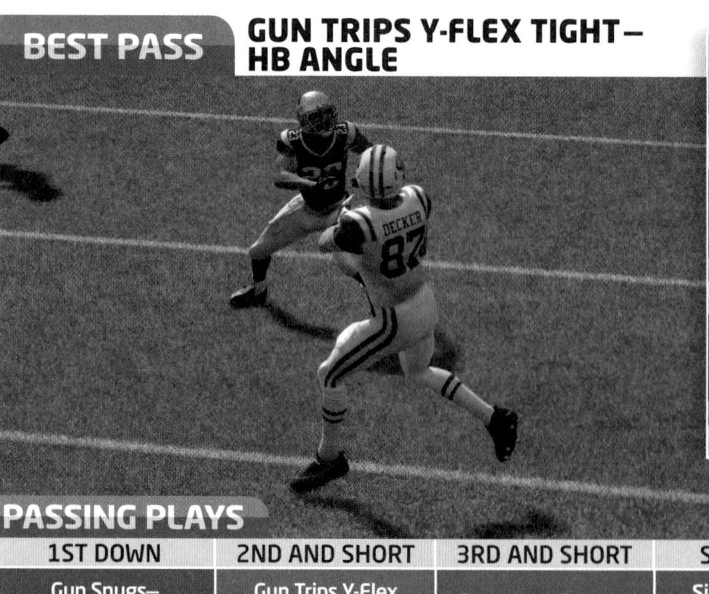

SETUP/READS:

- If the slot WR gets pressed, it can really mess up the timing and spacing of the play. Consider clearing him out if you play a physical team.
- Against man-to-man coverage look to the side with the TE and HB and throw on their cuts.
- Against the blitz hit the zig route or consider taking a shot downfield if you have the matchup advantage.

ADVANCED SETUP:

- Slant the inside WR (optional).
- Flip the play.

PASSING PLAYS

1ST DOWN	2ND AND SHORT	3RD AND SHORT	SHOT PLAYS	2ND AND LONG	3RD AND LONG
Gun Snugs—Jet Slot Post	Gun Trips Y-Flex Tight—Scat	I-Form Pro—Mid Attack	Singleback Ace—PA Shot Post	Gun Split Jet—Jets Go's	Gun Bunch Quads—Drag Under
Gun Bunch Wk—Jets DBL Trail	Gun Doubles—TE Stick	Strong Pro—F Angle	Gun Trips Open Left—PA Boot Over	Singleback Ace—Inside Cross	Gun Empty Spread—Four Verticals
Gun Split Jet—Jets Slot Cross	Strong Pro—Spacing	Gun Trips Y-Flex Tight—TE In	Pistol Wing Trips—PA Double Post	Singleback Bunch Ace—Verticals	Gun Trey Open—Strong Flood

BASE PLAY | MAN BEATER | ZONE BEATER | BLITZ BEATER

 For more plays and strategies for this team, visit your eGuide using the access code sheet provided.

BEST DEFENSIVE PLAYS

PRO TIPS

- If you want to win more games in *Madden NFL 16*, rely on these defensive plays to lock up the run and pass.
- Always try to have your three best defensive linemen in the game, even on passing downs.
- Your CBs are your biggest advantage; don't be afraid to blitz and leave them on an island.

BEST RUN D: 3-4 SOLID–TRIO SKY ZONE

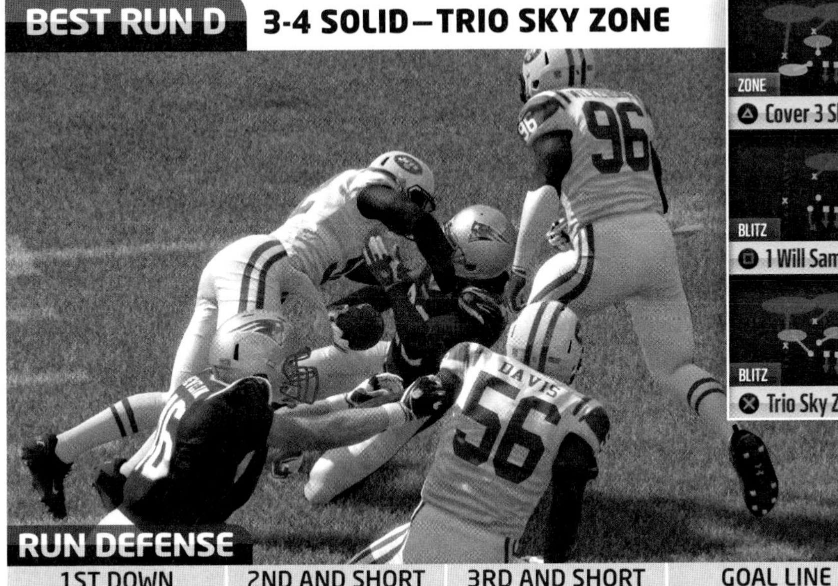

- ZONE — Cover 3 Sky
- BLITZ — 1 Will Sam Go
- BLITZ — Trio Sky Zone

SETUP:

- This run plugs the middle with your three best linemen, and your LBs will stay wide and do the rest.
- The blitzing LB can often sneak past linemen to get tackles in the backfield. Smart teams will run outside and away from him, so don't get greedy.

PLAYER TO CONTROL:

- Any defensive lineman

RUN DEFENSE

1ST DOWN	2ND AND SHORT	3RD AND SHORT	GOAL LINE	2ND AND LONG	3RD AND LONG
3-4 Solid–Cover 2 Man	3-4 Over–Cover 1 Hole	3-4 Over–Sting Pinch	Goal Line 5-4-2–Jam Cover 1	Nickel 2-4-5 Prowl–Cover 2 Man	Big Dime 2-3-6–1 Robber Show 2
3-4 Solid–Cover 2 Press	3-4 Over–Sam Mike 3	3-4 Over–Sting Pinch Zone	Goal Line 5-4-2–Flat Buzz	Nickel 2-4-5 Prowl–Cover 2 Drop	Big Dime 2-3-6–Cover 6 Show 2

MAN COVERAGE | ZONE COVERAGE | MAN BLITZ | ZONE BLITZ

BEST PASS D: NICKEL 3-3-5 WIDE–COVER 1 ROBBER

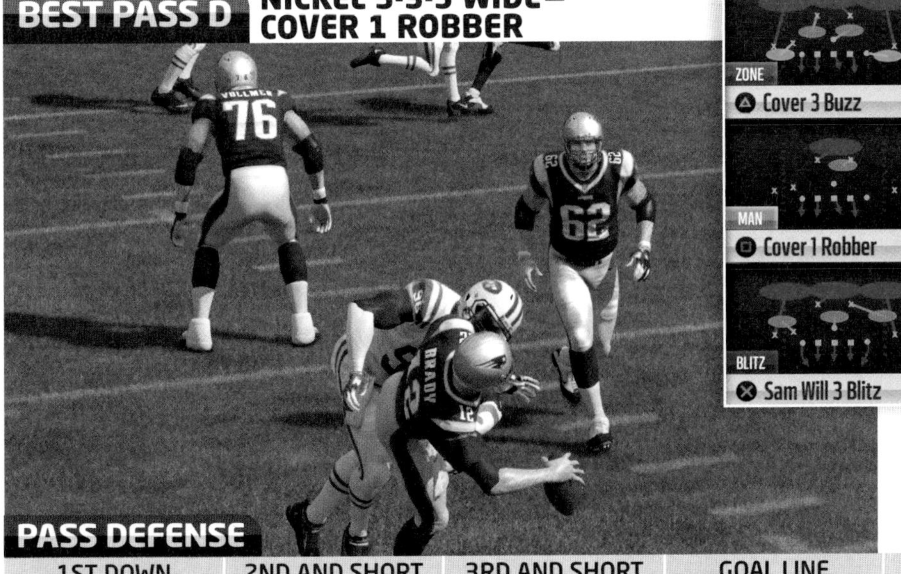

- ZONE — Cover 3 Buzz
- MAN — Cover 1 Robber
- BLITZ — Sam Will 3 Blitz

SETUP:

- The OLB in man coverage is your biggest vulnerability on this play, so help out with your user safety.
- Try using a package to flip your two safeties, this will take advantage of their skill sets.
- If the HB doesn't run a route, you will have an extra defender in coverage over the middle.

PLAYER TO CONTROL:

- Safety in a hook zone

PASS DEFENSE

1ST DOWN	2ND AND SHORT	3RD AND SHORT	GOAL LINE	2ND AND LONG	3RD AND LONG
3-4 Solid–Cover 2 Man	Nickel 2-4-5 Even–Cover 2 Sink	Nickel 3-3-5 Wide–Cover 1 Robber	Goal Line 5-3-3–GL Man	3-4 Even–1 QB Contain	Big Dime 1-4-6–DB Sting
3-4 Solid–Cover 4	Nickel 2-4-5 Even–Cover 2	Nickel 3-3-5 Wide–Sam Will 3 Blitz	Goal Line 5-3-3–Pinch Zone	3-4 Even–SS Scrape 3	Big Dime 1-4-6–Spinner Dog 3

MAN COVERAGE | ZONE COVERAGE | MAN BLITZ | ZONE BLITZ

DETROIT LIONS

GAMEPLAY RATING 83

CONNECTED FRANCHISE MODE STRATEGY

CFM TEAM RATING: **86**
OFFENSE: **85**
DEFENSE: **89**
OFFENSIVE SCHEME: **Vertical**
DEFENSIVE SCHEME: **Attacking 4-3**
STRENGTHS: **QB, WR, FS**
WEAKNESSES: **LE, HB, C**

2014 TEAM RANKINGS

2nd NFC North (11-5-0)
PASSING OFFENSE: **12th**
RUSHING OFFENSE: **28th**
PASSING DEFENSE: **13th**
RUSHING DEFENSE: **1st**

2014 TEAM LEADERS

PASSING: **Matthew Stafford: 4,257**
RUSHING: **Joique Bell: 860**
RECEIVING: **Golden Tate: 1,331**
TACKLES: **DeAndre Levy: 151**
SACKS: **Ndamukong Suh: 8.5**
INTS: **Glover Quin: 7**

KEY ADDITIONS

WR Lance Moore
CB Rashean Mathis
DT Tyrunn Walker

KEY ROOKIES

G Laken Tomlinson
HB Ameer Abdullah
CB Alex Carter

OWNER: **Edward Crocker**
LEGACY SCORE: **0**

COACH: **Jim Caldwell**
LEVEL: **19**
LEGACY SCORE: **700**
OFFENSIVE SCHEME: **Vertical**
DEFENSIVE SCHEME: **Attacking 4-3**

OFFENSIVE SCOUTING REPORT

- QB Matt Stafford still has one of the biggest arms in the NFL, but he will need to be more consistent on short passes to lead the Lions to the promised land. There is no use in upgrading his Play Action rating, since the Lions rarely run the ball.
- HB Reggie Bush moves on from the Lions; however, Joique Bell is ready to step in and take over in the passing game. While he doesn't have the top end speed, he is a reliable option for a pass-heavy team.
- WR Calvin Johnson got some help last year with the emergence of Golden Tate from Seattle, who actually out-gained him in yards. Make no mistake: This is still Johnson's team, and he should be targeted downfield anytime there is single coverage. To really get the most from the Lions, keep developing their young talent at TE, which will hurt teams who focus solely on the outside receiving options.

DEFENSIVE SCOUTING REPORT

- The defensive line has a whole new look for the Lions with Nick Fairley and Ndamukong Suh leaving town. This creates more opportunity for Ezekiel Ansah, who is already one of the best young pass rushers in the league.
- ROLB DeAndre Levy is an excellent option beside MLB Stephen Tulloch, who is coming off an injury. These players may not be household names, but they perform very well on the field.
- The Lions' secondary deserves to be considered in the league's top 10 after solid seasons by both safeties. Your best bet is to play lots of zone coverage with Darius Slay and Rashean Mathis, who both have pretty good size for the position.

SCHEDULE

Week	Date	Time	Network	Opponent
1	SEP 13	4:05 PM ET	FOX	CHARGERS
2	SEP 20	1:00 PM ET	FOX	VIKINGS
3	SEP 27	8:30 PM ET	NBC	BRONCOS
4	OCT 05	8:30 PM ET	ESPN	SEAHAWKS
5	OCT 11	4:05 PM ET	FOX	CARDINALS
6	OCT 18	1:00 PM ET	FOX	BEARS
7	OCT 25	1:00 PM ET	FOX	VIKINGS
8	NOV 01	9:30 AM ET	FOX	CHIEFS
9	BYE WEEK			
10	NOV 15	1:00 PM ET	FOX	PACKERS
11	NOV 22	1:00 PM ET		RAIDERS
12	NOV 26	12:30 PM ET	FOX	EAGLES
13	DEC 03	8:25 PM ET		PACKERS
14	DEC 13	1:00 PM ET	FOX	RAMS
15	DEC 21	8:30 PM ET	ESPN	SAINTS
16	DEC 27	1:00 PM ET	FOX	49ERS
17	JAN 03	1:00 PM ET	FOX	BEARS

KEY PLAYERS

KEY OFFENSIVE PLAYER

CALVIN JOHNSON #81

WR #81 HT 6'5" WT 236 COLLEGE Georgia Tech EXP 8

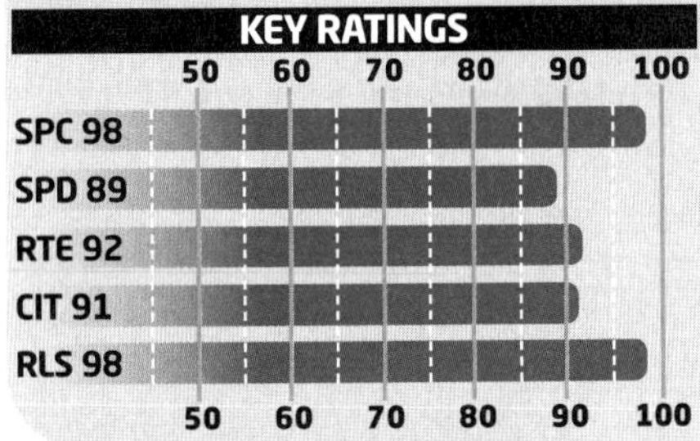

- Johnson should be your main target in the red zone with a high throw and aggressive catch.
- What makes Megatron so good is his ability to line up in so many different positions and still rack up catches.

KEY DEFENSIVE PLAYER

EZEKIEL ANSAH

RE #94 HT 6'6" WT 270 COLLEGE BYU EXP 2

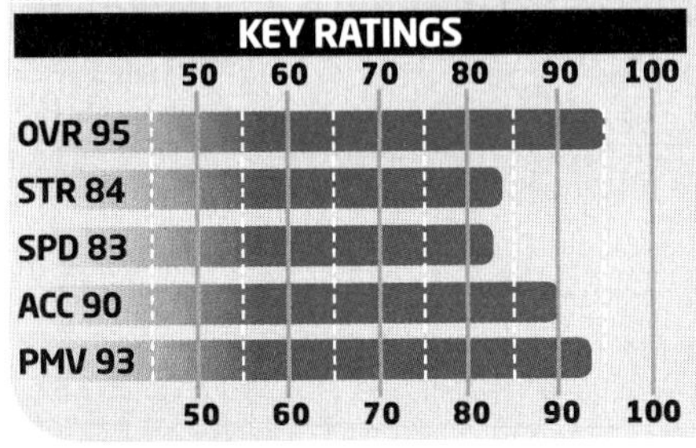

- As if the size and speed weren't enough, Ansah can also knock balls loose with big hits because he has a 90 Hit Power rating.
- Keep developing Ansah's block shedding so he won't be a liability in the run game; for now keep a linebacker behind him.

KEY ROOKIE

LAKEN TOMLINSON

LG #72 HT 6'3" WT 323 COLLEGE Duke EXP Rookie

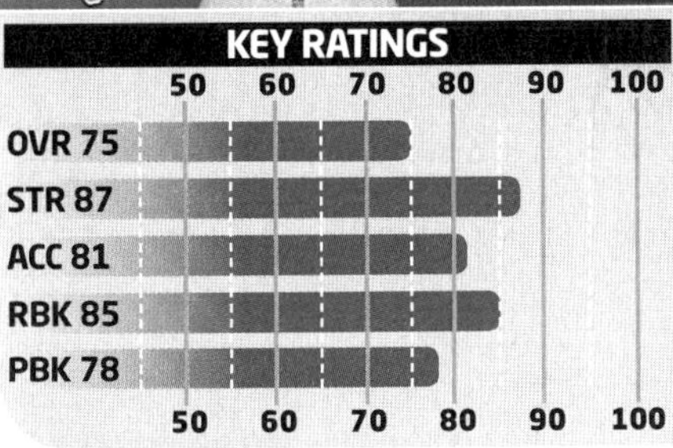

- Tomlinson is more of a run blocker, but he should have plenty of time to develop into an all-around starter.
- Utilize Tomlinson's Acceleration rating on plays like counters, where he will be pulling to the edge.

KEY SLEEPER

JOSEPH FAURIA

TE #80 HT 6'7" WT 255 COLLEGE UCLA EXP 2

KEY RATINGS

Rating	Value
OVR	75
SPD	80
SPC	88
CIT	81
JMP	88

- Fauria needs an upgrade to either his run blocking or route running to be a true threat on an every-down basis.
- Big Joe is a TD machine in the red zone; line him up on the side opposite Calvin Johnson.

OFFENSIVE DEPTH CHART

POS	FIRST	LAST	OVR
QB	MATTHEW	STAFFORD	84
QB	KELLEN	MOORE	71
QB	DAN	ORLOVSKY	70
HB	JOIQUE	BELL	80
HB	THEO	RIDDICK	75
HB	AMEER	ABDULLAH	74
HB	GEORGE	WINN	69
FB	MICHAEL	BURTON	64
WR	CALVIN	JOHNSON	95
WR	GOLDEN	TATE	88
WR	COREY	FULLER	72
WR	JEREMY	ROSS	72
WR	RYAN	BROYLES	71
WR	T.J.	JONES	67
TE	JOSEPH	FAURIA	77
TE	BRANDON	PETTIGREW	77
TE	ERIC	EBRON	75
LT	RILEY	REIFF	82
LT	CORNELIUS	LUCAS	65
LT	COREY	ROBINSON	63
LG	MANNY	RAMIREZ	79
LG	LAKEN	TOMLINSON	74
C	TRAVIS	SWANSON	73
C	TAYLOR	BOGGS	67
RG	LARRY	WARFORD	87
RG	AL	BOND	62
RT	LAADRIAN	WADDLE	79
RT	MICHAEL	WILLIAMS	66

DEFENSIVE DEPTH CHART

POS	FIRST	LAST	OVR
LE	JASON	JONES	80
LE	DEVIN	TAYLOR	72
LE	LARRY	WEBSTER	69
DT	HALOTI	NGATA	92
DT	TYRUNN	WALKER	79
DT	JERMELLE	CUDJO	70
DT	CARAUN	REID	68
DT	GABE	WRIGHT	65
RE	EZEKIEL	ANSAH	88
RE	DARRYL	TAPP	72
RE	XAVIER	PROCTOR	62
LOLB	JOSH	BYNES	75
LOLB	KYLE	VAN NOY	72
MLB	STEPHEN	TULLOCH	87
MLB	TAHIR	WHITEHEAD	82
MLB	TRAVIS	LEWIS	65
ROLB	DEANDRE	LEVY	93
ROLB	JULIAN	STANFORD	72
CB	RASHEAN	MATHIS	84
CB	DARIUS	SLAY	84
CB	JOSH	WILSON	78
CB	BILL	BENTLEY	72
CB	NEVIN	LAWSON	72
FS	GLOVER	QUIN	90
FS	DON	CAREY	73
SS	JAMES	IHEDIGBO	85
SS	ISA	ABDUL-QUDDUS	71

SPECIAL TEAMS

POS	FIRST	LAST	OVR
K	MATT	PRATER	85
KR	THEO	RIDDICK	75
KR	JEREMY	ROSS	72
P	SAM	MARTIN	91
PR	JEREMY	ROSS	72

BEST OFFENSIVE PLAYS

PRO TIPS

- These are the best two offensive plays in your playbook. They will get your playmakers in position to win you games.
- Use the new "shot plays" to look for a big throw downfield once per half.
- Try your best to "hide" WR Calvin Johnson in some formation—he doesn't always have to line up outside.

BEST RUN: STRONG CLOSE—HB OFF TACKLE

SETUP:

- This is always one of our favorite formations, and the HB Off Tackle is a rare but excellent run.
- This run will only be successful if you are patient. Don't turn on the gas until your HB has his blocks set and is beyond the line.

ADVANCED SETUP:

- Sub in a tackle at TE.

RUNNING PLAYS

1ST DOWN	2ND AND SHORT	3RD AND SHORT	GOAL LINE	2ND AND LONG	3RD AND LONG
Singleback Jumbo—HB Stretch	Weak Pro—HB Dive	I-Form Tight Pair—FB Dive	I-Form Twins Flex—FB Dive Strong	Pistol Y-Trips—Strong Power	Gun Trey Open Lion—HB Base
Strong Close—HB Dive	I-Form Pro—HB Blast	Pistol Strong—HB Stretch	Goal Line—HB Sting	Gun Doubles—Inside Zone	Gun Spread Y-Flex—HB Delay
Strong Close—HB Off Tackle	Singleback Doubles—HB Cutback	Pistol Strong—HB Power O	Goal Line—Power O	Gun Snugs Flip—HB Quick Base	Gun Doubles—HB Counter

INSIDE RUN | OUTSIDE RUN | SHOTGUN RUN | QB RUN

BEST PASS: PISTOL ACE—SKINNY POSTS

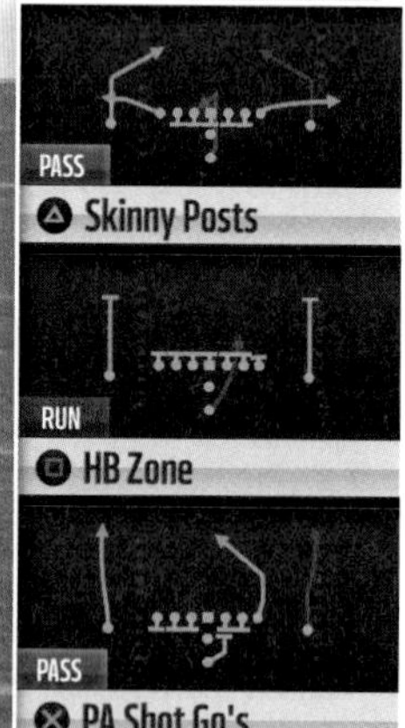

SETUP/READS:

- The timing of the posts is crucial; if it's not right you will see far too many passes batted down by LBs.
- Against man-to-man coverage utilize those TE hot routes, which should get a free release off the line.
- Against the blitz, you can easily max protect this formation and pick up nearly any pressure in the game.

ADVANCED SETUP:

- Slant either TE.
- Wheel the HB.

PASSING PLAYS

1ST DOWN	2ND AND SHORT	3RD AND SHORT	SHOT PLAYS	2ND AND LONG	3RD AND LONG
Pistol Ace—Skinny Posts	Strong Close—WR Out	Strong Close—PA Scissors	Singleback Doubles—Goaline Fade	Pistol Y-Trips—PA All Go	Gun Trey Open Lion—HB Cross Screen
Gun Ace Twins—Posts	Pistol Y-Trips—Y Trail	I-Form Pro—Angle	Singleback Jumbo—PA Y-Drag Wheel	Pistol Slot Flex Lion—PA Boot	Gun Empty Trey—Verts Y Shake
Gun Snugs Flip—Drive Trail	Singleback Y-Trips Lion—Lions Drags	I-Form Twins Flex—PA Divide	Gun Y-Trips Wk—PA Shot Go's	Gun Split Lion—Lions Sail	Gun Empty Lion—Lions Deep In

BASE PLAY | MAN BEATER | ZONE BEATER | BLITZ BEATER

 For more plays and strategies for this team, visit your eGuide using the access code sheet provided.

BEST DEFENSIVE PLAYS

PRO TIPS

- **Rely on these defensive plays to lock up the run and pass.**
- The 5-2 formation might be overkill, but it is a simple run defense that effectively stops under-center runs and is great in the red zone.
- The Big Dime 4-1-6 has some excellent plays to stop the pass, but your optimal lineup has two LBs on the field (Nickel). Use formation subs to get your best talent on the field.

BEST RUN D 5-2 NORMAL—COVER 1

BLITZ
Cover 3

BLITZ
Cover 1

BLITZ
Trio Sky Zone

SETUP:

- Learning to shift your defensive line in the direction of the TE will turn this from a good run defense into a great one.
- If the offense starts running outside runs from shotgun formations, dump the 5-2 for something with better pass coverage.
- The Lions don't quite have the same level of talent on the defensive line, but they still have plenty of options for the 5-2.

PLAYER TO CONTROL:

- Any defensive lineman

RUN DEFENSE

1ST DOWN	2ND AND SHORT	3RD AND SHORT	GOAL LINE	2ND AND LONG	3RD AND LONG
5-2 Normal—Trio Sky Zone	5-2 Normal—Cover 1	5-2 Normal—Pinch	Goal Line 5-4-2—Jam Cover 1	Nickel Wide 9—Cov 1 Hole Press	Nickel Double A Gap—Nickel Dog Meg
5-2 Normal—Cover 3	5-2 Normal—Cover 2	5-2 Normal—Fire Zone 2	Goal Line 5-4-2—Flat Buzz	Nickel Wide 9—Cov 3 Sky Press	Nickel Double A Gap—Nickel Dog 3 Buzz

MAN COVERAGE | ZONE COVERAGE | MAN BLITZ | ZONE BLITZ

BEST PASS D BIG DIME 4-1-6—BUCK SLANT 3

ZONE
Cover 2

BLITZ
Buck Slant 3

ZONE
Cover 2 Sink

SETUP:

- The flats will be left open on this play. If it is a third and short situation, switch to man coverage.
- Don't always rush with the blitzing LB; start towards the line and drop over the middle to confuse the QB.
- If your opponent starts to catch on to the pressure, flip the play or switch to a Cover 3 defense.

PLAYER TO CONTROL:

- Blitzing LB on the left of the screen

PASS DEFENSE

1ST DOWN	2ND AND SHORT	3RD AND SHORT	GOAL LINE	2ND AND LONG	3RD AND LONG
4-3 Wide 9—Cover 2 Man	4-3 Over Plus—Cover 2 Sink	Nickel Normal—Overload Blitz	Goal Line 5-3-3—GL Man	Dime Normal—Mike Dime Blitz	Big Dime 4-1-6—Corner Blitz 3
4-3 Wide 9—Cover 4 Press	4-3 Over Plus—Mike Sam 2	Nickel Normal—Cover 2 Show 4	Goal Line 5-3-3—GL Zone	Dime Normal—Fox FZ Press	Big Dime 4-1-6—Buck Slant 3

MAN COVERAGE | ZONE COVERAGE | MAN BLITZ | ZONE BLITZ

GREEN BAY PACKERS

GAMEPLAY RATING 90

CONNECTED FRANCHISE MODE STRATEGY

CFM TEAM RATING: **88**
OFFENSE: **97**
DEFENSE: **83**
OFFENSIVE SCHEME: **West Coast**
DEFENSIVE SCHEME: **Attacking 3-4**
STRENGTHS: **QB, HB, WR**
WEAKNESSES:

2014 TEAM RANKINGS

1st NFC North (12-4-0)
PASSING OFFENSE: **8th**
RUSHING OFFENSE: **11th**
PASSING DEFENSE: **10th**
RUSHING DEFENSE: **23rd**

2014 TEAM LEADERS

PASSING: **Aaron Rodgers: 4,381**
RUSHING: **Eddie Lacy: 1,139**
RECEIVING: **Jordy Nelson: 1,519**
TACKLES: **Morgan Burnett: 130**
SACKS: **Clay Matthews: 11**
INTS: **Casey Hayward: 3**

KEY ADDITIONS

FB John Kuhn (re-signed)

KEY ROOKIES

CB Damarious Randall
CB Quinten Rollins
WR Ty Montgomery

OWNER: **Mark Murphy**
LEGACY SCORE: **1,450**

COACH: **Mike McCarthy**
LEVEL: **25**
LEGACY SCORE: **3,000**
OFFENSIVE SCHEME: **West Coast**
DEFENSIVE SCHEME: **Attacking 3-4**

OFFENSIVE SCOUTING REPORT

- QB Aaron Rodgers is the best QB in football and consistently keeps the Packers in the playoff hunt. While he doesn't have the same speed any longer, he can still pick up some first downs if teams forget to contain or spy him.
- HB Eddie Lacy is an amazing back who is capable of carrying the offense at times. Take advantage of his talents in the passing game, because most defenders in the secondary can't tackle him.
- The WR combo of Jordy Nelson and Randall Cobb is more than most teams can handle. The Packers were very smart to keep those two together for the long term.

DEFENSIVE SCOUTING REPORT

- The Packers' linebacking corps will have to absorb the loss of veteran A.J. Hawk, but they still can still get it done. Allow Julius Peppers and Mike Neal to rush the passer while Matthews and the young Carl Bradford hold down the middle.
- RE Mike Daniels is an excellent pass rusher on the defensive line. Support him in the run game with a strong LB like Mike Neal.
- CBs Sam Shields and Casey Hayward were smart choices to build around for the Green Bay Packers. Give Hayward a solid contract offer because you no longer have the depth without CB Tramon Williams in town.

SCHEDULE

Week	Date	Time	Network	Opponent
1	SEP 13	1:00 PM ET	FOX	BEARS
2	SEP 20	8:30 PM ET	NBC	SEAHAWKS
3	SEP 28	8:30 PM ET	ESPN	CHIEFS
4	OCT 04	4:25 PM ET	FOX	49ERS
5	OCT 11	1:00 PM ET		RAMS
6	OCT 18	4:25 PM ET		CHARGERS
7	BYE WEEK			
8	NOV 01	8:30 PM ET	NBC	BRONCOS
9	NOV 08	1:00 PM ET	FOX	PANTHERS
10	NOV 15	1:00 PM ET	FOX	LIONS
11	NOV 22	1:00 PM ET	FOX	VIKINGS
12	NOV 26	8:30 PM ET	NBC	BEARS
13	DEC 03	8:25 PM ET		LIONS
14	DEC 13	4:25 PM ET	FOX	COWBOYS
15	DEC 20	4:05 PM ET	FOX	RAIDERS
16	DEC 27	4:25 PM ET	FOX	CARDINALS
17	JAN 03	1:00 PM ET	FOX	VIKINGS

KEY PLAYERS

KEY OFFENSIVE PLAYER

AARON RODGERS #12

QB #12 HT 6'2" WT 225 COLLEGE California EXP 10

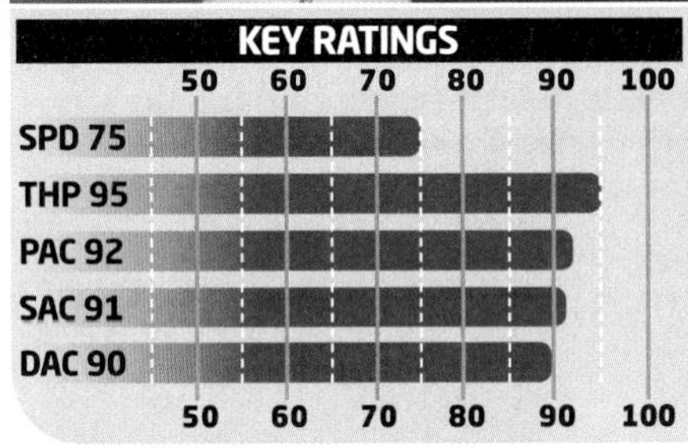

- Make sure to use all of the new throw types to take advantage of Rodgers's stunning accuracy.
- Aaron Rodgers is the best overall QB in the game and is capable of running any style of offense.

KEY DEFENSIVE PLAYER

CLAY MATTHEWS #52

MLB #52 HT 6'3" WT 255 COLLEGE USC EXP 6

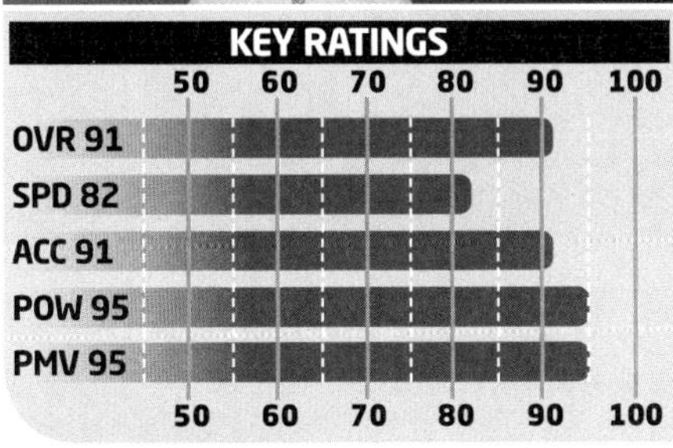

- Matthews has a great ability to recognize plays and avoid being faked out by play action.
- Learn to line up Clay Matthews all over your defense and that Hit Power rating will pay big dividends.

KEY ROOKIE

DAMARIOUS RANDALL #23

CB #23 HT 5'11" WT 196 COLLEGE Arizona St. EXP Rookie

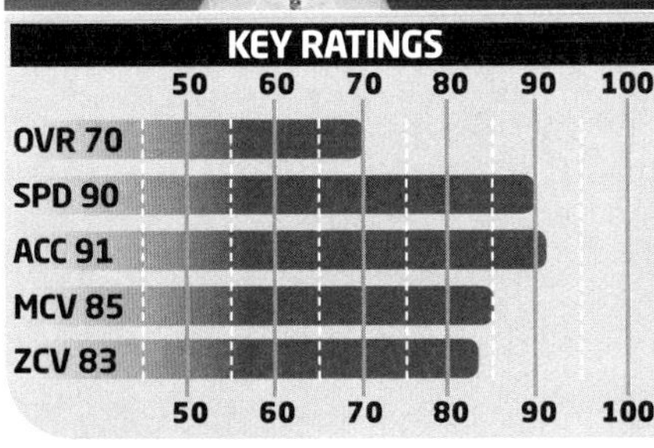

- Randall is a great addition to a secondary that had some turnover in the off-season.
- Randall has nice balance and will be a great combo with last year's first-round selection, FS Ha Ha Clinton-Dix.

KEY SLEEPER

JEFF JANIS #83

WR #83 HT 6'3" WT 219 COLLEGE Saginaw Valley EXP 1

- Janis will need some upgrades to route running, but he could be a nice player to fill in for Jarrett Boykin.
- Janis is 6'3" with a 90 Jump rating; if anyone can get him the ball in a good spot, it's Aaron Rodgers.

OFFENSIVE DEPTH CHART

POS	FIRST	LAST	OVR
QB	AARON	RODGERS	99
QB	SCOTT	TOLZIEN	71
QB	BRETT	HUNDLEY	70
HB	EDDIE	LACY	90
HB	JAMES	STARKS	78
HB	JOHN	CROCKETT	68
HB	RAJION	NEAL	66
FB	JOHN	KUHN	89
FB	AARON	RIPKOWSKI	65
WR	JORDY	NELSON	93
WR	RANDALL	COBB	91
WR	DAVANTE	ADAMS	79
WR	JEFF	JANIS	71
WR	JARED	ABBREDERIS	69
WR	TY	MONTGOMERY	69
TE	ANDREW	QUARLESS	77
TE	RICHARD	RODGERS	74
TE	JUSTIN	PERILLO	64
LT	DAVID	BAKHTIARI	79
LT	JEREMY	VUJNOVICH	60
LG	JOSH	SITTON	97
LG	GARTH	GERHART	70
C	COREY	LINSLEY	86
C	J.C.	TRETTER	73
RG	T.J.	LANG	92
RG	LANE	TAYLOR	66
RT	BRYAN	BULAGA	87
RT	DON	BARCLAY	75

DEFENSIVE DEPTH CHART

POS	FIRST	LAST	OVR
LE	JOSH	BOYD	76
LE	DATONE	JONES	74
LE	KHYRI	THORNTON	68
DT	B.J.	RAJI	81
DT	LETROY	GUION	74
DT	MIKE	PENNEL	69
RE	MIKE	DANIELS	89
RE	BRUCE	GASTON	63
LOLB	JULIUS	PEPPERS	88
LOLB	JAYRONE	ELLIOTT	68
LOLB	NATE	PALMER	66
MLB	CLAY	MATTHEWS	90
MLB	SAM	BARRINGTON	74
MLB	CARL	BRADFORD	71
MLB	JAKE	RYAN	65
ROLB	NICK	PERRY	79
ROLB	MIKE	NEAL	76
ROLB	ANDY	MULUMBA	68
CB	CASEY	HAYWARD	85
CB	SAM	SHIELDS	82
CB	DAMARIOUS	RANDALL	72
CB	DEMETRI	GOODSON	71
CB	QUINTEN	ROLLINS	67
FS	HA HA	CLINTON-DIX	81
FS	MICAH	HYDE	79
SS	MORGAN	BURNETT	86
SS	SEAN	RICHARDSON	73
SS	CHRIS	BANJO	69

SPECIAL TEAMS

POS	FIRST	LAST	OVR
K	MASON	CROSBY	84
KR	MICAH	HYDE	79
KR	JEFF	JANIS	71
P	TIM	MASTHAY	63
PR	MICAH	HYDE	79

BEST OFFENSIVE PLAYS

PRO TIPS

- These are the best two offensive plays in your playbook. They will get your playmakers in position to win you games.
- Eddie Lacy is an excellent power back who can also be a solid option in the passing game if you call well-timed plays.
- Don't think of Randall Cobb and Jordy Nelson as defined to one role. They can both do it all while lining up anywhere.

BEST RUN: WEAK SLOT–OFF TACKLE

SETUP:

- The focus of this formation will be on the slot WR to the right; if the defense aligns there, you should have the edge all game.
- This formation is a solid way to get Eddie Lacy more carries and to set up PA Boot plays for QB Aaron Rodgers, who is one of the best.

ADVANCED SETUP:

- Follow your lead blockers.

RUNNING PLAYS

1ST DOWN	2ND AND SHORT	3RD AND SHORT	GOAL LINE	2ND AND LONG	3RD AND LONG
Singleback Bunch–HB Ace Power	I-Form Pro–HB Blast	I-Form Pro–FB Dive Strong	Full House Wide–HB Slam	Pistol Slot Flex Packer–HB Zone	Gun Pack Trips–HB Base
Singleback Doubles Pack–0 1 Trap	Singleback Flex–HB Slash	I-Form Pro–Strech	Goal Line–FB Dive	Gun Doubles On–Inside Zone	Gun Trips Y Iso–HB Counter
Singleback Ace–HB Zone Wk	Full House Wide–Weak Zone	Weak Slot–Off Tackle	Goal Line–QB Sneak	Pistol Y-Trips–HB Counter	Gun Wing Offset Wk–Inside Zone Split

INSIDE RUN | OUTSIDE RUN | SHOTGUN RUN | QB RUN

BEST PASS: PISTOL Y TRIPS–Y TRAIL

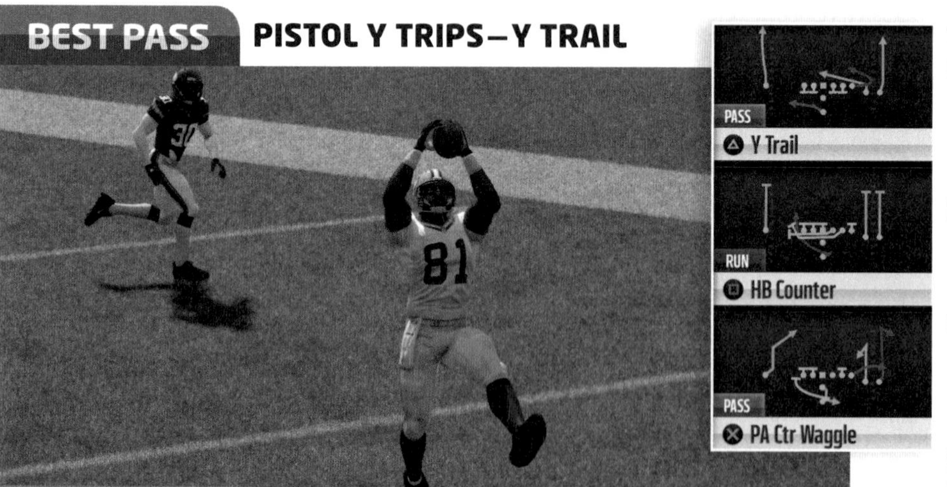

SETUP/READS:

- Against zone coverage look for the trail route, which should have plenty of space cleared out. Be patient and consider playmakering it upfield for an even bigger gain.
- Against man coverage, target the middle of the field, and make sure to get Randall Cobb in this position with the Strong Slot package.
- This play requires you to have confidence in going down the sideline to Nelson when you spot a favorable one-on-one matchup.

ADVANCED SETUP:

- Wheel the HB.

PASSING PLAYS

1ST DOWN	2ND AND SHORT	3RD AND SHORT	SHOT PLAYS	2ND AND LONG	3RD AND LONG
Singleback Ace Pair–TE Attack	Gun Double Flex–Deep Curl	Gun Bunch Wk–PA Post	Pistol Y-Trips–PA Zone Shot	Gun Trips Y Iso–Deep Attack	Singleback Ace Twins–Smash
Gun Bunch Wk–Double Trail	Singleback Ace Twins–PA FL Stretch	Singleback Tight Flex–Shallow Cross	Singleback Doubles Pack–PA Deep Cross	Gun Bunch Wk–Verticals	Gun Bunch Wk–HB Cross Screen
Pistol Slot Flex Packer–Inside Cross	Singleback Flex–Packer Ins	Full House Wide–Angle Swing	Gun Pack Trips–Slot Fade Shot	Gun Empty Trey–Dbl Slot Cross	Gun Flex Trey–Four Verticals

BASE PLAY | MAN BEATER | ZONE BEATER | BLITZ BEATER

 For more plays and strategies for this team, visit your eGuide using the access code sheet provided.

BEST DEFENSIVE PLAYS

PRO TIPS

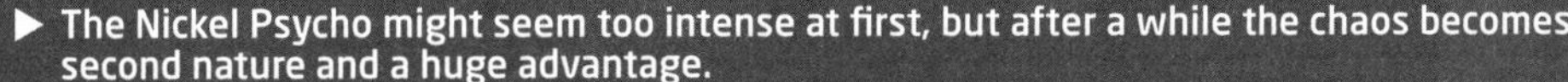
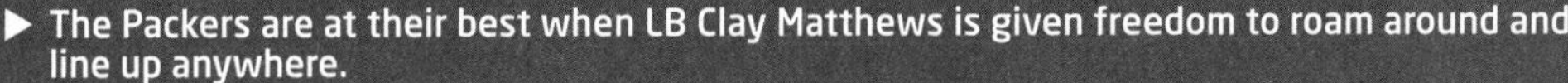

- **Rely on these defensive plays to lock up the run and pass.**
- The Nickel Psycho might seem too intense at first, but after a while the chaos becomes second nature and a huge advantage.
- The Packers are at their best when LB Clay Matthews is given freedom to roam around and line up anywhere.

BEST RUN D: NICKEL PSYCHO–OVERLOAD 3 SEAM

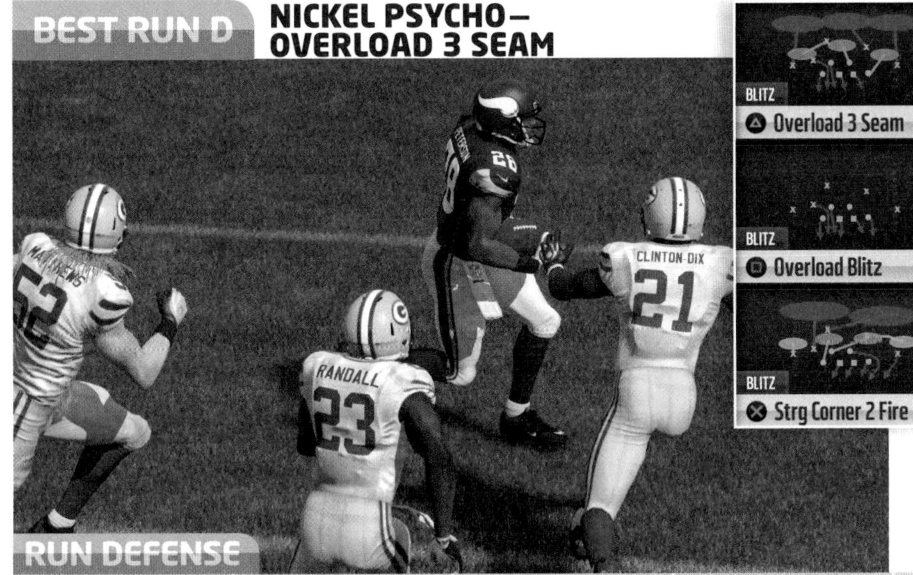

- BLITZ — Triangle: Overload 3 Seam
- BLITZ — Square: Overload Blitz
- BLITZ — X: Strg Corner 2 Fire

SETUP:

- This play doesn't have a specific lineup on every snap, so just grab onto a defender and be ready to plug holes against the run.
- You have great command off all your LBs in this formation and can use global adjustments to quickly zone or blitz everyone.

PLAYER TO CONTROL:

- Any roaming LB

RUN DEFENSE

1ST DOWN	2ND AND SHORT	3RD AND SHORT	GOAL LINE	2ND AND LONG	3RD AND LONG
3-4 Solid–Cover 2 Man	3-4 Solid–1 Will Sam Go	3-4 Over–Sting Pinch	Goal Line 5-4-2–Jam Cover 1	Nickel Psycho–Cover 1 Robber	Nickel 3-3-5 Wide–1 QB Contain
3-4 Solid–Cover 2 Press	3-4 Solid–Trio Sky Zone	3-4 Over–Sting Pinch Zone	Goal Line 5-4-2–Flat Buzz	Nickel Psycho–Cover 3 Sky	Nickel 3-3-5 Wide–Cover 4 Show 2

MAN COVERAGE ZONE COVERAGE MAN BLITZ ZONE BLITZ

BEST PASS D: BIG DIME 2-3-6 WILL–COVER 2

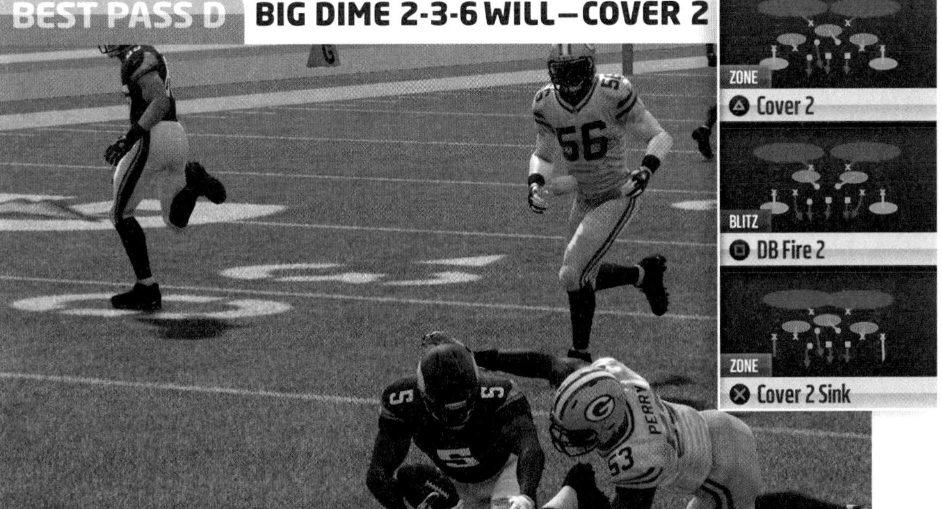

- ZONE — Triangle: Cover 2
- BLITZ — Square: DB Fire 2
- ZONE — X: Cover 2 Sink

SETUP:

- Switching between the Cover 2 and Cover 2 Sink will take advantage of the Packers' strength in the secondary.
- Have LB Julius Peppers in pass coverage, because his size makes it very tough for QBs to throw over.
- The blitzing LB on this play is under your control, so use him to take away your opponent's first read.

PLAYER TO CONTROL:

- Blitzing LB

PASS DEFENSE

1ST DOWN	2ND AND SHORT	3RD AND SHORT	GOAL LINE	2ND AND LONG	3RD AND LONG
3-4 Odd–Cover 1 Hole	3-4 Over–Cover 1 Hole	Nickel Psycho–OLB Fire	Goal Line 5-3-3–GL Man	Nickel 2-4-5–Overstorm Brave	Nickel 2-4-5 Dbl A Gap–Mid Blitz
3-4 Odd–Cover 3 Sky	3-4 Over–Sam Mike 3	Nickel Psycho–Overload 3 Seam	Goal Line 5-3-3–GL Zone	Nickel 2-4-5–Buck Slant 3	Nickel 2-4-5 Dbl A Gap–Buck Zone Blitz

MAN COVERAGE ZONE COVERAGE MAN BLITZ ZONE BLITZ

CAROLINA PANTHERS

GAMEPLAY RATING 80

CONNECTED FRANCHISE MODE STRATEGY

CFM TEAM RATING: **87**
OFFENSE: **89**
DEFENSE: **89**
OFFENSIVE SCHEME: **Balanced Offense**
DEFENSIVE SCHEME: **Base 4-3**
STRENGTHS: **QB, C, TE, WR, FB, MLB, DT**
WEAKNESSES: **ROLB, FS, RT, HB**

2014 TEAM RANKINGS

1st NFC South (7-8-1)
PASSING OFFENSE: **19th**
RUSHING OFFENSE: **7th**
PASSING DEFENSE: **11th**
RUSHING DEFENSE: **16th**

2014 TEAM LEADERS

PASSING: **Cam Newton: 3,127**
RUSHING: **Jonathan Stewart: 809**
RECEIVING: **Greg Olsen: 1,008**
TACKLES: **Luke Kuechly: 153**
SACKS: **Charles Johnson: 8.5**
INTS: **Roman Harper: 4**

KEY ADDITIONS

WR Jarrett Boykin
CB Charles Tillman
RT Jonathan Martin
FS Kurt Coleman

KEY ROOKIES

LB Shaq Thompson
WR Devin Funchess
G Daryl Williams

OWNER: **Jerry Richardson**
LEGACY SCORE: **950**

COACH: **Ron Rivera**
LEVEL: **9**
LEGACY SCORE: **165**
OFFENSIVE SCHEME: **Balanced**
DEFENSIVE SCHEME: **Base 4-3**

OFFENSIVE SCOUTING REPORT

- QB Cam Newton has been signed for the long term and gives the team not only a face for the franchise but the ability to utilize a unique scheme. Joe Webb is a decent backup who can spell Newton, but you should focus on keeping him upright and out of harm's way.
- HB Jonathan Stewart has a unique blend of strength and elusiveness that makes him a good back for the Panthers' scheme. The real key is keeping him healthy. FB Mike Tolbert is an excellent option to get the most out of your scheme, especially in the red zone and catching passes out of the backfield.
- The Panthers found a true #1 WR in Kelvin Benjamin. He is an excellent threat in the red zone with a 6'5" frame and a 97 CIT rating. He is also excellent against press coverage, so don't worry about facing physical corners. He is the only reliable target for QB Cam Newton; everyone else has flashes, but you need to put them in the best spot for their talent to take over. At TE, Greg Olsen is the best target you have for third downs and is also a solid run blocker.

DEFENSIVE SCOUTING REPORT

- The Panthers' defensive line is very balanced across the board. Players like Star Lotulelei will stuff the run while Charles Johnson and Kawann Short will get after the passer.
- Nothing needs to be said about MLB Luke Kuechly, as he is one of the best all-around players in football. Another one of our favorite players, however, is Thomas Davis, who has been playing at a high level for years now. He has excellent play recognition and won't get fooled on play-action fakes. Allow those two to roam free and focus on rookie Shaq Thompson to make plays and get him XP.
- The Panthers' secondary is actually built pretty nicely for a player who likes to use zone coverage. Tre Boston is quickly becoming a solid defender and should be much improved as you boost his play recognition. While the starting CBs might not be household names yet, they both have great size and should be rock solid in either flat or deep zone coverage.

SCHEDULE

Week	Date	Time	Network		Opponent
1	SEP 13	1:00 PM ET	FOX	AT	JAGUARS
2	SEP 20	1:00 PM ET			TEXANS
3	SEP 27	1:00 PM ET	FOX		SAINTS
4	OCT 04	1:00 PM ET	FOX	AT	BUCCANEERS
5	BYE WEEK				
6	OCT 18	4:05 PM ET	FOX	AT	SEAHAWKS
7	OCT 25	8:30 PM ET	NBC		EAGLES
8	NOV 02	8:30 PM ET	ESPN		COLTS
9	NOV 08	1:00 PM ET	FOX		PACKERS
10	NOV 15	1:00 PM ET	FOX	AT	TITANS
11	NOV 22	1:00 PM ET	FOX		REDSKINS
12	NOV 26	4:30 PM ET		AT	COWBOYS
13	DEC 06	1:00 PM ET	FOX	AT	SAINTS
14	DEC 13	1:00 PM ET	FOX		FALCONS
15	DEC 20	1:00 PM ET	FOX	AT	GIANTS
16	DEC 27	1:00 PM ET	FOX	AT	FALCONS
17	JAN 03	1:00 PM ET	FOX		BUCCANEERS

KEY PLAYERS

KEY OFFENSIVE PLAYER

CAM NEWTON

#1

QB #1 HT 6'5" WT 245 COLLEGE Auburn EXP 4

KEY RATINGS

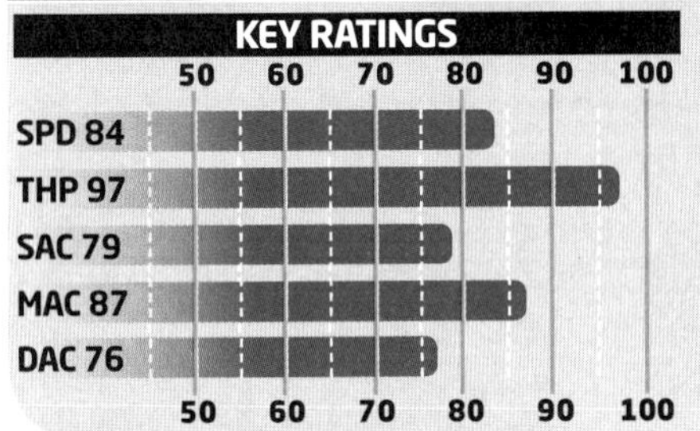

- Newton has excellent strength, agility, and acceleration, which allow him to be an excellent threat on the ground.
- Newton is best when throwing passes between 20 and 40 yards, so look to your TEs and WRs on crossing routes downfield.

KEY DEFENSIVE PLAYER

LUKE KUECHLY

MLB #59 HT 6'3" WT 238 COLLEGE Boston College EXP 3

KEY RATINGS

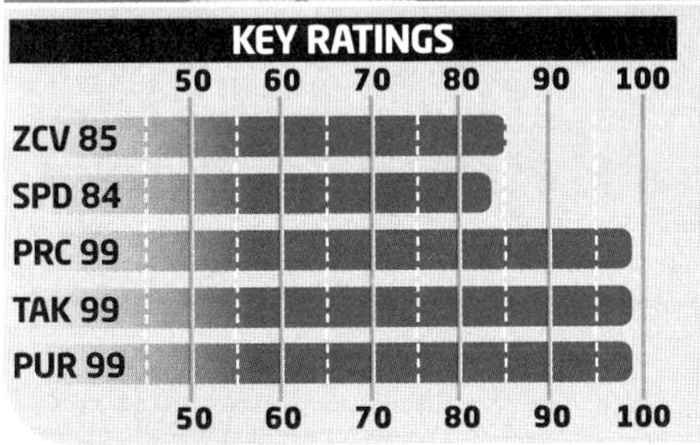

- Kuechly will get himself in position to make big plays for your defense consistently.
- The scary part is that he is still developing; add a little more hit power to his game for even more turnovers.

KEY ROOKIE

SHAQ THOMPSON

ROLB #54 HT 6'0" WT 228 COLLEGE Washington EXP Rookie

KEY RATINGS

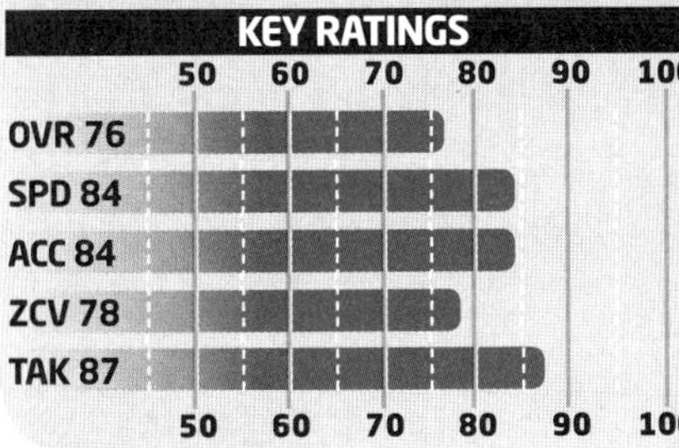

- Thompson is a major talent who will be solid in zone coverage and is a sure tackler.
- If you switch and play some nickel defense, utilize Thomas Davis and give Thompson a rest until you go back to the base 4-3.

KEY SLEEPER

DEVIN FUNCHESS

WR #17 HT 6'4" WT 232 COLLEGE Michigan EXP Rookie

KEY RATINGS

50 60 70 80 90 100

OVR 73

SPD 89

SPC 86

CIT 75

JMP 88

50 60 70 80 90 100

- Funchess will be a great complement to Kelvin Benjamin and can hopefully take some pressure off. Upgrade his Catch in Traffic and Route Running ratings.
- Work on developing the 6'4" Funchess over Stephen Hill, because there is more long-term upside.

OFFENSIVE DEPTH CHART

POS	FIRST	LAST	OVR
QB	CAM	NEWTON	90
QB	DEREK	ANDERSON	72
QB	JOE	WEBB	66
HB	JONATHAN	STEWART	84
HB	JORDAN	TODMAN	73
HB	CAMERON	ARTIS-PAYNE	69
HB	FOZZY	WHITTAKER	68
WR	KELVIN	BENJAMIN	86
WR	JERRICHO	COTCHERY	76
WR	TED	GINN JR.	75
WR	COREY	BROWN	73
WR	JARRETT	BOYKIN	72
WR	DEVIN	FUNCHESS	72
TE	GREG	OLSEN	92
TE	ED	DICKSON	76
TE	BRANDON	WILLIAMS	72
LT	MICHAEL	OHER	72
LT	JONATHAN	MARTIN	67
LT	MARTIN	WALLACE	59
LG	ANDREW	NORWELL	79
LG	AMINI	SILATOLU	74
C	RYAN	KALIL	87
C	BRIAN	FOLKERTS	67
RG	TRAI	TURNER	83
RG	CHRIS	SCOTT	72
RT	MIKE	REMMERS	77
RT	NATE	CHANDLER	76
RT	DARYL	WILLIAMS	70

DEFENSIVE DEPTH CHART

POS	FIRST	LAST	OVR
LE	CHARLES	JOHNSON	89
LE	MARIO	ADDISON	77
LE	FRANK	ALEXANDER	69
DT	STAR	LOTULELEI	87
DT	KAWANN	SHORT	83
DT	DWAN	EDWARDS	75
DT	COLIN	COLE	74
DT	KYLE	LOVE	73
RE	WES	HORTON	74
RE	KONY	EALY	72
LOLB	THOMAS	DAVIS	90
LOLB	ADARIUS	GLANTON	64
MLB	KUECHLY	LUKE	96
MLB	TRUSNIK	JASON	72
MLB	MAYO	DAVID	65
MLB	JACOBS	BEN	64
ROLB	A.J.	KLEIN	74
ROLB	SHAQ	THOMPSON	72
ROLB	KEVIN	REDDICK	69
CB	JOSH	NORMAN	84
CB	BENE	BENWIKERE	81
CB	CHARLES	TILLMAN	81
CB	MELVIN	WHITE	69
CB	CARRINGTON	BYNDOM	64
FS	TRE	BOSTON	81
FS	COLIN	JONES	72
FS	DEAN	MARLOWE	62
SS	KURT	COLEMAN	79
SS	ROMAN	HARPER	79
SS	ROBERT	LESTER	75

SPECIAL TEAMS

POS	FIRST	LAST	OVR
K	GRAHAM	GANO	87
KR	TED	GINN JR.	75
KR	FOZZY	WHITTAKER	68
P	BRAD	NORTMAN	81
PR	TED	GINN JR.	75

BEST OFFENSIVE PLAYS

PRO TIPS

- **These are the best two offensive plays in your playbook. They will get your playmakers in position to win you games.**
- The Panthers' scheme is at its best when the ground game has been established and play action comes naturally.
- The Panthers' playbook has some excellent Read Option plays to take advantage of overly aggressive defenses.

BEST RUN — STRONG H PRO—POWER O

SETUP:

- This is a staple run, but don't rely on Cam Newton to carry the ball all game long—use him as a surprise.
- On early downs, this run can go outside. On third down, take the sure yards up the middle.

ADVANCED SETUP:

- Motion the FB to the right (optional).

RUNNING PLAYS

1ST DOWN	2ND AND SHORT	3RD AND SHORT	GOAL LINE	2ND AND LONG	3RD AND LONG
Strong H Twins–Outside Zone	Singleback Ace–0 1 Trap	Weak Pro Twins–HB Gut	Gun Heavy Panther–QB Power	Pistol Weak–Triple Option	Gun Split Panther–Inside Zone Split
I-Form Pro–Inside Zone	Singleback Tight Slots–HB Cutback	I-Form Tight Pair–FB Dive	Gun Heavy Panther–QB Blast	Pistol Strong–Inside Zone Split	Gun Ace Twins–Read Option
Singleback Ace Pair Flex–Counter Weak	Strong H Pro–HB Blast	I-Form Tight Pair–FB Fake HB Flip	Goal Line–QB Sneak	Pistol Full Panther–Triple Option	Gun Ace Twins–QB Power

INSIDE RUN | OUTSIDE RUN | SHOTGUN RUN | QB RUN

BEST PASS — GUN TREY Y-FLEX—LEVELS SAIL

SETUP/READS:

- Against zone coverage one of the routes on the left will get open, so throw a bullet pass with confidence.
- Against man-to-man coverage target the TE cutting towards the sideline. Keep an eye out to see if a WR has a linebacker on him.
- Streak Kelvin Benjamin for high-point catches on the outside. Streak Ted Ginn Jr. if you sense a speed mismatch in the seam.

ADVANCED SETUP:

- Slant any WR on the left side.

PASSING PLAYS

1ST DOWN	2ND AND SHORT	3RD AND SHORT	SHOT PLAYS	2ND AND LONG	3RD AND LONG
Gun Ace Twins–Posts	Singleback Bunch Ace–Clearout SE Opt	Singleback Bunch Ace–Bunch Dig	Singleback Ace Pair Flex–PA Shot Post	Singleback Ace–PA Panther Seam	Gun Trey Y-Flex–Verticals
Gun Doubles Offset–Shark HB Wheel	Singleback Tight Slots–Mesh	Strong H Pro–Texas	Gun Trey Y-Flex–PA Crossers	Singleback Bunch–Panther Go's	Gun Bunch Wk–Verticals
Singleback Tight Slots–Deep Post	Pistol Strong–Spacing	I-Form Tight Pair–PA Spot	Gun Trips TE–PA Counter Go	Singleback Tight Slots–HB Wheel	Gun Y-Trips Open–Deep Dig

BASE PLAY | MAN BEATER | ZONE BEATER | BLITZ BEATER

 For more plays and strategies for this team, visit your eGuide using the access code sheet provided.

BEST DEFENSIVE PLAYS

PRO TIPS

- **Rely on these defensive plays to lock up the run and pass.**
- **The 5-2 is an excellent formation to have when facing an opponent with a power run game.**
- **The Nickel Double A Gap is an excellent way to fake some pressure over the interior of the offensive line.**

BEST RUN D 5-2 NORMAL—COVER 3

BLITZ △ Cover 3

BLITZ ▢ Cover 1

BLITZ ✕ Trio Sky Zone

SETUP:

- This is more of a short-yardage defense, but it should allow your LBs to make plays.
- Use the Trio Sky Zone to send pressure at any extra blockers the offense uses.
- Go with the Fire Zone 2 in the red zone and shade your coverage underneath.

PLAYER TO CONTROL:

- Either OLB in a hook zone

RUN DEFENSE

1ST DOWN	2ND AND SHORT	3RD AND SHORT	GOAL LINE	2ND AND LONG	3RD AND LONG
4-3 Stack—Cover 2 Man	4-3 Stack—Cover 1 Robber Press	5-2 Normal—Pinch	Goal Line 5-4-2—Jam Cover 1	Nickel Normal—Cover 2 Sink	Big Dime 4-1-6—Cov 1 Thief Press
4-3 Stack—Cover 2 Press	4-3 Stack—Aggie Cloud Star	5-2 Normal—Trio Sky Zone	Goal Line 5-4-2—Flat Buzz	Nickel Normal—Cover Show 4	Big Dime 4-1-6—Cov 3 Buzz Press

MAN COVERAGE | ZONE COVERAGE | MAN BLITZ | ZONE BLITZ

BEST PASS D NICKEL DOUBLE A GAP—BUCK ZONE BLITZ

MAN △ Cover 1 Hole

BLITZ ▢ Mid Blitz

BLITZ ✕ Buck Zone Blitz

SETUP:

- Consider QB spying the blitzing LB, because your rush angle is very wide and QBs could escape through the middle.
- This will give up some throws to the flat, but the offense has to be smart enough to make it consistently.
- Consider sending both LBs on a blitz to really ramp up the pressure on third and long.

PLAYER TO CONTROL:

- DT Star Lotulelei (power rush)

PASS DEFENSE

1ST DOWN	2ND AND SHORT	3RD AND SHORT	GOAL LINE	2ND AND LONG	3RD AND LONG
5-2 Normal—Cover 1	4-3 Wide 9—Cover 1 Hole	Nickel 4 D Ends—Cover 1 Hole	Goal Line 5-3-3—GL Man	Nickel Double A Gap—Mid Blitz	Nickel Double A Gap—Nickel Dog Meg
5-2 Normal—Cover 3	4-3 Wide 9—Sam Blitz 3	Nickel 4 D Ends—Odd Overload 2	Goal Line 5-3-3—GL Zone	Nickel Double A Gap—Buck Zone Blitz	Nickel Double A Gap—Nickel Dog 3 Buzz

MAN COVERAGE | ZONE COVERAGE | MAN BLITZ | ZONE BLITZ

NEW ENGLAND PATRIOTS

GAMEPLAY RATING 91

CONNECTED FRANCHISE MODE STRATEGY

CFM TEAM RATING: **87**
OFFENSE: **89**
DEFENSE: **91**
OFFENSIVE SCHEME: **Spread**
DEFENSIVE SCHEME: **Hybrid**
STRENGTHS: **QB, TE, WR, LB, FS**
WEAKNESSES: **CB, DT, LG, HB**

2014 TEAM RANKINGS

1st AFC East (12-4-0)
PASSING OFFENSE: **9th**
RUSHING OFFENSE: **18th**
PASSING DEFENSE: **17th**
RUSHING DEFENSE: **9th**

2014 TEAM LEADERS

PASSING: **Tom Brady: 4,109**
RUSHING: **Jonas Gray: 412**
RECEIVING: **Rob Gronkowski: 1,124**
TACKLES: **Jamie Collins: 116**
SACKS: **Rob Ninkovich: 8**
INTS: **Devin McCourty: 2**

KEY ADDITIONS

HB Travaris Cadet
TE Scott Chandler
DT Alan Branch

KEY ROOKIES

DT Malcom Brown
SS Jordan Richards
DE Geneo Grissom

OWNER: **Robert Kraft**
LEGACY SCORE: **11,700**

COACH: **Griffin Murphy**
LEVEL: **1**
LEGACY SCORE: **0**
OFFENSIVE SCHEME: **Spread**
DEFENSIVE SCHEME: **Hybrid**

OFFENSIVE SCOUTING REPORT

- The Patriots will be in the hunt for a Super Bowl every year that Tom Brady is the starting QB. Start looking to Jimmy Garoppolo, who will be the heir apparent once Brady decides to hang them up and head to Canton.
- The Patriots have what seems like a patchwork backfield, but all the players are there for a specific reason. Know how to get the most from them. Use Travaris Cadet as a third down back in the passing game while having Blount as your downhill runner. You never know who is going to have the next big game.
- The Patriots' receiving corps really came on strong during their Super Bowl run. WR Julian Edelman proved he is a special talent, while Brandon LaFell and Danny Amendola also contributed. Keep Gronk safe over the middle with conservative catches from time to time, as he is the key to the offense.

DEFENSIVE SCOUTING REPORT

- DE Chandler Jones is the star of the defensive line, but Rob Ninkovich's ability to line up anywhere is what really makes this hybrid front possible.
- The Patriots took a few drafts to build their LB corps, and it is now one of the most versatile in football. LOLB Jamie Collins is a athletic force who can play coverage or rush the passer at a high level.
- The Patriots' secondary was one of the best in football last season, but it is now time for the young talent to step up after the departure of Darrelle Revis, Brandon Browner, and Kyle Arrington. The good news is that veteran leader Devin McCourty is still the anchor, and they have promising young talent like Super Bowl hero Malcolm Butler.

SCHEDULE

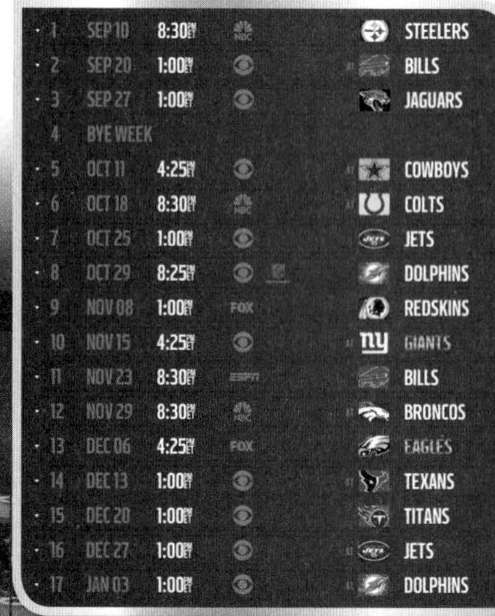

Week	Date	Time		Opponent
1	SEP 10	8:30 PM ET		STEELERS
2	SEP 20	1:00 PM ET	AT	BILLS
3	SEP 27	1:00 PM ET		JAGUARS
4	BYE WEEK			
5	OCT 11	4:25 PM ET	AT	COWBOYS
6	OCT 18	8:30 PM ET	AT	COLTS
7	OCT 25	1:00 PM ET		JETS
8	OCT 29	8:25 PM ET		DOLPHINS
9	NOV 08	1:00 PM ET		REDSKINS
10	NOV 15	4:25 PM ET	AT	GIANTS
11	NOV 23	8:30 PM ET		BILLS
12	NOV 29	8:30 PM ET	AT	BRONCOS
13	DEC 06	4:25 PM ET		EAGLES
14	DEC 13	1:00 PM ET	AT	TEXANS
15	DEC 20	1:00 PM ET		TITANS
16	DEC 27	1:00 PM ET	AT	JETS
17	JAN 03	1:00 PM ET	AT	DOLPHINS

KEY PLAYERS

KEY OFFENSIVE PLAYER

ROB GRONKOWSKI

TE #87 HT 6'6" WT 265 COLLEGE Arizona EXP 5

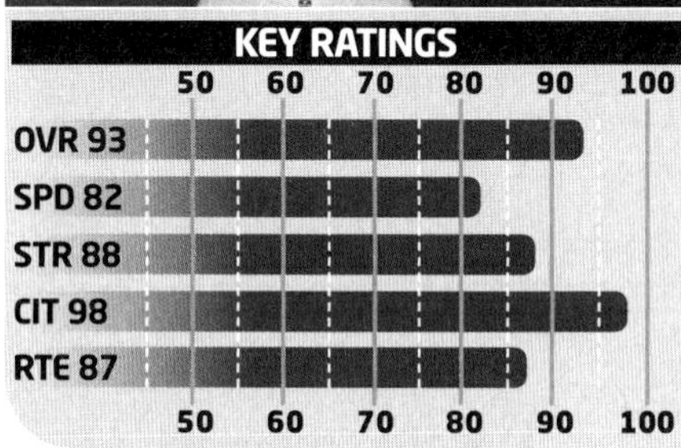

- Gronk will be able to run over most defenders in the secondary with an 88 Trucking rating.
- Gronk is an very solid run blocker, so keep developing him there if you plan to pound the rock.

KEY DEFENSIVE PLAYER

DEVIN MCCOURTY

#32

FS #32 HT 5'10" WT 195 COLLEGE Rutgers EXP 5

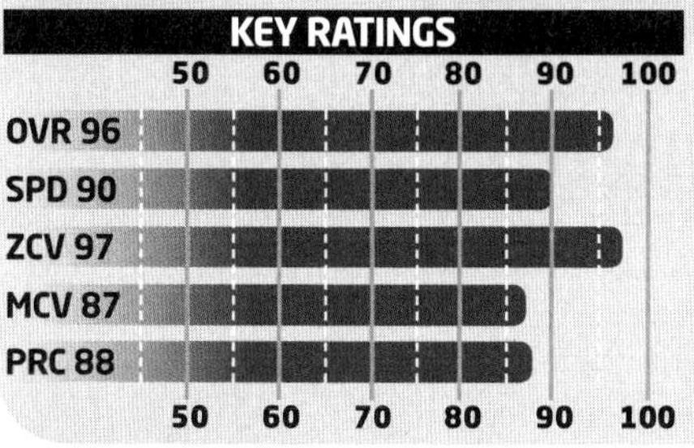

- The combination of speed, zone coverage, and play recognition separates McCourty from almost every other safety in the game.
- Spend any extra XP on boosts to strength and tackling; everything else is already up to par.

KEY ROOKIE

MALCOM BROWN

DT #59 HT 6'2" WT 319 COLLEGE Texas EXP Rookie

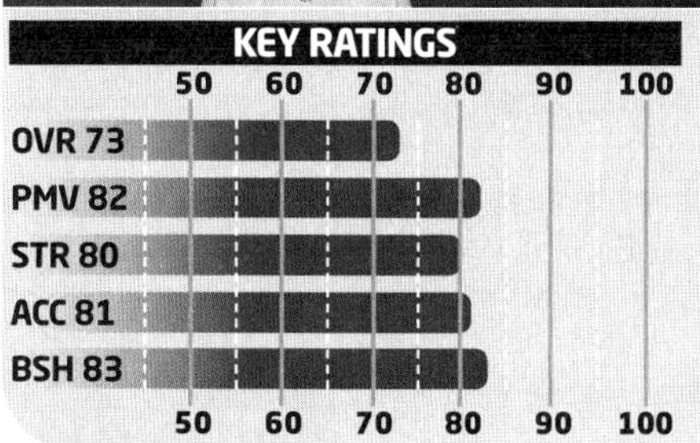

- This is back-to-back DT selections in the first round for New England, after Dominique Easley last year.
- Brown is a very balanced player, but don't expect him to stuff the run—you already have plenty of players to handle that duty.

KEY SLEEPER

DEKODA WATSON

ROLB #56 HT 6'2" WT 240 COLLEGE Florida State EXP 5

KEY RATINGS

OVR 72
SPD 89
ACC 90
FMV 80
ZCV 77

- Watson should be used on some passing downs as a zone defender or sent off the edge as a speedy blitzer.
- Watson probably won't develop into a Pro Bowl-caliber player, so use his strengths and get what you can.

OFFENSIVE DEPTH CHART

POS	FIRST	LAST	OVR
QB	TOM	BRADY	97
QB	MATT	FLYNN	73
QB	JIMMY	GAROPPOLO	73
HB	LEGARRETTE	BLOUNT	80
HB	BRANDON	BOLDEN	73
HB	JONAS	GRAY	72
HB	TRAVARIS	CADET	71
FB	JAMES	DEVELIN	87
WR	JULIAN	EDELMAN	89
WR	BRANDON	LAFELL	83
WR	DANNY	AMENDOLA	79
WR	AARON	DOBSON	75
WR	BRIAN	TYMS	70
WR	JOSH	BOYCE	67
TE	ROB	GRONKOWSKI	99
TE	SCOTT	CHANDLER	80
TE	MICHAEL	HOOMANAWANUI	77
LT	NATE	SOLDER	82
LT	MARCUS	CANNON	72
LG	JORDAN	DEVEY	73
LG	TRE	JACKSON	70
C	BRYAN	STORK	78
RG	RYAN	WENDELL	79
RG	JOSH	KLINE	73
RT	SEBASTIAN	VOLLMER	91
RT	CAYLIN	HAUPTMANN	67

DEFENSIVE DEPTH CHART

POS	FIRST	LAST	OVR
LE	ROB	NINKOVICH	87
LE	TREY	FLOWERS	72
DT	JABAAL	SHEARD	84
DT	ALAN	BRANCH	79
DT	SEALVER	SILIGA	79
DT	MALCOM	BROWN	72
DT	DOMINIQUE	EASLEY	75
RE	CHANDLER	JONES	88
RE	ZACH	MOORE	69
RE	GENEO	GRISSOM	63
LOLB	JAMIE	COLLINS	90
LOLB	JONATHAN	FREENY	71
LOLB	DARIUS	FLEMING	67
MLB	JEROD	MAYO	89
MLB	DANE	FLETCHER	69
MLB	ERIC	MARTIN	63
ROLB	DONT'A	HIGHTOWER	93
ROLB	DEKODA	WATSON	74
ROLB	CHRIS	WHITE	69
CB	LOGAN	RYAN	80
CB	BRADLEY	FLETCHER	77
CB	MALCOLM	BUTLER	76
CB	ROBERT	MCCLAIN	71
CB	JUSTIN	GREEN	69
FS	DEVIN	MCCOURTY	94
FS	TAVON	WILSON	75
FS	DURON	HARMON	73
SS	PATRICK	CHUNG	88
SS	NATE	EBNER	67
SS	JORDAN	RICHARDS	69

SPECIAL TEAMS

POS	FIRST	LAST	OVR
K	STEPHEN	GOSTKOWSKI	95
KR	BRANDON	LAFELL	83
KR	DANNY	AMENDOLA	79
P	RYAN	ALLEN	72
PR	JULIAN	EDELMAN	89

BEST OFFENSIVE PLAYS

PRO TIPS

- These are the best two offensive plays in your playbook. They will get your playmakers in position to win you games.
- It doesn't matter who is carrying the ball for the Patriots. Keep straight ahead and pick up as many yards as possible.
- Use the Trips Y Iso formation in the red zone; Gronk can't be stopped outside.

BEST RUN: SINGLEBACK ACE OVERLOAD–HB BELLY WEAK

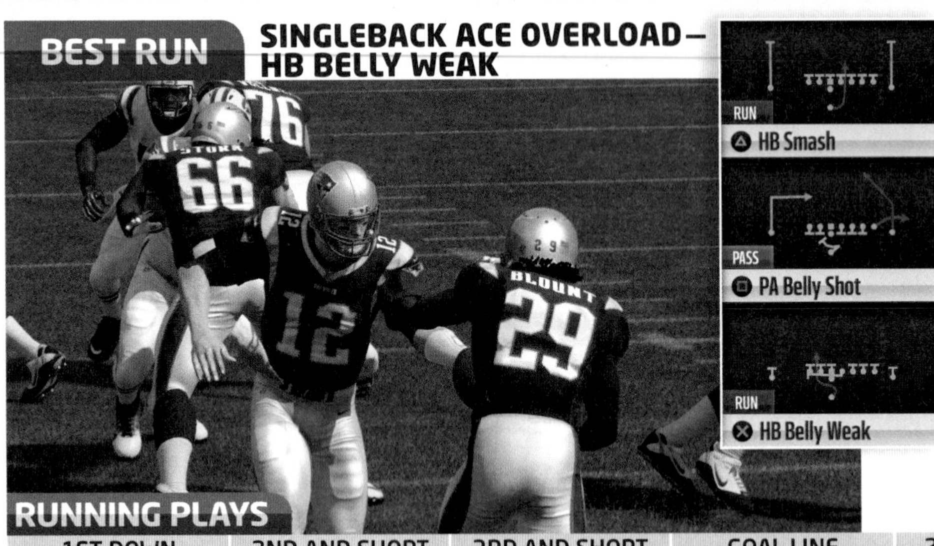

SETUP:

- This is a unique formation that could give smaller defenses problems. Otherwise, stick with passing as your main attack and mix in shotgun runs.
- In short yardage, go with the HB Smash from this formation and keep it behind the right guard.

ADVANCED SETUP:

- Playmaker the run to the right.

RUNNING PLAYS

1ST DOWN	2ND AND SHORT	3RD AND SHORT	GOAL LINE	2ND AND LONG	3RD AND LONG
Singleback Ace Pair Twins–HB Toss Strong	Singleback Bunch Ace–Inside Zone	I-Form Tight Pair–Iso	Goal Line–QB Sneak	Gun Tight Doubles On–HB Off Tackle	Gun Split Close Pats–HB Draw
Singleback Ace–0 1 Trap	Singleback Normal Patriots–0 1 Trap	I-Form Tight Pair–FB Dive	Singleback Ace Overload–HB Smash	Singleback Ace–HB Pump Draw	Gun Pats Wing Trips–5 6 Trap
Singleback Ace–HB Stretch	Singleback Tight Slots–HB Cutback	I-Form Tight Pair–FB Fake HB Flip	Singleback Ace Overload HB Stretch	Gun Trips Y Iso–HB Counter	Gun Bunch Wk–HB Base

INSIDE RUN | OUTSIDE RUN | SHOTGUN RUN | QB RUN

BEST PASS: GUN SPLIT CLOSE PATS–Z SPOT

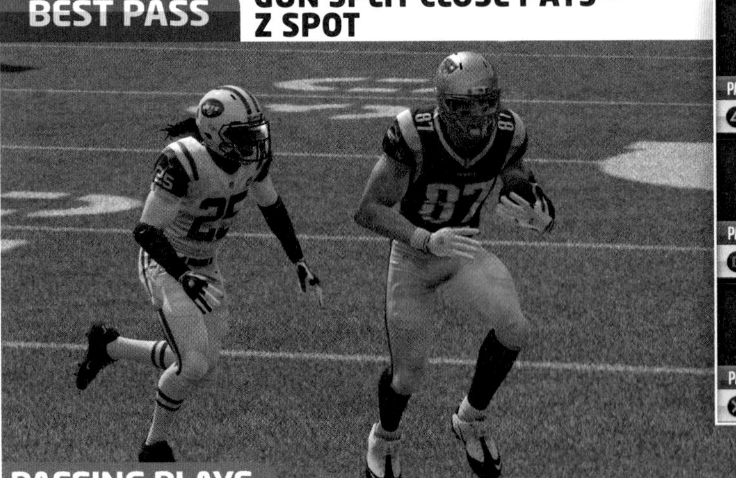

PASS
Z Spot
PASS
WR Corners
PASS
Y Out

SETUP/READS:

- Against zone coverage look to the short curl route sitting underneath. The HB Slip Screen can be solid vs consistent zone coverage teams.
- Against man-to-man coverage you should have two options getting open on their cut to the outside.
- Against the blitz, quickly send the ball out to the HB in the flat.

ADVANCED SETUP:

- Drag or slant the far right WR (optional).

PASSING PLAYS

1ST DOWN	2ND AND SHORT	3RD AND SHORT	SHOT PLAYS	2ND AND LONG	3RD AND LONG
Gun Trips TE–Drive Post	Singleback Tight Slots–Y Flood	Gun Normal Y-Slot–Slot Outs	Singleback Ace Overload–PA LT Sneak	Gun Trips Y Iso–PA Deep Outs	Gun Pats Wing Trips–Pats Y Out
Gun Pats Wing Trips–Wheel Mesh	Gun Bunch Wk–PA Post	Gun Tight Doubles On–DBL Stick	Gun Trips Y Iso–Smash Y Fade	Gun Empty Ace Patriot–Empty Stick Nod	Gun Tight Doubles On–Cross Wheels
Singleback Bunch Ace–TE Angle	Gun Trips TE–HB Angle	Gun Empty Ace Patriot–Spacing	Gun Split Close Pats–PA Y Shot	Gun Trips TE–Slot Swing	Gun Split Close Pats–HB WheelFrankie31

BASE PLAY | MAN BEATER | ZONE BEATER | BLITZ BEATER

 For more plays and strategies for this team, visit your eGuide using the access code sheet provided.

BEST DEFENSIVE PLAYS

PRO TIPS

- If you want to win more games in *Madden NFL 16*, rely on these defensive plays to lock up the run and pass.
- The Patriots' defense is one of the few playbooks in the game with both 3-4 and 4-3 fronts.
- Make sure to use FS Devin McCourty as an all-around player who can move around to create confusion.

BEST RUN D: 4-3 UNDER—WILL 3 PRESS

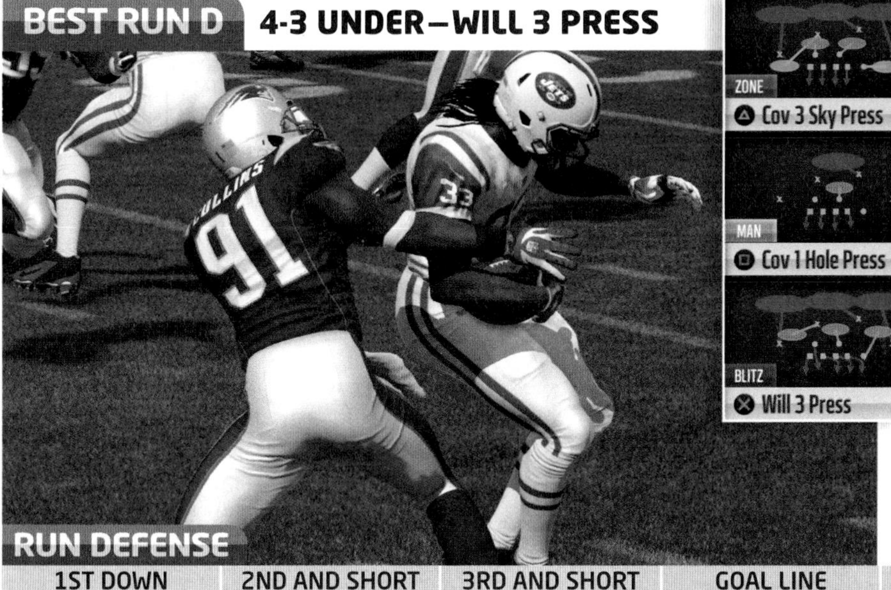

ZONE — △ Cov 3 Sky Press

MAN — □ Cov 1 Hole Press

BLITZ — ✕ Will 3 Press

SETUP:

- If your opponent is running to the right side, try the Sam 3 Press.
- The 4-3 Over also has Will 3 Press, which will protect the left side slightly better if you keep getting attacked there.

PLAYER TO CONTROL:

- FS up off the left edge

RUN DEFENSE

1ST DOWN	2ND AND SHORT	3RD AND SHORT	GOAL LINE	2ND AND LONG	3RD AND LONG
3-4 Odd—Sam Mike 1	4-3 Under—Free Fire	4-3 Over—Cov 1 Hole Press	Goal Line 5-4-2—Jam Cover 1	Big Dime 2-3-6—Sam—Mike Edge 1	Nickel 3-3-5 Odd—Cover 1 Hole
3-4 Odd—Will Sam 3	4-3 Under—Will 3 Press	4-3 Over—Strong Slant 3	Goal Line 5-4-2—Flat Buzz	Big Dime 2-3-6—Sam Overload 3 Press	Nickel 3-3-5 Odd—3 Buzz Sting Press

MAN COVERAGE ZONE COVERAGE MAN BLITZ ZONE BLITZ

BEST PASS D: NICKEL 3-3-5 ODD—3 SKY WK SHOW 4

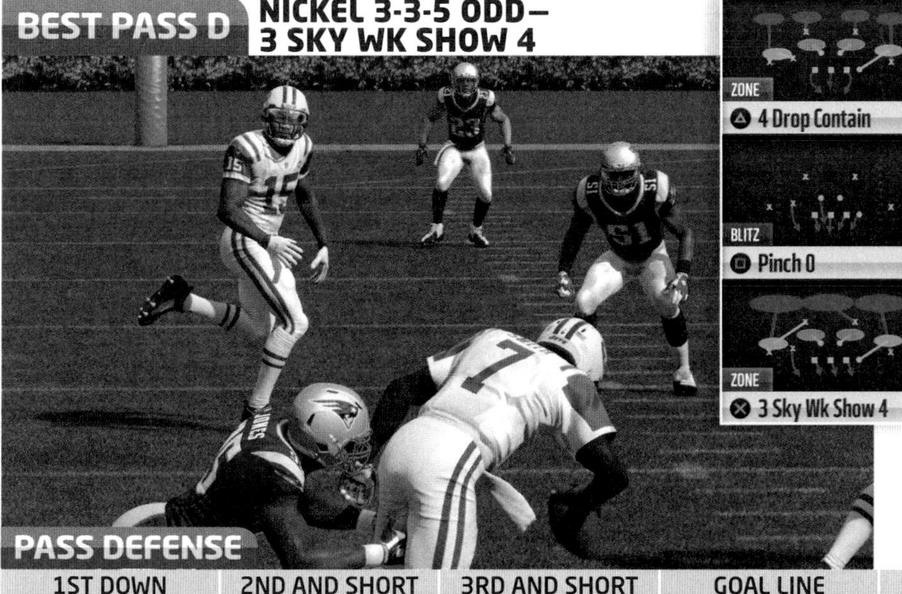

ZONE — △ 4 Drop Contain

BLITZ — □ Pinch 0

ZONE — ✕ 3 Sky Wk Show 4

SETUP:

- Look to add some extra heat off the edge by timing the snap with the slot CB.
- Get LB Jamie Collins in the game for his speed and zone coverage combo.
- If you think the opposing QB might try to sneak out of the pocket, call a QB contain before the snap.

PLAYER TO CONTROL:

- Blitzing CB off the left edge

PASS DEFENSE

1ST DOWN	2ND AND SHORT	3RD AND SHORT	GOAL LINE	2ND AND LONG	3RD AND LONG
4-3 Over—Cover 2 Man	3-4 Solid—1 Will Sam Go	Nickel 2-4-5—Over Storm Brave	Goal Line 5-3-3—GL Man	Nickel 3-3-5 Odd—Sam Mike 1	Big Dime 1-4-6—DB Sting
4-3 Over—Cover 4	3-4 Solid—Trio Sky Zone	Nickel 2-4-5—Nickel Blitz 2	Goal Line 5-3-3—GL Zone	Nickel 3-3-5 Odd—3 Sky Wk Show 4	Big Dime 1-4-6—Mike SS 3 Seam

MAN COVERAGE ZONE COVERAGE MAN BLITZ ZONE BLITZ

OAKLAND RAIDERS

GAMEPLAY RATING 74

CONNECTED FRANCHISE MODE STRATEGY

CFM TEAM RATING: **78**
OFFENSE: **81**
DEFENSE: **79**
OFFENSIVE SCHEME: **Power Run**
DEFENSIVE SCHEME: **Base 4-3**
STRENGTHS: **FB, LOLB, LT, C**
WEAKNESSES: **HB, QB, RE**

2014 TEAM RANKINGS

4th AFC West (3-13-0)
PASSING OFFENSE: **26th**
RUSHING OFFENSE: **32nd**
PASSING DEFENSE: **16th**
RUSHING DEFENSE: **22nd**

2014 TEAM LEADERS

PASSING: **Derek Carr: 3,270**
RUSHING: **Darren McFadden: 534**
RECEIVING: **Andre Holmes: 693**
TACKLES: **Charles Woodson: 113**
SACKS: **Justin Tuck: 5**
INTS: **Charles Woodson: 4**

KEY ADDITIONS

WR Michael Crabtree
LB Malcolm Smith
QB Christian Ponder
HB Trent Richardson
HB Roy Helu Jr.

KEY ROOKIES

WR Amari Cooper
DT Mario Edwards Jr.
TE Clive Walford

OWNER: **Mark Davis**
LEGACY SCORE: **0**

COACH: **Jack Del Rio**
LEVEL: **4**
LEGACY SCORE: **50**
OFFENSIVE SCHEME: **Power Run**
DEFENSIVE SCHEME: **Base 4-3**

OFFENSIVE SCOUTING REPORT

- QB Derek Carr stepped in and showed promise during his rookie season. Continue to develop his Deep Accuracy rating, or his big arm won't lead to many big plays.
- The Raiders have moved on from two veterans in their backfield, but that can't hurt their rushing attack, which ranked worst in the league last season. Give Latavius Murray the bulk of the carries and run behind the left side of the line, because it is your strong suit.
- The Raiders don't have much stability in their WR corps, but the signing of Michael Crabtree and the drafting of Amari Cooper could change that. Build chemistry between Cooper and Carr to really change the dynamic of the offense. Don't forget about FB Marcel Reece. He is the most dynamic FB in the game, so find clever ways to get him involved.

DEFENSIVE SCOUTING REPORT

- LE Justin Tuck is the pass rusher of the bunch on the defensive line. On the other side, allow RE Mario Edwards to develop into an all-around player. Currently his best purpose is to stop the run.
- The Raiders nailed their draft pick last season with LB Khalil Mack. Continue to get him on the field no matter what the situation or position and reap the rewards.
- The Raiders have an extremely young secondary that has some solid talent on the corners. Allow FS Charles Woodson to be the veteran leader and help develop the youngsters into stars.

SCHEDULE

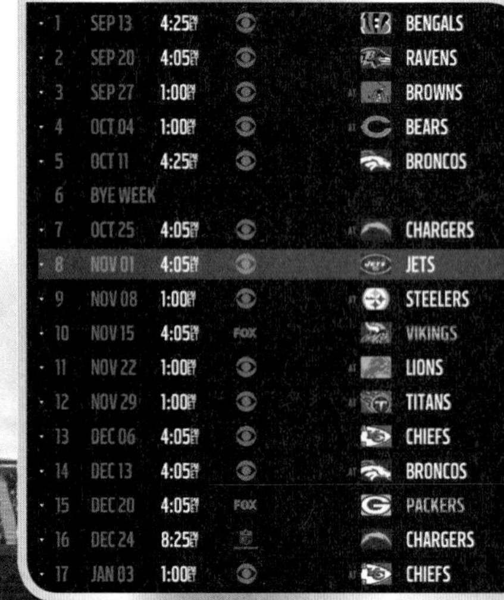

Week	Date	Time	Network		Opponent
1	SEP 13	4:25 PM ET			BENGALS
2	SEP 20	4:05 PM ET			RAVENS
3	SEP 27	1:00 PM ET		AT	BROWNS
4	OCT 04	1:00 PM ET		AT	BEARS
5	OCT 11	4:25 PM ET			BRONCOS
6	BYE WEEK				
7	OCT 25	4:05 PM ET		AT	CHARGERS
8	NOV 01	4:05 PM ET			JETS
9	NOV 08	1:00 PM ET		AT	STEELERS
10	NOV 15	4:05 PM ET	FOX		VIKINGS
11	NOV 22	1:00 PM ET		AT	LIONS
12	NOV 29	1:00 PM ET		AT	TITANS
13	DEC 06	4:05 PM ET			CHIEFS
14	DEC 13	4:05 PM ET		AT	BRONCOS
15	DEC 20	4:05 PM ET	FOX		PACKERS
16	DEC 24	8:25 PM ET			CHARGERS
17	JAN 03	1:00 PM ET		AT	CHIEFS

KEY PLAYERS

KEY OFFENSIVE PLAYER

MARCEL REECE #45

FB #45 HT 6'1" WT 255 COLLEGE Washington EXP 7

KEY RATINGS

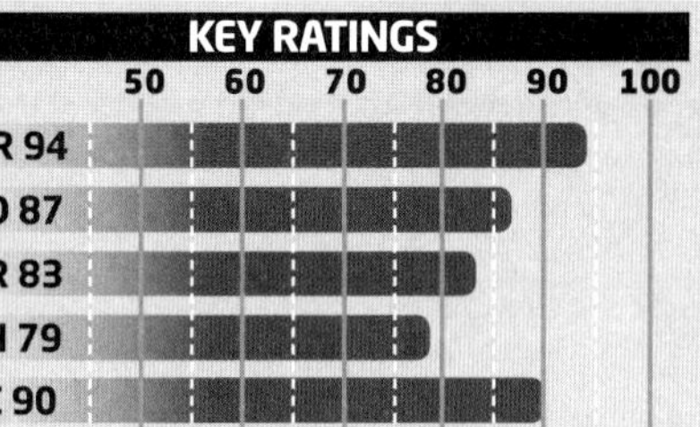

- The value you get from a player like Reece is up to the play caller. Don't forget to sub him in at TE and even HB—otherwise trade him.
- Reece is like a Swiss army knife and has the skill set to do multiple jobs.

KEY DEFENSIVE PLAYER

KHALIL MACK #52

LOLB #52 HT 6'3" WT 252 COLLEGE Buffalo EXP 1

KEY RATINGS

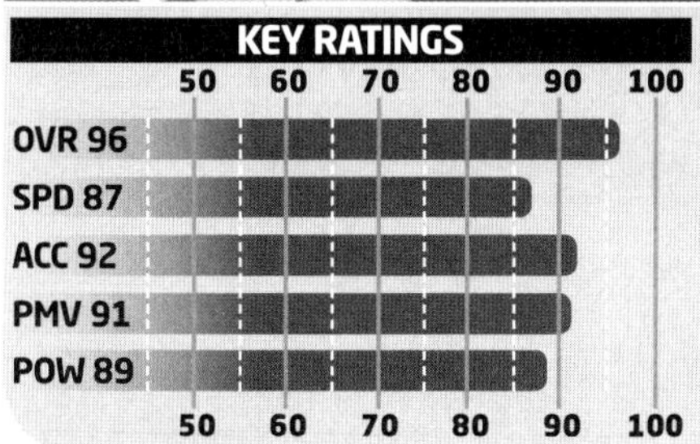

- Mack is an incredible talent that fits perfectly into the Raiders' scheme. Allow him to be the centerpiece of your defense.
- Keep working on the play recognition for Khalil Mack so teams won't be able to use his speed against him with play action.

KEY ROOKIE

AMARI COOPER #89

WR #89 HT 6'1" WT 211 COLLEGE Alabama EXP Rookie

KEY RATINGS

50 60 70 80 90 100

OVR 82
SPD 92
AGI 94
CIT 89
RTE 84

- Cooper not only will go for some amazing catches, but also he will hang onto them with his high Spectacular Catch and Catch in Traffic ratings.
- Continue to develop Amari Cooper's Release rating if you want him to be a matchup nightmare vs any CB.

KEY SLEEPER

MICHAEL DYER #37

HB #37 HT 5'8" WT 218 COLLEGE Louisville EXP Rookie

KEY RATINGS

50 60 70 80 90 100

OVR 62
SPD 86
TRK 85
ACC 88
BCV 79

- Spend more time upgrading Dyer than Trent Richardson at this stage. Dyer can be a short-yardage option.
- Dyer doesn't have much value until you upgrade his agility, but thankfully there is plenty of time.

OFFENSIVE DEPTH CHART

POS	FIRST	LAST	OVR
QB	DEREK	CARR	79
QB	CHRISTIAN	PONDER	73
QB	MATT	MCGLOIN	70
HB	LATAVIUS	MURRAY	78
HB	ROY	HELU JR.	77
HB	TRENT	RICHARDSON	75
HB	GEORGE	ATKINSON III	65
FB	MARCEL	REECE	82
WR	AMARI	COOPER	82
WR	MICHAEL	CRABTREE	82
WR	ROD	STREATER	78
WR	ANDRE	HOLMES	75
WR	BRICE	BUTLER	73
WR	KENBRELL	THOMPKINS	72
TE	LEE	SMITH	77
TE	MYCHAL	RIVERA	75
TE	CLIVE	WALFORD	72
LT	DONALD	PENN	89
LT	J'MARCUS	WEBB	70
LT	MATTHEW	MCCANTS	67
LG	GABE	JACKSON	84
LG	LAMAR	MADY	70
C	RODNEY	HUDSON	89
RG	RYAN	WENDELL	79
RG	JOSH	KLINE	73
RT	AUSTIN	HOWARD	78
RT	MENELIK	WATSON	73

DEFENSIVE DEPTH CHART

POS	FIRST	LAST	OVR
LE	JUSTIN	TUCK	85
LE	DENICO	AUTRY	65
LE	MAX	VALLES	61
DT	DAN	WILLIAMS	88
DT	JUSTIN	ELLIS	74
DT	STACY	MCGEE	71
DT	RICKY	LUMPKIN	69
RE	C.J.	WILSON	74
RE	MARIO	EDWARDS JR.	71
RE	BENSON	MAYOWA	69
LOLB	KHALIL	MACK	91
LOLB	NEIRON	BALL	62
MLB	CURTIS	LOFTON	79
MLB	BEN	HEENEY	63
ROLB	SIO	MOORE	80
ROLB	MALCOLM	SMITH	77
ROLB	RAY RAY	ARMSTRONG	67
CB	T.J.	CARRIE	81
CB	D.J.	HAYDEN	78
CB	KEITH	MCGILL	71
CB	JAMES	DOCKERY	67
CB	NEIKO	THORPE	64
FS	CHARLES	WOODSON	85
SS	NATE	ALLEN	82
SS	BRANDIAN	ROSS	72
SS	JONATHAN	DOWLING	64

SPECIAL TEAMS

POS	FIRST	LAST	OVR
K	SEBASTIAN	JANIKOWSKI	87
KR	T.J.	CARRIE	81
KR	ANDRE	DEBOSE	55
P	MARQUETTE	KING	80
PR	T.J.	CARRIE	81

BEST OFFENSIVE PLAYS

PRO TIPS

- These are the best two offensive plays in your playbook. They will get your playmakers in position to win you games.
- The Raiders' offensive playbook features 20 shotgun formations, but you should stick with your best 3-5.
- The Raiders added some new runs in the off-season, but your best bet is still straight ahead.

BEST RUN: SINGLEBACK ACE PAIR SLOT—INSIDE ZONE SPLIT

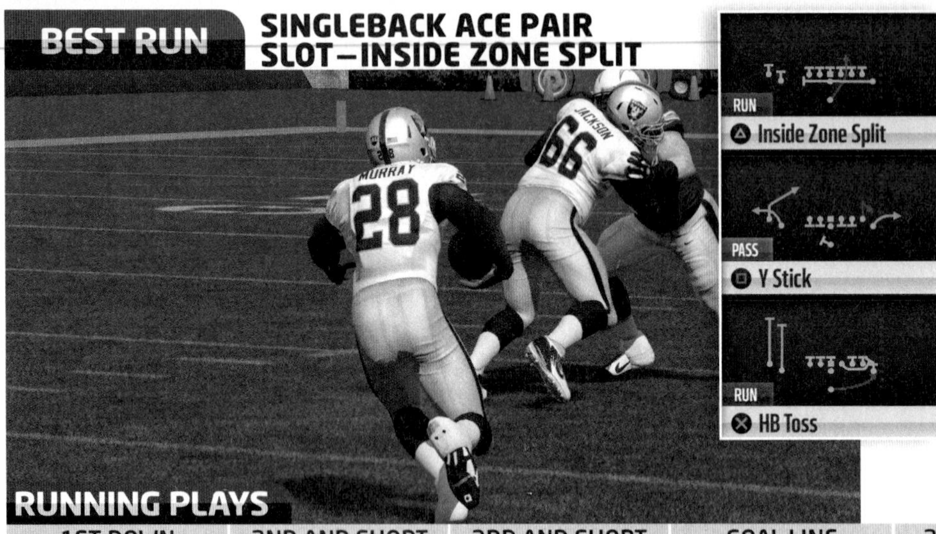

SETUP:

- Get your highest-rated impact blocker into the game at TE.
- If the defense loses contain off the left edge, make a quick juke and get outside. It won't happen often, but it makes for a big gain.
- This is a simple run up the middle, which should help the Raiders improve on their last ranked rushing attack from last season.

ADVANCED SETUP:

- Motion the far right TE to the right (optional).

RUNNING PLAYS

1ST DOWN	2ND AND SHORT	3RD AND SHORT	GOAL LINE	2ND AND LONG	3RD AND LONG
Singleback Ace Wing—HB Stretch	Singleback Ace Wing—0 1 Trap	Pistol Doubles—HB Zone	Goal Line—QB Sneak	Gun Flip Trips Raider—Read Option	Gun Bunch Offset—HB Draw
Singleback Ace Pair—Inside Zone Split	I-Form Tight Pair—OAK Off Tackle	Singleback Doubles—HB Cutback	Goal Line—FB Dive	Gun Trey Open Offset—Read Option	Gun Dbls Y-Flex Offset—0 1 Trap
I-Form Pro—OAK Zone Wk	Singleback Wing Trips Open—Inside Zone Split	Singleback Ace Pair Slot—HB Stretch	Goal Line—Strong Toss	Gun Dbls Y-Flex Offset—Outside Zone	Gun Y-Trips Offset—HB Counter

INSIDE RUN | OUTSIDE RUN | SHOTGUN RUN | QB RUN

BEST PASS: GUN BUNCH OPEN OFFSET—Y TRAIL

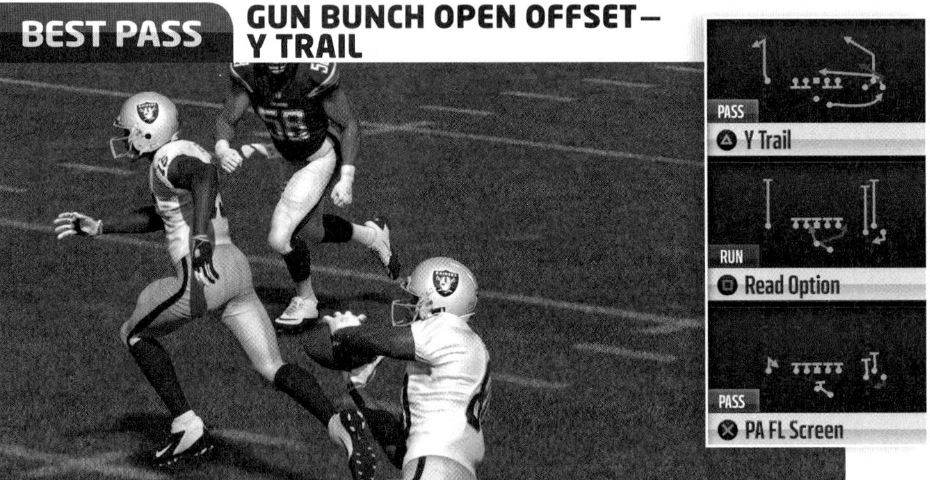

SETUP/READS:

- Against zone coverage hang onto the ball and look for the post; otherwise, dump it to the flat if you see pressure.
- Against man-to-man coverage one of the routes across the middle will open up, even against a strong user defender.
- Your options for the far left WR are nearly endless, and the smoke screen or comeback route is good if there is no flat zone.

ADVANCED SETUP:

- Streak the far left WR.

PASSING PLAYS

1ST DOWN	2ND AND SHORT	3RD AND SHORT	SHOT PLAYS	2ND AND LONG	3RD AND LONG
Gun Ace Twins Offset—Posts	Gun Ace Twins Offset—Raiders Sail	Gun Dbls Y-Flex Offset—Angle Smash	Singleback Ace Wing—PA Cross Shot	Singleback Ace Pair—TE Attack	Gun Wing Trips Raider—Four Verticals
Gun Bunch Open Offset—Y Trail	Gun Trio Offset—Mesh	Gun Wing Trips Raider Wk—PA Slide	Gun Ace Twins Offset—PA Verts	Gun Empty Trey—Dbl Slot Cross	Gun Doubles Wing Offset—Texas Verticals
Gun Flip Trips Raider—OAK Verticals	Gun Wing Trips Raider Wk—Post N Cross	Gun Wing Trips Raider—OAK Y Screen	Gun Wing Trips Raider Wk—Mtn Pump and Go	Gun Flip Trips Raider—OAK Post Shot	Gun Empty Trey—Under Seams

BASE PLAY | MAN BEATER | ZONE BEATER | BLITZ BEATER

BEST DEFENSIVE PLAYS

PRO TIPS

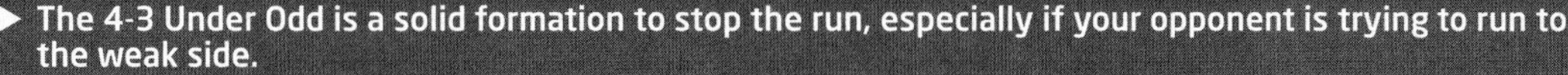

- If you want to win more games in *Madden NFL 16*, rely on these defensive plays to lock up the run and pass.
- The 4-3 Under Odd is a solid formation to stop the run, especially if your opponent is trying to run to the weak side.
- Find a way to get Khalil Mack on the field and rushing the passer; it doesn't matter if it is at LB or DE.

BEST RUN D: 4-3 UNDER ODD – WILL GO FIRE 3

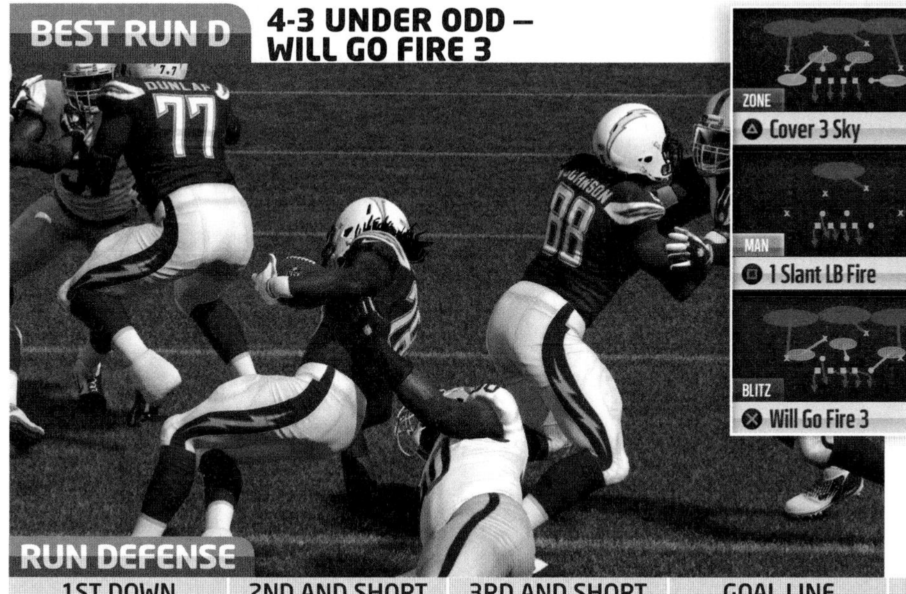

ZONE — Cover 3 Sky

MAN — 1 Slant LB Fire

BLITZ — Will Go Fire 3

SETUP:

- Consider crashing your line down and showing blitz in short-yardage situations.
- While your blitzing LB might not shoot the gap, he will take out any lead blockers and allow your teammates to make the play.

PLAYER TO CONTROL:

- The FS (drop into the box vs run-heavy formations)

RUN DEFENSE

1ST DOWN	2ND AND SHORT	3RD AND SHORT	GOAL LINE	2ND AND LONG	3RD AND LONG
4-3 Under Odd–Cover 2 Man	4-3 Over–Sam Will Blitz	4-3 Stack–Thunder Smoke	Goal Line 5-4-2–Jam Cover 1	Nickel 4 D Ends–Odd 1 Contain	Nickel Normal–Cover 2 Man
4-3 Under Odd–Will Go Fire 3	4-3 Over–Strong Slant 3	4-3 Stack–Free Fire 3	Goal Line 5-4-2–Flat Buzz	Nickel 4 D Ends–Odd Overload 3	Nickel Normal–Cov 3 Buzz Press

MAN COVERAGE | ZONE COVERAGE | MAN BLITZ | ZONE BLITZ

BEST PASS D: NICKEL DOUBLE A GAP – RUSH 3 BUZZ

ZONE — 3 Cloud Show 2

BLITZ — Dog 3 Show 2

BLITZ — Rush 3 Buzz

SETUP:

- Make sure to get Khalil Mack into the game off the left edge, because his speed will help generate pressure.
- Your DEs in this formation should have solid Zone Coverage ratings since they will be asked to drop into coverage at times.
- Crashing your line can help ramp up the pressure, but you will give up the quick throw, especially to the flat.

PLAYER TO CONTROL:

- DE on the right side of the screen dropping into hook zone

PASS DEFENSE

1ST DOWN	2ND AND SHORT	3RD AND SHORT	GOAL LINE	2ND AND LONG	3RD AND LONG
4-3 Wide 9–1 Contain QB Spy	Nickel Normal–Cov 1 Hole Press	Nickel Double A Gap–Nickel Dog Meg	Goal Line 5-3-3–GL Man	Dime Normal–Mike Dime Blitz	Quarter Normal–DB Strike
4-3 Wide 9–Cover 2 Invert	Nickel Normal–Cov 3 Sky Press	Nickel Double A Gap–3 Cloud Show 2	Goal Line 5-3-3–GL Zone	Dime Normal–ox FZ Press	Quarter Normal–FZ 3 Sky

MAN COVERAGE | ZONE COVERAGE | MAN BLITZ | ZONE BLITZ

ST. LOUIS RAMS

GAMEPLAY RATING 78

CONNECTED FRANCHISE MODE STRATEGY

CFM TEAM RATING: **84**
OFFENSE: **81**
DEFENSE: **89**
OFFENSIVE SCHEME: **Power Run**
DEFENSIVE SCHEME: **Base 4-3**
STRENGTHS: **DT, DE, TE, LT**
WEAKNESSES: **HB, WR, C, RG**

2014 TEAM RANKINGS

4th NFC West (6-10-0)
PASSING OFFENSE: **23rd**
RUSHING OFFENSE: **20th**
PASSING DEFENSE: **19th**
RUSHING DEFENSE: **14th**

2014 TEAM LEADERS

PASSING: **Austin Davis: 2,001**
RUSHING: **Tre Mason: 765**
RECEIVING: **Kenny Britt: 748**
TACKLES: **Alec Ogletree: 111**
SACKS: **Robert Quinn: 10.5**
INTS: **Trumaine Johnson: 3**

KEY ADDITIONS

DT Nick Fairley
QB Nick Foles
LB Akeem Ayers

KEY ROOKIES

HB Todd Gurley
T Rob Havenstein
T Jamon Brown

OWNER: **Stan Kroenke**
LEGACY SCORE: **0**

COACH: **Jeff Fisher**
LEVEL: **18**
LEGACY SCORE: **3,700**
OFFENSIVE SCHEME: **Power Run**
DEFENSIVE SCHEME: **Base 4-3**

OFFENSIVE SCOUTING REPORT

- The Rams made a move to get QB Nick Foles in the off-season, which should help solidify the position. Keep Foles healthy by utilizing a short passing game and upgrading the right side of your offensive line.
- The young combination of Tre Mason and Todd Gurley at HB will really take the pressure off the offense. Give the ball to the hot hand and go with Gurley for power and Mason for elusive moves.
- Don't let the speed and agility of WR Tavon Austin go to waste. Beyond special teams, Austin needs to have the ball in his hands once per half, even if you need to hand it to him.

DEFENSIVE SCOUTING REPORT

- Look for DE Chris Long to rebound this season. Otherwise, keep focusing on building the youth on the defensive line. You have plenty of talent locked up long term with Robert Quinn and Aaron Donald.
- MLB James Laurinaitis is a solid defender in the middle of the defense, but look to build some depth behind him for the long term. There is a good amount of speed at the OLB positions that you can get creative with for a defensive scheme.
- The Rams' CBs are solid in man-to-man coverage, but the rest of your starters lean towards zone. This means the Cover 2 Sink might be a perfect scheme to try out against your opponents early in the game. E.J. Gaines and Janoris Jenkins should be solid against most WRs.

SCHEDULE

Week	Date	Time	Network		Opponent
1	SEP 13	1:00 PM ET	FOX		SEAHAWKS
2	SEP 20	1:00 PM ET	FOX	AT	REDSKINS
3	SEP 27	1:00 PM ET			STEELERS
4	OCT 04	4:25 PM ET	FOX	AT	CARDINALS
5	OCT 11	1:00 PM ET		AT	PACKERS
6	BYE WEEK				
7	OCT 25	1:00 PM ET			BROWNS
8	NOV 01	1:00 PM ET	FOX		49ERS
9	NOV 08	1:00 PM ET	FOX	AT	VIKINGS
10	NOV 15	1:00 PM ET	FOX		BEARS
11	NOV 22	1:00 PM ET	FOX	AT	RAVENS
12	NOV 29	1:00 PM ET	FOX	AT	BENGALS
13	DEC 06	1:00 PM ET	FOX		CARDINALS
14	DEC 13	1:00 PM ET	FOX		LIONS
15	DEC 17	8:25 PM ET			BUCCANEERS
16	DEC 27	4:25 PM ET	FOX	AT	SEAHAWKS
17	JAN 03	4:25 PM ET	FOX	AT	49ERS

KEY PLAYERS

KEY OFFENSIVE PLAYER

JARED COOK #89

TE #89 HT 6'5" WT 254 COLLEGE South Carolina EXP 6

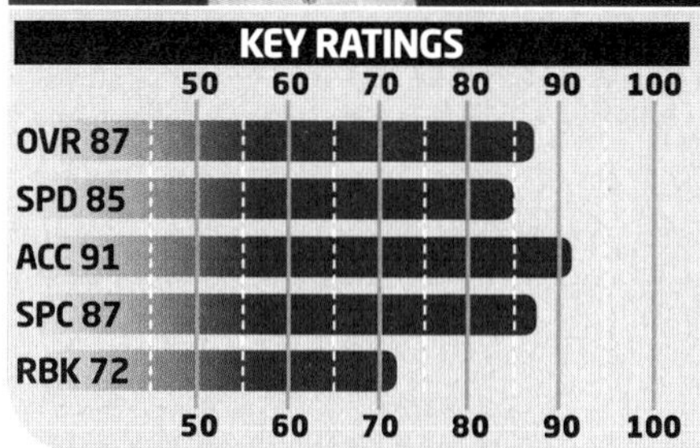

- Cook is an athletic threat who can get vertical in a hurry, so make sure to stretch the seam with him.
- Work on upgrades to his Catch in Traffic rating to make him an all-around player who hangs on to clutch catches.

KEY DEFENSIVE PLAYER

AARON DONALD #99

DT #99 HT 6'1" WT 285 COLLEGE Pittsburgh EXP 1

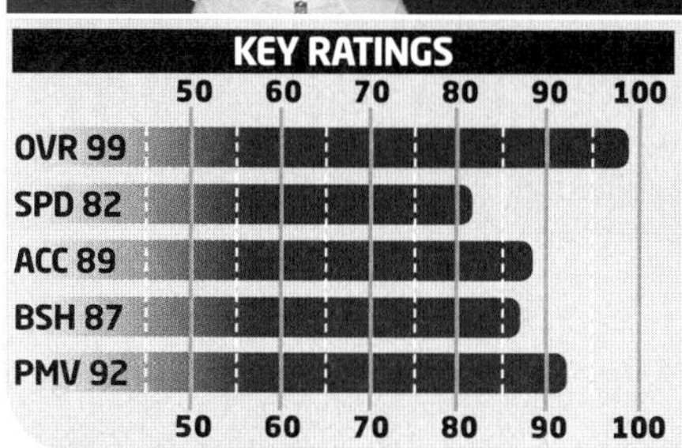

- Donald had an excellent rookie season. However, teams will be more aware of his presence in the lineup now.
- The depth of the defensive line is a real strength. Keep a rotation going to keep your players fresh.

KEY ROOKIE

TODD GURLEY #30

HB #30 HT 6'1" WT 222 COLLEGE Georgia EXP Rookie

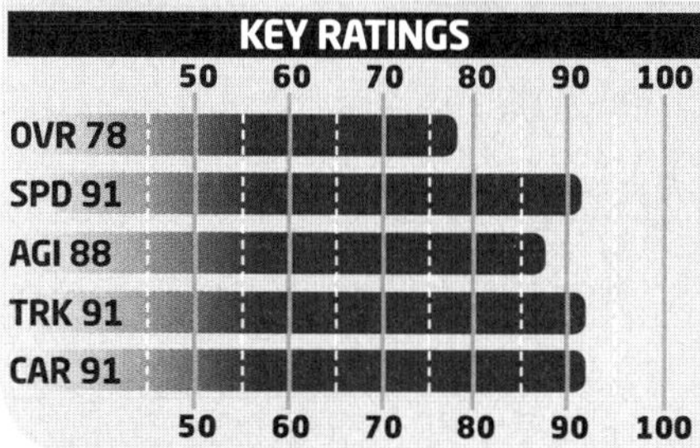

- Gurley fits perfectly into the power run mentality of the Rams' offense.
- Make sure to split carries until you can spend some XP to boost his Injury rating.

KEY SLEEPER

LAMARCUS JOYNER #20

FS #20 HT 5'8" WT 184 COLLEGE Florida State EXP 1

KEY RATINGS

50 60 70 80 90 100

OVR 77
SPD 87
ACC 93
MCV 76
PUR 85

- Joyner is the best option for man-to-man coverage in the secondary, so sub him in for Cover 0 blitzes.
- Mark Barron is the best run stopper in the secondary, but if his confidence slips, give Joyner a role on passing downs.

OFFENSIVE DEPTH CHART

POS	FIRST	LAST	OVR
QB	NICK	FOLES	78
QB	AUSTIN	DAVIS	73
QB	CASE	KEENUM	72
HB	TODD	GURLEY	80
HB	TRE	MASON	79
HB	BENNY	CUNNINGHAM	73
HB	ISAIAH	PEAD	67
FB	CORY	HARKEY	79
WR	KENNY	BRITT	82
WR	BRIAN	QUICK	79
WR	STEDMAN	BAILEY	76
WR	TAVON	AUSTIN	75
WR	CHRIS	GIVENS	68
WR	DEVON	WYLIE	62
TE	JARED	COOK	84
TE	LANCE	KENDRICKS	78
TE	ALEX	BAYER	67
LT	GREG	ROBINSON	74
LT	JAMON	BROWN	65
LG	RODGER	SAFFOLD	83
LG	CODY	WICHMANN	64
C	TIM	BARNES	72
C	DEMETRIUS	RHANEY	63
RG	BARRETT	JONES	74
RG	ANDREW	DONNAL	66
RT	GARRETT	REYNOLDS	77
RT	BRANDON	WASHINGTON	72
RT	ROB	HAVENSTEIN	70

DEFENSIVE DEPTH CHART

POS	FIRST	LAST	OVR
LE	WILLIAM	HAYES	86
LE	CHRIS	LONG	84
LE	ETHAN	WESTBROOKS	64
DT	AARON	DONALD	92
DT	NICK	FAIRLEY	86
DT	MICHAEL	BROCKERS	80
DT	DOUG	WORTHINGTON	69
RE	ROBERT	QUINN	93
RE	EUGENE	SIMS	74
LOLB	ALEC	OGLETREE	81
LOLB	MARSHALL	MCFADDEN	64
MLB	JAMES	LAURINAITIS	79
MLB	BRYCE	HAGER	63
MLB	DAREN	BATES	60
ROLB	AKEEM	AYERS	81
ROLB	JO-LONN	DUNBAR	76
ROLB	KOREY	TOOMER	63
CB	JANORIS	JENKINS	81
CB	E.J.	GAINES	79
CB	TRUMAINE	JOHNSON	75
CB	BRANDON	MCGEE	69
CB	MARCUS	ROBERSON	64
FS	RODNEY	MCLEOD	79
FS	MARK	BARRON	78
FS	LAMARCUS	JOYNER	77
SS	T.J.	MCDONALD	82
SS	CODY	DAVIS	68
SS	MAURICE	ALEXANDER	66

SPECIAL TEAMS

POS	FIRST	LAST	OVR
K	GREG	ZUERLEIN	81
KR	BENNY	CUNNINGHAM	73
KR	CHRIS	GIVENS	68
P	JOHNNY	HEKKER	93
PR	TAVON	AUSTIN	75

BEST OFFENSIVE PLAYS

PRO TIPS

- **These are the best two offensive plays in your playbook. They will get your playmakers in position to win you games.**
- **Try to run the bulk of your power runs to the left for better blocking.**
- **Stick with Todd Gurley for up-the-middle runs, and bring in Tre Mason to take it outside.**

BEST RUN: STRONG Y-FLEX—INSIDE ZONE LEAD

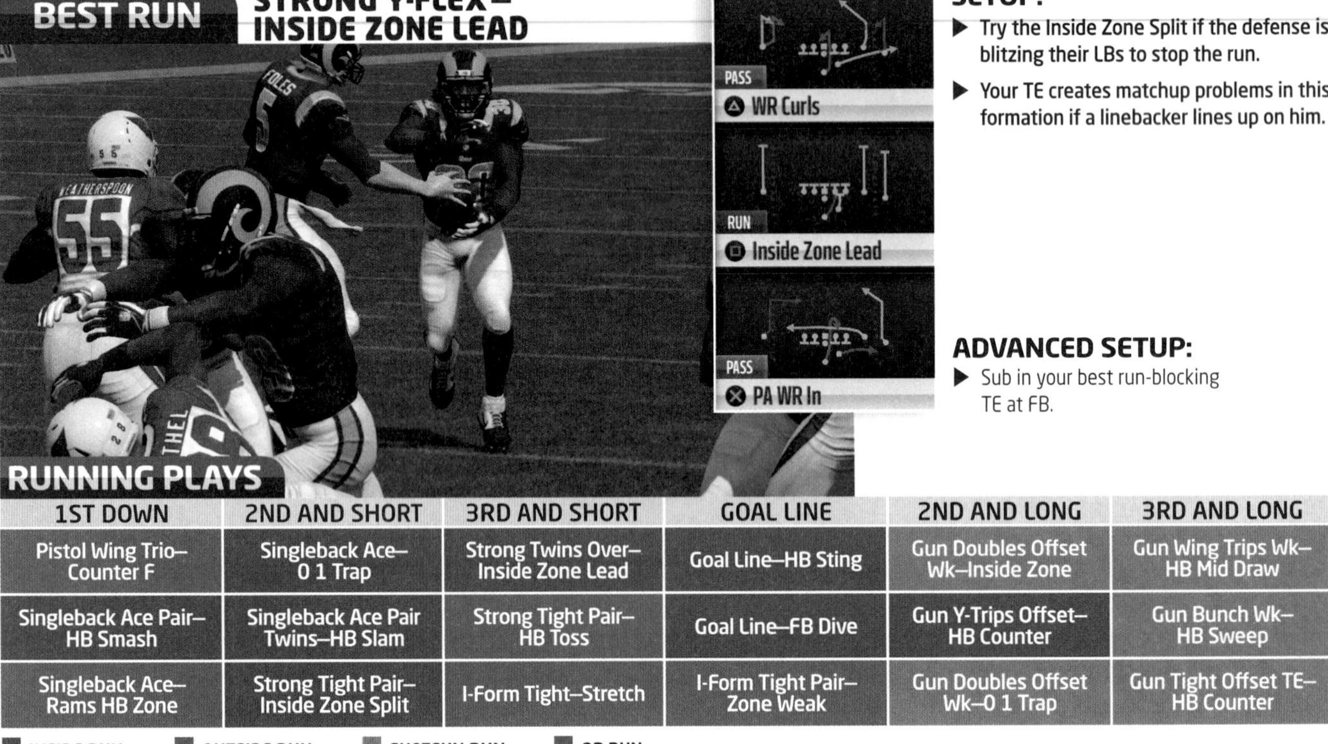

SETUP:

- Try the Inside Zone Split if the defense is blitzing their LBs to stop the run.
- Your TE creates matchup problems in this formation if a linebacker lines up on him.

ADVANCED SETUP:

- Sub in your best run-blocking TE at FB.

RUNNING PLAYS

1ST DOWN	2ND AND SHORT	3RD AND SHORT	GOAL LINE	2ND AND LONG	3RD AND LONG
Pistol Wing Trio—Counter F	Singleback Ace—0 1 Trap	Strong Twins Over—Inside Zone Lead	Goal Line—HB Sting	Gun Doubles Offset Wk—Inside Zone	Gun Wing Trips Wk—HB Mid Draw
Singleback Ace Pair—HB Smash	Singleback Ace Pair Twins—HB Slam	Strong Tight Pair—HB Toss	Goal Line—FB Dive	Gun Y-Trips Offset—HB Counter	Gun Bunch Wk—HB Sweep
Singleback Ace—Rams HB Zone	Strong Tight Pair—Inside Zone Split	I-Form Tight—Stretch	I-Form Tight Pair—Zone Weak	Gun Doubles Offset Wk—0 1 Trap	Gun Tight Offset TE—HB Counter

INSIDE RUN | OUTSIDE RUN | SHOTGUN RUN | QB RUN

BEST PASS: GUN WING TRIPS WK—ISO DRAG

SETUP/READS:

- Against zone coverage look to hit the TE after he gets behind the LBs.
- Against man-to-man coverage consider taking a shot downfield if you have the size advantage on the outside.
- Against the blitz dump it over the middle to the drag and use the new RAC (run after catch) option it to turn upfield.

ADVANCED SETUP:

- Playmaker the drag upfield after the snap.

PASSING PLAYS

1ST DOWN	2ND AND SHORT	3RD AND SHORT	SHOT PLAYS	2ND AND LONG	3RD AND LONG
Singleback Bunch—Clearout SE Opt	Weak Close—Bench Switch	I-Form Pro—Texas	Singleback Doubles—Goaline Fade	Gun Doubles Offset Wk—Switch	Gun Empty Base—Verticals
Gun Tight Offset TE—Drive Out	Gun Tight Offset TE—Mesh	Strong Pro—F Angle	Singleback Doubles—Z-Close Cross	Gun Trey Open Offset—Y Cross Flood	Gun Trey Open Offset—Curls Dig
Singleback Doubles—PA Slot Cross	Singleback Ace—Ace Posts	Gun Split Ram—PA F Slide	Gun Tight Offset TE—PA Seams Shot	Gun Trey Open Offset—PA Read	Gun Normal Y-Flex Tight—HB Slip Screen

BASE PLAY | MAN BEATER | ZONE BEATER | BLITZ BEATER

 For more plays and strategies for this team, visit your eGuide using the access code sheet provided.

BEST DEFENSIVE PLAYS

PRO TIPS

- **Rely on these defensive plays to lock up the run and pass.**
- **The Rams should be able to slow down most rushing attacks without having to get super aggressive.**
- **While the Rams DEs are excellent, the DTs should really contribute to the rush this year, so pay attention to packages.**

BEST RUN D: 4-3 STACK—COVER 2 SINK

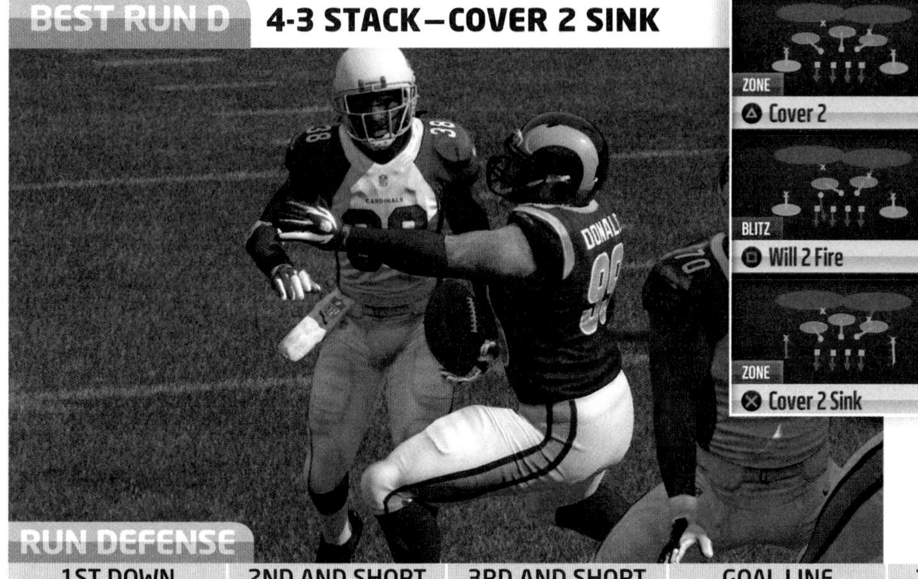

ZONE
△ Cover 2

BLITZ
□ Will 2 Fire

ZONE
✕ Cover 2 Sink

SETUP:

- This scheme takes advantage of your team's strengths and isn't too aggressive. Blitz your LBs in short yardage.
- This defense looks similar to your man-to-man pass defense and could fool your opponent.

PLAYER TO CONTROL:

- Either DT (try to get in the backfield)

RUN DEFENSE

1ST DOWN	2ND AND SHORT	3RD AND SHORT	GOAL LINE	2ND AND LONG	3RD AND LONG
4-3 Over–1 QB Contain	4-3 Under–Cover 1 Hole	46 Bear Under–LB Dogs	Goal Line 5-4-2–Jam Cover 1	Nickel 4 D Ends–Cover 1 LB Blitz	Dime Normal–Cov 1 Robber Press
4-3 Over–Strong Slant 3	4-3 Under–Will Go Fire 3	46 Bear Under–LB Dogs 3	Goal Line 5-4-2–Flat Buzz	Nickel 4 D Ends–Cover 3 Sky	Dime Normal–Cover 3 Cloud

MAN COVERAGE | ZONE COVERAGE | MAN BLITZ | ZONE BLITZ

BEST PASS D: NICKEL 4 D ENDS—COVER 2 MAN

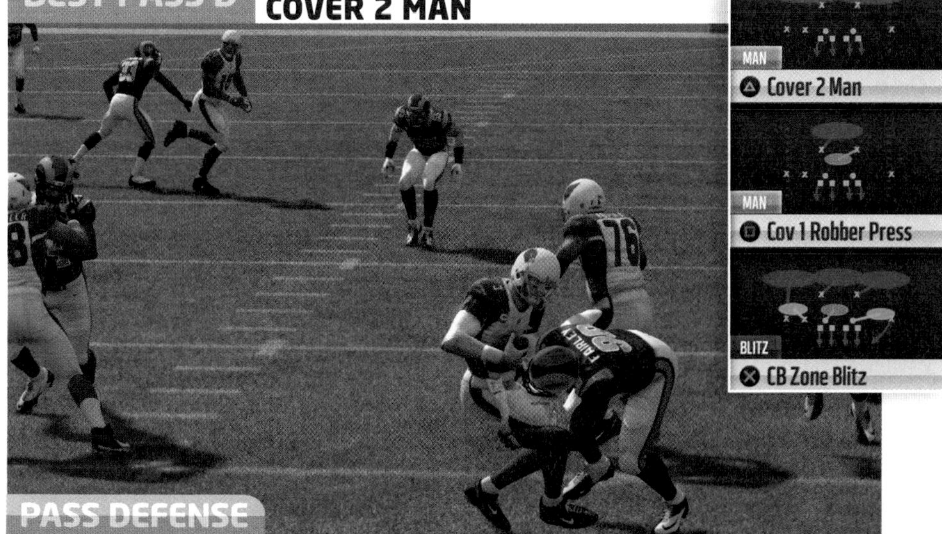

MAN
△ Cover 2 Man

MAN
□ Cov 1 Robber Press

BLITZ
✕ CB Zone Blitz

SETUP:

- Make sure to sub DTs Aaron Donald and Nick Fairley into the game at defensive tackle.
- If your rush isn't getting there, try the CB Zone Blitz once per drive.
- Bring a safety down to stop any throws to the tight end.

PLAYER TO CONTROL:

- MLB on the left of the screen

PASS DEFENSE

1ST DOWN	2ND AND SHORT	3RD AND SHORT	GOAL LINE	2ND AND LONG	3RD AND LONG
46 Bear Under–Cover 1	Nickel Normal–2 QB Contain	Nickel 4 D Ends–Odd 1 Contain	Goal Line 5-3-3–GL Man	Nickel Double A Gap–Nickel Dog Meg	Nickel 4 D Ends–Odd LB Dogs
46 Bear Under–Cover 3	Nickel Normal–Under Smoke 2	Nickel 4 D Ends–Odd Overload 2	Goal Line 5-3-3–Pinch Zone	Nickel Double A Gap–Nickel Dog 3 Buzz	Nickel 4 D Ends–Odd 4 Blitz Show 2

MAN COVERAGE | ZONE COVERAGE | MAN BLITZ | ZONE BLITZ

BALTIMORE RAVENS

GAMEPLAY RATING 85

CONNECTED FRANCHISE MODE STRATEGY

CFM TEAM RATING: **89**
OFFENSE: **91**
DEFENSE: **89**
OFFENSIVE SCHEME: **Vertical Offense**
DEFENSIVE SCHEME: **Hybrid**
STRENGTHS: **QB, RG, ROLB, MLB, CB**
WEAKNESSES: **FS, LE, WR, HB**

2014 TEAM RANKINGS

3rd AFC North (10-6-0)
PASSING OFFENSE: **13th**
RUSHING OFFENSE: **8th**
PASSING DEFENSE: **23rd**
RUSHING DEFENSE: **4th**

2014 TEAM LEADERS

PASSING: **Joe Flacco: 3,986**
RUSHING: **Justin Forsett: 1,266**
RECEIVING: **Steve Smith: 1,065**
TACKLES: **C.J. Mosley: 133**
SACKS: **Elvis Dumervil: 17**
INTS: **C.J. Mosley: 2**

KEY ADDITIONS

CB Kyle Arrington
QB Matt Schaub

KEY ROOKIES

WR Breshad Perriman
TE Maxx Williams
DT Carl Davis

OWNER: **Steve Bisciotti**
LEGACY SCORE: **3,325**

COACH: **John Harbaugh**
LEVEL: **22**
LEGACY SCORE: **2,500**
OFFENSIVE SCHEME: **Vertical**
DEFENSIVE SCHEME: **Hybrid**

OFFENSIVE SCOUTING REPORT

- QB Joe Flacco nearly led the Ravens to a playoff upset in Foxborough last season. Expect nothing less than another solid season, where he will look to build on that 27/12 touchdown/interception ratio. The Ravens' offensive line should give Flacco plenty of time to look downfield this year.
- HB Justin Forsett proved that he deserves not only the starting spot in Baltimore but also a new contract. Even if Forsett can repeat his success, start building some more options at the backup spot.
- WR Steve Smith showed he still had some gas left in the tank with another solid season. Develop some young talent at the receiving corps to replace the veteran in a few seasons.

DEFENSIVE SCOUTING REPORT

- Finding a solid player like Brandon Williams at DT allowed the Ravens to get younger and save money on veterans like Haloti Ngata and Terrance Cody. Those players were excellent, so keep developing Williams.
- The Ravens have had some fresh talent injected in their LB corps over the last few seasons. Keep getting whatever is left from Terrell Suggs and Daryl Smith, but never bet against them.
- Jimmy Smith is a physical press corner who can excel in any scheme. On the other side, Lardarius Webb is a good man-to-man CB who lacks the ability to play all-out press coverage. Note your matchups and keep Smith lined up vs any star wideouts.

SCHEDULE

Week	Date	Time	Opponent
1	SEP 13	4:25 PM ET	AT BRONCOS
2	SEP 20	4:05 PM ET	AT RAIDERS
3	SEP 27	1:00 PM ET	BENGALS
4	OCT 01	8:25 PM ET	AT STEELERS
5	OCT 11	1:00 PM ET	BROWNS
6	OCT 18	4:25 PM ET	AT 49ERS
7	OCT 26	8:30 PM ET	AT CARDINALS
8	NOV 01	1:00 PM ET	CHARGERS
9	BYE WEEK		
10	NOV 15	1:00 PM ET	JAGUARS
11	NOV 22	1:00 PM ET	RAMS
12	NOV 30	8:30 PM ET	AT BROWNS
13	DEC 06	1:00 PM ET	AT DOLPHINS
14	DEC 13	8:30 PM ET	SEAHAWKS
15	DEC 20	1:00 PM ET	CHIEFS
16	DEC 27	8:30 PM ET	STEELERS
17	JAN 03	1:00 PM ET	AT BENGALS

KEY PLAYERS

KEY OFFENSIVE PLAYER

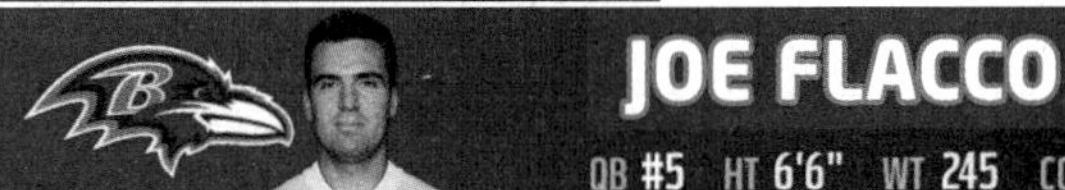

JOE FLACCO #5

QB #5 HT 6'6" WT 245 COLLEGE Delaware EXP 7

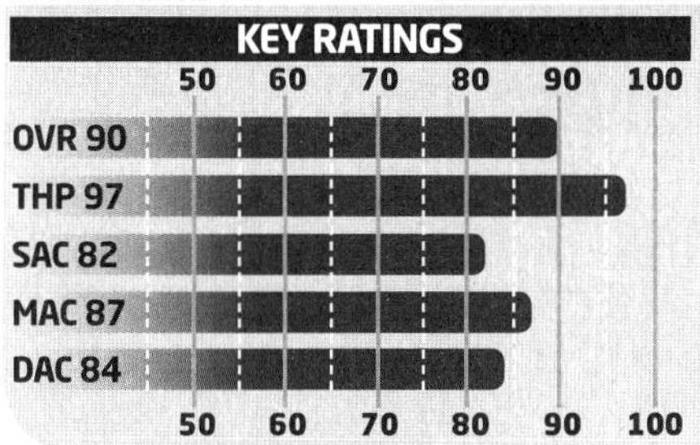

- Touch up Flacco's Play Action and Throw On Run ratings with some XP.
- There is nothing flashy about Joe Flacco; he just makes every throw out there.

KEY DEFENSIVE PLAYER

JIMMY SMITH #22

CB #22 HT 6'2" WT 210 COLLEGE Colorado EXP 4

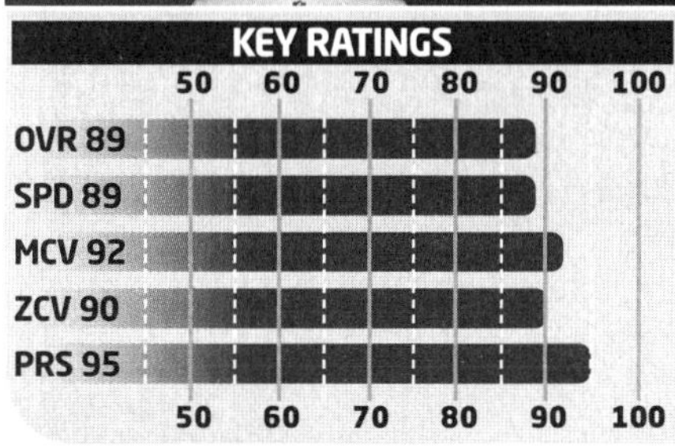

- Smith has quickly become one of the Ravens' best defenders. Continue to upgrade his Play Recognition rating to make him one of the league's best.
- Smith should be able to go up with nearly any WR and knock the ball out.

KEY ROOKIE

BRESHAD PERRIMAN

WR #18 HT 6'2" WT 212 COLLEGE UCF EXP Rookie

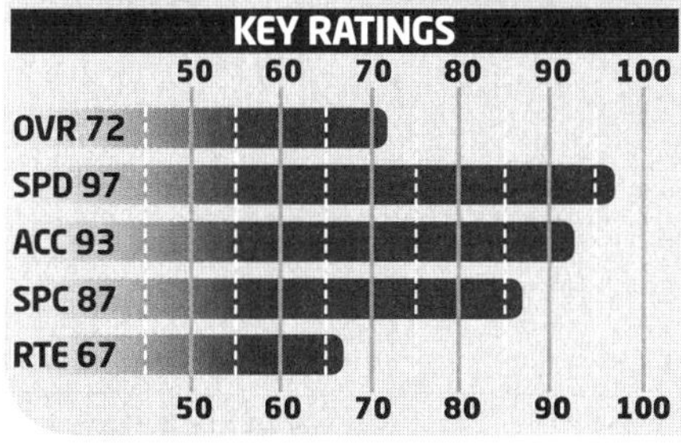

- Don't try to replace Torrey Smith—let Perriman develop into his own role.
- The combination of speed with Flacco's throwing power should be excellent.

KEY SLEEPER

MATT ELAM

SS #26 HT 5'10" WT 206 COLLEGE Florida EXP 2

KEY RATINGS

50	60	70	80	90	100

OVR 69
SPD 86
ACC 89
POW 90
TAK 67

- There is always a place in the lineup for 90 Hit Power, even if it means special teams.
- Elam looked to be a promising talent, so don't give up on him even if means you must user-control him.

OFFENSIVE DEPTH CHART

POS	FIRST	LAST	OVR
QB	JOE	FLACCO	89
QB	MATT	SCHAUB	74
QB	BRYN	RENNER	65
HB	JUSTIN	FORSETT	87
HB	LORENZO	TALIAFERRO	73
HB	JAVORIUS	ALLEN	71
HB	TERRENCE	MAGEE	67
FB	KYLE	JUSZCZYK	86
WR	STEVE	SMITH SR.	86
WR	MARLON	BROWN	76
WR	BRESHAD	PERRIMAN	73
WR	KAMAR	AIKEN	72
WR	MICHAEL	CAMPANARO	71
WR	ALDRICK	ROBINSON	69
TE	DENNIS	PITTA	83
TE	CROCKETT	GILLMORE	76
TE	MAXX	WILLIAMS	74
LT	EUGENE	MONROE	82
LT	JAMES	HURST	59
LG	KELECHI	OSEMELE	90
LG	JAH	REID	74
LG	ROBERT	MYERS	60
C	JEREMY	ZUTTAH	82
C	RYAN	JENSEN	67
RG	MARSHAL	YANDA	98
RG	JOHN	URSCHEL	78
RT	RICK	WAGNER	86
RT	MARCEL	JONES	70

DEFENSIVE DEPTH CHART

POS	FIRST	LAST	OVR
LE	TIMMY	JERNIGAN	79
LE	LAWRENCE	GUY	74
LE	CASEY	WALKER	61
DT	BRANDON	WILLIAMS	85
DT	CARL	DAVIS	71
DT	CHRISTO	BILUKIDI	70
RE	CHRIS	CANTY	82
RE	DEANGELO	TYSON	66
RE	KAPRON	LEWIS-MOORE	65
LOLB	ELVIS	DUMERVIL	88
LOLB	COURTNEY	UPSHAW	80
MLB	DARYL	SMITH	90
MLB	C.J.	MOSLEY	88
MLB	ARTHUR	BROWN	73
MLB	ALBERT	MCCLELLAN	69
ROLB	TERRELL	SUGGS	93
ROLB	ZA'DARIUS	SMITH	61
CB	JIMMY	SMITH	88
CB	LARDARIUS	WEBB	82
CB	ANTHONY	LEVINE	73
CB	RASHAAN	MELVIN	71
CB	ASA	JACKSON	68
FS	KENDRICK	LEWIS	81
FS	TERRENCE	BROOKS	72
FS	QUINTON	POINTER	68
SS	WILL	HILL	88
SS	MATT	ELAM	72
SS	BRYNDEN	TRAWICK	65

SPECIAL TEAMS

POS	FIRST	LAST	OVR
K	JUSTIN	TUCKER	95
KR	LARDARIUS	WEBB	82
KR	MICHAEL	CAMPANARO	71
P	SAM	KOCH	85
PR	MICHAEL	CAMPANARO	71

BEST OFFENSIVE PLAYS

PRO TIPS

- **These are the best two offensive plays in your playbook. They will get your playmakers in position to win you games.**
- Justin Forsett has enough agility to change lanes in the running game, although he can't outrun most players in the secondary.
- Breshad Perriman is a matchup nightmare due to his speed. He can open everything up underneath.

BEST RUN: SINGLEBACK DOUBLES–ZONE WEAK

SETUP:

- You can sub in a better blocking TE at the inside WR position if you want to cut the run outside more.
- There are lots of great rollout plays built off this handoff fake, so make sure to set it up early.

ADVANCED SETUP:

- Motion the far inside slot WR on the left

RUNNING PLAYS

1ST DOWN	2ND AND SHORT	3RD AND SHORT	GOAL LINE	2ND AND LONG	3RD AND LONG
Singleback Deuce Wing–HB Stretch	Weak Tight Twins–HB Dive	I-Form Pro–FB Dive Strong	Goal Line–HB Sting	Gun Spread Y-Flex–HB Draw	Gun Trips Y-Flex Tight–HB Draw
Singleback Deuce Wing–Zone Weak	I-Form Close–Zone Weak	I-Form Pro–FB Fake HB Flip	Goal Line–FB Dive	Weak Tight Twins–HB Draw	Gun Bunch Wk–HB Sweep
I-Form Close–HB Stretch	Singleback Deuce Wing–Inside Zone Split	Strong Pro Twins–HB Stretch	I-Form Tight Pair–HB Stretch	Gun Trips Y-Flex Tight–Outside Zone	Gun Y-Trips HB Wk–HB Off Tackle

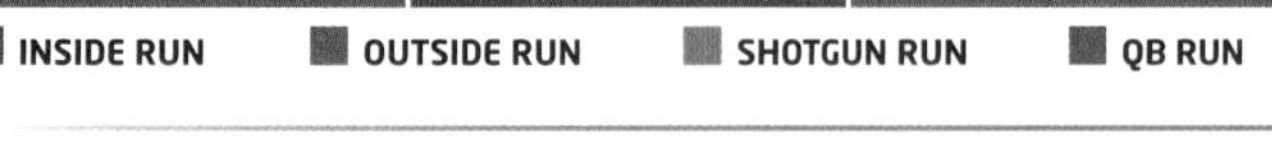
INSIDE RUN | OUTSIDE RUN | SHOTGUN RUN | QB RUN

BEST PASS: GUN FLIP TRIPS RAVEN–SLOT TRAIL

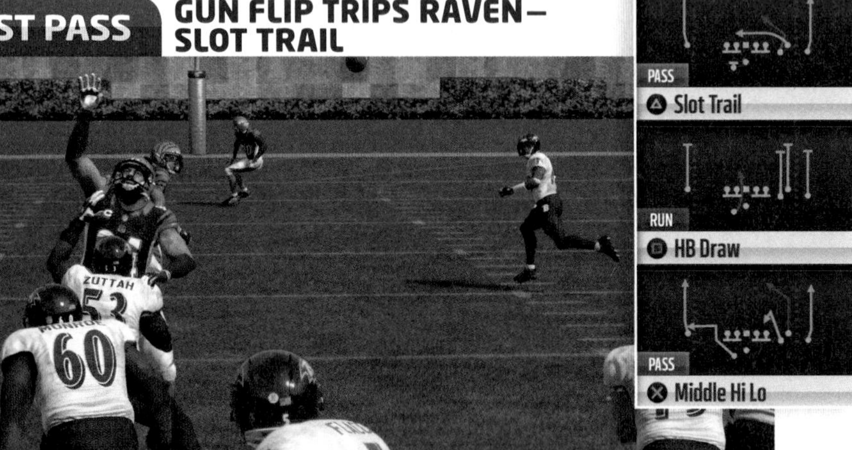

SETUP/READS:

- Against zone coverage wait for the drag to clear the LBs and then catch it and run (RAC). This formation has many great flood concepts.
- Against man-to-man coverage the route running of the trail route should create some separation on the cut.
- This play will only be a success if you sub in Steve Smith to go over the middle and Perriman to go deep on the outside.

ADVANCED SETUP:

- Wheel or flat the HB.

PASSING PLAYS

1ST DOWN	2ND AND SHORT	3RD AND SHORT	SHOT PLAYS	2ND AND LONG	3RD AND LONG
I-Form Close–Ravens Drag	Gun Trips Y-Flex Tight–Levels Sail	Strong Pro–F Angle	Singleback Ace Pair–Close PA Cross	Gun Flip Trips Raven–HB Slip Screen	Gun Empty Base Flex–Verticals
Weak Tight Twins–PA Cross F Wheel	I-Form Pro–Cross In	Strong Tight–FB Angle	Gun Trips Y-Flex Tight–PA Crossers	Singleback Deuce Wing–Corner	Singleback Tight Doubles–Drag In
Gun Flip Trips Raven–Slot Trail	Gun Y-Trips HB Wk–DBL Under	Gun Bunch Wk–PA Post	I-Form Pro–PA Draw Shot	Singleback Tight Doubles–Close Deep Cop	Gun Bunch Wk–Verticals

BASE PLAY | MAN BEATER | ZONE BEATER | BLITZ BEATER

 For more plays and strategies for this team, visit your eGuide using the access code sheet provided.

BEST DEFENSIVE PLAYS

PRO TIPS

- **Rely on these defensive plays to lock up the run and pass.**
- **The Ravens' run defense lost some strength in their interior, but thankfully they still have Terrell Suggs off the edge.**
- **The 3-3-5 is a nice balanced formation to spend the first half of the game in. Adjust at halftime for a more specific formation.**

BEST RUN D 3-4 OVER ED—SAM CRASH 3

- ZONE △ Cover 3 Sky
- MAN □ Cover 1 Hole
- BLITZ ✕ Sam Crash 3

SETUP:

- Blitzing a quick LB off the right edge is a great way to pick up some tackles in the backfield.
- Make sure Suggs is the LB on the opposite side of the blitzer, since he doesn't need much support behind him.

PLAYER TO CONTROL:

- DT over the center

RUN DEFENSE

1ST DOWN	2ND AND SHORT	3RD AND SHORT	GOAL LINE	2ND AND LONG	3RD AND LONG
3-4 Bear—Cover 1 Hole	3-4 Bear—Sam Mike 1	3-4 Predator—Safety Blitz	Goal Line 5-4-2—Jam Cover 1	Nickel 2-4-5 Even—1 Inside Blitz Cop	Big Dime 2-3-6 Will—Cov 1 Robber Press
3-4 Bear—Cover 2 Invert	3-4 Bear—Buck SS 3	3-4 Predator—SS Scrape 3	Goal Line 5-4-2—Flat Buzz	Nickel 2-4-5 Even—Cover 3 Cloud	Big Dime 2-3-6 Will—SS Zone Blitz

MAN COVERAGE | ZONE COVERAGE | MAN BLITZ | ZONE BLITZ

BEST PASS D NICKEL 3-3-5—COVER 4 DROP

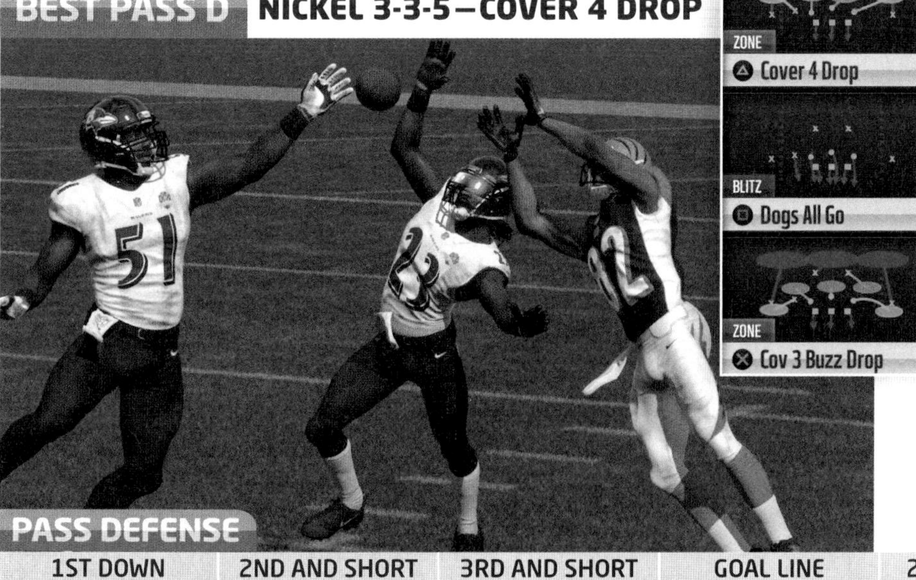

- ZONE △ Cover 4 Drop
- BLITZ □ Dogs All Go
- ZONE ✕ Cov 3 Buzz Drop

SETUP:

- The Cover 4 Drop is actually a very tough defense to move the ball against, especially if you tackle well.
- Shading your coverage underneath will give your defenders an extra step towards breaking in and knocking down a pass.
- The combinations of rushers and blitzers off of this play are nearly unlimited, so don't be afraid to send some heat on third down.

PLAYER TO CONTROL:

- Suggs (power rush off the edge)

PASS DEFENSE

1ST DOWN	2ND AND SHORT	3RD AND SHORT	GOAL LINE	2ND AND LONG	3RD AND LONG
Nickel 2-4-5 Even—Cover 2 Man	3-4 Odd—2 Sink QB Contain	3-4 Bear—Will Sam 1	Goal Line 5-3-3—GL Man	Big Dime 2-3-6—Over Storm Brave	Quarter 1-3-7—DB Strike
Nickel 2-4-5 Even—Cover 3 Cloud	3-4 Odd—3 Drop QB Contain	3-4 Bear—Pinch Dog 3	Goal Line 5-3-3—GL Zone	Big Dime 2-3-6—3 Seam Press	Quarter 1-3-7—FZ 3 Sky

MAN COVERAGE | ZONE COVERAGE | MAN BLITZ | ZONE BLITZ

WASHINGTON REDSKINS

GAMEPLAY RATING 75

CONNECTED FRANCHISE MODE STRATEGY

CFM TEAM RATING: **80**
OFFENSE: **85**
DEFENSE: **81**
OFFENSIVE SCHEME: **West Coast**
DEFENSIVE SCHEME: **Base 3-4**
STRENGTHS: **FB, WR, OLB, DL**
WEAKNESSES: **LG, SS, TE**

2014 TEAM RANKINGS

4th NFC East (4-12-0)
PASSING OFFENSE: **11th**
RUSHING OFFENSE: **19th**
PASSING DEFENSE: **24th**
RUSHING DEFENSE: **12th**

2014 TEAM LEADERS

PASSING: **Kirk Cousins: 1,710**
RUSHING: **Alfred Morris: 1,074**
RECEIVING: **DeSean Jackson: 1,169**
TACKLES: **Keenan Robinson: 109**
SACKS: **Ryan Kerrigan: 13.5**
INTS: **Bashaud Breeland: 2**

KEY ADDITIONS

DT Terrance Knighton
DE Stephen Paea
CB Chris Culliver

KEY ROOKIES

T Brandon Scherff
DE Preston Smith
RB Matt Jones

OWNER: **Dan Snyder**
LEGACY SCORE: **150**

COACH: **Jay Gruden**
LEVEL: **2**
LEGACY SCORE: **0**
OFFENSIVE SCHEME: **West Coast**
DEFENSIVE SCHEME: **Base 3-4**

OFFENSIVE SCOUTING REPORT

- QB Robert Griffin III is still looking to return to the form of his incredible rookie season. The scheme should allow him to make the easy throws to get his confidence up. While his speed is still amazing, it can lead to injury, and you need him on the field.
- Don't forget about FB Darrel Young, who is an excellent all-around player. The more you can get him on the field in those pistol sets, the better.
- The Redskins' receiving corps is still one of the fastest in the league, but make sure to round it out with some size via the draft.

DEFENSIVE SCOUTING REPORT

- The Redskins transformed their defensive line seemingly overnight and should now be able to shut down the run without sending much help.
- With veteran LB Brian Orakpo moving to the Titans, the defense is now in the control of LB Ryan Kerrigan. Lock him up for the long term, because you can't live without his 97 Power Moves rating.
- The Redskins' secondary is average but has a real chance to develop into a solid man-coverage unit led by CB Chris Culliver. Start to develop the young talent, even if they take some bumps early.

SCHEDULE

Week	Date	Time	TV		Opponent
1	SEP 13	1:00 PM ET			DOLPHINS
2	SEP 20	1:00 PM ET	FOX		RAMS
3	SEP 24	8:25 PM ET		AT	GIANTS
4	OCT 04	1:00 PM ET	FOX		EAGLES
5	OCT 11	1:00 PM ET	FOX	AT	FALCONS
6	OCT 18	1:00 PM ET	FOX	AT	JETS
7	OCT 25	1:00 PM ET	FOX		BUCCANEERS
8	BYE WEEK				
9	NOV 08	1:00 PM ET	FOX	AT	PATRIOTS
10	NOV 15	1:00 PM ET	FOX		SAINTS
11	NOV 22	1:00 PM ET	FOX	AT	PANTHERS
12	NOV 29	1:00 PM ET	FOX		GIANTS
13	DEC 07	8:30 PM ET	ESPN		COWBOYS
14	DEC 13	1:00 PM ET	FOX	AT	BEARS
15	DEC 20	1:00 PM ET			BILLS
16	DEC 26	8:25 PM ET		AT	EAGLES
17	JAN 03	1:00 PM ET	FOX	AT	COWBOYS

KEY PLAYERS

KEY OFFENSIVE PLAYER

ALFRED MORRIS #46

HB #46 HT 5'10" WT 218 COLLEGE FAU EXP 3

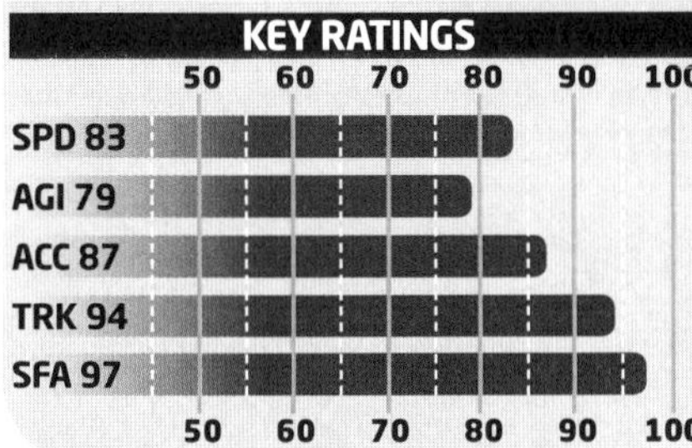

- Morris is great at securing the football and picking up as many yards as possible in this scheme.
- He is best when put on a straight line ahead—it doesn't matter who is in his way.

KEY DEFENSIVE PLAYER

TERRANCE KNIGHTON #98

DT #98 HT 6'3" WT 335 COLLEGE Temple EXP 6

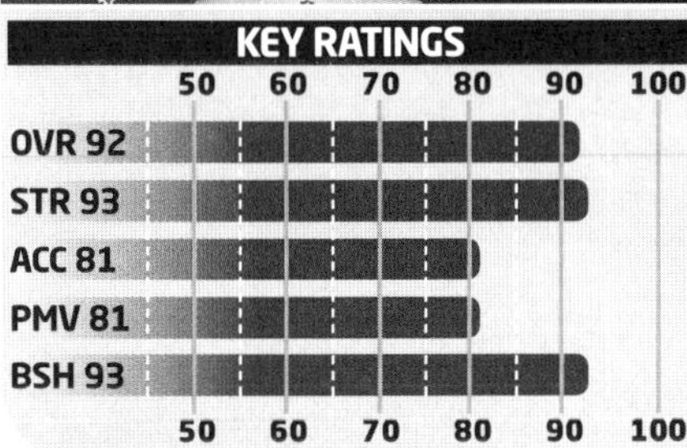

- With Knighton and LE Stephen Paea, the Redskins have one of the strongest fronts in the entire game.
- Knighton is one of the best pure run stuffers in the league. He will anchor your defense.

KEY ROOKIE

BRANDON SCHERFF 

RT #75 HT 6'5" WT 319 COLLEGE Iowa EXP Rookie

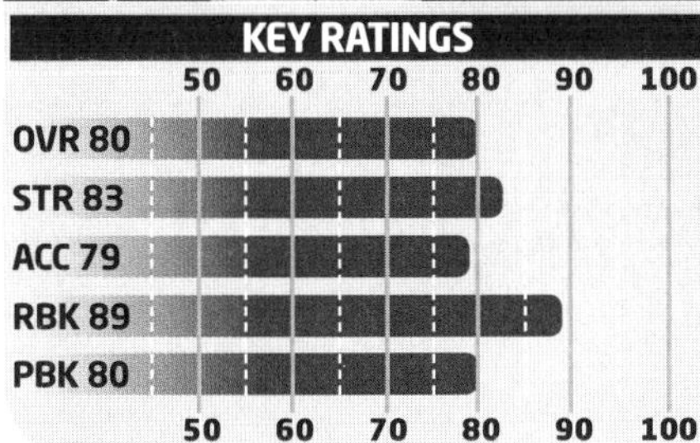

- Scherff is a promising player for the future and will seal the edge in the run game.
- Scherff needs upgrades to strength and pass blocking, but unfortunately you can't afford to wait to start him.

KEY SLEEPER

MATT JONES 

HB #31 HT 6'2" WT 231 COLLEGE Florida EXP Rookie

- Jones is an excellent choice to spell HB Alfred Morris. They are very similar players.
- Jones will need an upgrade to ball carrier vision if he plans on taking over the bulk of the carries in the future.

OFFENSIVE DEPTH CHART

POS	FIRST	LAST	OVR
QB	ROBERT	GRIFFIN III	78
QB	KIRK	COUSINS	73
QB	COLT	MCCOY	73
HB	ALFRED	MORRIS	84
HB	MATT	JONES	71
HB	SILAS	REDD	71
HB	CHRIS	THOMPSON	69
WR	DESEAN	JACKSON	88
WR	PIERRE	GARCON	83
WR	ANDRE	ROBERTS	74
WR	JAMISON	CROWDER	70
WR	RYAN	GRANT	68
WR	EVAN	SPENCER	60
TE	JORDAN	REED	82
TE	NILES	PAUL	74
TE	LOGAN	PAULSEN	71
LT	TRENT	WILLIAMS	87
LT	MORGAN	MOSES	70
LG	SHAWN	LAUVAO	80
LG	JOSH	LERIBEUS	73
LG	ARIE	KOUANDJIO	62
C	KORY	LICHTENSTEIGER	86
C	TYLER	LARSEN	65
RG	SPENCER	LONG	71
RT	BRANDON	SCHERFF	80
RT	TOM	COMPTON	76
RT	TY	NSEKHE	69

DEFENSIVE DEPTH CHART

POS	FIRST	LAST	OVR
LE	STEPHEN	PAEA	83
LE	RICKY	JEAN FRANCOIS	77
LE	KEDRIC	GOLSTON	72
DT	TERRANCE	KNIGHTON	88
DT	CHRIS	BAKER	77
DT	JERRELL	POWE	71
DT	ROBERT	THOMAS	62
RE	JASON	HATCHER	87
RE	FRANK	KEARSE	67
RE	TRAVIAN	ROBERTSON	60
LOLB	RYAN	KERRIGAN	90
LOLB	TRENT	MURPHY	76
LOLB	JACKSON	JEFFCOAT	63
MLB	PERRY	RILEY JR.	76
MLB	KEENAN	ROBINSON	75
MLB	WILL	COMPTON	70
MLB	ADAM	HAYWARD	70
ROLB	PRESTON	SMITH	70
ROLB	TREVARDO	WILLIAMS	64
CB	CHRIS	CULLIVER	85
CB	DEANGELO	HALL	77
CB	BASHAUD	BREELAND	72
CB	DAVID	AMERSON	71
FS	DASHON	GOLDSON	74
FS	TRENTON	ROBINSON	72
FS	KYSHOEN	JARRETT	63
SS	DUKE	IHENACHO	76
SS	JERON	JOHNSON	76
SS	PHILLIP	THOMAS	72

SPECIAL TEAMS

POS	FIRST	LAST	OVR
K	KAI	FORBATH	78
KR	ANDRE	ROBERTS	74
KR	CHRIS	THOMPSON	69
P	TRESS	WAY	85
PR	ANDRE	ROBERTS	74

BEST OFFENSIVE PLAYS

PRO TIPS

- **These are the best two offensive plays in your playbook. They will get your playmakers in position to win you games.**
- **If you would rather utilize a pocket passer, check out the Pistol Slot Wing instead of the Pistol Slot for some good power running plays.**
- **The Pistol Bunch is an excellent formation to free up your WRs from press coverage at the line.**

BEST RUN PISTOL SLOT—READ OPTION

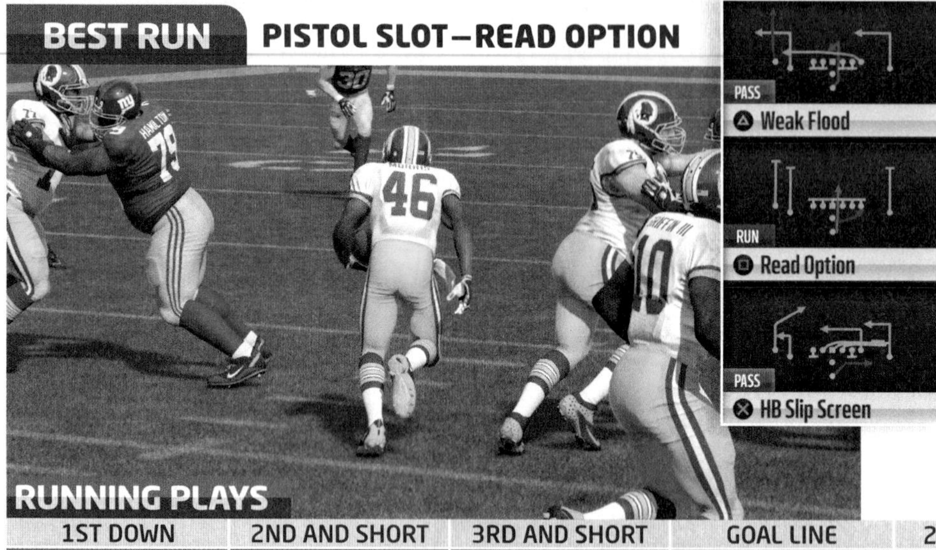

SETUP:

- Don't worry about making a huge gain; this play should pick up 4 yards nearly every time.
- The biggest mistake that average players make is wanting to keep the ball with the QB rather than making a good read.
- There are lots of good "shot plays" off this handoff fake, so don't be afraid to use your speed on the outside to go long.

ADVANCED SETUP:

- None

RUNNING PLAYS

1ST DOWN	2ND AND SHORT	3RD AND SHORT	GOAL LINE	2ND AND LONG	3RD AND LONG
Singleback Doubles—HB Misdirection	Singleback Doubles—0 1 Trap	Pistol Slot—Read Option	I-Form Tight Pair—FB Dive	Pistol Y-Trips—Strong Power	Pistol Strong—Tr Option Slip
Singleback Ace Close—Zone Weak	Weak Pro—Inside Zone Split	Strong Pro Twins—HB Stretch	I-Form Tight—Zone Weak	Pistol Slot Wing—Inside Zone Split	Gun Doubles Wk—HB Base
Strong Pro—HB Stretch	Pistol Strong—Lead Read Option	Gun Y-Trips Open—5 6 Trap	Goal Line—QB Sneak	Gun Trips Y-Flex Tight—Read Option	Gun Empty Trey Flex—QB Draw

INSIDE RUN · OUTSIDE RUN · SHOTGUN RUN · QB RUN

BEST PASS PISTOL BUNCH—SEATTLE

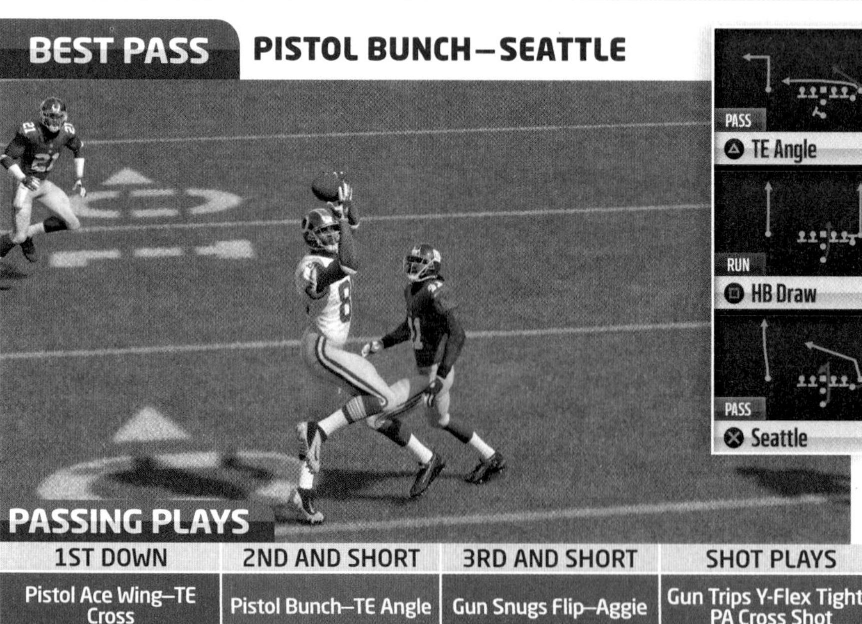

SETUP/READS:

- Against zone coverage attack the seam, because most defenders will worry about the outside WR.
- Against man-to-man, audible to a play like TE Angle to smash the defense over the middle. It is a perfect combo play!
- This formation has some great play action plays that can allow you to beat the blitz with quick dump-off throws.

ADVANCED SETUP:

- Wheel the HB.

PASSING PLAYS

1ST DOWN	2ND AND SHORT	3RD AND SHORT	SHOT PLAYS	2ND AND LONG	3RD AND LONG
Pistol Ace Wing—TE Cross	Pistol Bunch—TE Angle	Gun Snugs Flip—Aggie	Gun Trips Y-Flex Tight—PA Cross Shot	Gun Empty Trey Flex—Stick N Nod	Singleback Wing Trio—PA Verticals
Gun Tight Doubles On—Cross Wheels	Gun Tight Doubles On—Flood Drive	Gun Dbls Y-Flex Offset—Angle Smash	Pistol Ace Wing—PA Deep Cross	Gun Dbls Y-Flex Offset—Fork Wheel	Pistol Bunch—Seattle
Singleback Ace Close—Tight Slots TE Angle	Strong Pro—F Angle	Gun Bunch Offset—Skins Trail	Singleback Ace Pair Slot—PA Misdirect Shot	Gun Y-Trips Open—Verticals X Shallow	Gun Wing Trips Offset Wk—Four Verticals

BASE PLAY · MAN BEATER · ZONE BEATER · BLITZ BEATER

BEST DEFENSIVE PLAYS

PRO TIPS

- **If you want to win more games in *Madden NFL 16*, rely on these defensive plays to lock up the run and pass.**
- The Redskins' defense is anchored by LB Ryan Kerrigan. Protect the opposite edge by blitzing or adding extra defenders over there.
- The Nickel 2-4-5 Even is a formation crucial to the success of your defense. Learn to live in it.

BEST RUN D 3-4 ODD—WILL BUCK 3 PRESS

MAN
Cover 2 Man

BLITZ
Will Buck 3 Press

BLITZ
Pinch Dog 2 Press

SETUP:

- This is an excellent defense against teams that like to attack the weak side with runs like Counter or Misdirection.
- When you call QB contain before the snap, your defenders will look to play even wider, which helps lock up the edge.

PLAYER TO CONTROL:

- FS in a hook zone

RUN DEFENSE

1ST DOWN	2ND AND SHORT	3RD AND SHORT	GOAL LINE	2ND AND LONG	3RD AND LONG
3-4 Odd—2 Sink QB Contain	3-4 Over—Sting Pinch	3-4 Even—1 QB Contain	Goal Line 5-4-2—Jam Cover 1	Nickel 2-4-5 Prowl—Cover 2 Man	Nickel 3-3-5 Wide—Cover 1 Robber
3-4 Odd—4 Drop QB Contain	3-4 Over—Sting Pinch Zone	3-4 Even—Will Fire 3 Seam	Goal Line 5-4-2—Flat Buzz	Nickel 2-4-5 Prowl—Cover 2 Drop	Nickel 3-3-5 Wide—Cover 3 Buzz

MAN COVERAGE ZONE COVERAGE MAN BLITZ ZONE BLITZ

BEST PASS D NICKEL 2-4-5 EVEN—COVER 4

ZONE
Cover 4

BLITZ
Silver Shoot Pinch

BLITZ
Cross Fire 3 Seam

SETUP:

- The Cover 4 is thought of as a deep-pass coverage, but it can often result in turnovers to the flat.
- By using coverage shading before the snap, you can make your zones play more aggressively, and they should jump more routes.

PLAYER TO CONTROL:

- Any lineman (rush)

PASS DEFENSE

1ST DOWN	2ND AND SHORT	3RD AND SHORT	GOAL LINE	2ND AND LONG	3RD AND LONG
3-4 Solid—Cover 2 Man	3-4 Solid—Cover 1 Robber	Nickel 2-4-5 Even—1 Inside Blitz Cop	Goal Line 5-3-3—MLB Gap A Zone	Big Dime 1-4-6—Mike SS 1 Dog	Nickel 2-4-5 Dbl A Gap—Buck Zone Blitz
3-4 Solid—Cover 4	3-4 Solid—Cover 6	Nickel 2-4-5 Even—3 Seam Show 2	Goal Line 5-3-3—Pinch Zone	Big Dime 1-4-6—Mike SS 3 Seam	Nickel 2-4-5 Dbl A Gap—Will 3 Buzz

MAN COVERAGE ZONE COVERAGE MAN BLITZ ZONE BLITZ

NEW ORLEANS SAINTS

GAMEPLAY RATING 78

CONNECTED FRANCHISE MODE STRATEGY

CFM TEAM RATING: **80**
OFFENSE: **85**
DEFENSE: **81**
OFFENSIVE SCHEME: **Vertical**
DEFENSIVE SCHEME: **Attacking 3-4**
STRENGTHS: **QB, C, FS**
WEAKNESSES: **HB, DT, CB, TE**

2014 TEAM RANKINGS

2nd NFC South (7-9-0)
PASSING OFFENSE: **3rd**
RUSHING OFFENSE: **13th**
PASSING DEFENSE: **25th**
RUSHING DEFENSE: **29th**

2014 TEAM LEADERS

PASSING: **Drew Brees: 4,952**
RUSHING: **Mark Ingram: 964**
RECEIVING: **Kenny Stills: 931**
TACKLES: **Curtis Lofton: 144**
SACKS: **Junior Galette: 10**
INTS: **Pierre Warren: 2**

KEY ADDITIONS

HB C.J. Spiller
CB Brandon Browner
C Max Unger

KEY ROOKIES

T Andrus Peat
LB Stephone Anthony
LB Hau'oli Kikaha

OWNER: **Tom Benson**
LEGACY SCORE: **1,600**

COACH: **Brady Leland**
LEVEL: **1**
LEGACY SCORE: **0**
OFFENSIVE SCHEME: **Vertical**
DEFENSIVE SCHEME: **Attacking 3-4**

OFFENSIVE SCOUTING REPORT

- QB Drew Brees may feel some effect from losing his main target in TE Jimmy Graham. However, he is too talented to let it affect him over the course of a whole season. Take the first few games to learn which receivers to trust on big downs.
- The Saints have a nice combination of power and speed in the backfield with Mark Ingram and C.J. Spiller. Both have shown flashes at times, but neither has proven to be an every-down back, so use them in a rotation.
- Marques Colston will have to continue to be the safety blanket for his QB. With a 97 Catch in Traffic rating, he should hang onto most balls, but his 83 Speed rating means he won't be running away from too many defenders.

DEFENSIVE SCOUTING REPORT

- On the defensive line, DT John Jenkins has the strength you need for a 3-4 scheme. Monitor the play of RE Cameron Jordan, who no doubt has the talent, but who might not fit in at 3-4 end. Get creative with formation subs to get the most out of him.
- The Saints' LBs don't have blazing speed, so play a zone scheme to maximize their range. If you feel yourself unable to keep up with another team, try playing rookie LB Stephone Anthony, who is raw but very quick.
- The Saints' secondary finally has some solid pieces back, especially if Jairus Byrd can remain healthy and lead the unit. New CB Brandon Browner will really help against some of the league's big receiving threats, like those division rival Tampa Bay has built around.

SCHEDULE

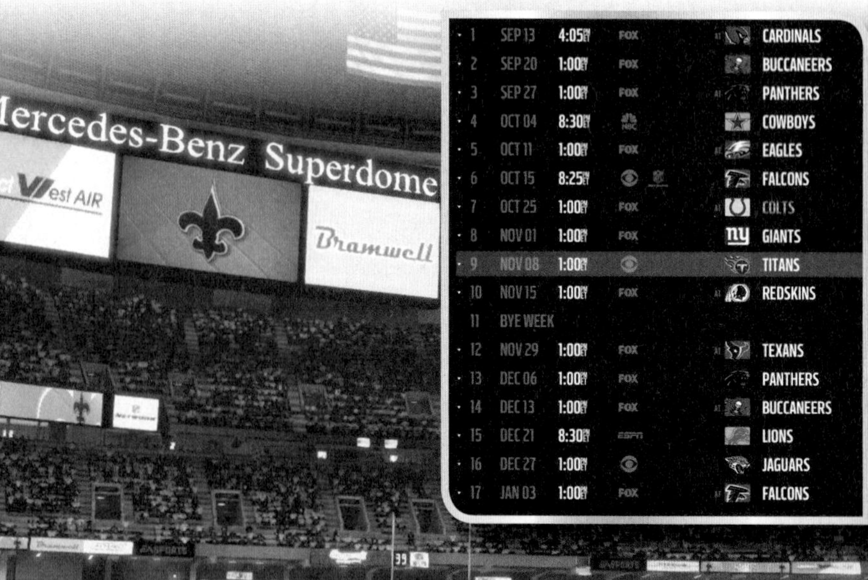

Week	Date	Time	Network		Opponent
1	SEP 13	4:05 PM ET	FOX	AT	CARDINALS
2	SEP 20	1:00 PM ET	FOX		BUCCANEERS
3	SEP 27	1:00 PM ET	FOX	AT	PANTHERS
4	OCT 04	8:30 PM ET	NBC		COWBOYS
5	OCT 11	1:00 PM ET	FOX	AT	EAGLES
6	OCT 15	8:25 PM ET			FALCONS
7	OCT 25	1:00 PM ET	FOX	AT	COLTS
8	NOV 01	1:00 PM ET	FOX		GIANTS
9	NOV 08	1:00 PM ET			TITANS
10	NOV 15	1:00 PM ET	FOX	AT	REDSKINS
11	BYE WEEK				
12	NOV 29	1:00 PM ET	FOX	AT	TEXANS
13	DEC 06	1:00 PM ET	FOX		PANTHERS
14	DEC 13	1:00 PM ET	FOX	AT	BUCCANEERS
15	DEC 21	8:30 PM ET	ESPN		LIONS
16	DEC 27	1:00 PM ET			JAGUARS
17	JAN 03	1:00 PM ET	FOX	AT	FALCONS

KEY PLAYERS

KEY OFFENSIVE PLAYER

DREW BREES #9

QB #9 HT 6'0" WT 209 COLLEGE Purdue EXP 14

KEY RATINGS

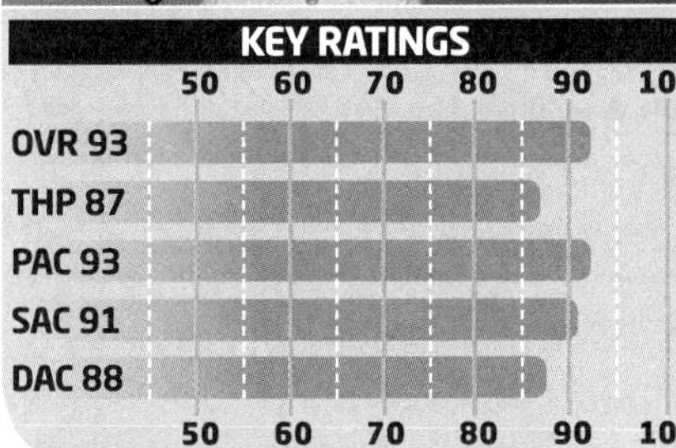

- Brees's accuracy across the board is what separates him from other QBs in the league.
- Be sure to utilize play action, as Brees is one of the best at it.

KEY DEFENSIVE PLAYER

JAIRUS BYRD #31

FS #31 HT 5'10" WT 203 COLLEGE Oregon EXP 6

KEY RATINGS

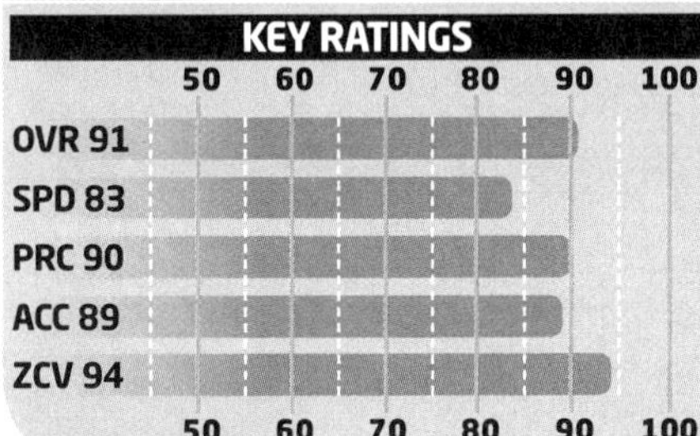

- Byrd has outstanding play recognition for his position and should be left to roam free over the middle.
- Keep boosting Byrd's speed and hit power to make him one of the best players in the league.

KEY ROOKIE

ANDRUS PEAT #75

LT #75 HT 6'7" WT 313 COLLEGE Stanford EXP Rookie

KEY RATINGS

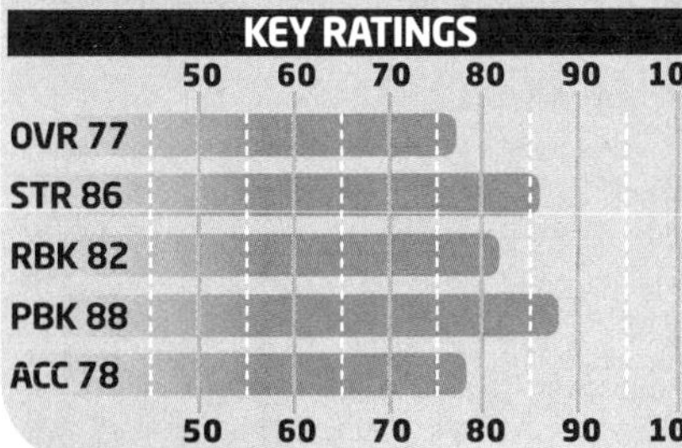

- Peat will be ready to start early in his career if you can get him some confidence.
- Peat is a versatile player who can play most positions on the line, but having him at tackle is the most valuable for the future.

KEY SLEEPER

BRANDON COLEMAN #16

WR #16 HT 6'6" WT 225 COLLEGE Rutgers EXP 1

KEY RATINGS

50 60 70 80 90 100

OVR 65

SPD 86

CIT 81

SPC 84

RTE 53

50 60 70 80 90 100

- Without a threat like TE Jimmy Graham in the red zone, Brees will need a big target like 6'6" Coleman, who can only run a few routes.
- The higher you can build ratings like Spectacular Catch and Catch in Traffic, the better Coleman will be on aggressive catches downfield.

OFFENSIVE DEPTH CHART

POS	FIRST	LAST	OVR
QB	DREW	BREES	95
QB	LUKE	MCCOWN	72
QB	GARRETT	GRAYSON	71
HB	MARK	INGRAM	83
HB	C.J.	SPILLER	82
HB	KHIRY	ROBINSON	74
HB	TIM	HIGHTOWER	72
FB	AUSTIN	JOHNSON	73
FB	ERIK	LORIG	72
WR	MARQUES	COLSTON	86
WR	BRANDIN	COOKS	82
WR	NICK	TOON	72
WR	JALEN	SAUNDERS	65
WR	BRANDON	COLEMAN	63
TE	JOSH	HILL	78
TE	BENJAMIN	WATSON	78
TE	ORSON	CHARLES	76
LT	TERRON	ARMSTEAD	81
LT	ANDRUS	PEAT	75
LG	SENIO	KELEMETE	71
C	MAX	UNGER	90
C	TIM	LELITO	77
C	MICHAEL	BREWSTER	68
RG	JAHRI	EVANS	78
RT	ZACH	STRIEF	85
RT	BRYCE	HARRIS	71
RT	NICK	BECTON	65

DEFENSIVE DEPTH CHART

POS	FIRST	LAST	OVR
LE	AKIEM	HICKS	81
LE	KEVIN	WILLIAMS	76
LE	TYELER	DAVISON	64
DT	BRODRICK	BUNKLEY	80
DT	JOHN	JENKINS	75
DT	LAWRENCE	VIRGIL	63
RE	CAMERON	JORDAN	87
RE	GLENN	FOSTER	73
LOLB	KASIM	EDEBALI	66
LOLB	HAU'OLI	KIKAHA	66
MLB	DAVID	HAWTHORNE	77
MLB	DANNELL	ELLERBE	75
MLB	STEPHONE	ANTHONY	71
MLB	RAMON	HUMBER	67
ROLB	PARYS	HARALSON	79
ROLB	ANTHONY	SPENCER	76
ROLB	RONALD	POWELL	64
CB	KEENAN	LEWIS	80
CB	BRANDON	BROWNER	82
CB	KYLE	WILSON	74
CB	STANLEY	JEAN-BAPTISTE	68
CB	BRIAN	DIXON	67
FS	JAIRUS	BYRD	91
FS	RAFAEL	BUSH	79
FS	KENNY	PHILLIPS	77
SS	JAMARCA	SANFORD	78
SS	KENNY	VACCARO	77
SS	VINNIE	SUNSERI	69

SPECIAL TEAMS

POS	FIRST	LAST	OVR
K	DUSTIN	HOPKINS	66
KR	MARCUS	MURPHY	65
KR	JALEN	SAUNDERS	65
P	THOMAS	MORSTEAD	91
PR	JALEN	SAUNDERS	65

BEST OFFENSIVE PLAYS

PRO TIPS

- These are the best two offensive plays in your playbook. They will get your playmakers in position to win you games.
- Starting out a series with some simple crossing patterns can help you build some confidence early.
- Use HB Mark Ingram as your main option on up-the-middle runs and bring in HB C.J. Spiller when you want to hit the outside.

BEST RUN: SINGLEBACK DOUBLES–HB SMASH

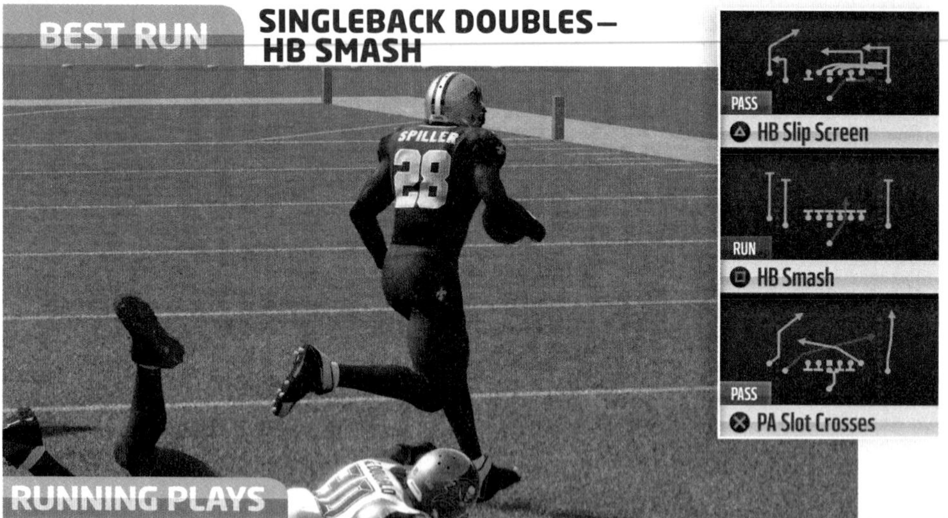

SETUP:

- Your backup TE, Orson Charles, is a solid run blocker who can hold the edge if you want to cut it outside.
- Make this run have more risk but more reward by taking out the powerful Mark Ingram and subbing in C.J. Spiller.

ADVANCED SETUP:

- Sub in your backup HB.

RUNNING PLAYS

1ST DOWN	2ND AND SHORT	3RD AND SHORT	GOAL LINE	2ND AND LONG	3RD AND LONG
Singleback Twin TE Flex–HB Toss Strong	Singleback Ace–0 1 Trap	I-Form Close–HB Lead Dive	Goal Line–FB Dive	Pistol Slot Wing–HB Stretch	Pistol Bunch TE–HB Counter
Singleback Doubles–HB Smash	Singleback Twin TE Flex–HB Zone Wk	I-Form Pro–Off Tackle	Goal Line–QB Sneak	Pistol Slot Wing–Inside Zone Split	Gun Trey Open Saint–Inside Zone
Strong Close–HB Off Tackle	I-Form Twins Flex–FB Dive Strong	Singleback Snugs Flip–HB Pitch	I-Form Tight–HB Off Tackle	Pistol Slot Wing–HB Counter	Gun Trips Y Iso–HB Draw

INSIDE RUN | OUTSIDE RUN | SHOTGUN RUN | QB RUN

BEST PASS: PISTOL BUNCH TE–CROSS DRAG

SETUP/READS:

- Against zone coverage make the easy throw. Not every pass has to go deep downfield on this play.
- Against man-to-man your speed advantage on the crossing patterns should get big separation.
- Against the blitz either dump it off to the HB or wait for the TE to get some separation over the middle.

ADVANCED SETUP:

- Streak or curl the far left WR.
- Wheel the HB.

PASSING PLAYS

1ST DOWN	2ND AND SHORT	3RD AND SHORT	SHOT PLAYS	2ND AND LONG	3RD AND LONG
Gun Tight Offset TE–Saints Drive Out	I-Form Pro–Texas	Singleback Twin TE Flex–Quick Slant	Gun Empty Saint–Saints Shot Post	Gun DBL Y-Flex Off Wk–Saints Mesh Wheel	Pistol Slot Wing–Fade Smash
Gun Tight Offset TE–Saints Wheel Spot	Strong Close–Mesh	I-Form Tight–Angle	Gun Tight Offset TE–PA Shot Seams	Singleback Bunch Base–Seattle	Singleback Snugs Flip–HB Wheel
Pistol Bunch TE–Curl Flat	Pistol Bunch TE–Fk Screen	Gun Empty Trey–All Hitch	Singleback Twin TE Flex–PA Saints Shot	Gun Empty Y-Saints–Saints Go's Whip	Gun Empty Y-Saints–Saints Under

BASE PLAY | MAN BEATER | ZONE BEATER | BLITZ BEATER

 For more plays and strategies for this team, visit your eGuide using the access code sheet provided.

BEST DEFENSIVE PLAYS

PRO TIPS

- Rely on these defensive plays to lock up the run and pass.
- Consider switching Jairus Byrd out with Rafael Bush on the 3-4 Bear to add some more hit power to the field.
- The Saints' best overall defensive lineup is the 2-4-5.

BEST RUN D: 3-4 BEAR—COVER 2 INVERT

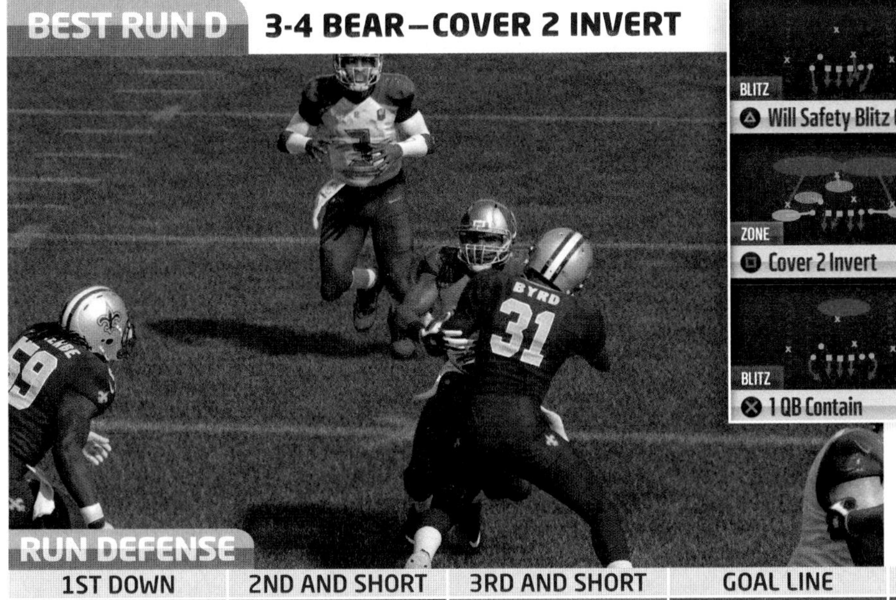

SETUP:

- The 3-4 Bear is a solid run defense, especially in short yardage.
- Feel free to play very aggressively with the free safety; he has no deep responsibility on the play.

PLAYER TO CONTROL:

- FS in a hook zone

RUN DEFENSE

1ST DOWN	2ND AND SHORT	3RD AND SHORT	GOAL LINE	2ND AND LONG	3RD AND LONG
3-4 Even—Cov1 Robber Press	3-4 Bear—Sam Mike 1	3-4 Bear—1 QB Contain	Goal Line 5-4-2—Jam Cover 1	Nickel 3-3-5 Wide—Cover 2 Man	Nickel 2-4-5—Cover 2 Sink
3-4 Even—Mike Scrape 3 Press	3-4 Bear—Pinch Dog 3	3-4 Bear—Cover 2 Invert	Goal Line 5-4-2—Flat Buzz	Nickel 3-3-5 Wide—Cover 4 Show 2	Nickel 2-4-5—Cover 2

MAN COVERAGE | ZONE COVERAGE | MAN BLITZ | ZONE BLITZ

BEST PASS D: NICKEL 2-4-5—COVER 2 PRESS

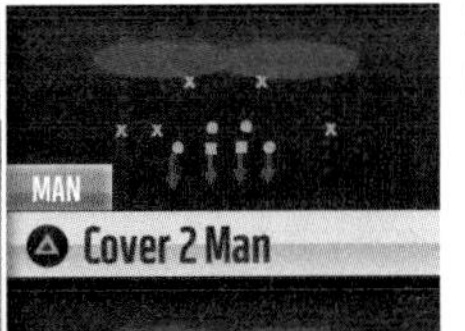

SETUP:

- Make sure to shade your coverage over the top to make this more of an every-down defense.
- If you expect the offense to try a verticals concept, switch to Cover 4 or 2 Man Under.
- CB Brandon Browner has the size to make his zones very tough to throw over.

PLAYER TO CONTROL:

- The LOLB off the right edge (finesse rush)

PASS DEFENSE

1ST DOWN	2ND AND SHORT	3RD AND SHORT	GOAL LINE	2ND AND LONG	3RD AND LONG
3-4 Odd—Cover 2 Sink QB Contain	3-4 Predator—Cover 1 Hole	Dollar 3-2-6—Cov 1 Robber Press	Goal Line 5-3-3—GL Man	Quarter 1-3-7—Under Smoke	Big Dime 1-4-6—Mike SS 1 Dog
3-4 Odd—3 Drop QB Contain	3-4 Predator—Will Fire 3 Seam	Dollar 3-2-6—DB Fire 2 Press	Goal Line 5-3-3—GL Zone	Quarter 1-3-7—FZ 3 Sky	Big Dime 1-4-6—Mike SS 3 Seam

MAN COVERAGE | ZONE COVERAGE | MAN BLITZ | ZONE BLITZ

SEATTLE SEAHAWKS

GAMEPLAY RATING 91

CONNECTED FRANCHISE MODE STRATEGY

CFM TEAM RATING: **92**
OFFENSE: **89**
DEFENSE: **97**
OFFENSIVE SCHEME: **Power Run**
DEFENSIVE SCHEME: **Attacking 4-3**
STRENGTHS: **QB, TE, HB, CB, FS, SS, MLB**
WEAKNESSES: **C, DT, RG, RT**

2014 TEAM RANKINGS

1st NFC West (12-4-0)
PASSING OFFENSE: **27th**
RUSHING OFFENSE: **1st**
PASSING DEFENSE: **1st**
RUSHING DEFENSE: **3rd**

2014 TEAM LEADERS

PASSING: **Russell Wilson: 3,475**
RUSHING: **Marshawn Lynch: 1,306**
RECEIVING: **Doug Baldwin: 825**
TACKLES: **K.J. Wright: 107**
SACKS: **Michael Bennett: 7**
INTS: **Richard Sherman: 4**

KEY ADDITIONS

TE Jimmy Graham
CB Cary Williams
C Lemuel Jeanpierre

KEY ROOKIES

DE Frank Clark
WR Tyler Lockett
G Terry Poole

OWNER: **Paul Allen**
LEGACY SCORE: **1,725**

COACH: **Pete Carroll**
LEVEL: **25**
LEGACY SCORE: **2,150**
OFFENSIVE SCHEME: **Balanced**
DEFENSIVE SCHEME: **Attacking 4-3**

OFFENSIVE SCOUTING REPORT

- QB Russell Wilson has become an incredible talent during his first contract, make sure to save money for him in the off-season.
- HB Marshawn Lynch still deserves all the carries, but choose one backup to develop when you get a lead or he needs a rest.
- The Seattle receiving corps is built around solid talent, but the true superstar is the newly acquired TE Jimmy Graham.

DEFENSIVE SCOUTING REPORT

- There are so many combinations to rush the passer for Seattle that it makes it nearly impossible for offensive teams to match up.
- Make sure that Bobby Wagner is anchoring the defense on every snap, and Bruce Irvin should be in to rush anytime a pass is suspected.
- The Seattle defense is the perfect blend of size and speed to shut down all the playmakers in the NFC.

SCHEDULE

Week	Date	Time	Network	Opponent
1	SEP 13	1:00 PM ET	FOX	AT RAMS
2	SEP 20	8:30 PM ET	NBC	AT PACKERS
3	SEP 27	4:25 PM ET		BEARS
4	OCT 05	8:30 PM ET	ESPN	LIONS
5	OCT 11	1:00 PM ET	FOX	AT BENGALS
6	OCT 18	4:05 PM ET	FOX	PANTHERS
7	OCT 22	8:25 PM ET		AT 49ERS
8	NOV 01	4:25 PM ET	FOX	AT COWBOYS
9	BYE WEEK			
10	NOV 15	8:30 PM ET	NBC	CARDINALS
11	NOV 22	4:25 PM ET	FOX	49ERS
12	NOV 29	4:25 PM ET		STEELERS
13	DEC 06	1:00 PM ET	FOX	AT VIKINGS
14	DEC 13	8:30 PM ET	NBC	AT RAVENS
15	DEC 20	4:05 PM ET	FOX	BROWNS
16	DEC 27	4:25 PM ET	FOX	RAMS
17	JAN 03	4:25 PM ET	FOX	AT CARDINALS

KEY PLAYERS

KEY OFFENSIVE PLAYER

JIMMY GRAHAM #88

TE #88 HT 6'7" WT 265 COLLEGE Miami EXP 5

KEY RATINGS

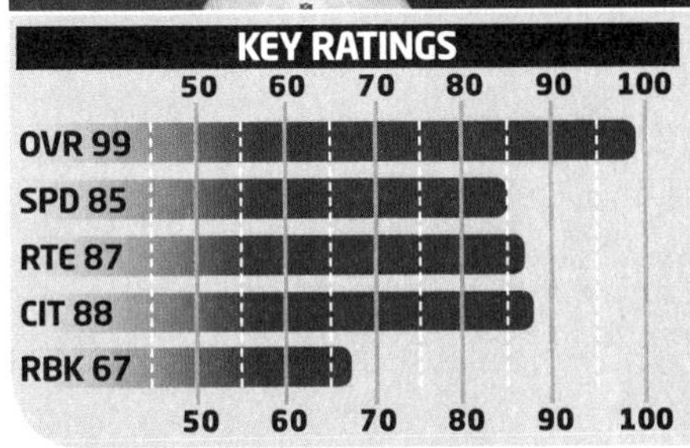

- Graham also has an elite Release rating, which means he can be split out wide and still beat the press.
- Spend some XP on run blocking to turn Graham into an all-around player.

KEY DEFENSIVE PLAYER

RICHARD SHERMAN #25

CB #25 HT 6'3" WT 195 COLLEGE Stanford EXP 4

KEY RATINGS

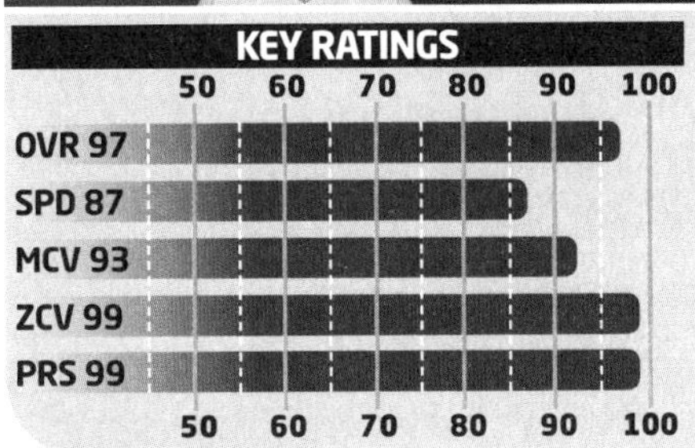

- If an opponent is looking to utilize the high-point throw, quickly shut them down with the 6'3" Sherman.
- Sherman is an amazing defender who can read plays quickly with his 99 Play Recognition.

KEY ROOKIE

FRANK CLARK #55

RE #55 HT 6'3" WT 271 COLLEGE Michigan EXP Rookie

KEY RATINGS

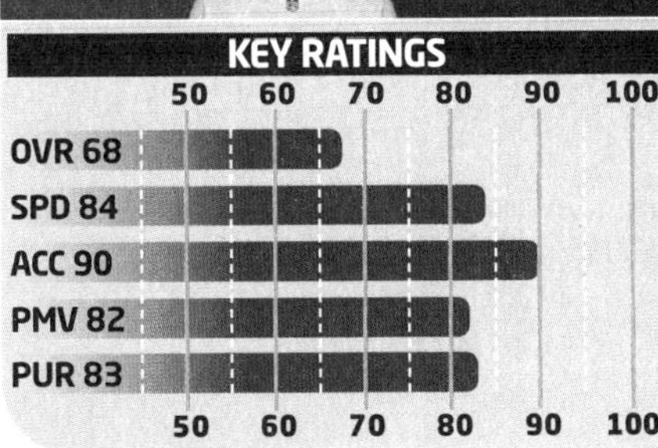

- Clark has solid hit power and could be a nice backup to Bruce Irvin while he develops.
- Spend XP on upgrading Awareness and Play Recognition ratings for Clark, because he is a very raw talent.

KEY SLEEPER

CHRIS MATTHEWS #13

WR #13 HT 6'5" WT 218 COLLEGE Kentucky EXP 2

KEY RATINGS

50 60 70 80 90 100

OVR 78

SPD 86

AGI 89

SPC 88

JMP 92

50 60 70 80 90 100

- Matthews had a huge game in Super Bowl, but some Madden NFL players already knew about his talent.
- Take advantage of his big frame in the red zone, especially if your TE is attracting a double team.

OFFENSIVE DEPTH CHART

POS	FIRST	LAST	OVR
QB	RUSSELL	WILSON	89
QB	TARVARIS	JACKSON	73
QB	B.J.	DANIELS	63
HB	MARSHAWN	LYNCH	96
HB	ROBERT	TURBIN	78
HB	CHRISTINE	MICHAEL	76
HB	THOMAS	RAWLS	66
FB	DERRICK	COLEMAN	80
FB	WILL	TUKUAFU	74
WR	DOUG	BALDWIN	84
WR	JERMAINE	KEARSE	81
WR	RICARDO	LOCKETTE	74
WR	CHRIS	MATTHEWS	74
WR	TYLER	LOCKETT	72
TE	JIMMY	GRAHAM	95
TE	LUKE	WILLSON	81
TE	COOPER	HELFET	74
TE	ANTHONY	MCCOY	74
LT	RUSSELL	OKUNG	85
LT	TERRY	POOLE	63
LG	ALVIN	BAILEY	80
LG	MARK	GLOWINSKI	71
C	LEMUEL	JEANPIERRE	72
C	PATRICK	LEWIS	64
RG	J.R.	SWEEZY	79
RG	KEAVON	MILTON	65
RT	JUSTIN	BRITT	76
RT	GARRY	GILLIAM	69

DEFENSIVE DEPTH CHART

POS	FIRST	LAST	OVR
LE	MICHAEL	BENNETT	95
LE	DEMARCUS	DOBBS	73
LE	GREG	SCRUGGS	67
DT	BRANDON	MEBANE	86
DT	TONY	MCDANIEL	79
DT	AHTYBA	RUBIN	78
DT	JORDAN	HILL	76
DT	JESSE	WILLIAMS	71
RE	CLIFF	AVRIL	87
RE	CASSIUS	MARSH	66
RE	FRANK	CLARK	64
LOLB	BRUCE	IRVIN	84
LOLB	MIKE	MORGAN	73
MLB	BOBBY	WAGNER	92
MLB	BROCK	COYLE	66
ROLB	K.J.	WRIGHT	86
ROLB	KEVIN	PIERRE-LOUIS	70
CB	RICHARD	SHERMAN	97
CB	CARY	WILLIAMS	82
CB	JEREMY	LANE	79
CB	MARCUS	BURLEY	76
CB	THAROLD	SIMON	73
FS	EARL	THOMAS III	95
FS	DESHAWN	SHEAD	71
SS	KAM	CHANCELLOR	94
SS	DION	BAILEY	72

SPECIAL TEAMS

POS	FIRST	LAST	OVR
K	STEVEN	HAUSCHKA	87
KR	DOUG	BALDWIN	84
KR	TYLER	LOCKETT	72
P	JON	RYAN	90
PR	DOUG	BALDWIN	84

BEST OFFENSIVE PLAYS

PRO TIPS

- These are the best two offensive plays in your playbook. They will get your playmakers in position to win you games.
- Getting Jimmy Graham split out on an island is one of the strengths of the Seahawks' playbook .
- The alignment of their shotgun sets can open up huge running lanes.

BEST RUN I-FORM H PRO—INSIDE ZONE

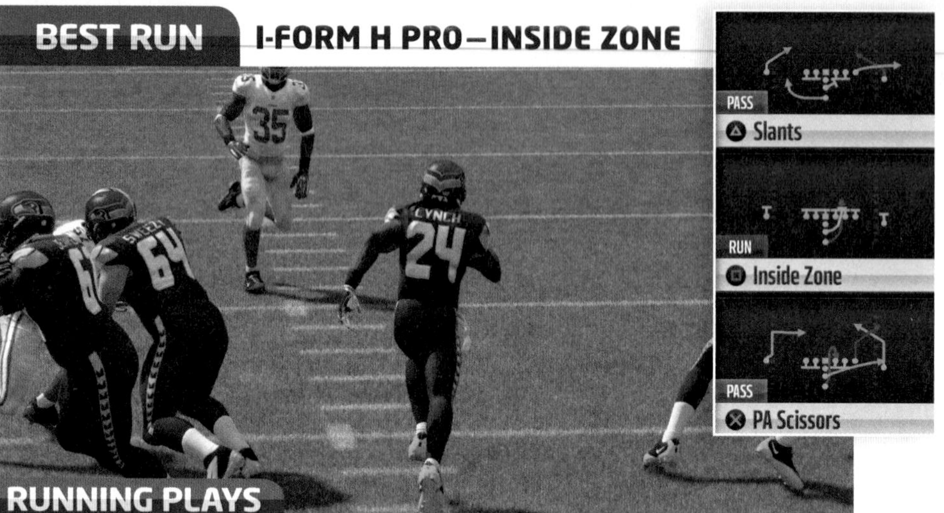

SETUP:

- The Seahawks have some excellent shotgun runs, but this is a no-nonsense power running set.
- While it can be fun to run with your QB, Lynch is the best option available—feed him.

ADVANCED SETUP:

- Sub a tackle in at TE.

RUNNING PLAYS

1ST DOWN	2ND AND SHORT	3RD AND SHORT	GOAL LINE	2ND AND LONG	3RD AND LONG
Singleback Deuce Wing–HB Stretch	Singleback Hawk Doubles–0 1 Trap	Gun Trips Y Iso–Inside Zone	Goal Line Normal–HB Sting	Gun Doubles Stack–Inside Zone	Pistol Ace–Read Option
Singleback Deuce Wing–Zone Weak	Singleback Deuce Wing–Inside Zone Split	Strong H TE Flip–HB Stretch	Goal Line Normal–QB Sneak	Pistol Strong Slot–Triple Option	Gun Wing Offset Wk–Read Option
I-Form H Slot–HB Stretch	I-Form H Slot–HB Iso	Singleback Ace Pair–HB Stretch	Singleback Deuce Wing–Split Belly	Gun Trio Offset–Speed Option	Gun Trips Y Iso–HB Draw

INSIDE RUN | OUTSIDE RUN | SHOTGUN RUN | QB RUN

BEST PASS GUN TREY Y-FLEX—PA CROSSERS

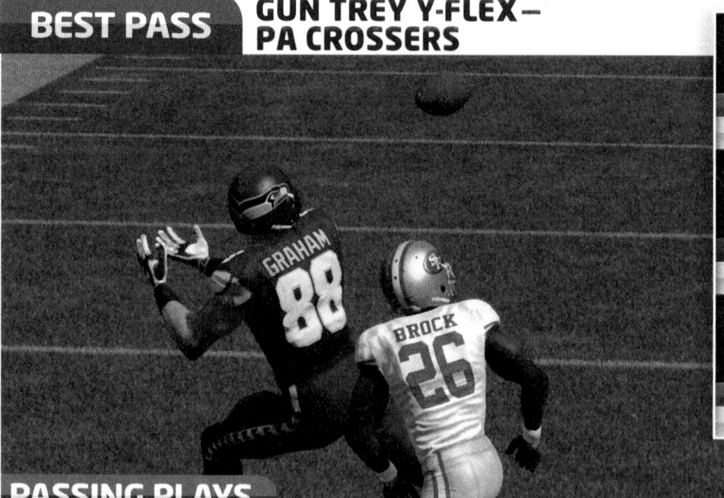

SETUP/READS:

- Against zone coverage read the play from left to right, and look for the short crosser before looking deep.
- Against man-to-man target TE Jimmy Graham when he cuts to the outside.
- Make sure to run the ball from this set first to set up the fake and slow down blitzers.

ADVANCED SETUP:

- Put the HB on a flat to either side to cancel play action.

PASSING PLAYS

1ST DOWN	2ND AND SHORT	3RD AND SHORT	SHOT PLAYS	2ND AND LONG	3RD AND LONG
Gun Trey Y-Flex–Levels Sail	Gun Empty Hawk–Slants Stay	Pistol Strong Slot–Under	Singleback Bunch Ace–PA Fork Shot	Gun Trips Y Iso–Verticals	Gun Trips Y Iso–Hawks Y Stutter
Singleback Hawk Doubles–Z Spot	Singleback Deuce Wing–Quick Slant	Singleback Bunch Ace–TE Angle	Singleback Hawk Doubles–PA Zone Shot	Gun Spread Y-Slot–Slot Post	Gun Trips Y Iso–HB Slip Screen
Gun Split Hawk–Slot Cross	I-Form H Pro–Texas	Gun Doubles Wing Offset–HB Angle	Gun Trey Y-Flex–PA Crosser	Gun Trey Y-Flex–PA Crosser	Gun Tight Slots–Bench

BASE PLAY | MAN BEATER | ZONE BEATER | BLITZ BEATER

BEST DEFENSIVE PLAYS

PRO TIPS

- **If you want to win more games in *Madden NFL 16*, rely on these defensive plays to lock up the run and pass.**
- Try shifting your LBs to the right with 4-3 Over Plus if the opponent has a twin TE set.
- Make sure to sub your DE to DT in dollar, then bring an OLB to the DE spot.

BEST RUN D: 4-3 OVER PLUS–MIKE BLITZ 3

ZONE – Cover 3
MAN – Cover 1
BLITZ – Mike Blitz 3

SETUP:

- If you need to get a stop on 3rd and short, consider calling "show blitz" before the snap.
- Because of their hit power, Bobby Wagner and Kam Chancellor are the players you want making tackles.

PLAYER TO CONTROL:

- Left-of-screen LB on a hook zone

RUN DEFENSE

1ST DOWN	2ND AND SHORT	3RD AND SHORT	GOAL LINE	2ND AND LONG	3RD AND LONG
46 Bear Under–Cover 1	4-3 Stack–Cover 1 Press	4-6 Bear Under–LB Dogs	Goal Line 5-3-3–GL Man	Nickel Normal–2 QB Contain	Dollar 3-2-6–Cover2 Man
46 Bear Under–Cover 3	4-3 Stack–Wk Slant 3 Press	4-6 Bear Under–LB Dogs 3	Goal Line 5-3-3–Pinch Zone	Nickel Normal–Cover 4	Dollar 3-2-6–Cov 3 Sky Press

MAN COVERAGE | ZONE COVERAGE | MAN BLITZ | ZONE BLITZ

BEST PASS D: BEST PASS D–COVER 1 ROBBER PRESS

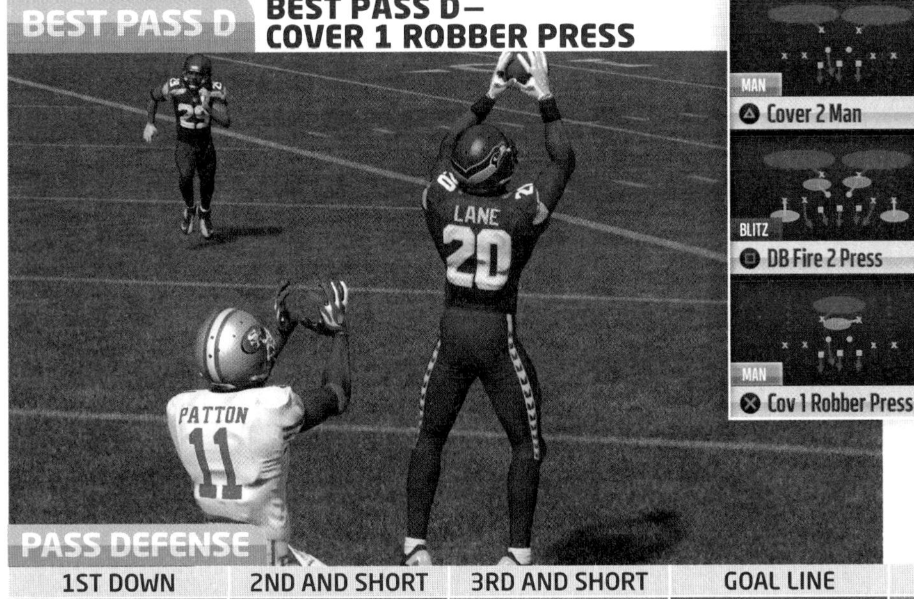

MAN – Cover 2 Man
BLITZ – DB Fire 2 Press
MAN – Cov 1 Robber Press

SETUP:

- Try putting the blitzing LB on a QB spy to contain mobile QBs.
- Safety Earl Thomas makes this entire play viable, because he can cover huge amounts of ground.
- Use the matchup stick to look for a speed disadvantage at CB/WR; don't get burned deep.

PLAYER TO CONTROL:

- Blitzing LB on left of screen

PASS DEFENSE

1ST DOWN	2ND AND SHORT	3RD AND SHORT	GOAL LINE	2ND AND LONG	3RD AND LONG
46 Bear Under–Cover 1	4-3 Over–Cov 1 Hole Press	4-3 Over Plus–Corner Dog 1	Goal Line 5-4-2–Jam Cover 1	Nickel Wide 9–Odd LB Dogs	Dollar 3-2-6–Spinner
46 Bear Under–Cover 3	4-3 Over–Will 3 Press	4-3 Over Plus–Mike Blitz 3	Goal Line 5-4-2–Flat Buzz	Nickel Wide 9–Odd Overload 3	Dollar 3-2-6–Overload 3 Seam

MAN COVERAGE | ZONE COVERAGE | MAN BLITZ | ZONE BLITZ

PITTSBURGH STEELERS

GAMEPLAY RATING **84**

CONNECTED FRANCHISE MODE STRATEGY

CFM TEAM RATING: **84**
OFFENSE: **93**
DEFENSE: **81**
OFFENSIVE SCHEME: **Balanced**
DEFENSIVE SCHEME: **Base 3-4**
STRENGTHS: **HB, WR, QB, C, RG, MLB**
WEAKNESSES: **S, CB, RE**

2014 TEAM RANKINGS

1st AFC North (11-5-0)
PASSING OFFENSE: **2nd**
RUSHING OFFENSE: **16th**
PASSING DEFENSE: **27th**
RUSHING DEFENSE: **6th**

2014 TEAM LEADERS

PASSING: **Ben Roethlisberger: 4,952**
RUSHING: **Le'Veon Bell: 1,361**
RECEIVING: **Antonio Brown: 1,698**
TACKLES: **Lawrence Timmons: 132**
SACKS: **Cameron Heyward: 7.5**
INTS: **William Gay: 3**

KEY ADDITIONS

LB James Harrison (re-signed)
LB Arthur Moats (re-signed)
TE Matt Spaeth (re-signed)

KEY ROOKIES

LB Bud Dupree
CB Senquez Golson
WR Sammie Coates

OWNER: **Dan Rooney**
LEGACY SCORE: **6,075**

COACH: **Mike Tomlin**
LEVEL: **15**
LEGACY SCORE: **2,300**
OFFENSIVE SCHEME: **Balanced**
DEFENSIVE SCHEME: **Base 3-4**

OFFENSIVE SCOUTING REPORT

- QB Ben Roethlisberger has excellent strength, which allows him to keep plays alive until he finds an open target. With the emergence of a great HB, his Play Action rating and ability to throw on the run should come in handy.
- Le'Veon Bell has absolutely turned into an every-down back for the Steelers. Not only does he have excellent agility, but he rarely fumbles and is a solid pass catcher. Start saving up because he will command a huge payday soon.
- In the WR corps, Antonio Brown has an amazing ability to hang onto balls in traffic, so go to him any time you need a clutch catch and let him do the work after the grab. Martavis Bryant is the next player you should focus on developing, because his size will make him a real threat in the red zone.

DEFENSIVE SCOUTING REPORT

- The Steelers' defensive line is perfect for their 3-4 scheme. Continue to work on pass-rushing skills for Stephon Tuitt. He is young and still developing. Expect Cameron Heyward and Steve McLendon to perform well, as they are in the prime of their careers.
- Last season, rookie LB Ryan Shazier stepped in and showed incredible speed. Improve his coverage skills, or consider switching him to a role where he can blitz on an every-down basis.
- The Steelers lost their veteran leader with the retirement of Troy Polamalu. However, they have the young talent ready to replace him in Shamarko Thomas. Focus your scouting on finding a CB in the upcoming draft.

SCHEDULE

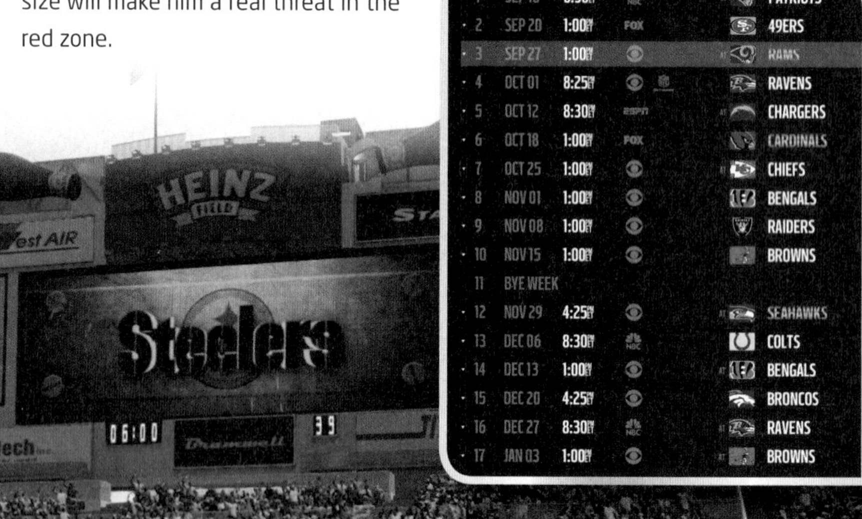

Week	Date	Time	Network		Opponent
1	SEP 10	8:30 PM ET	NBC	AT	PATRIOTS
2	SEP 20	1:00 PM ET	FOX		49ERS
3	SEP 27	1:00 PM ET		AT	RAMS
4	OCT 01	8:25 PM ET			RAVENS
5	OCT 12	8:30 PM ET	ESPN	AT	CHARGERS
6	OCT 18	1:00 PM ET	FOX		CARDINALS
7	OCT 25	1:00 PM ET		AT	CHIEFS
8	NOV 01	1:00 PM ET			BENGALS
9	NOV 08	1:00 PM ET			RAIDERS
10	NOV 15	1:00 PM ET			BROWNS
11	BYE WEEK				
12	NOV 29	4:25 PM ET		AT	SEAHAWKS
13	DEC 06	8:30 PM ET	NBC		COLTS
14	DEC 13	1:00 PM ET		AT	BENGALS
15	DEC 20	4:25 PM ET			BRONCOS
16	DEC 27	8:30 PM ET	NBC	AT	RAVENS
17	JAN 03	1:00 PM ET		AT	BROWNS

KEY PLAYERS

KEY OFFENSIVE PLAYER

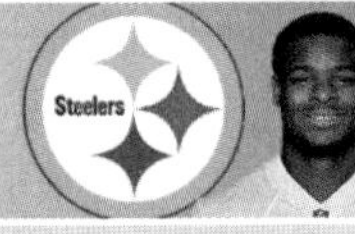

LE'VEON BELL #26

HB #26 HT 6'1" WT 244 COLLEGE Michigan St. EXP 2

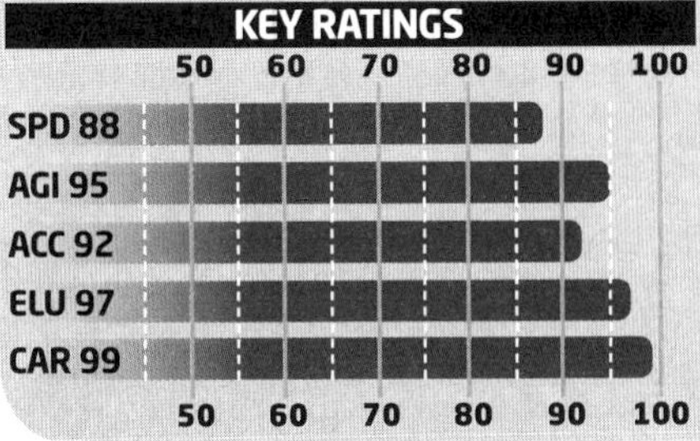

- To get the most out of Bell, target him in the passing game, because he can break screen passes for huge gains.
- Juke is a great option in the open field, but spin and stiff arm moves are close seconds.

KEY DEFENSIVE PLAYER

CAMERON HEYWARD #97

LE #97 HT 6'5" WT 288 COLLEGE Ohio State EXP 4

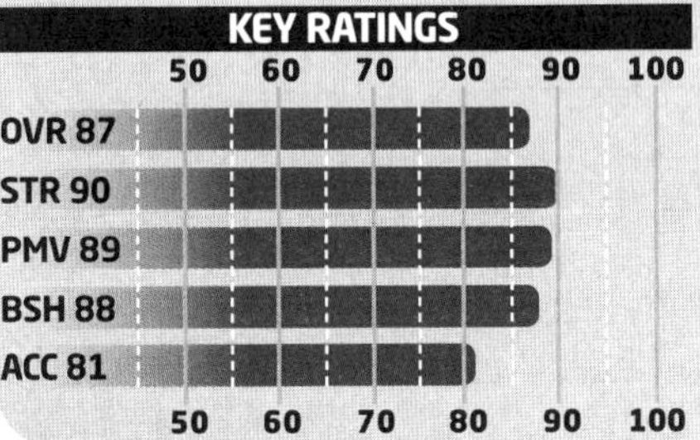

- Model the development of the younger DE Stephon Tuitt after Heyward, who can slide inside and rush on passing downs.
- Heyward has developed into an all-around defensive star and should remain in black and yellow for a long time.

KEY ROOKIE

BUD DUPREE #48

ROLB #48 HT 6'4" WT 269 COLLEGE Kentucky EXP Rookie

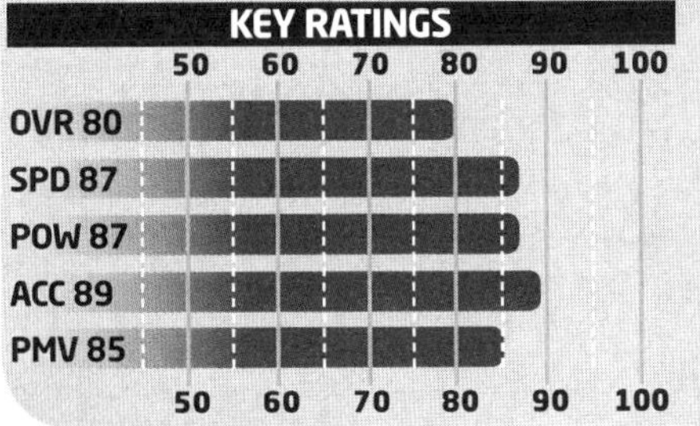

- This marks the second straight season the Steelers have gone for a linebacker early in the draft, and both times they have nailed it.
- Dupree is a pure pass rusher, so make sure to protect him against the run game until you beef up his 67 Block Shed rating.

KEY SLEEPER

DRI ARCHER #13

HB #13 HT 5'8" WT 173 COLLEGE Kent State EXP 1

KEY RATINGS

OVR 68
SPD 96
AGI 92
ACC 95
ELU 87

- There is rarely a reason to take your starter off the field, but 96 Speed would be one time to try to hit a big play.
- Don't forget to cover up the ball or get out of bounds. Archer has only a 69 Carry rating and needs an upgrade.

OFFENSIVE DEPTH CHART

POS	FIRST	LAST	OVR
QB	BEN	ROETHLISBERGER	95
QB	BRUCE	GRADKOWSKI	74
QB	LANDRY	JONES	68
HB	LE'VEON	BELL	94
HB	DEANGELO	WILLIAMS	78
HB	DRI	ARCHER	68
HB	JOSH	HARRIS	66
FB	WILL	JOHNSON	83
WR	ANTONIO	BROWN	97
WR	MARTAVIS	BRYANT	80
WR	MARKUS	WHEATON	75
WR	SAMMIE	COATES	71
WR	DARRIUS	HEYWARD-BEY	69
TE	HEATH	MILLER	83
TE	MATT	SPAETH	78
TE	JESSE	JAMES	64
LT	KELVIN	BEACHUM	87
LT	MIKE	ADAMS	66
LG	RAMON	FOSTER	82
LG	CHRIS	HUBBARD	72
C	MAURKICE	POUNCEY	90
C	CODY	WALLACE	71
C	B.J.	FINNEY	65
RG	DAVID	DECASTRO	87
RT	MARCUS	GILBERT	84
RT	MITCHELL	VAN DYK	67

DEFENSIVE DEPTH CHART

POS	FIRST	LAST	OVR
LE	CAMERON	HEYWARD	88
LE	CAM	THOMAS	71
LE	L.T.	WALTON	61
DT	STEVE	MCLENDON	84
DT	DANIEL	MCCULLERS	68
RE	STEPHON	TUITT	73
RE	CLIFTON	GEATHERS	70
LOLB	ARTHUR	MOATS	80
LOLB	JORDAN	ZUMWALT	65
LOLB	ANTHONY	CHICKILLO	64
MLB	LAWRENCE	TIMMONS	90
MLB	RYAN	SHAZIER	76
MLB	VINCE	WILLIAMS	75
MLB	SEAN	SPENCE	71
ROLB	JAMES	HARRISON	84
ROLB	BUD	DUPREE	73
ROLB	JARVIS	JONES	71
CB	WILLIAM	GAY	84
CB	CORTEZ	ALLEN	76
CB	ANTWON	BLAKE	70
CB	SENQUEZ	GOLSON	70
CB	B.W.	WEBB	70
FS	MIKE	MITCHELL	78
FS	ROBERT	GOLDEN	68
FS	GEROD	HOLLIMAN	66
SS	SHAMARKO	THOMAS	76
SS	WILL	ALLEN	75
SS	ROSS	VENTRONE	66

SPECIAL TEAMS

POS	FIRST	LAST	OVR
K	SHAUN	SUISHAM	86
KR	MARKUS	WHEATON	75
KR	DRI	ARCHER	68
P	BRAD	WING	64
PR	ANTONIO	BROWN	97

BEST OFFENSIVE PLAYS

PRO TIPS

- These are the best two offensive plays in your playbook. They will get your playmakers in position to win you games.
- Le'Veon Bell is one of the better all-around backs in the game, so don't forget to get him involved in the passing game.
- Antonio Brown is one of the best receivers in the game after the catch.

BEST RUN: PISTOL SLOT WING–INSIDE ZONE SPLIT

PASS — △ Corner Strike

RUN — ▢ Inside Zone Split

PASS — ✕ PA Zone Shot

SETUP:

- This run is designed to hit the middle, but Bell is explosive enough to take it outside if you see a lane.
- This is one of our favorite runs in the entire game. Use it until defenses proves they can stop it.

ADVANCED SETUP:

- None

RUNNING PLAYS

1ST DOWN	2ND AND SHORT	3RD AND SHORT	GOAL LINE	2ND AND LONG	3RD AND LONG
Singleback Ace–HB Stretch	Pistol Y-Trips–HB Zone	I-Form Tight Pair–FB Dive	Goal Line–QB Sneak	Gun Split Close–Power O	Gun Wing Trio Steeler–HB Base
Singleback Pitt Doubles–HB Cutback	Singleback Ace–0 1 Trap	I-Form Tight Pair–Zone Weak	Goal Line–HB Sting	Pistol Slot Wing–Inside Zone Split	Gun Y-Trips Wk–Inside Zone
I-Form Pro–Outside Zone	Strong Close–HB Dive	Singleback Ace Pair Flex–HB Stretch	Weak Pro–HB Gut	Gun Bunch Wk–HB Counter	Gun Doubles–HB Counter

INSIDE RUN | OUTSIDE RUN | SHOTGUN RUN | QB RUN

BEST PASS: GUN TIGHT DOUBLES ON–CROSS WHEELS

PASS — △ Z Spot

PASS — ▢ HB Slip Screen

PASS — ✕ Cross Wheels

SETUP/READS:

- Against zone coverage be patient and keep your eyes over the middle of the field.
- Against man-to-man coverage the two crossing routes should work well with each other to free one receiver up.
- Against the blitz look to quickly hit the HB in the flat for a back-breaking gain.

ADVANCED SETUP:

- Streak the far left WR.

PASSING PLAYS

1ST DOWN	2ND AND SHORT	3RD AND SHORT	SHOT PLAYS	2ND AND LONG	3RD AND LONG
Gun Split Close–Y Trail	Strong Close–Y Trail	I-Form Pro–HB Angle	Gun Split Close–Vertical Shots	Gun Empty Trey–Dbl Slot Cross	Gun Doubles–Y-Sail
Singleback Ace–Ace Posts	Pistol Y-Trips–Stick N Nod	Strong Close–HB Slip Screen	I-Form Pro–All Fade	Gun Trio–Steeler Dig	Singleback Pitt Doubles–Pitt Slot Post
Singleback Ace Pair Flex–WR Clown Cross	Gun Snugs–Steeler Crosses	Pistol Slot Wing–PA Slot Cross	Gun Tight Doubles On–Shot Fade Cross	Gun Bunch Wk–Verticals	Gun Trips HB Wk–Four Verticals

BASE PLAY | MAN BEATER | ZONE BEATER | BLITZ BEATER

 For more plays and strategies for this team, visit your eGuide using the access code sheet provided.

BEST DEFENSIVE PLAYS

PRO TIPS

- If you want to win more games in *Madden NFL 16*, rely on these defensive plays to lock up the run and pass.
- The Steelers still have plenty of LBs to stay in a 3-4 for most of the game.
- Look for chances to make a big play with SS Shamarko Thomas, and keep an eye on his position during the game.

BEST RUN D: 3-4 OVER—SAM MIKE 3

ZONE — Cover 3 Sky

MAN — Cover 1 Hole

BLITZ — Sam Mike 3

SETUP:

- Try to get a double team along the defensive line to help give your blitzing LB a gap to shoot through.
- Don't forget to base align against formations that try to spread you out.

PLAYER TO CONTROL:

- DT over the center

RUN DEFENSE

1ST DOWN	2ND AND SHORT	3RD AND SHORT	GOAL LINE	2ND AND LONG	3RD AND LONG
3-4 Over–Cover 1 Hole	3-4 Under–Cov 1 Robber Press	3-4 Solid–1 Will Sam Go	Goal Line 5-4-2–Jam Cover 1	Nickel 3-3-5 Wide–Cover 2 Man	Nickel 2-4-5–Cover 2 Man
3-4 Odd–Cover 3 Sky	3-4 Over–Sam Mike 3	3-4 Solid–Trio Sky Zone	Goal Line 5-4-2–Flat Buzz	Nickel 3-3-5 Wide–Cover 2 Sink	Nickel 2-4-5–Cover 4

MAN COVERAGE | ZONE COVERAGE | MAN BLITZ | ZONE BLITZ

BEST PASS D: NICKEL 2-4-5 PROWL—COVER 2 DROP

ZONE — Cover 2 Drop

BLITZ — Dbl Loop

BLITZ — Dbl Loop 3

SETUP:

- Shading your defensive coverage over the top can help defend against vertical concepts.
- Shading your defensive coverage underneath on third and short will help against concepts like spacing.
- If your defensive line can't get a rush, the opponent will pick you apart along the deep sideline. Consider blitzing some LBs on long-yardage situations.

PLAYER TO CONTROL:

- Either MLB in a hook zone

PASS DEFENSE

1ST DOWN	2ND AND SHORT	3RD AND SHORT	GOAL LINE	2ND AND LONG	3RD AND LONG
3-4 Even–Cov1 Robber Press	Nickel 2-4-5 Prowl–OLB Fire	Nickel 2-4-5 Prowl–Dbl Loop	Goal Line 5-3-3–GL Man	Big Dime 2-3-6 Will–Mike Edge 1	Nickel 2-4-5 Dbl A Gap–Mid Blitz
3-4 Even–Mike Scrape 3 Press	Nickel 2-4-5 Prowl–Overload 3 Seam	Nickel 2-4-5 Prowl–Dbl Loop 3	Goal Line 5-3-3–GL Zone	Big Dime 2-3-6 Will–3 Cloud Press	Nickel 2-4-5 Dbl A Gap–Will 3 Buzz

MAN COVERAGE | ZONE COVERAGE | MAN BLITZ | ZONE BLITZ

HOUSTON TEXANS

GAMEPLAY RATING 79

CONNECTED FRANCHISE MODE STRATEGY

CFM TEAM RATING: **82**
OFFENSE: **85**
DEFENSE: **85**
OFFENSIVE SCHEME: **Power Run**
DEFENSIVE SCHEME: **Attacking 3-4**
STRENGTHS: **DT, HB, LT, DE, RE, CB**
WEAKNESSES: **QB, TE, C, SS, LE**

2014 TEAM RANKINGS

2nd AFC South (9-7-0)
PASSING OFFENSE: **24th**
RUSHING OFFENSE: **5th**
PASSING DEFENSE: **21st**
RUSHING DEFENSE: **10th**

2014 TEAM LEADERS

PASSING: **Ryan Fitzpatrick: 2,483**
RUSHING: **Arian Foster: 1,246**
RECEIVING: **DeAndre Hopkins: 1,210**
TACKLES: **Kendrick Lewis: 84**
SACKS: **J.J. Watt: 20.5**
INTS: **A.J. Bouye: 3**

KEY ADDITIONS

S Rahim Moore
QB Brian Hoyer
DT Vince Wilfork
WR Nate Washington
WR Cecil Shorts
S Stevie Brown

KEY ROOKIES

CB Kevin Johnson
LB Benardrick McKinney
WR Jaelen Strong

OWNER: **Bob McNair**
LEGACY SCORE: **450**

COACH: **Bill O'Brien**
LEVEL: **7**
LEGACY SCORE: **0**
OFFENSIVE SCHEME: **Power Run**
DEFENSIVE SCHEME: **Attacking 3-4**

OFFENSIVE SCOUTING REPORT

- The Texans still need to find a long-term option at starting QB. Although they brought in Brian Hoyer, we would still give Ryan Mallett the nod and try to develop that strong arm into a viable option. Make sure to scout plenty of QBs in the upcoming draft and try another option.
- HB Arian Foster rebounded to have a strong season and prove his long-term value. Fight against his declining Speed rating; otherwise, in a few seasons he will only be a great option on up-the-middle runs.
- With the departure of Andre Johnson, the Texans' WR corps will need a new leader. Thankfully, DeAndre Hopkins has shown excellent skill and just needs a more consistent chemistry at QB to really take things to the next level.

DEFENSIVE SCOUTING REPORT

- J.J. Watt was the defensive player of the year last season and made a strong case for MVP. This should make life for his teammates easy on the defensive side of the ball. Keep moving him around to keep offenses guessing.
- The LBs for the Texans are solid pass rushers off the edge and should continue to improve nicely. Build around Brian Cushing in the middle; that is one spot that can't afford to take an injury.
- The Texans have the makings of a solid secondary but lack a true identity. Try playing heavy Cover 2 early in the season and using shading to get the most out of your players.

SCHEDULE

Week	Date	Time	TV		Opponent
1	SEP 13	1:00 PM ET			CHIEFS
2	SEP 20	1:00 PM ET		AT	PANTHERS
3	SEP 27	1:00 PM ET	FOX		BUCCANEERS
4	OCT 04	1:00 PM ET		AT	FALCONS
5	OCT 08	8:25 PM ET			COLTS
6	OCT 18	1:00 PM ET		AT	JAGUARS
7	OCT 25	1:00 PM ET		AT	DOLPHINS
8	NOV 01	1:00 PM ET			TITANS
9	BYE WEEK				
10	NOV 16	8:30 PM ET	ESPN	AT	BENGALS
11	NOV 22	1:00 PM ET			JETS
12	NOV 29	1:00 PM ET	FOX		SAINTS
13	DEC 06	1:00 PM ET		AT	BILLS
14	DEC 13	1:00 PM ET			PATRIOTS
15	DEC 20	1:00 PM ET		AT	COLTS
16	DEC 27	1:00 PM ET		AT	TITANS
17	JAN 03	1:00 PM ET			JAGUARS

KEY PLAYERS

KEY OFFENSIVE PLAYER

ARIAN FOSTER

HB #23 HT 6'1" WT 227 COLLEGE Tennessee EXP 6

KEY RATINGS

OVR 92
SPD 82
CTH 78
AGI 91
CAR 95

- Don't let the slower speed fool you; the Strength and Ball Carrier Vision ratings are what make Foster excellent.
- Foster is a solid back who can consistently truck his way to 1,000 yards per season.

KEY DEFENSIVE PLAYER

J.J. WATT

#99

RE #99 HT 6'5" WT 289 COLLEGE Wisconsin EXP 4

KEY RATINGS

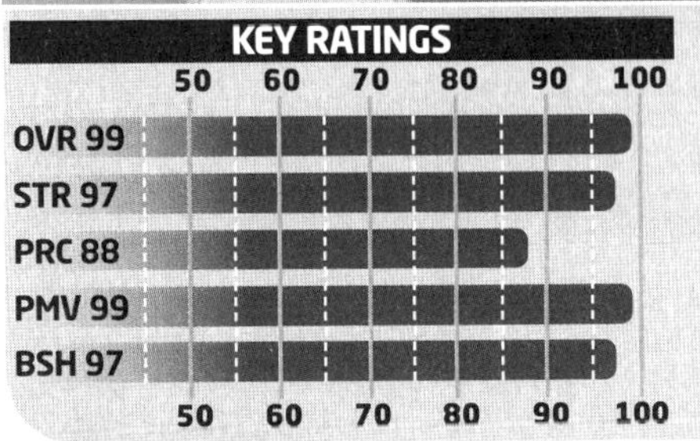

- Watt not only is one of the best but also is one of the most versatile linemen in the game.
- Continue to build your defense around him. He is locked up for the long term.

KEY ROOKIE

KEVIN JOHNSON

CB #30 HT 6'0" WT 188 COLLEGE Wake Forest EXP Rookie

KEY RATINGS

OVR 75
SPD 88
AGI 92
MCV 82
ZCV 87

- Continue to develop Johnson's Press rating if you want to make him a better overall fit.
- Johnson will be a solid CB in the slot with his size and zone coverage.

KEY SLEEPER

CHARLES JAMES

CB #31 HT 5'9" WT 179 COLLEGE Charleston S. EXP 2

KEY RATINGS

OVR 64
SPD 88
AGI 89
MCV 74
ZCV 82

- James is a smart player who is well balanced. Keep developing his zone coverage and find him some time on the field in Quarter formations.
- James can also be used as a returner on special teams if you need an option back there.

OFFENSIVE DEPTH CHART

POS	FIRST	LAST	OVR
QB	RYAN	MALLETT	74
QB	BRIAN	HOYER	73
QB	TOM	SAVAGE	70
HB	ARIAN	FOSTER	91
HB	ALFRED	BLUE	74
HB	CHRIS	POLK	74
HB	JONATHAN	GRIMES	71
FB	JAY	PROSCH	77
WR	DEANDRE	HOPKINS	88
WR	CECIL	SHORTS	78
WR	NATE	WASHINGTON	78
WR	JAELEN	STRONG	72
WR	DAMARIS	JOHNSON	71
WR	KESHAWN	MARTIN	69
TE	GARRETT	GRAHAM	74
TE	RYAN	GRIFFIN	73
TE	C.J.	FIEDOROWICZ	71
LT	DUANE	BROWN	90
LT	JEFF	ADAMS	67
LT	WILL	YEATMAN	66
LG	XAVIER	SU'A-FILO	74
LG	CHAD	SLADE	65
C	BEN	JONES	75
C	CODY	WHITE	68
C	JAMES	FERENTZ	67
RG	BRANDON	BROOKS	87
RG	DAVID	QUESSENBERRY	73
RT	DEREK	NEWTON	87
RT	BRYAN	WITZMANN	68

DEFENSIVE DEPTH CHART

POS	FIRST	LAST	OVR
LE	JEOFFREY	PAGAN	66
LE	LYNDEN	TRAIL	60
DT	VINCE	WILFORK	91
DT	LOUIS	NIX III	74
DT	BRANDON	DEADERICK	69
RE	J.J.	WATT	99
RE	TEVITA	FINAU	66
RE	CHRISTIAN	COVINGTON	62
LOLB	BENARDRICK	MCKINNEY	72
LOLB	JOHN	SIMON	72
LOLB	KOURTNEI	BROWN	62
MLB	BRIAN	CUSHING	82
MLB	AKEEM	DENT	75
MLB	JUSTIN	TUGGLE	72
MLB	JEFF	TARPINIAN	68
ROLB	WHITNEY	MERCILUS	80
ROLB	JADEVEON	CLOWNEY	78
ROLB	JASON	ANKRAH	64
CB	JOHNATHAN	JOSEPH	88
CB	KAREEM	JACKSON	84
CB	KEVIN	JOHNSON	74
CB	A.J.	BOUYE	73
CB	ANDRE	HAL	72
FS	RAHIM	MOORE	85
FS	LONNIE	BALLENTINE	66
SS	STEVIE	BROWN	80
SS	EDDIE	PLEASANT	75

SPECIAL TEAMS

POS	FIRST	LAST	OVR
K	RANDY	BULLOCK	80
KR	DAMARIS	JOHNSON	71
KR	KESHAWN	MARTIN	69
P	SHANE	LECHLER	84
PR	KESHAWN	MARTIN	69

BEST OFFENSIVE PLAYS

PRO TIPS

- These are the best two offensive plays in your playbook. They will get your playmakers in position to win you games.
- The Texans' offensive playbook isn't the most creative in the game, but it has plenty of effective plays.
- The running game is built for a back who can make one cut, find a lane, and then get up to full speed quickly.

BEST RUN: SINGLEBACK ACE TWINS–HB STRETCH

SETUP:

- This run is all about what you read before the snap. One side should almost always be open.
- Don't forget to add some fake playmakers in from time to time, to make the defense think you are switching the run direction before the snap.

ADVANCED SETUP:

- Playmaker the run left (optional)

RUNNING PLAYS

1ST DOWN	2ND AND SHORT	3RD AND SHORT	GOAL LINE	2ND AND LONG	3RD AND LONG
I-Form Tight Pair–Strong Stretch	Singleback Ace Twins–HB Dive	Singleback Ace–0 1 Trap	Goal Line–QB Sneak	Gun Normal Y-Slot–HB Quick Base	Gun Snugs Flip–HB Mid Draw
Singleback Y-Trips Texan–HB Wk Dive	Strong Pro–HB Dive	Strong Pro–HB Off Tackle	Goal Line–HB Sting	Gun Wing Trips Wk–Inside Zone	Gun Bunch Wk–HB Sweep
Singleback Doubles–HB Misdirection	Weak Pro Twins–HB Blast	Singleback Jumbo Z–HB Smash	I-Form Tight Pair–FB Dive	Gun Y-Trips HB Wk–Inside Zone	Gun Tight Doubles On–HB Draw

INSIDE RUN | OUTSIDE RUN | SHOTGUN RUN | QB RUN

BEST PASS: GUN SNUGS FLIP–DRIVE TRAIL

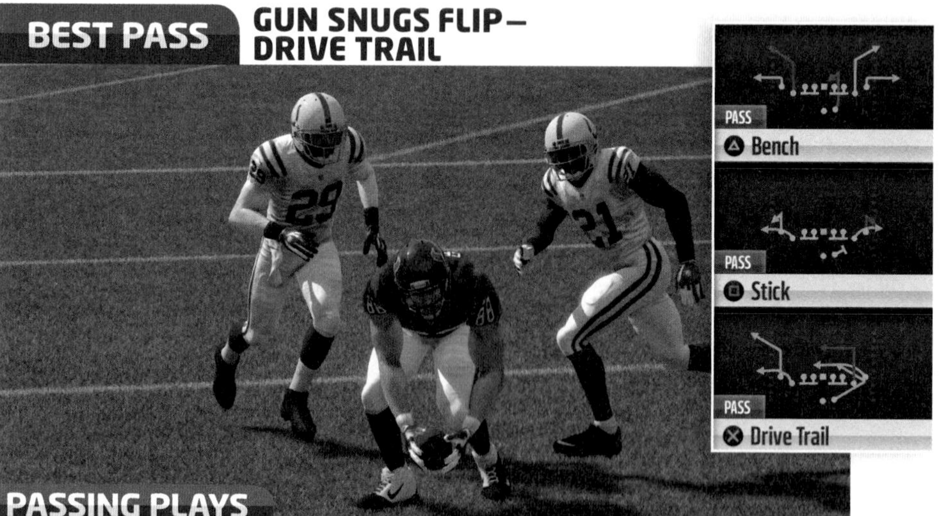

SETUP/READS:

- To make this play work against zone coverage, you must learn to master the possession catch in the seam.
- Against man-to-man coverage there is simply too much going on over the middle of the field for defenders to stick with their man.
- Make aggressive defenses pay by looking to the left side and going to the flat or taking a chance downfield to your number one WR.

ADVANCED SETUP:

- Streak or curl the TE.

PASSING PLAYS

1ST DOWN	2ND AND SHORT	3RD AND SHORT	SHOT PLAYS	2ND AND LONG	3RD AND LONG
Gun Y-Trips HB Wk–Texans Under	Gun Wing Trips Wk–Wheel Mesh	I-Form Pro–PA Scissors	Singleback Ace Twins–PA FL Stretch	Gun Tight Doubles On–Tight Curl	Gun Empty Y-Flex–Verticals
Gun Ace Pair Flex–TE Spot	Singleback Tight Doubles–Texan Under	Gun Bunch Wk–PA Post	Gun Tight Doubles On–Shot Fade Cross	Gun Ace Pair Flex–PA Slot Post	Gun Empty Texan–Stick Nod
Singleback Ace Twins–Texan Y-Drag	Singleback Doubles–PA Slot Crosses	Gun Bunch Wk–Texans Trail	Gun Trips TE–PA Shot Wheel	Gun Snugs Flip–Drive Trail	Gun Bunch Wk–Verticals

BASE PLAY | MAN BEATER | ZONE BEATER | BLITZ BEATER

 For more plays and strategies for this team, visit your eGuide using the access code sheet provided.

BEST DEFENSIVE PLAYS

PRO TIPS

- **Rely on these defensive plays to lock up the run and pass.**
- The Texans have the reigning defensive player of the year in J.J. Watt, and he will draw lots of attention from opposing offenses.
- The 3-4 scheme is solidified in Houston with the addition of Vince Wilfork over the nose. Expect teams to run outside.

BEST RUN D — NICKEL 3-3-5 WILL—COVER 2

SETUP:

- Alternate between the Cover 2 and Cover 2 Sink to help protect against any play-action fakes from the offense.
- Shade underneath if you expect the run, and consider blitzing your LBs on short-yardage situations.

PLAYER TO CONTROL:

- MLB in a hook zone

RUN DEFENSE

1ST DOWN	2ND AND SHORT	3RD AND SHORT	GOAL LINE	2ND AND LONG	3RD AND LONG
3-4 Under–1 QB Contain	3-4 Under–Cov1 Robber Press	3-4 Solid–Sting Pinch	Goal Line 5-4-2–Jam Cover 1	Nickel 3-3-5 Wide–Cover 1 Robber	Nickel 3-3-5 Will–Cover 2 Man
3-4 Under–Cover 3 Cloud	3-4 Under–Mike Scrape 3 Press	3-4 Solid–Trio Sky Zone	Goal Line 5-4-2–Flat Buzz	Nickel 3-3-5 Wide–Sam Will 3 Blitz	Nickel 3-3-5 Wide–Cover 4 Show 2

MAN COVERAGE ZONE COVERAGE MAN BLITZ ZONE BLITZ

BEST PASS D — NICKEL 2-4-5 DBL A GAP—COVER 3 SKY

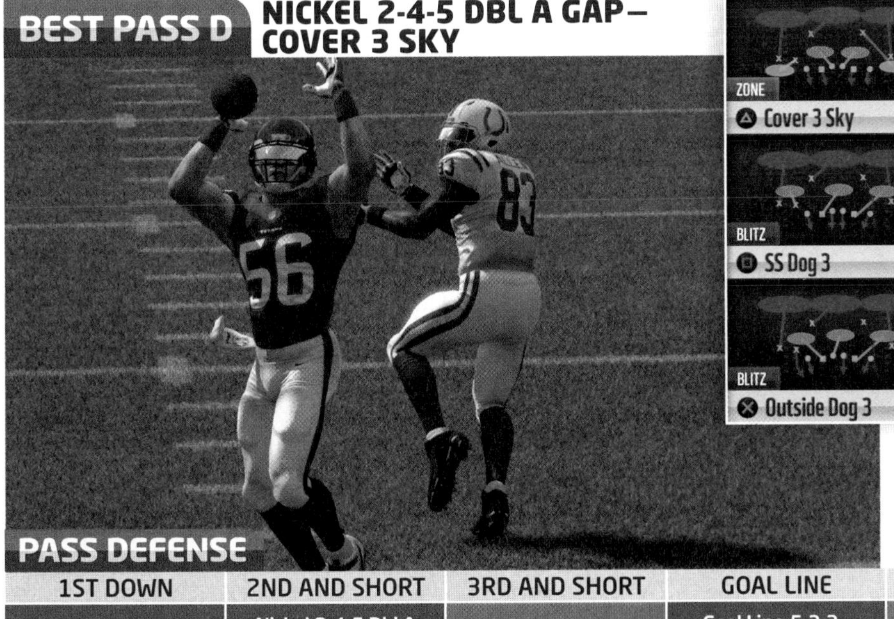

SETUP:

- Sub in ROLB Jadeveon Clowney and manually rush him off the edge. He is an excellent complement to Watt.
- Try getting pressure with the Cover 3 Sky first. If you're not having any luck, go to the Outside Dog 3.
- The LBs dropping over the middle will hopefully help generate some turnovers for your defense.

PLAYER TO CONTROL:

- ROLB (rush)

PASS DEFENSE

1ST DOWN	2ND AND SHORT	3RD AND SHORT	GOAL LINE	2ND AND LONG	3RD AND LONG
3-4 Even–Cover 2 Man	Nickel 2-4-5 Dbl A Gap–Mid Blitz	3-4 Over–Cover 1 Hole	Goal Line 5-3-3–GL Man	Big Dime 1-4-6–Cover 1 Robber	Quarter 1-3-7–DB Strike
3-4 Even–Cover 4	Nickel 2-4-5 Dbl A Gap–Buck Zone Blitz	3-4 Over–Sam Mike 3	Goal Line 5-3-3–GL Zone	Big Dime 1-4-6–Cover 3 Sky	Quarter 1-3-7–FZ 3 Sky

MAN COVERAGE ZONE COVERAGE MAN BLITZ ZONE BLITZ

TENNESSEE TITANS

GAMEPLAY RATING 72

CONNECTED FRANCHISE MODE STRATEGY

CFM TEAM RATING: **82**
OFFENSE: **83**
DEFENSE: **85**
OFFENSIVE SCHEME: **Spread**
DEFENSIVE SCHEME: **Zone Blitz 3-4**
STRENGTHS: **RG, TE, DE**
WEAKNESSES: **C, FS, RT**

2014 TEAM RANKINGS

4th AFC South (2-14-0)
PASSING OFFENSE: **22nd**
RUSHING OFFENSE: **26th**
PASSING DEFENSE: **15th**
RUSHING DEFENSE: **31st**

2014 TEAM LEADERS

PASSING: **Zach Mettenberger: 1,412**
RUSHING: **Bishop Sankey: 569**
RECEIVING: **Delanie Walker: 890**
TACKLES: **Michael Griffin: 112**
SACKS: **Derrick Morgan: 6.5**
INTS: **Jason McCourty: 3**

KEY ADDITIONS

WR Hakeem Nicks
LB Brian Orakpo
CB Perrish Cox

KEY ROOKIES

QB Marcus Mariota
WR Dorial Green-Beckham
G Jeremiah Poutasi

OWNER: **Steve Fowler**
LEGACY SCORE: **0**

COACH: **Ken Whisenhunt**
LEVEL: **3**
LEGACY SCORE: **650**
OFFENSIVE SCHEME: **Spread**
DEFENSIVE SCHEME: **Zone Blitz 3-4**

OFFENSIVE SCOUTING REPORT

- While three QBs split snaps last season, there is only one player who should take them this season. Invest all of your resources into making rookie QB Marcus Mariota the face of the franchise. His unique talent will allow you to run a unique offensive scheme.
- Bishop Sankey turned in a decent rookie campaign at HB last season, and hopefully the new QB and offensive system will allow him to continue to improve. Remember that he is an elusive-style back with some hands despite his solid strength.
- Hakeem Nicks and Justin Hunter are good physical receivers, but give the snaps to Green-Beckham and see what he can become. Use Kendall Wright and Harry Douglas as your best targets over the middle, and look to pick up yards after the catch.

DEFENSIVE SCOUTING REPORT

- Derrick Morgan rushing off the edge as an LB should be a nice change of pace for the defense. Use his power moves and acceleration to get after the QB. Pairing him with LE Ropati Pitoitua will protect him in the run game, and they will make a great combo.
- Bringing in veteran LB Brian Orakpo was a great move. He is the perfect fit for the Titans' defensive scheme. Keep him together with Jurrell Casey to give extra support in the run game. Don't give up on your young MLBs, because their speed is excellent.
- The Titans' secondary is average, so try to draft a safety who can allow your defense to take more chances. CB Jason McCourty is still the leader and has solid speed. He can even get in on the run game and make some tackles.

SCHEDULE

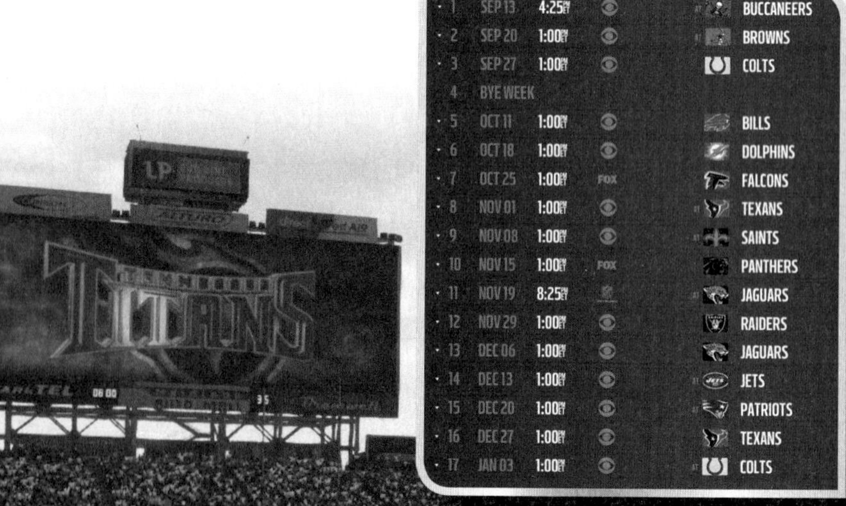

1	SEP 13	4:25 PM ET		AT BUCCANEERS
2	SEP 20	1:00 PM ET		AT BROWNS
3	SEP 27	1:00 PM ET		COLTS
4	BYE WEEK			
5	OCT 11	1:00 PM ET		BILLS
6	OCT 18	1:00 PM ET		DOLPHINS
7	OCT 25	1:00 PM ET	FOX	FALCONS
8	NOV 01	1:00 PM ET		AT TEXANS
9	NOV 08	1:00 PM ET		AT SAINTS
10	NOV 15	1:00 PM ET	FOX	PANTHERS
11	NOV 19	8:25 PM ET		AT JAGUARS
12	NOV 29	1:00 PM ET		RAIDERS
13	DEC 06	1:00 PM ET		JAGUARS
14	DEC 13	1:00 PM ET		AT JETS
15	DEC 20	1:00 PM ET		AT PATRIOTS
16	DEC 27	1:00 PM ET		TEXANS
17	JAN 03	1:00 PM ET		AT COLTS

KEY PLAYERS

KEY OFFENSIVE PLAYER

DELANIE WALKER #82

TE #82 HT 6'0" WT 248 COLLEGE Central Missouri EXP 9

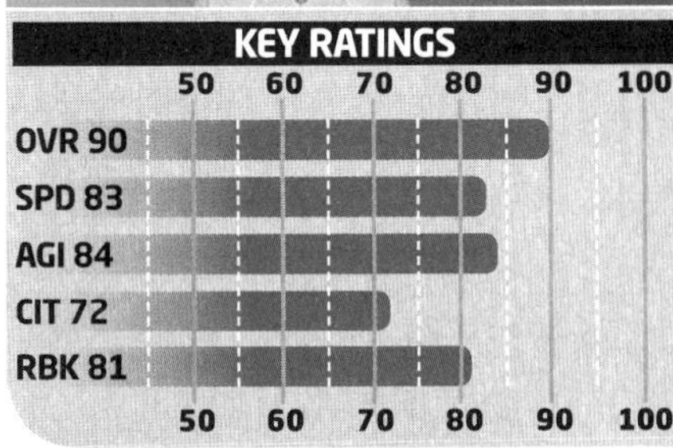

- Walker isn't the biggest or fastest target, but he can consistently find holes in the defense.
- Walker is one of the best run blockers in the game at the TE spot.

KEY DEFENSIVE PLAYER

JURRELL CASEY #99

RE #99 HT 6'1" WT 305 COLLEGE USC EXP 4

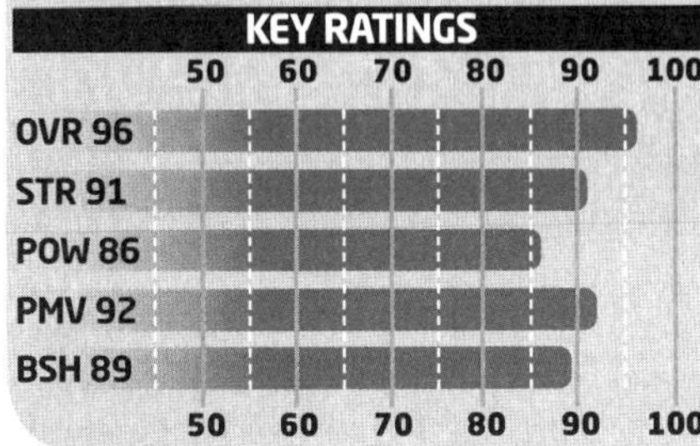

- Casey doesn't have the biggest frame on the team, but he is still extremely strong against the run and pass.
- Slide Casey inside on passing situations to keep him on the field.

KEY ROOKIE

MARCUS MARIOTA #8

QB #8 HT 6'3" WT 222 COLLEGE Oregon EXP Rookie

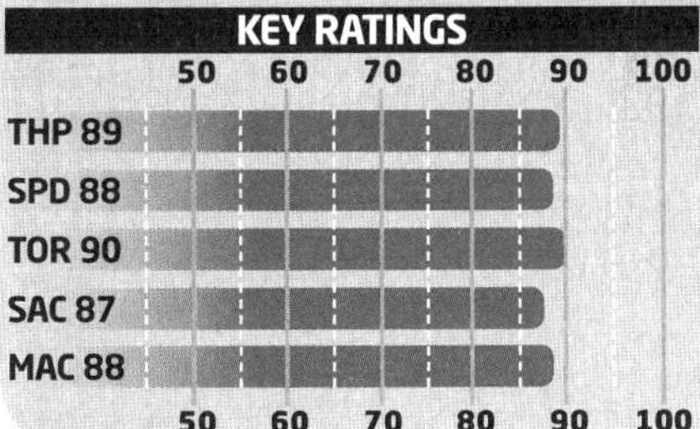

- Mariota's 90 Acceleration rating is important for roll-outs and the read option.
- He will need to work on his deep accuracy to keep the defense away from the line of scrimmage.

KEY SLEEPER

DORIAL GREEN-BECKHAM #17

WR #17 HT 6'5" WT 237 COLLEGE Oklahoma EXP Rookie

KEY RATINGS

50 60 70 80 90 100

OVR 76
SPD 89
AGI 91
CIT 87
SPC 90

- Green-Beckham has the size to become a TD-scoring machine at the next level.
- Continue to develop his route running to turn him into a threat all over the field.

OFFENSIVE DEPTH CHART

POS	FIRST	LAST	OVR
QB	MARCUS	MARIOTA	78
QB	ZACH	METTENBERGER	76
QB	CHARLIE	WHITEHURST	74
HB	BISHOP	SANKEY	75
HB	DEXTER	MCCLUSTER	73
HB	DAVID	COBB	71
HB	ANTONIO	ANDREWS	63
FB	JALSTON	FOWLER	68
FB	CONNOR	NEIGHBORS	62
WR	KENDALL	WRIGHT	83
WR	HARRY	DOUGLAS	79
WR	HAKEEM	NICKS	78
WR	JUSTIN	HUNTER	75
WR	DORIAL	GREEN-BECKHAM	74
WR	TRE	MCBRIDE	68
TE	DELANIE	WALKER	87
TE	CRAIG	STEVENS	78
TE	TAYLOR	THOMPSON	70
LT	TAYLOR	LEWAN	81
LT	JAMON	MEREDITH	66
LG	ANDY	LEVITRE	82
LG	JUSTIN	MCCRAY	69
LG	JOSUE	MATIAS	65
C	BRIAN	SCHWENKE	72
C	GABE	IKARD	67
C	ANDY	GALLIK	65
RG	CHANCE	WARMACK	84
RG	QUINTON	SPAIN	66
RT	BYRON	STINGILY	74
RT	BYRON	BELL	73
RT	JEREMIAH	POUTASI	68

DEFENSIVE DEPTH CHART

POS	FIRST	LAST	OVR
LE	ROPATI	PITOITUA	77
LE	MIKE	MARTIN	74
LE	DAQUAN	JONES	68
DT	SAMMIE	HILL	78
DT	AL	WOODS	76
DT	ANGELO	BLACKSON	65
RE	JURRELL	CASEY	92
RE	KARL	KLUG	75
LOLB	DERRICK	MORGAN	87
LOLB	KAELIN	BURNETT	70
LOLB	DEIONTREZ	MOUNT	59
MLB	AVERY	WILLIAMSON	77
MLB	WESLEY	WOODYARD	77
MLB	ZACH	BROWN	75
MLB	ZAVIAR	GOODEN	68
ROLB	BRIAN	ORAKPO	87
ROLB	JONATHAN	MASSAQUOI	73
CB	JASON	MCCOURTY	86
CB	PERRISH	COX	79
CB	BLIDI	WREH-WILSON	72
CB	COTY	SENSABAUGH	69
CB	JEMEA	THOMAS	66
FS	MICHAEL	GRIFFIN	75
FS	MARQUESTON	HUFF	74
SS	DA'NORRIS	SEARCY	86
SS	DAIMION	STAFFORD	71
SS	CODY	PREWITT	65

SPECIAL TEAMS

POS	FIRST	LAST	OVR
K	RYAN	SUCCOP	79
KR	DEXTER	MCCLUSTER	73
KR	CLYDE	GATES	67
P	BRETT	KERN	88
PR	DEXTER	MCCLUSTER	73

BEST OFFENSIVE PLAYS

PRO TIPS

- These are the best two offensive plays in your playbook. They will get your playmakers in position to win you games.
- Pistol Y-Trips has so many options that Flood is just the start of your scheme.
- Marcus Mariota brings a new element to the offense; learn how to get the most out of it

BEST RUN — GUN DBLS Y-FLEX OFFSET–TITANS READ OPTION

SETUP:

- Learning to make the correct read on the handoff will determine your success with this play.
- This play mixed with PA Titans Combo will really make for a tough scheme to stop.

ADVANCED SETUP:

- Motion the TE to the right (optional).

RUNNING PLAYS

1ST DOWN	2ND AND SHORT	3RD AND SHORT	GOAL LINE	2ND AND LONG	3RD AND LONG
Singleback Ace Wing–HB Stretch	Singleback Ace Wing–HB Stretch	Weak Close–FB Dive	I-Form Tight Pair–FB Dive	Gun DBLS Y-Flex Offset–Titans Read Option	Gun Double Stack–Inside Zone
Singleback Ace Close–Zone Weak	Strong H TE Flip–Zone Split Lead	Singleback Wing Trips Open–Inside Zone Split	Goal Line–QB Sneak	Pistol Y-Trips–Inside Zone	Gun Trey Y-Flex–Read Option
I-Form Tight–Power O	Weak Close–HB Gut	Singleback Bunch Ace–Inside Zone Split	I-Form Tight Pair–FB Fake HB Flip	Gun Wing Trips Titan Wk–Y Lead Read Option	Gun Trey Open–HB Counter

INSIDE RUN | OUTSIDE RUN | SHOTGUN RUN | QB RUN

BEST PASS — PISTOL Y-TRIPS–FLOOD

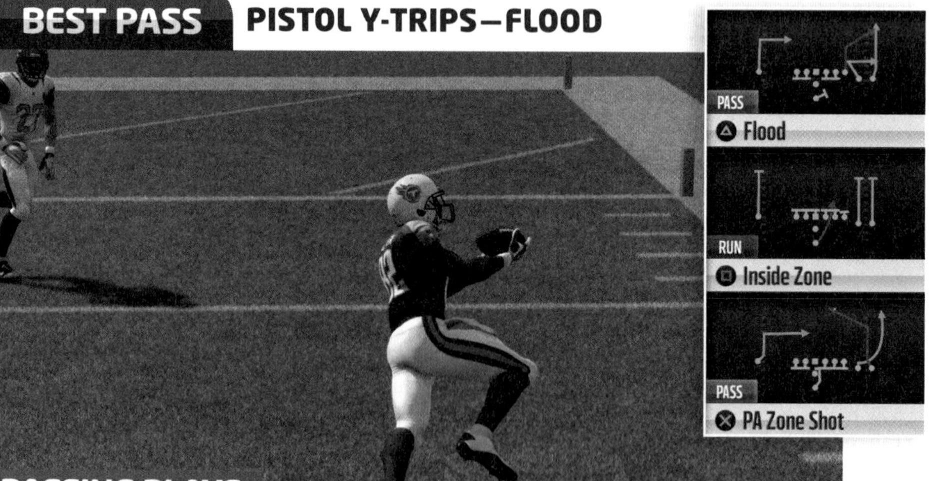

SETUP/READS:

- Against zone coverage, wait for the corner route to clear the flat zone and then throw a high pass.
- Against man-to-man coverage target the in route on the back side or wait for the slot to cut back outside.
- Against the blitz either leak the ball to the HB or block him and take a shot downfield.

ADVANCED SETUP:

- Flat or wheel the HB.
- Slant the slot WR (optional).

PASSING PLAYS

1ST DOWN	2ND AND SHORT	3RD AND SHORT	SHOT PLAYS	2ND AND LONG	3RD AND LONG
Gun Tight Flex–Cross	I-Form Tight–Y-Dig	Gun Dbls Y-Flex Offset–Angle Smash	Pistol Y-Trips–PA Zone Shot	Gun Wing Trips Titan Wk–Post N Cross	Singleback Ace Wing–Corner Strike
Singleback Ace Close–Tight Slots TE Angle	Strong H TE Flip–Texas	Gun Trey Y-Flex–PA WR Screen	I-Form Tight Pair–Goal Line Fade	Singleback Ace Pair Slot–PA Y-Drag Wheel	Singleback Bunch Ace–Verticals
Gun Trey Open–Trail Shake	Pistol Y-Trips–X Post	Gun Dbls Y-Flex Offset–HB Slip Screen	Gun Trips TE–PA Boot Shot	Pistol Y-Trips–PA All Go	Gun Empty Base Flex–Verticals

BASE PLAY | MAN BEATER | ZONE BEATER | BLITZ BEATER

BEST DEFENSIVE PLAYS

PRO TIPS

- If you want to win more games in *Madden NFL 16*, rely on these defensive plays to lock up the run and pass.
- The 3-3-5 Wide is a an excellent set for the Titans, especially with Jurrell Casey's pass-rush ability.
- The Pinch Buck 0 is best against runs from under center; it can be more risky against shotgun runs because of that formation's better passing ability.

BEST RUN D: 3-4 ODD–WILL BUCK 3 PRESS

- MAN — △ Cover 2 Man
- BLITZ — □ Will Buck 3 Press
- BLITZ — ✕ Pinch Dog 2 Press

SETUP:

- Calling QB contain on this play can keep your defenders wide and shut down runs like HB Counter.
- Brian Orakpo is a solid edge defender who doesn't need much help—send any extra defenders to the other side of the field.

PLAYER TO CONTROL:

- Either blitzing LB on the left of the screen

RUN DEFENSE

1ST DOWN	2ND AND SHORT	3RD AND SHORT	GOAL LINE	2ND AND LONG	3RD AND LONG
3-4 Solid–Cover 1 Robber	3-4 Odd–Sam Mike 1	3-4 Solid–Sting Pinch	Goal Line 5-4-2–Jam Cover 1	Nickel 2-4-5 Prowl–Cover 2 Man	Big Dime 1-4-6–Cover 1 Robber
3-4 Solid–Trio Sky Zone	3-4 Odd–Cover 3 Buzz	3-4 Solid–Clamp Double Go	Goal Line 5-4-2–Flat Buzz	Nickel 2-4-5 Prowl–Cover 2 Drop	Big Dime 1-4-6–Cover 3 Sky

MAN COVERAGE | ZONE COVERAGE | MAN BLITZ | ZONE BLITZ

BEST PASS D: NICKEL 3-3-5 WIDE–SAM WILL 3 BLITZ

- ZONE — △ Cover 3 Buzz
- MAN — □ Cover 1 Robber
- BLITZ — ✕ Sam Will 3 Blitz

SETUP:

- If you don't feel like you have a great matchup on the outside, consider adding an extra defender on a man assignment.
- Feel free to drop one of the edge blitzers into a flat zone, especially towards the open side of the field.
- Some teams that lack a power run game won't be able to beat this as a run defense. If so, stay in it.

PLAYER TO CONTROL:

- DT on the right of the screen

PASS DEFENSE

1ST DOWN	2ND AND SHORT	3RD AND SHORT	GOAL LINE	2ND AND LONG	3RD AND LONG
3-4 Under–Cover 2 Man	Nickel 3-3-5 Wide–1 QB Contain	Big Dime 2-3-6 Will–1 QB Contain	Goal Line 5-3-3–GL Man	Nickel 2-4-5 Dbl A Gap–Mid Blitz	Quarter 1-3-7–DB Strike
3-4 Under–Cover 4 Show 2	Nickel 3-3-5 Wide–Mike 3 Show 2	Big Dime 2-3-6 Will–Mike Edge 3 Seam	Goal Line 5-3-3–GL Zone	Nickel 2-4-5 Dbl A Gap–Buck Zone Blitz	Quarter 1-3-7–FZ 3 Sky

MAN COVERAGE | ZONE COVERAGE | MAN BLITZ | ZONE BLITZ

MINNESOTA VIKINGS

GAMEPLAY RATING 77

CONNECTED FRANCHISE MODE STRATEGY

CFM TEAM RATING: **85**
OFFENSE: **85**
DEFENSE: **91**
OFFENSIVE SCHEME: **Balanced**
DEFENSIVE SCHEME: **Attacking 4-3**
STRENGTHS: **HB, CB, FS, DL**
WEAKNESSES: **MLB, WR, LG**

2014 TEAM RANKINGS

3rd NFC North (7-9-0)
PASSING OFFENSE: **28th**
RUSHING OFFENSE: **14th**
PASSING DEFENSE: **7th**
RUSHING DEFENSE: **25th**

2014 TEAM LEADERS

PASSING: **Teddy Bridgewater: 2,919**
RUSHING: **Matt Asiata: 570**
RECEIVING: **Greg Jennings: 742**
TACKLES: **Robert Blanton: 106**
SACKS: **Everson Griffen: 12**
INTS: **Harrison Smith: 5**

KEY ADDITIONS

CB Terence Newman
HB DuJuan Harris
QB Mike Kafka

KEY ROOKIES

CB Trae Waynes
LB Eric Kendricks
DE Danielle Hunter

OWNER: **Zygi Wilf**
LEGACY SCORE: **175**

COACH: **Mike Zimmer**
LEVEL: **4**
LEGACY SCORE: **0**
OFFENSIVE SCHEME: **Power Run**
DEFENSIVE SCHEME: **Attacking 4-3**

OFFENSIVE SCOUTING REPORT

- QB Teddy Bridgewater had a solid rookie season and proved he has accuracy across all ranges of the field. Develop his throwing power to allow him to take shots downfield to your speedy WRs.
- HB Adrian Peterson will take all the pressure off the offense this season and should be allowed to carry the load. For the future, allow Jerick McKinnon the chance to spell Peterson. He showed some flashes of speed last season.
- The Vikings picked up speedy WR Mike Wallace, who has the ability to run every route in the playbook. He still has what it takes to run by defenders at times and will need to lead a young group. Work on improving the route running of Charles Johnson, Jarius Wright, and Cordarrelle Patterson if they are going to excel in this scheme. They all have the speed. This is a big season for Kyle Rudolph, who must justify a big contract. Let him become a go-to option on third down.

DEFENSIVE SCOUTING REPORT

- The Vikings' defensive line might have some trouble winning the trench battle against power run teams, but they will generate plenty of pressure in the passing game without blitzing anyone. Move DT Linval Joseph to wherever the point of attack is in the run game and he will slow it down.
- While rookie MLB Eric Kendricks is a scheme fit for the Vikings' defense, consider giving him some time to develop before he starts. Play mostly nickel coverage and allow young and athletic LB Anthony Barr to play next to Gerald Hodges.
- FS Harrison Smith has turned into a legit star with a nose for the football. Let him use his tremendous zone coverage to help out his teammates, who are all a perfect scheme fit for the Vikings.

SCHEDULE

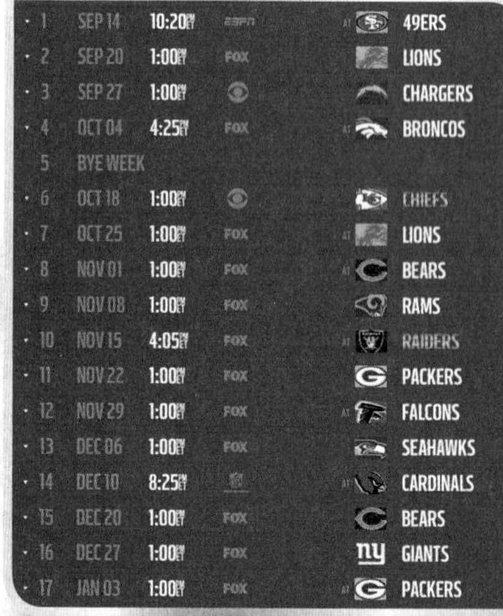

Week	Date	Time	Network		Opponent
1	SEP 14	10:20 PM ET	ESPN	AT	49ERS
2	SEP 20	1:00 PM ET	FOX		LIONS
3	SEP 27	1:00 PM ET			CHARGERS
4	OCT 04	4:25 PM ET	FOX	AT	BRONCOS
5	BYE WEEK				
6	OCT 18	1:00 PM ET			CHIEFS
7	OCT 25	1:00 PM ET	FOX	AT	LIONS
8	NOV 01	1:00 PM ET	FOX	AT	BEARS
9	NOV 08	1:00 PM ET	FOX		RAMS
10	NOV 15	4:05 PM ET	FOX	AT	RAIDERS
11	NOV 22	1:00 PM ET	FOX		PACKERS
12	NOV 29	1:00 PM ET	FOX	AT	FALCONS
13	DEC 06	1:00 PM ET	FOX		SEAHAWKS
14	DEC 10	8:25 PM ET		AT	CARDINALS
15	DEC 20	1:00 PM ET	FOX		BEARS
16	DEC 27	1:00 PM ET	FOX		GIANTS
17	JAN 03	1:00 PM ET	FOX	AT	PACKERS

KEY PLAYERS

KEY OFFENSIVE PLAYER

ADRIAN PETERSON #28

HB #28 HT 6'1" WT 217 COLLEGE Oklahoma EXP 8

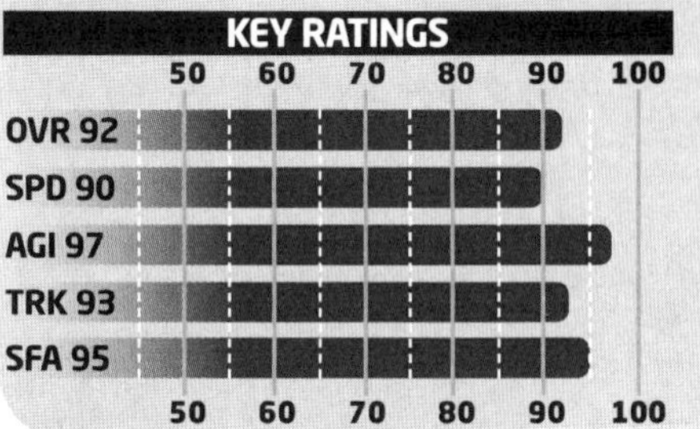

KEY RATINGS

- OVR 92
- SPD 90
- AGI 97
- TRK 93
- SFA 95

- Adrian Peterson is still an extremely physical runner, and the stiff arm is still his best move when taking on a tackler.
- Peterson's agility allows him to change holes after the handoff, which is unusual for a back with 88 Strength.

KEY DEFENSIVE PLAYER

HARRISON SMITH #22

FS #22 HT 6'2" WT 214 COLLEGE Notre Dame EXP 3

KEY RATINGS

- OVR 94
- SPD 86
- ACC 80
- PUR 90
- ZCV 92

- Smith is a transformative safety for the Vikings; he allows their CBs to take chances.
- Continue to improve on Smith's play recognition, which will allow you to focus on the SS position instead.

KEY ROOKIE

TRAE WAYNES #26

CB #26 HT 6'0" WT 186 COLLEGE Michigan St. EXP Rookie

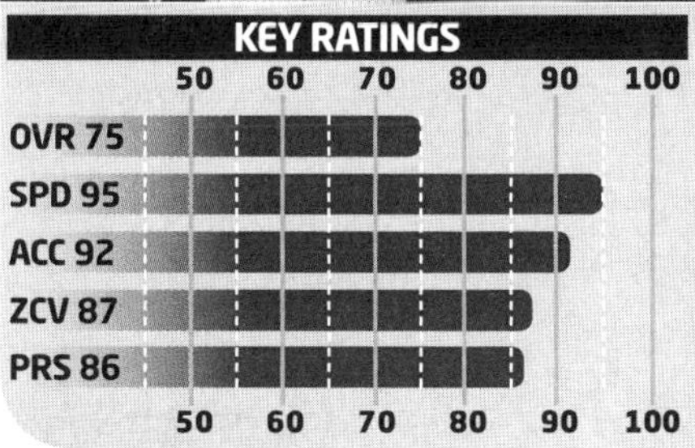

KEY RATINGS

- OVR 75
- SPD 95
- ACC 92
- ZCV 87
- PRS 86

- Waynes is just one of many great zone CBs for the Vikings. Use them all to blanket the field with their coverage.
- Agility is the first thing to improve for Waynes, which should help him be better in the rare times you call man coverage.

KEY SLEEPER

BRANDON WATTS #58

ROLB #58 HT 6'2" WT 231 COLLEGE Georgia Tech EXP 1

KEY RATINGS

- OVR 75
- SPD 91
- ACC 93
- POW 76
- PMV 64

- Watts needs to find a pass-rushing move quickly to take advantage of his speed off the edge.
- Pair Watts with Barr off the edge and you will have one of the fastest pass-rushing combos in the league.

OFFENSIVE DEPTH CHART

POS	FIRST	LAST	OVR
QB	TEDDY	BRIDGEWATER	82
QB	SHAUN	HILL	74
QB	MIKE	KAFKA	68
HB	ADRIAN	PETERSON	95
HB	JERICK	MCKINNON	76
HB	MATT	ASIATA	72
HB	DUJUAN	HARRIS	72
FB	ZACH	LINE	72
WR	MIKE	WALLACE	86
WR	CHARLES	JOHNSON	78
WR	JARIUS	WRIGHT	76
WR	CORDARRELLE	PATTERSON	73
WR	STEFON	DIGGS	71
WR	ADAM	THIELEN	71
TE	KYLE	RUDOLPH	81
TE	CHASE	FORD	75
TE	RHETT	ELLISON	74
LT	MATT	KALIL	73
LT	TYRUS	THOMPSON	64
LG	DAVID	YANKEY	73
LG	AUSTIN	SHEPHERD	62
C	JOHN	SULLIVAN	87
C	JOE	BERGER	77
RG	BRANDON	FUSCO	82
RG	BOBBY	VARDARO	65
RT	PHIL	LOADHOLT	85
RT	T.J.	CLEMMINGS	71
RT	MIKE	HARRIS	67

DEFENSIVE DEPTH CHART

POS	FIRST	LAST	OVR
LE	BRIAN	ROBISON	82
LE	JUSTIN	TRATTOU	67
LE	B.J.	DUBOSE	63
DT	SHARRIF	FLOYD	87
DT	LINVAL	JOSEPH	84
DT	TOM	JOHNSON	79
DT	SHAMAR	STEPHEN	70
DT	CHIGBO	ANUNOBY	69
RE	EVERSON	GRIFFEN	89
RE	SCOTT	CRICHTON	72
RE	DANIELLE	HUNTER	65
LOLB	ANTHONY	BARR	85
LOLB	GERALD	HODGES	80
MLB	ERIC	KENDRICKS	72
MLB	AUDIE	COLE	71
MLB	CASEY	MATTHEWS	66
ROLB	CHAD	GREENWAY	80
ROLB	MICHAEL	MAUTI	66
ROLB	BRANDON	WATTS	61
CB	XAVIER	RHODES	86
CB	CAPTAIN	MUNNERLYN	81
CB	TERENCE	NEWMAN	81
CB	JOSH	ROBINSON	78
CB	TRAE	WAYNES	75
FS	HARRISON	SMITH	93
FS	ANDREW	SENDEJO	75
SS	ROBERT	BLANTON	86
SS	ANTONE	EXUM JR.	71

SPECIAL TEAMS

POS	FIRST	LAST	OVR
K	BLAIR	WALSH	79
KR	CORDARRELLE	PATTERSON	73
KR	MARCUS	SHERELS	69
P	JEFF	LOCKE	66
PR	MARCUS	SHERELS	69

BEST OFFENSIVE PLAYS

PRO TIPS

- These are the best two offensive plays in your playbook. They will get your playmakers in position to win you games.
- The Vikings are one team that should commit to running the ball early in the game to set up your rollout fakes in the second half.
- The Vikings have some excellent Gun Empty formations that can be used to pick up short chunks of yards and to keep the chains moving.

BEST RUN: SINGLEBACK ACE PAIR TWINS—INSIDE ZONE SPLIT

SETUP:

- This run can open up huge holes in the middle of the line, so try to keep it inside for consistency.
- To help prevent fumbles, cover up the ball if the defense is swarming.

ADVANCED SETUP:

- Motion the outside TE one step left.

RUNNING PLAYS

1ST DOWN	2ND AND SHORT	3RD AND SHORT	GOAL LINE	2ND AND LONG	3RD AND LONG
Singleback Jumbo Pair—HB Stretch	Weak Pro—HB Inside	Strong Close—HB Dive	I-Form Pro—Inside Zone	Gun Ace Twins Offset—Read Option	Gun Trey Open—Inside Zone
Singleback Ace Close—HB Blunt Dive	Singleback Doubles—HB Misdirection	Singleback Jumbo Pair—HB Counter Wk	Goal Line—HB Sting	Gun Split Viking—Inside Zone Split	Gun Trey Y-Flex—QB Slot Option
Weak Pro—Inside Zone Split	Singleback Tight Doubles On—HB Zone Wk	Full House Normal Wide—HB Sweep	Goal Line—QB Sneak	Gun Split Viking—Shovel Option	Gun Trey Y-Flex—0 1 Trap

INSIDE RUN | OUTSIDE RUN | SHOTGUN RUN | QB RUN

BEST PASS: SINGLEBACK TIGHT DOUBLES ON—SHAKES

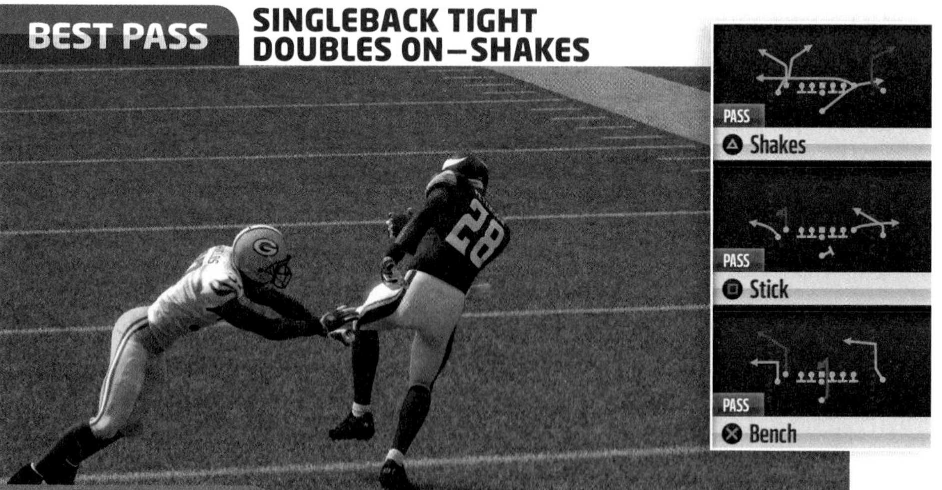

SETUP/READS:

- Against zone coverage, target either sideline route if the zones get pulled down by the flat. Otherwise, check down.
- Against man-to-man your underneath route combinations should create too much confusion for the defense to stick with.
- Vary the direction in which you release your HB to the flat to try to get him towards the most space available.

ADVANCED SETUP:

- Slant the far right WR (optional).

PASSING PLAYS

1ST DOWN	2ND AND SHORT	3RD AND SHORT	SHOT PLAYS	2ND AND LONG	3RD AND LONG
Gun Split Viking—Slot Post Angle	Gun Empty Bunch—Divide Wheel	Strong Close—WR DBL Outs	Gun Trey Y-Flex Wk—PA Cross Shot	Gun Ace Twins—PA Verts Shot	Singleback Ace Pair—TE Attack
Gun Double Flex—Deep Curl	Singleback Tight Doubles On—Shakes	Gun Trey Y-Flex Wk—PA Vikes Y Pop	Gun Trips TE Offset—PA Shot Crossers	Gnu Dbls Y-Flex Offset—Vikes Y Cross	Singleback Bunch—Four Verticals
Singleback Ace Pair Twins—Y-Go	Singleback Ace Close—Tight Slots TE Angle	I-Form Pro—Mid Attack	I-Form Pro—Vikings Fades	Gnu Dbls Y-Flex Offset—Fork Wheel	Gun Empty Base Flex—Verticals

BASE PLAY | MAN BEATER | ZONE BEATER | BLITZ BEATER

 For more plays and strategies for this team, visit your eGuide using the access code sheet provided.

BEST DEFENSIVE PLAYS

PRO TIPS

- If you want to win more games in *Madden NFL 16*, rely on these defensive plays to lock up the run and pass.
- The Vikings have a pretty stout front with just four defensive linemen in the game.
- The Vikings are best as a zone coverage team. Learn to use shading to really maximize your pre-snap options.

BEST RUN D: 46 NORMAL—COVER 2 INVERT

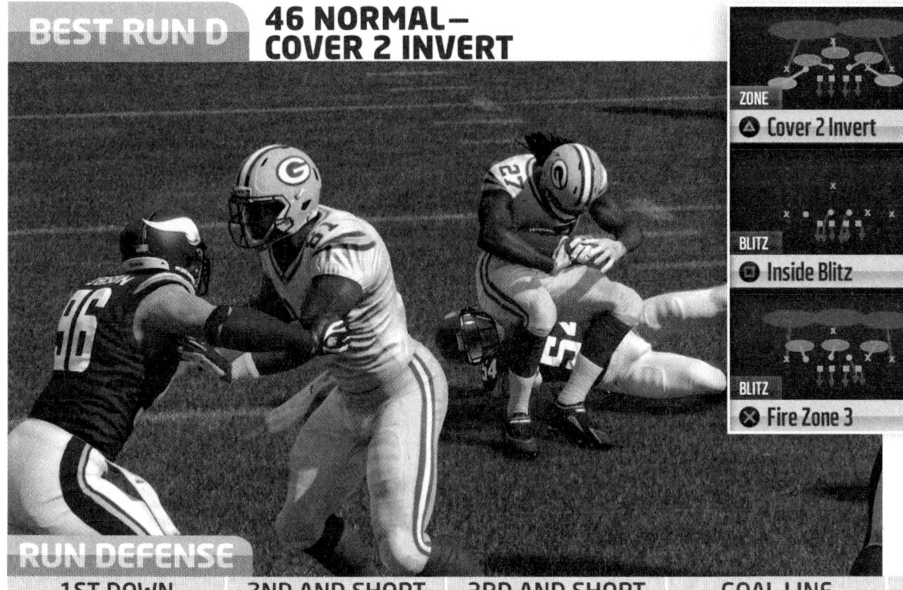

ZONE △ Cover 2 Invert

BLITZ □ Inside Blitz

BLITZ ⊗ Fire Zone 3

SETUP:

- Winning run defense starts with a numbers advantage in the box; bring the FS even closer to the line to spook your opponent.
- The Cover 2 Invert should be ample, but if your opponent brings out a heavy formation, call the Fire Zone 3.
- Your FS might not always make the play, but if he can take on blockers, it will free up a teammate to haul down the back.

PLAYER TO CONTROL:

- FS in a hook zone

RUN DEFENSE

1ST DOWN	2ND AND SHORT	3RD AND SHORT	GOAL LINE	2ND AND LONG	3RD AND LONG
4-3 Wide 9—1 QB Contain Spy	46 Normal—Cover 1 Hole	46 Normal—1 Rush Outside	Goal Line 5-4-2—Jam Cover 1	Nickel Double A Gap—Nickel Dog Meg	Nickel 3-3-5 Wide—Cover 2 Man
4-3 Wide 9—Cover 2 Invert	46 Normal—Cover 2 Invert	46 Normal—Zone Blitz	Goal Line 5-4-2—Flat Buzz	Nickel Double A Gap—Rush 3 Buzz	Nickel 3-3-5 Wide—Cover 4 Show 2

MAN COVERAGE | ZONE COVERAGE | MAN BLITZ | ZONE BLITZ

BEST PASS D: DIME NORMAL—FOX FZ PRESS

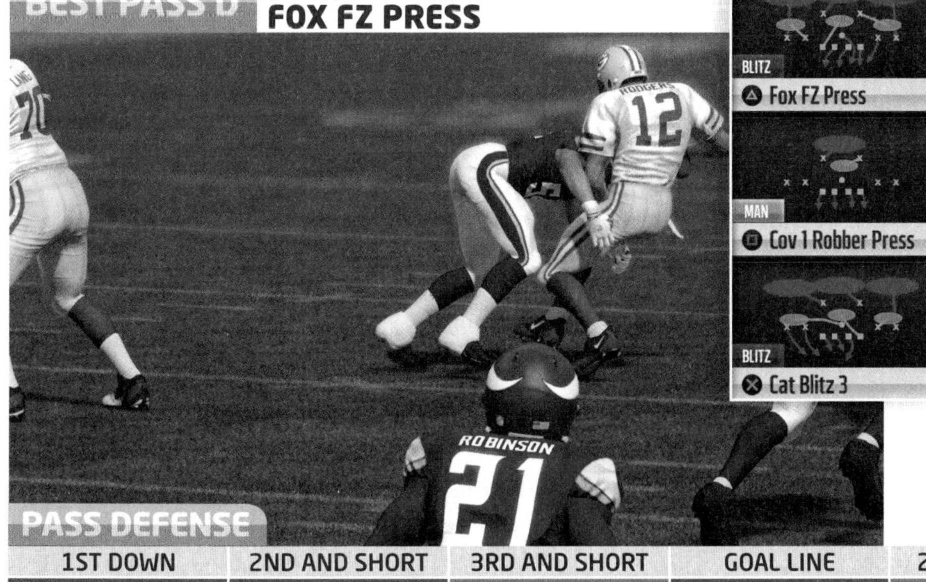

BLITZ △ Fox FZ Press

MAN □ Cov 1 Robber Press

BLITZ ⊗ Cat Blitz 3

SETUP:

- Getting Anthony Barr into the game with this formation is one of the smartest ways to maximize it.
- This play sends solid pressure off the right edge. Use it until your opponent starts to target the flat with quick passes.
- If the offense likes to keep extra backs and TEs in to block, this turns into an even better playcall.

PLAYER TO CONTROL:

- Hook zone on the left of the screen

PASS DEFENSE

1ST DOWN	2ND AND SHORT	3RD AND SHORT	GOAL LINE	2ND AND LONG	3RD AND LONG
46 Normal—1 QB Contain	46 Normal—1 QB Contain	Nickel 3-3-5 Wide—Mike Blitz 0	Goal Line 5-3-3—GL Man	Nickel Wide 9—Odd LB Dogs	Dime Normal—Mike Dime Blitz
46 Normal—Cover 2 Invert	46 Normal—Fire Zone 3	Nickel 3-3-5 Wide—Mike 3 Show 2	Goal Line 5-3-3—GL Zone	Nickel Wide 9—Odd Overload 3	Dime Normal—Fox FZ Press

MAN COVERAGE | ZONE COVERAGE | MAN BLITZ | ZONE BLITZ

FANTASY FOOTBALL

What Is Fantasy Football?

Do you have what it takes to put together a winning football franchise? **NFL.com Fantasy Football** gives you the perfect chance to find out. Fantasy football, like other fantasy games, puts you in the front office and on the sidelines as general manager and coach of your team. You select from a list of the best players in the NFL, and they compete on a weekly basis for your team. Their on-field performance drives your fantasy point total and overall success.

Specifically, fantasy football works like this: You decide what type of league you want to participate in, acquire a roster of players (either through a draft or through autopick assignment), then set your lineup each week during the season and watch as touchdowns, field goals, yards gained, sacks, interceptions, and much, much more generate fantasy points for or against your team. Whether you win or lose and climb or fall on the leaderboard all depends on how well you maximize the talent on your roster each week. Will you make a risky move to start that backup running back, or will you play it safe and keep your starting lineup consistent?

From prize-eligible NFL-Managed leagues to fully customizable Custom leagues, NFL.com provides ample options to start your fantasy season. Want to compete to win official NFL prizes, including trips to the Pro Bowl and Super Bowl XLIX? Join an NFL-Managed league, where you will go head-to-head against other NFL fans across the country for the right to be called a league champion. Or are you looking to fully customize your fantasy experience, from the league and scoring settings to the users you will compete with on a weekly basis? Create your Custom league today and invite friends, family, coworkers and anyone else to compete in a season-long fantasy battle on NFL.com. Exclusive NFL.com Fantasy Football features, including instant video highlights and free Fantasy Game Center Live Scoring, await in all NFL.com fantasy leagues.

Will your team earn the title of NFL.com Fantasy Football Champion this season? Find the right settings to suit your interests and start building your winning franchise today!

EXCLUSIVE FEATURES

- Free Live Scoring with Instant Video Highlights
- Free, Mobile Apps
- Upgraded Draft Client with iPad Support
- Expanded Mock Drafts
- Roster Options
- Fantasy Guru
- Ultimate Experience Leagues
- Advanced Stats and Data
- Alerts and Notifications
- League Power Rankings

UPGRADED FEATURES

- All-New Mobile Apps
- Fresh Look and Faster Gameplay
- Interactive Fantasy Genius Community
- Improved Research Section
- And More Coming Soon

Why Choose NFL.com Fantasy?

If you want football, then go to the NFL. You will experience the *only* fantasy football game with exclusive NFL access through Instant Video Highlights, Player Comparison Tool using SAP technology, and more. NFL.com Fantasy Football brings you closer to the sport you love, because here at the NFL, football is all we do.

Completely redesigned, the new NFL.com Fantasy Football experience was built from the ground up to suit all types of fantasy players, regardless of experience or skill. Fantasy rookies will enjoy the user-friendly experience, and fantasy football fanatics will enjoy ground-breaking features. Sign-up is easy, and NFL.com Fantasy Football is absolutely *free* to play.

Scoring Settings (NFL-Managed)

NFL-Managed leagues feature NFL.com default scoring and league settings, including standard roster sizes, starting positions, and head-to-head scoring. All NFL-Managed leagues are free to join, and team owners can opt-in to be eligible to win great prizes based on their season performance. NFL.com will act as league manager for NFL-Managed leagues, ensuring a fair, fun game for fantasy players of all skill levels. Users can join either Live Draft NFL-Managed leagues from the League Directory or create an Autopick team that will be placed in a league and drafted when you are ready.

These are the default scoring settings used in all NFL-Managed Leagues:

OFFENSE

- **Passing Yards: 1 point per 25 yards passing**
- **Passing Touchdowns: 4 points**
- **Interceptions: -2 points**
- **Rushing Yards: 1 point per 10 yards**
- **Rushing Touchdowns: 6 points**
- **Receiving Yards: 1 point per 10 yards**
- **Receiving Touchdowns: 6 points**
- **Fumble Recovered for a Touchdown: 6 points**
- **2-Point Conversions: 2 points**
- **Fumbles Lost: -2 points**

KICKING

- **PAT Made: 1 point**
- **FG Made (0-49 yards): 3 points**
- **FG Made (50+ yards): 5 points**

DEFENSE

- **Sacks: 1 point**
- **Interceptions: 2 points**
- **Fumbles Recovered: 2 points**
- **Safeties: 2 points**
- **Defensive Touchdowns: 6 points**
- **Kick and Punt Return Touchdowns: 6 points**
- **Points Allowed (0): 10 points**
- **Points Allowed (1-6): 7 points**
- **Points Allowed (7-13): 4 points**
- **Points Allowed (14-20): 1 points**
- **Points Allowed (21-27): 0 points**
- **Points Allowed (28-34): -1 points**
- **Points Allowed (35+): -4 points**

Head-to-Head Scoring Format

All NFL.com Fantasy Football leagues feature head-to-head scoring. As in the games that take place across the NFL each Sunday, your team will be matched up against another team within your league. Similar to an NFL game being decided on the field with the team scoring the most points earning a win, your fantasy matchup behaves accordingly.

Based on your NFL-Managed league scoring settings, your team will earn points based on the actual statistics and results played out in the NFL that week. If your team earns more points than your opponent, you earn a win in the league standings. Fewer points? Take a loss. And if your game ends in a tie (you guessed it) it's a tie in the overall standings.

League Settings

These default league settings are used in all NFL-Managed leagues.

- **Teams: 10**
- **Divisions: None**
- **League Viewable by Public: No**
- **Undroppable List: NFL.com Fantasy Default List**
- **Maximum Acquisitions per Season: No Maximum**
- **Maximum Acquisitions per Week: No Maximum**
- **Trade Limit per Season: No Limit**
- **Trade Review Type: League Votes**
- **Waiver Period: 1 Day**
- **Waiver Type: Weekly Reset, Inverse Order of Standings**
- **Post-Draft Players: Follow Waiver Rules**
- **Roster Lock Type: Players Lock at Individual Game Time**
- **2015 Keeper Settings: None**
- **Starting Positions and Roster Size: Nine Starters (QB, RB, RB, WR, WR, W/R Flex, TE, K, DEF) and Six Bench Players**

NFL-Managed Draft Types

Live Online Draft and Autopick Draft are the only draft types used in NFL-Managed Leagues.

LIVE DRAFT

The Live Online Draft feature allows you to select a full fantasy team, *live*, round-by-round in an interactive environment. The draft client features comprehensive stats, analysis, and chat functionality, all packaged in a user-friendly interface. In this draft application you can rank your players in real time, adding them to a queue that will update as players are taken by other teams in the league. You can search for players or filter the available players by position so that you can make fast, easy, and informed decisions to fill out your roster. When you have found the perfect selection, click "Draft Now" and the player you selected will be assigned to your team. You can track all of the action by round and by individual team, all in one place inside the draft application.

AUTOPICK DRAFT

The Autopick Draft operates based on NFL.com fantasy experts' default rankings or a team owner's established pre-rankings. This draft type is an excellent choice for beginners as well as for leagues that can't agree on a live draft time. In an Autopick Draft, players are assigned to your team automatically. NFL.com helps you fill your roster, either by going strictly off your Pre-Rank Draft list and Excluded Players list or by selecting the best available player at an open position of need on your roster. Select a day and time for your Autopick Draft, and that is all you need to produce a league full of fantasy teams for owners to manage as they see fit.

TOP 5 Must-Have Players

5 DEANDRE HOPKINS (WR), HOUSTON TEXANS

Hopkins is entering the season when he could potentially explode into a superstar and household name. Since veteran WR Andre Johnson left in free agency, Hopkins will have all the opportunities he can handle. All signs, including his 74 catches last season, point to him being able to handle it, and he just needs to increase his TDs to make him a must-have fantasy asset.

4 RUSSELL WILSON (QB), SEATTLE SEAHAWKS

QB Russell Wilson added a new weapon in the off-season in TE Jimmy Graham, who is looking to rebound with a big season. Wilson now has some excellent threats in the red zone and should see his passing totals increase. Wilson has slowly developed from a QB who can manage games to one who can fully take them over. The Seahawks still have all the pieces, and Wilson also racks up yardage with his legs, which is a bonus. If you don't land Luck, Rodgers, or Romo, Wilson is a great option.

3 JULIO JONES (WR), ATLANTA FALCONS

Julio Jones had an excellent rebound season last year and proved he is worth your consideration as a top fantasy wideout. His pairing with QB Matt Ryan makes him a consistent option, and he should get more chances to cash in on TDs this season. When selecting Jones, you should expect over 100 catches once again and hopefully double-digit scores to make it really pay off.

2 BRANDIN COOKS (WR), NEW ORLEANS SAINTS

The New Orleans Saints always put up huge passing numbers, led by QB Drew Brees. This season, they won't have TE Jimmy Graham or WR Kenny Stills to catch passes, so somebody will need to pick up the slack. The main candidate is WR Brandin Cooks, who should be a breakout candidate and not someone you will need to spend too early of a selection on. This is Cooks's big change to capitalize, and you want to buy before he hits it big.

1 DEZ BRYANT (WR), DALLAS COWBOYS

The Cowboys' secret ingredient is their offensive line, as it makes everything so much easier. It creates big holes in the running game and also gives QB Tony Romo time to create in the pocket. While most defenses can't cover Dez Bryant, no defense can cover him when he has time to get free downfield when a play breaks down. He has the full trust of his QB in the red zone, and his ability to consistently haul in touchdowns makes him a must-have player.

Top 5 Sleepers

5 DAVANTE ADAMS (WR), GREEN BAY PACKERS

The Green Bay Packers always seem to sneak a sleeper player onto this list, and with good reason. QB Aaron Rodgers can seemingly turn any player into a star. Last season, Jarrett Boykin came up a little short of expectations, but WR Davante Adams showed some flashes. This could be his year to explode and help out this already-loaded WR corps. While Jordy Nelson and Randall Cobb will always be the main targets, Rodgers and the Packers' offense put up plenty of passing stats to go around.

4 BISHOP SANKEY (RB), TENNESSEE TITANS

Sankey was listed on most sleeper and top rookie lists last season but never quite became a top performer. This year, his competition in the backfield is gone and the job will be his to win. With a year under his belt, this could be the season that Sankey lives up to his projections from last year. The best part is that the expectations have calmed, and he should be available for a reasonable value.

3 TEDDY BRIDGEWATER (QB), MINNESOTA VIKINGS

During his rookie season, QB Teddy Bridgewater showed excellent promise even without star HB Adrian Peterson in the lineup. Bridgewater got plenty of experience and proved he could consistently complete passes and keep drives going. With more time to develop this off-season, Bridgewater and the Vikings should continue to improve, and the numbers could be solid with a full season of games. While Bridgewater may not crack the top 5 quite yet, he should be pretty consistent and should be a great player against the right defense.

2 MARTAVIS BRYANT (WR), PITTSBURGH STEELERS

Martavis Bryant is another talent that we projected for a stellar rookie campaign last year. While he got out of the gate slowly, he rewarded owners by proving he could make huge plays and find the end zone. This year, a full season should really amplify those numbers, and while defenses will be more aware of him and his big frame, Pittsburgh has too many weapons to focus only on him. Expect Bryant to be the benefactor of stellar WR Antonio Brown lining up next to him.

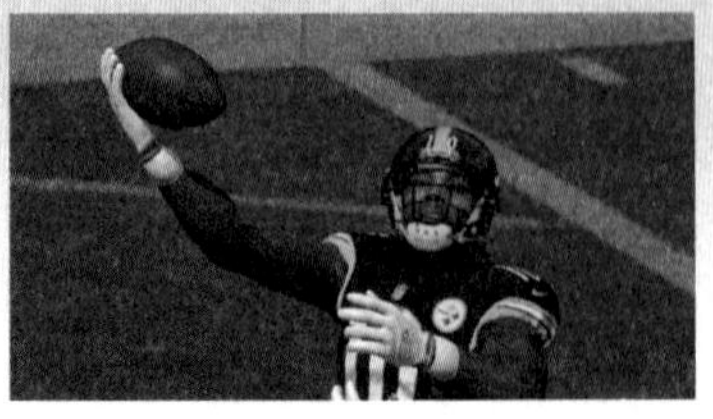

1 NELSON AGHOLOR (WR), PHILADELPHIA EAGLES

The Eagles' offense has put up big numbers both running and passing the ball since the debut of coach Chip Kelly. This season, they should continue to have balance and will rely on rookie WR Nelson Agholor to fill in the production of veteran WR Jeremy Maclin, who left in free agency. Kelly has already proven that a rookie WR can post big numbers in his system—WR Jordan Matthews had a great season last year.

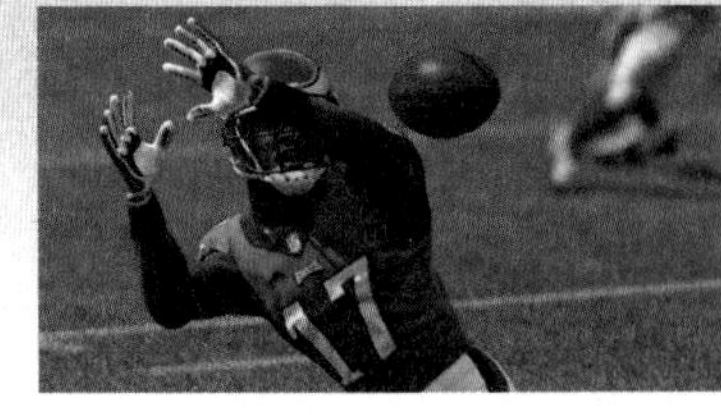

TOP 5 Overrated Players

5 DREW BREES (QB), NEW ORLEANS SAINTS

Drew Brees has been a top fantasy QB for what feels like the last decade. The Saints' QB has always put up huge numbers in a pass-heavy scheme that can turn seemingly average players into stars. While the yardage and completion percentage was there last season, the TD/INT ratio approached a more mortal 2/1. Brees also lost his main red zone target in TE Jimmy Graham, which could also hurt his numbers. Don't take Brees off your board, but don't select him based on past performance only.

4 LESEAN MCCOY (RB), BUFFALO BILLS

McCoy was good but not great in his first season after winning the rushing title. Now, he will be taking handoffs in Buffalo rather than Philadelphia and must prove he can get back to that level of performance. Buffalo needs to show they have a QB who can take the pressure off the run game; otherwise, yards may be tough for McCoy. Let someone else draft McCoy, and once he gets settled in the scheme, look for a mid-season trade if you think he is going to hit his stride.

3 DEMARCO MURRAY (RB), PHILADELPHIA EAGLES

Murray delivered a monster fantasy season last year and should be high atop most draft boards. The key will be staying healthy and learning to fit in a new scheme, because he left Dallas for Philadelphia. Dallas has an excellent offensive line, so it will be interesting to see if Murray can deliver another huge season. Philly has some great depth in the backfield and a versatile scheme, so don't expect him to carry the full load again this season.

2 OWEN DANIELS (TE), DENVER BRONCOS

Daniels had a good season in Baltimore last year and will now be tasked with filling in for TE Julius Thomas in Denver. Daniels is a legit option but must prove he can be explosive and stay healthy. Most of your league members will be eyeing him, so try to grab his teammate, Virgil Green, who could deliver big value. QB Peyton Manning makes any receiving option a potential fantasy stud, so take the player with the most upside.

1 LEGARRETTE BLOUNT (HB), NEW ENGLAND PATRIOTS

Blount delivered big-time performances for the Patriots last season in some crucial games. Although he should be the option for the Patriots on running downs, nobody can be certain how many attempts that will deliver. New England is known for keeping a good rotation of backs and picked up some good pass catchers to fill in for Shane Vereen, who left during free agency and was a staple on third down. Blount is best when he is under the radar, so only grab him with the right expectations.

Top 5 Rookies

5 KEVIN WHITE (WR), CHICAGO BEARS

Kevin White is in an excellent position from a fantasy football perspective. He is a talented rookie who will get a chance early with the departure of WR Brandon Marshall. However, defenses will mainly be worried about his teammate, WR Alshon Jeffery. This could mean big numbers if QB Jay Cutler, who still has a big arm, can get the offense back on track.

4 T.J. YELDON (RB), JACKSONVILLE JAGUARS

The Jaguars made Yeldon their second-round pick and hope to pair him with QB Blake Bortles to help turn the franchise around. While the Jaguars do have a solid stable of backs, Yeldon has the talent to get the bulk of the carries during his rookie season. In a point-per-reception (PPR) league, Yeldon should be even more valuable, as he should be an every-down back who can catch some passes out of the backfield.

3 JAMEIS WINSTON (QB), TAMPA BAY BUCCANEERS

Winston was the number one overall selection in the draft and is the top QB on our list. His big arm fits perfectly with his big targets on the outside, including WR Mike Evans. During his rookie season, Evans was a TD scoring machine in the red zone and should give Winston a big target that he can trust. The Bucs may not make a playoff run, but they should certainly be more competitive this season, and Winston will be a big part of it.

2 MELVIN GORDON (RB), SAN DIEGO CHARGERS

Gordon was the top back in college football last season and even finished second for the Heisman trophy. The Chargers moved up two spots in the draft to select him, and they will need him to deliver after losing RB Ryan Mathews in free agency. San Diego has an excellent leader at QB in Philip Rivers, who always has the Chargers near the top of the rankings. Look for Gordon to get off to a good start, because he is going to a team that consistently wins more than half its games.

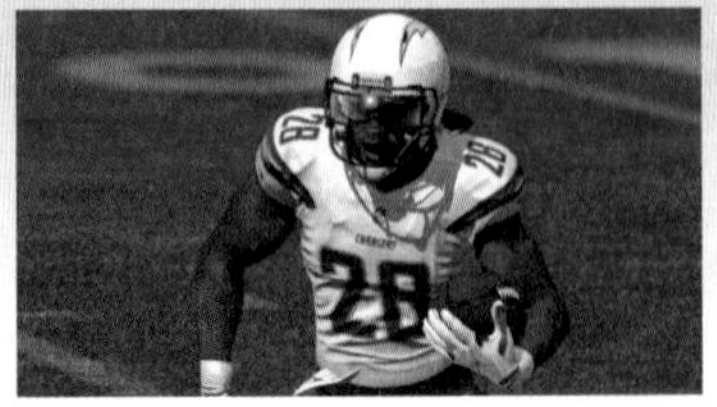

1 AMARI COOPER (WR), OAKLAND RAIDERS

Last season, rookie WR Odell Beckham Jr. exploded on the field and even onto the cover of *Madden NFL 16*. While it is hard to imagine another rookie WR making those incredible plays, the statistical production is possible. Amari Cooper joins the Raiders, and although they don't have an explosive offense, they do have a young QB who needs to find a go-to option at receiver. Oakland struggled to run the ball last season, so they will need the passing game to help take the pressure off. Keep an eye on this combo early in camp to see if they can develop some chemistry that could lead to numbers like Bills' WR Sammy Watkins posted last season.

Fantasy Football 2015 Mock Draft

QB RB WR TE PK DEF

Rnd	Player 1	Player 2	Player 3	Player 4	Player 5	Player 6	Player 7	Player 8	Player 9	Player 10
1	JAMAAL CHARLES RB (KC)	EDDIE LACY RB (GB)	ADRIAN PETERSON RB (MIN)	LE'VEON BELL RB (PIT)	ANTONIO BROWN WR (PIT)	ARIAN FOSTER RB (HOU)	MARSHAWN LYNCH RB (SEA)	MATT FORTE HB (CHI)	AARON RODGERS QB (GB)	LESEAN MCCOY RB (BUF)
2	ANDREW LUCK QB (IND)	JULIO JONES WR (ATL)	JORDY NELSON WR (GB)	DEMARYIUS THOMAS WR (DEN)	ODELL BECKHAM JR. WR (NYG)	C.J. ANDERSON RB (DEN)	DEZ BRYANT WR (DAL)	CALVIN JOHNSON WR (DET)	ROB GRONKOWSKI TE (NE)	JEREMY HILL RB (CIN)
3	T.Y. HILTON WR (IND)	DEMARCO MURRAY RB (DAL)	A.J. GREEN WR (CIN)	ALSHON JEFFERY WR (CHI	JUSTIN FORSETT RB (BAL)	RANDALL COBB WR (GB)	MIKE EVANS WR (TB)	MARK INGRAM RB (NO)	LAMAR MILLER RB (MIA)	KELVIN BENJAMIN WR (CAR)
4	JOIQUE BELL RB (DET)	JORDAN MATTHEWS WR (PHI)	CARLOS HYDE RB (SF)	BRANDIN COOKS WR (NO)	JONATHAN STEWART RB (CAR)	RUSSELL WILSON QB (SEA)	ALFRED MORRIS RB (WAS)	JIMMY GRAHAM TE (SEA)	EMMANUEL SANDERS WR (DEN)	DEANDRE HOPKINS WR (HOU)
5	ANDRE ELLINGTON RB (ARI)	PEYTON MANNING QB (DEN)	FRANK GORE RB (IND)	LATAVIUS MURRAY RB (OAK)	JULIAN EDELMAN WR (NE)	DESEAN JACKSON WR (WAS)	DREW BREES QB (NO)	MATT RYAN QB (ATL)	JARVIS LANDRY WR (MIA)	SAMMY WATKINS WR (BUF)
6	AMARI COOPER WR (OAK)	GREG OLSEN TE (CAR)	TOM BRADY QB (NE)	TONY ROMO QB (DAL)	RYAN TANNEHILL QB (MIA)	KEVIN WHITE WR (CHI)	MELVIN GORDON RB (SD)	DARREN MCFADDEN RB (DAL)	ANDRE JOHNSON WR (IND)	MATTHEW STAFFORD QB (DET)
7	TRAVIS KELCE TE (KC)	KEENAN ALLEN WR (SD)	JULIUS THOMAS TE (JAC)	DWAYNE ALLEN TE (IND)	ANTONIO GATES TE (SD)	COBY FLEENER TE (IND)	MARTELLUS BENNETT TE (CHI)	BRANDON LAFELL WR (NE)	RASHAD JENNINGS RB (NYG)	CHARLES CLAY TE (BUF)
8	RANDY BULLOCK PK (HOU)	DAN CARPENTER PK (BUF)	ARIZONA DEFENSE DEF (ARI)	GREEN BAY DEFENSE DEF (GB)	ADAM VINATIERI PK (IND)	CODY PARKEY PK (PHI)	STEPHEN GOSTKOWSKI PK (NE)	HOUSTON DEFENSE DEF (HOU)	BUFFALO DEFENSE DEF (BUF)	SEATTLE DEFENSE DEF (SEA)
9	PHILADELPHIA DEFENSE DEF (PHI)	BALTIMORE DEFENSE DEF (BAL	DAN BAILEY PK (DAL)	MATT BRYANT PK (ATL)	NEW ENGLAND DEFENSE DEF (NE)	ST. LOUIS DEFENSE DEF (STL)	INDIANAPOLIS DEFENSE DEF (IND)	JUSTIN TUCKER PK (BAL)	MASON CROSBY PK (GB)	NICK FOLK PK (NYJ)
10	JOSEPH RANDLE HB (DAL)	CAM NEWTON QB (CAR)	CHRIS IVORY RB (NYJ)	TORREY SMITH WR (SF)	GIOVANI BERNARD RB (CIN)	TODD GURLEY RB (STL)	JEREMY MACLIN WR (KC)	PHILIP RIVERS QB (SD	BEN ROETHLISBERGER QB (PIT)	LEGARRETTE BLOUNT RB (NE)
11	T.J. YELDON RB (JAC)	C.J. SPILLER RB (NO)	GOLDEN TATE WR (DET)	VINCENT JACKSON WR (TB)	BRANDON MARSHALL WR (NYJ)	STEVE SMITH WR (BAL)	ELI MANNING QB (NYG)	BRESHAD PERRIMAN WR (BAL)	STEVAN RIDLEY RB (NYJ)	JAY CUTLER QB (CHI)
12	NICK FOLES QB (STL)	FRED JACKSON RB (BUF)	TEDDY BRIDGEWATER QB (MIN)	COLIN KAEPERNICK QB (SF)	CARSON PALMER QB (ARI)	JOE FLACCO QB (BAL)	DEANGELO WILLIAMS RB (PIT)	RYAN MATHEWS RB (PHI)	TRE MASON RB (STL)	JAELEN STRONG WR (HOU
13	RODDY WHITE WR (ATL)	MICHAEL FLOYD WR (ARI)	CHARLES JOHNSON WR (MIN)	NELSON AGHOLOR WR (PHI)	KENDALL WRIGHT WR (TEN)	MICHAEL CRABTREE WR (OAK)	CODY LATIMER WR (DEN)	MIKE WALLACE WR (MIN)	ISAIAH CROWELL RB (CLE)	JOHN BROWN WR (ARI)
14	DORIAL GREEN-BECKHAM WR (TEN)	DAVANTE PARKER WR (MIA)	DEVONTA FREEMAN RB (ATL)	TERRANCE WEST RB (CLE)	CHARLES SIMS RB (TB)	DAVID JOHNSON RB (ARI)	VICTOR CRUZ WR (NG)	BOBBY RAINEY RB (TB)	DONTE MONCRIEF WR (IND)	TEVIN COLEMAN RB (ATL)
15	ALFRED BLUE RB (HOU)	SHANE VEREEN RB (NYG)	BISHOP SANKEY RB (TEN)	ANDRE WILLIAMS RB (NYG)	DELANIE WALKER TE (TEN)	JORDAN CAMERON TE (MIA)	BRANDEN OLIVER RB (SD)	KENNY STILLS WR (MIA)	ALLEN ROBINSON WR (JAX)	LORENZO TALIAFERRO RB (BAL)

Fantasy Football 2015 Draft Guide

Here is a handy chart to bring to your fantasy draft so you are ready to build a great team. Make sure to take your time, stay focused, and find great value. Check out NFL.com for even more rankings

QUARTERBACKS

QB	PLAYER	TEAM	BYE WEEK	TD PROJECTIONS	PROJECTED POINTS
		LOCKS			
1	Aaron Rodgers	Packers	7	41	368
2	Andrew Luck	Colts	10	39	353
3	Russell Wilson	Seahawks	9	30	335
4	Ben Roethlisberger	Steelers	11	31	300
5	Matt Ryan	Falcons	10	29	286
		OVERVALUED			
1	Peyton Manning	Broncos	7	35	296
2	Drew Brees	Saints	11	33	291
3	Tony Romo	Cowboys	6	32	280
4	Joe Flacco	Ravens	9	27	255
5	Carson Palmer	Cardinals	9	25	239
		UNDERVALUED			
1	Cam Newton	Panthers	5	26	285
2	Philip Rivers	Chargers	10	31	275
3	Matt Stafford	Lions	9	27	273
4	Eli Manning	Giants	11	27	251
5	Colin Kaepernick	49ers	10	22	248
		SLEEPERS			
1	Ryan Tannehill	Dolphins	5	27	275
2	Derek Carr	Raiders	6	20	217
3	Jameis Winston	Buccaneers	6	20	209
4	Teddy Bridgewater	Vikings	5	19	217
5	Sam Bradford	Eagles	8	25	225

HALFBACKS

HB	PLAYER	TEAM	BYE WEEK	TOTAL TDS	PROJECTED POINTS
		LOCKS			
1	Eddie Lacy	Packers	7	12	244
2	Adrian Peterson	Vikings	5	15	244
3	Jamaal Charles	Chiefs	9	12	228
4	Matt Forte	Bears	7	10	210
5	Marshawn Lynch	Seahawks	9	12	215
		OVERVALUED			
1	LeGarrette Blount	Patriots	4	12	239
2	DeMarco Murray	Eagles	7	10	200
3	C.J. Anderson	Broncos	7	11	206
4	Alfred Morris	Redskins	8	8	189
5	Rashad Jennings	Giants	11	7	175
		UNDERVALUED			
1	Joique Bell	Lions	9	7	173
2	Justin Forsett	Ravens	9	10	198
3	Darren McFadden	Dallas	6	9	177
4	Carlos Hyde	49ers	10	6	138
5	Lamar Miller	Dolphins	5	5	135
		SLEEPERS			
1	Tevin Coleman	Falcons	10	5	106
2	T.J. Yeldon	Jaguars	8	6	115
3	Melvin Gordon	Chargers	10	5	123
4	Duke Johnson	Browns	11	3	87
5	David Cobb	Titans	4	6	89

WIDE RECEIVERS

WR	PLAYER	TEAM	BYE WEEK	PROJECTED PTS
		LOCKS		
1	Dez Bryant	Cowboys	6	226
2	Calvin Johnson	Lions	9	218
3	Demaryius Thomas	Broncos	7	216
4	Julio Jones	Falcons	10	207
5	Jordy Nelson	Packers	7	209
		OVERVALUED		
1	Antonio Brown	Steelers	11	226
2	Odell Beckham Jr.	Giants	11	208
3	DeAndre Hopkins	Texans	9	186
4	Jordan Matthews	Eagles	8	180
5	Jeremy Maclin	Chiefs	9	157
		UNDERVALUED		
1	Jarvis Landry	Dolphins	5	137
2	Michael Floyd	Cardinals	9	130
3	Keenan Allen	Chargers	10	114
4	Kendall Wright	Titans	4	109
5	A.J. Green	Bengals	7	194
		SLEEPERS		
1	Davante Adams	Packers	7	82
2	Kevin White	Bears	7	125
3	Nelson Agholor	Eagles	8	103
4	Martavis Bryant	Steelers	11	96
5	Jaelen Strong	Texans	9	91

TIGHT ENDS

TE	PLAYER	TEAM	BYE WEEK	PROJECTED PTS
		LOCKS		
1	Rob Gronkowski	Patriots	4	173
2	Jimmy Graham	Seahawks	9	141
3	Greg Olsen	Panthers	5	137
4	Julius Thomas	Jaguars	8	120
5	Travis Kelce	Chiefs	9	136
		OVERVALUED		
1	Antonio Gates	Chargers	10	111
2	Dwayne Allen	Colts	10	96
3	Vernon Davis	49ers	10	90
4	Charles Clay	Bills	8	89
5	Jared Cook	Rams	6	79
		UNDERVALUED		
1	Owen Daniels	Broncos	7	102
2	Maxx Williams	Ravens	9	80
3	Kyle Rudolph	Vikings	5	77
4	Martellus Bennett	Bears	7	93
5	Heath Miller	Steelers	11	86
		SLEEPERS		
1	Josh Hill	Saints	11	75
2	Garrett Graham	Texans	9	64
3	Mychal Rivera	Raiders	6	65
4	Eric Ebron	Lions	9	71
5	Levine Toilolo	Falcons	10	39

DEFENSE

DEF	TEAM	BYE WEEK	PROJECTED POINTS
	DEFENSIVE LOCKS		
1	Seahawks	9	165
2	Texans	9	170
3	Bills	8	165
4	Chiefs	9	127
5	Rams	6	157
	DEFENSIVE SPOT STARTERS		
1	Jets	5	92
2	Panthers	5	107
3	Falcons	10	90
4	Raiders	6	68
5	Browns	11	113

KICKERS

	PLAYER	TEAM	BYE WEEK	PROJECTED POINTS
		KICKER LOCKS		
1	Stephen Gostkowski	Patriots	4	152
2	Adam Vinatieri	Colts	10	148
3	Cody Parkey	Eagles	8	146
4	Mason Crosby	Packers	7	144
5	Dan Bailey	Cowboys	6	143
		KICKER SPOT STARTERS		
1	Sebastian Janikowski	Raiders	6	106
2	Robbie Gould	Bears	7	109
3	Blair Walsh	Vikings	5	114
4	Greg Zuerlein	Rams	6	112
5	Mike Nugent	Bengals	7	115

APPENDIX / GLOSSARY

Many players watch football on Sunday and quickly learn the rules and strengths of the players. *Madden NFL 16* is the most authentic simulation of football action, and there is plenty to learn even for a veteran player. Start with the basics and quickly add a few new adjustments to your game each week. Keep this page as a reference to make sure you understand the basics of football. The Skills Trainer is your best friend when it comes to learning all the mechanics in *Madden NFL 16*. There is also a list of full list of controls for each situation in the Game Settings menu.

A Gap—The gaps in the offensive line between the center and the guards are the A gaps. There is one to the right and one to the left. The fastest way to the QB is through the A gap since it's right up the middle.

Aggressive Catch – This catch mechanic allows computer players to go up and attack the ball at its highest point. It can be triggered manually by using Ⓨ (Xbox) or △ (PS) when the ball is in the air; you do not need to be clicked on the receiver.

Audible/Audibling—The act of coming to the line and then changing your play. If you call something in the huddle and get to the line of scrimmage and realize the defense is doing something different than you expected, you want to call an audible. This allows you to change your play to something you think will work better. You can set up to five audibles before the game to make sure you are ready for any situation.

B Gap—The gaps in the offensive line between the guards and tackles are the B gaps. There is one on each side of the line, and the B gap is the second quickest way to get pressure (after the A gap).

Blitz—On offense, the defense may look to blitz you by bringing more defenders towards your QB than you can block. On defense, you blitz by rushing more players at the QB than your opponent can block. This leaves your coverage vulnerable, but you may force the offense into a bad decision or get a sack.

Block a Halfback—Blocking a halfback is done by putting a player behind the line into a blocking hot route. This will help if you sense a blitz coming at your offense and want your HB to stay in and block.

Blue Route—This is a "block-and-release" route, which tells your offensive player (whose route is blue) to help block before releasing out on his route for a pass.

The Box—The area on defense before the snap where the defensive line and LBs line up. Looking at "the box" can help you decide if the defense is defending a run and has "eight defenders in the box" or not.

Bunch Set—Three players stacked tightly together on one-half of the field makes a bunch set. A bunch is great for flooding certain areas of the field. An example is Ace Bunch.

C gap—The C gap refers to the offensive line and is just outside of either tackle. It can be thought of as "the edge"; however, if a TE lines up there, it becomes another gap like the A or B gap. This is the slowest way to get pressure on the QB and generally is where offensive lines want to allow rushers.

Check Down—To dump off a short pass to the halfback or last option on a play, especially after seeing that your other options are covered.

Chew Clock—This setting in the play-calling screen allows you to run off additional seconds on the clock in between snaps. This speeds up the end of a game when the score isn't close.

Clicking onto a Player—This is the act of switching your player mid-play to control someone close to the action. "I clicked onto the WR and tried to make the catch."

Concept—A specific set of routes that work together to beat a specific defense. For example, a mesh concept is having two crossing drag routes on a play.

Conservative Catch—A catch mechanic that allows a receiver to focus on catching the ball and securing it rather than picking up more yards after the catch. This is a smart idea on the sideline and near the back of the end zone.

Depth Chart—The area of the game where you set your lineup. Access this by pressing the Pause menu to set which players play where.

Draw—This is a run play that pretends the offense is passing. The QB drops back and the receivers start to run routes. Once the defense is fooled, the QB hands off to the running back, who looks for open running lanes.

Dropping a Lineman—Placing a defender on the line of scrimmage into a zone assignment. This is most common with a zone blitz play.

Empty Set—A common formation with an empty set is Gun Empty. The backfield is "empty" because there are five WRs in on the play.

Flat—The area of the field near the sideline in line with the line of scrimmage. The most common term is a "pass to the flat," which means a short pass to the halfback who is running towards the sideline from out of the backfield.

Flood—When you send more receivers into a certain area of the field than the opponent has coverage. One example is Four Verticals against a Cover 3 defense. You have four receivers downfield and the opponent only has three defenders deep—therefore one must be open.

Formation—The formation is how players line up before the snap of the football. There are offensive formations and defensive formations. Singleback and Gun are offensive formations, for example.

Horizontal Passing Concepts—Attacking the field with a short-to-medium passing game that uses safe throws to keep the chains moving. This offense lacks the big plays of a vertical passing game but should yield a higher percentage of completed throws. The mesh concept is a horizontal passing concept.

Hot Route—Before the snap, you can change any of your players' route assignments to one of eight pre-set routes based on his position. If you read that the defense is weak in a certain area, call a hot route or use multiple hot routes to create a new play on the fly.

Hurry-Up Offense—After a play you can call your players back to the line of scrimmage without going back to the play-calling screen. The last play you called will be selected, and the defense won't be able to substitute. This up-tempo offense can be used to tire out the defense and keep them off balance. It is also known as a no-huddle offense.

Juke—Use the right stick to have your offensive player make a move to fake out the defender.

Line of Scrimmage—A line parallel to the yard lines where the ball is spotted right before it's snapped. The linemen blocking the defense take their places along this line.

Motion a WR—Before the snap, you can highlight an offensive player (WR, TE, or HB) and have him move to a new position. When the blue circle is underneath him, use the D-pad to move him to a new position. This can create new formations and forces the defense to watch where you move your player.

Option Run—A play where the QB can either hand off the ball to his teammate or keep it for himself depending on what he sees with the defense. Also known as Read Option.

Packaging—Using packages at the play-calling screen with the right stick can sub specific players into the game for special situations. For example, the Dual HB package will take out the FB and place another HB into the game at his position.

Pistol—This is a unique formation where the QB takes a shotgun snap but the HB still lines up behind him. You'll find the Pistol in the Redskins' playbook, for example.

Play-Action Pass—Play action involves faking a handoff to the back to try to fool the defense into thinking it's a run. The QB still has the ball and looks to throw.

Play Ball—This defensive mechanic allows the defender to try to play the ball at its highest point. This can force a knockout and is the best way to go for an interception.

Play Man—This defensive mechanic allows the defender to play the receiver as he is catching the ball to improve the chance that he can knock it out or force a drop.

Press Coverage—When press coverage is called, your defensive back will stand close to the WR and play physical at the snap. This forces the receiver to use his hands to get off the jam at the line and can throw off timing with the QB. The danger is that if the WR can get free, he will often get good separation from the defender. This is also known as bump-n-run coverage.

Quick Audible—Before the snap, you can quickly audible to another play if you read that the defense is weak against something. You can call a quick pass, deep pass, play-action pass, or run from any formation by using the right stick in a specific direction.

RAC—The "run after catch" mechanic allows a receiver to turn upfield as he is catching the ball to pick up as many yards as possible. It's controlled by Ⓧ (Xbox) or ▢ (PS).

Read Option—An option run in which the QB either hands the ball off to his HB or keeps it. The QB must "read" the defender and make a quick decision!

Screen Pass—Screen passes are most often used when facing an aggressive defense. They look to hit the HB near the flat and try to get the offensive linemen out in front to block.

Set—Once you select a formation, the set is how your players will align within it. For example, 4-3 is a defensive formation, and then Over Plus is the set.

Shot Play—This is a specific play concept that the offense calls when they want to look for a big play downfield in the passing game.

Shotgun Snap—Any formation where the QB lines up 4-5 yards behind the center, who snaps the ball to the QB in the air. This increases chances for bad snaps and most commonly is used with formations that lean heavily towards the pass. The QB catches the snap and doesn't have to backpedal, so he is all set up to throw.

Slide Protection—Before the snap, you can tell your linemen to slide left, right, or pinch into the middle. This will help them pick up blitzers if you sense them coming from a specific area.

Stiff Arm—A stiff arm is a move by the ball carrier where he puts a straight arm out to prevent the tackler from getting in range to make a hit. This is generally a more effective move for power back than for elusive backs. Make sure to check a player's Stiff Arm rating to see how effective he will be at performing the move.

Strafe—On defense, strafing will square your hips to the line of scrimmage and give you better control of your player. You will not be able to move as fast when strafing.

Strip—A tackle who is running for a ball carrier can go for a "strip," where he tries to knock the ball loose, rather than a tackle. This can force a turnover, but it can also result in a broken tackle. It is best to go for a strip only when you have lots of teammates in the area.

Swat—Having your defender try to knock the ball down rather than go for the interception. He looks to knock away the pass, which gives him more range and can be safer than trying for an interception.

Tight Set—Tight sets bring your receivers into the middle of the field rather than out wide as in most formations. This will create a lot of action in the middle of the field and force the defense to bump into each other as they try to cram into a tight area. Shotgun Tight Flex is a tight set.

Trips Set—These formations place three WRs onto one side of the field. This forces your opponents to shift their attention towards that side since there are more players on that side of the field. Trips sets are great for flooding zone coverages. Shotgun Trips is one example.

Truck—A ball carrier who tries to run over a defender when being tackled is a truck. Trucking is most common with power backs, especially near the goal line.

Under Center—Any formation where the QB lines up directly behind the center and takes a handoff directly from him. This is the opposite of a shotgun snap.

Usering/User Control—When you actively control a player during a play. Whatever player you use on defense is who you are "user-controlling." The best players believe they can make more plays than if the computer were controlling the same player.

User Catch—The act of clicking onto a WR and holding the Catch button to go after a pass.

Verticals Passing Concept—This passing concept looks to stretch the field aggressively towards your opponent's end zone. Most often the deep pass audible, by flicking the right stick right, will give you this style of play. The most common way to attack the defense is with Four Verticals, which floods coverage deep by sending all four receivers deep downfield.

YAC—Yards after catch for a receiver or yards after contact for a running back.

Zone Blitz—The art of bringing pressure from one area of the field while dropping defenders into another. This is a tactic used to confuse the offense.

DEFENSIVE PRE-SNAP ADJUSTMENTS

Blitz—You can make any selected player blitz by using this hot route command, a.k.a. a blitz straight down since the player's rush angle will appear straight down on the screen.

Bluff Blitz—This hot route makes your defender attack the line of scrimmage before dropping into his zone. You can fake pressure with a linebacker before he drops over the middle.

Curl to Flat —The "buzz zone" zone defender will drop 8-10 yards deep and defend the curl; if there is no route threatening that area, he will move to the flat. A buzz zone is also known as a purple zone because of the zone color.

Deep Zone—This dark blue zone will drop back and play deep assignments.

Flat Zone—This light blue zone will drop down and play the flat. It is great for guarding short-throwing offenses and players who like to dump off passes to the halfback.

Guess Play—Predict a pass or commit to a run to one side or up the middle. Use LT (Xbox) or L2 (PS) and the right stick before the snap.

Hook Zone—This yellow zone will guard a 3- to 5-yard radius around wherever it is assigned. It is great for covering the middle of the field.

Option Adjustment—Contain the QB or RB on option plays depending on your pre-snap command.

QB Contain—You can place your defensive ends in contains by using LT (Xbox) or L2 (PS) before the snap and pressing RB (Xbox) or R1 (PS).

QB Spy—A QB spy tells your defender to watch the QB and attack him if he runs past the line of scrimmage. This is a great way to stop scrambling QBs. This route also helps stop short throws right over the middle.

Shift Defense—Pinch, spread, or shift your defense in either direction with LT (Xbox) or L2 (PS) and the left stick.

Quick Adjustments—These allow you to control your secondary players without clicking onto them before the snap.

DEFENSIVE COVERAGE ADJUSTMENTS

Base Align—This allows defenses to align their defenders in the general settings of the formation. As offensive formations change they can alter how a formation looks and plays. To prevent that from happening we use base align.

Give Cushion—If you want to play bend-but-don't-break defense, use "give cushion" coverage. This moves your defenders farther away from the line of scrimmage and puts them in a "prevent" defensive position.

Inside—Your defenders will attempt to get inside position against the receivers and jump routes like ins and slants.

Man Align—Your defenders, especially LBs and safeties, will line up closer to their assignments, which is useful on Cover 0 blitzes.

Outside—Your defenders will play the receiver outside and jump routes like corners and outs.

Over Top—Your defensive zones will stay back against the receivers. They won't get beaten deep by vertical concepts but won't be able to break down on routes as easily.

Press—This will jam receivers at the line of scrimmage. Pressing slows down offenses and allows blitzes more time to get after the quarterback. It can leave your defense vulnerable if the WR beats the press.

Protect the Sticks (Sticks) —Your defenders will keep in mind the down and distance and drop their zones to that depth. This is a great adjustment for third and long.

Quick Adjust—Allows you to make adjustments to defenders before the snap without clicking onto them.

Show Blitz—A great way to load the box up with defenders is to utilize show blitz. Most formations in the game will create a Bear front, which is great for stopping the run and blitzing your opponent.

Underneath—Your defensive zones will play underneath their targets. This is great for clamping down on the horizontal passing game.

OFFENSIVE HOT ROUTES

Remember that you can only make one hot route before getting to the line in *Madden NFL 16*. For all other offensive hot routes, you must wait until the QB finishes his animation before inputting another.

Check-and-Release—This blue route tells your back to help block before releasing to the flat.

Comeback—A route for outside WRs that runs about 15 yards downfield before turning around.

Curl—The WR starts out on a straight pattern and turns around sharply after 8-10 yards.

Drag—A drag runs straight across the field after a 2-yard move forward.

Fade—This route starts the WR moving a few steps towards the sideline and then runs straight downfield.

Flat—A short route by the HB that runs to the flat and gives the QB a short option near the sideline.

Hitch—Similar to the curl route but runs shorter and is only available on the inside.

In—The receiver runs straight for 8 yards before cutting 90 degrees towards the middle of the field. This is the opposite of an out route.

Option—A route by the HB that gives the player the option to sit underneath zone or continue towards the sideline against man-to-man.

Out—The receiver runs straight for 8 yards before cutting 90 degrees towards the sideline. This is the opposite of an in route.

Slant—This route starts like a streak for a few steps and then breaks sharply at an angle across the field.

Smart Route—By pressing down on the right stick, you can tell your WR to run his route to the first down marker. This is great for third-and-long plays where the standard route won't run far enough downfield.

Smoke Screen—The WR on the outside turns towards the QB to quickly catch the pass and get upfield. This route is best against defenses that are playing far back off the receiver.

Streak—This route runs straight downfield (a.k.a. a "go" or "9" route).

Swing—The back in the backfield will swing out to the left or right.

Wheel—This route starts like a flat route but cuts upfield on a streak once it reaches the sideline.

Zig—A zig appears to start like a slant route, but the receiver pivots and cuts back to the outside towards the sideline.

POSITIONS

OFFENSE

Quarterback (QB)—The player who takes the snap from the lineman and either hands off, passes, or runs the ball.

Halfback (HB)—The player who usually lines up behind the QB and takes handoffs on run plays (a.k.a. RB—running back). On pass plays he can either run a route and become a receiver or stay in to help block.

Fullback (FB)—Lines up in front of the HB and looks to block players trying to tackle the HB. Can also catch and block on pass plays.

Wide Receiver (WR)—Receivers line up outside the linemen and look to get open downfield on pass plays. The QB throws them the ball and they can run after they catch it.

Tight End (TE)—Most commonly lines up outside the linemen and can either block on run plays or go out on pass plays.

Slot Receiver—This receiver lines up outside the tackles and is a receiver but lines up inside the farthest WR. These players most often run routes over the middle of the field or use their speed to get deep.

Offensive Linemen (OL)—These players block for the QB and HB. The center (C) is in the middle and snaps the ball to the QB on every play. There are guards on either side of the center (RG and LG) and two tackles (RT and LT) flanking the guards.

DEFENSE

Defensive End (DE)—The defensive end matches up against the other team's lineman on the outside and is most known for trying to sack the QB on passing plays. You have two DEs on the field in most situations (3-4 and 4-3 defenses).

Defensive Tackle (DT)—The DT plays in the middle of the defensive line, usually closest to the center. He is mostly known for plugging up the middle and is usually one of the biggest players on the team (there's one DT in a 3-4, two in a 4-3 defense).

Outside Linebacker (OLB)—These LBs line up outside and can cover receivers or blitz on pass plays. They must tackle anything that gets past the line on a run play. You have two OLBs on the field in a 3-4 or a 4-3 defense.

Middle Linebacker (MLB)—This player controls the middle of the field for the defense. He stands behind the defensive tackle and must tackle everything that comes through the middle. You have two MLBs in 3-4 and one in a 4-3 defense.

Cornerback (CB)—These players play outside and must cover the WRs on passing plays.

Free Safety (FS)—This player backs up the cornerbacks and helps give them support in the passing game.

Strong Safety (SS)—This player helps in the passing game but can also be brought towards the line of scrimmage to help in the run game as well.

SPECIAL TEAMS

Kicker (K)—The kicker (or placekicker) is responsible for a team's field goal or extra-point kicks.

Punter (P)—The punter's role is to catch the ball from the long snapper and kick it downfield to the opposing team on fourth down to help his team's field position.

Long Snapper (LS)—The long snapper is a specialized player who snaps the ball to the holder on field goals or to the punter so they can set up to kick it.

Kick Returner (KR)—The kick returner catches the kickoff from the opposing team and tries to return it for as many yards as possible to set his team up with good field position.

Punt Returner (PR)—The punt returner is an elusive-style player who catches punts from the opposing team and works to get return yardage.

Third Down Running Back (3DRB)—The third-down running back is often a specialized back who is strong in the passing game as a route runner or a pass blocker against blitzes.

Kickoff Specialist (KOS): The kickoff specialist's only job is to kick the ball off to the other team. Often the kicker shares this duty, but teams will sometimes bring in a player with a stronger leg, since accuracy isn't as important in this role.

PLAYER RATINGS

Ratings have never had such a huge effect over the results of gameplay as they do in *Madden NFL 16*. Make sure to test your assumptions and get players with high ratings in positions to make plays.

Acceleration (ACC)—How quickly a player gets to top speed.

Key Position: HB, WR, DE, OLB, CB

Agility (AGI)—How quickly and tightly a player is able to cut.

Key Position: HB, WR, CB

Awareness (AWR)—How smart a player is on the field; a good Awareness rating is great for CPU-controlled players.

Key Position: All positions

Ball Carrier Vision (BCV)—How well a CPU-controlled player can find holes in the defense and use moves.

Key Position: HB, WR, QB

Block Shedding (BSH)—How good a player is at getting off a block while trying to defending the run.

Key Position: DE, DT, OLB

Break Tackle (BTK)—How well a ball carrier can break tackles against a defender. This plays against a defender's Tackle rating.

Key Position: QB, HB, FB, WR

Carry (CAR)—How well a ball carrier holds onto the ball; a higher number means a lower chance of a fumble.

Key Position: HB, FB, QB, WR

Catch (CTH)—How well a receiver can catch and hold onto the ball; a higher number means fewer dropped passes.

Key Position: WR, TE, HB

Catch in Traffic (CIT)—How well a receiver is able to catch and hold onto a ball in traffic. A higher number means a better chance of hanging onto the ball when being tackled by a defender.

Key Position: TE, WR, HB

Deep Accuracy (DAC)—This affects how accurate a quarterback is on throws over 40 yards.

Key Position: QB

Elusiveness (ELU)—How good a player is at using elusive moves to get away from defenders. Elusiveness is more common in speed backs.

Key Position: HB, WR, QB

Finesse Moves (FMV)—How good a player rushing the QB is at using a finesse move to get off blocks. An example is a swim move.

Key Position: DE, DT, OLB

Hit Power (POW)—How hard a defensive player can tackle a ball carrier. A higher number means more hit stick and fumble chances.

Key Position: OLB, MLB, FS, SS

Impact Blocking (IBL)—How good a player is at making blocks in the open field. The higher the rating, the bigger the chance for a big block that can knock an opponent off his feet. These are more common in the special teams return game.

Key Position: Offensive linemen, FB, TE

Injury (INJ)—How good a player is at staying healthy. The higher the rating, the less of a chance a player will get injured during the game and over the course of a season.

Key Position: All Positions

Juke Move (JKM)—How well a player can use a fake step juke move to get away from defenders. The rating can affect the tightness of the move and the amount of ground covered when juking.

Key Position: HB, WR, QB

Jumping (JMP)—How high a player can jump.

Key Position: WR, TE, CB

Kick Accuracy (KAC)—How accurate a player is when kicking a field goal, punting the ball, or kicking off.

Key Position: K, P

Kick Power (KPW)—How far a player can kick a field goal, punt the ball, or kick off.

Key Position: K, P

Man Coverage (MCV)—How well a defender can stick with his receiver while he is running his route. The higher the number, the closer he will play his assignment. This rating goes up against a receiver's Route Running rating.

Medium Accuracy (MAC)—This affects how accurate a quarterback is on throws between 20 and 40 yards.

Key Position: QB

Key Position: CB, FS, SS

Overall (OVR)—This rating provides a great snapshot of a player's attributes. Although you need to dig deeper to find out exactly what type of player you have, this will allow you to make quick decisions about whom to start.

Key Position: All players

Pass Blocking (PBK)—How well an offensive lineman is at blocking a defender who is rushing the QB on a passing play.

Key Position: Offensive line

Play Recognition (PRC)—How quickly a defensive player identifies what type of play the offense is running. A higher rating means less of a chance to be fooled on play action and the quicker the player will attack the line on run plays.

Key Position: OLB, MLB, FS, SS

Power Moves (PMV)—How good a player rushing the QB is at using a power-style move to get off blocks. An example is a bull rush move.

Key Position: DE, DT, OLB

Press (PRS)—How good a defender is at lining up in front of a WR and not letting him off the line of scrimmage. The higher the number, the better the defender will be at playing bump-n-run coverage. This goes against a receiver's Release rating.

Key Position: CB, FS, SS

Pursuit (PUR)—How good a player is at taking proper angles to track down a ball carrier.

Key Position: OLB, MLB, FS, SS

Release (RLS)—How good a receiver is at getting off of press coverage. The higher the rating, the better chance he has to beat press coverage. This matches up against a defender's Press rating.

Key Position: WR

Return (RET)—How good a player is at catching the ball on special teams.

Key Position: KR, PR

Route Running (RTE)—How well a receiver can run sharp routes that can get him space from the defender. This will determine separation against a man-to-man defender based on the defender's Man Coverage rating.

Key Position: WR, TE, HB

Run Blocking (RBK)—How good an offensive lineman is at blocking a defender on a rushing play.

Key Position: Offensive line, FB, TE

Run Block Strength (RBS), Run Block Footwork (RBF), Pass Block Strength (PBS), and Pass Block Footwork (PBF) are no longer used in MUT or gameplay. They are used only in CFM simulation games.

Short Accuracy (SAC)—This affects how accurate a quarterback is on throws under 20 yards.

Key Position: QB

Spectacular Catch (SPC)—How well a receiver is able to go up and make jumping or unique catches. A higher number means a better chance of amazing catches over defenders.

Speed (SPD)—How fast a player runs.

Key Position: All players except offensive linemen

Spin Move (SPM)—How well a ball carrier can use a spin style move to get away from defenders. The rating can affect the tightness of the spin radius.

Key Position: HB, WR, QB

Stamina (STA)—This affects how long a player can stay in the game before becoming tired. The higher the rating, the more snaps a player will have before having to rest.

Key Position: All positions

Stiff Arm (SFA)—How good a ball carrier is at using his free hand to ward off tacklers.

Key Position: HB, WR, QB

Strength (STR)—How strong a player is and how well he can stand his ground or get pushed during a line battle.

Key Position: Offensive and defensive lines

Tackle (TAK)—How well a defensive player can tackle a ball carrier. A higher number means a lower chance of broken tackles.

Key Position: OLB, MLB, FS, SS

Throw Accuracy (THA)—How accurate a QB is when throwing the ball. A higher number means more consistent throws downfield.

Key Position: QB

Throw Accuracy (THA) is important only in games that are simulated.

Throw Power (THP)—How fast and far a QB can throw the ball. A higher number means better downfield throws.

Key Position: QB

Trucking (TRK)—How good a player is at using power moves to run over defenders. Trucking is more common in power backs.

Key Position: HB, FB, QB

Zone Coverage (ZCV)—How well a player will track his receiver in zone coverage. The higher the number, the more he will be able to cover a play in his zone during a pass play.

Key Position: OLB, MLB, CB, FS, SS

ACHIEVEMENTS

ACHIEVEMENT NAME	DESCRIPTION	XBOX POINTS	PS TROPHY	PS POINTS
GOING FOR GOLD	Earn gold from a drill inside the Skills Trainer.	100	Gold	90
UNDERSTANDING	Earn at least one bronze medal in all drills inside of Skills Trainer.	140	Silver	30
THREW DOWN THE GAUNTLET AGAIN	Defeat the level 25 boss of the Skills Trainer Gauntlet.	50	Gold	90
RUN DEGREE	Earn at least a bronze medal in all six run concepts inside of Skills Trainer.	20	Bronze	15
EARLY BIRD	Get hit with a neutral zone infraction penalty (no SuperSim or Practice mode).	10	Bronze	15
ASSISTED	Record four assisted tackles in one game (no SuperSim or Practice mode).	25	Bronze	15
LAB RAT	Change one or more penalty sliders in the Settings menu.	10	Bronze	15
TURN DOWN FOR WATT	Make a user-pick with J.J. Watt (no SuperSim or Practice mode).	20	Silver	30
PUT SOME TOUCH ON IT	Throw a TD using the touch pass (no SuperSim or Practice mode).	10	Bronze	15
PEANUT PUNCH	Successfully use the strip ball mechanic (no SuperSim or Practice mode).	10	Bronze	15
NOW DO IT AGAIN	Complete your first draft.	10	Bronze	15
GOOD ON PAPER	Draft a team with an Overall rating greater than 82 in Draft Champions.	50	Gold	90
DRAFT WITH STYLE	Build a team style (five players of a particular team style).	35	Silver	30
THE CHAMPION	Complete a draft without losing a single game.	20	Bronze	15
SNICKERS YOU'RE NOT YOU WHEN YOU'RE LOSING	Come back and win when trailing by 17+ points (no SuperSim or Co-op).	30	Silver	30
THAT WAS EASY	Enter Draft Champions mode.	5	Bronze	15
GRINDIN' SOLOS	Win a MUT solo challenge.	20	Bronze	15
NEGOTIATOR	Win a MUT auction.	15	Bronze	15
BEYOND A HOBBY	Complete a MUT set.	20	Bronze	15
WHY NOT ME IN THE SUPER BOWL?	Make it to a MUT seasons' Super Bowl.	50	Gold	90
THIS IS MY ULTIMATE TEAM	Create a MUT team.	10	Bronze	15
STAY FOCUSED	Earn a first-round bye in Ultimate Team seasons.	25	Bronze	15
LAY IT ALL ON THE LINE	Make the playoffs in Ultimate Team seasons.	20	Bronze	15
SAMMY WATKINS LEGACY AWARD	Using a created player, coach, or owner, surpass a legacy score of 25.	10	Bronze	15
HA-HA CLINTON-DIX LEGACY AWARD	Using a created player, coach, or owner, surpass a legacy score of 125.	10	Bronze	15
TEDDY BRIDGEWATER LEGACY AWARD	Using a created player, coach, or owner, surpass a legacy score of 300.	10	Bronze	15
LE'VEON BELL LEGACY AWARD	Using a created player, coach, or owner, surpass a legacy score of 800.	10	Bronze	15
MATT RYAN LEGACY AWARD	Using a created player, coach, or owner, surpass a legacy score of 1,500.	10	Bronze	15
NDAMUKONG SUH LEGACY AWARD	Using a created player, coach, or owner, surpass a legacy score of 3,600.	20	Bronze	15
MARSHAWN LYNCH LEGACY AWARD	Using a created player, coach, or owner, surpass a legacy score of 6,500.	25	Bronze	15
DARRELLE REVIS LEGACY AWARD	Using a created player, coach, or owner, surpass a legacy score of 9,500.	30	Bronze	15
WALTER PAYTON LEGACY AWARD	Using a created player, coach, or owner, surpass a legacy score of 15,450.	50	Silver	30
PEYTON MANNING LEGACY AWARD	Using a created player, coach, or owner, surpass a legacy score of 20,000.	75	Gold	90
ONLINE NEXT?	Complete a single-player Draft Champions event.	10	Bronze	15
GREAT PICK	Draft a player with an Overall rating at least 10 points higher than the base team.	10	Bronze	15
DRAFTAHOLIC	Complete five Draft Champions events.	25	Silver	30

Written by Zach "ZFARLS" Farley

DK/Prima Games, a division of Penguin Random House LLC
6081 East 82nd Street, Suite #400
Indianapolis, IN 46250

Standard Guide ISBN: 978-0-7440-1634-5

Mini Guide ISBN: 978-0-7440-1655-0

Printing Code: The rightmost double-digit number is the year of the book's printing; the rightmost single-digit number is the number of the book's printing. For example, 15-1 shows that the first printing of the book occurred in 2015.

18 17 16 15 4 3 2 1

Printed in the USA.

CREDITS

Project Manager
Jesse Anderson

Book Designer
Tim Amrhein

Production Designer
Wil Cruz

Copy Editor
Deana Shields

PRIMA GAMES STAFF

VP & Publisher
Mike Degler

Editorial Manager
Tim Fitzpatrick

Design and Layout Manager
Tracy Wehmeyer

Licensing
Aaron Lockhart
Christian Sumner

Marketing
Katie Hemlock
Paul Giacomotto

Digital Publishing
Julie Asbury
Tim Cox
Shaida Boroumand

Operations Manager
Stacey Beheler

ACKNOWLEDGMENTS

This guide would not be possible without extraordinary contributions from the team at EA SPORTS. Special thanks to Josh Rabenovets, Jennica Pearson, Allan Chiu, Seann Graddy, Kolbe Launchbaugh, Ben Haumiller, Patrick Bellanca, Jake Stein, Jon Hanson, Rex Dickson, Larry Richart, Mike Scantlebury, Clint Oldenburg, Danny Doeberling, Markus Frieske, Andrew Johnson, Stephen Gibbons, John Coleman, Tom Lischke, Joe Alread, Billy Schautz, Jeff Younger, Andrew Hoffman, Christian Casas, Ryan Glick, Justin Chow, Devin Peden, Will Sykes, and many others for all their help along the way.